BATMAN
THE JIRO KUWATA
BATMANGA
VOLUME 3

Written & Illustrated by **JIRO KUWATA**
Translation by **SHELDON DRZKA**
Lettered by **WES ABBOTT**
BATMAN created by **BOB KANE** with **BILL FINGER**

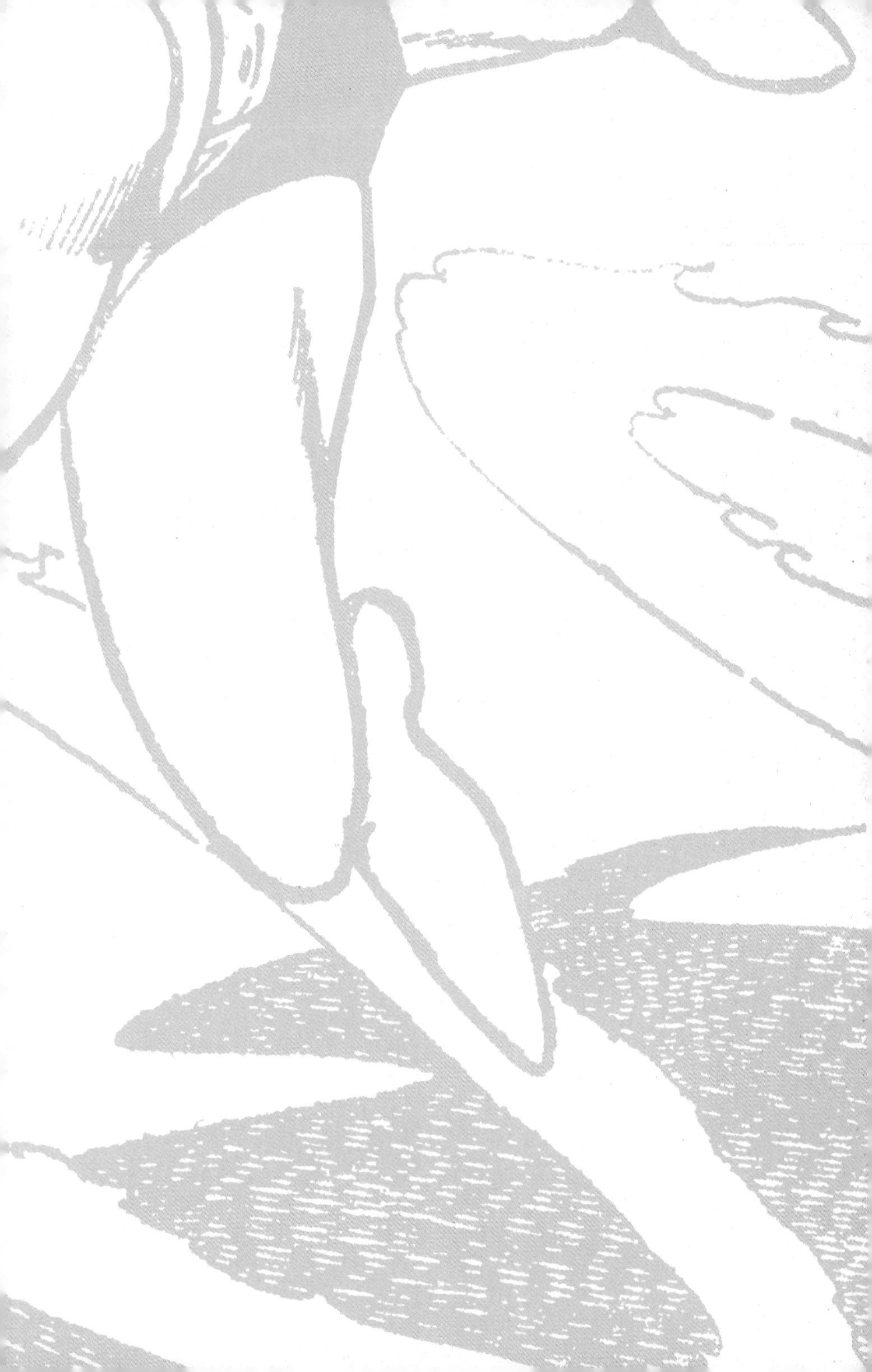

TABLE OF CONTENTS

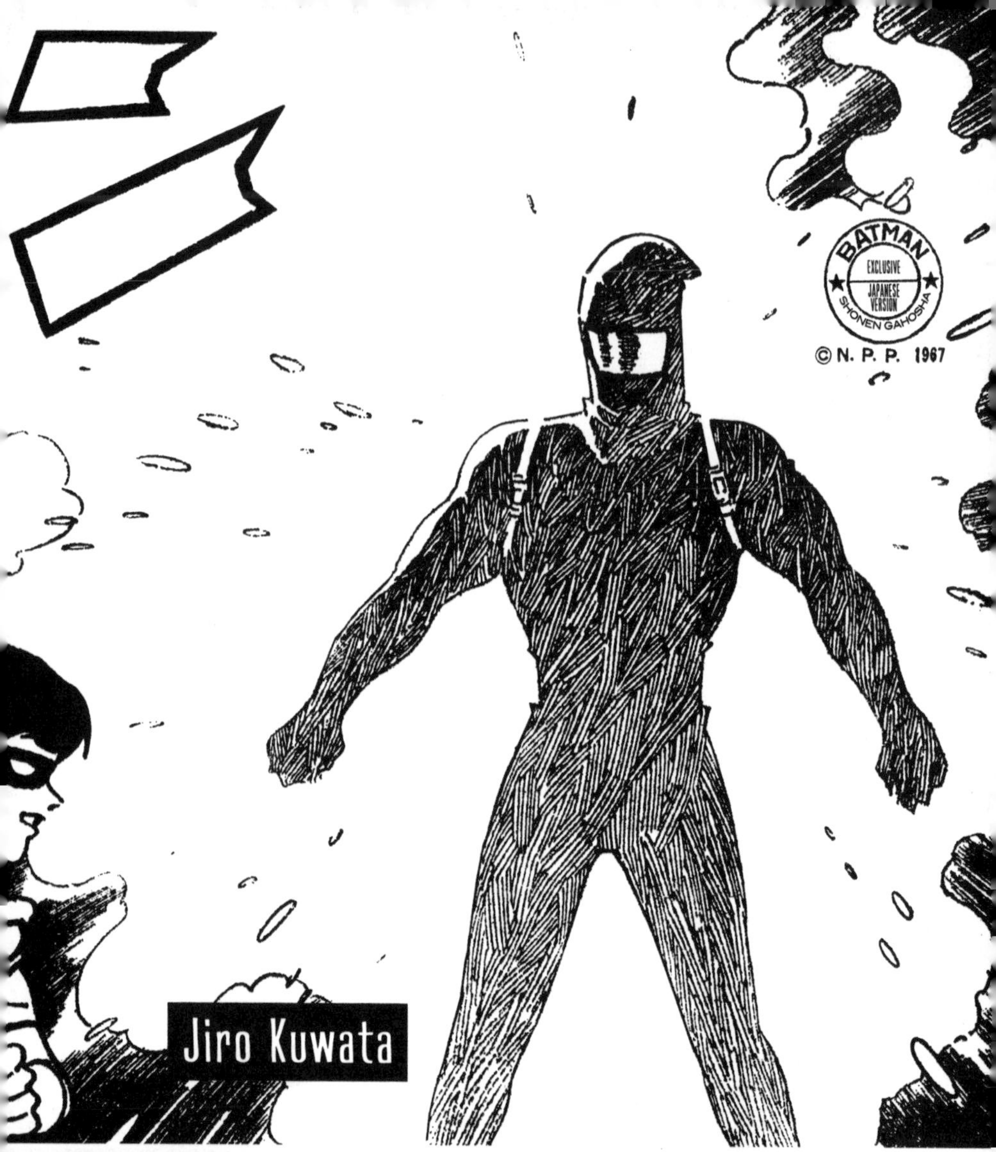
BATMAN
EXCLUSIVE
JAPANESE VERSION
SHONEN GAHOSHA
© N. P. P. 1967
Jiro Kuwata
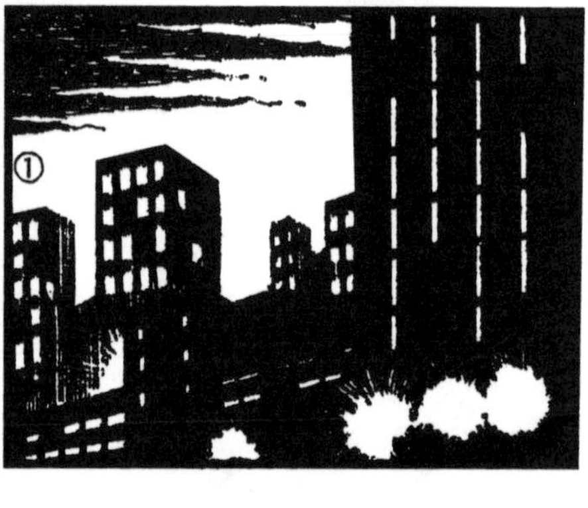
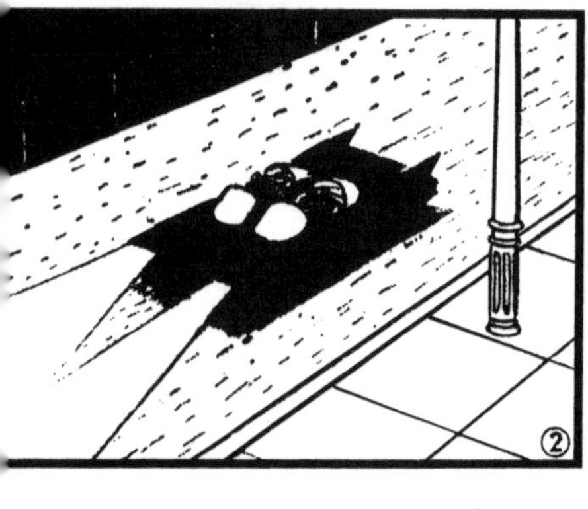

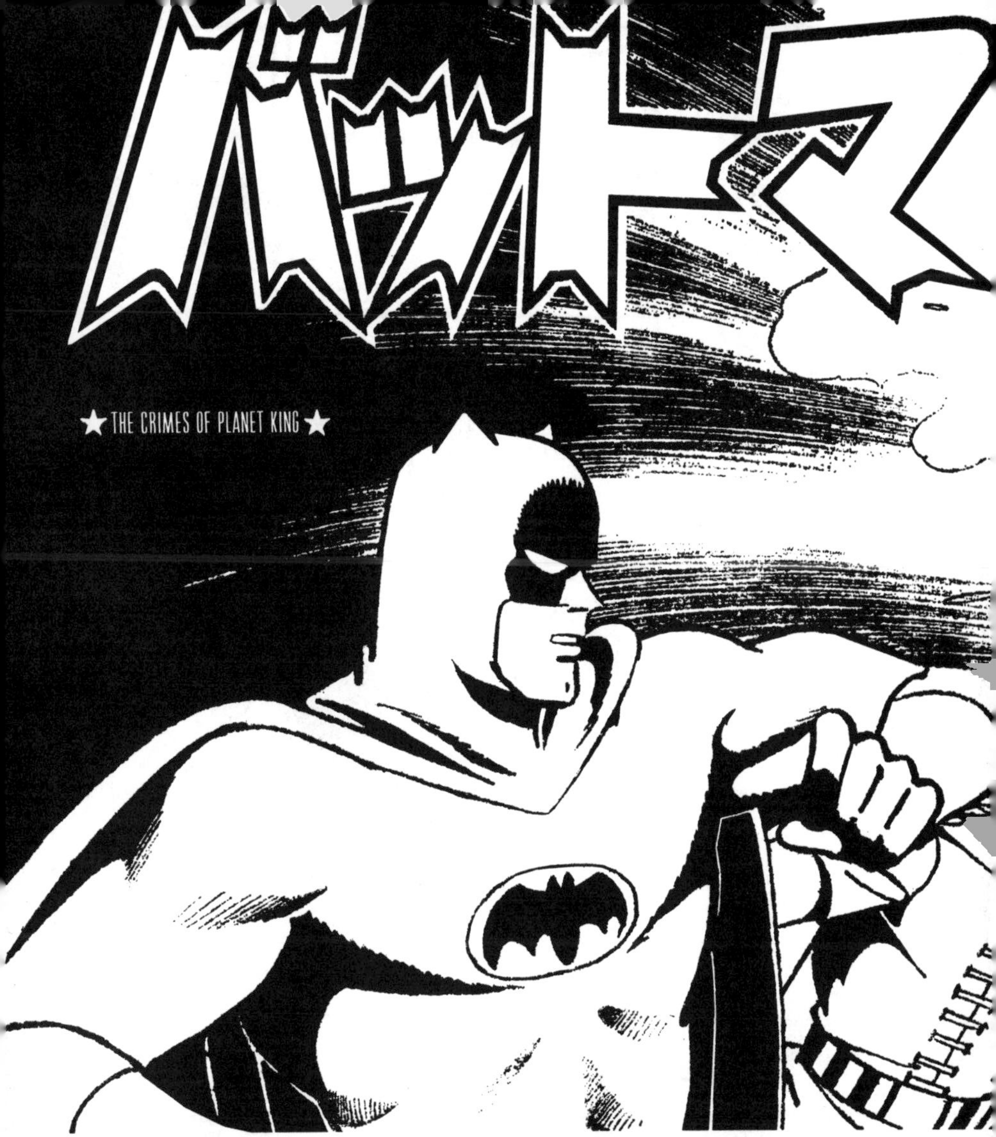
★THE CRIMES OF PLANET KING★

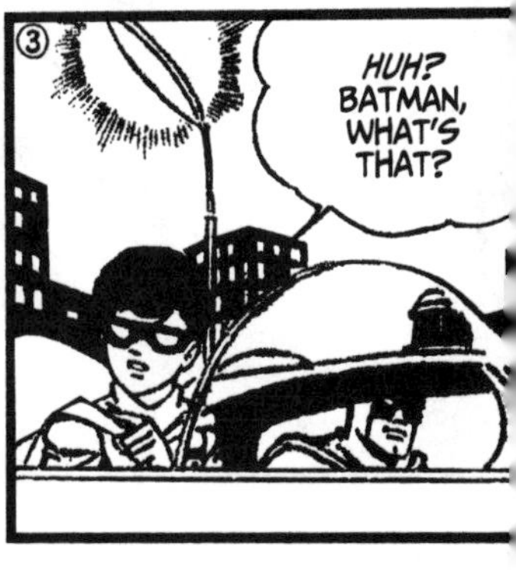
③
HUH? BATMAN, WHAT'S THAT?

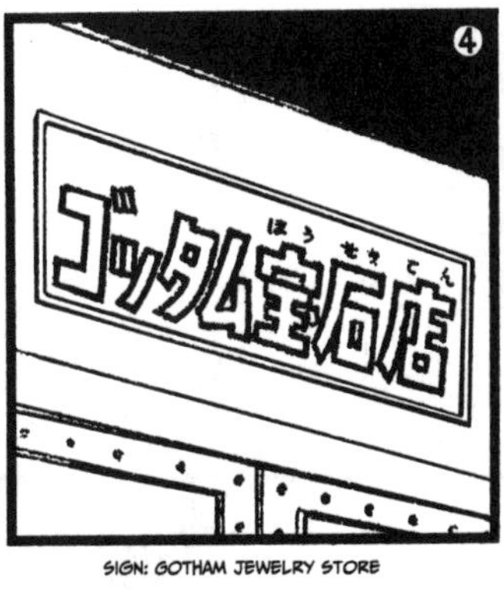
④
ゴッタム宝石店

SIGN: GOTHAM JEWELRY STORE

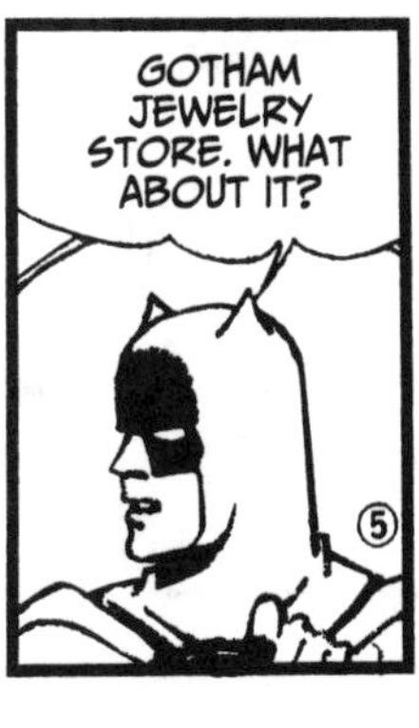
GOTHAM JEWELRY STORE. WHAT ABOUT IT?
⑤

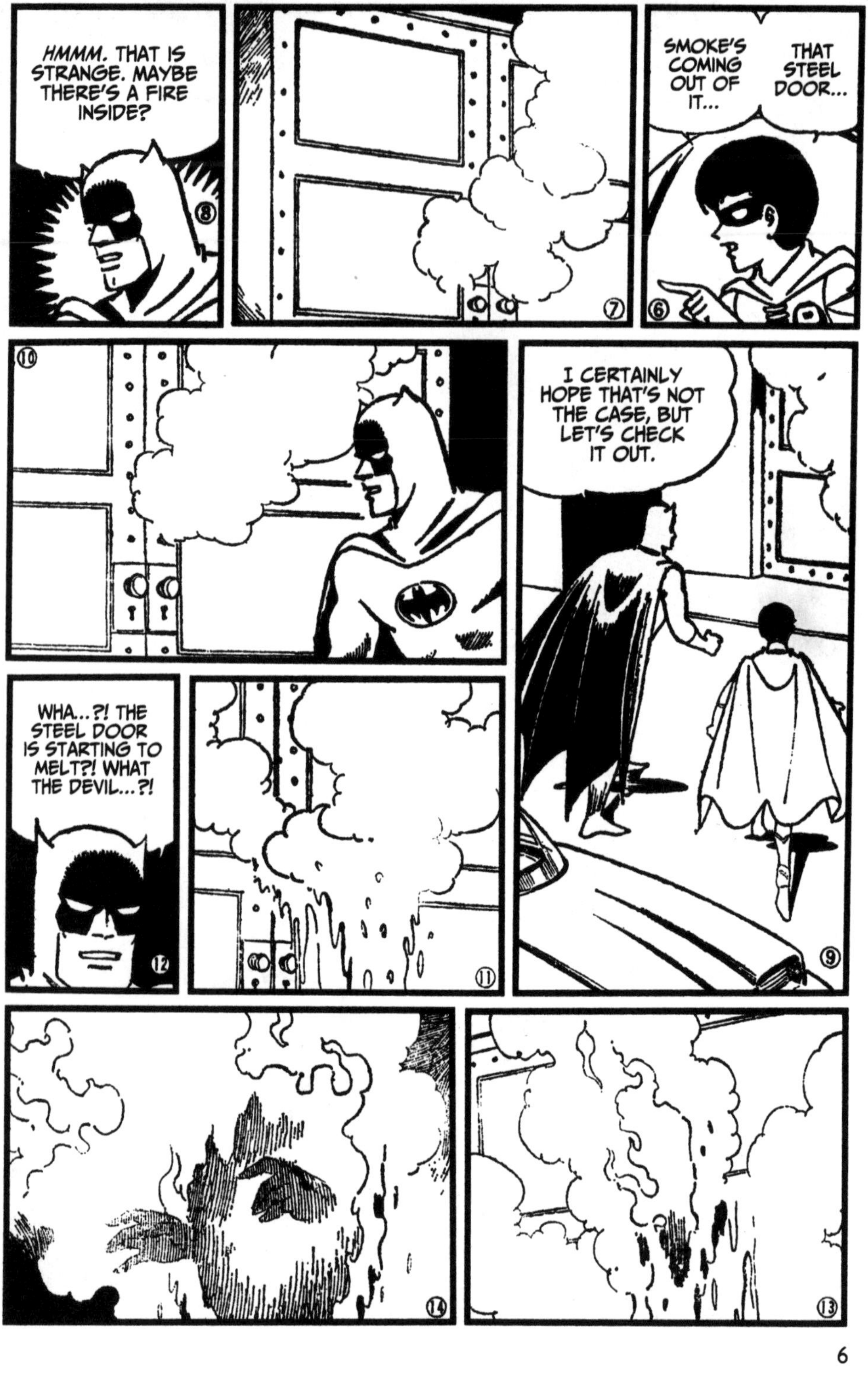
THAT STEEL DOOR...
SMOKE'S COMING OUT OF IT...
HMMM. THAT IS STRANGE. MAYBE THERE'S A FIRE INSIDE?
I CERTAINLY HOPE THAT'S NOT THE CASE, BUT LET'S CHECK IT OUT.
WHA...?! THE STEEL DOOR IS STARTING TO MELT?! WHAT THE DEVIL...?!

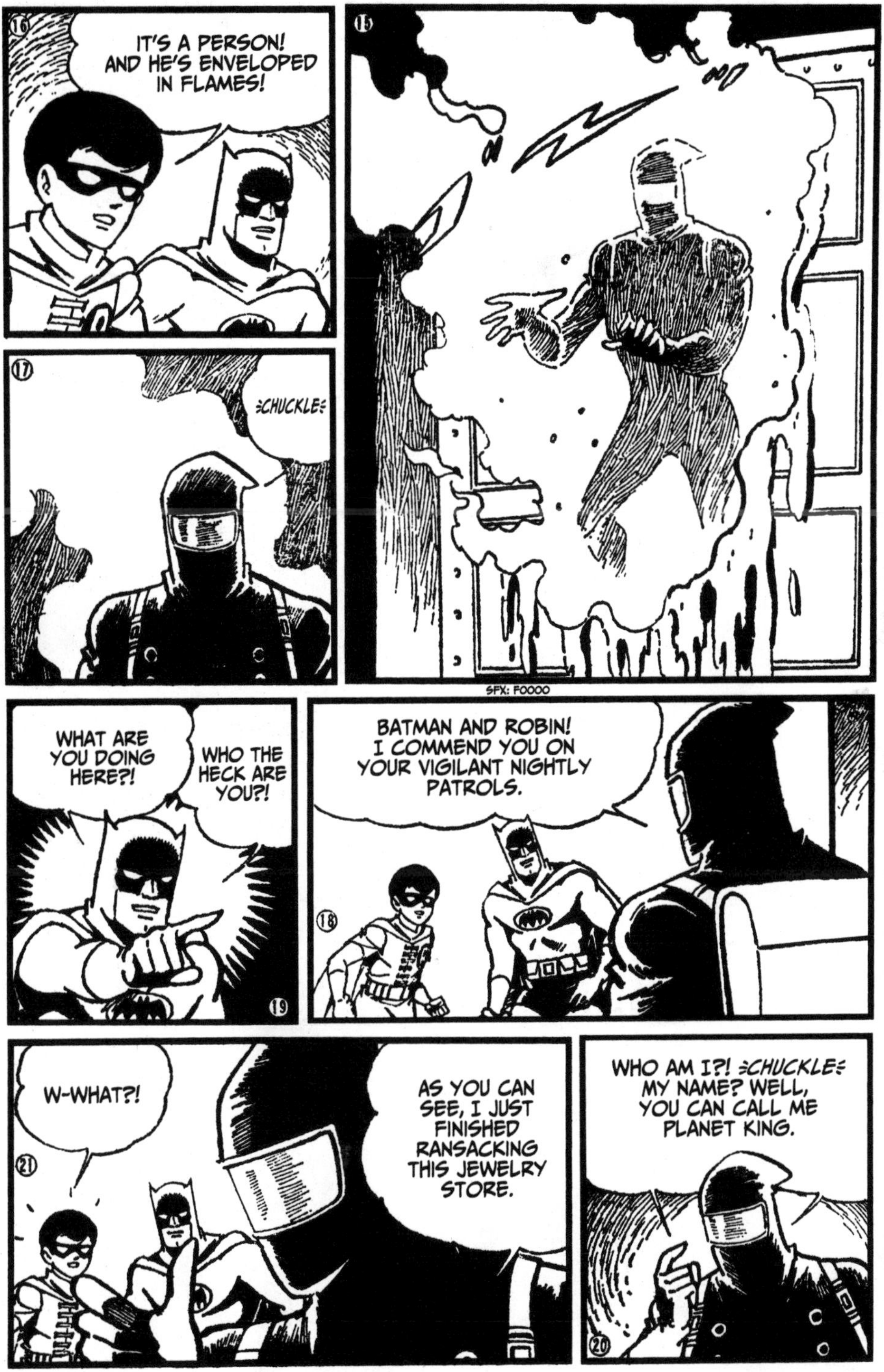
SFX: FOOOO
IT'S A PERSON! AND HE'S ENVELOPED IN FLAMES!
≈CHUCKLE≈
BATMAN AND ROBIN! I COMMEND YOU ON YOUR VIGILANT NIGHTLY PATROLS.
WHO THE HECK ARE YOU?!
WHAT ARE YOU DOING HERE?!
WHO AM I?! ≈CHUCKLE≈ MY NAME? WELL, YOU CAN CALL ME PLANET KING.
AS YOU CAN SEE, I JUST FINISHED RANSACKING THIS JEWELRY STORE.
W-WHAT?!

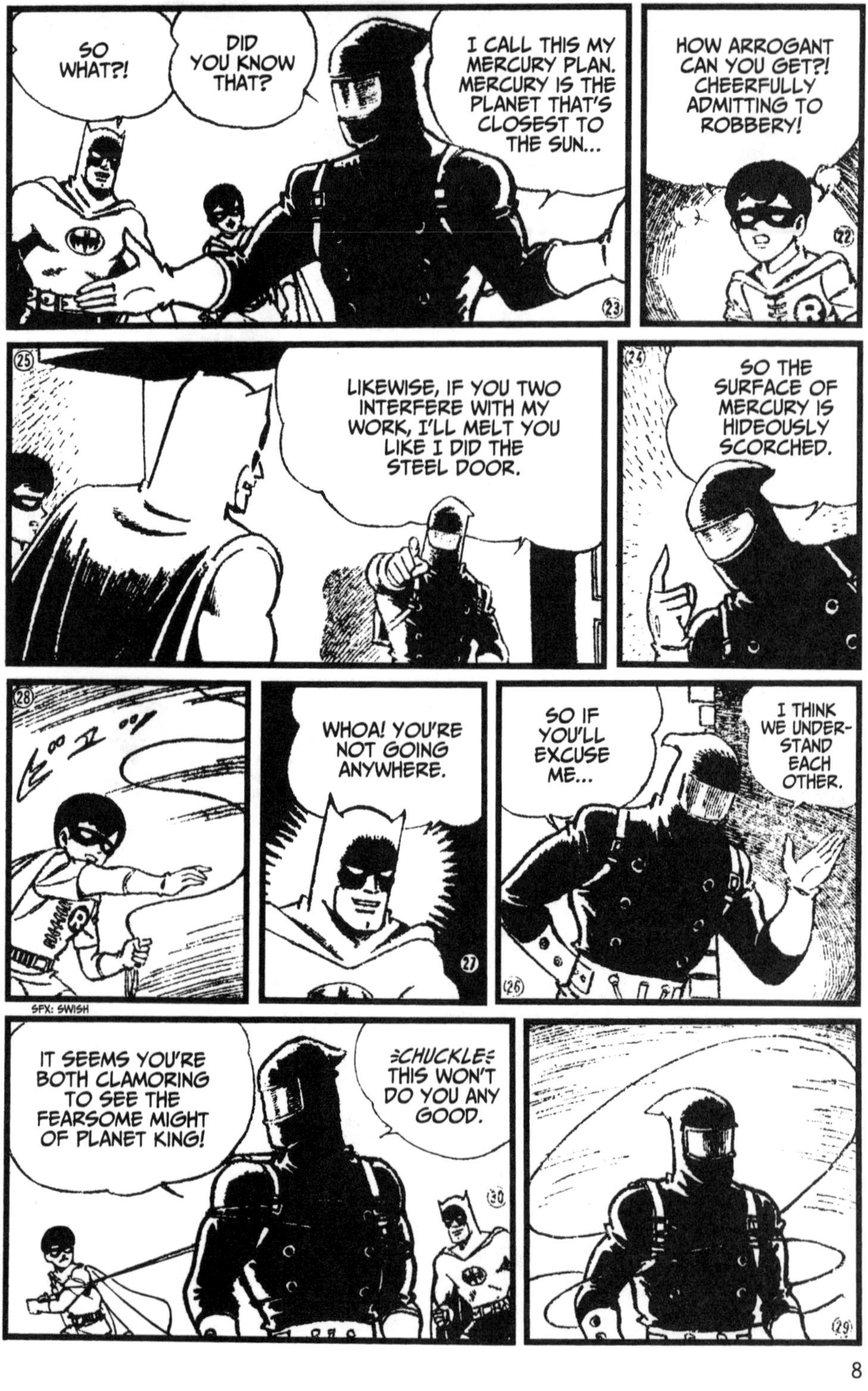
HOW ARROGANT CAN YOU GET?! CHEERFULLY ADMITTING TO ROBBERY!
I CALL THIS MY MERCURY PLAN. MERCURY IS THE PLANET THAT'S CLOSEST TO THE SUN...
DID YOU KNOW THAT?
SO WHAT?!
SO THE SURFACE OF MERCURY IS HIDEOUSLY SCORCHED.
LIKEWISE, IF YOU TWO INTERFERE WITH MY WORK, I'LL MELT YOU LIKE I DID THE STEEL DOOR.
I THINK WE UNDER-STAND EACH OTHER.
SO IF YOU'LL EXCUSE ME...
WHOA! YOU'RE NOT GOING ANYWHERE.
SFX: SWISH
≈CHUCKLE≈ THIS WON'T DO YOU ANY GOOD.
IT SEEMS YOU'RE BOTH CLAMORING TO SEE THE FEARSOME MIGHT OF PLANET KING!

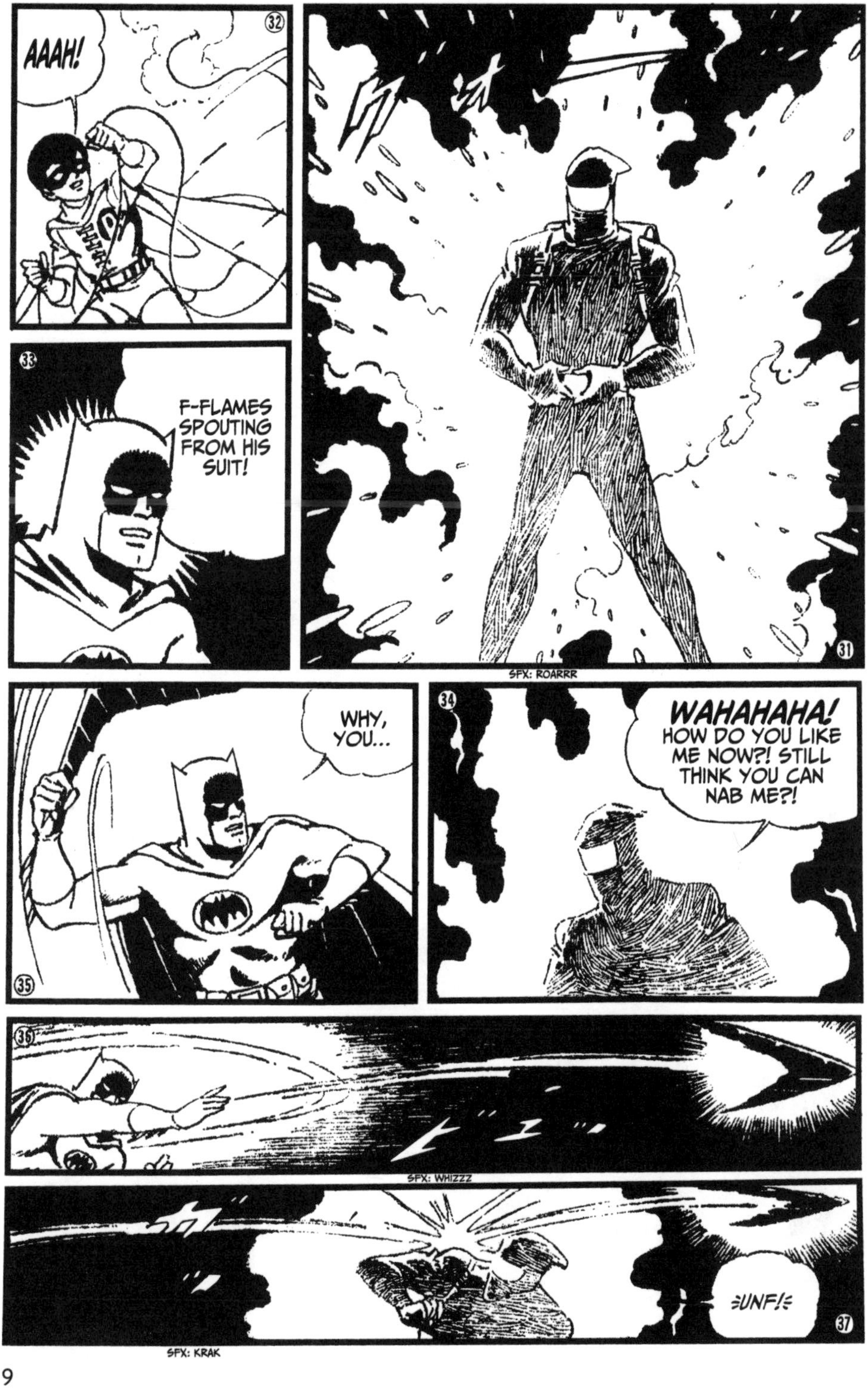
SFX: ROARRR
AAAH!
F-FLAMES SPOUTING FROM HIS SUIT!
WAHAHAHA! HOW DO YOU LIKE ME NOW?! STILL THINK YOU CAN NAB ME?!
WHY, YOU...
SFX: WHIZZZ
UNF!
SFX: KRAK

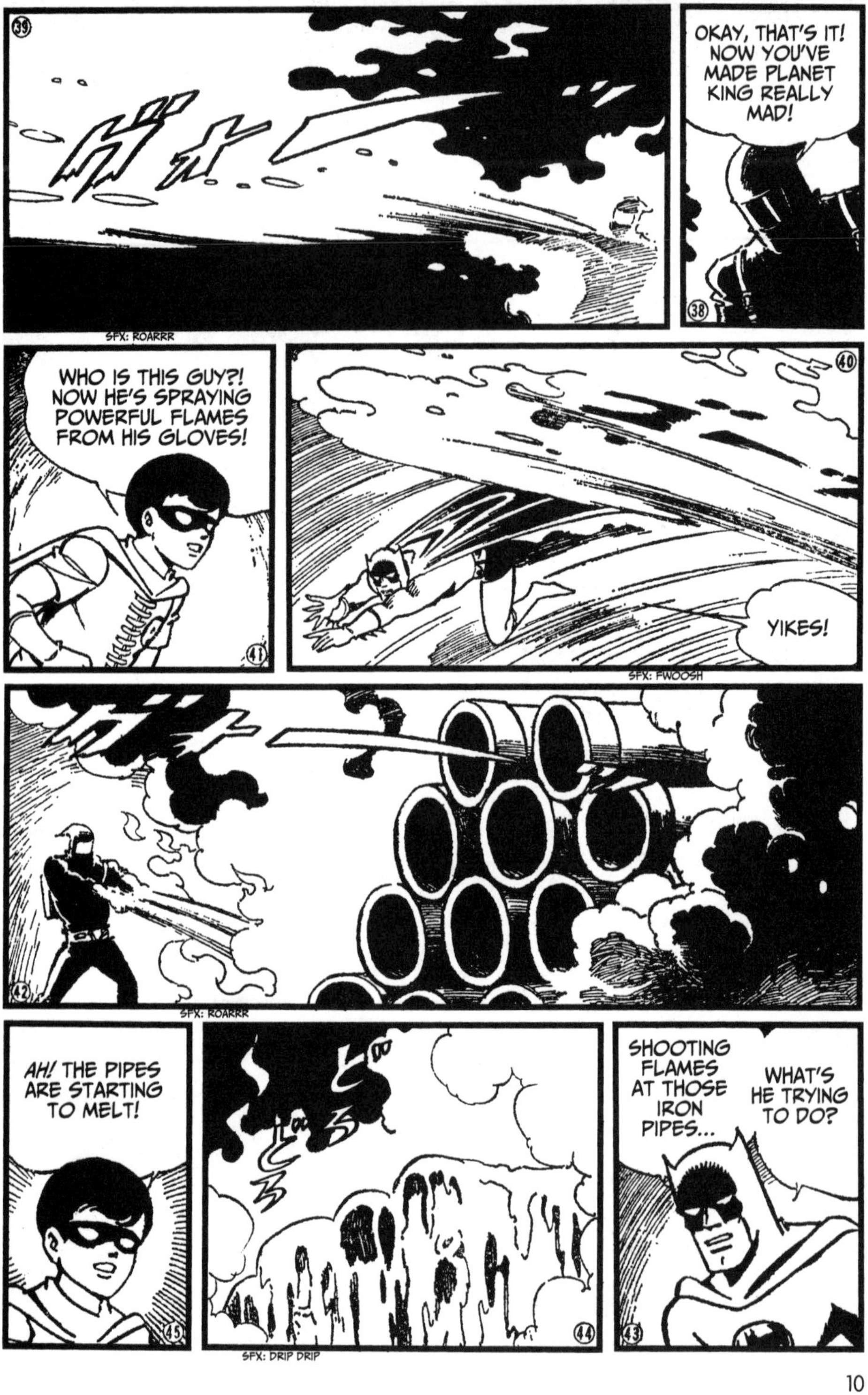
OKAY, THAT'S IT! NOW YOU'VE MADE PLANET KING REALLY MAD!
SFX: ROARRR
YIKES!
SFX: FWOOSH
WHO IS THIS GUY?! NOW HE'S SPRAYING POWERFUL FLAMES FROM HIS GLOVES!
SFX: ROARRR
SHOOTING FLAMES AT THOSE IRON PIPES...
WHAT'S HE TRYING TO DO?
SFX: DRIP DRIP
AH! THE PIPES ARE STARTING TO MELT!

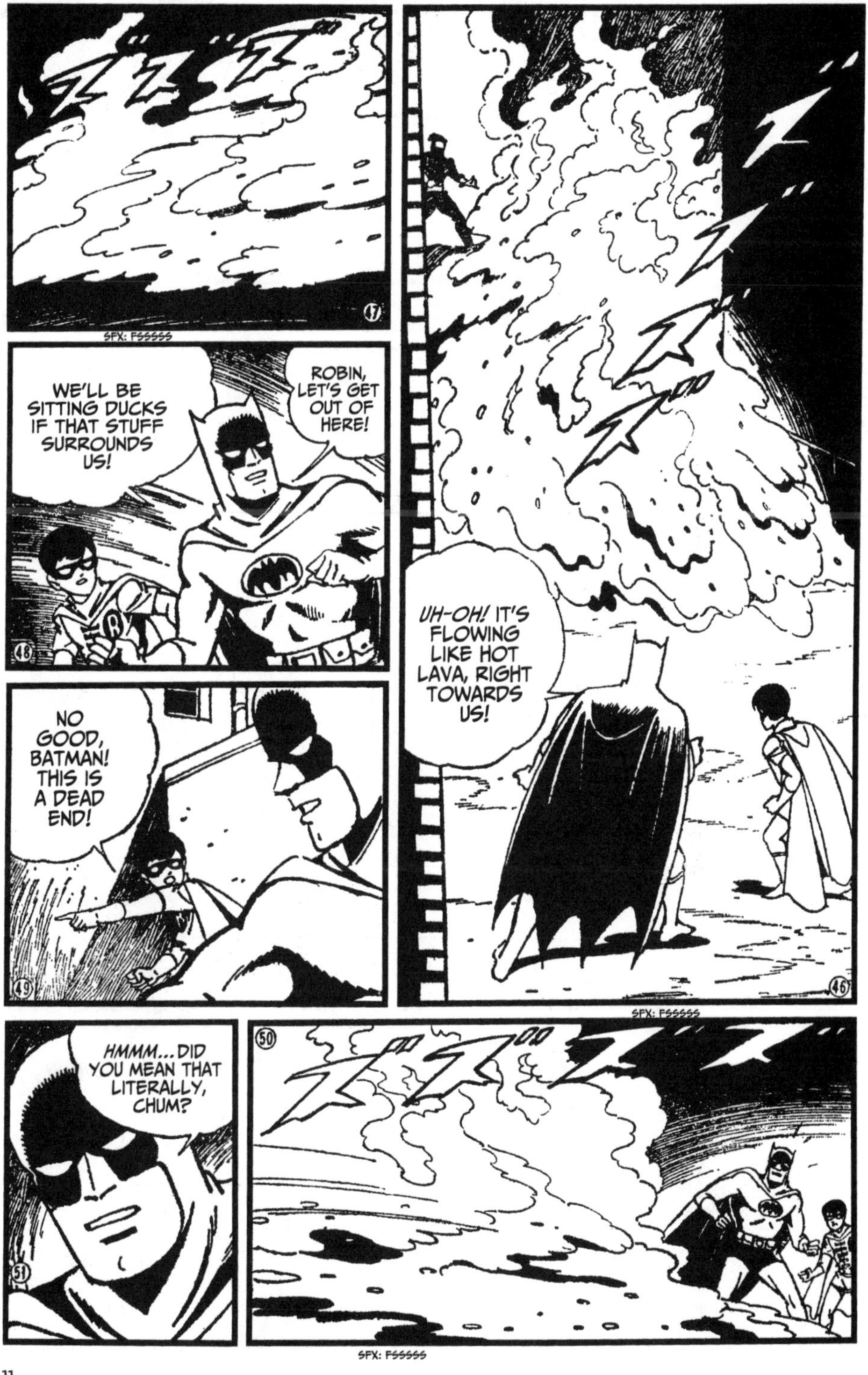
UH-OH! IT'S FLOWING LIKE HOT LAVA, RIGHT TOWARDS US!
ROBIN, LET'S GET OUT OF HERE!
WE'LL BE SITTING DUCKS IF THAT STUFF SURROUNDS US!
NO GOOD, BATMAN! THIS IS A DEAD END!
HMMM...DID YOU MEAN THAT LITERALLY, CHUM?

SFX: FSSSSS

SFX: FSSSSS

SFX: FSSSSS

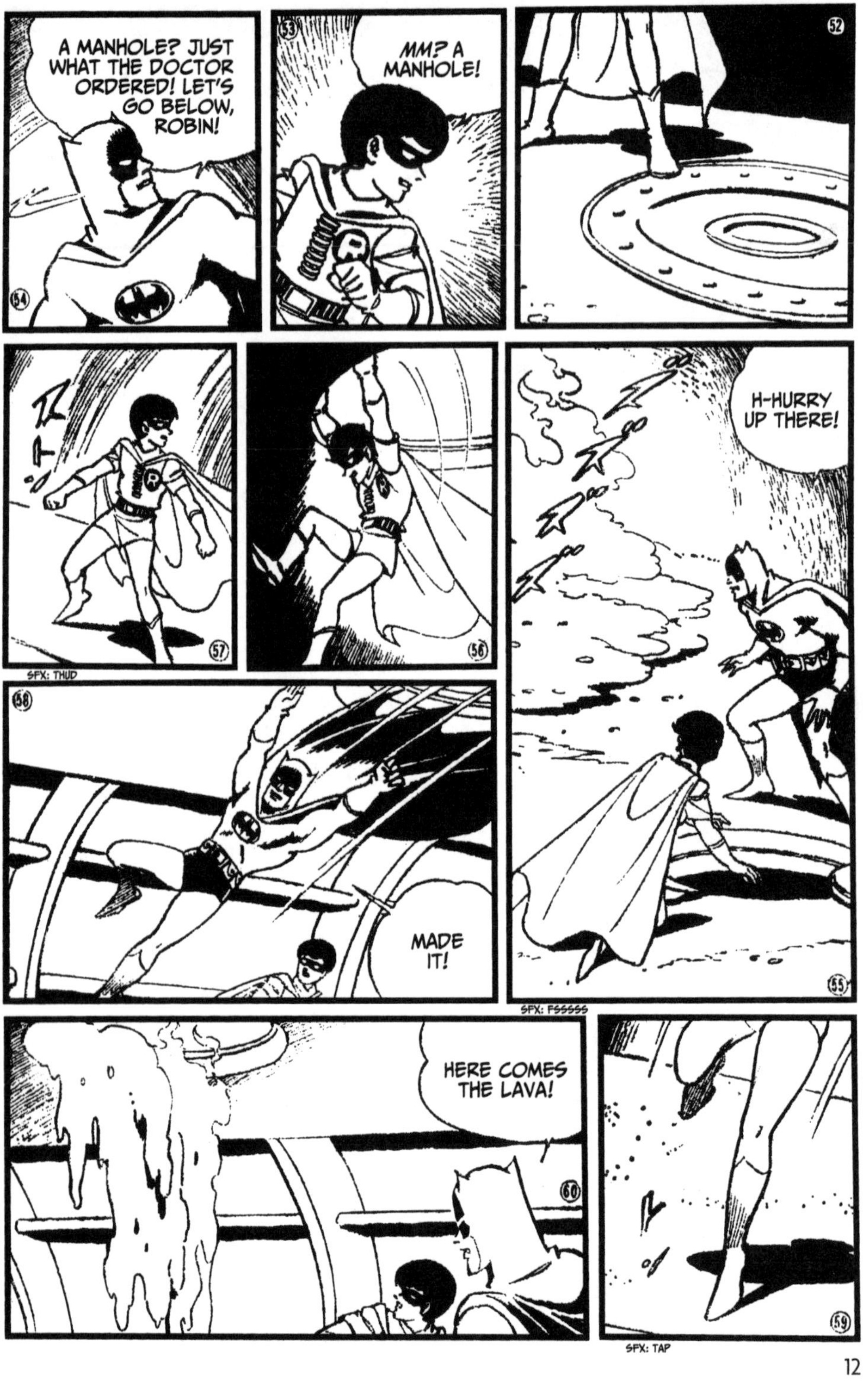
MM? A MANHOLE!
A MANHOLE? JUST WHAT THE DOCTOR ORDERED! LET'S GO BELOW, ROBIN!
H-HURRY UP THERE!
SFX: FSSSSS
SFX: THUD
MADE IT!
SFX: TAP
HERE COMES THE LAVA!

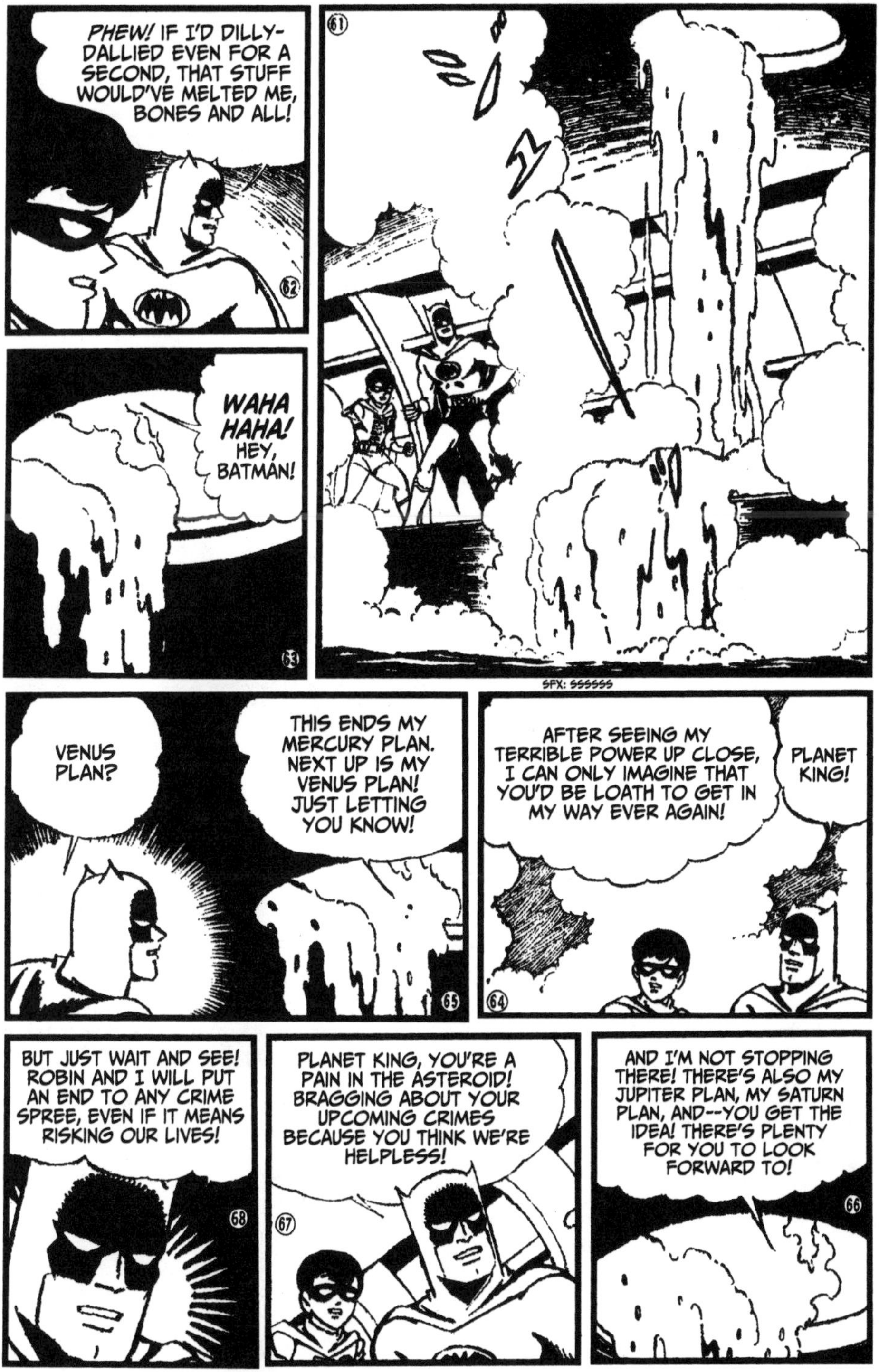
SFX: SSSSSS
PHEW! IF I'D DILLY-DALLIED EVEN FOR A SECOND, THAT STUFF WOULD'VE MELTED ME, BONES AND ALL!
WAHA HAHA! HEY, BATMAN!
PLANET KING!
AFTER SEEING MY TERRIBLE POWER UP CLOSE, I CAN ONLY IMAGINE THAT YOU'D BE LOATH TO GET IN MY WAY EVER AGAIN!
THIS ENDS MY MERCURY PLAN. NEXT UP IS MY VENUS PLAN! JUST LETTING YOU KNOW!
VENUS PLAN?
AND I'M NOT STOPPING THERE! THERE'S ALSO MY JUPITER PLAN, MY SATURN PLAN, AND--YOU GET THE IDEA! THERE'S PLENTY FOR YOU TO LOOK FORWARD TO!
PLANET KING, YOU'RE A PAIN IN THE ASTEROID! BRAGGING ABOUT YOUR UPCOMING CRIMES BECAUSE YOU THINK WE'RE HELPLESS!
BUT JUST WAIT AND SEE! ROBIN AND I WILL PUT AN END TO ANY CRIME SPREE, EVEN IF IT MEANS RISKING OUR LIVES!

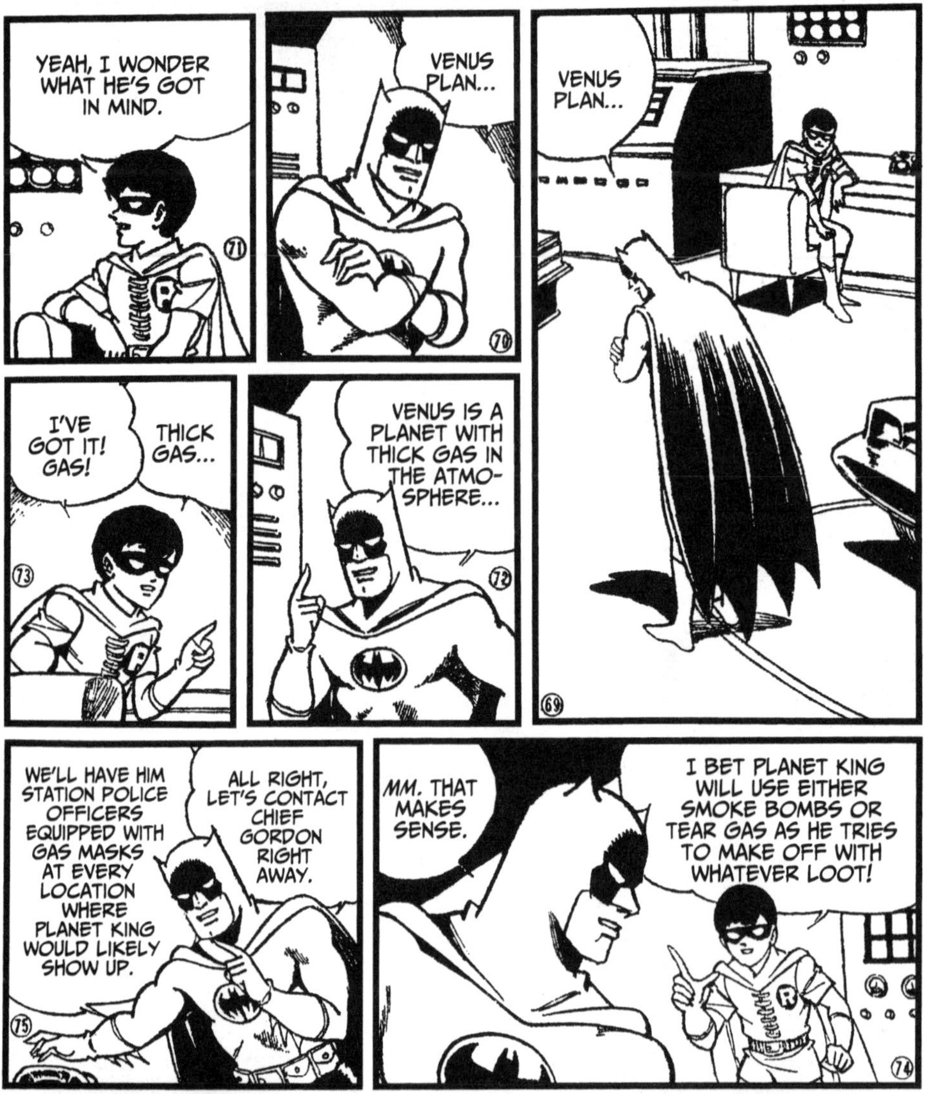
VENUS PLAN...
VENUS PLAN...
YEAH, I WONDER WHAT HE'S GOT IN MIND.
VENUS IS A PLANET WITH THICK GAS IN THE ATMO- SPHERE...
THICK GAS...
I'VE GOT IT! GAS!
I BET PLANET KING WILL USE EITHER SMOKE BOMBS OR TEAR GAS AS HE TRIES TO MAKE OFF WITH WHATEVER LOOT!
MM. THAT MAKES SENSE.
ALL RIGHT, LET'S CONTACT CHIEF GORDON RIGHT AWAY.
WE'LL HAVE HIM STATION POLICE OFFICERS EQUIPPED WITH GAS MASKS AT EVERY LOCATION WHERE PLANET KING WOULD LIKELY SHOW UP.

However, at that moment, Planet King was already about to set his evil plan into motion...

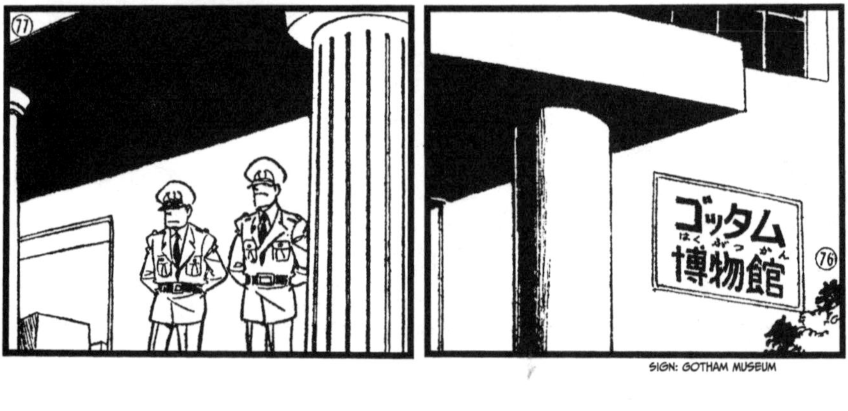
ゴッタム
はくぶつかん
博物館

SIGN: GOTHAM MUSEUM

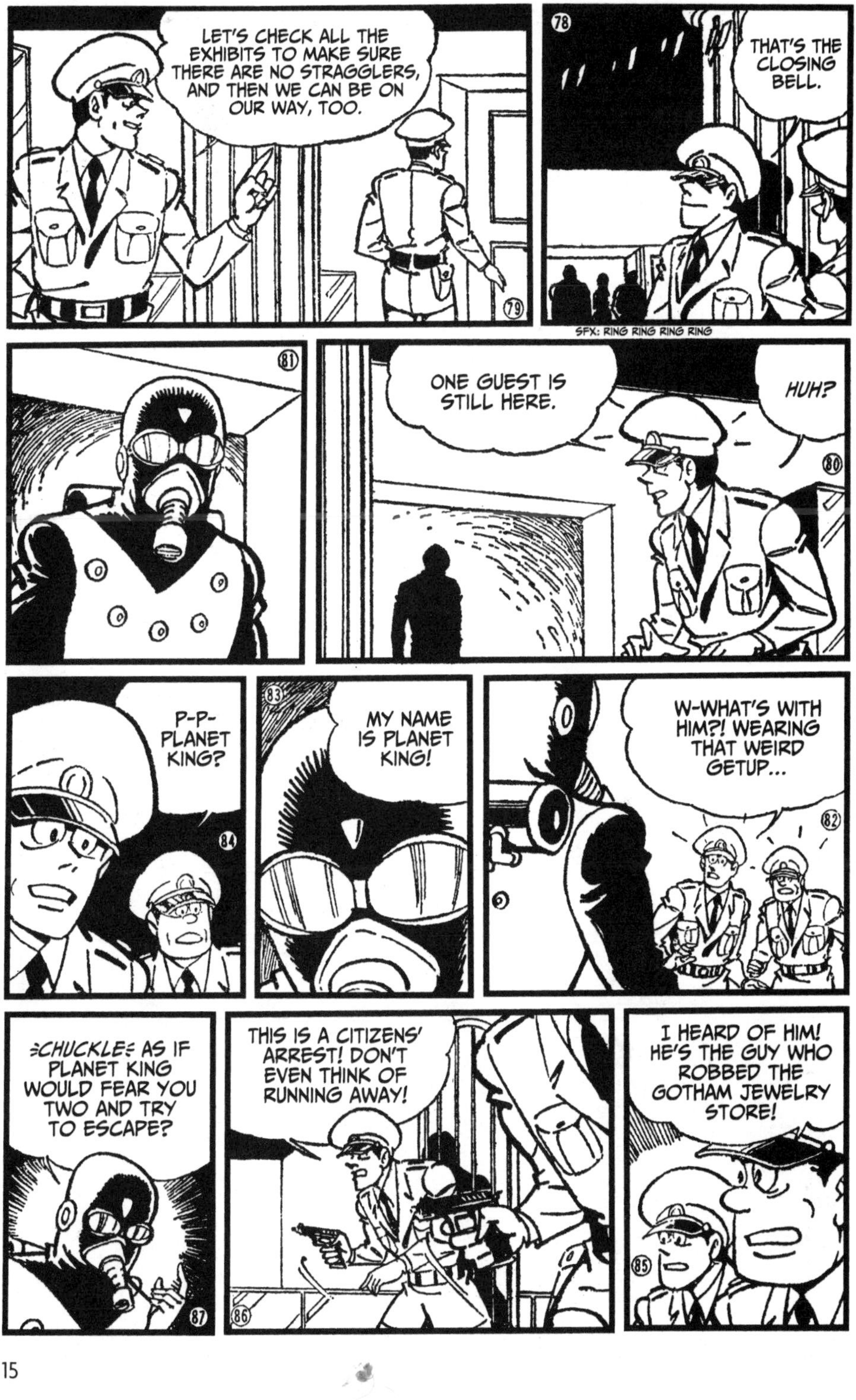
78
THAT'S THE CLOSING BELL.
SFX: RING RING RING RING
LET'S CHECK ALL THE EXHIBITS TO MAKE SURE THERE ARE NO STRAGGLERS, AND THEN WE CAN BE ON OUR WAY, TOO.
79
HUH?
ONE GUEST IS STILL HERE.
80
81
W-WHAT'S WITH HIM?! WEARING THAT WEIRD GETUP...
82
83
MY NAME IS PLANET KING!
P-P-PLANET KING?
84
I HEARD OF HIM! HE'S THE GUY WHO ROBBED THE GOTHAM JEWELRY STORE!
85
THIS IS A CITIZENS' ARREST! DON'T EVEN THINK OF RUNNING AWAY!
86
=CHUCKLE= AS IF PLANET KING WOULD FEAR YOU TWO AND TRY TO ESCAPE?
87

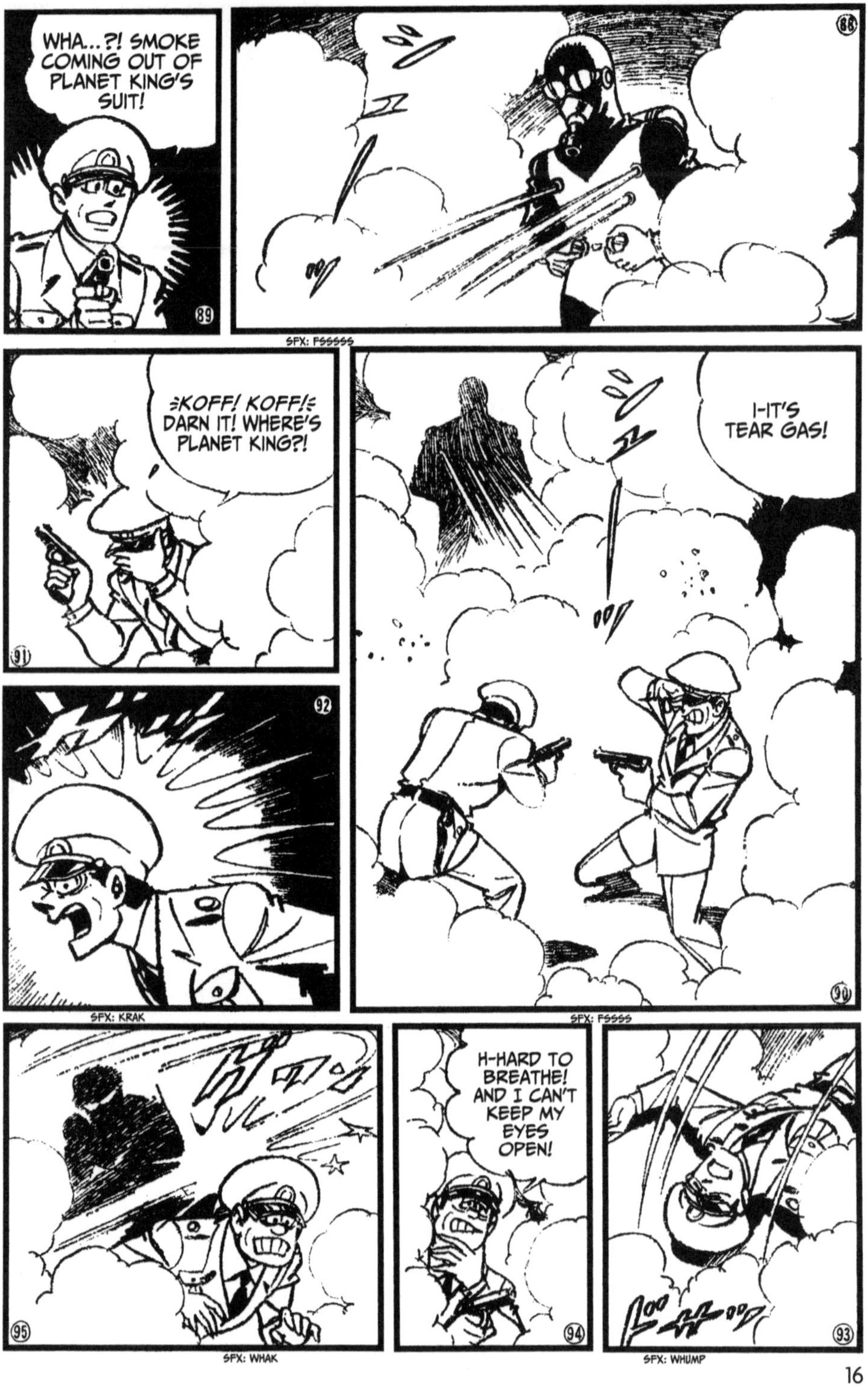
SFX: FSSSSS
WHA...?! SMOKE COMING OUT OF PLANET KING'S SUIT!
I-IT'S TEAR GAS!
SFX: FSSSS
≈KOFF! KOFF!≈ DARN IT! WHERE'S PLANET KING?!
SFX: KRAK
SFX: WHUMP
H-HARD TO BREATHE! AND I CAN'T KEEP MY EYES OPEN!
SFX: WHAK

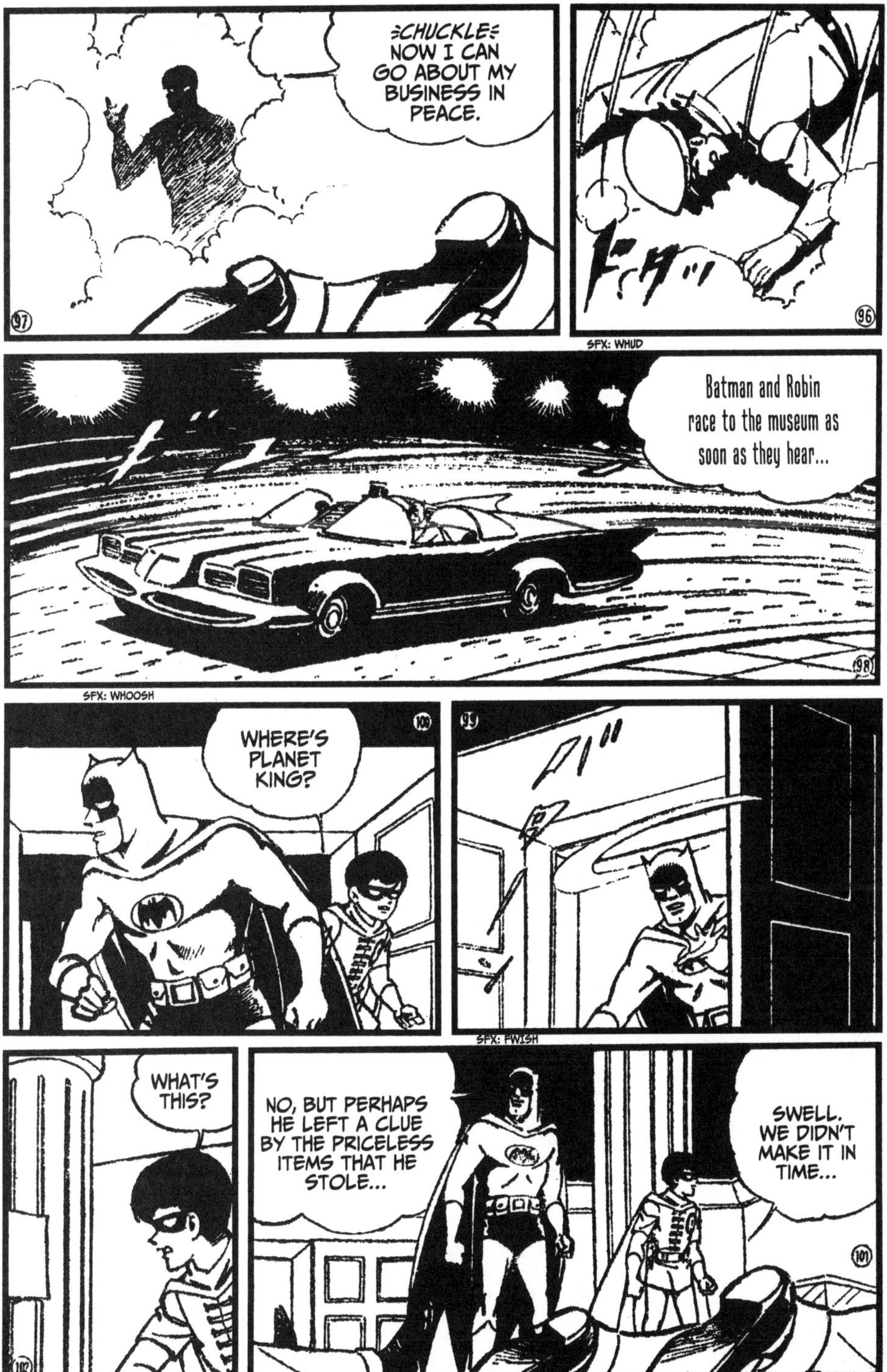
SFX: WHUD
≈CHUCKLE≈ NOW I CAN GO ABOUT MY BUSINESS IN PEACE.
Batman and Robin race to the museum as soon as they hear...
SFX: WHOOSH
SFX: FWISH
WHERE'S PLANET KING?
SWELL. WE DIDN'T MAKE IT IN TIME...
NO, BUT PERHAPS HE LEFT A CLUE BY THE PRICELESS ITEMS THAT HE STOLE...
WHAT'S THIS?

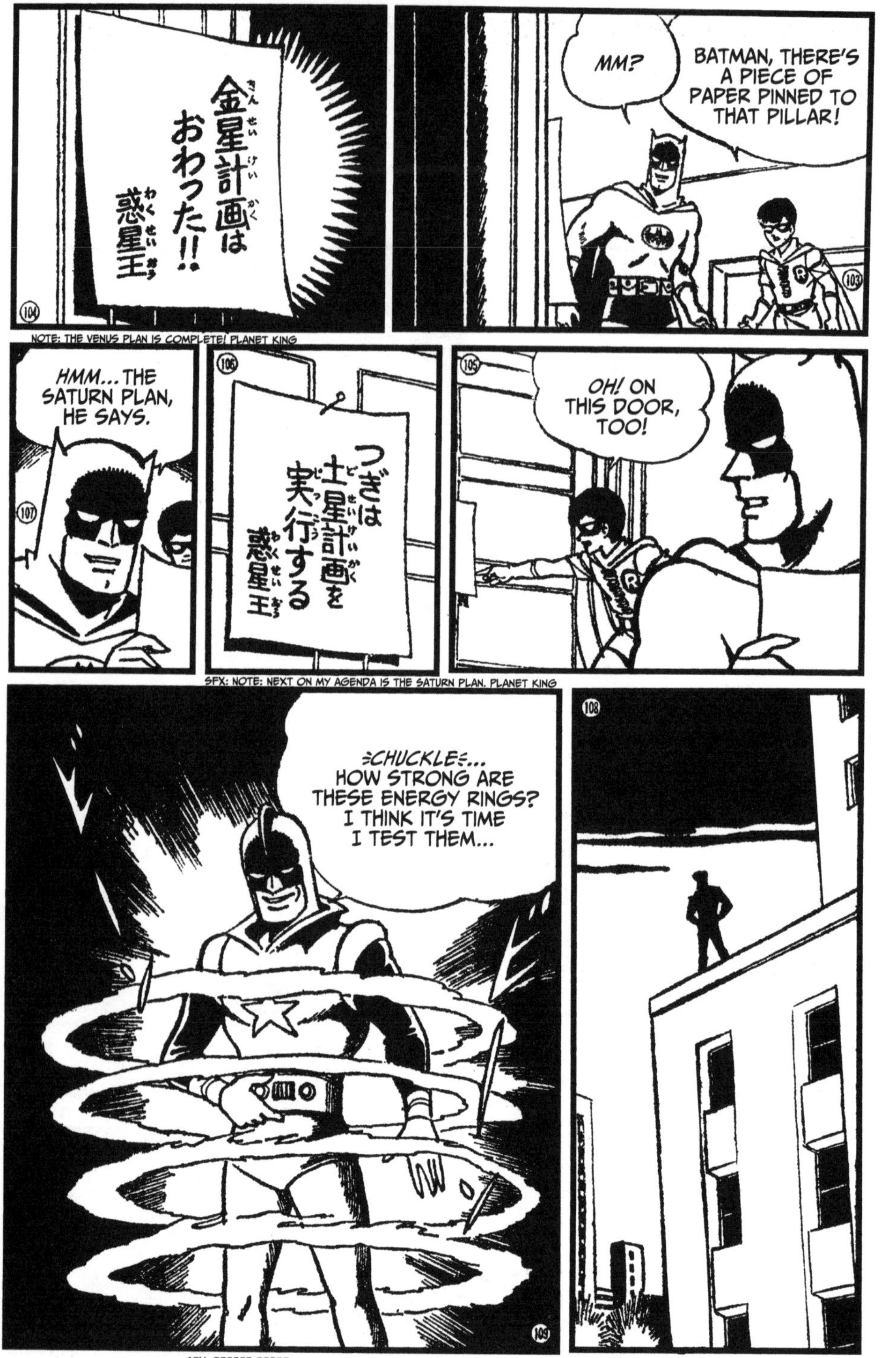
BATMAN, THERE'S A PIECE OF PAPER PINNED TO THAT PILLAR!
MM?
金星計画はおわった!! 惑星王
OH! ON THIS DOOR, TOO!
つぎは土星計画を実行する 惑星王
HMM... THE SATURN PLAN, HE SAYS.
≡CHUCKLE≡... HOW STRONG ARE THESE ENERGY RINGS? I THINK IT'S TIME I TEST THEM...

NOTE: THE VENUS PLAN IS COMPLETE! PLANET KING

SFX: NOTE: NEXT ON MY AGENDA IS THE SATURN PLAN. PLANET KING

SFX: BEEEEE BEEEE

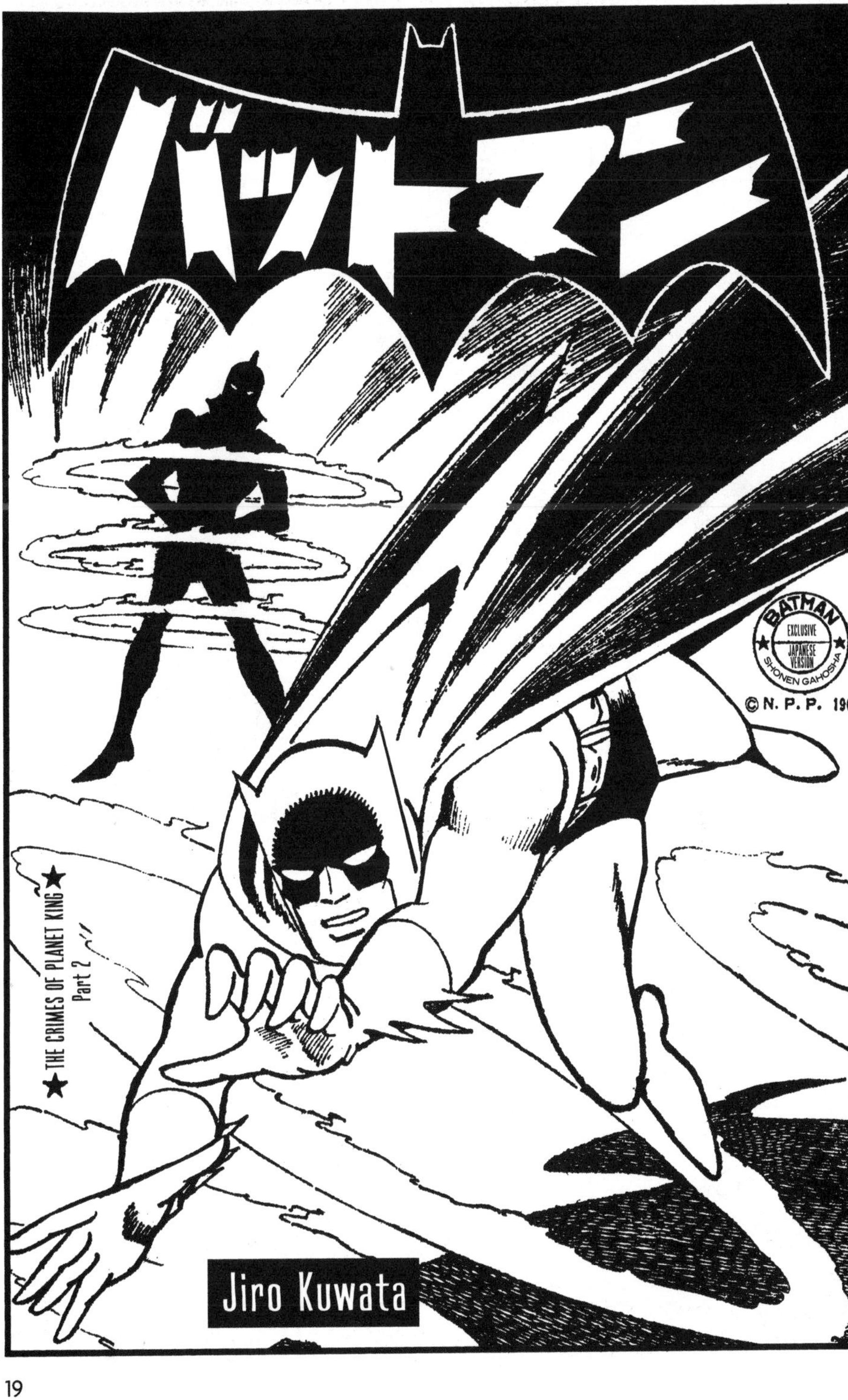
バットマン
★THE CRIMES OF PLANET KING★
Part 2
BATMAN
EXCLUSIVE
JAPANESE VERSION
SHONEN GAHOSHA
© N. P. P. 1967
Jiro Kuwata

LAST EPISODE...

A mysterious person calling himself "Planet King" appeared in Gotham City. He committed one crime after another, naming each evil deed after planets like Mercury and Venus. Next on Planet King's agenda is the "Saturn plan"...

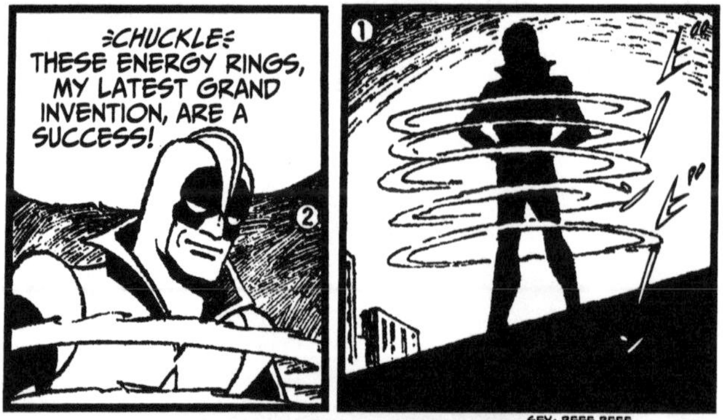

SFX: BEEE BEEE
≈CHUCKLE≈
THESE ENERGY RINGS, MY LATEST GRAND INVENTION, ARE A SUCCESS!

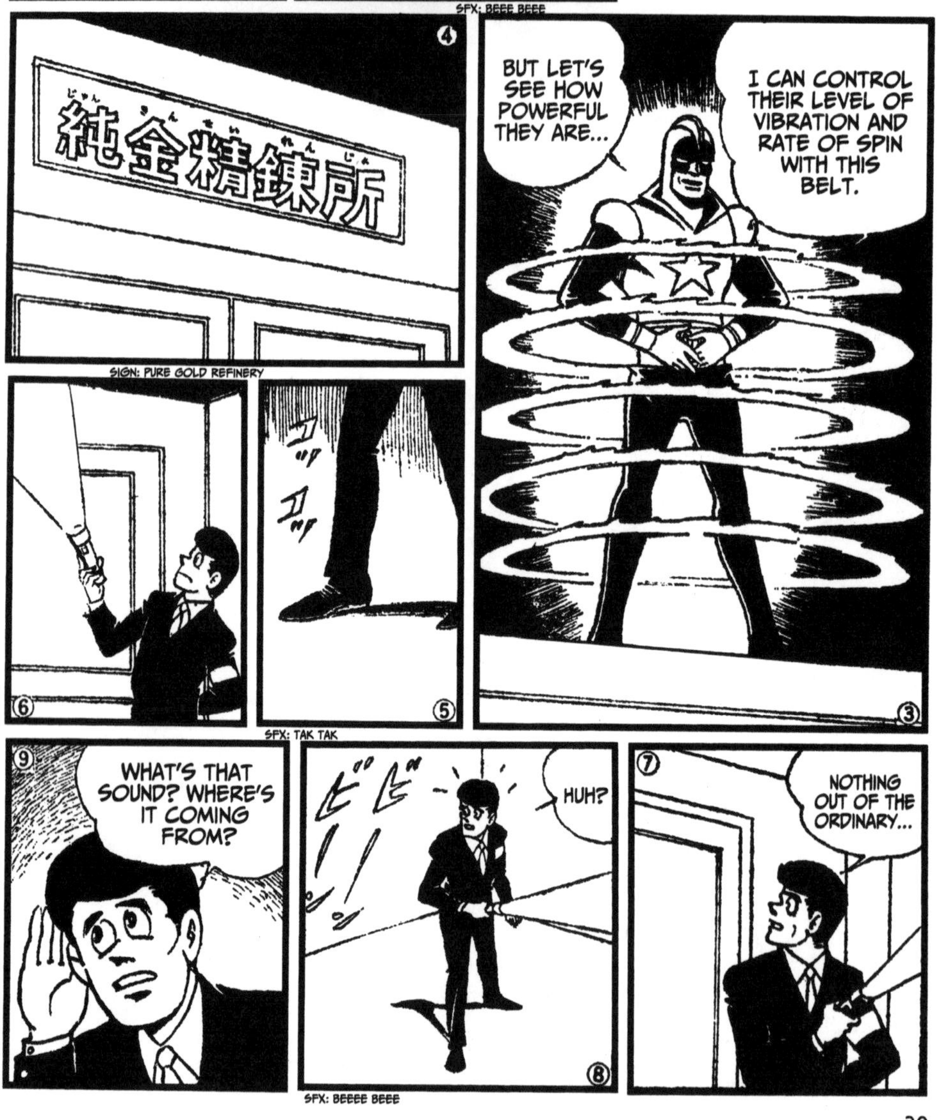

I CAN CONTROL THEIR LEVEL OF VIBRATION AND RATE OF SPIN WITH THIS BELT.
BUT LET'S SEE HOW POWERFUL THEY ARE...
純金精錬所
SIGN: PURE GOLD REFINERY
SFX: TAK TAK
NOTHING OUT OF THE ORDINARY...
HUH?
SFX: BEEEE BEEE
WHAT'S THAT SOUND? WHERE'S IT COMING FROM?

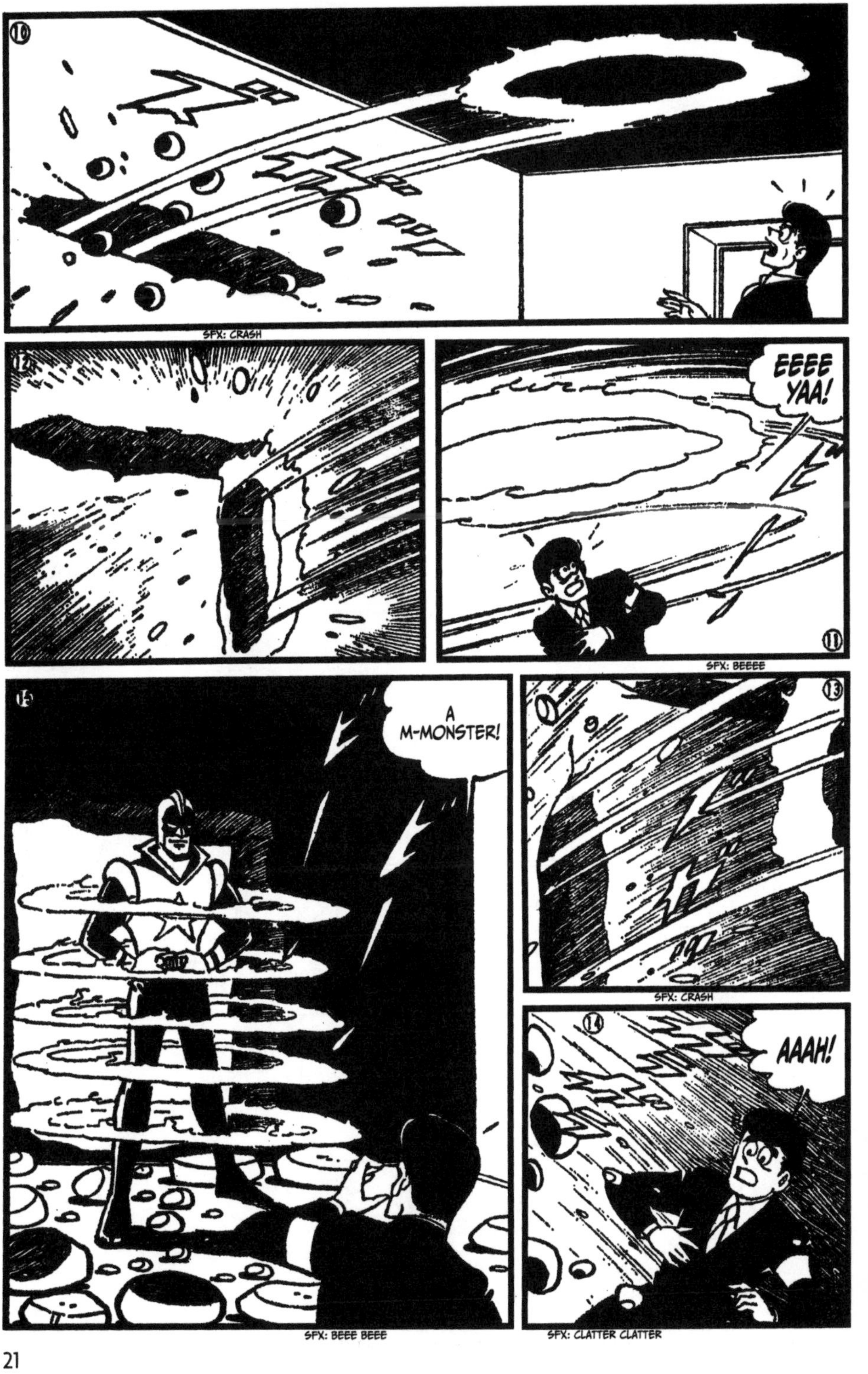
SFX: CRASH
EEEE YAA!
SFX: BEEEE
SFX: CRASH
AAAH!
SFX: CLATTER CLATTER
A M-MONSTER!
SFX: BEEE BEEE

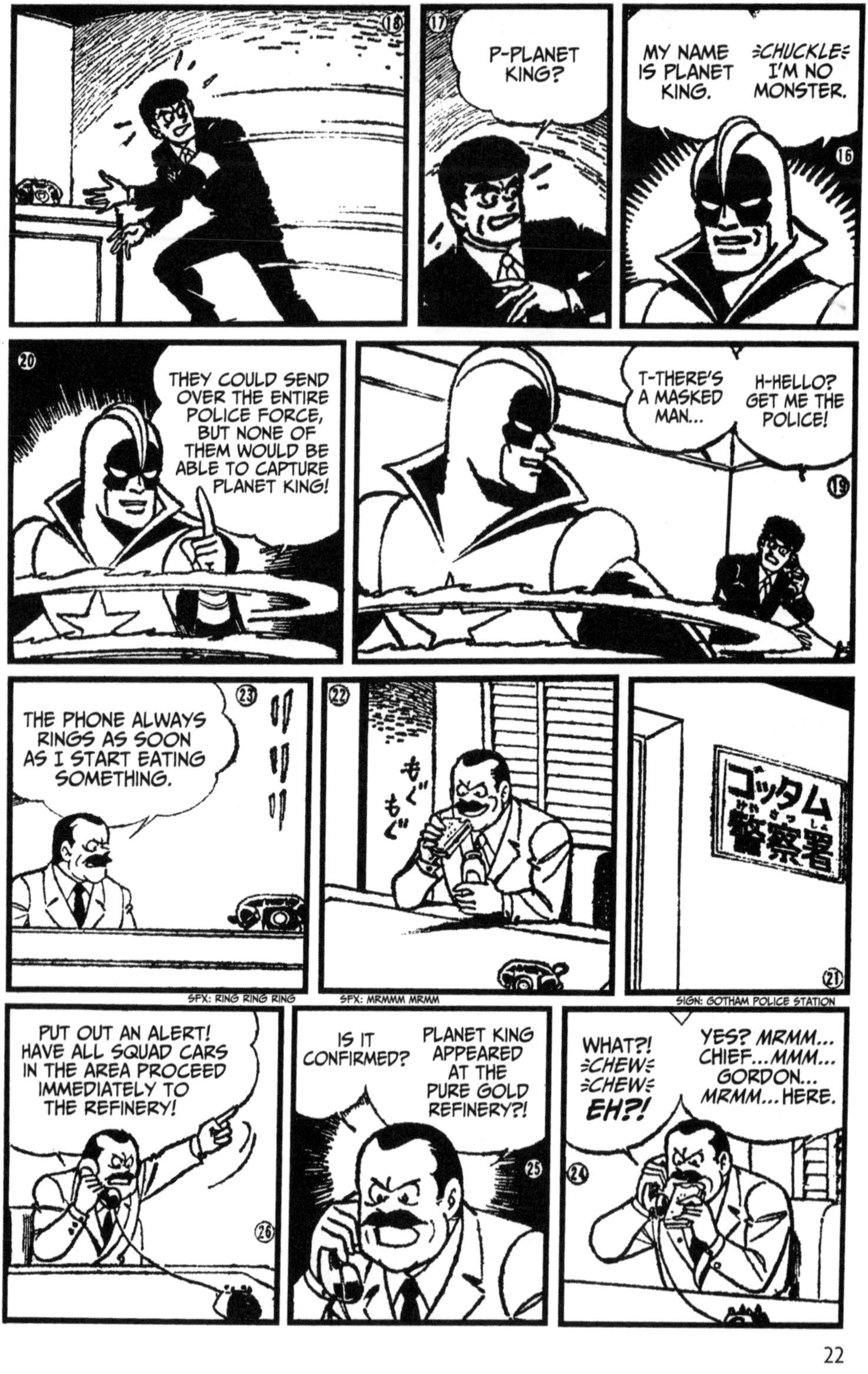
=CHUCKLE= I'M NO MONSTER.
MY NAME IS PLANET KING.
P-PLANET KING?
H-HELLO? GET ME THE POLICE!
T-THERE'S A MASKED MAN...
THEY COULD SEND OVER THE ENTIRE POLICE FORCE, BUT NONE OF THEM WOULD BE ABLE TO CAPTURE PLANET KING!
ゴッタム警察署
SIGN: GOTHAM POLICE STATION
もぐもぐ
SFX: MRMMM MRMM
THE PHONE ALWAYS RINGS AS SOON AS I START EATING SOMETHING.
SFX: RING RING RING
YES? MRMM... CHIEF...MMM... GORDON... MRMM...HERE.
WHAT?! =CHEW= =CHEW= EH?!
PLANET KING APPEARED AT THE PURE GOLD REFINERY?!
IS IT CONFIRMED?
PUT OUT AN ALERT! HAVE ALL SQUAD CARS IN THE AREA PROCEED IMMEDIATELY TO THE REFINERY!

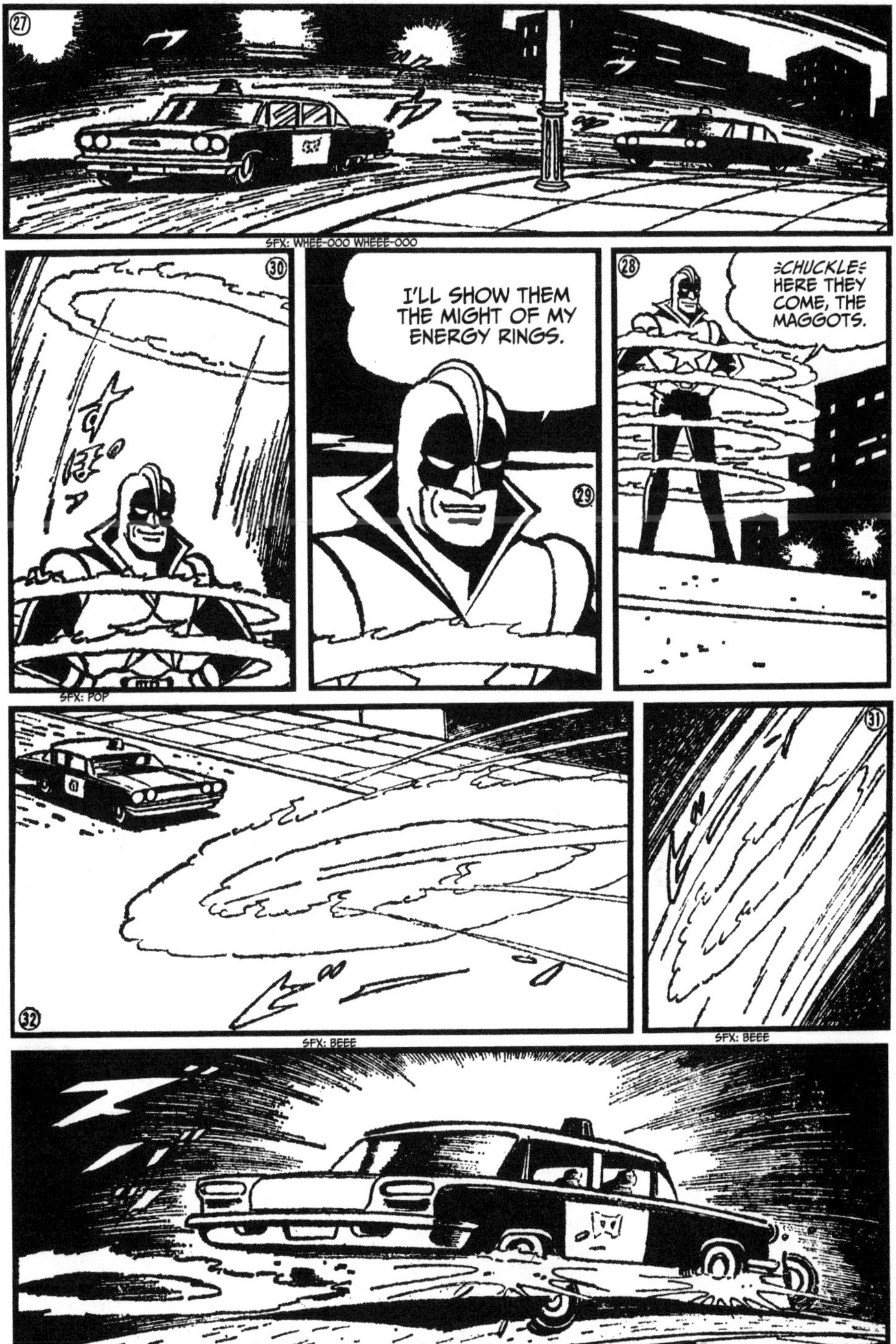
SFX: WHEE-OOO WHEEE-OOO
=CHUCKLE= HERE THEY COME, THE MAGGOTS.
I'LL SHOW THEM THE MIGHT OF MY ENERGY RINGS.
SFX: POP
SFX: BEEE
SFX: BEEE
SFX: SLASH

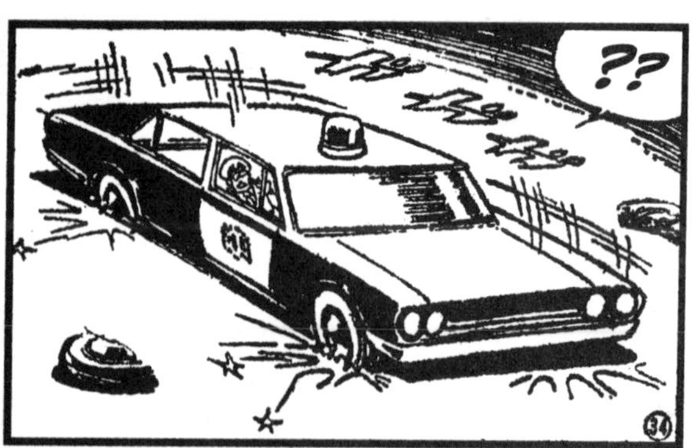
??
SFX: BAM BAM BAM

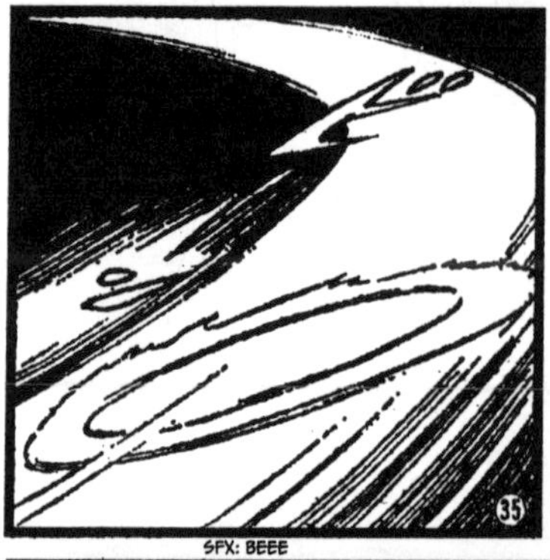
SFX: BEEE

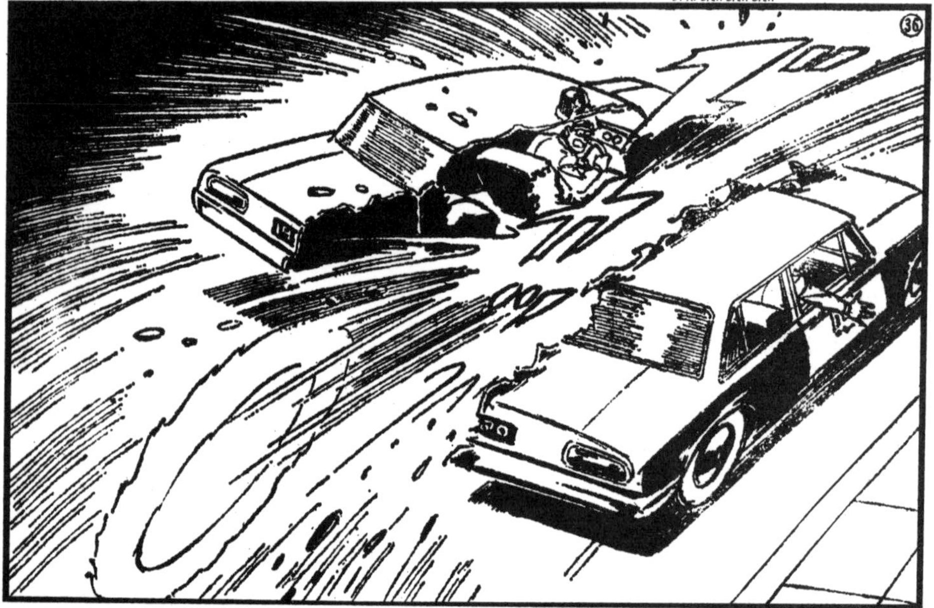
SFX: SKRISH

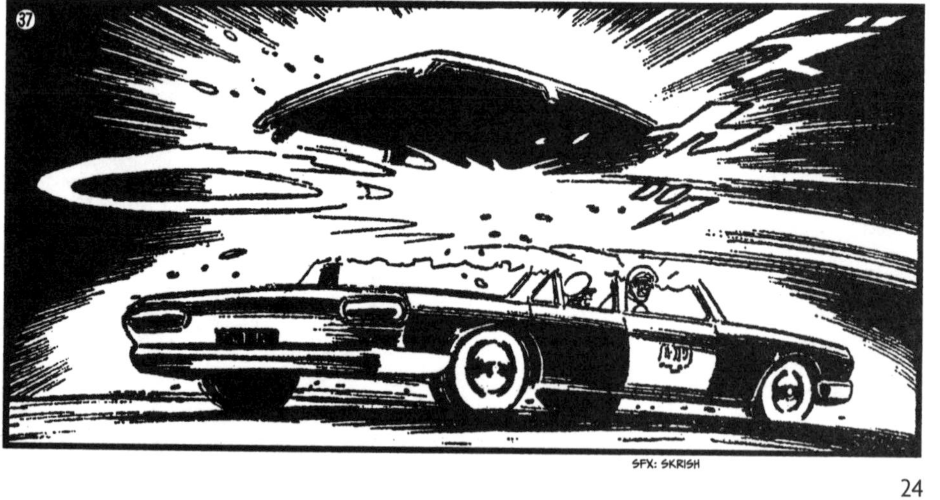
SFX: SKRISH

Batman and Robin also got the summons and speed towards the scene.

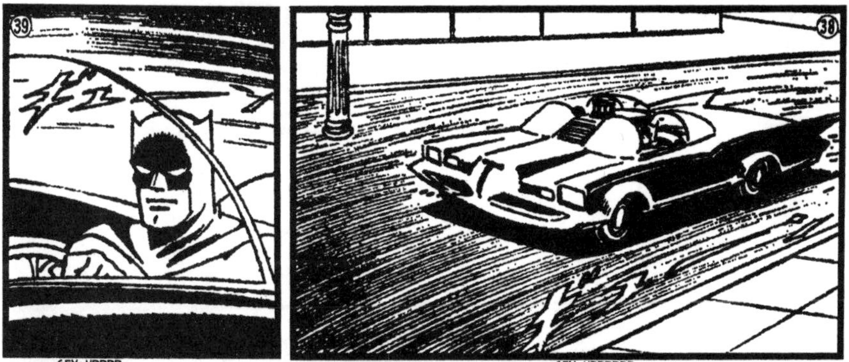

SFX: VRRRRRR

SFX: VRRRR

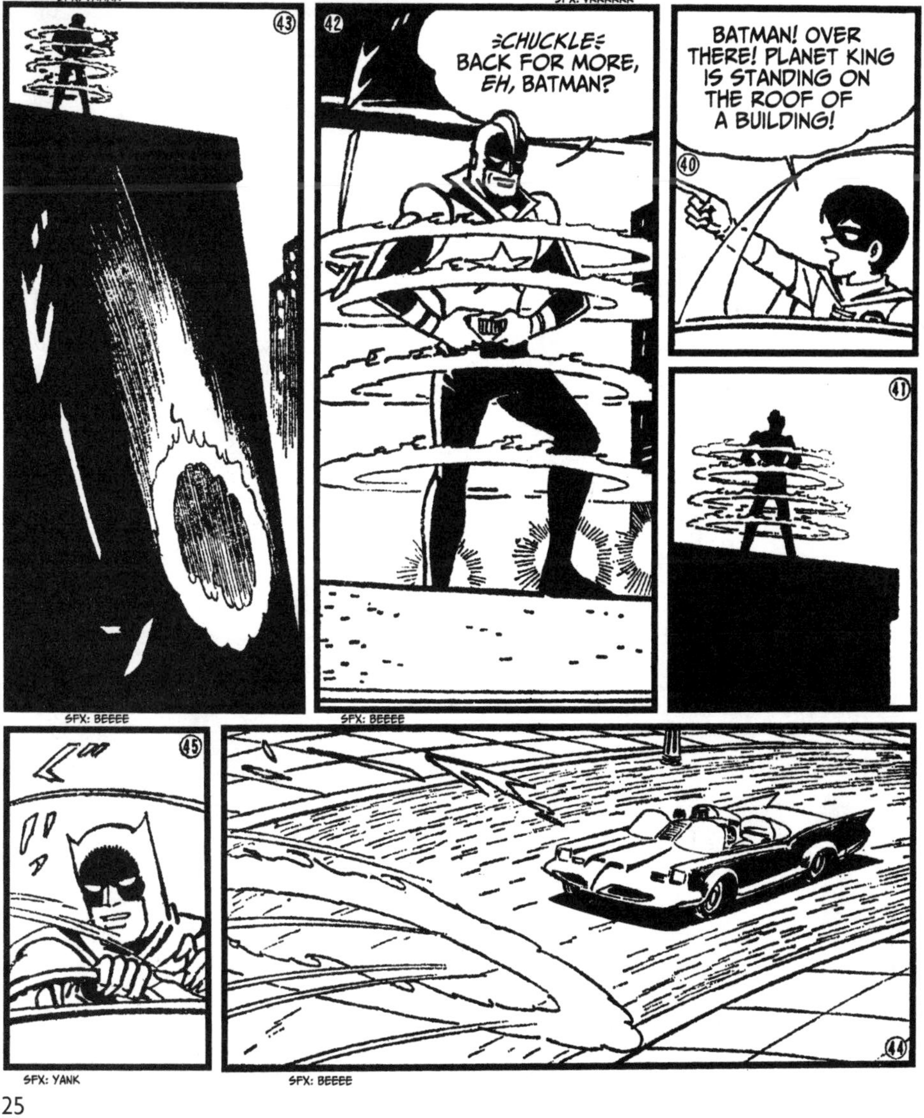
BATMAN! OVER THERE! PLANET KING IS STANDING ON THE ROOF OF A BUILDING!
=CHUCKLE= BACK FOR MORE, EH, BATMAN?

SFX: BEEEE

SFX: BEEEE

SFX: BEEEE

SFX: YANK

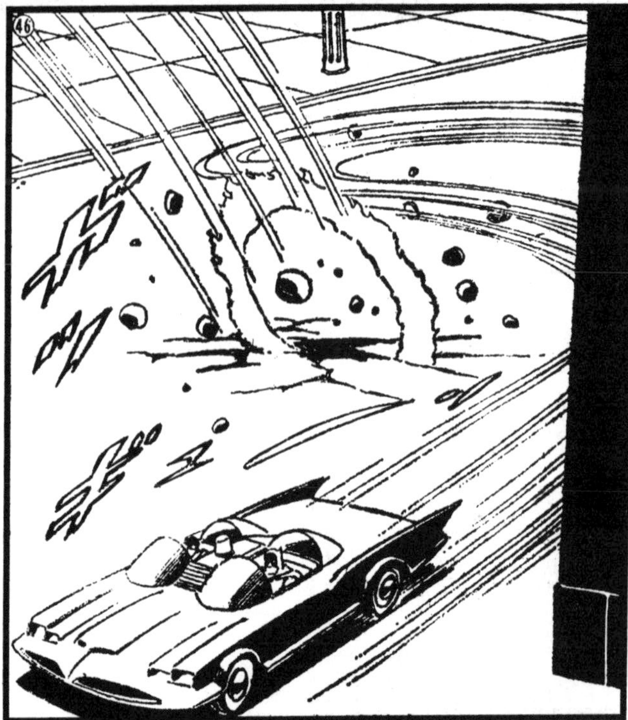

TOP SFX: CRASH BOTTOM SFX: SKREEE

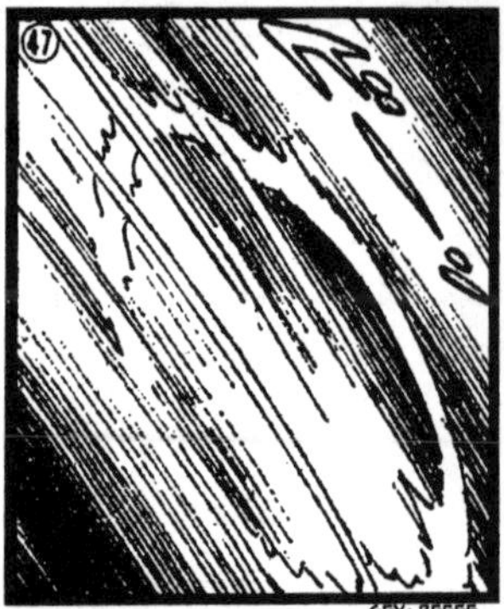

SFX: BEEEE

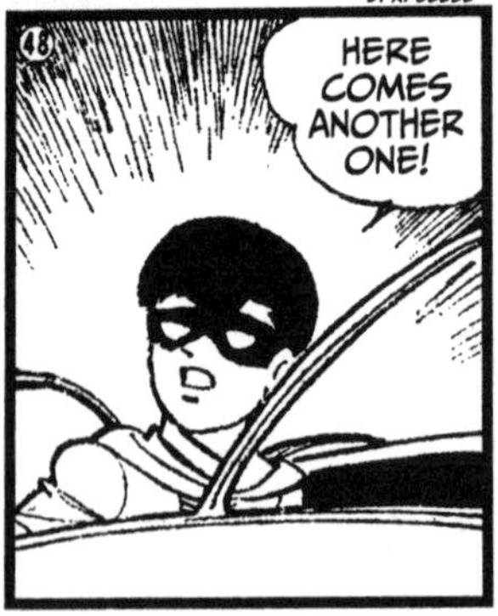
HERE COMES ANOTHER ONE!

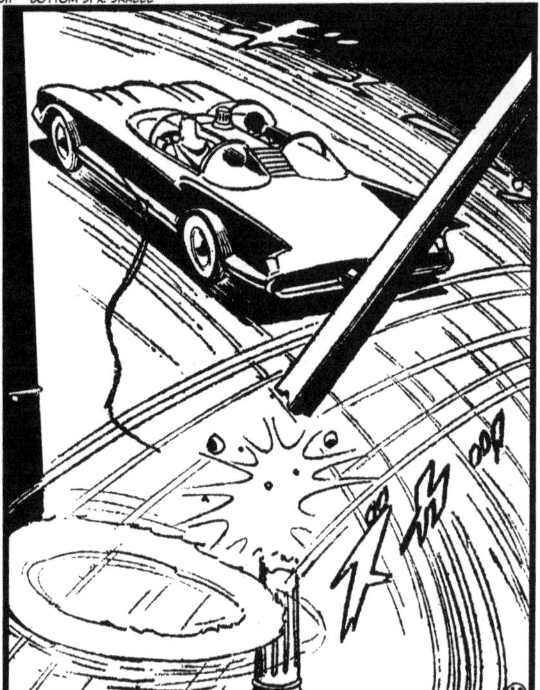

TOP SFX: SKREEE BOTTOM SFX: SHIK

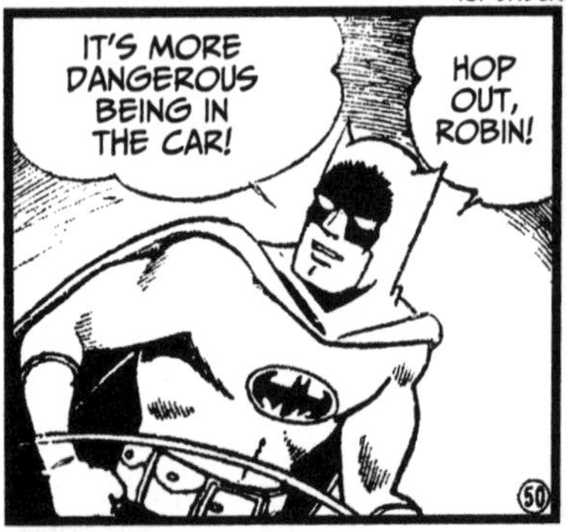
HOP OUT, ROBIN!
IT'S MORE DANGEROUS BEING IN THE CAR!

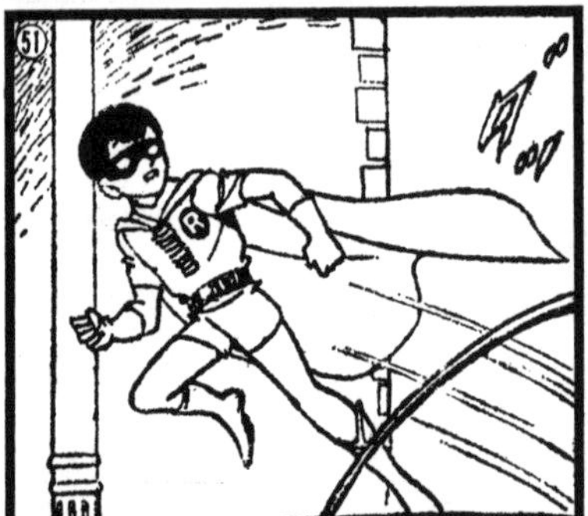

SFX: SWISH

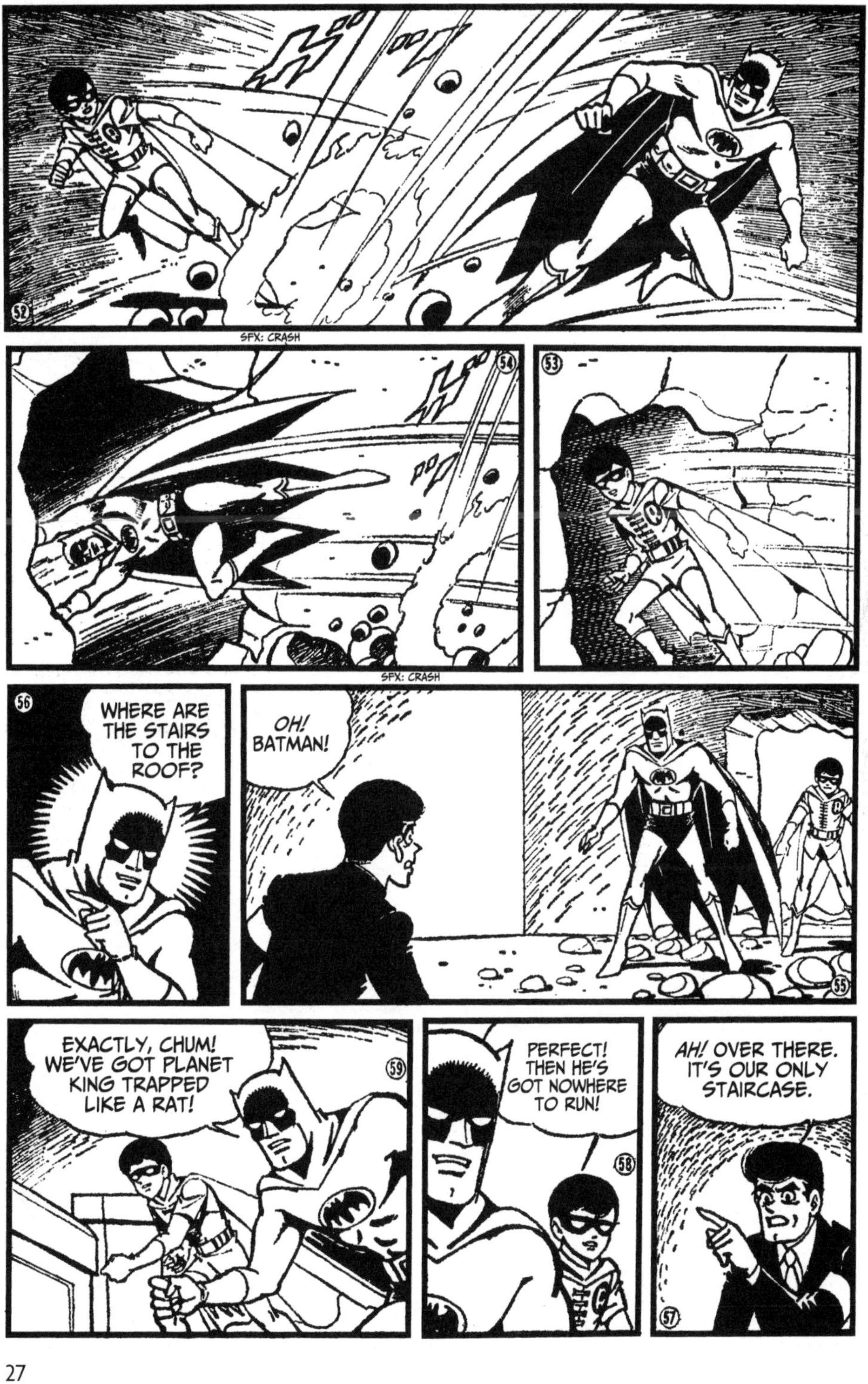
SFX: CRASH
SFX: CRASH
OH! BATMAN!
WHERE ARE THE STAIRS TO THE ROOF?
AH! OVER THERE. IT'S OUR ONLY STAIRCASE.
PERFECT! THEN HE'S GOT NOWHERE TO RUN!
EXACTLY, CHUM! WE'VE GOT PLANET KING TRAPPED LIKE A RAT!

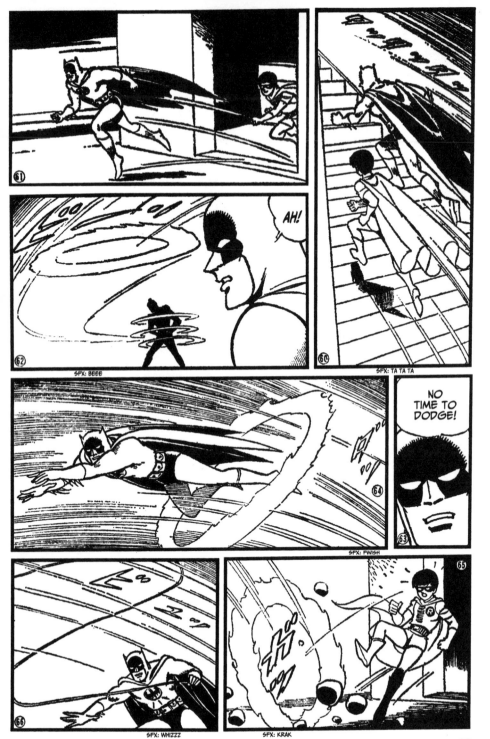

SFX: BEEE

SFX: TA TA TA

NO TIME TO DODGE!

SFX: FWISH

SFX: WHIZZZ

SFX: KRAK

28

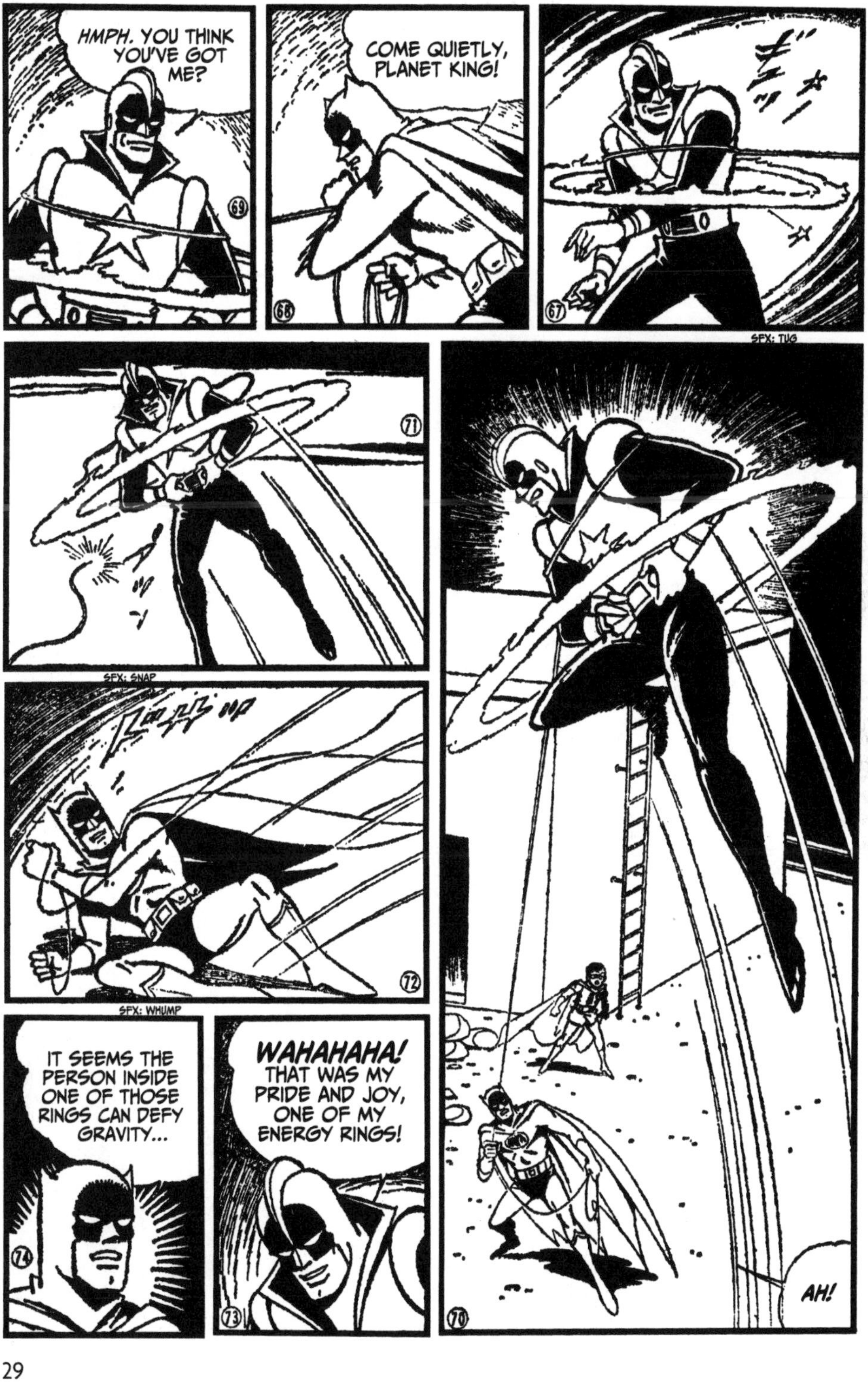
SFX: TUG
COME QUIETLY, PLANET KING!
HMPH. YOU THINK YOU'VE GOT ME?
AH!
SFX: SNAP
SFX: WHUMP
WAHAHAHA! THAT WAS MY PRIDE AND JOY, ONE OF MY ENERGY RINGS!
IT SEEMS THE PERSON INSIDE ONE OF THOSE RINGS CAN DEFY GRAVITY...

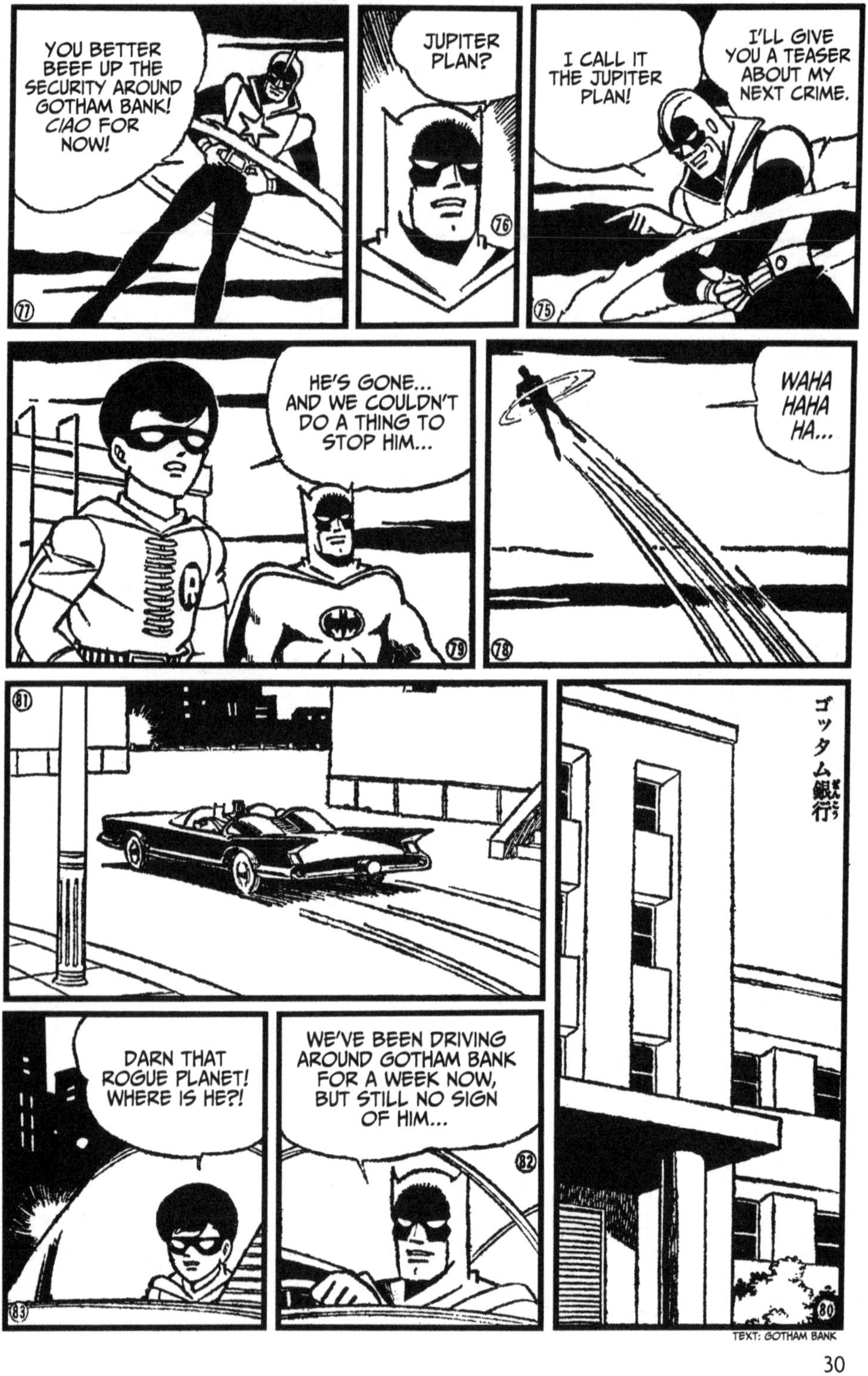
I'LL GIVE YOU A TEASER ABOUT MY NEXT CRIME.
I CALL IT THE JUPITER PLAN!
JUPITER PLAN?
YOU BETTER BEEF UP THE SECURITY AROUND GOTHAM BANK! *CIAO* FOR NOW!
WAHA HAHA HA...
HE'S GONE... AND WE COULDN'T DO A THING TO STOP HIM...
ゴッタム銀行
WE'VE BEEN DRIVING AROUND GOTHAM BANK FOR A WEEK NOW, BUT STILL NO SIGN OF HIM...
DARN THAT ROGUE PLANET! WHERE IS HE?!
TEXT: GOTHAM BANK

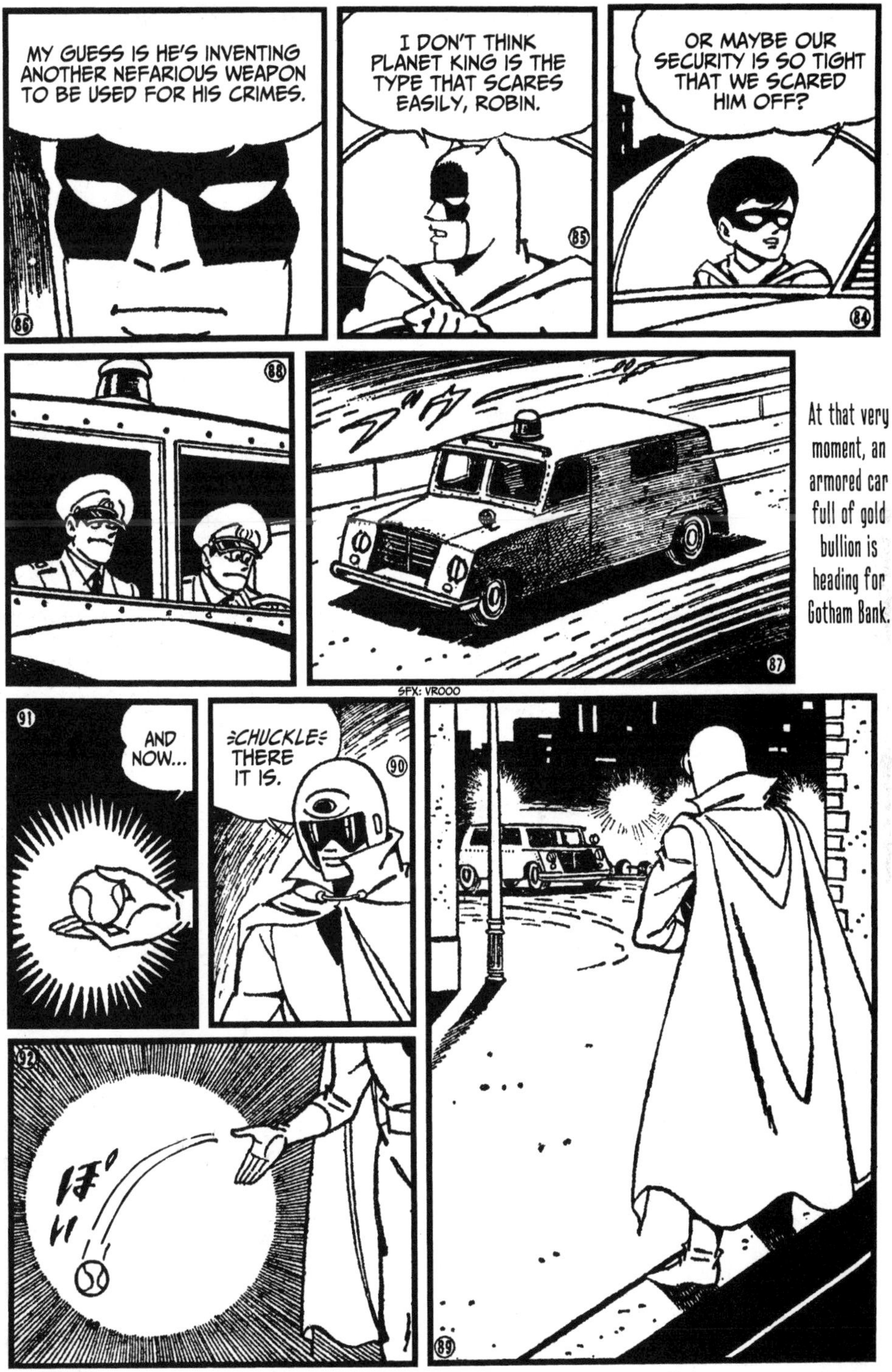
OR MAYBE OUR SECURITY IS SO TIGHT THAT WE SCARED HIM OFF?
I DON'T THINK PLANET KING IS THE TYPE THAT SCARES EASILY, ROBIN.
MY GUESS IS HE'S INVENTING ANOTHER NEFARIOUS WEAPON TO BE USED FOR HIS CRIMES.
At that very moment, an armored car full of gold bullion is heading for Gotham Bank.
SFX: VROOO
≈CHUCKLE≈ THERE IT IS.
AND NOW...
ぽい
SFX: TOSS

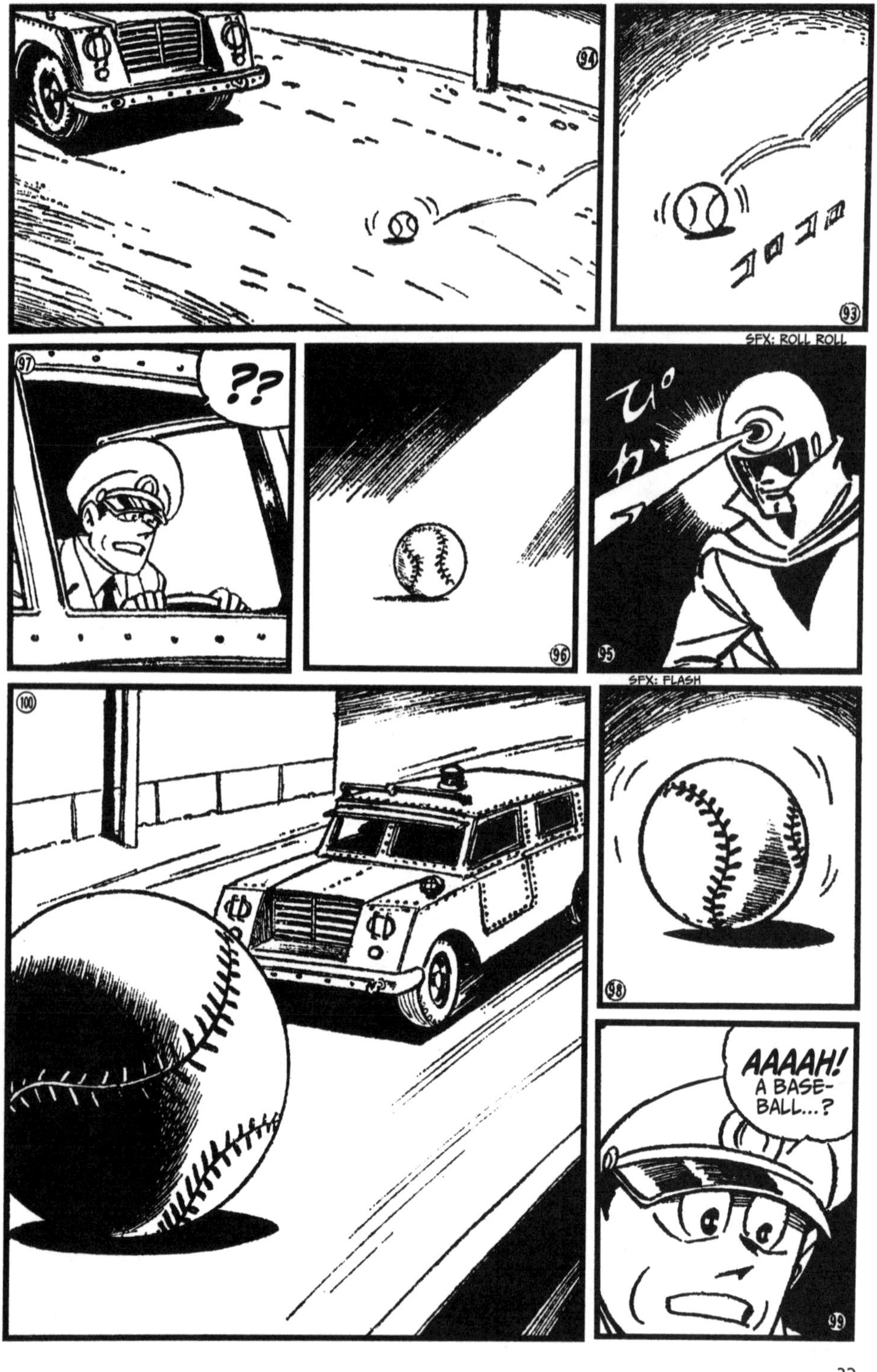

コロコロ
SFX: ROLL ROLL
ぴか
SFX: FLASH
??
AAAAH!
A BASE-
BALL...?

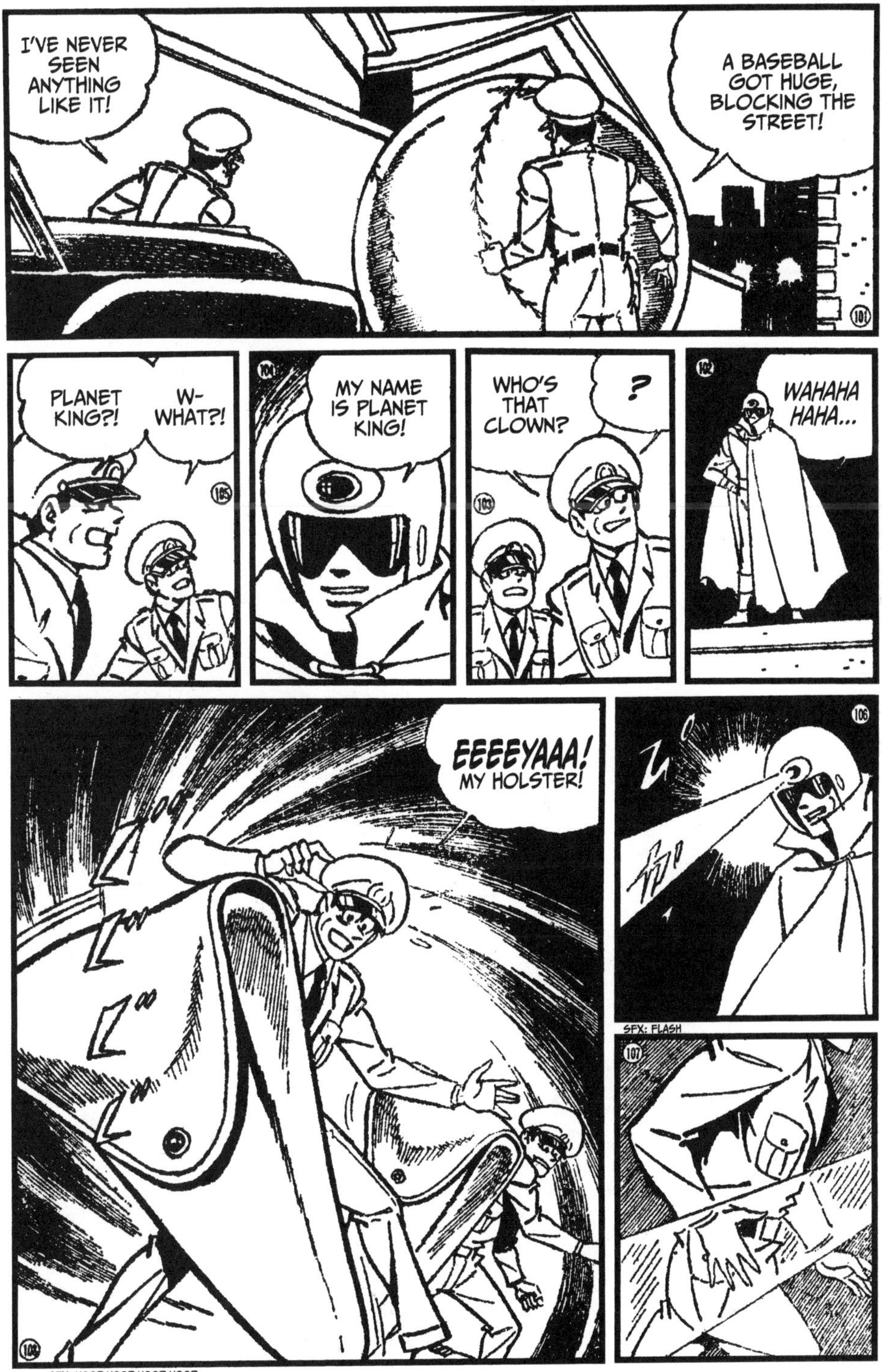
A BASEBALL GOT HUGE, BLOCKING THE STREET!
I'VE NEVER SEEN ANYTHING LIKE IT!
WAHAHA HAHA...
?
WHO'S THAT CLOWN?
MY NAME IS PLANET KING!
W-WHAT?!
PLANET KING?!
SFX: FLASH
EEEEYAAA! MY HOLSTER!
SFX: VOOP VOOP VOOP VOOP

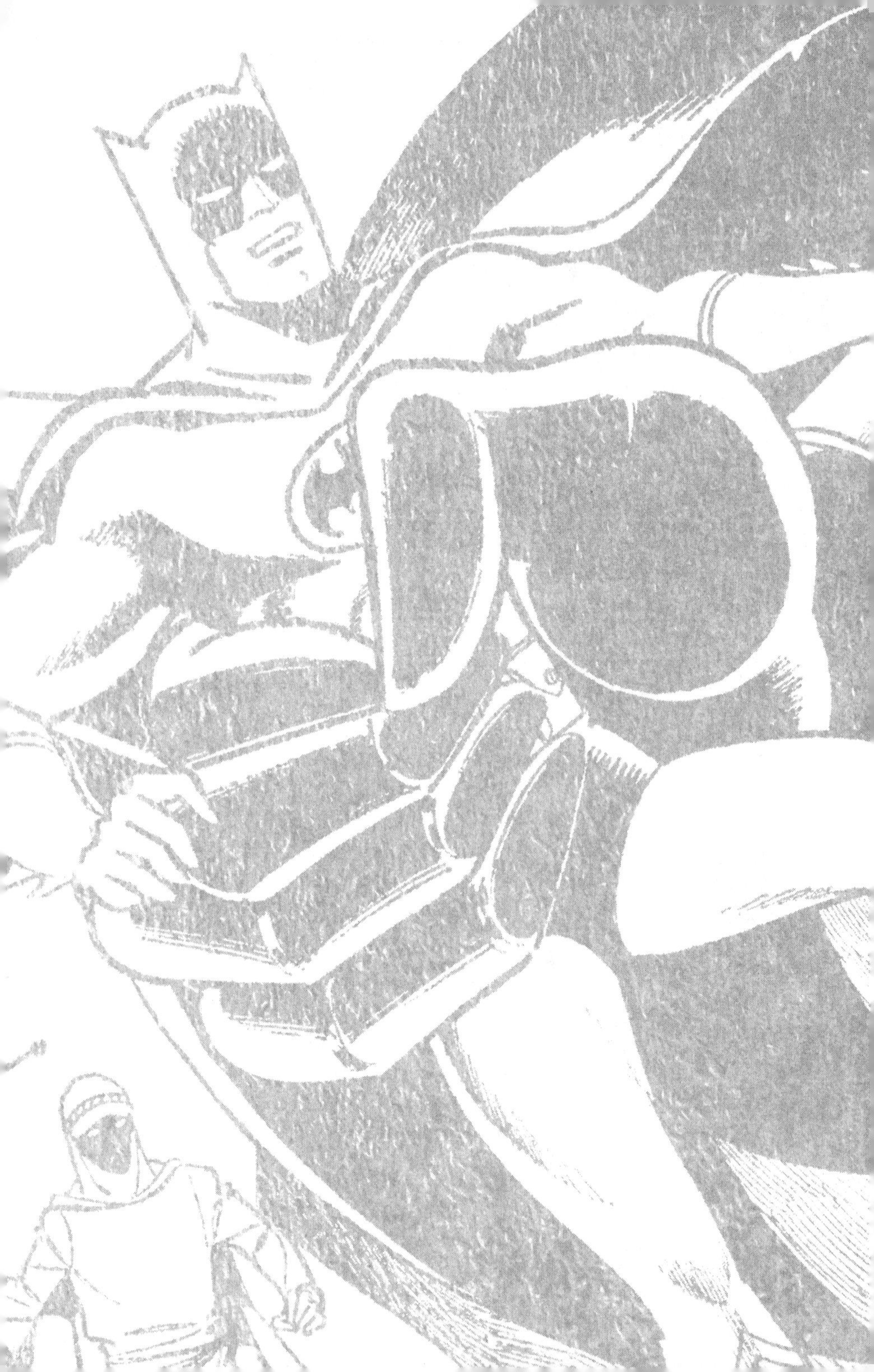

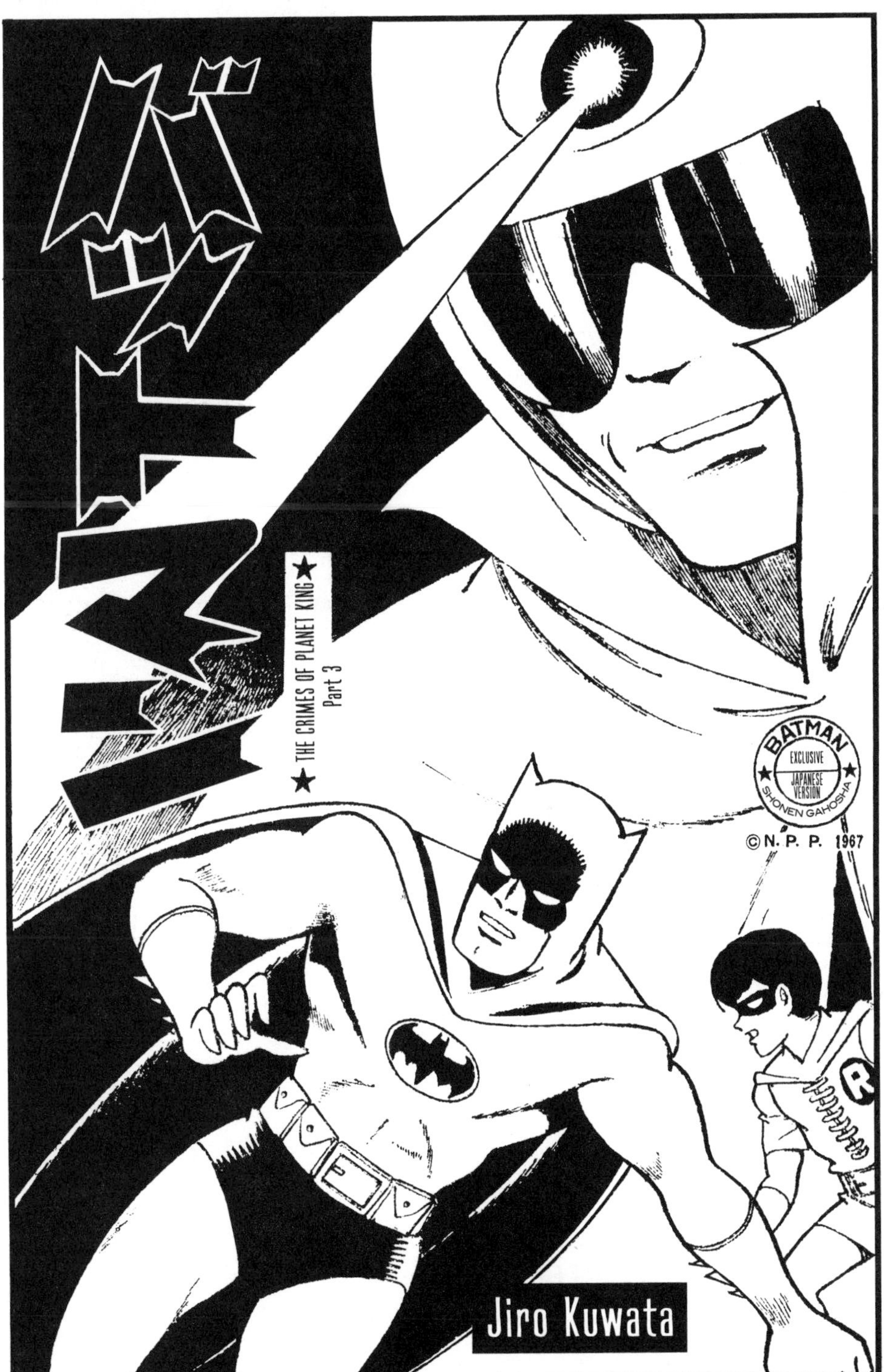
★THE CRIMES OF PLANET KING★
Part 3
BATMAN
EXCLUSIVE
JAPANESE VERSION
SHONEN GAHOSHA
©N. P. P. 1967
Jiro Kuwata

LAST EPISODE...

Planet King continued his rampage of planned crimes named after planets. An armored truck was on its way to Gotham Bank bearing gold bullion when a baseball rolled out in front of it. A ray of light hit the ball and suddenly the ball grew to enormous size. When the shocked guards came out of the truck, the mysterious light hit their holsters, making them grow right before their eyes...

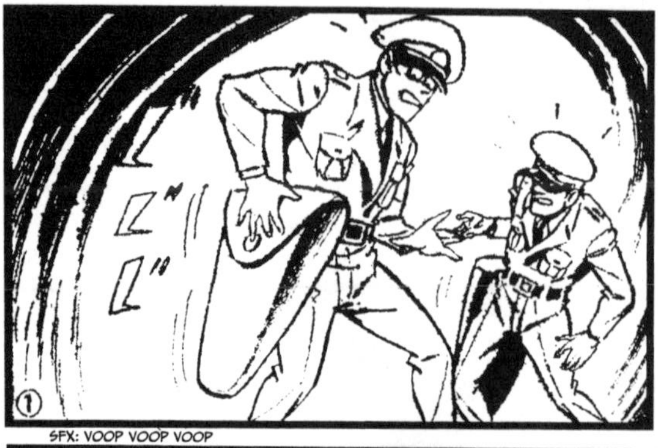
SFX: VOOP VOOP VOOP

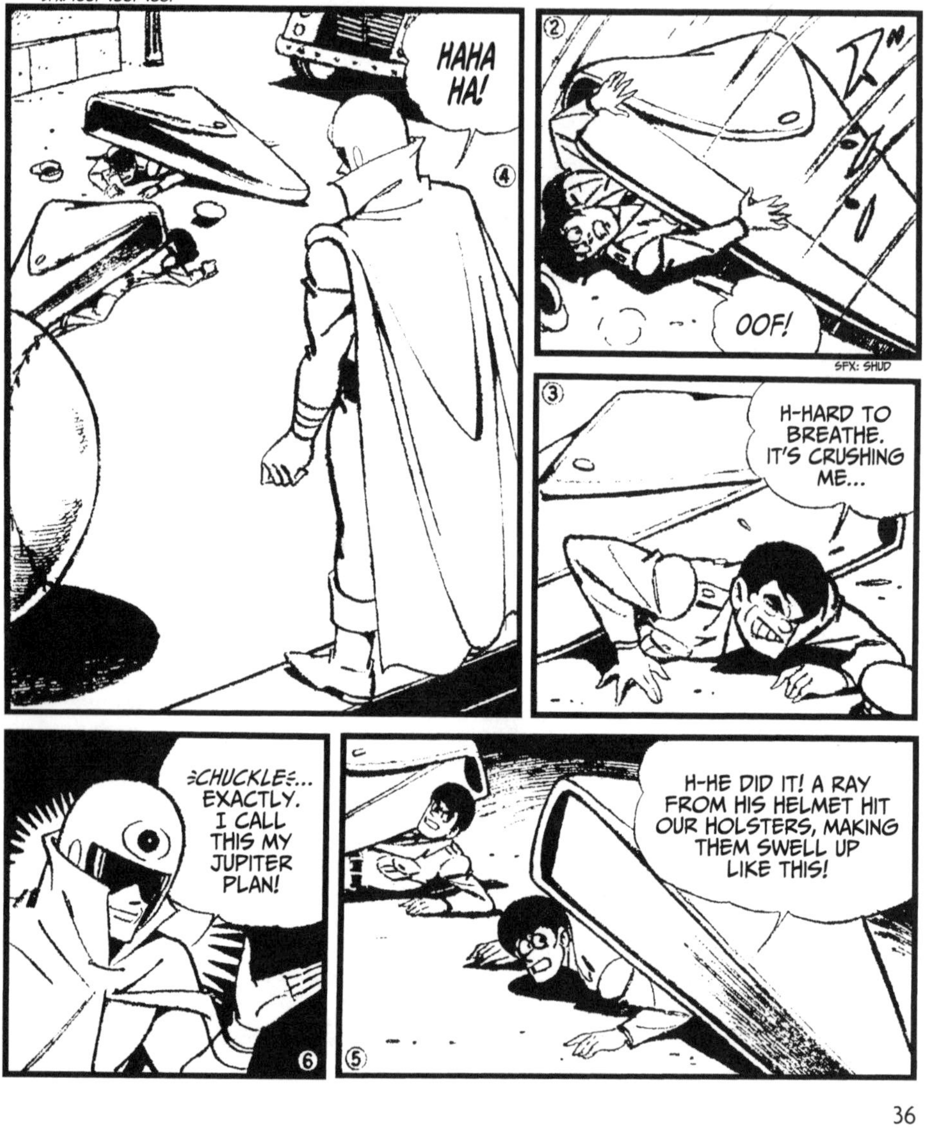
OOF!
SFX: SHUD
H-HARD TO BREATHE. IT'S CRUSHING ME...
HAHA HA!
H-HE DID IT! A RAY FROM HIS HELMET HIT OUR HOLSTERS, MAKING THEM SWELL UP LIKE THIS!
=CHUCKLE=... EXACTLY. I CALL THIS MY JUPITER PLAN!

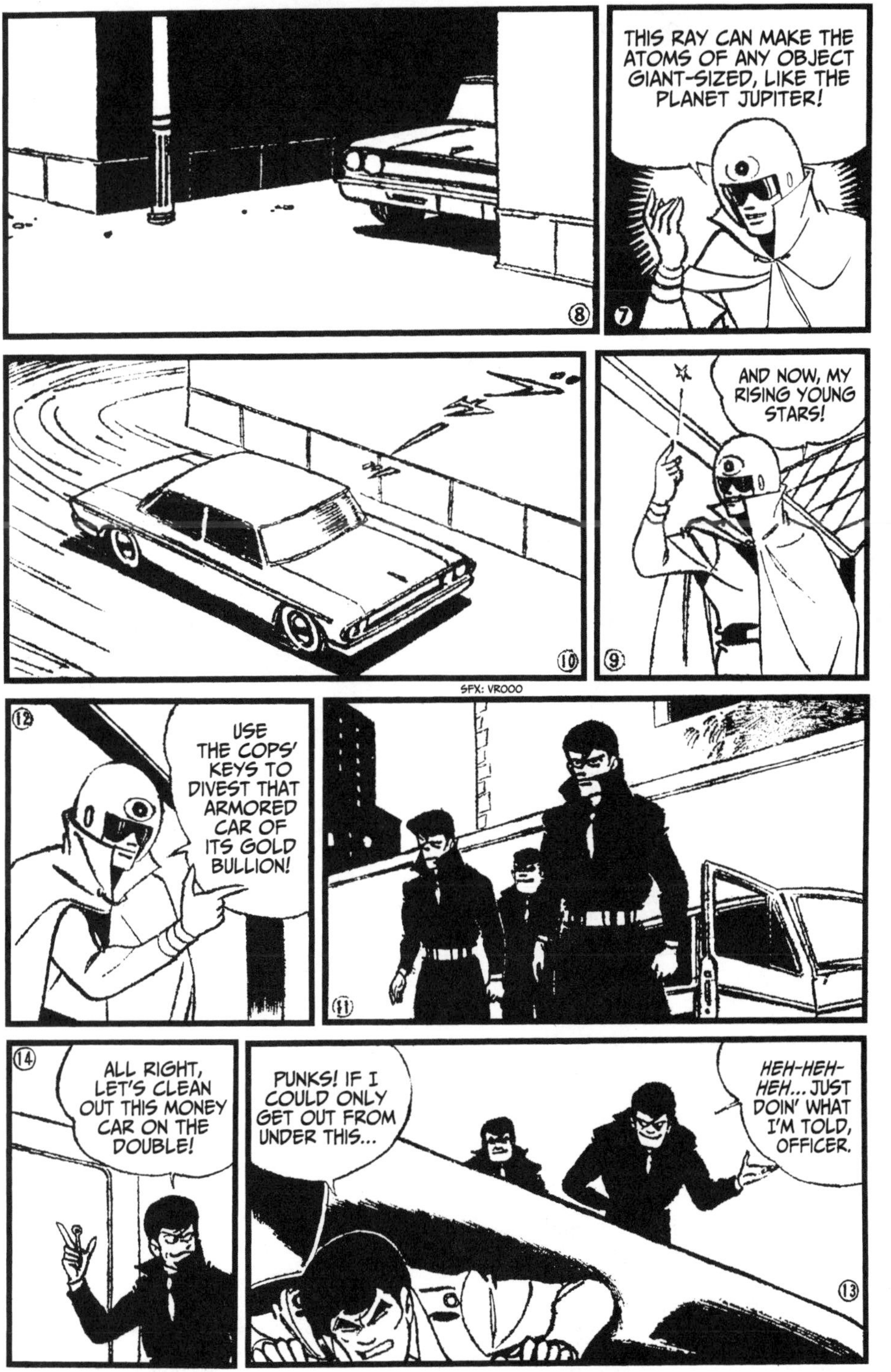

THIS RAY CAN MAKE THE ATOMS OF ANY OBJECT GIANT-SIZED, LIKE THE PLANET JUPITER!
AND NOW, MY RISING YOUNG STARS!
SFX: VROOO
USE THE COPS' KEYS TO DIVEST THAT ARMORED CAR OF ITS GOLD BULLION!
HEH-HEH-HEH... JUST DOIN' WHAT I'M TOLD, OFFICER.
PUNKS! IF I COULD ONLY GET OUT FROM UNDER THIS...
ALL RIGHT, LET'S CLEAN OUT THIS MONEY CAR ON THE DOUBLE!

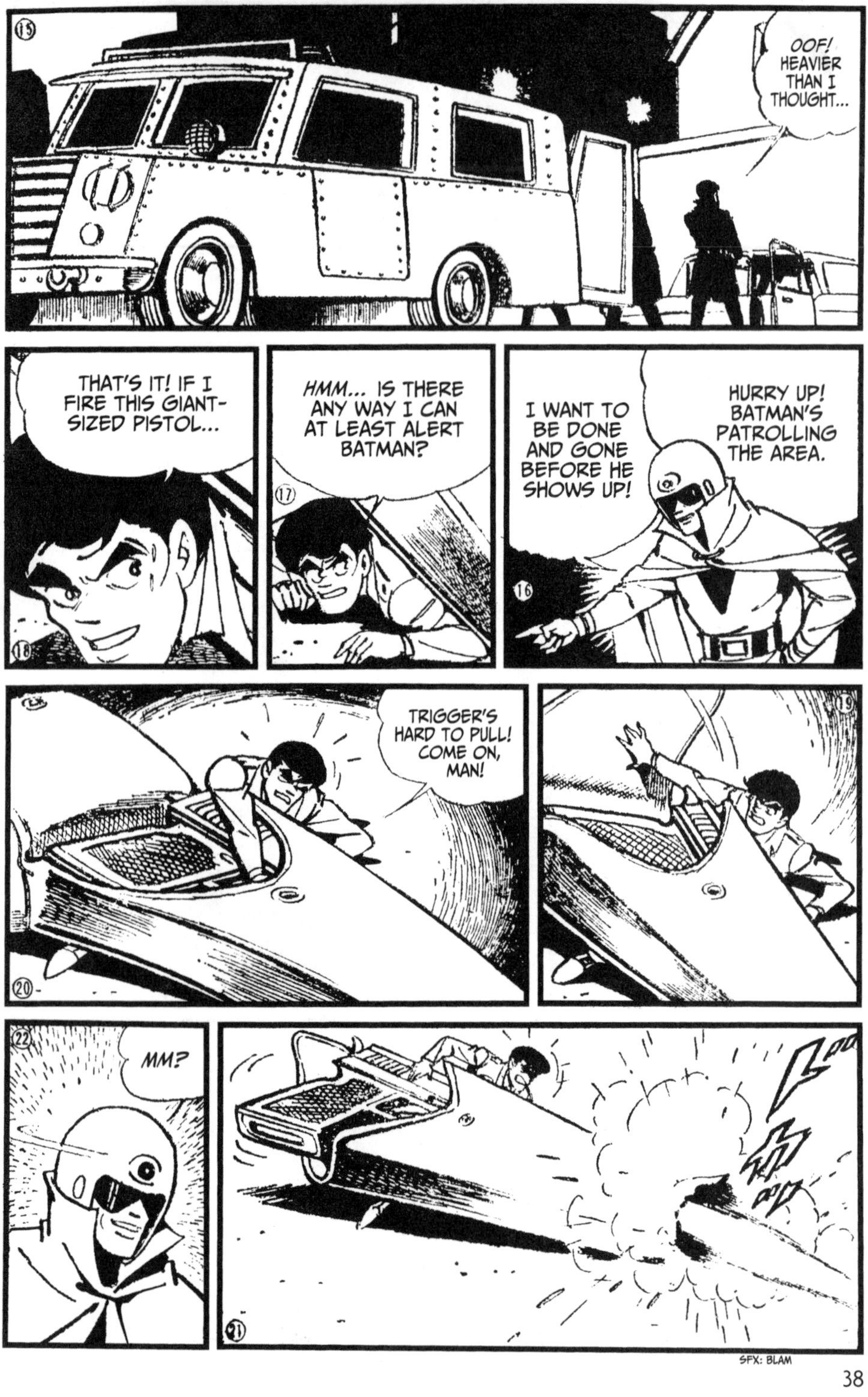
OOF! HEAVIER THAN I THOUGHT...
HURRY UP! BATMAN'S PATROLLING THE AREA.
I WANT TO BE DONE AND GONE BEFORE HE SHOWS UP!
HMM... IS THERE ANY WAY I CAN AT LEAST ALERT BATMAN?
THAT'S IT! IF I FIRE THIS GIANT-SIZED PISTOL...
TRIGGER'S HARD TO PULL! COME ON, MAN!
MM?

SFX: BLAM

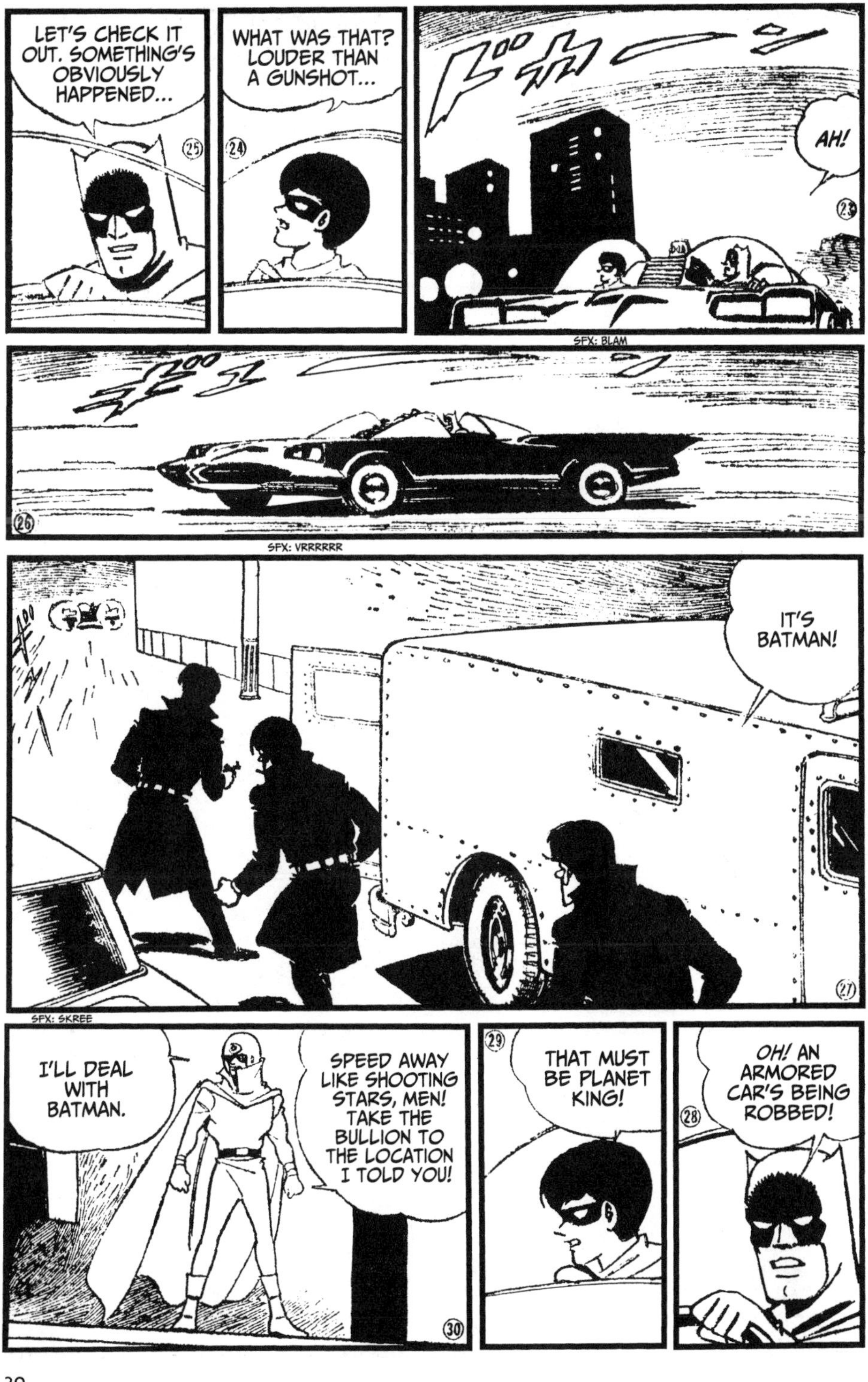
AH!
SFX: BLAM
WHAT WAS THAT? LOUDER THAN A GUNSHOT...
LET'S CHECK IT OUT. SOMETHING'S OBVIOUSLY HAPPENED...
SFX: VRRRRRR
IT'S BATMAN!
SFX: SKREE
OH! AN ARMORED CAR'S BEING ROBBED!
THAT MUST BE PLANET KING!
SPEED AWAY LIKE SHOOTING STARS, MEN! TAKE THE BULLION TO THE LOCATION I TOLD YOU!
I'LL DEAL WITH BATMAN.

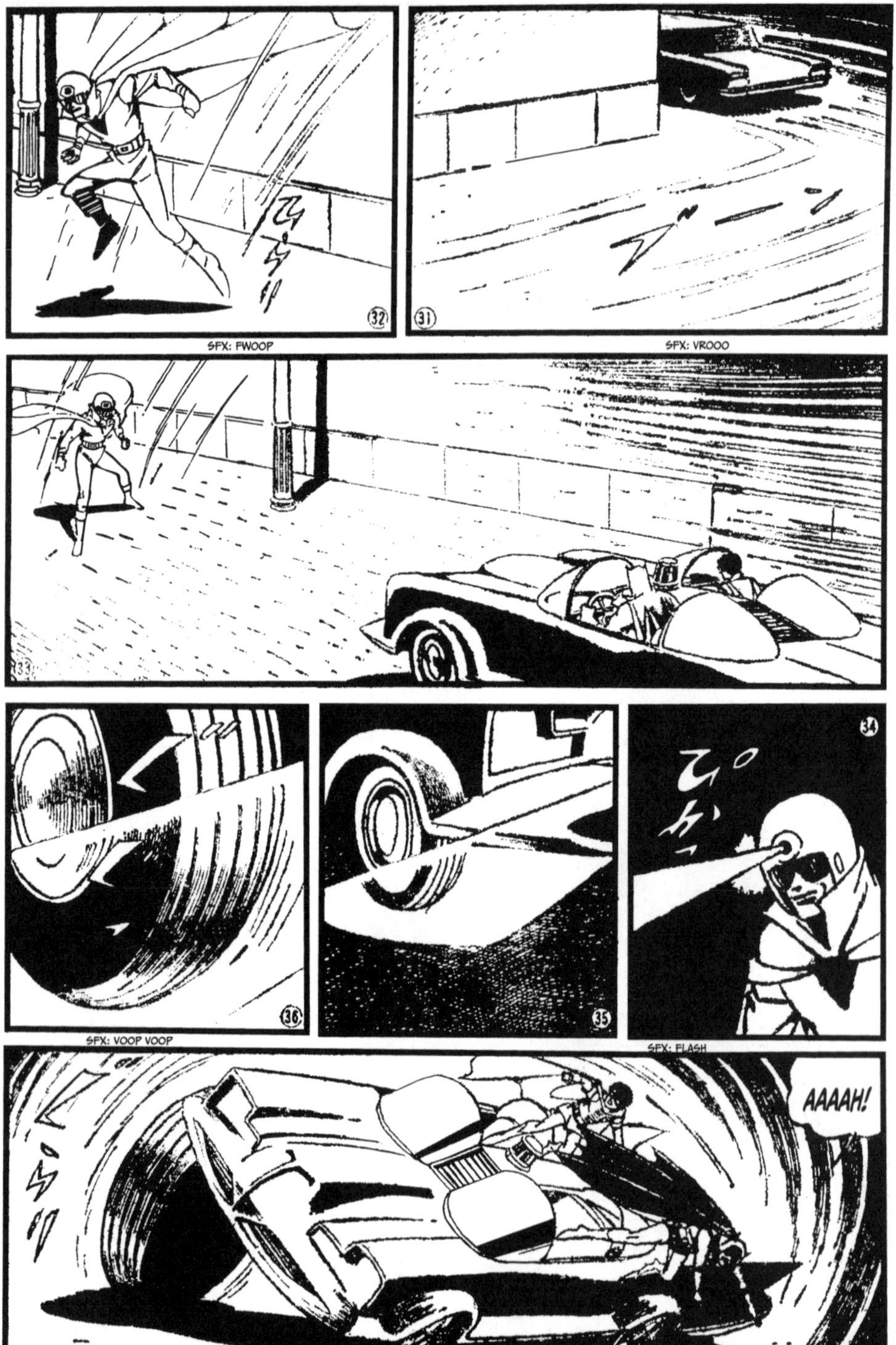
SFX: VROOO
SFX: FWOOP
ぴかっ
SFX: FLASH
SFX: VOOP VOOP
AAAAH!
SFX: WOBBLE

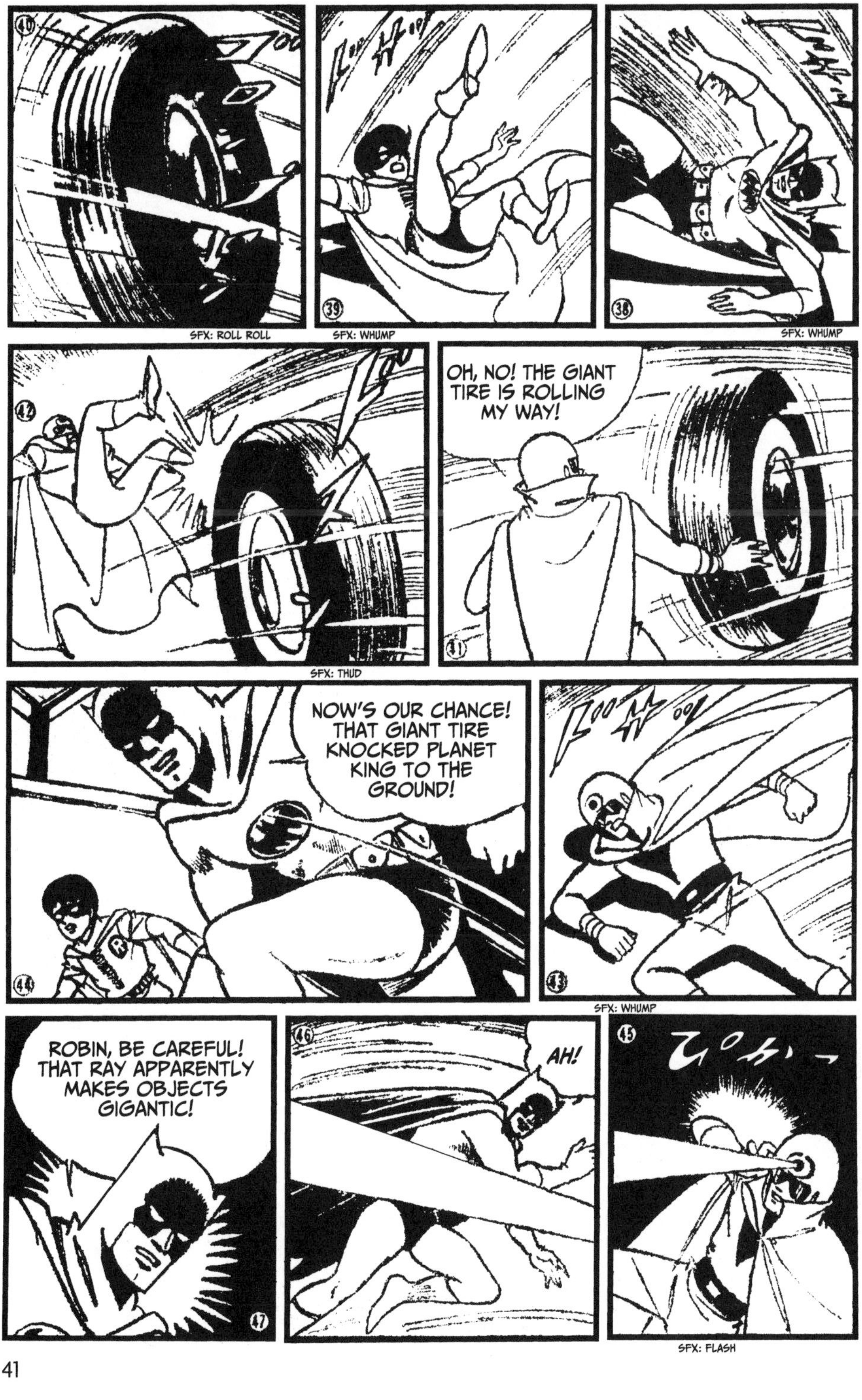
SFX: WHUMP
SFX: WHUMP
SFX: ROLL ROLL
OH, NO! THE GIANT TIRE IS ROLLING MY WAY!
SFX: THUD
SFX: WHUMP
NOW'S OUR CHANCE! THAT GIANT TIRE KNOCKED PLANET KING TO THE GROUND!
SFX: FLASH
AH!
ROBIN, BE CAREFUL! THAT RAY APPARENTLY MAKES OBJECTS GIGANTIC!

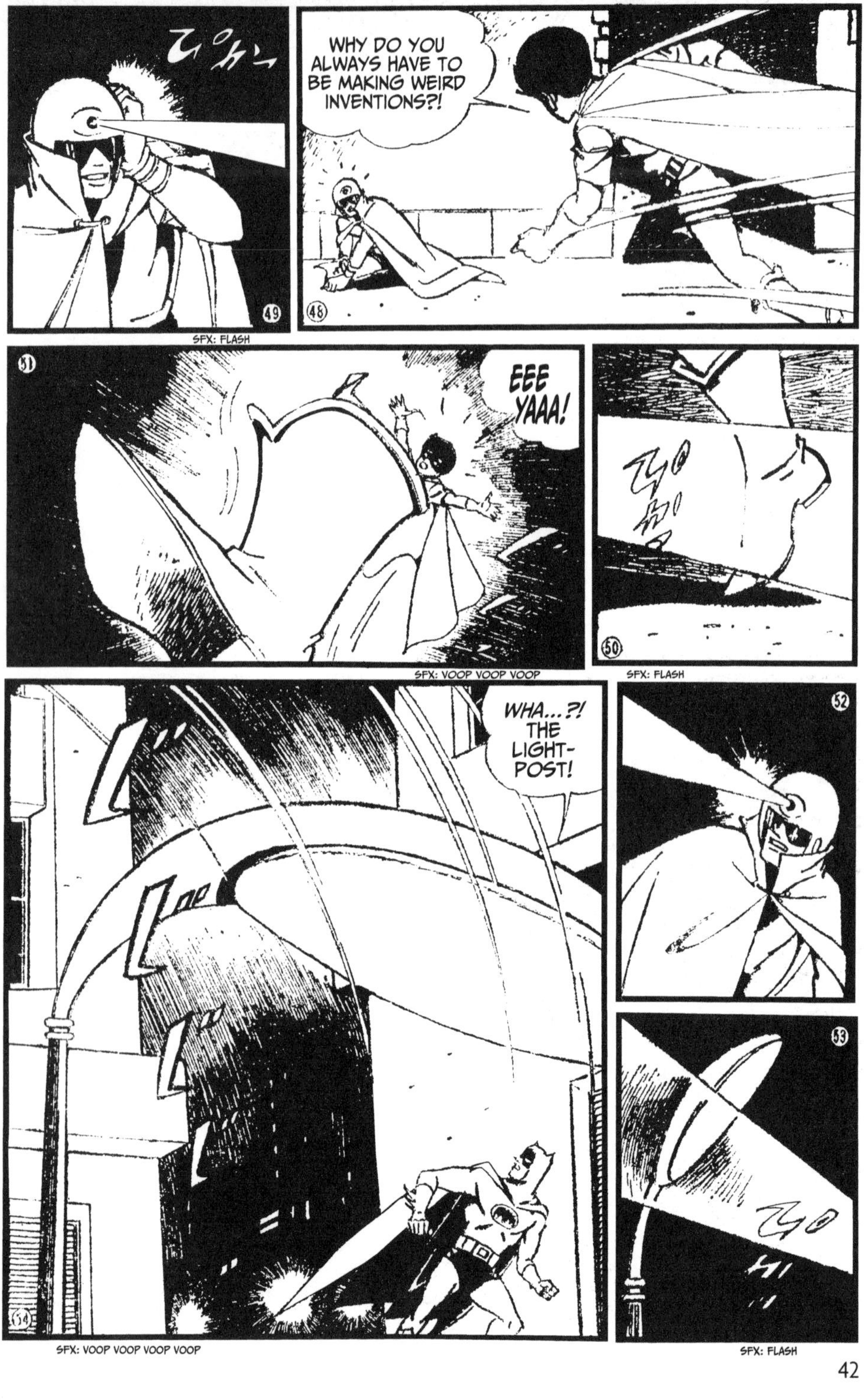
WHY DO YOU ALWAYS HAVE TO BE MAKING WEIRD INVENTIONS?!
SFX: FLASH
SFX: FLASH
EEE YAAA!
SFX: VOOP VOOP VOOP
SFX: FLASH
WHA...?! THE LIGHT-POST!
SFX: VOOP VOOP VOOP VOOP

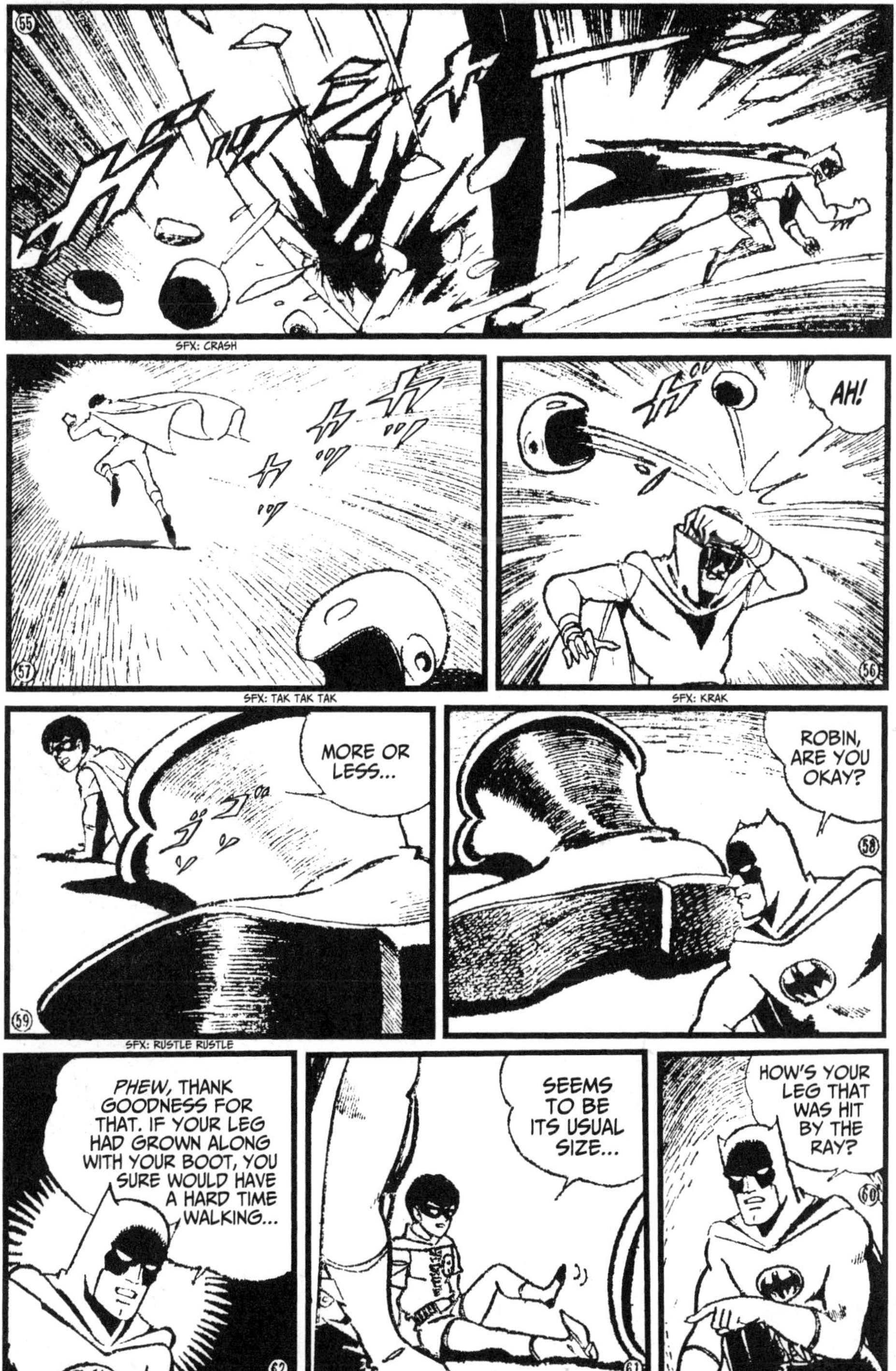
SFX: CRASH
AH!
SFX: KRAK
SFX: TAK TAK TAK
ROBIN, ARE YOU OKAY?
MORE OR LESS...
SFX: RUSTLE RUSTLE
HOW'S YOUR LEG THAT WAS HIT BY THE RAY?
SEEMS TO BE ITS USUAL SIZE...
PHEW, THANK GOODNESS FOR THAT. IF YOUR LEG HAD GROWN ALONG WITH YOUR BOOT, YOU SURE WOULD HAVE A HARD TIME WALKING...

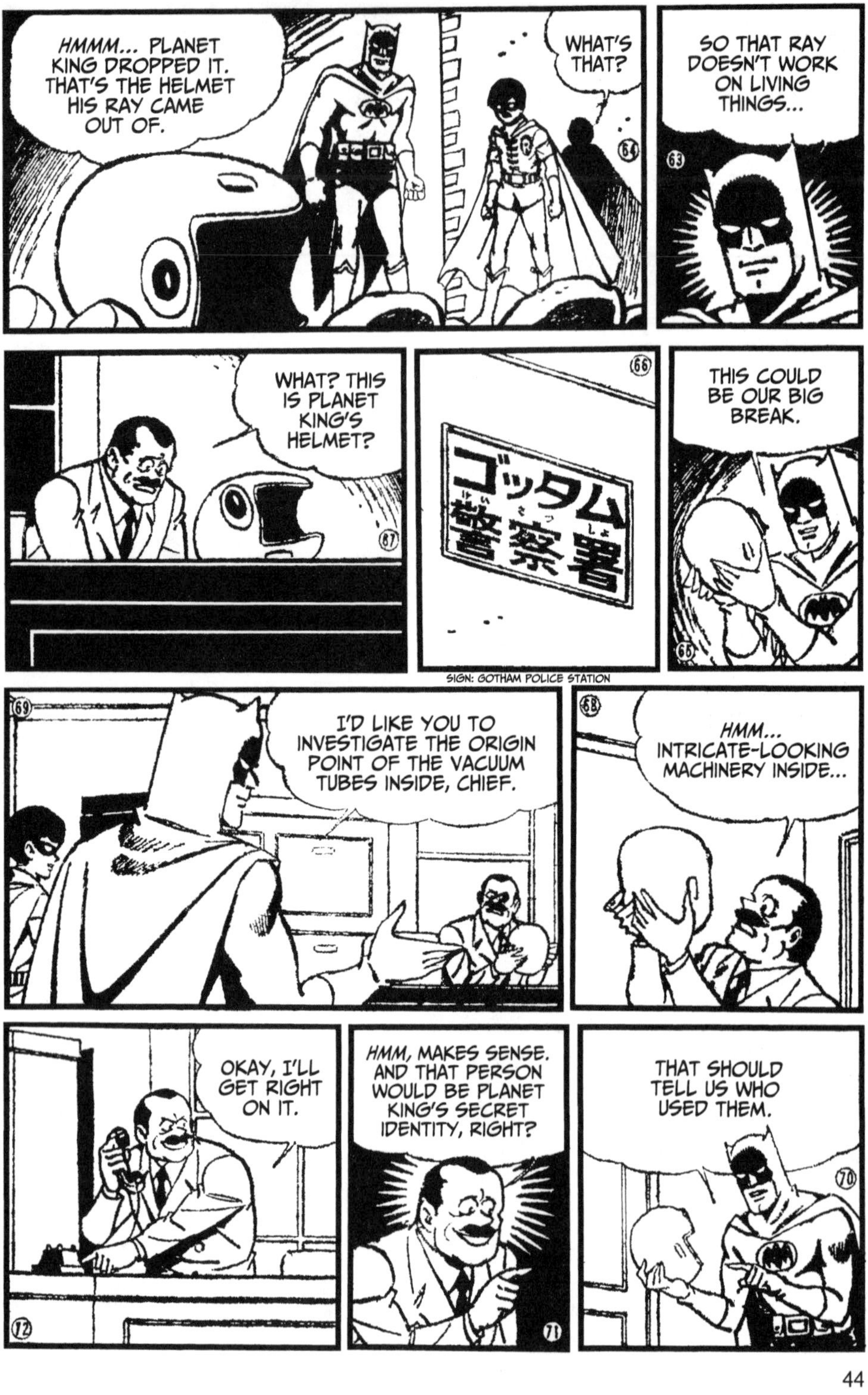
SO THAT RAY DOESN'T WORK ON LIVING THINGS...
WHAT'S THAT?
HMMM... PLANET KING DROPPED IT. THAT'S THE HELMET HIS RAY CAME OUT OF.
THIS COULD BE OUR BIG BREAK.
ゴッタム警察署
SIGN: GOTHAM POLICE STATION
WHAT? THIS IS PLANET KING'S HELMET?
HMM... INTRICATE-LOOKING MACHINERY INSIDE...
I'D LIKE YOU TO INVESTIGATE THE ORIGIN POINT OF THE VACUUM TUBES INSIDE, CHIEF.
THAT SHOULD TELL US WHO USED THEM.
HMM, MAKES SENSE. AND THAT PERSON WOULD BE PLANET KING'S SECRET IDENTITY, RIGHT?
OKAY, I'LL GET RIGHT ON IT.

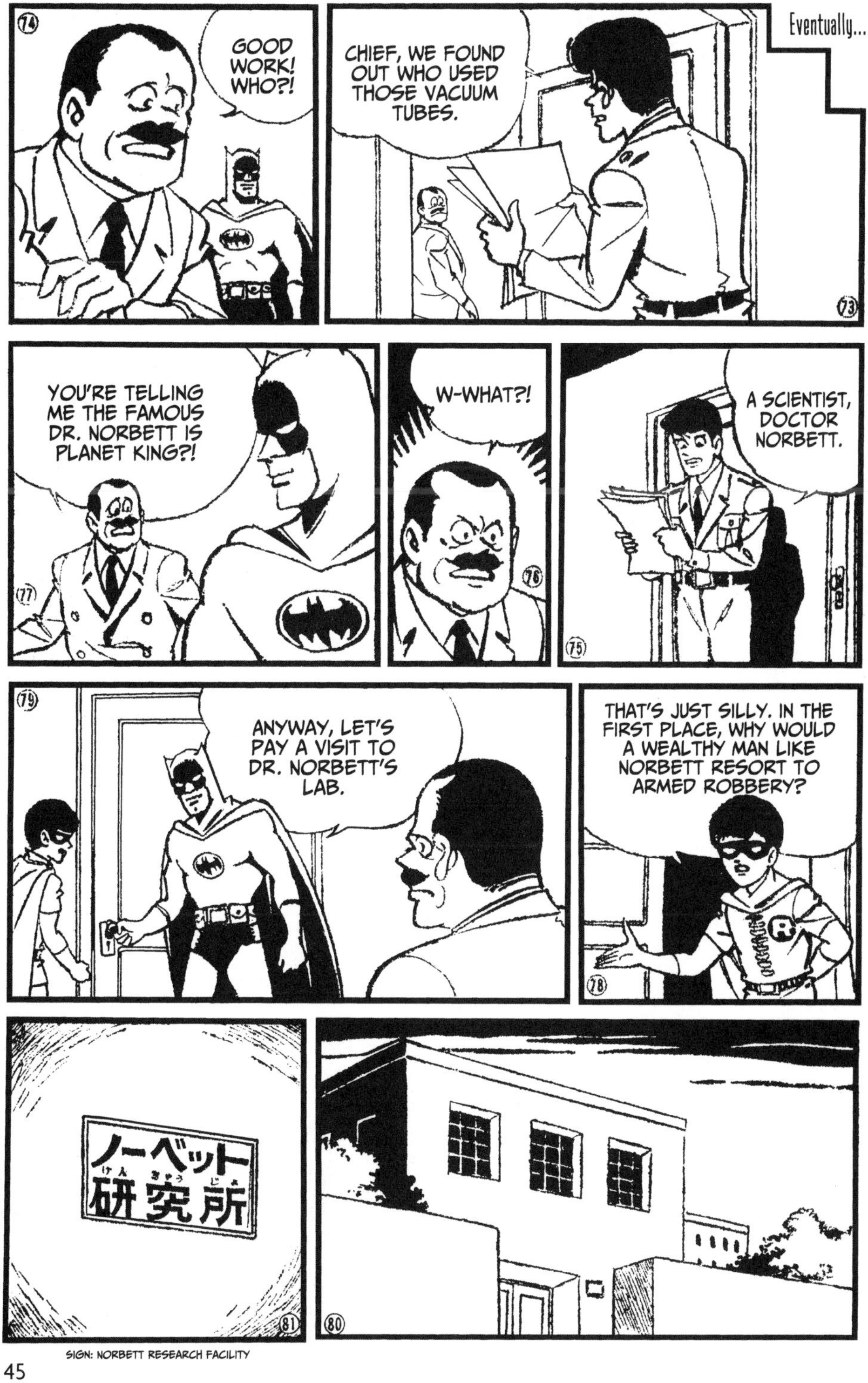
Eventually...
CHIEF, WE FOUND OUT WHO USED THOSE VACUUM TUBES.
GOOD WORK! WHO?!
A SCIENTIST, DOCTOR NORBETT.
W-WHAT?!
YOU'RE TELLING ME THE FAMOUS DR. NORBETT IS PLANET KING?!
THAT'S JUST SILLY. IN THE FIRST PLACE, WHY WOULD A WEALTHY MAN LIKE NORBETT RESORT TO ARMED ROBBERY?
ANYWAY, LET'S PAY A VISIT TO DR. NORBETT'S LAB.
ノーベット研究所

SIGN: NORBETT RESEARCH FACILITY

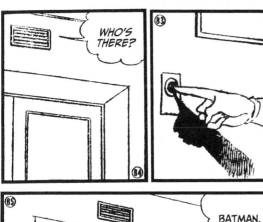

WHO'S THERE?
BATMAN.
I DON'T KNOW WHAT YOU'RE HERE FOR, BUT I'M SICK IN BED...
I HAVE A COUPLE OF QUESTIONS FOR YOU, DR. NORBETT.
ALL RIGHT, FINE. COME IN.

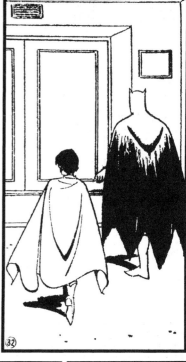

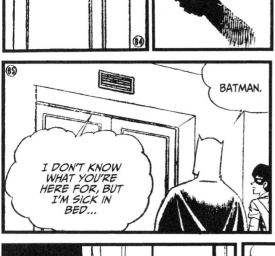

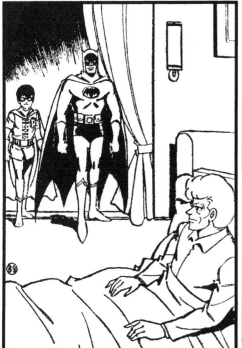

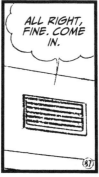

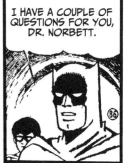

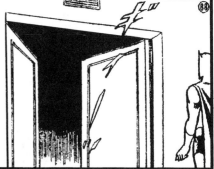

SFX: CREAK

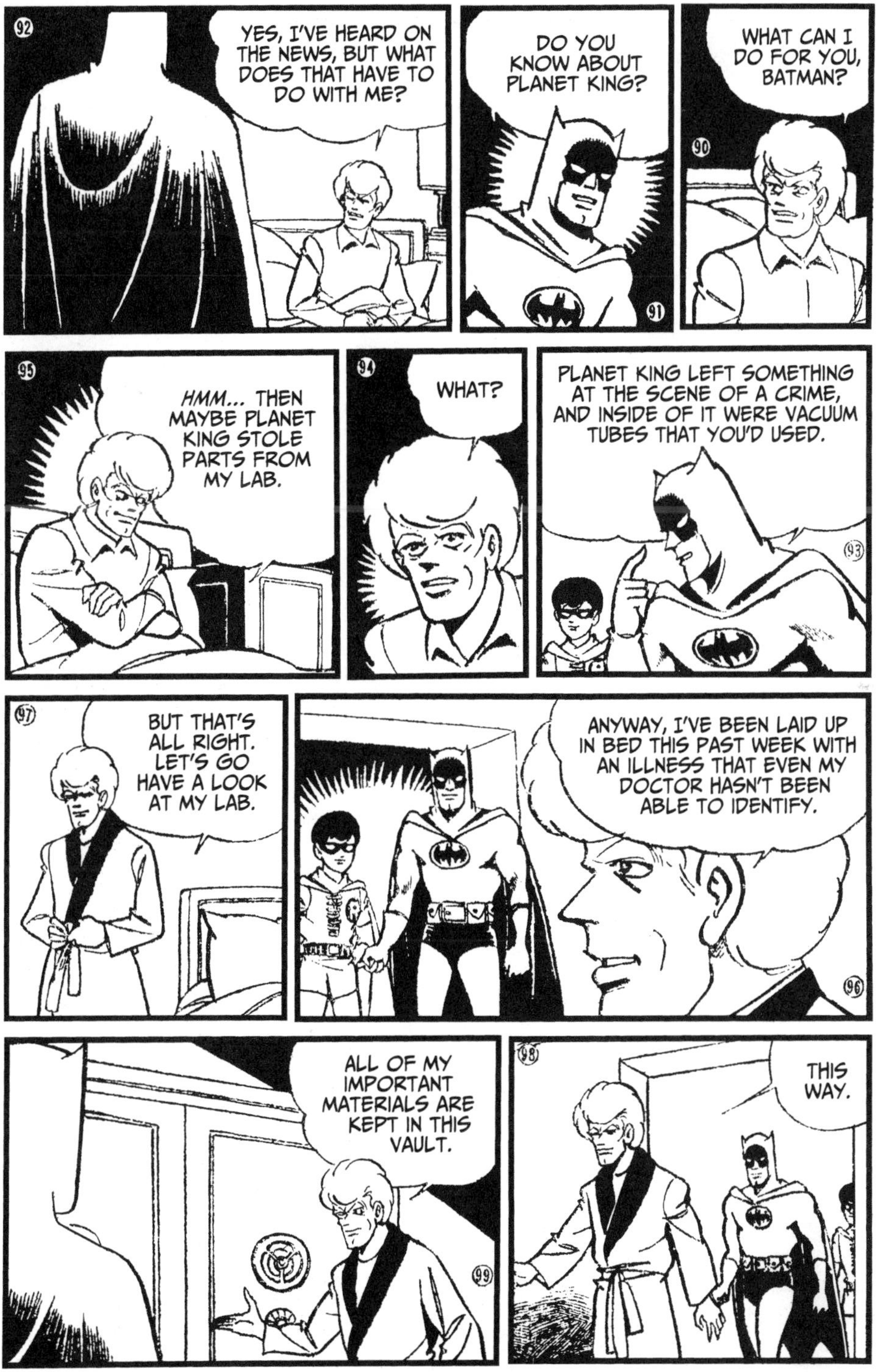
WHAT CAN I DO FOR YOU, BATMAN?
DO YOU KNOW ABOUT PLANET KING?
YES, I'VE HEARD ON THE NEWS, BUT WHAT DOES THAT HAVE TO DO WITH ME?
PLANET KING LEFT SOMETHING AT THE SCENE OF A CRIME, AND INSIDE OF IT WERE VACUUM TUBES THAT YOU'D USED.
WHAT?
HMM... THEN MAYBE PLANET KING STOLE PARTS FROM MY LAB.
ANYWAY, I'VE BEEN LAID UP IN BED THIS PAST WEEK WITH AN ILLNESS THAT EVEN MY DOCTOR HASN'T BEEN ABLE TO IDENTIFY.
BUT THAT'S ALL RIGHT. LET'S GO HAVE A LOOK AT MY LAB.
THIS WAY.
ALL OF MY IMPORTANT MATERIALS ARE KEPT IN THIS VAULT.

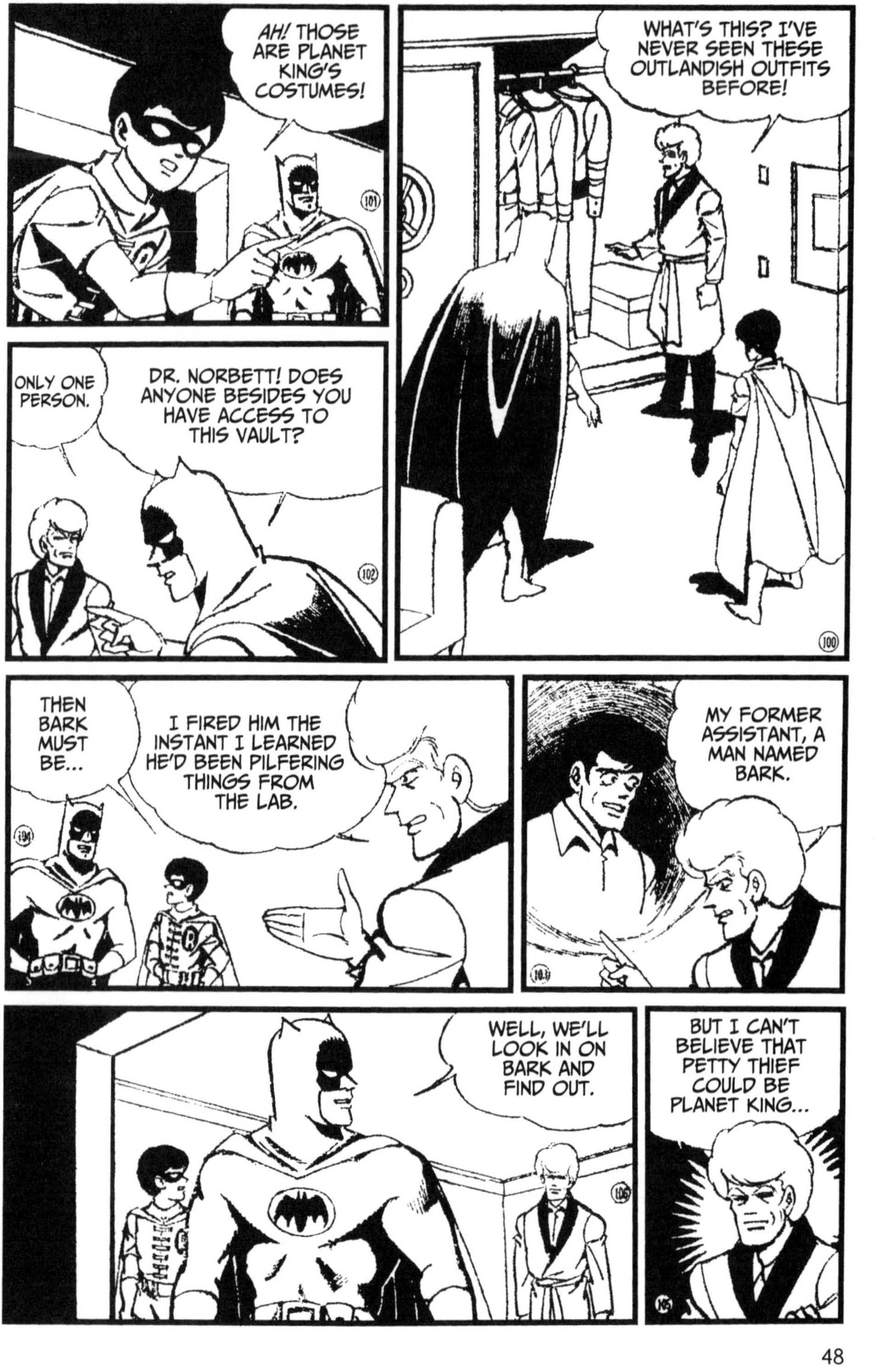
WHAT'S THIS? I'VE NEVER SEEN THESE OUTLANDISH OUTFITS BEFORE!
AH! THOSE ARE PLANET KING'S COSTUMES!
DR. NORBETT! DOES ANYONE BESIDES YOU HAVE ACCESS TO THIS VAULT?
ONLY ONE PERSON.
MY FORMER ASSISTANT, A MAN NAMED BARK.
I FIRED HIM THE INSTANT I LEARNED HE'D BEEN PILFERING THINGS FROM THE LAB.
THEN BARK MUST BE...
BUT I CAN'T BELIEVE THAT PETTY THIEF COULD BE PLANET KING...
WELL, WE'LL LOOK IN ON BARK AND FIND OUT.

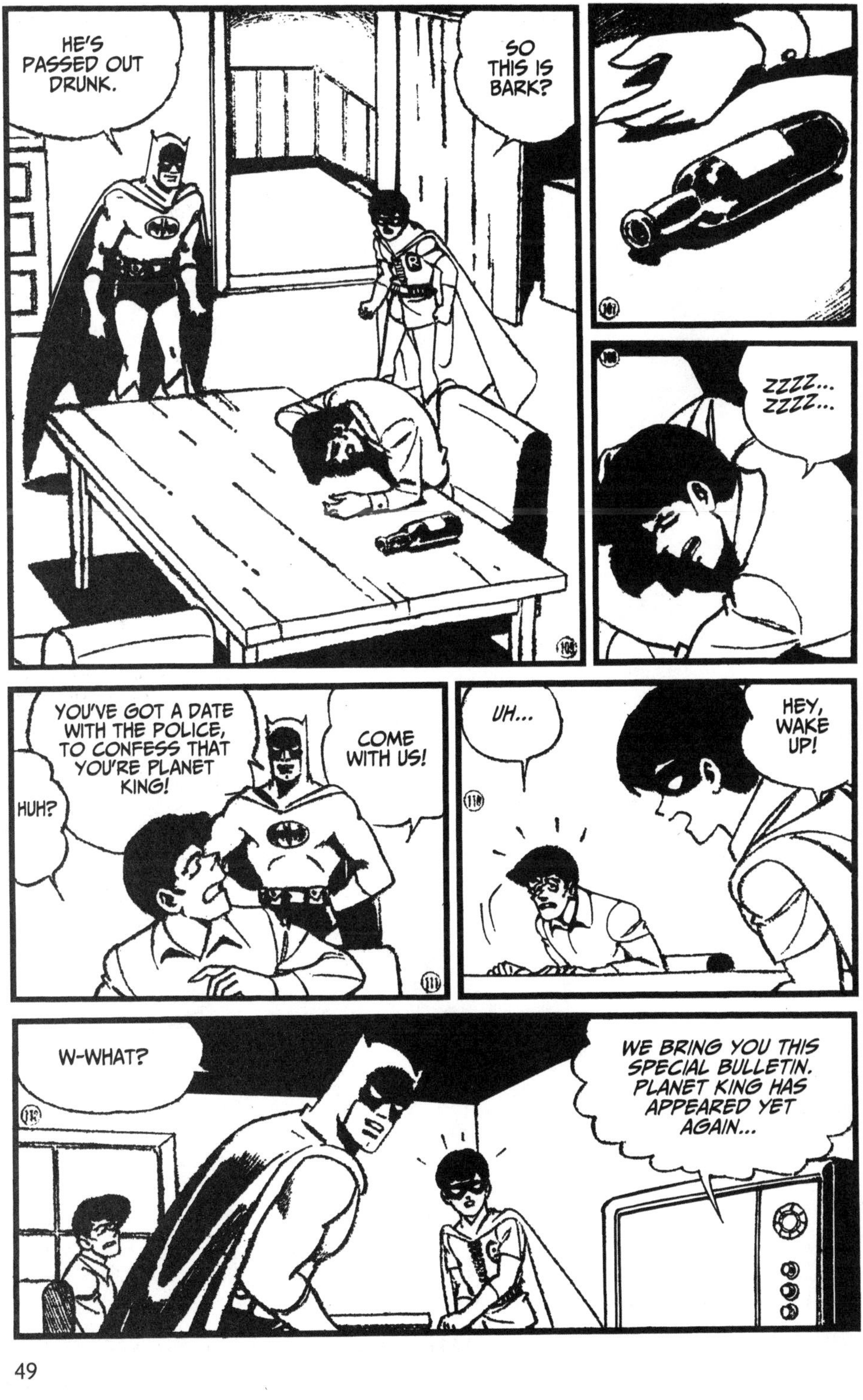
ZZZZ... ZZZZ...
SO THIS IS BARK?
HE'S PASSED OUT DRUNK.
HEY, WAKE UP!
UH...
COME WITH US!
YOU'VE GOT A DATE WITH THE POLICE, TO CONFESS THAT YOU'RE PLANET KING!
HUH?
WE BRING YOU THIS SPECIAL BULLETIN. PLANET KING HAS APPEARED YET AGAIN...
W-WHAT?

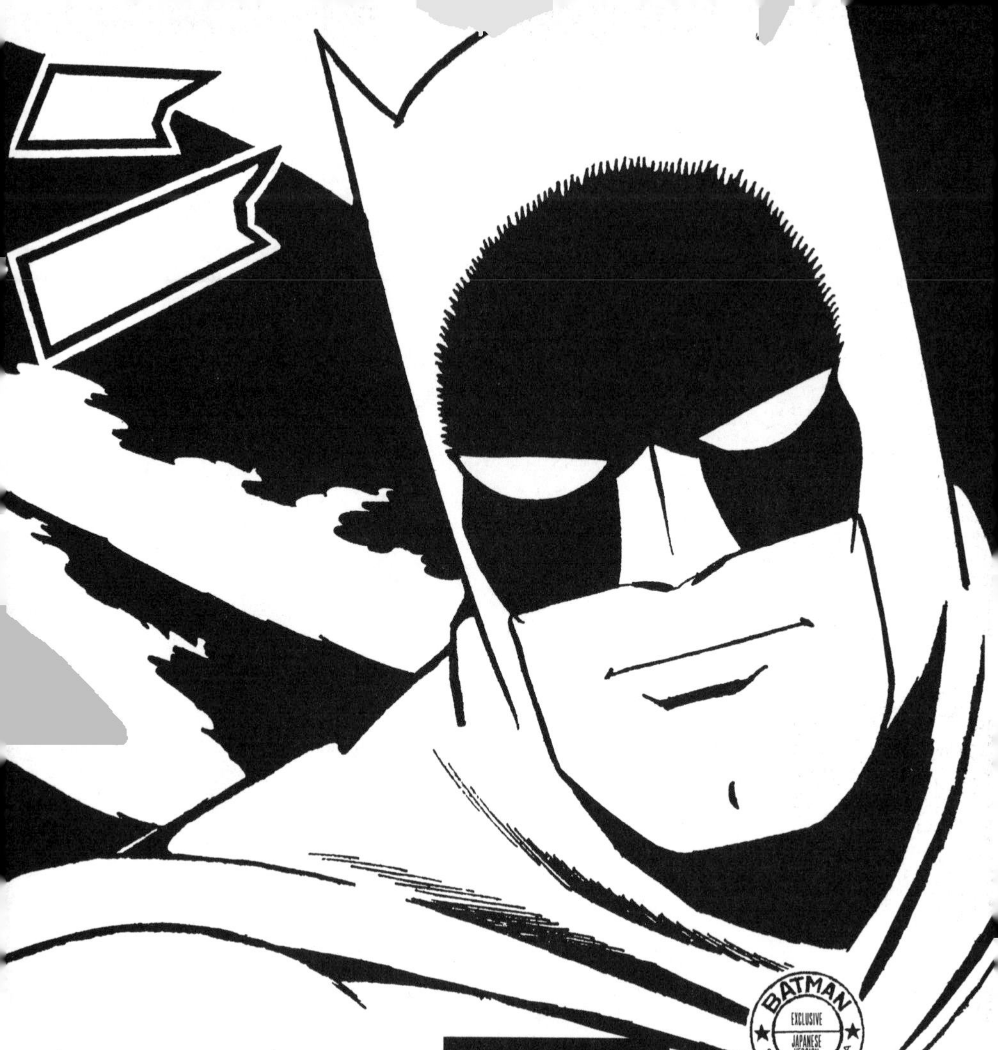
BATMAN
EXCLUSIVE
JAPANESE VERSION
SHONEN GAHOSHA

★ THE CRIMES OF PLANET KING ★
Part 4

Jiro Kuwata

LAST EPISODE...
Suspecting Bark, Dr. Norbett's assistant, of being Planet King, Batman and Robin barge in on the man in his apartment, only to find him intoxicated. Just then, a special bulletin on the radio announces that Planet King has struck again!

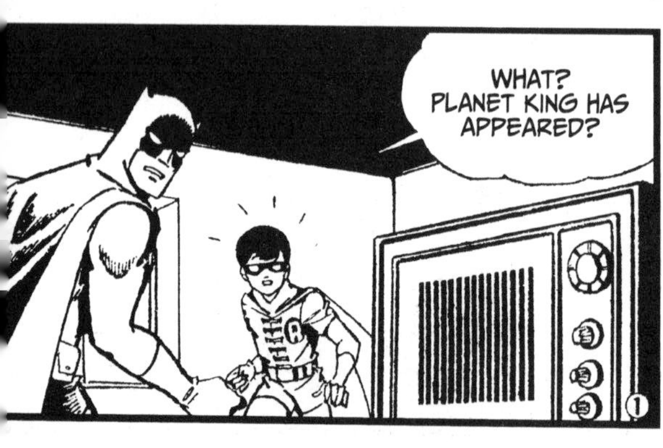
WHAT? PLANET KING HAS APPEARED?
1

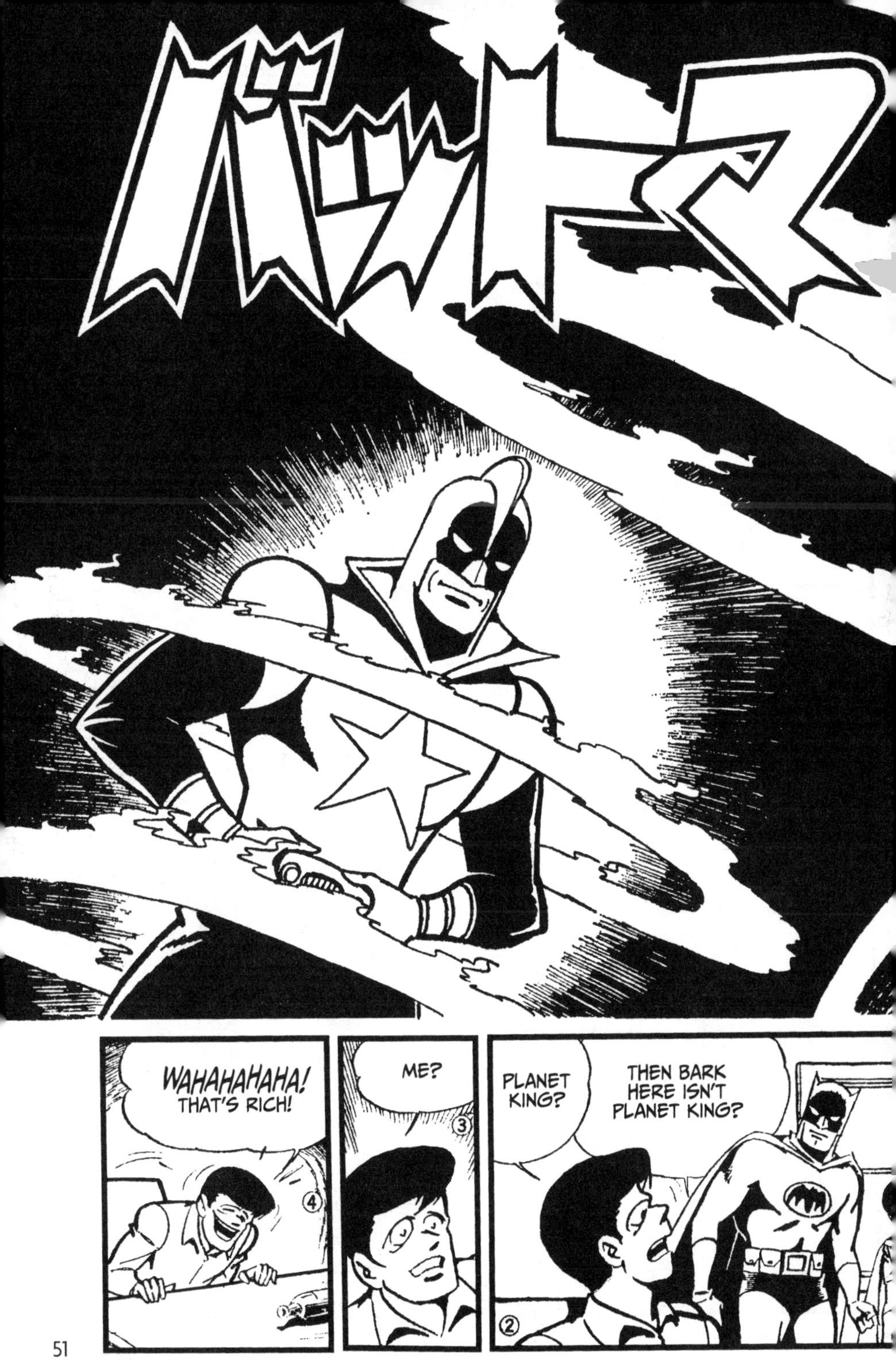

THEN BARK HERE ISN'T PLANET KING?
PLANET KING?
ME?
WAHAHAHAHA! THAT'S RICH!

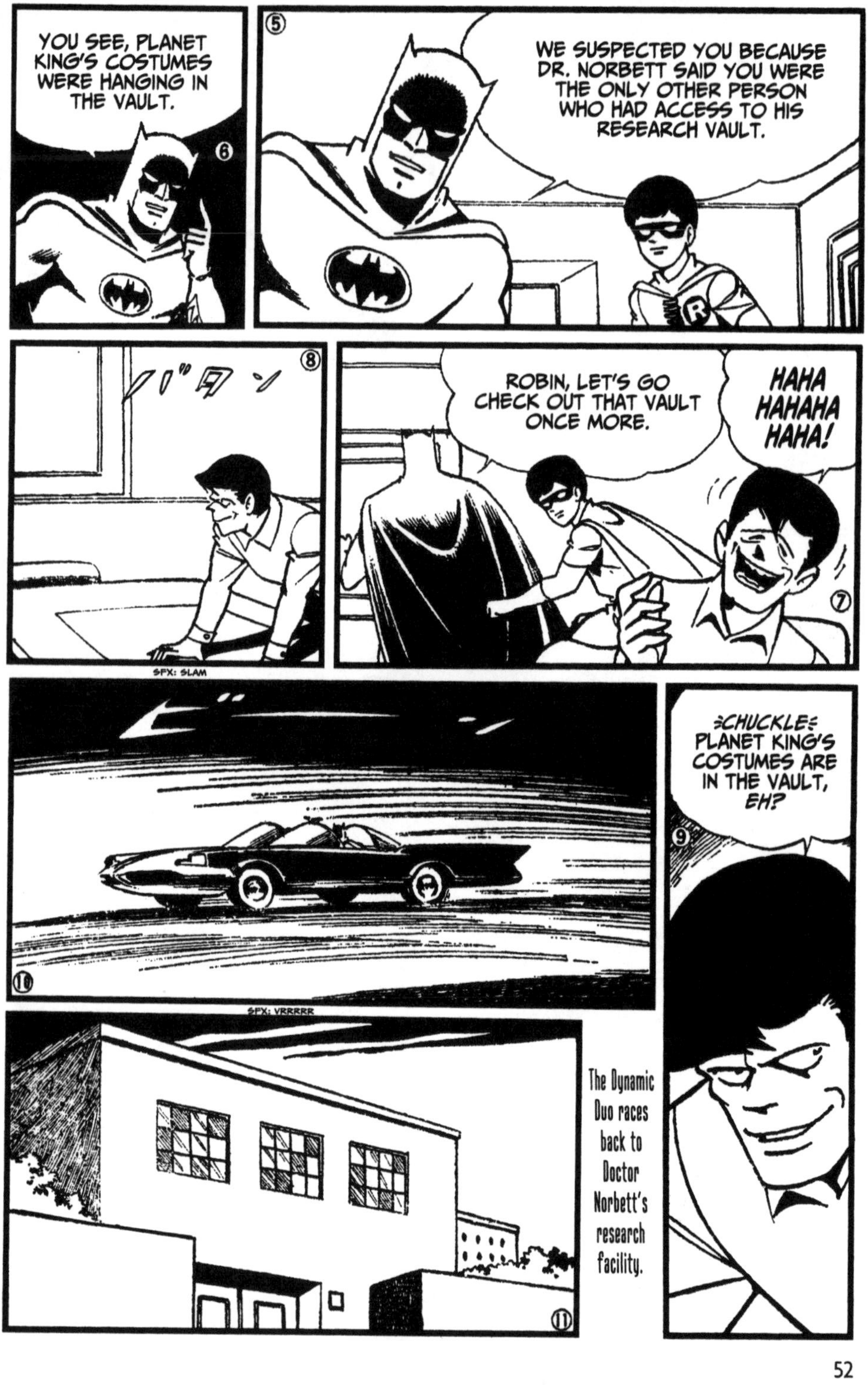
WE SUSPECTED YOU BECAUSE DR. NORBETT SAID YOU WERE THE ONLY OTHER PERSON WHO HAD ACCESS TO HIS RESEARCH VAULT.
YOU SEE, PLANET KING'S COSTUMES WERE HANGING IN THE VAULT.
HAHA HAHAHA HAHA!
ROBIN, LET'S GO CHECK OUT THAT VAULT ONCE MORE.
SFX: SLAM
≈CHUCKLE≈ PLANET KING'S COSTUMES ARE IN THE VAULT, EH?
SFX: VRRRRR
The Dynamic Duo races back to Doctor Norbett's research facility.

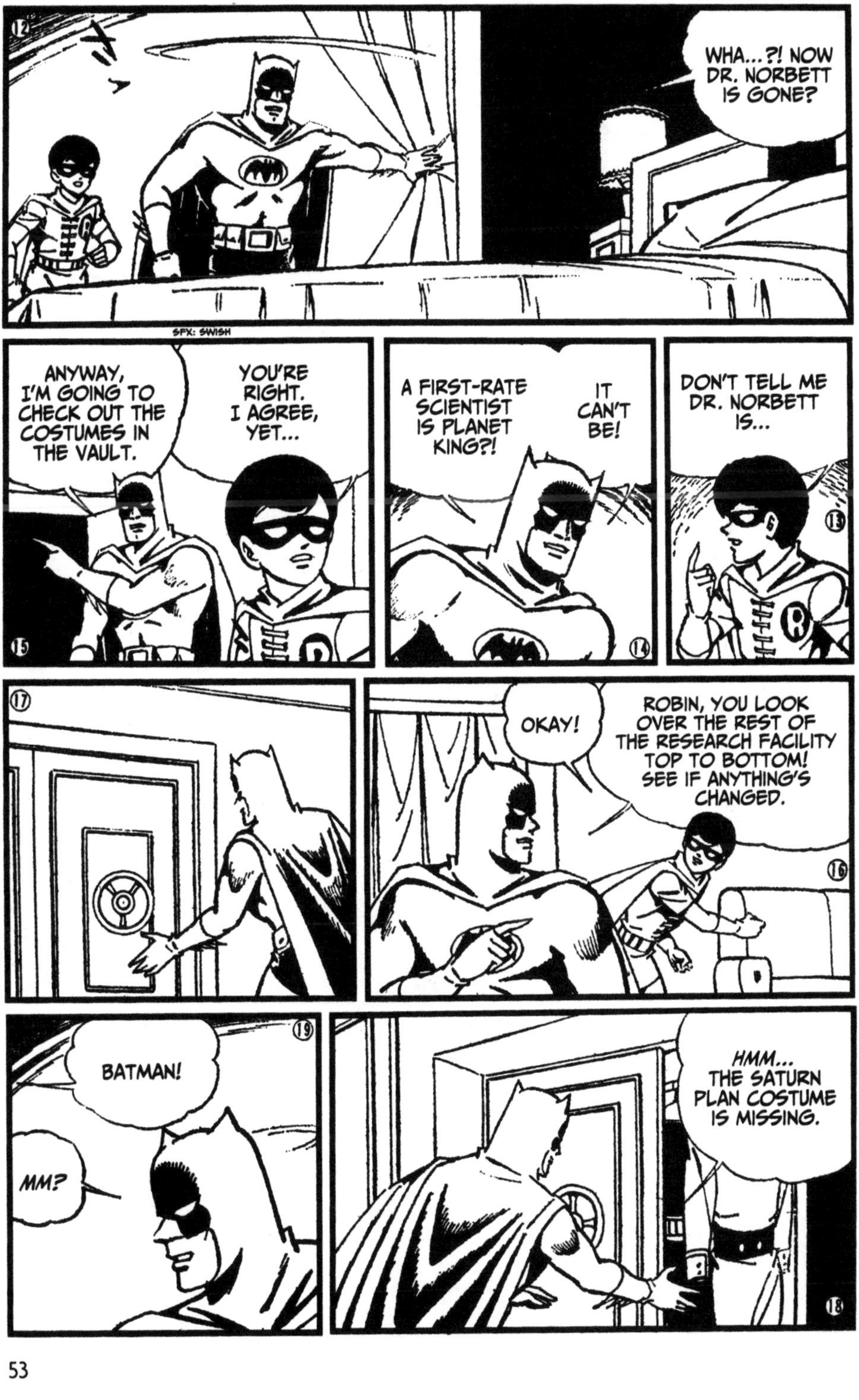
WHA...?! NOW DR. NORBETT IS GONE?
SFX: SWISH
DON'T TELL ME DR. NORBETT IS...
IT CAN'T BE!
A FIRST-RATE SCIENTIST IS PLANET KING?!
YOU'RE RIGHT. I AGREE, YET...
ANYWAY, I'M GOING TO CHECK OUT THE COSTUMES IN THE VAULT.
ROBIN, YOU LOOK OVER THE REST OF THE RESEARCH FACILITY TOP TO BOTTOM! SEE IF ANYTHING'S CHANGED.
OKAY!
HMM... THE SATURN PLAN COSTUME IS MISSING.
BATMAN!
MM?

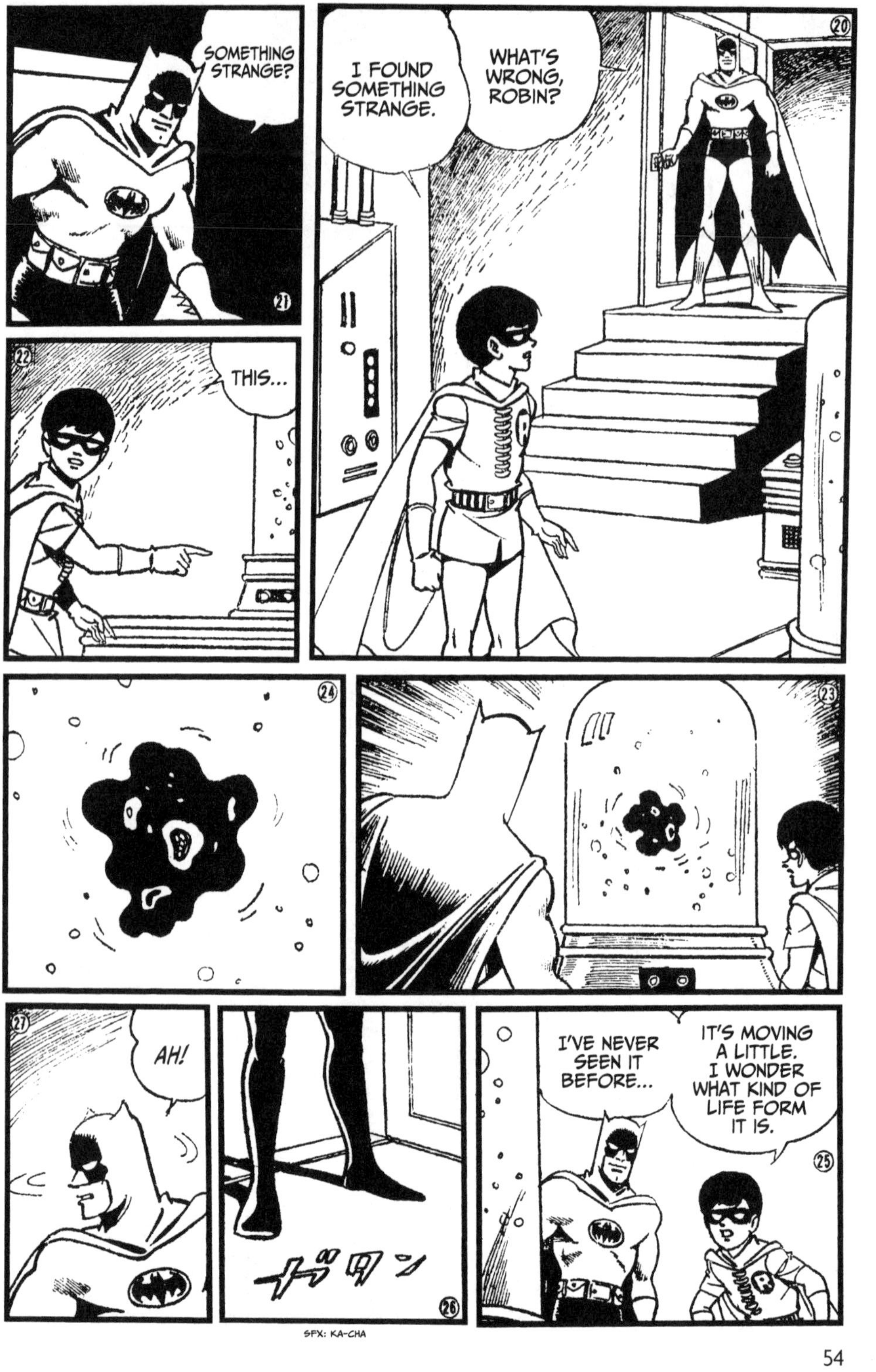
WHAT'S WRONG, ROBIN?
I FOUND SOMETHING STRANGE.
SOMETHING STRANGE?
THIS...
IT'S MOVING A LITTLE. I WONDER WHAT KIND OF LIFE FORM IT IS.
I'VE NEVER SEEN IT BEFORE...
AH!
SFX: KA-CHA

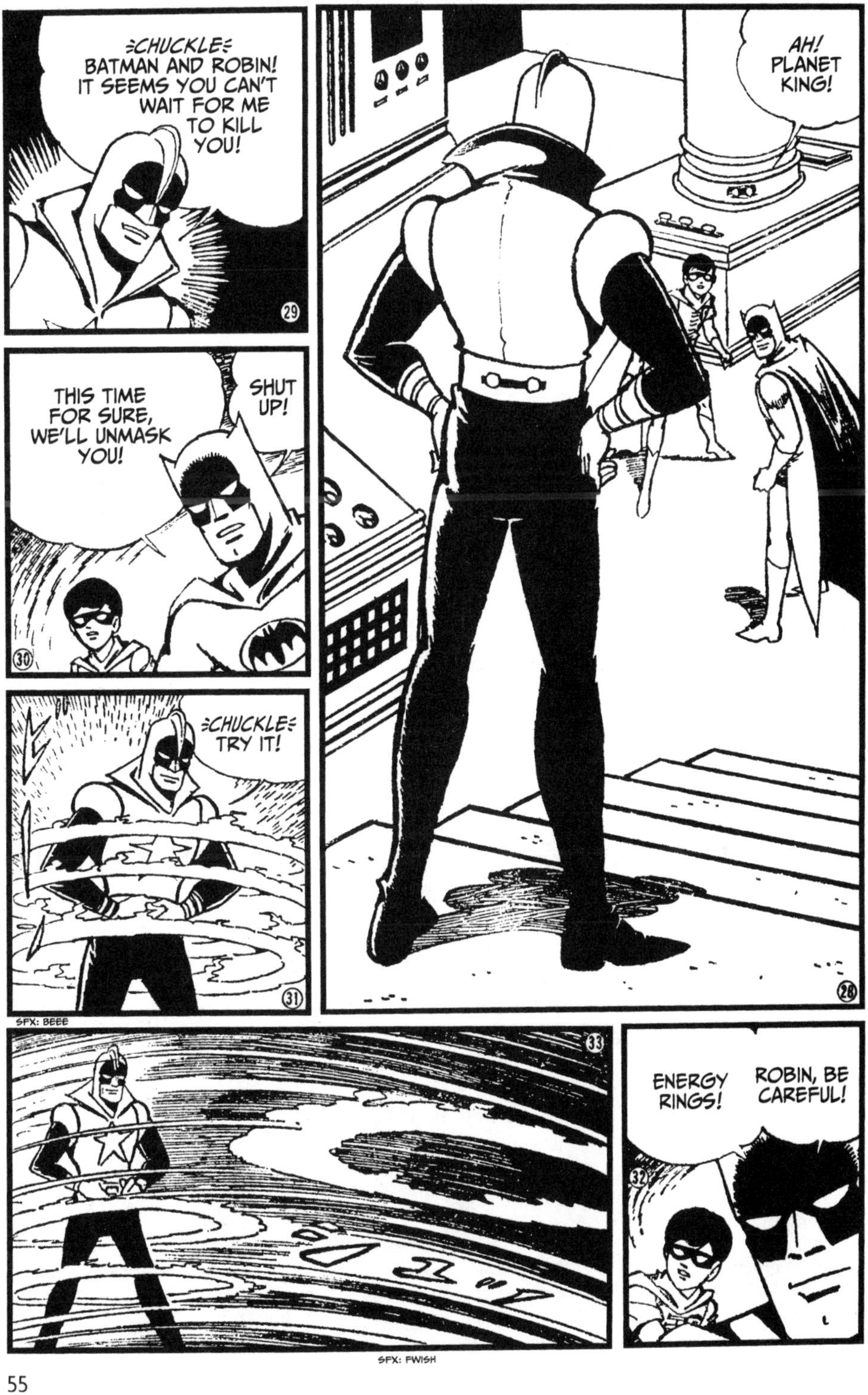
AH! PLANET KING!
≈CHUCKLE≈ BATMAN AND ROBIN! IT SEEMS YOU CAN'T WAIT FOR ME TO KILL YOU!
SHUT UP!
THIS TIME FOR SURE, WE'LL UNMASK YOU!
≈CHUCKLE≈ TRY IT!
SFX: BEEE
ROBIN, BE CAREFUL!
ENERGY RINGS!
SFX: FWISH

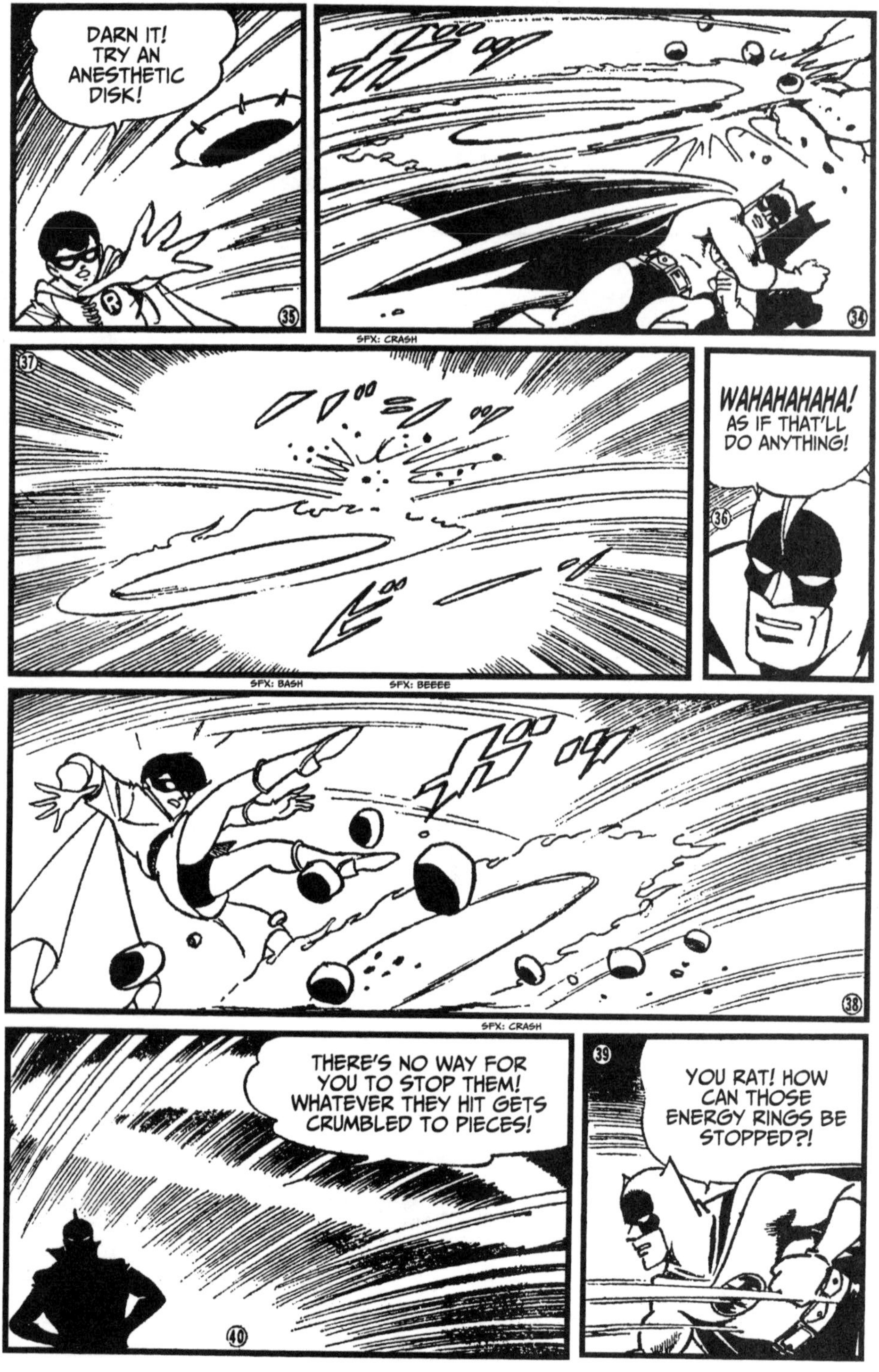
SFX: CRASH
DARN IT! TRY AN ANESTHETIC DISK!
WAHAHAHAHA! AS IF THAT'LL DO ANYTHING!
SFX: BASH
SFX: BEEEE
SFX: CRASH
YOU RAT! HOW CAN THOSE ENERGY RINGS BE STOPPED?!
THERE'S NO WAY FOR YOU TO STOP THEM! WHATEVER THEY HIT GETS CRUMBLED TO PIECES!

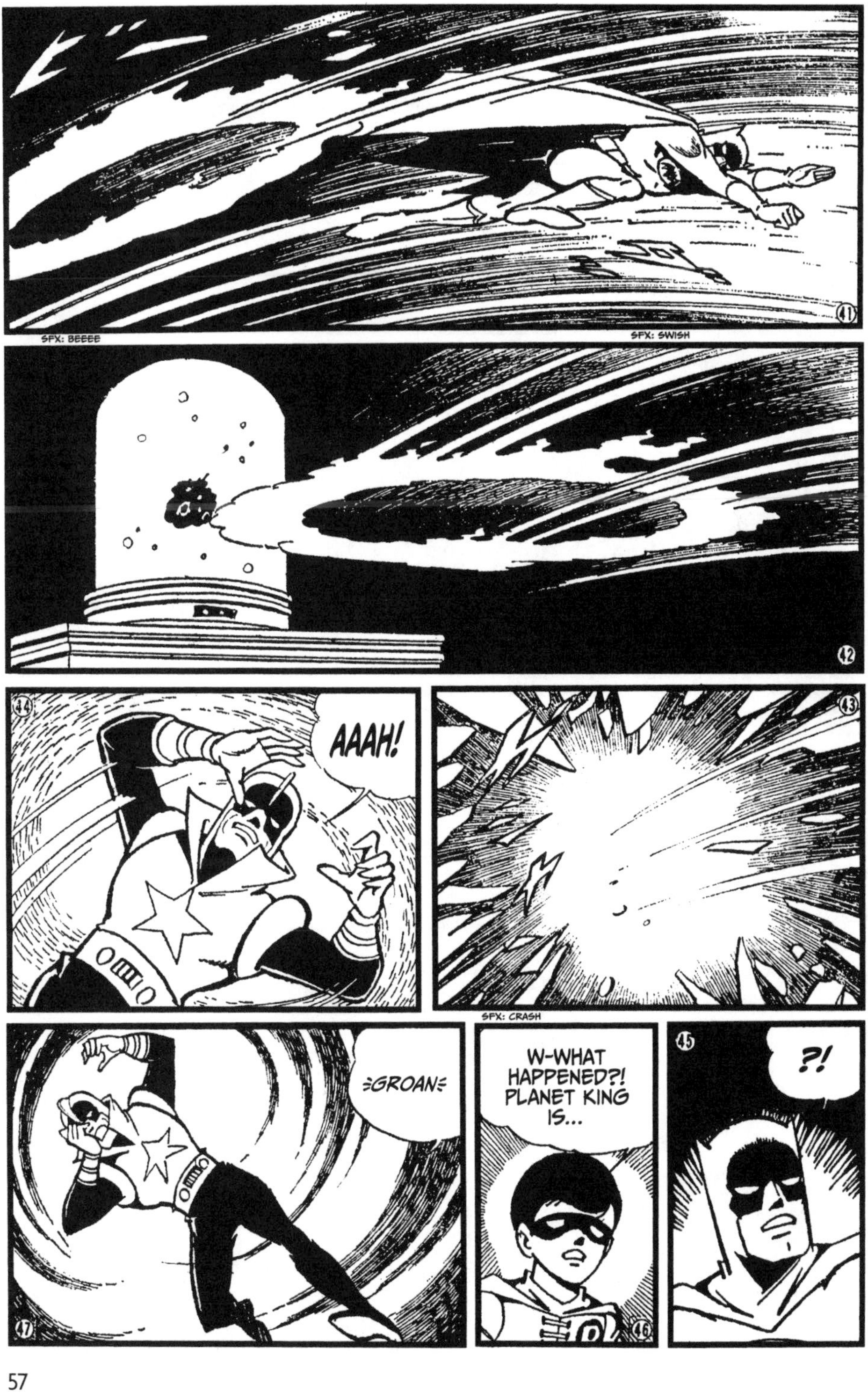
SFX: SWISH
SFX: BEEEE
SFX: CRASH
AAAH!
?!
W-WHAT HAPPENED?! PLANET KING IS...
GROAN

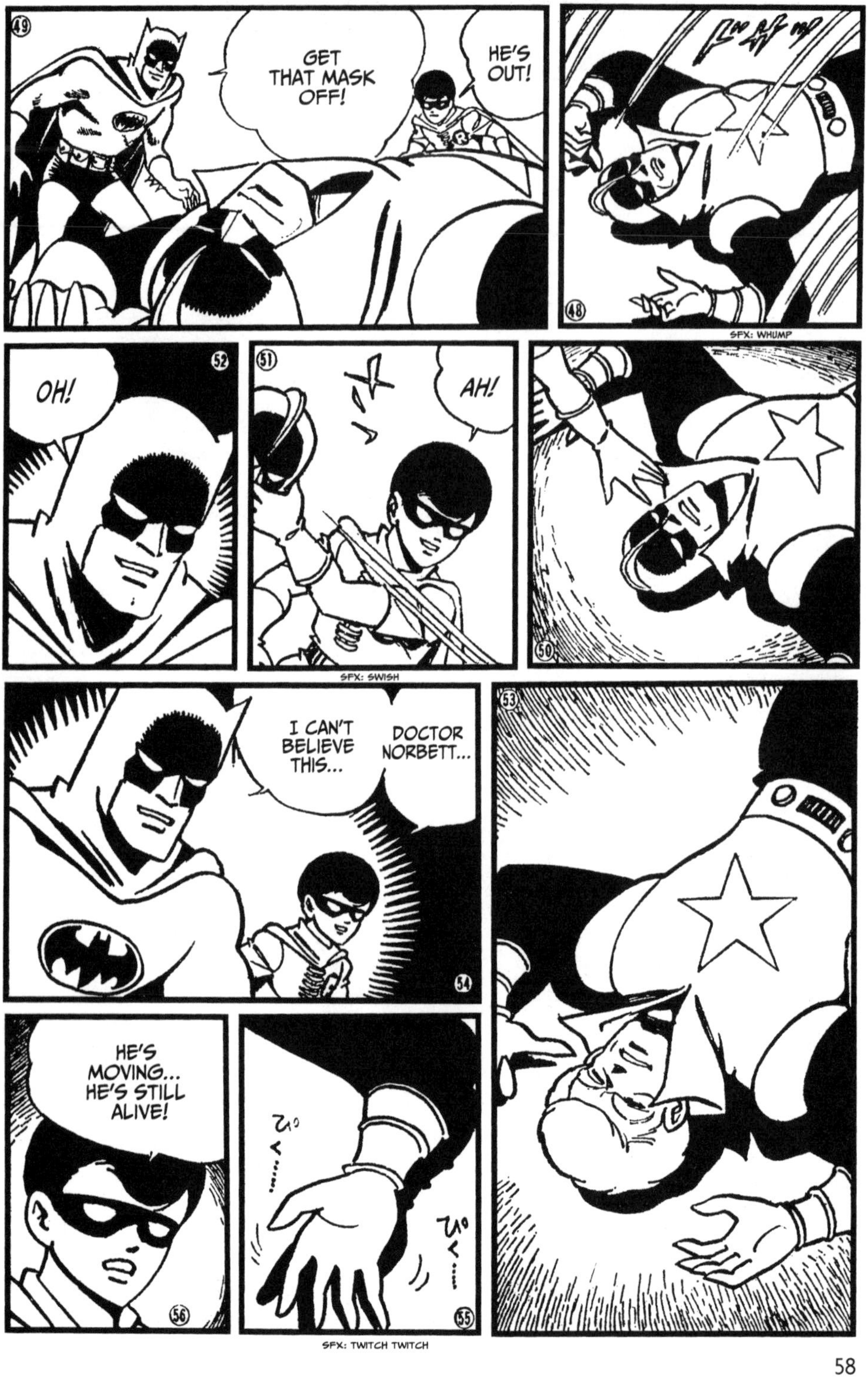
SFX: WHUMP
HE'S OUT!
GET THAT MASK OFF!
AH!
SFX: SWISH
OH!
DOCTOR NORBETT...
I CAN'T BELIEVE THIS...
SFX: TWITCH TWITCH
HE'S MOVING... HE'S STILL ALIVE!

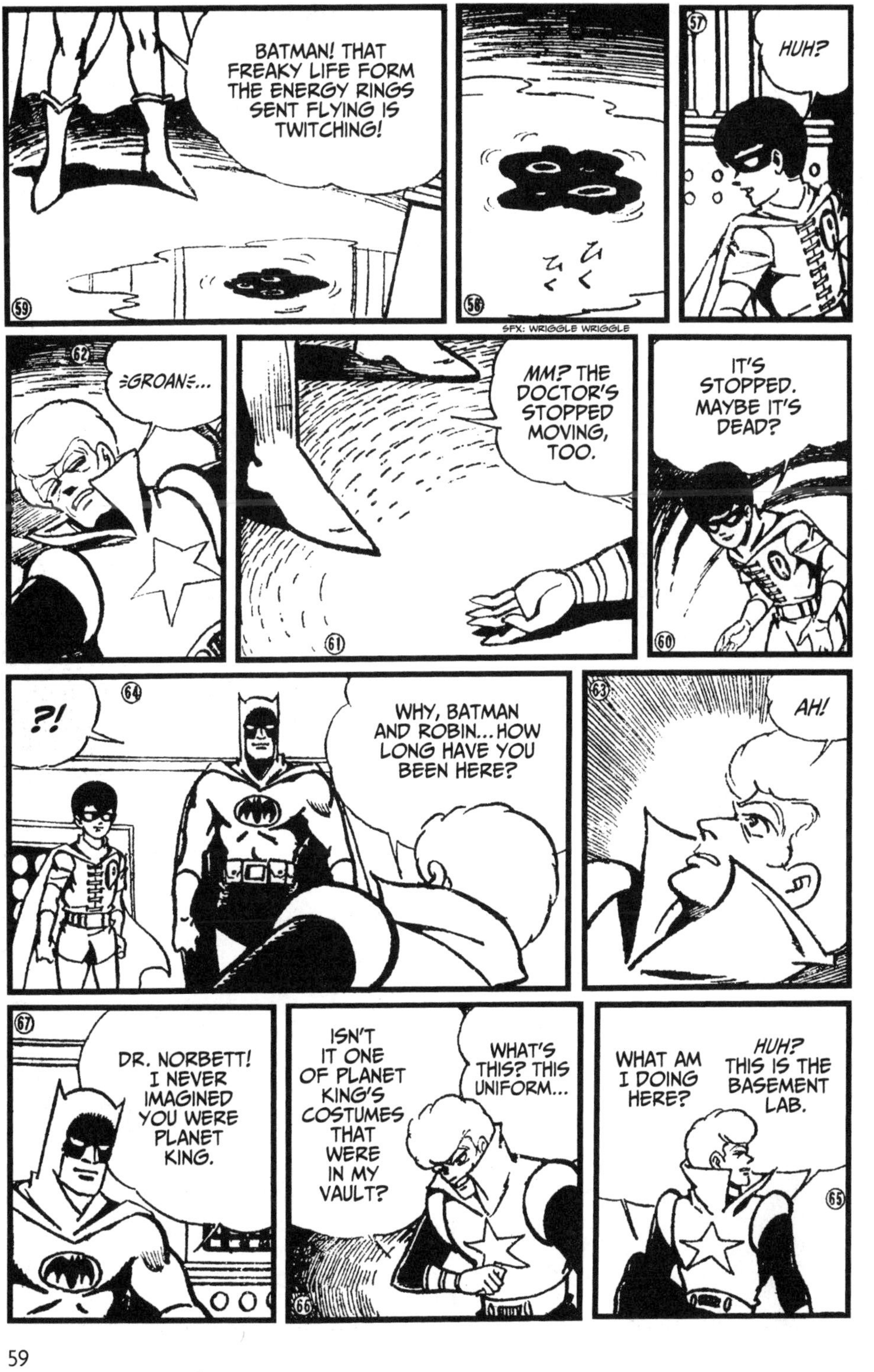
HUH?
ひくひく
SFX: WRIGGLE WRIGGLE
BATMAN! THAT FREAKY LIFE FORM THE ENERGY RINGS SENT FLYING IS TWITCHING!
IT'S STOPPED. MAYBE IT'S DEAD?
MM? THE DOCTOR'S STOPPED MOVING, TOO.
≷GROAN≶...
AH!
WHY, BATMAN AND ROBIN... HOW LONG HAVE YOU BEEN HERE?
?!
HUH? THIS IS THE BASEMENT LAB.
WHAT AM I DOING HERE?
WHAT'S THIS? THIS UNIFORM...
ISN'T IT ONE OF PLANET KING'S COSTUMES THAT WERE IN MY VAULT?
DR. NORBETT! I NEVER IMAGINED YOU WERE PLANET KING.

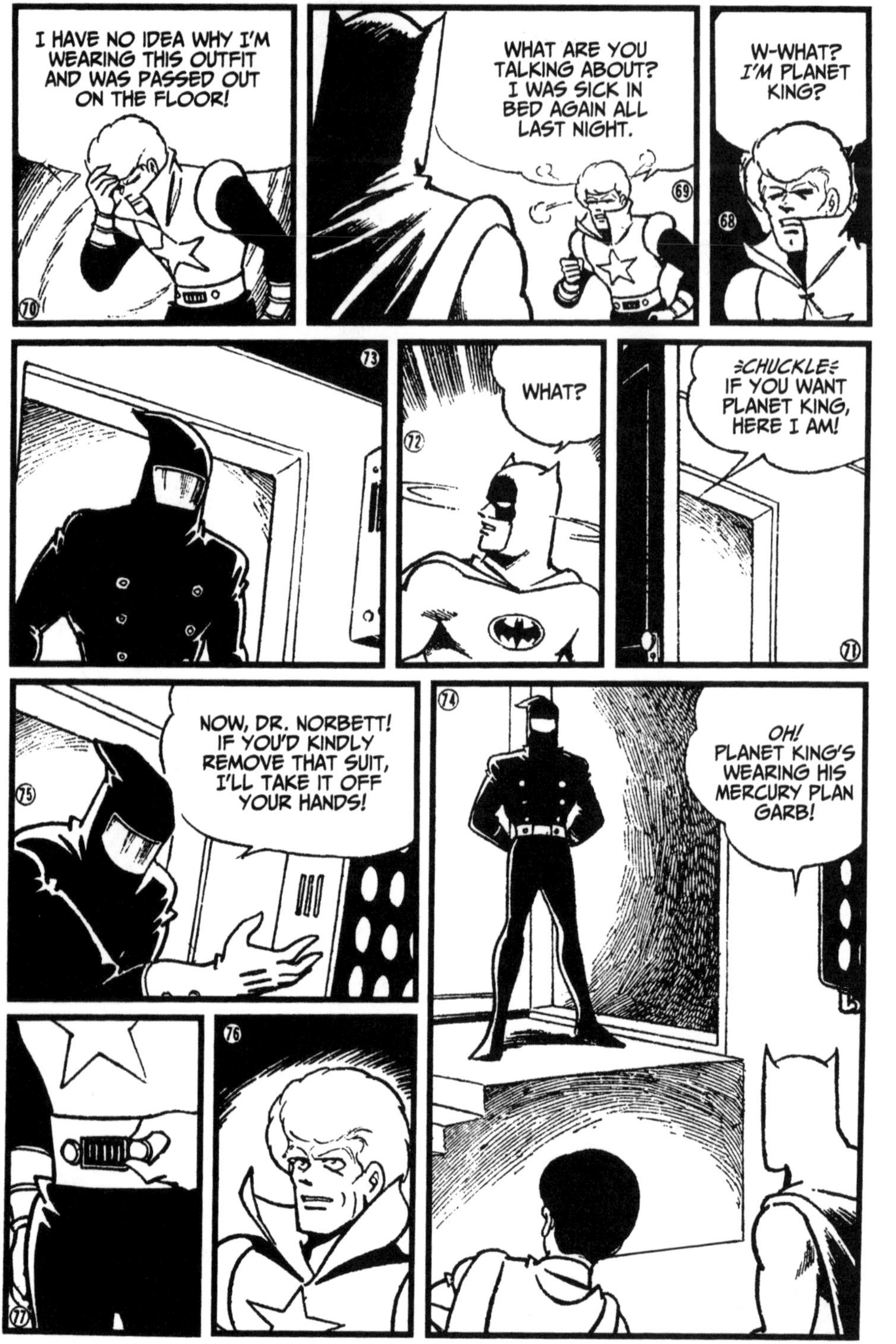
W-WHAT? *I'M* PLANET KING?
WHAT ARE YOU TALKING ABOUT? I WAS SICK IN BED AGAIN ALL LAST NIGHT.
I HAVE NO IDEA WHY I'M WEARING THIS OUTFIT AND WAS PASSED OUT ON THE FLOOR!
=CHUCKLE= IF YOU WANT PLANET KING, HERE I AM!
WHAT?
OH! PLANET KING'S WEARING HIS MERCURY PLAN GARB!
NOW, DR. NORBETT! IF YOU'D KINDLY REMOVE THAT SUIT, I'LL TAKE IT OFF YOUR HANDS!

SFX: BEEEE

AAAH!

SFX: CRASH

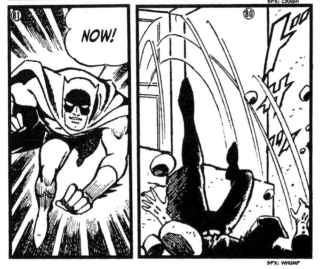

NOW!

SFX: WHUMP

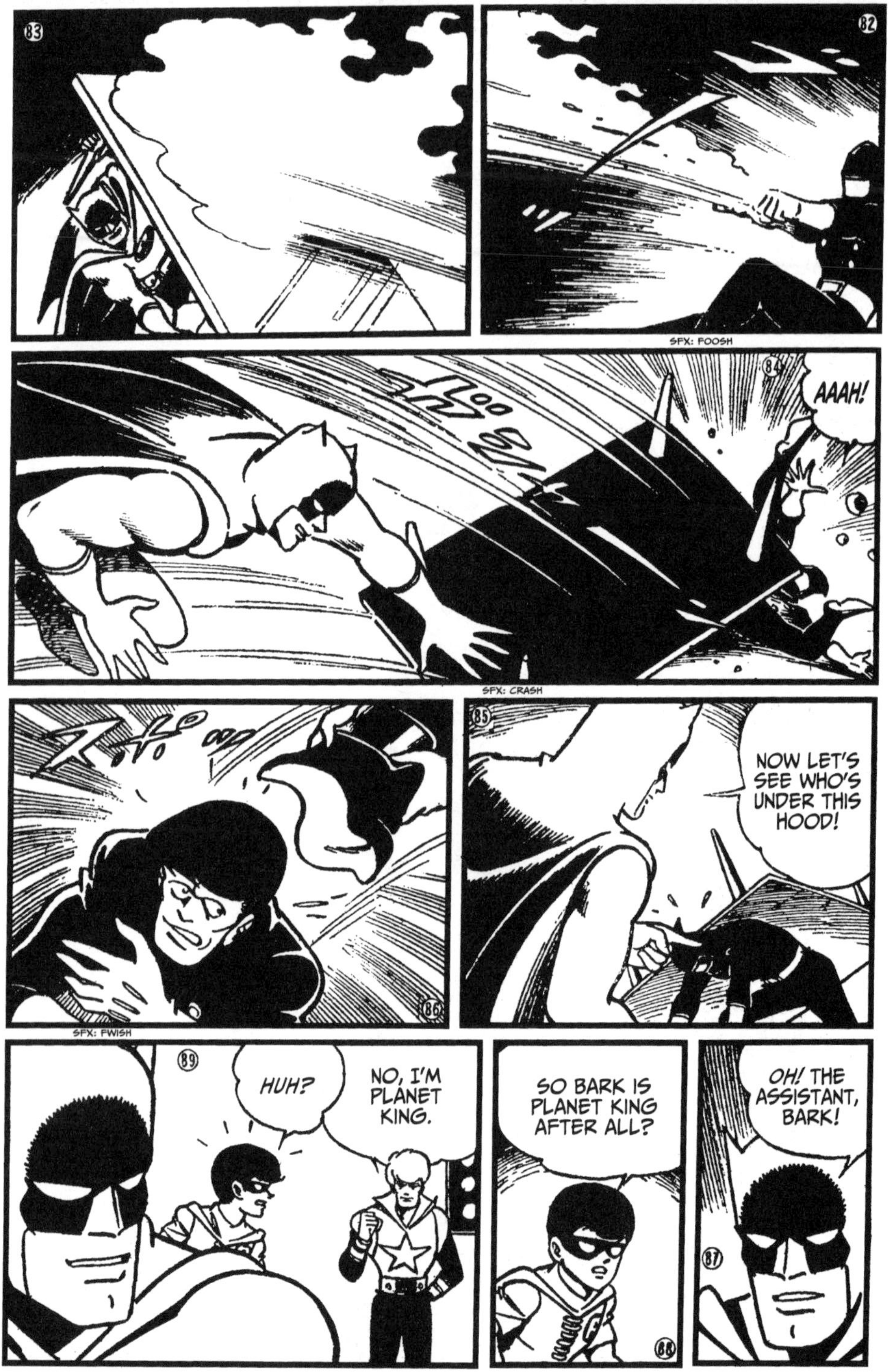
SFX: FOOSH
AAAH!
SFX: CRASH
NOW LET'S SEE WHO'S UNDER THIS HOOD!
SFX: FWISH
OH! THE ASSISTANT, BARK!
SO BARK IS PLANET KING AFTER ALL?
NO, I'M PLANET KING.
HUH?

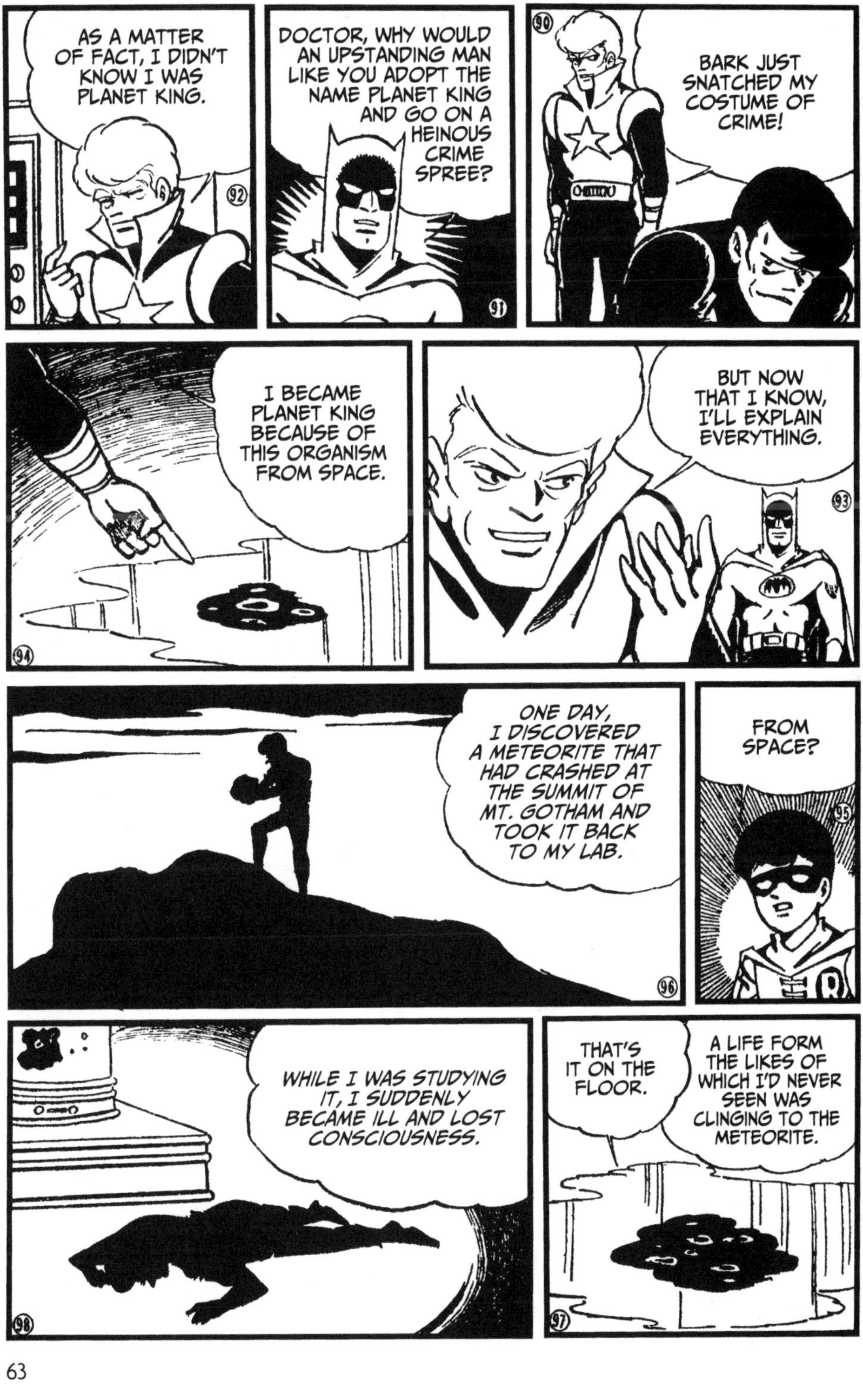
BARK JUST SNATCHED MY COSTUME OF CRIME!
DOCTOR, WHY WOULD AN UPSTANDING MAN LIKE YOU ADOPT THE NAME PLANET KING AND GO ON A HEINOUS CRIME SPREE?
AS A MATTER OF FACT, I DIDN'T KNOW I WAS PLANET KING.
BUT NOW THAT I KNOW, I'LL EXPLAIN EVERYTHING.
I BECAME PLANET KING BECAUSE OF THIS ORGANISM FROM SPACE.
FROM SPACE?
ONE DAY, I DISCOVERED A METEORITE THAT HAD CRASHED AT THE SUMMIT OF MT. GOTHAM AND TOOK IT BACK TO MY LAB.
A LIFE FORM THE LIKES OF WHICH I'D NEVER SEEN WAS CLINGING TO THE METEORITE.
THAT'S IT ON THE FLOOR.
WHILE I WAS STUDYING IT, I SUDDENLY BECAME ILL AND LOST CONSCIOUSNESS.

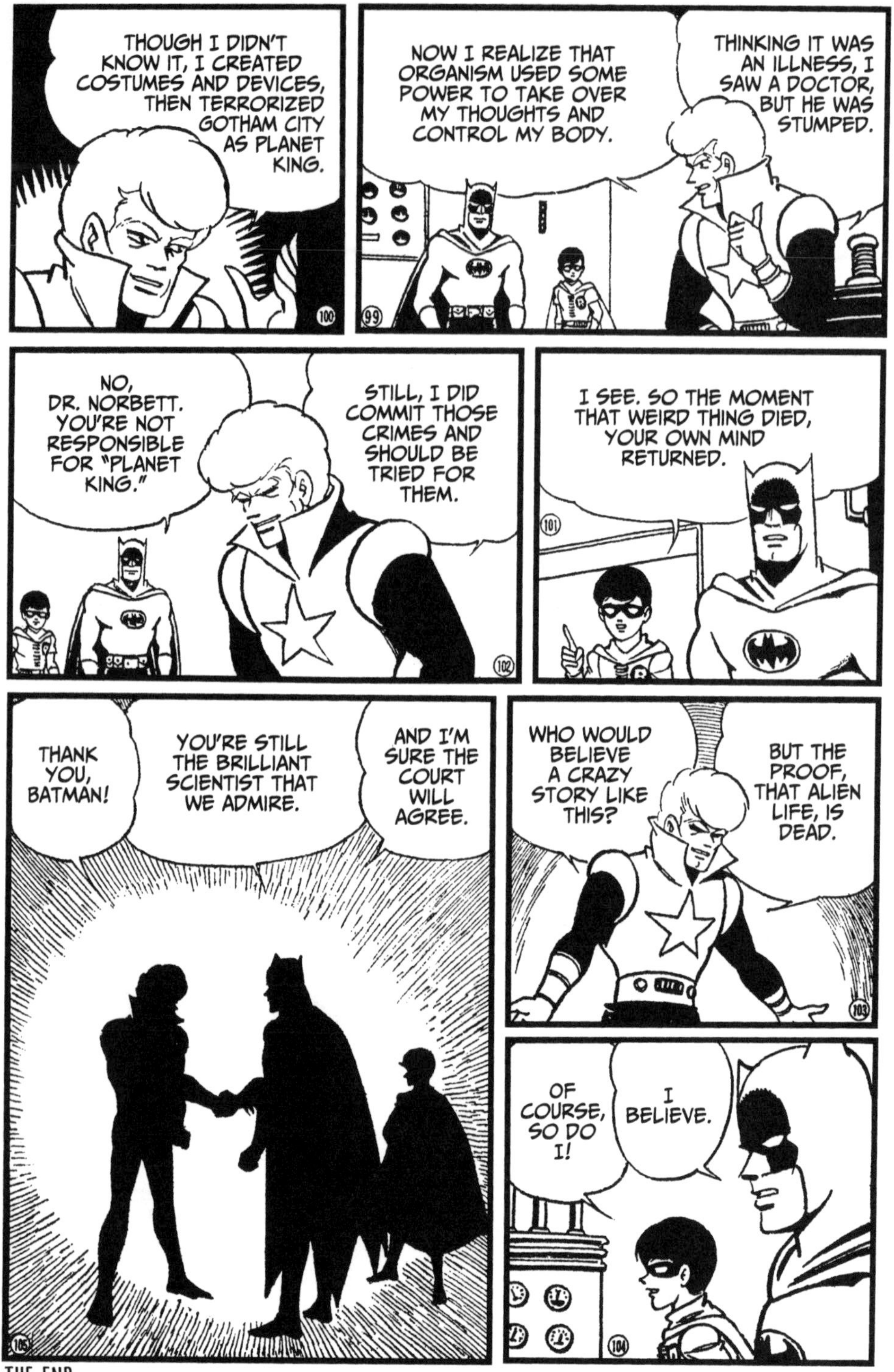
THINKING IT WAS AN ILLNESS, I SAW A DOCTOR, BUT HE WAS STUMPED.
NOW I REALIZE THAT ORGANISM USED SOME POWER TO TAKE OVER MY THOUGHTS AND CONTROL MY BODY.
THOUGH I DIDN'T KNOW IT, I CREATED COSTUMES AND DEVICES, THEN TERRORIZED GOTHAM CITY AS PLANET KING.
I SEE. SO THE MOMENT THAT WEIRD THING DIED, YOUR OWN MIND RETURNED.
STILL, I DID COMMIT THOSE CRIMES AND SHOULD BE TRIED FOR THEM.
NO, DR. NORBETT. YOU'RE NOT RESPONSIBLE FOR "PLANET KING."
BUT THE PROOF, THAT ALIEN LIFE, IS DEAD.
WHO WOULD BELIEVE A CRAZY STORY LIKE THIS?
I BELIEVE.
OF COURSE, SO DO I!
AND I'M SURE THE COURT WILL AGREE.
YOU'RE STILL THE BRILLIANT SCIENTIST THAT WE ADMIRE.
THANK YOU, BATMAN!

THE END

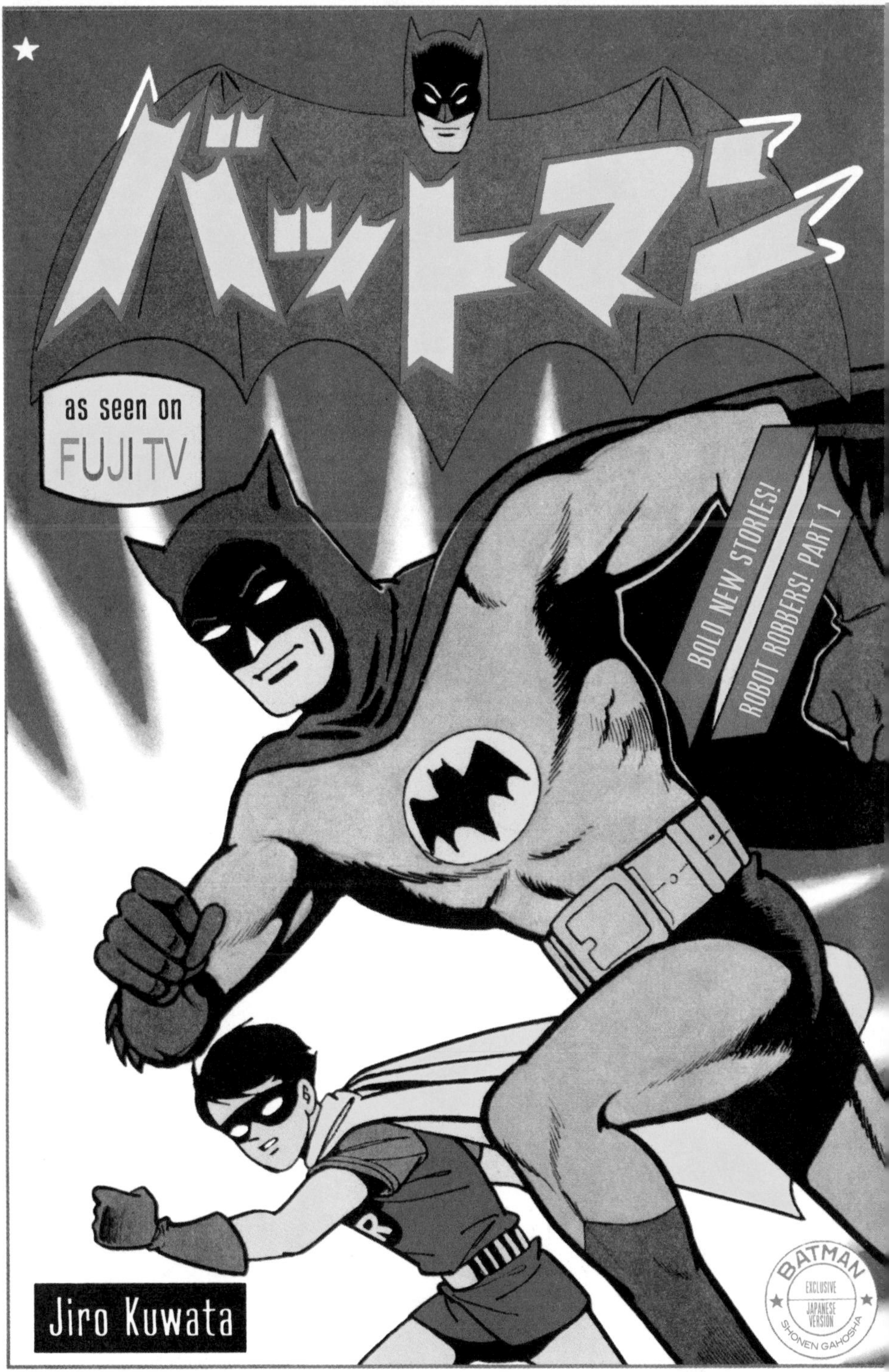
バットマン
as seen on
FUJI TV
BOLD NEW STORIES!
ROBOT ROBBERS! PART 1
Jiro Kuwata
BATMAN
EXCLUSIVE
JAPANESE VERSION
SHONEN GAHOSHA

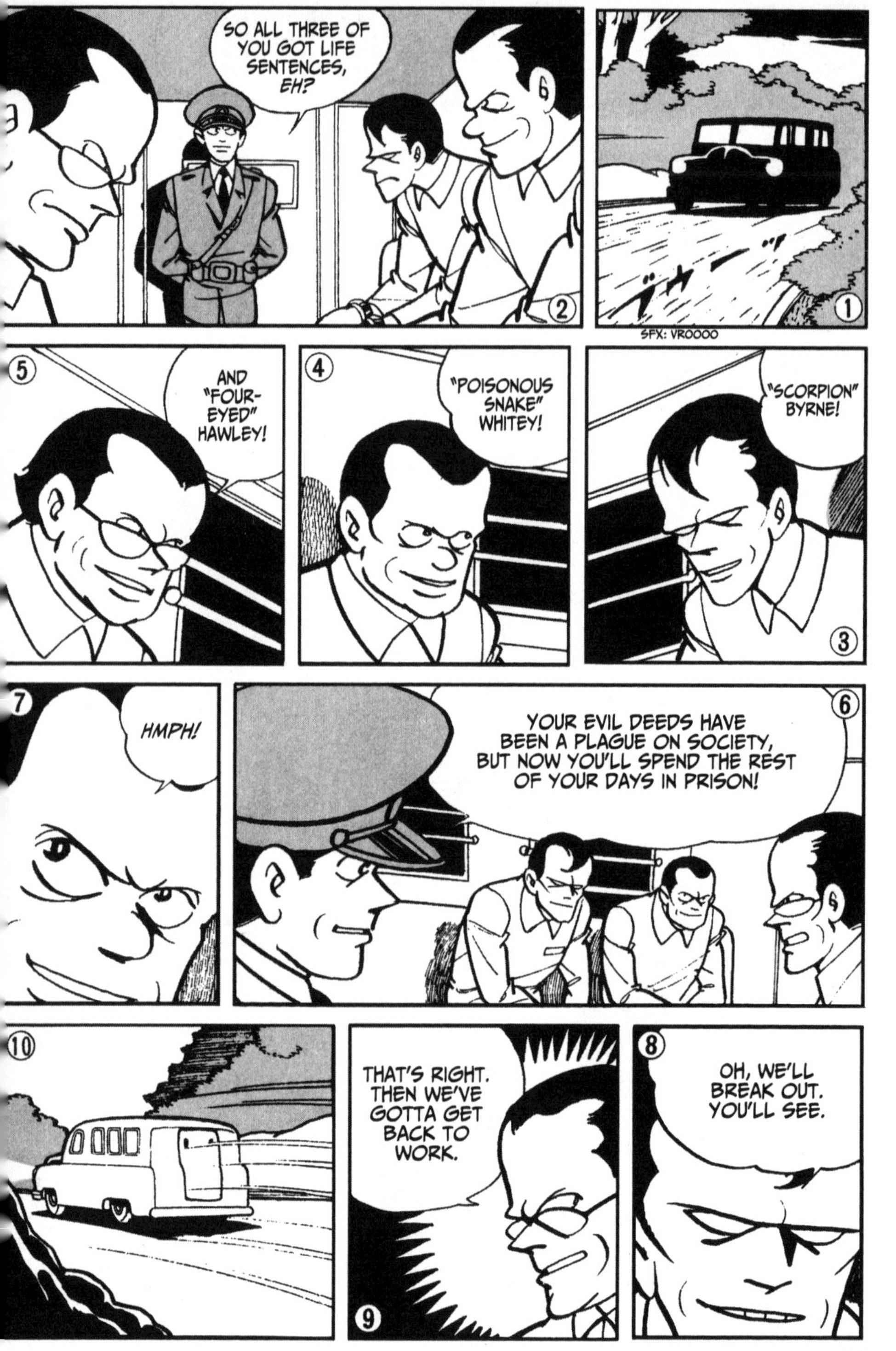
SFX: VROOOO
SO ALL THREE OF YOU GOT LIFE SENTENCES, EH?
"SCORPION" BYRNE!
"POISONOUS SNAKE" WHITEY!
AND "FOUR-EYED" HAWLEY!
YOUR EVIL DEEDS HAVE BEEN A PLAGUE ON SOCIETY, BUT NOW YOU'LL SPEND THE REST OF YOUR DAYS IN PRISON!
HMPH!
OH, WE'LL BREAK OUT. YOU'LL SEE.
THAT'S RIGHT. THEN WE'VE GOTTA GET BACK TO WORK.

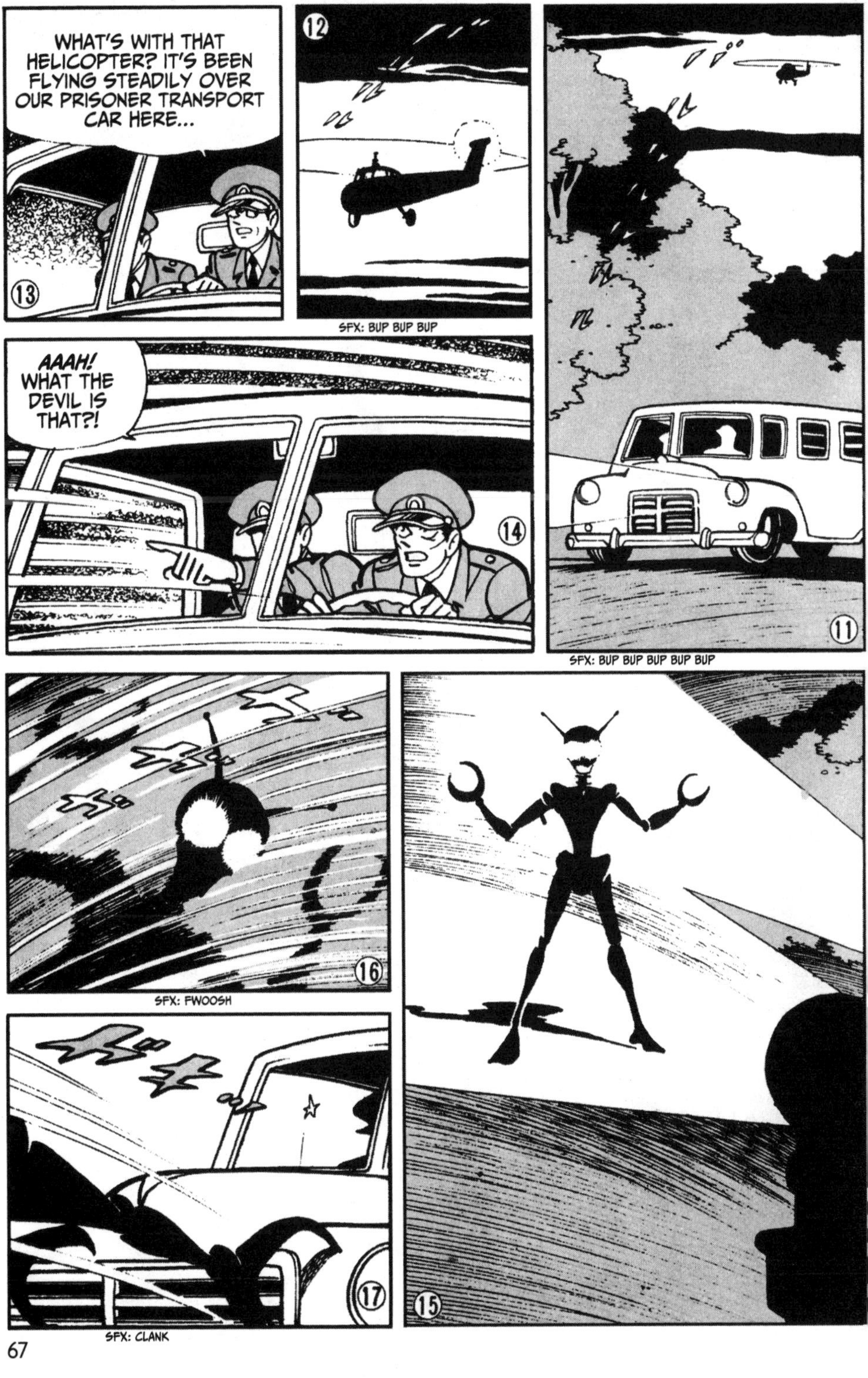
SFX: BUP BUP BUP BUP BUP
SFX: BUP BUP BUP
WHAT'S WITH THAT HELICOPTER? IT'S BEEN FLYING STEADILY OVER OUR PRISONER TRANSPORT CAR HERE...
AAAH! WHAT THE DEVIL IS THAT?!
SFX: FWOOSH
SFX: CLANK

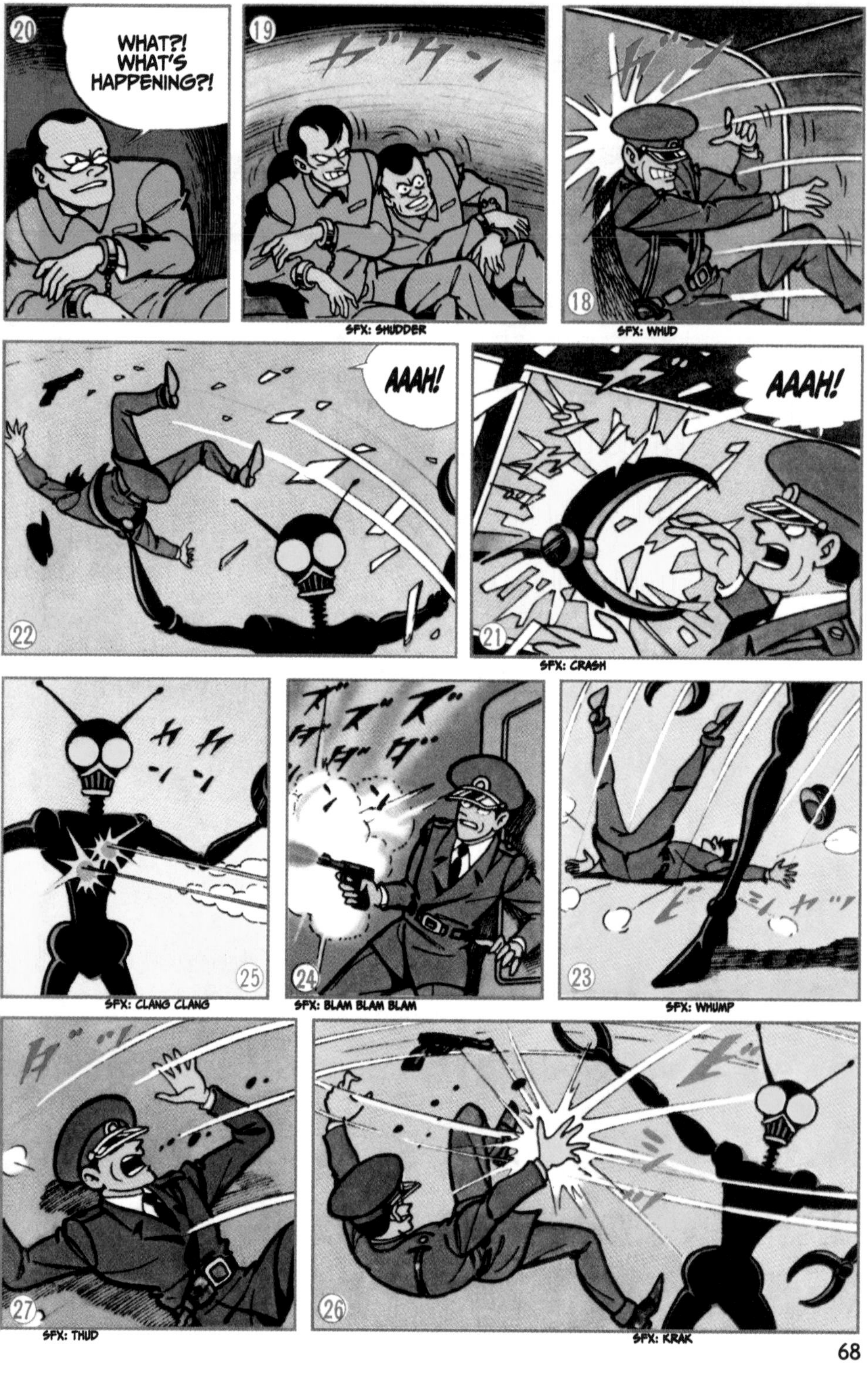
SFX: WHUD
SFX: SHUDDER
WHAT?! WHAT'S HAPPENING?!
AAAH!
SFX: CRASH
AAAH!
SFX: WHUMP
SFX: BLAM BLAM BLAM
SFX: CLANG CLANG
SFX: KRAK
SFX: THUD

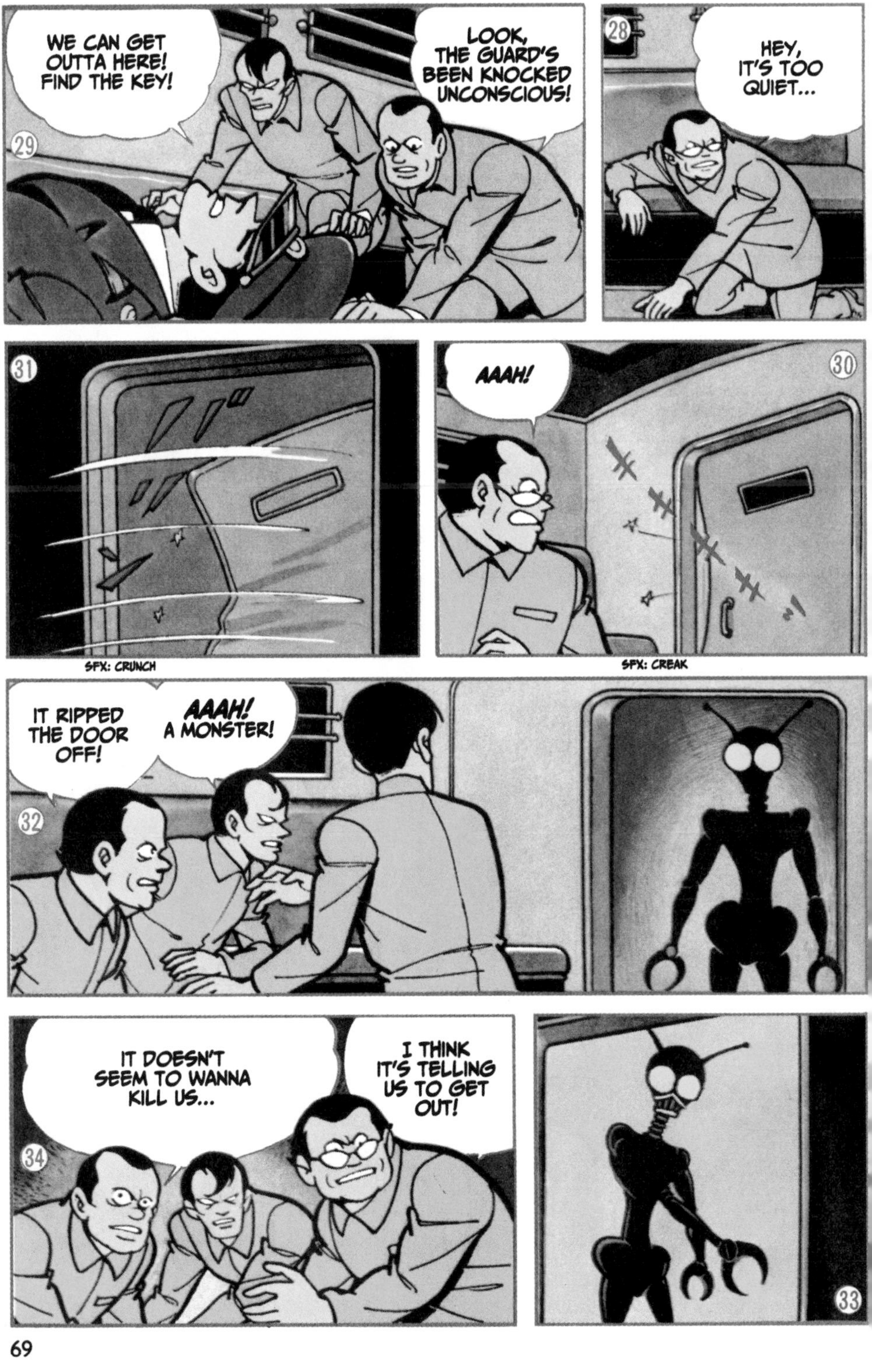
HEY, IT'S TOO QUIET...
LOOK, THE GUARD'S BEEN KNOCKED UNCONSCIOUS!
WE CAN GET OUTTA HERE! FIND THE KEY!
AAAH!
SFX: CREAK
SFX: CRUNCH
AAAH! A MONSTER!
IT RIPPED THE DOOR OFF!
I THINK IT'S TELLING US TO GET OUT!
IT DOESN'T SEEM TO WANNA KILL US...

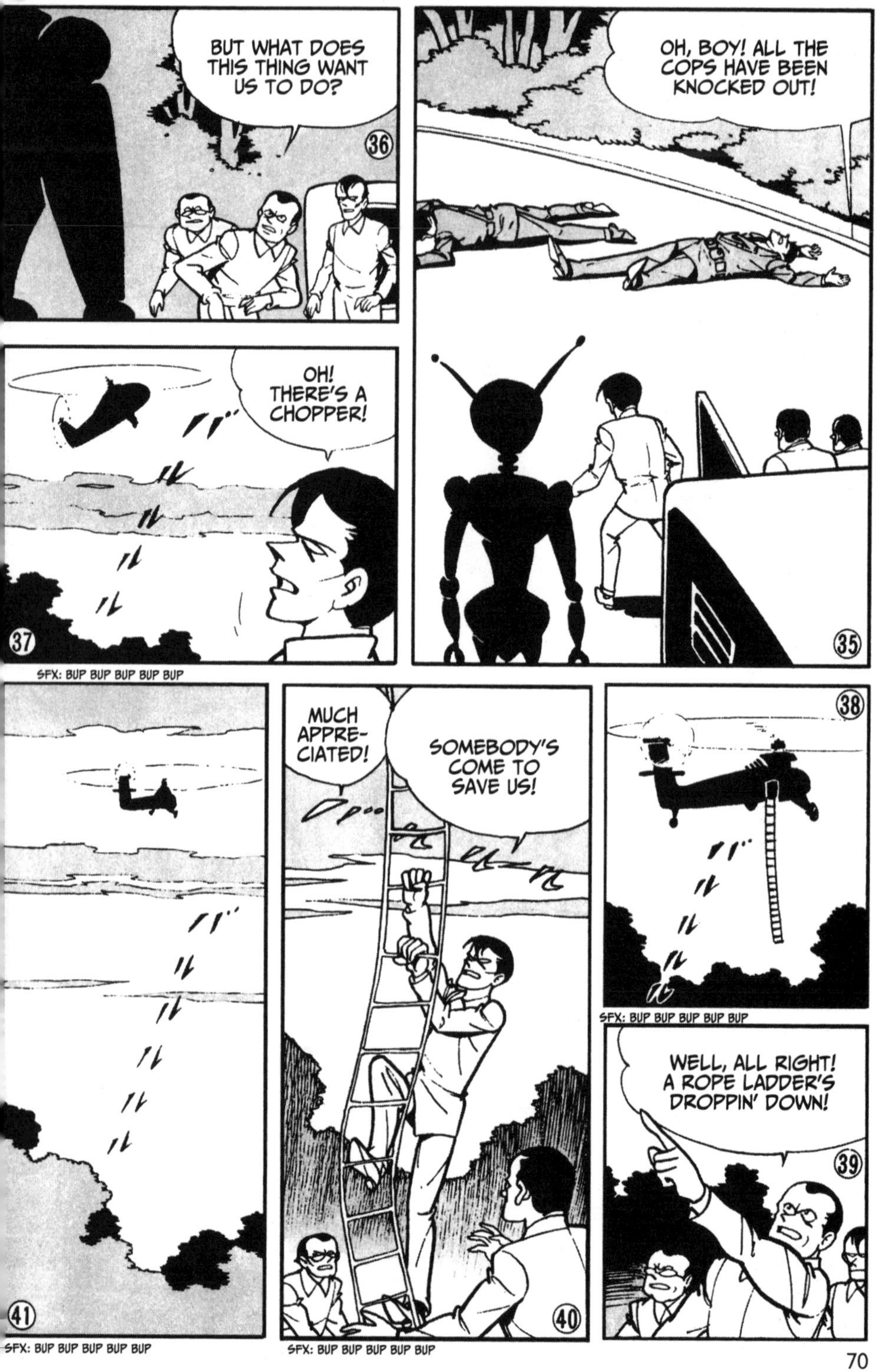
OH, BOY! ALL THE COPS HAVE BEEN KNOCKED OUT!
BUT WHAT DOES THIS THING WANT US TO DO?
OH! THERE'S A CHOPPER!
SFX: BUP BUP BUP BUP BUP
SFX: BUP BUP BUP BUP BUP
WELL, ALL RIGHT! A ROPE LADDER'S DROPPIN' DOWN!
SOMEBODY'S COME TO SAVE US!
MUCH APPRECIATED!
SFX: BUP BUP BUP BUP BUP
SFX: BUP BUP BUP BUP BUP

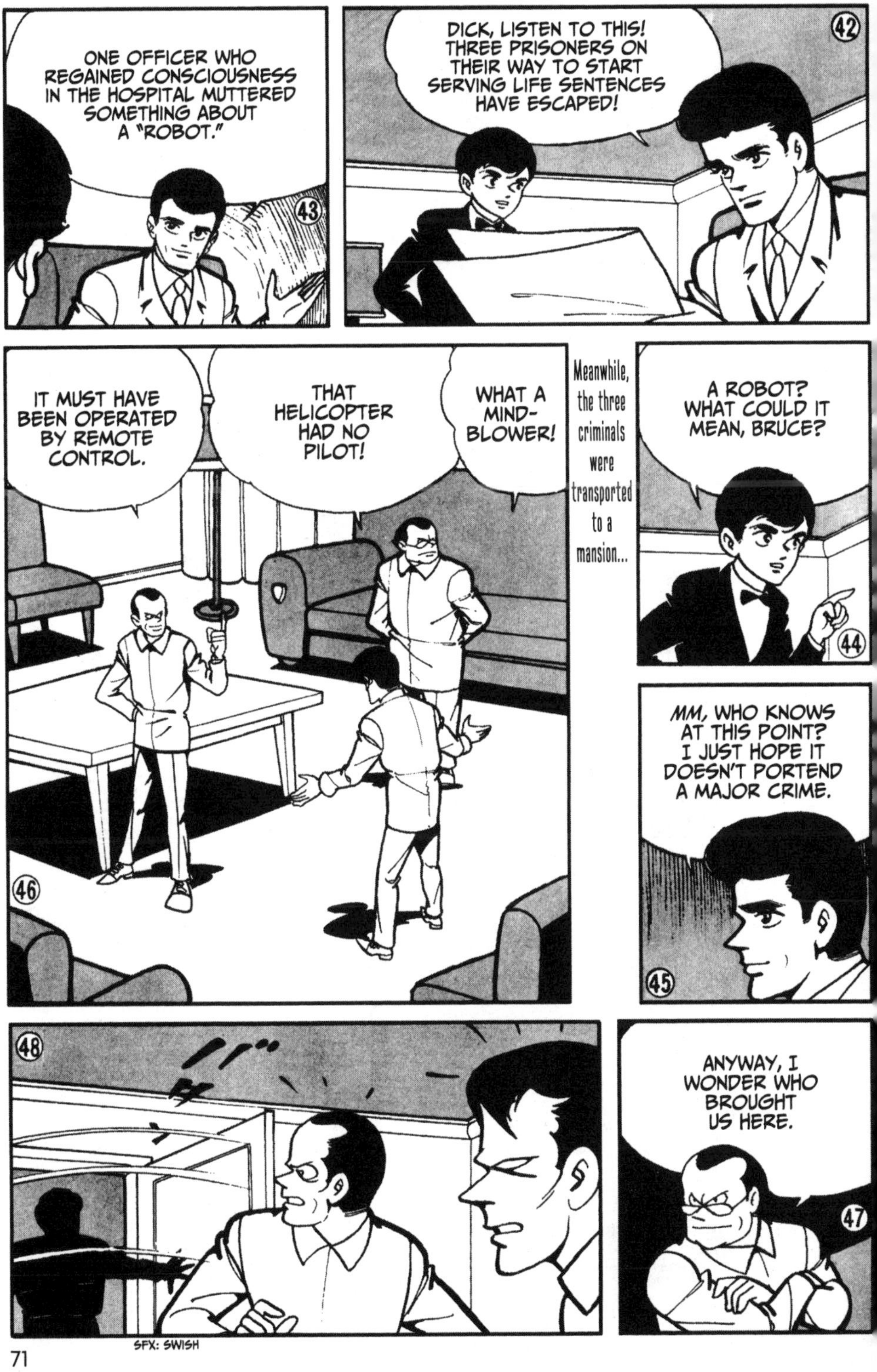
DICK, LISTEN TO THIS! THREE PRISONERS ON THEIR WAY TO START SERVING LIFE SENTENCES HAVE ESCAPED!
ONE OFFICER WHO REGAINED CONSCIOUSNESS IN THE HOSPITAL MUTTERED SOMETHING ABOUT A "ROBOT."
A ROBOT? WHAT COULD IT MEAN, BRUCE?
MM, WHO KNOWS AT THIS POINT? I JUST HOPE IT DOESN'T PORTEND A MAJOR CRIME.
Meanwhile, the three criminals were transported to a mansion...
WHAT A MIND-BLOWER!
THAT HELICOPTER HAD NO PILOT!
IT MUST HAVE BEEN OPERATED BY REMOTE CONTROL.
ANYWAY, I WONDER WHO BROUGHT US HERE.
SFX: SWISH

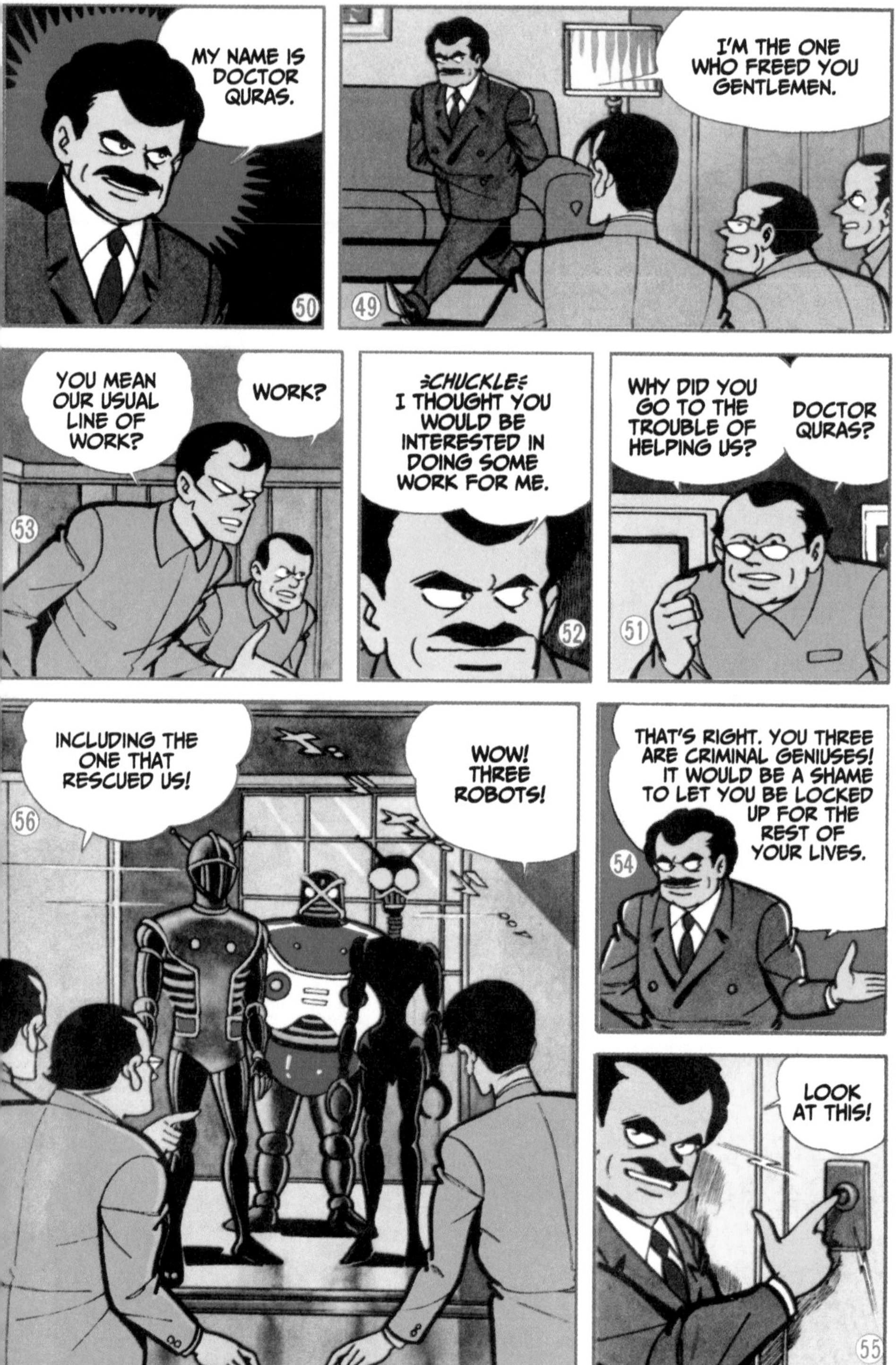
I'M THE ONE WHO FREED YOU GENTLEMEN.
MY NAME IS DOCTOR QURAS.
DOCTOR QURAS?
WHY DID YOU GO TO THE TROUBLE OF HELPING US?
⋞CHUCKLE⋟ I THOUGHT YOU WOULD BE INTERESTED IN DOING SOME WORK FOR ME.
WORK?
YOU MEAN OUR USUAL LINE OF WORK?
THAT'S RIGHT. YOU THREE ARE CRIMINAL GENIUSES! IT WOULD BE A SHAME TO LET YOU BE LOCKED UP FOR THE REST OF YOUR LIVES.
LOOK AT THIS!
WOW! THREE ROBOTS!
INCLUDING THE ONE THAT RESCUED US!

SFX: RATTLE RATTLE RATTLE

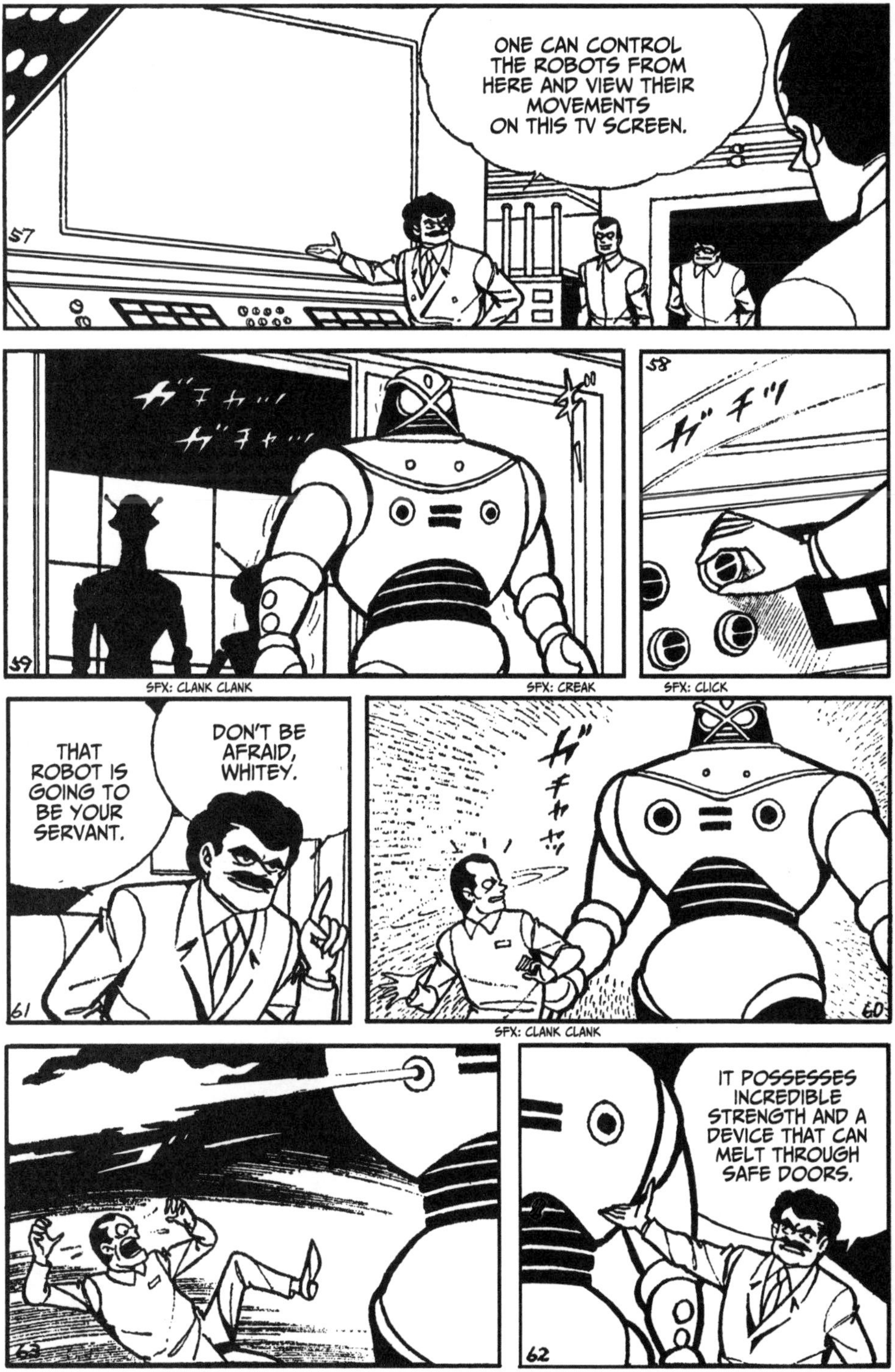
ONE CAN CONTROL THE ROBOTS FROM HERE AND VIEW THEIR MOVEMENTS ON THIS TV SCREEN.
SFX: CLICK
SFX: CREAK
SFX: CLANK CLANK
SFX: CLANK CLANK
DON'T BE AFRAID, WHITEY.
THAT ROBOT IS GOING TO BE YOUR SERVANT.
IT POSSESSES INCREDIBLE STRENGTH AND A DEVICE THAT CAN MELT THROUGH SAFE DOORS.
SFX: FOOSH

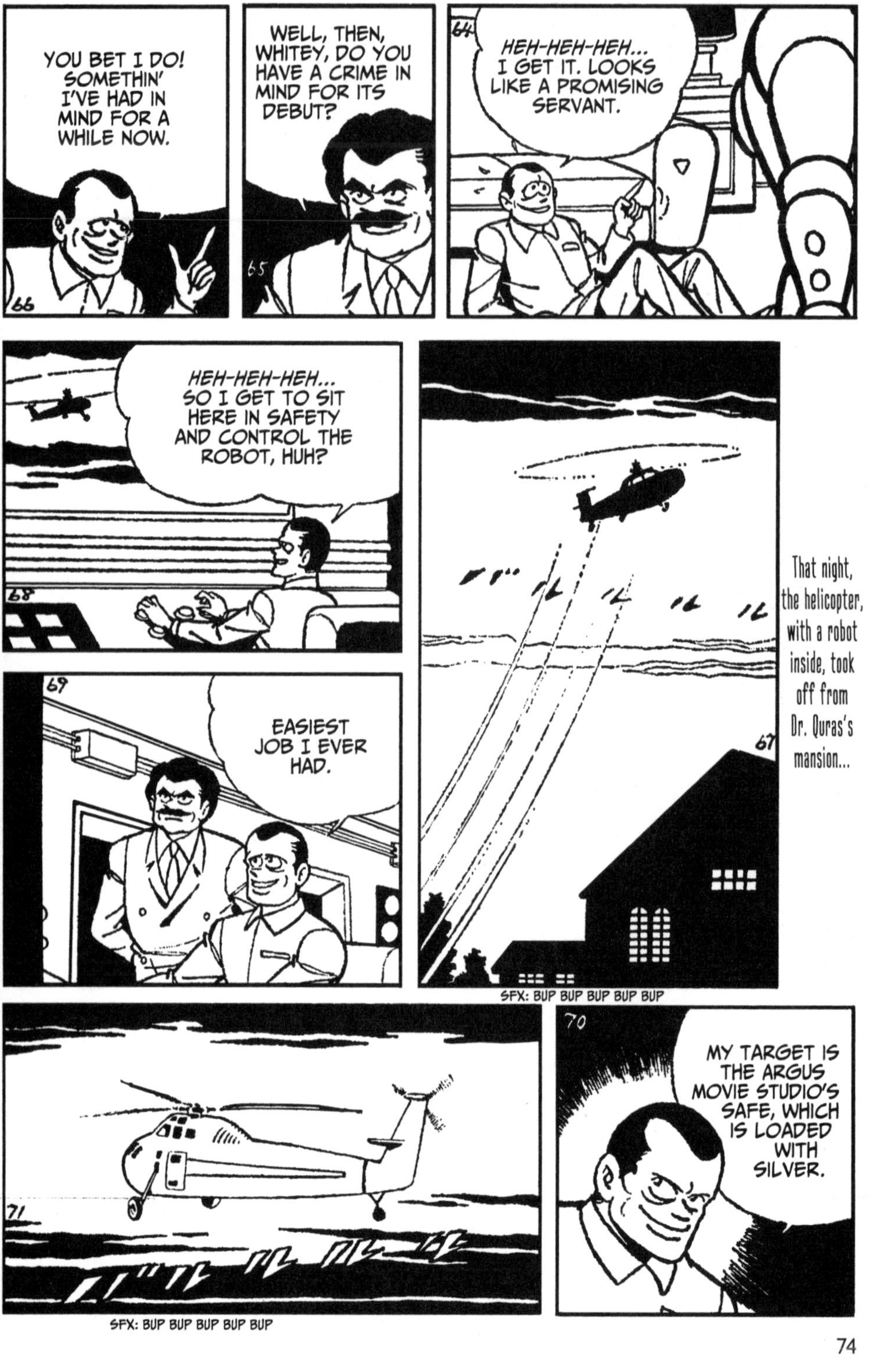
HEH-HEH-HEH... I GET IT. LOOKS LIKE A PROMISING SERVANT.
WELL, THEN, WHITEY, DO YOU HAVE A CRIME IN MIND FOR ITS DEBUT?
YOU BET I DO! SOMETHIN' I'VE HAD IN MIND FOR A WHILE NOW.
That night, the helicopter, with a robot inside, took off from Dr. Quras's mansion...
SFX: BUP BUP BUP BUP BUP
HEH-HEH-HEH... SO I GET TO SIT HERE IN SAFETY AND CONTROL THE ROBOT, HUH?
EASIEST JOB I EVER HAD.
MY TARGET IS THE ARGUS MOVIE STUDIO'S SAFE, WHICH IS LOADED WITH SILVER.
SFX: BUP BUP BUP BUP BUP

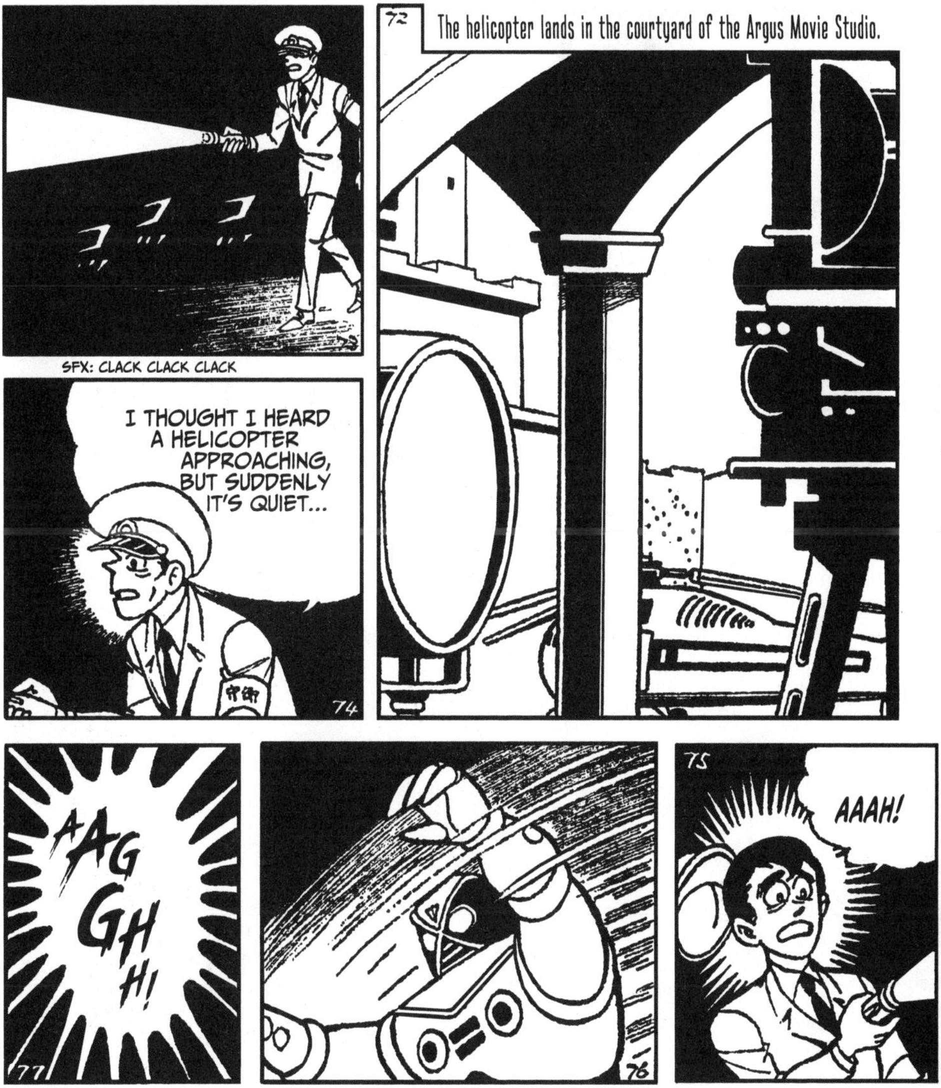
The helicopter lands in the courtyard of the Argus Movie Studio.
SFX: CLACK CLACK CLACK
I THOUGHT I HEARD A HELICOPTER APPROACHING, BUT SUDDENLY IT'S QUIET...
AAAH!
AAGGHH!

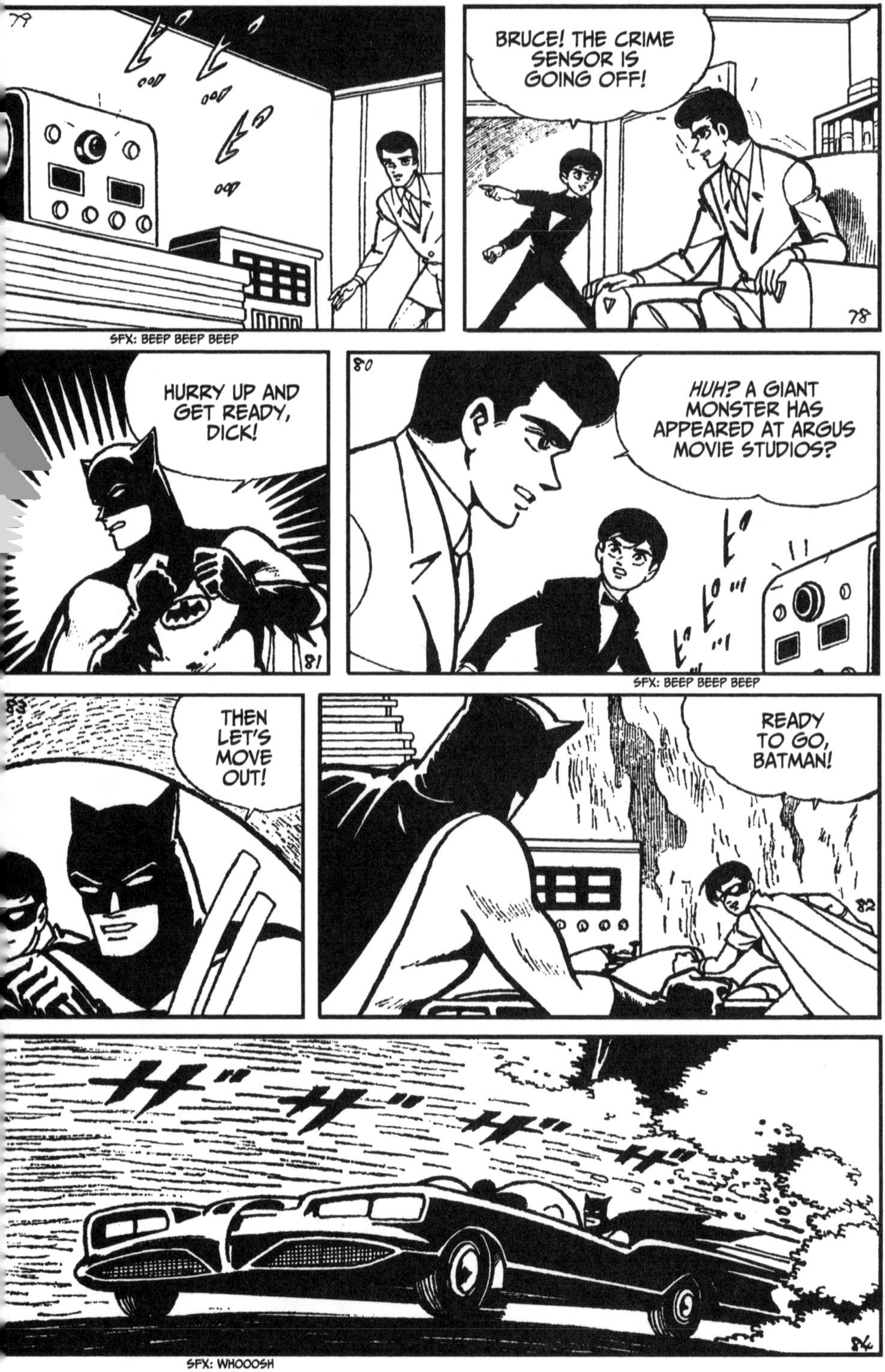
BRUCE! THE CRIME SENSOR IS GOING OFF!
SFX: BEEP BEEP BEEP
HUH? A GIANT MONSTER HAS APPEARED AT ARGUS MOVIE STUDIOS?
SFX: BEEP BEEP BEEP
HURRY UP AND GET READY, DICK!
READY TO GO, BATMAN!
THEN LET'S MOVE OUT!
SFX: WHOOOSH

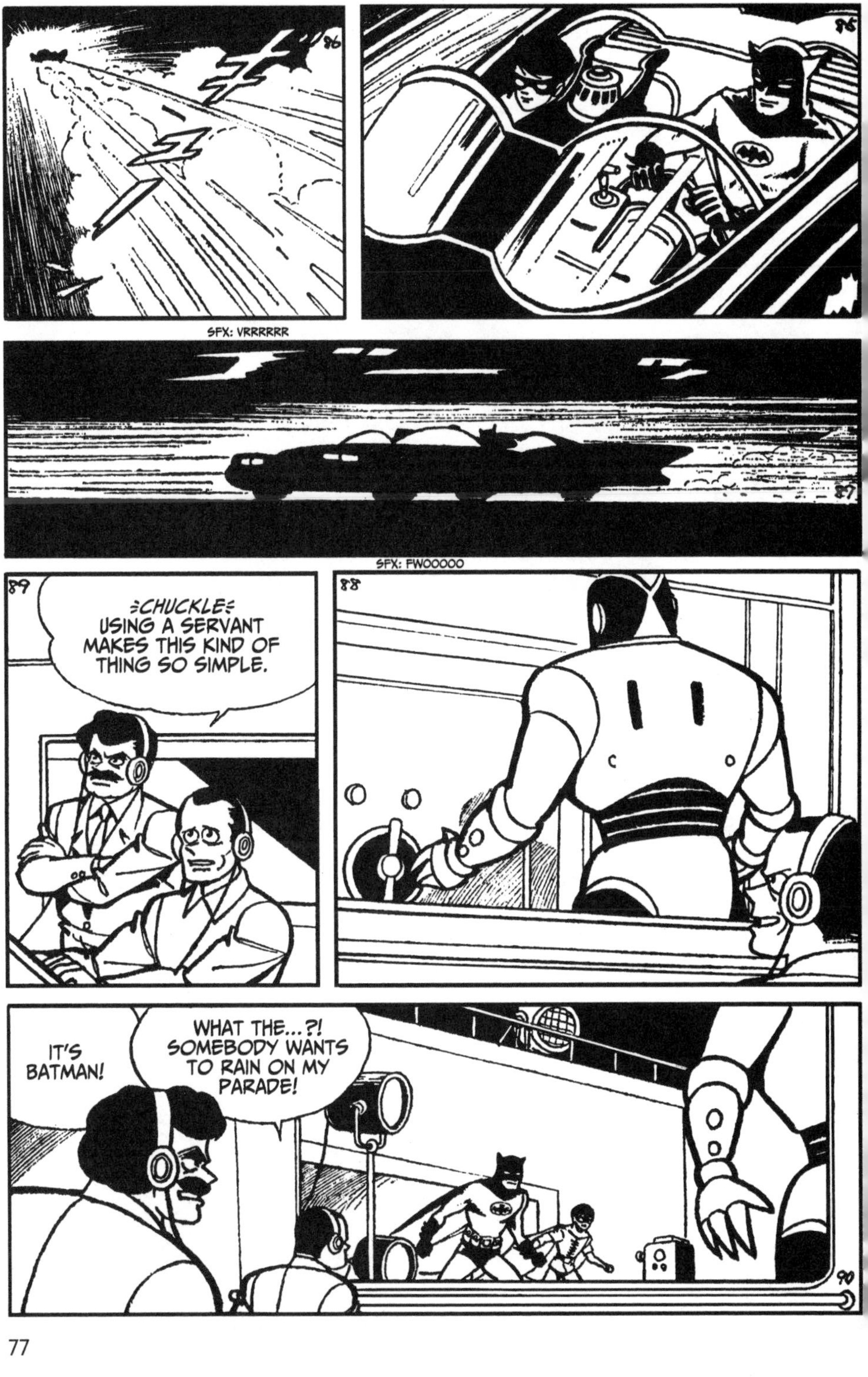
SFX: VRRRRRR
SFX: FWOOOOO
≡CHUCKLE≡ USING A SERVANT MAKES THIS KIND OF THING SO SIMPLE.
WHAT THE...?! SOMEBODY WANTS TO RAIN ON MY PARADE!
IT'S BATMAN!

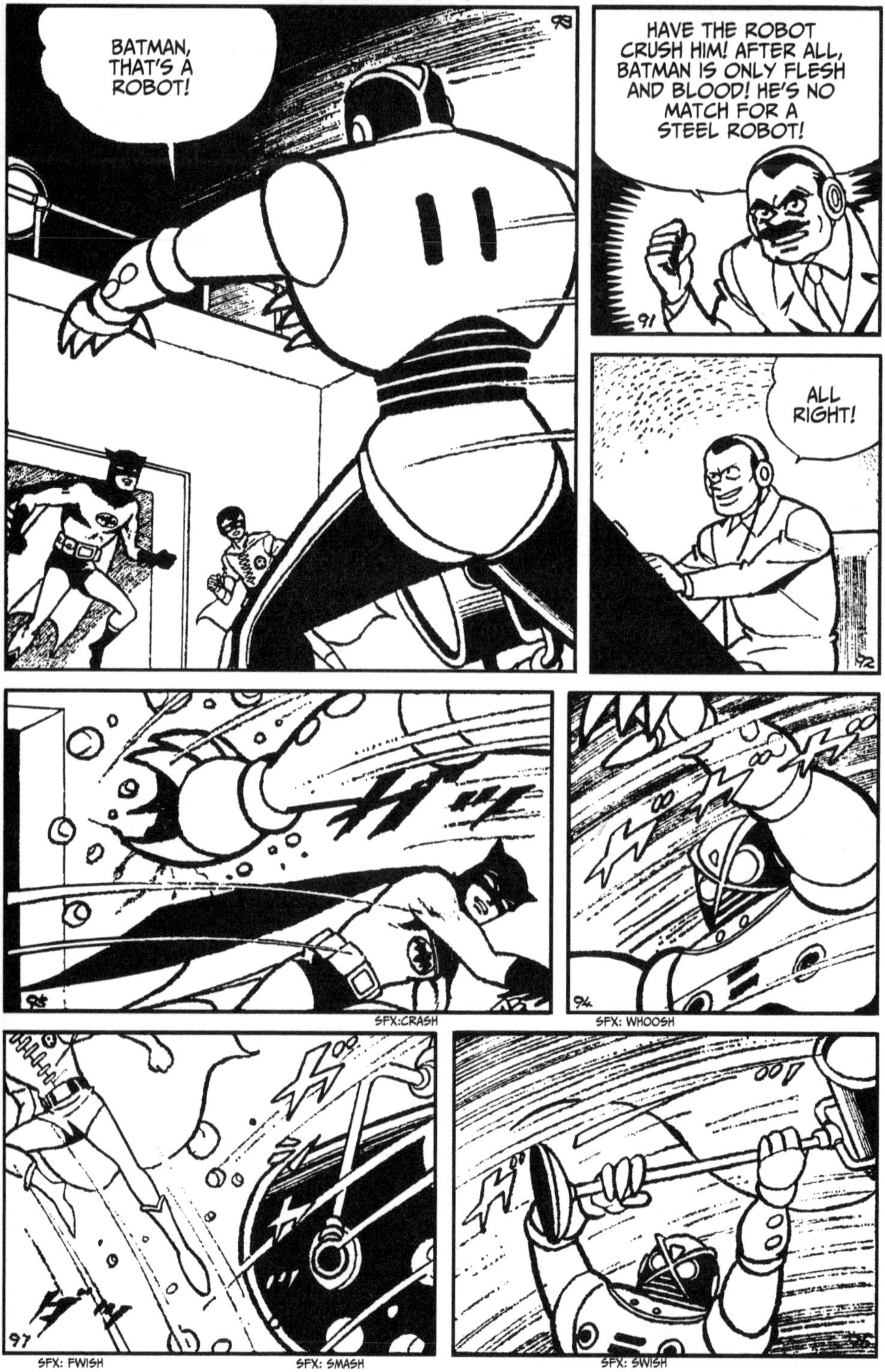
HAVE THE ROBOT CRUSH HIM! AFTER ALL, BATMAN IS ONLY FLESH AND BLOOD! HE'S NO MATCH FOR A STEEL ROBOT!
ALL RIGHT!
BATMAN, THAT'S A ROBOT!
SFX: WHOOSH
SFX:CRASH
SFX: SWISH
SFX: SMASH
SFX: FWISH

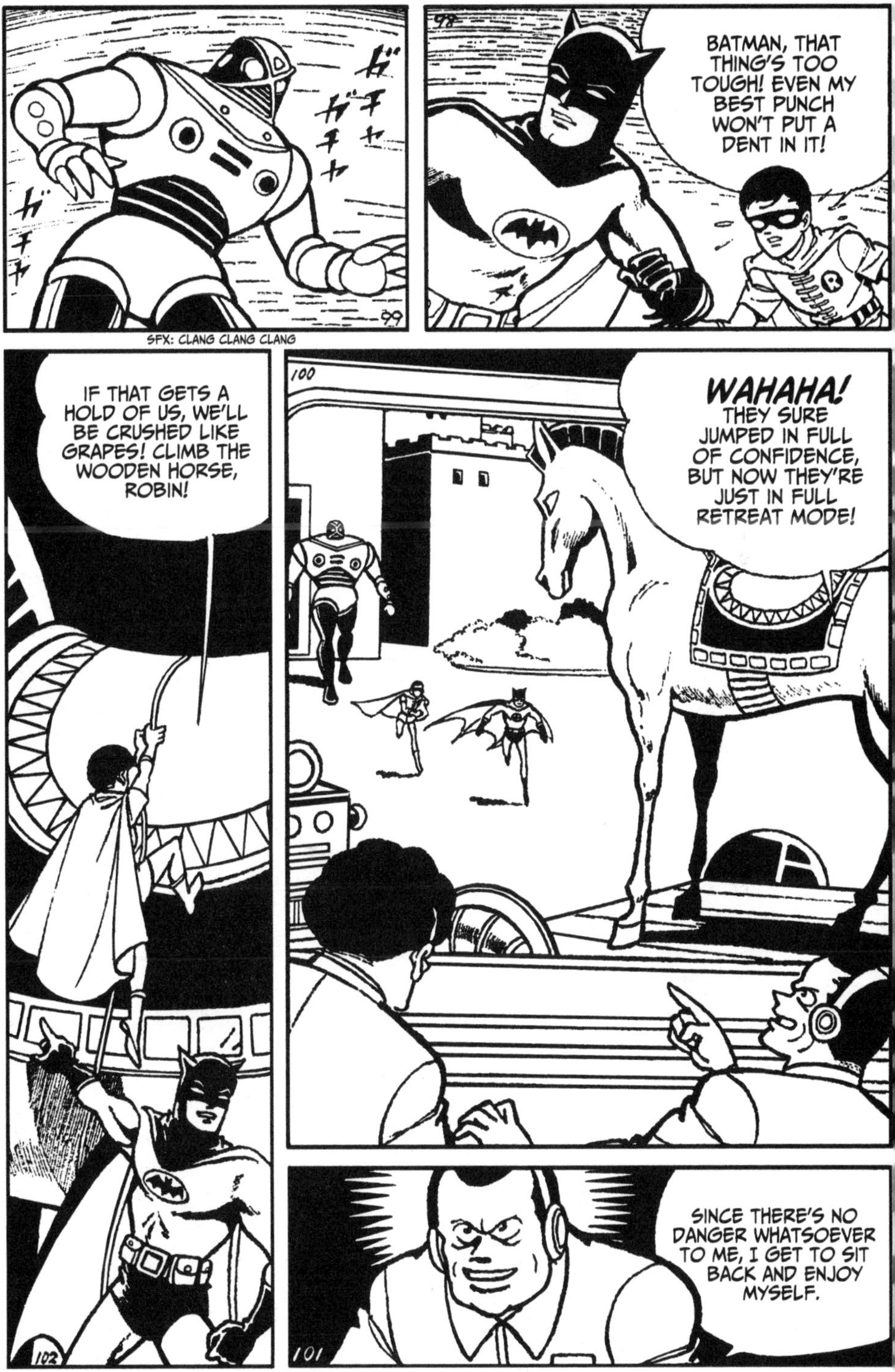

BATMAN, THAT THING'S TOO TOUGH! EVEN MY BEST PUNCH WON'T PUT A DENT IN IT!
SFX: CLANG CLANG CLANG
WAHAHA! THEY SURE JUMPED IN FULL OF CONFIDENCE, BUT NOW THEY'RE JUST IN FULL RETREAT MODE!
SINCE THERE'S NO DANGER WHATSOEVER TO ME, I GET TO SIT BACK AND ENJOY MYSELF.
IF THAT GETS A HOLD OF US, WE'LL BE CRUSHED LIKE GRAPES! CLIMB THE WOODEN HORSE, ROBIN!

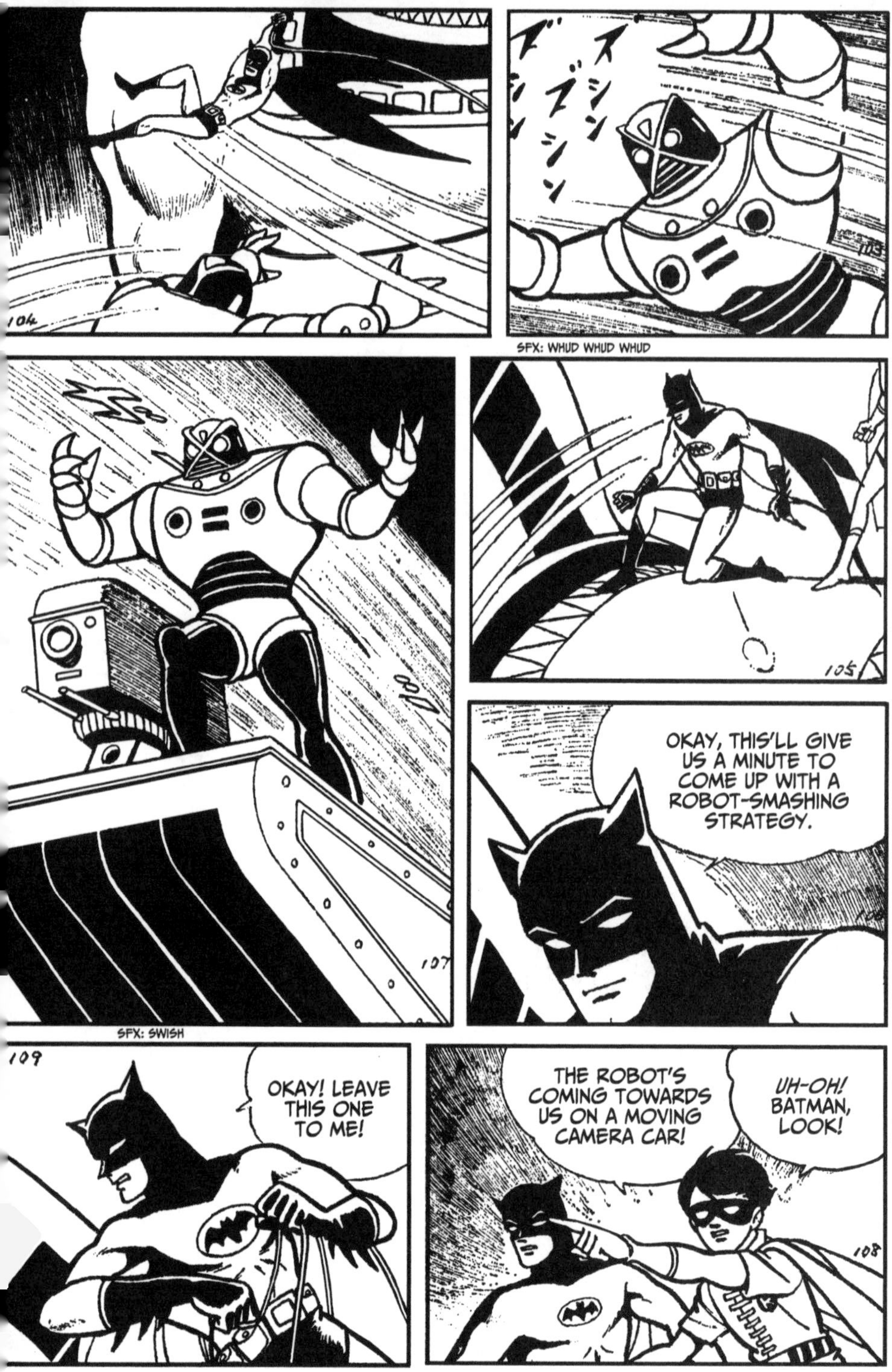
ズシン ズシン ズシン
SFX: WHUD WHUD WHUD
OKAY, THIS'LL GIVE US A MINUTE TO COME UP WITH A ROBOT-SMASHING STRATEGY.
SFX: SWISH
UH-OH! BATMAN, LOOK!
THE ROBOT'S COMING TOWARDS US ON A MOVING CAMERA CAR!
OKAY! LEAVE THIS ONE TO ME!

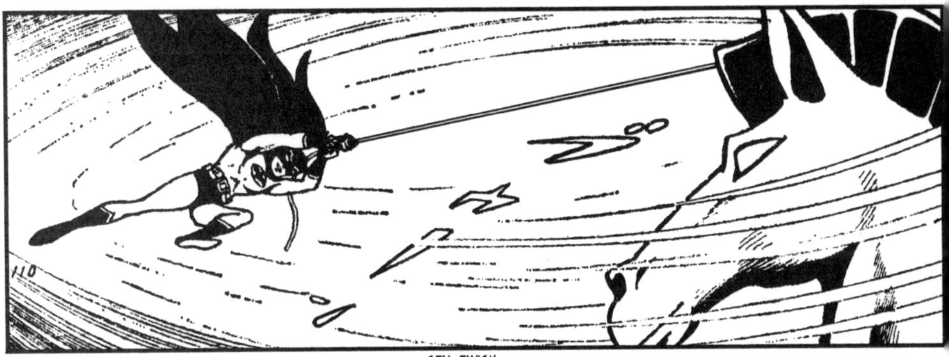

SFX: FWISH

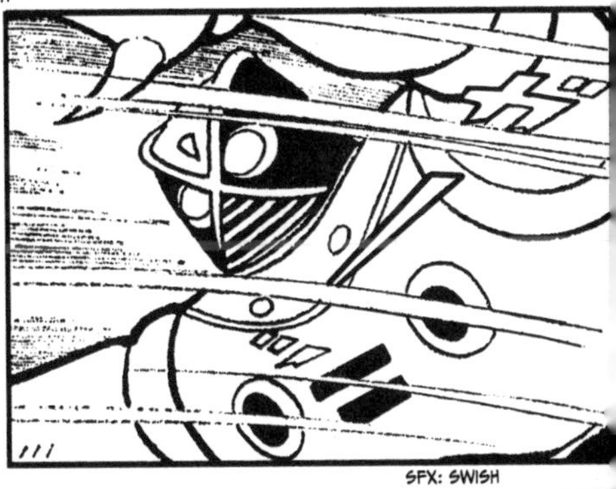

SFX: SWISH

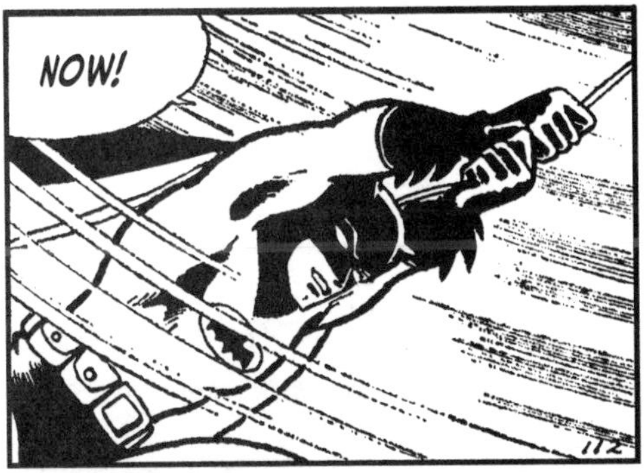
NOW!

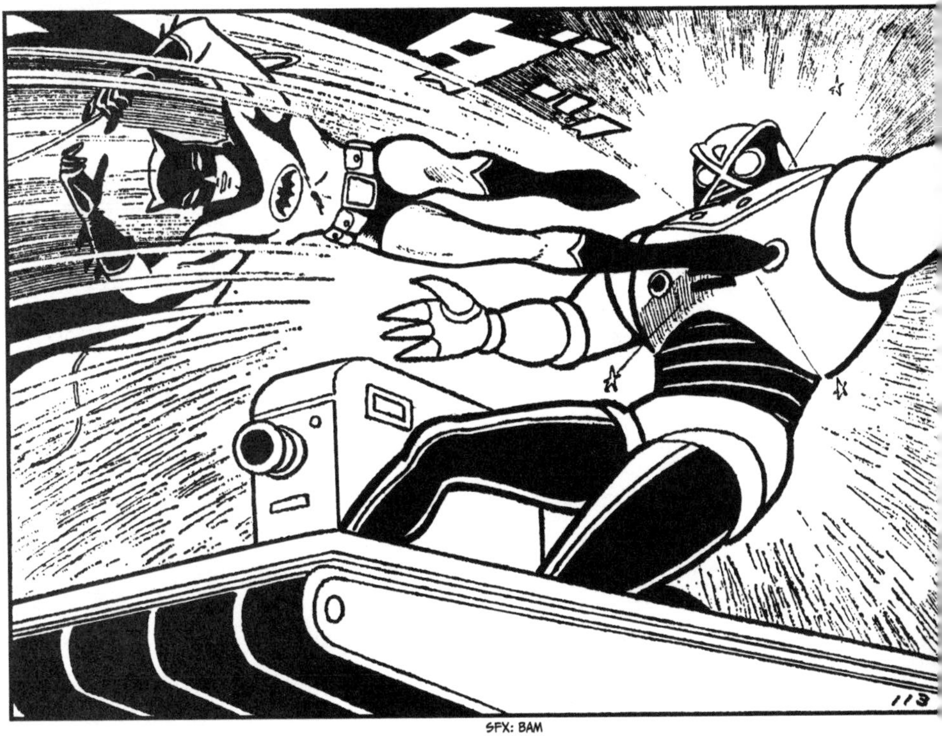

SFX: BAM

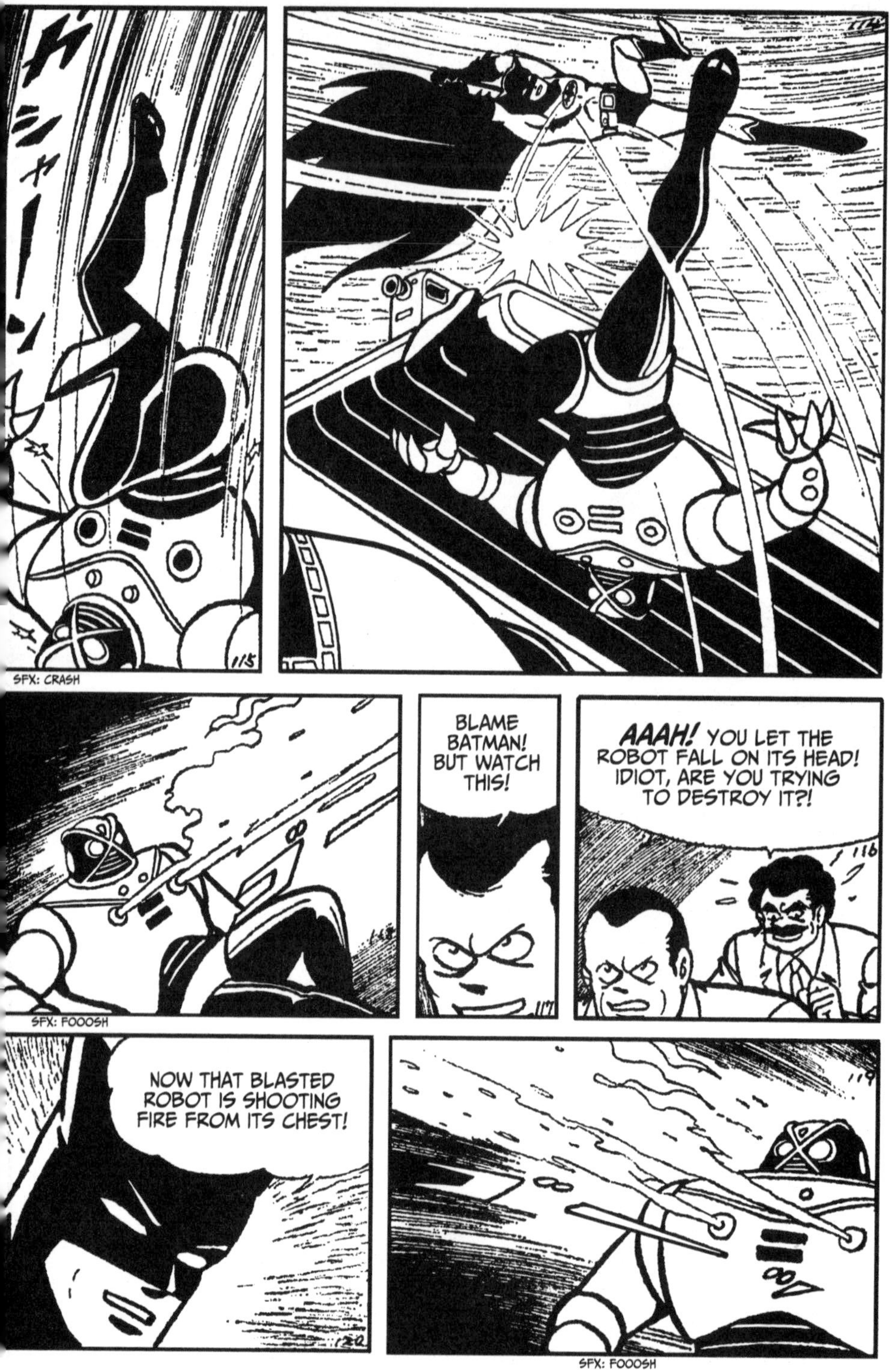
SFX: CRASH
AAAH! YOU LET THE ROBOT FALL ON ITS HEAD! IDIOT, ARE YOU TRYING TO DESTROY IT?!
BLAME BATMAN! BUT WATCH THIS!
SFX: FOOOSH
SFX: FOOOSH
NOW THAT BLASTED ROBOT IS SHOOTING FIRE FROM ITS CHEST!

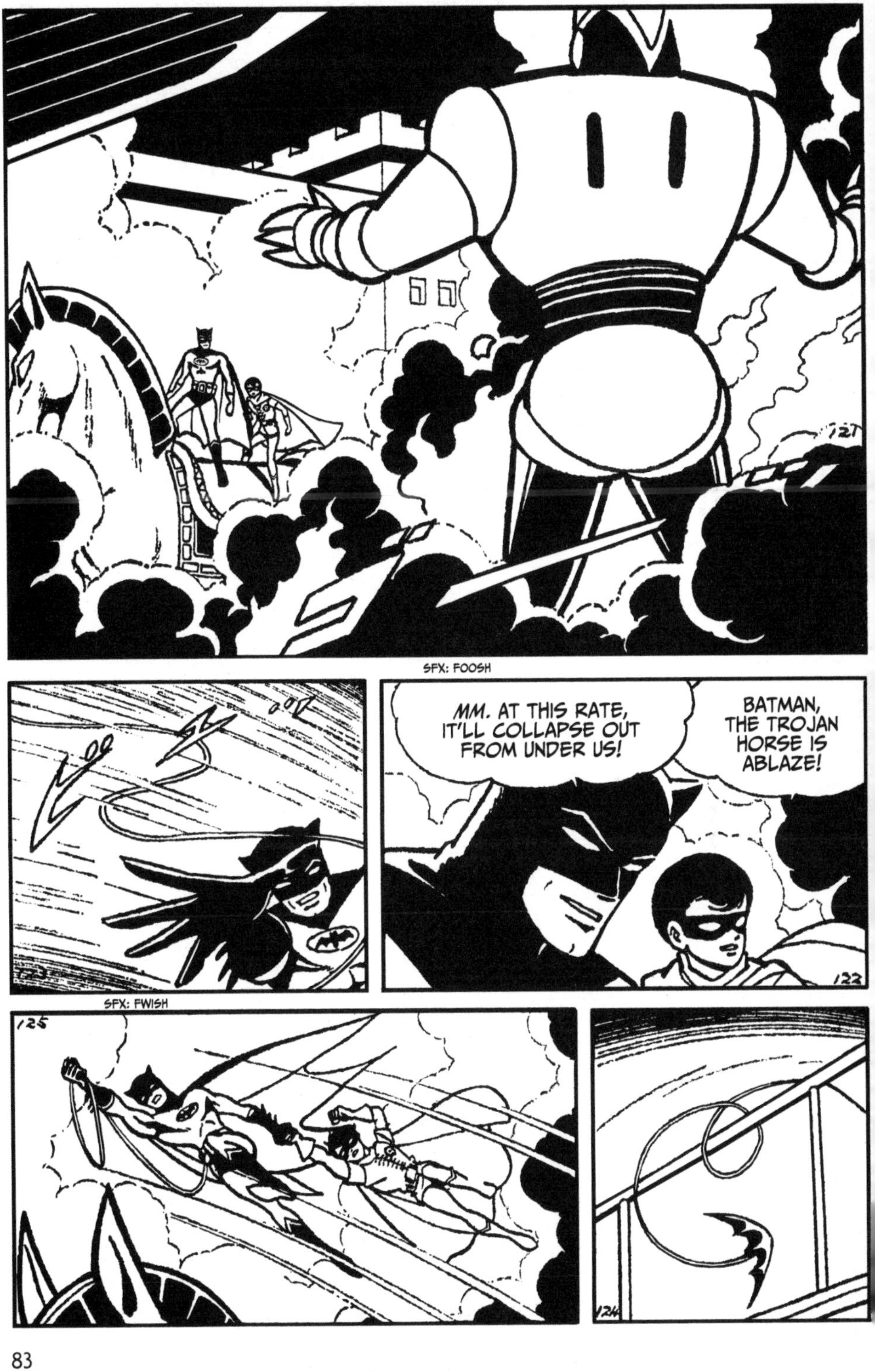
SFX: FOOSH
BATMAN, THE TROJAN HORSE IS ABLAZE!
MM. AT THIS RATE, IT'LL COLLAPSE OUT FROM UNDER US!
SFX: FWISH

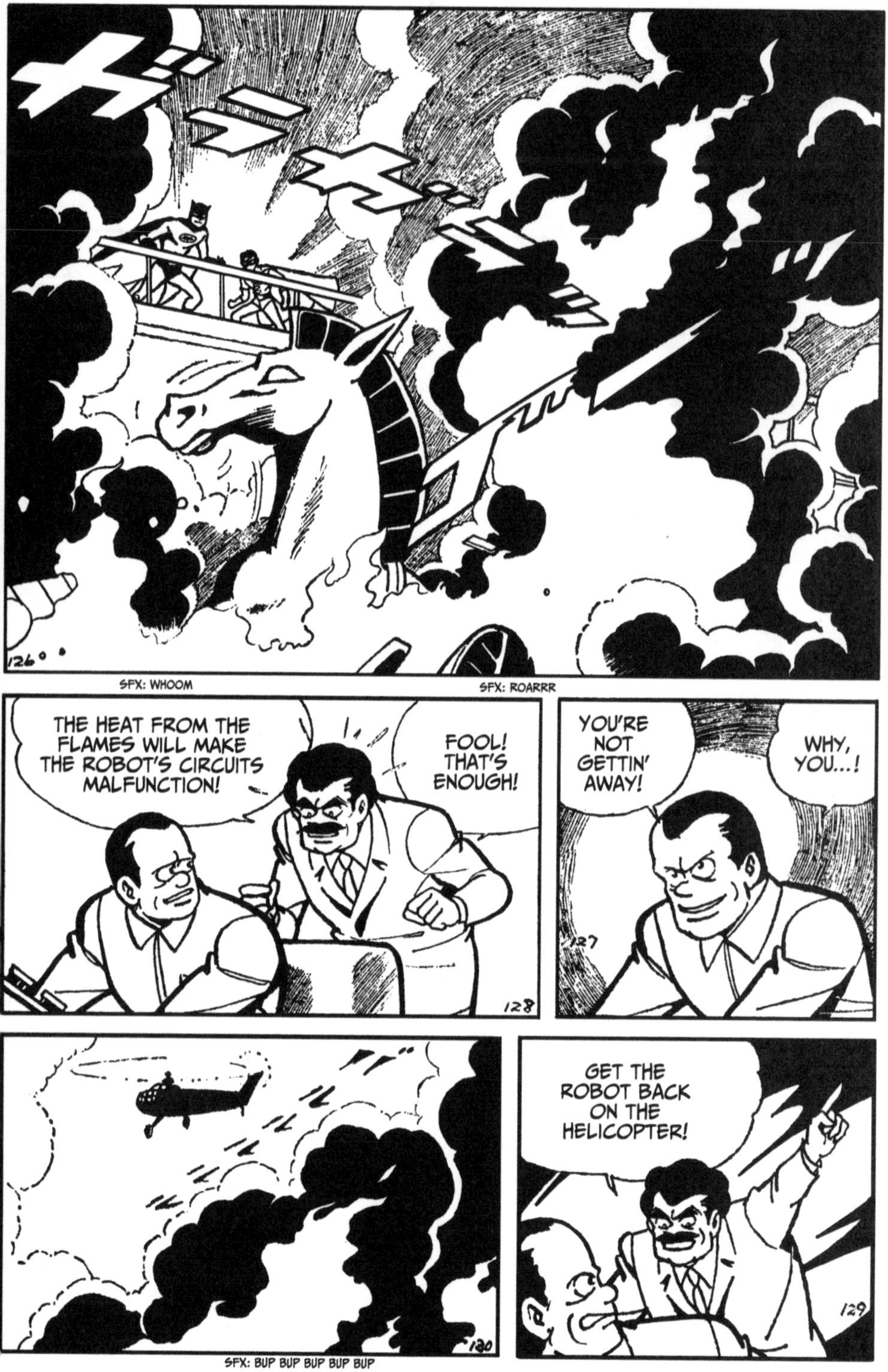
SFX: ROARRR
SFX: WHOOM
WHY, YOU...!
YOU'RE NOT GETTIN' AWAY!
FOOL! THAT'S ENOUGH!
THE HEAT FROM THE FLAMES WILL MAKE THE ROBOT'S CIRCUITS MALFUNCTION!
GET THE ROBOT BACK ON THE HELICOPTER!
SFX: BUP BUP BUP BUP BUP

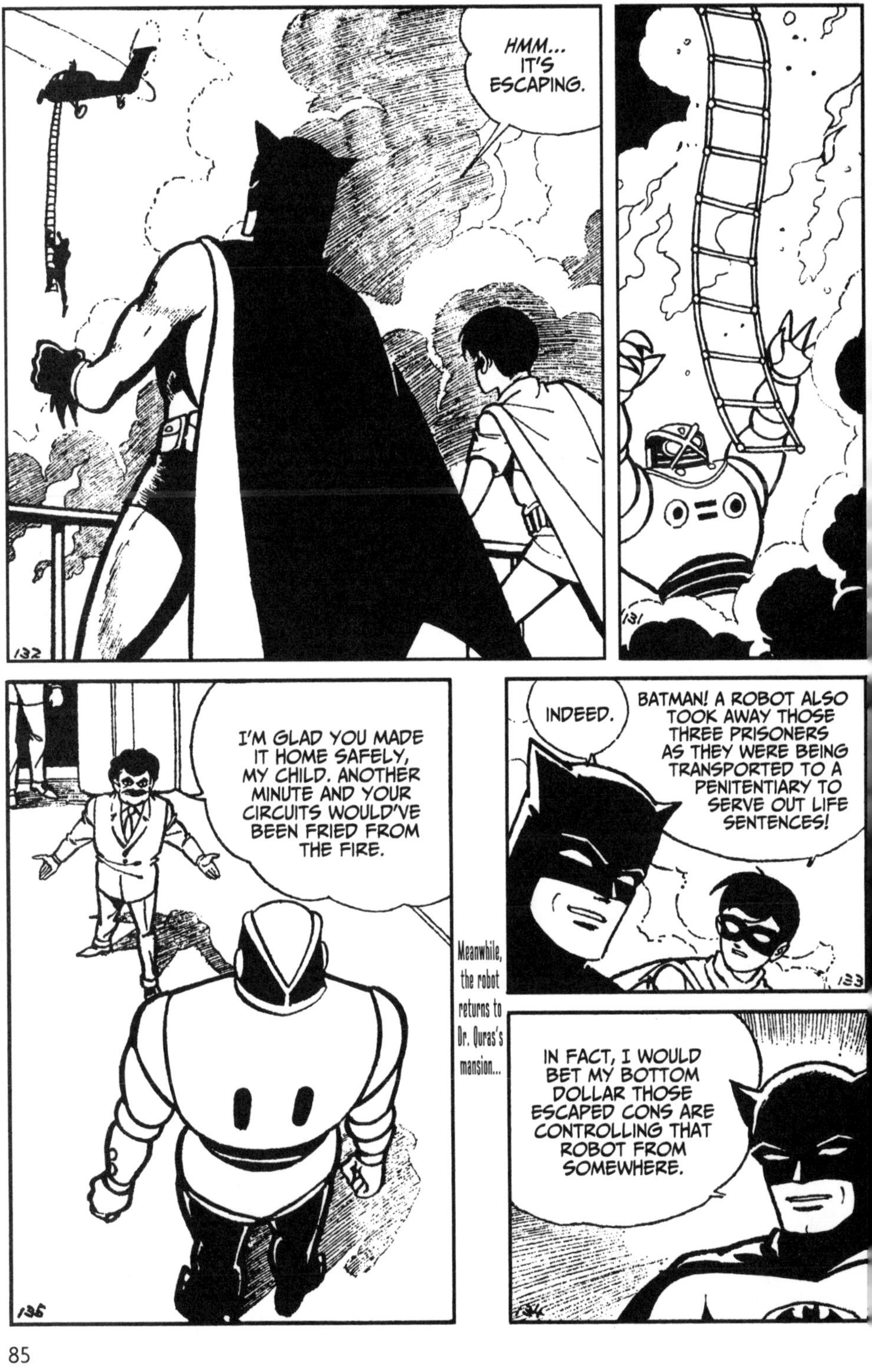
HMM... IT'S ESCAPING.
BATMAN! A ROBOT ALSO TOOK AWAY THOSE THREE PRISONERS AS THEY WERE BEING TRANSPORTED TO A PENITENTIARY TO SERVE OUT LIFE SENTENCES!
INDEED.
IN FACT, I WOULD BET MY BOTTOM DOLLAR THOSE ESCAPED CONS ARE CONTROLLING THAT ROBOT FROM SOMEWHERE.
Meanwhile, the robot returns to Dr. Quras's mansion...
I'M GLAD YOU MADE IT HOME SAFELY, MY CHILD. ANOTHER MINUTE AND YOUR CIRCUITS WOULD'VE BEEN FRIED FROM THE FIRE.

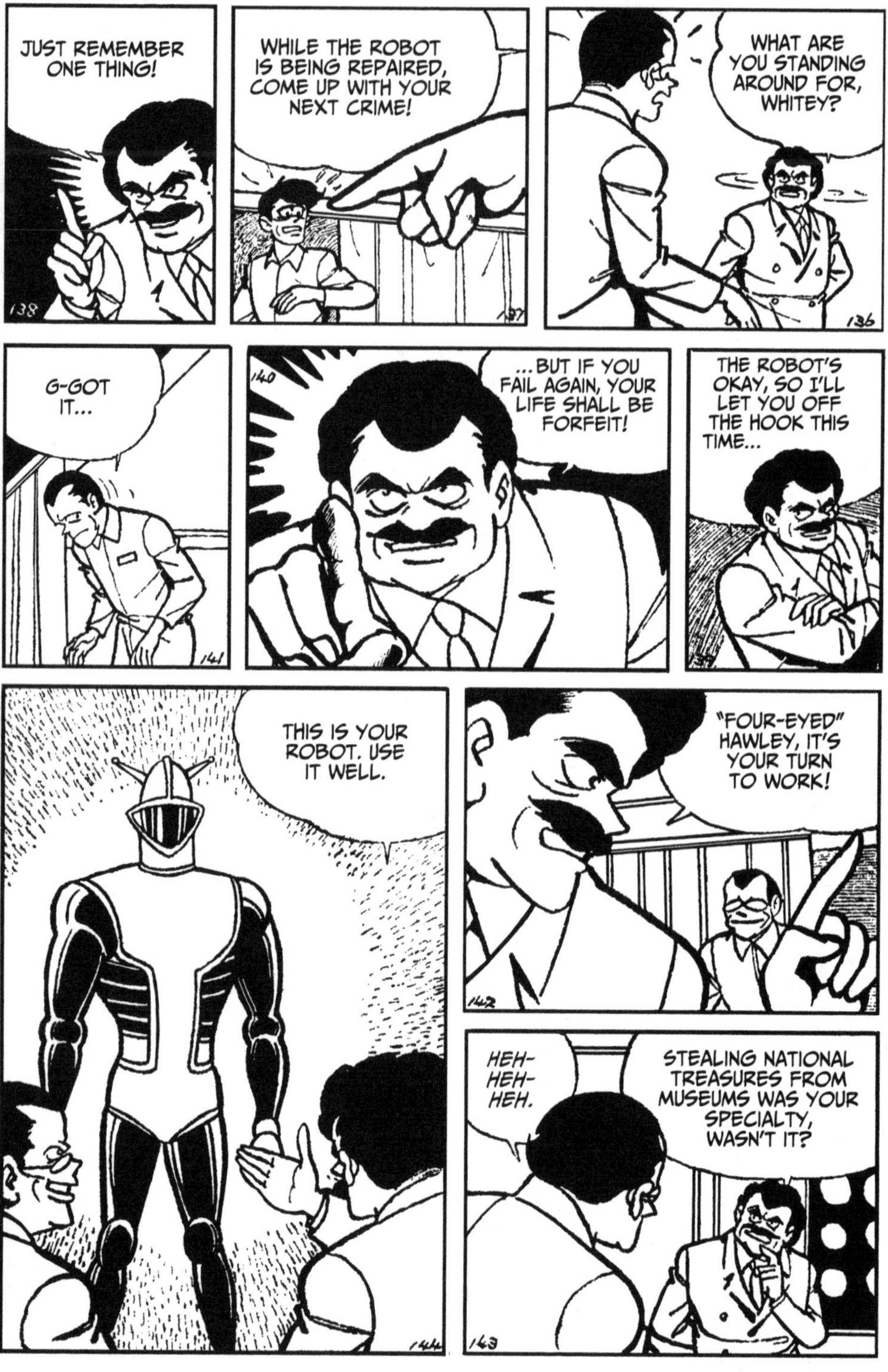
WHAT ARE YOU STANDING AROUND FOR, WHITEY?
WHILE THE ROBOT IS BEING REPAIRED, COME UP WITH YOUR NEXT CRIME!
JUST REMEMBER ONE THING!
THE ROBOT'S OKAY, SO I'LL LET YOU OFF THE HOOK THIS TIME...
...BUT IF YOU FAIL AGAIN, YOUR LIFE SHALL BE FORFEIT!
G-GOT IT...
"FOUR-EYED" HAWLEY, IT'S YOUR TURN TO WORK!
STEALING NATIONAL TREASURES FROM MUSEUMS WAS YOUR SPECIALTY, WASN'T IT?
HEH-HEH-HEH.
THIS IS YOUR ROBOT. USE IT WELL.

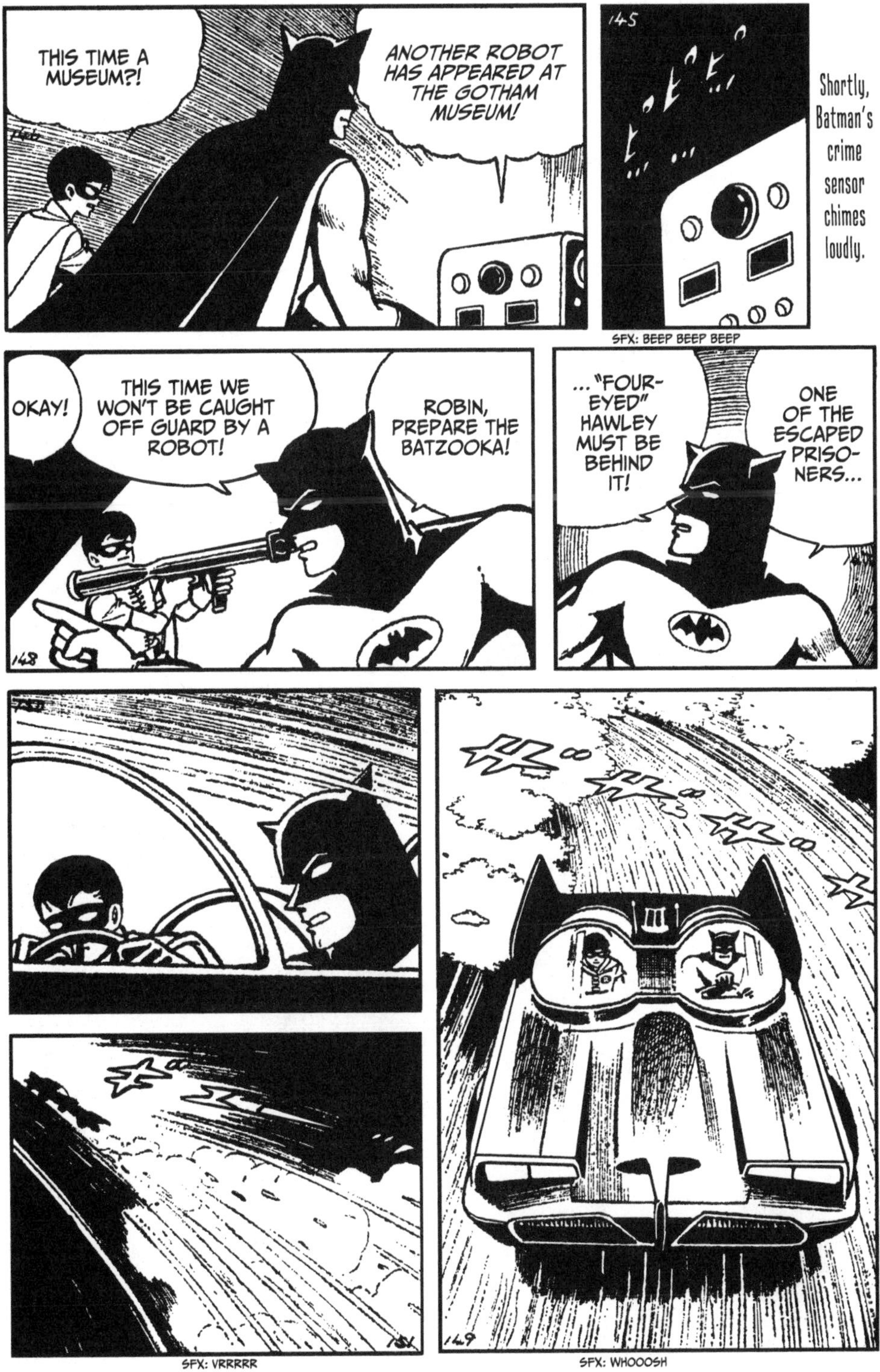
Shortly, Batman's crime sensor chimes loudly.
SFX: BEEP BEEP BEEP
ANOTHER ROBOT HAS APPEARED AT THE GOTHAM MUSEUM!
THIS TIME A MUSEUM?!
ONE OF THE ESCAPED PRISONERS...
..."FOUR-EYED" HAWLEY MUST BE BEHIND IT!
ROBIN, PREPARE THE BATZOOKA!
THIS TIME WE WON'T BE CAUGHT OFF GUARD BY A ROBOT!
OKAY!
SFX: WHOOOSH
SFX: VRRRRR

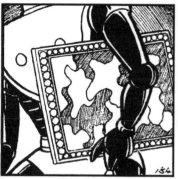

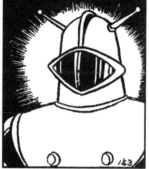

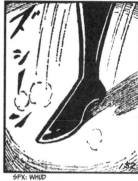

SFX: WHUD
THE ROBOT JUST CAME OUT! I'LL BLOW IT TO SMITHEREENS WITH THE BATZOOKA!
AH! BATMAN! YOU CAN'T SHOOT IT RIGHT NOW!
BLAST IT! YOU'RE RIGHT, ROBIN, NOT AS LONG AS THE ROBOT'S CARRYING VALUABLE PAINTINGS FROM THE MUSEUM!
SFX: CLANK CLANK

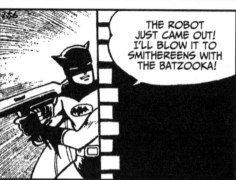

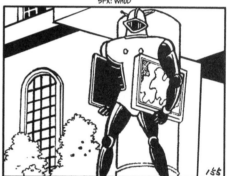

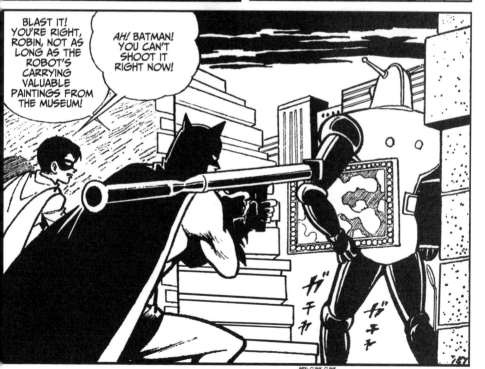

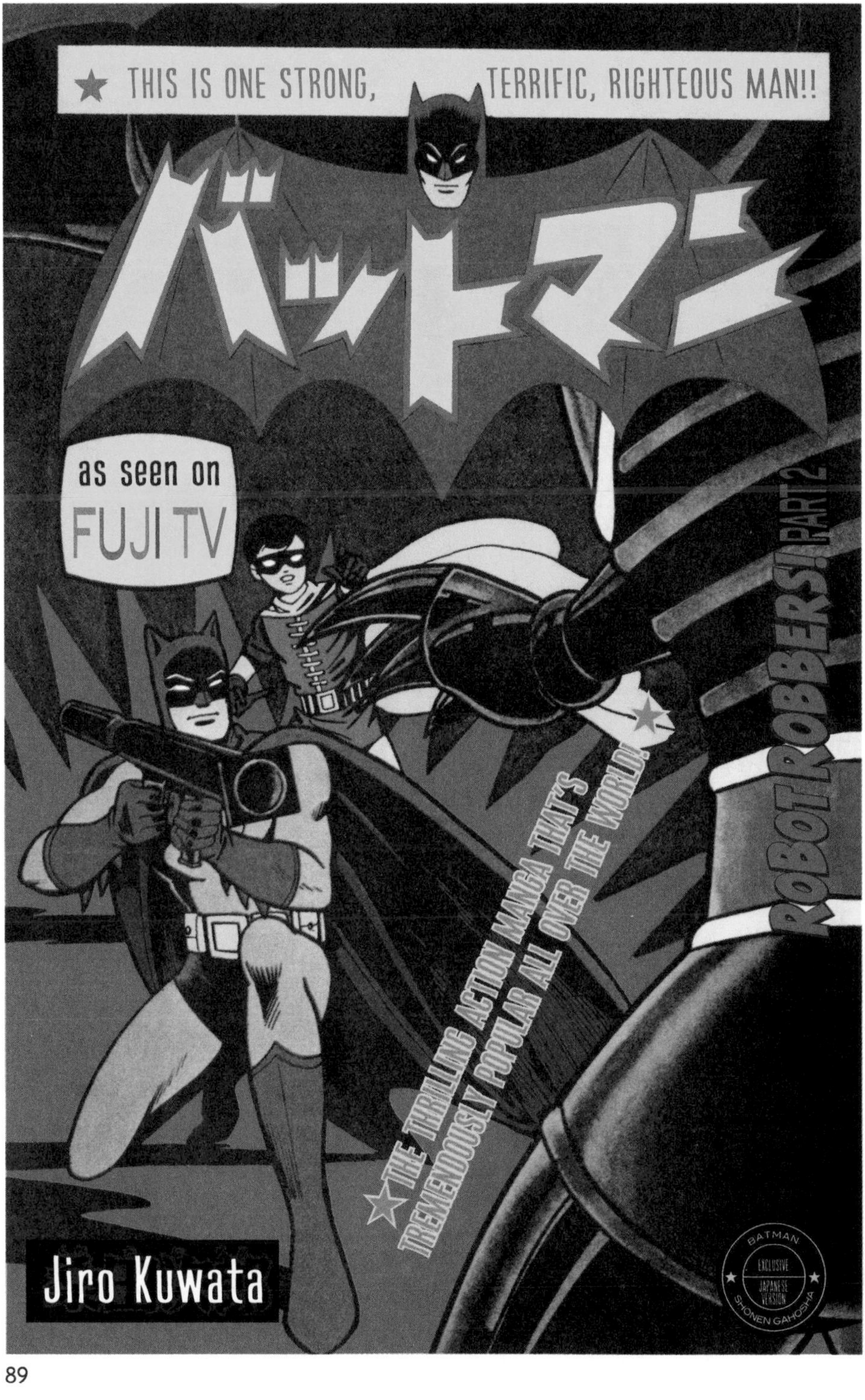
★ THIS IS ONE STRONG, TERRIFIC, RIGHTEOUS MAN!!
バットマン
as seen on
FUJI TV
ROBOT ROBBERS! PART 2
★ THE THRILLING ACTION MANGA THAT'S TREMENDOUSLY POPULAR ALL OVER THE WORLD! ★
Jiro Kuwata
BATMAN
EXCLUSIVE
JAPANESE VERSION
SHONEN GAHOSHA

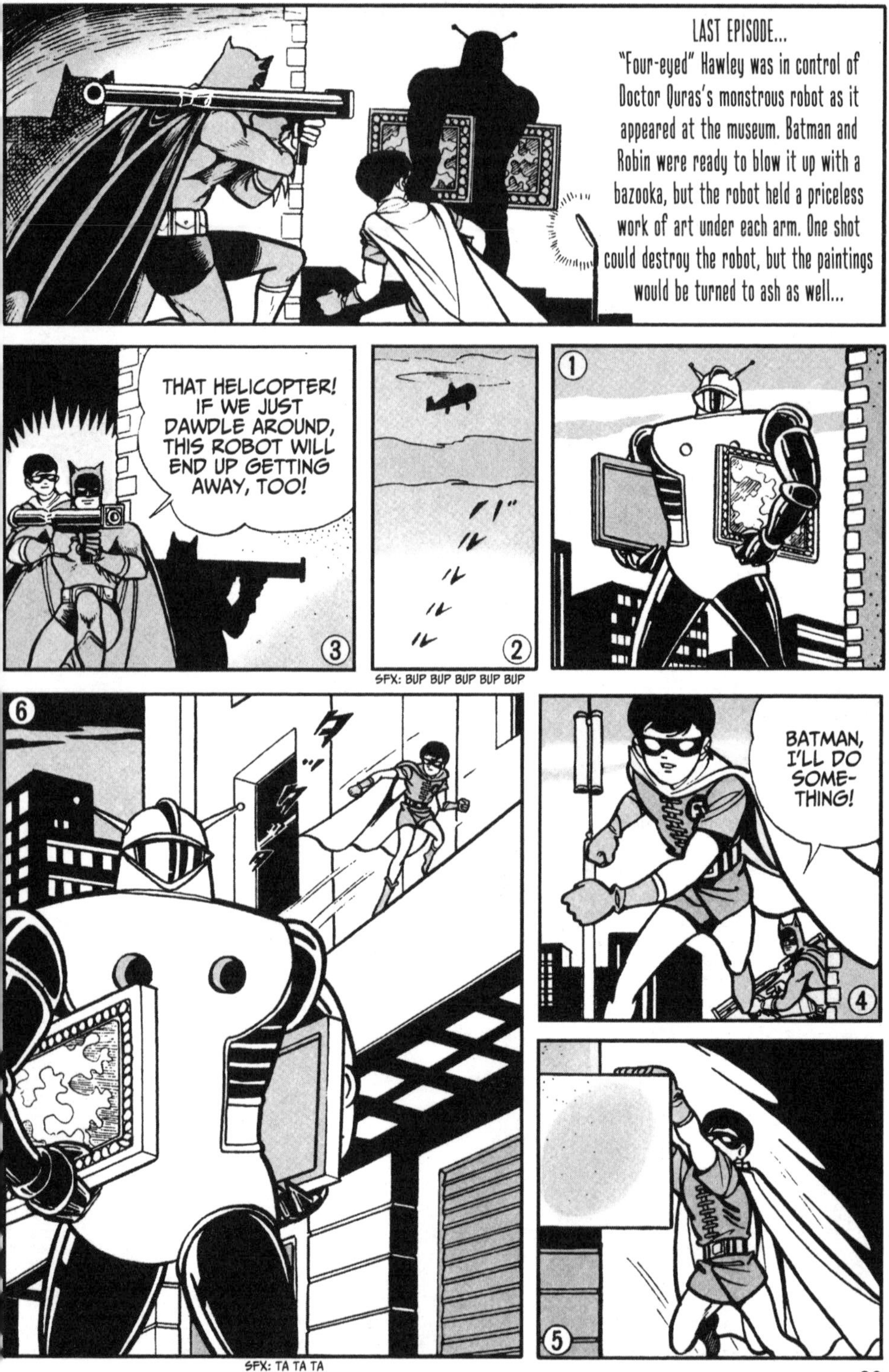
LAST EPISODE...
"Four-eyed" Hawley was in control of Doctor Quras's monstrous robot as it appeared at the museum. Batman and Robin were ready to blow it up with a bazooka, but the robot held a priceless work of art under each arm. One shot could destroy the robot, but the paintings would be turned to ash as well...
SFX: BUP BUP BUP BUP BUP
THAT HELICOPTER! IF WE JUST DAWDLE AROUND, THIS ROBOT WILL END UP GETTING AWAY, TOO!
BATMAN, I'LL DO SOME-THING!
SFX: TA TA TA

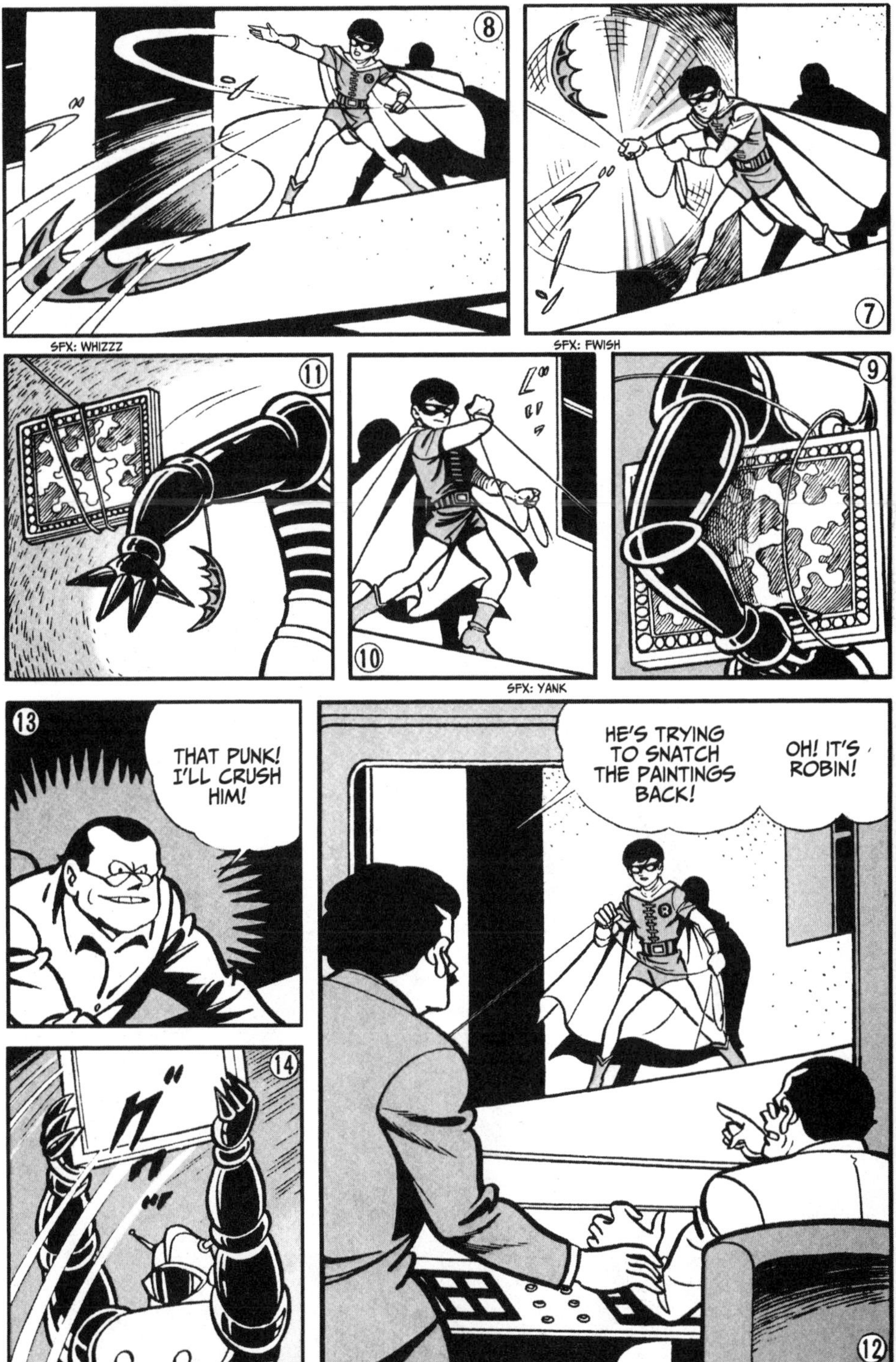
SFX: FWISH
SFX: WHIZZZ
SFX: YANK
OH! IT'S ROBIN!
HE'S TRYING TO SNATCH THE PAINTINGS BACK!
THAT PUNK! I'LL CRUSH HIM!
SFX: FWISH

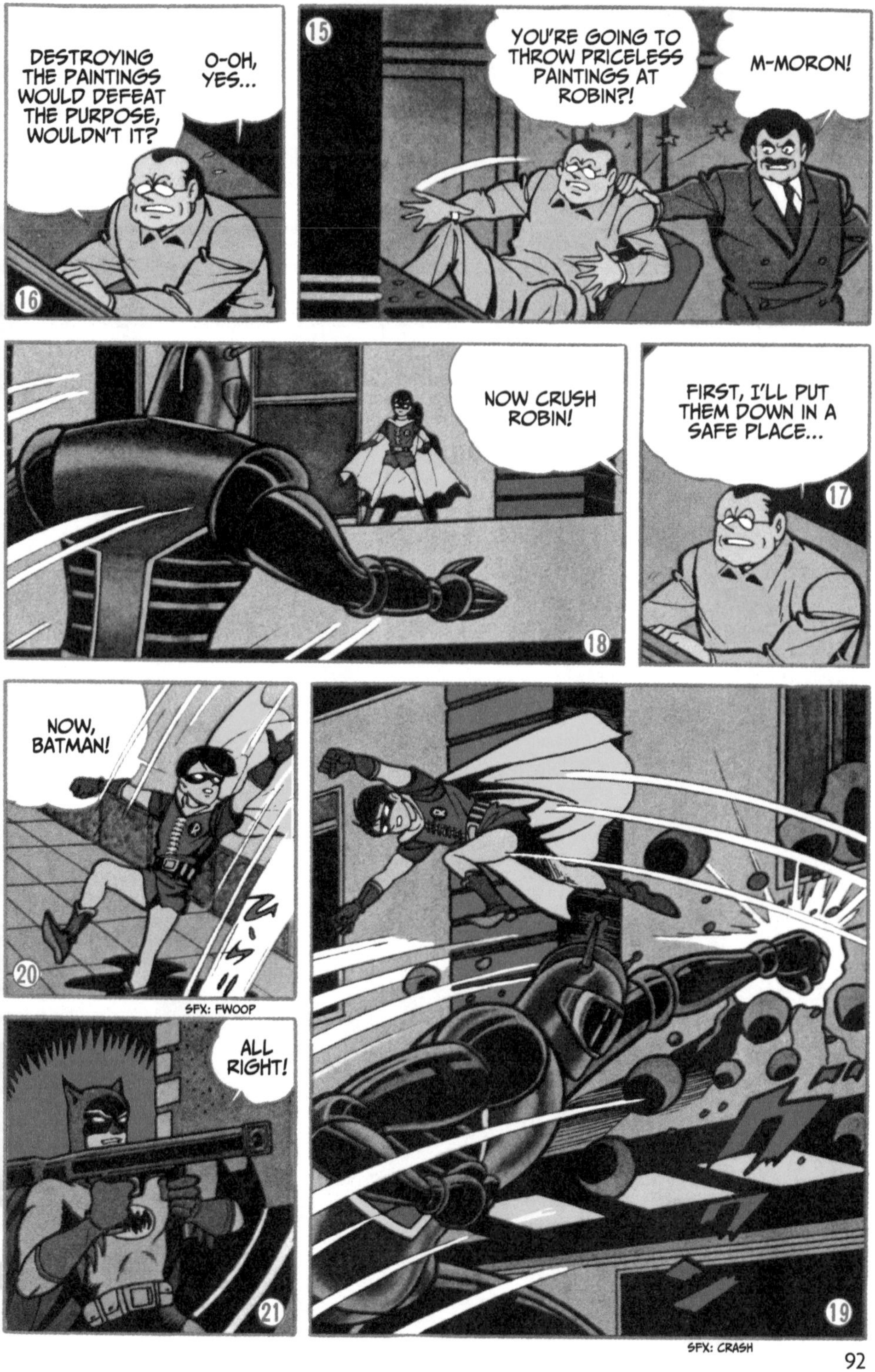
M-MORON!
YOU'RE GOING TO THROW PRICELESS PAINTINGS AT ROBIN?!
O-OH, YES...
DESTROYING THE PAINTINGS WOULD DEFEAT THE PURPOSE, WOULDN'T IT?
FIRST, I'LL PUT THEM DOWN IN A SAFE PLACE...
NOW CRUSH ROBIN!
SFX: CRASH
NOW, BATMAN!
SFX: FWOOP
ALL RIGHT!

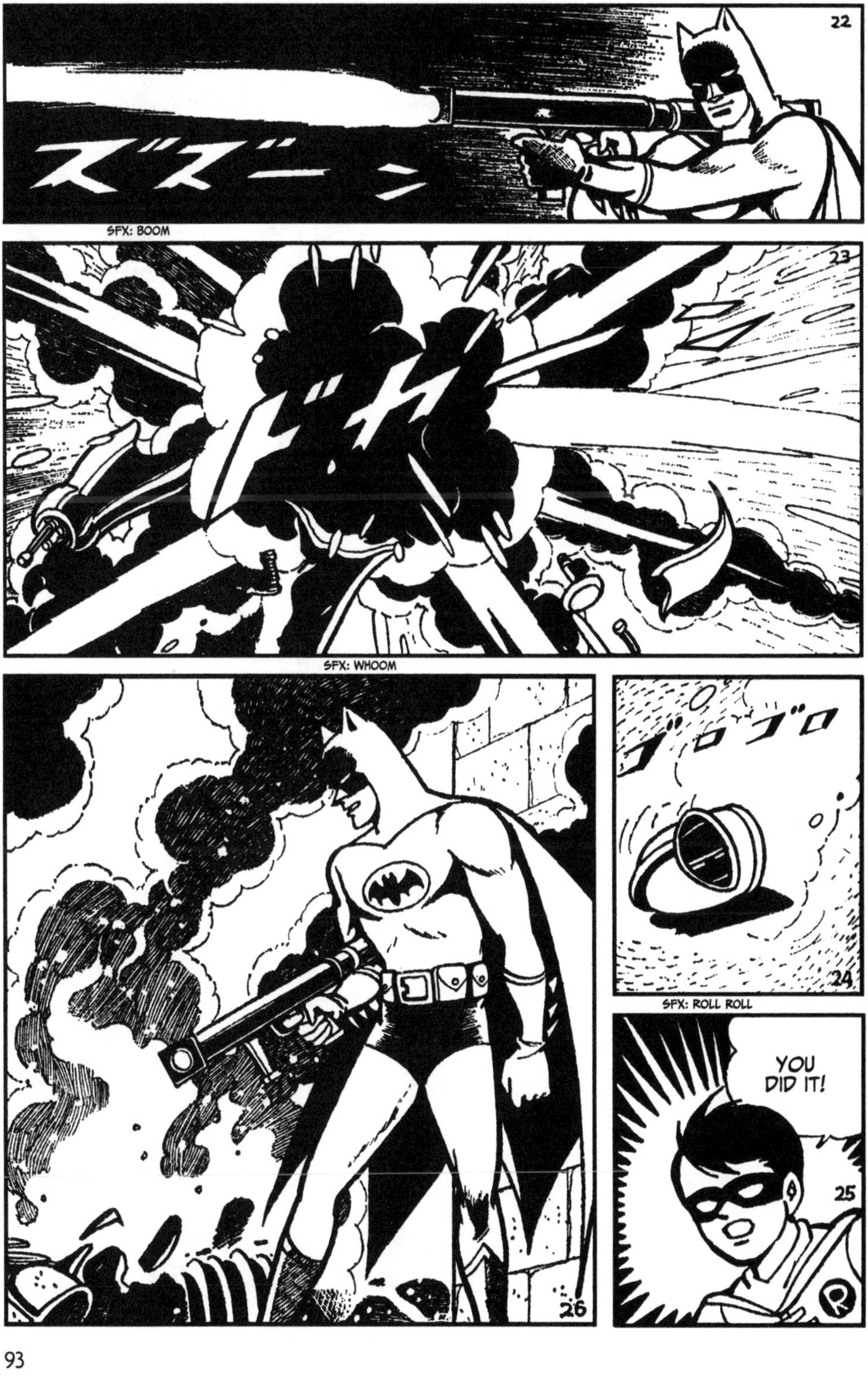
ズズーン
SFX: BOOM
SFX: WHOOM
ゴロゴロ
SFX: ROLL ROLL
YOU DID IT!

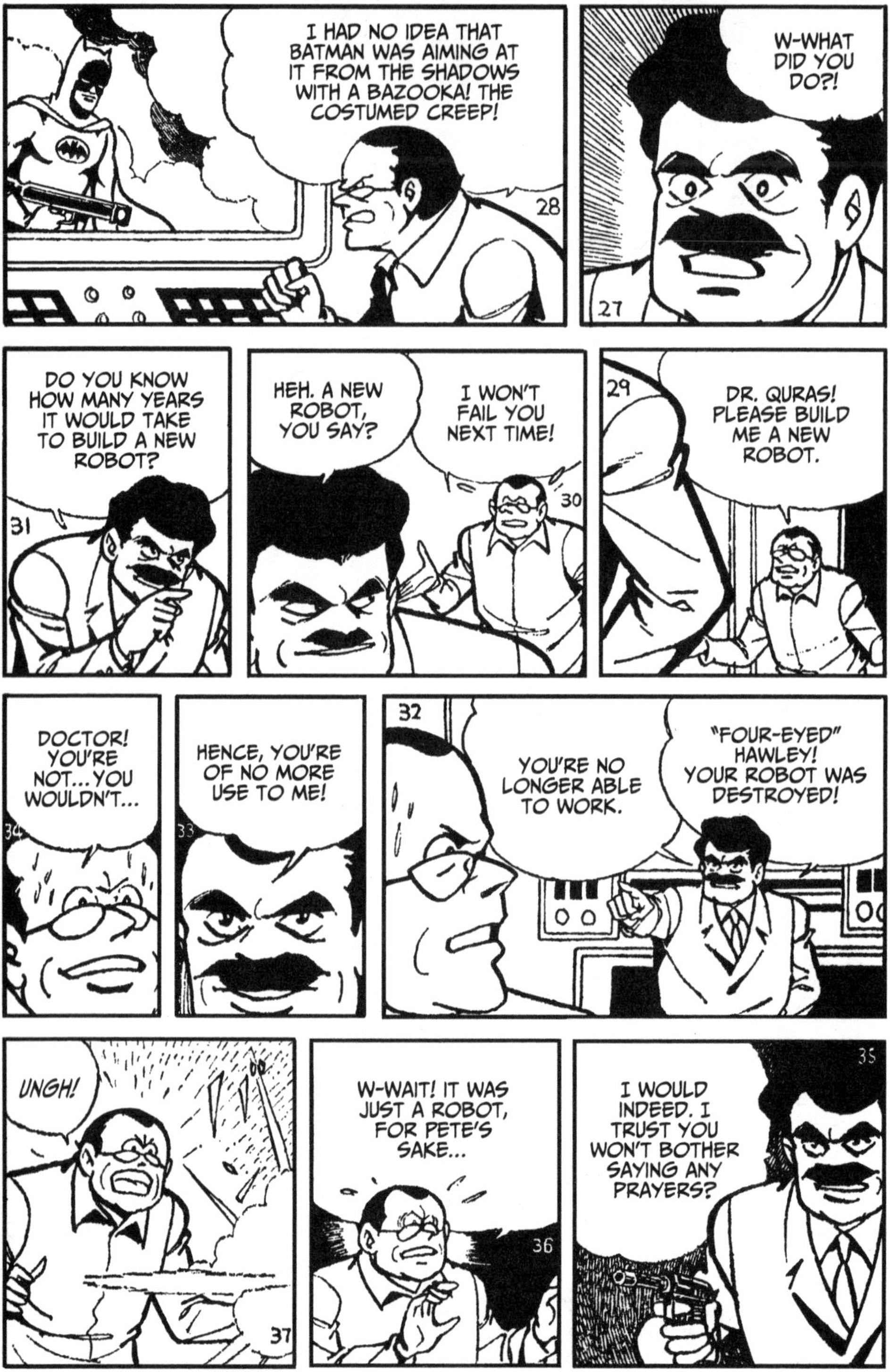
W-WHAT DID YOU DO?!
I HAD NO IDEA THAT BATMAN WAS AIMING AT IT FROM THE SHADOWS WITH A BAZOOKA! THE COSTUMED CREEP!
DR. QURAS! PLEASE BUILD ME A NEW ROBOT.
I WON'T FAIL YOU NEXT TIME!
HEH. A NEW ROBOT, YOU SAY?
DO YOU KNOW HOW MANY YEARS IT WOULD TAKE TO BUILD A NEW ROBOT?
"FOUR-EYED" HAWLEY! YOUR ROBOT WAS DESTROYED!
YOU'RE NO LONGER ABLE TO WORK.
HENCE, YOU'RE OF NO MORE USE TO ME!
DOCTOR! YOU'RE NOT...YOU WOULDN'T...
I WOULD INDEED. I TRUST YOU WON'T BOTHER SAYING ANY PRAYERS?
W-WAIT! IT WAS JUST A ROBOT, FOR PETE'S SAKE...
UNGH!

SFX: BLAM

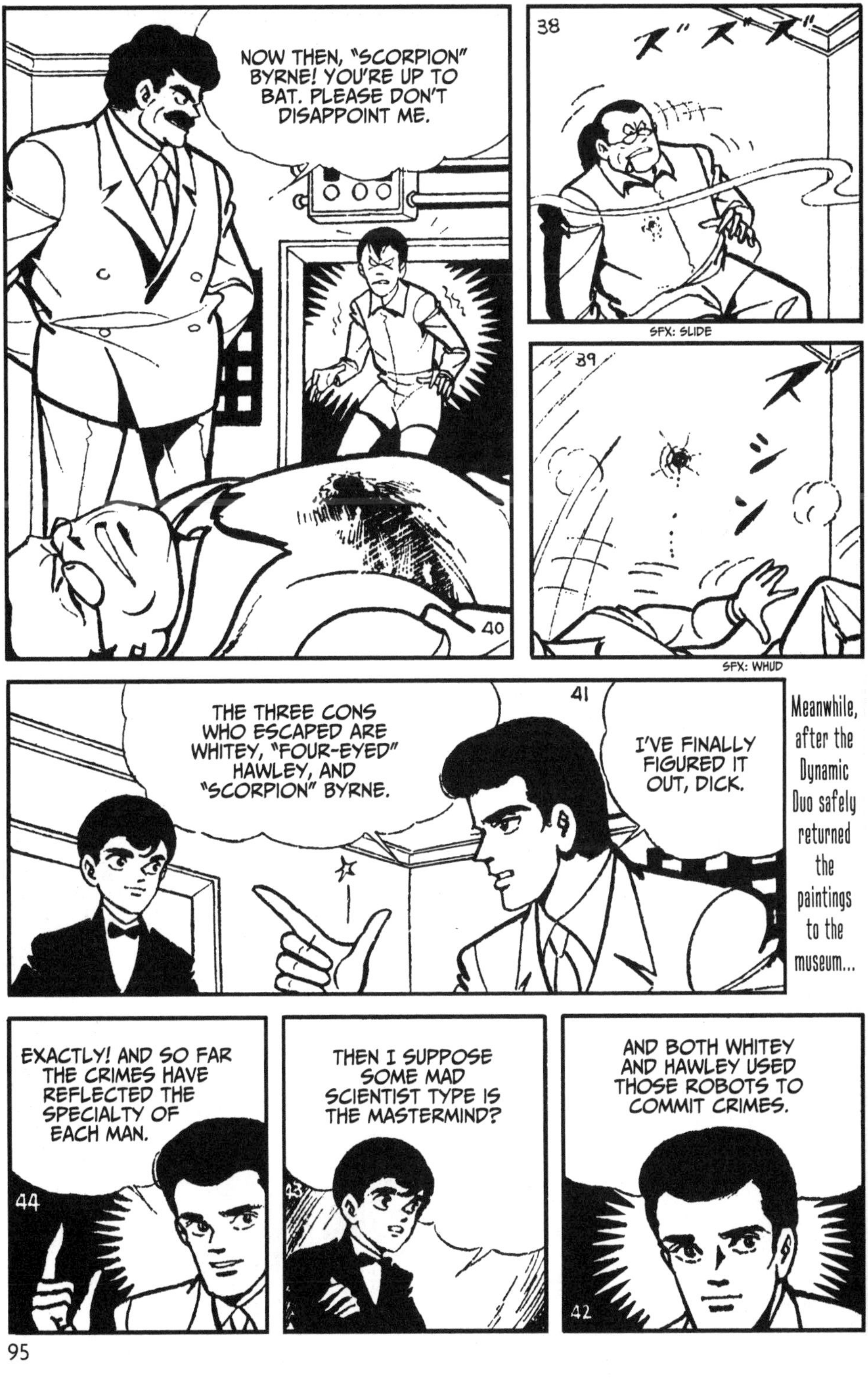
SFX: SLIDE
SFX: WHUD
NOW THEN, "SCORPION" BYRNE! YOU'RE UP TO BAT. PLEASE DON'T DISAPPOINT ME.
Meanwhile, after the Dynamic Duo safely returned the paintings to the museum...
I'VE FINALLY FIGURED IT OUT, DICK.
THE THREE CONS WHO ESCAPED ARE WHITEY, "FOUR-EYED" HAWLEY, AND "SCORPION" BYRNE.
AND BOTH WHITEY AND HAWLEY USED THOSE ROBOTS TO COMMIT CRIMES.
THEN I SUPPOSE SOME MAD SCIENTIST TYPE IS THE MASTERMIND?
EXACTLY! AND SO FAR THE CRIMES HAVE REFLECTED THE SPECIALTY OF EACH MAN.

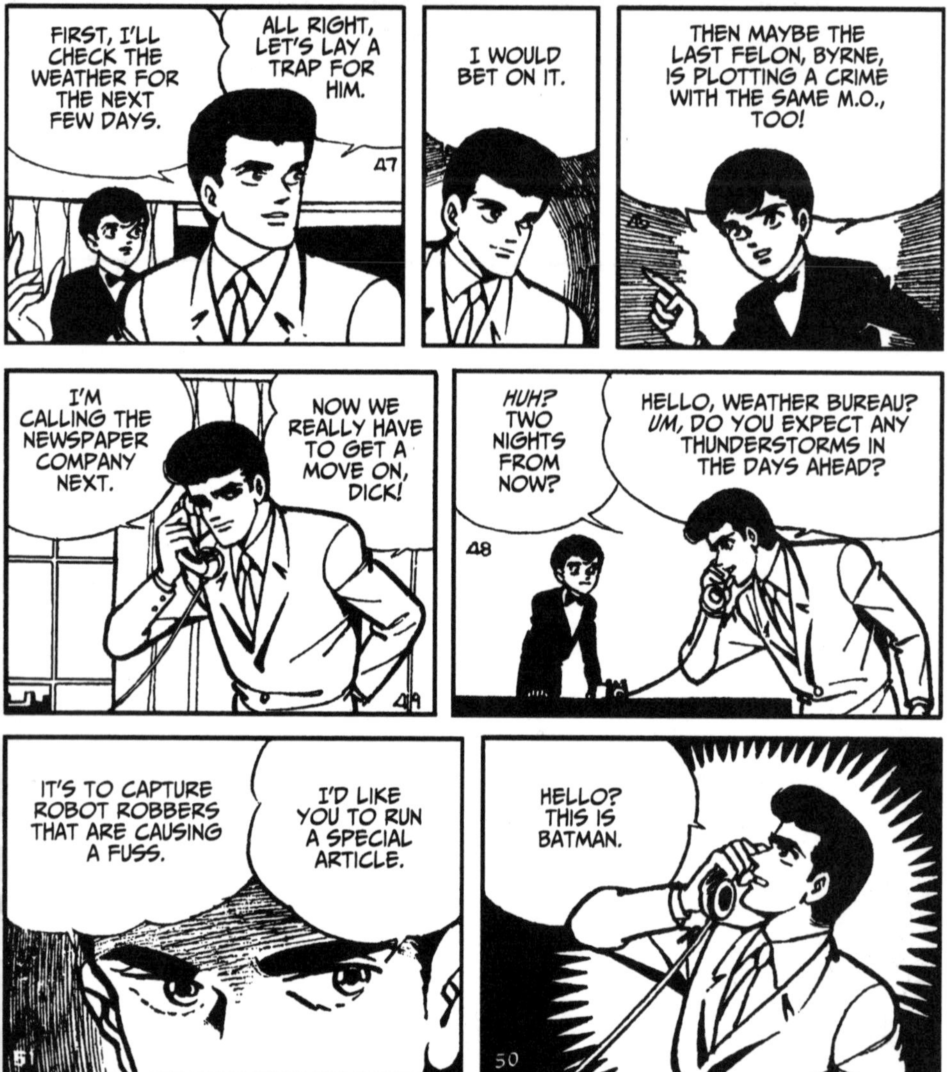
THEN MAYBE THE LAST FELON, BYRNE, IS PLOTTING A CRIME WITH THE SAME M.O., TOO!
I WOULD BET ON IT.
ALL RIGHT, LET'S LAY A TRAP FOR HIM.
FIRST, I'LL CHECK THE WEATHER FOR THE NEXT FEW DAYS.
HELLO, WEATHER BUREAU? *UM*, DO YOU EXPECT ANY THUNDERSTORMS IN THE DAYS AHEAD?
HUH? TWO NIGHTS FROM NOW?
NOW WE REALLY HAVE TO GET A MOVE ON, DICK!
I'M CALLING THE NEWSPAPER COMPANY NEXT.
HELLO? THIS IS BATMAN.
I'D LIKE YOU TO RUN A SPECIAL ARTICLE.
IT'S TO CAPTURE ROBOT ROBBERS THAT ARE CAUSING A FUSS.

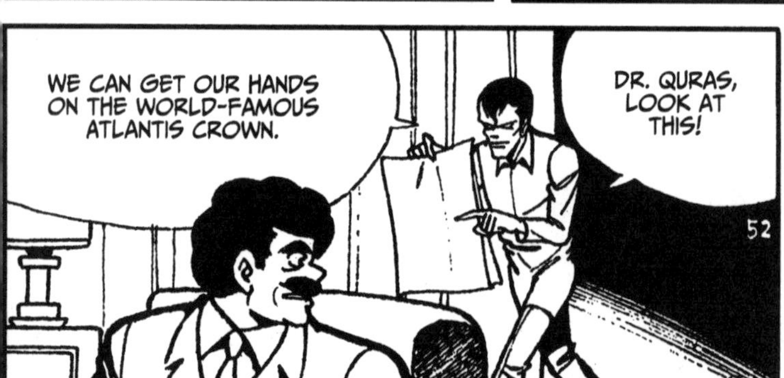
DR. QURAS, LOOK AT THIS!
WE CAN GET OUR HANDS ON THE WORLD-FAMOUS ATLANTIS CROWN.

Just what kind of article did Batman ask the newspaper to publish? The next day, "Scorpion" Byrne rushed into Dr. Quras's study with a newspaper in his hand.

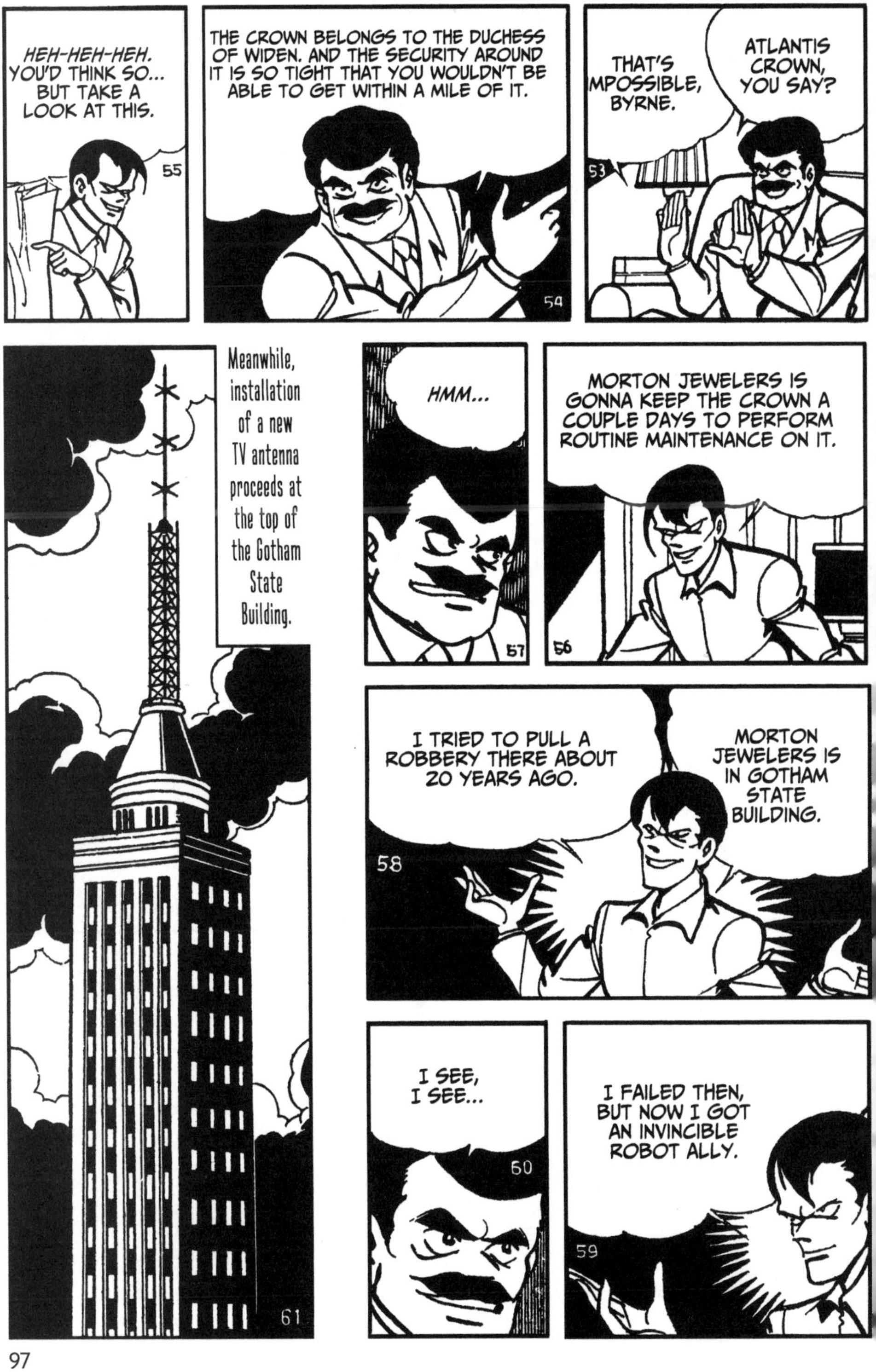
ATLANTIS CROWN, YOU SAY?
THAT'S IMPOSSIBLE, BYRNE.
THE CROWN BELONGS TO THE DUCHESS OF WIDEN. AND THE SECURITY AROUND IT IS SO TIGHT THAT YOU WOULDN'T BE ABLE TO GET WITHIN A MILE OF IT.
HEH-HEH-HEH. YOU'D THINK SO... BUT TAKE A LOOK AT THIS.
MORTON JEWELERS IS GONNA KEEP THE CROWN A COUPLE DAYS TO PERFORM ROUTINE MAINTENANCE ON IT.
HMM...
MORTON JEWELERS IS IN GOTHAM STATE BUILDING.
I TRIED TO PULL A ROBBERY THERE ABOUT 20 YEARS AGO.
I FAILED THEN, BUT NOW I GOT AN INVINCIBLE ROBOT ALLY.
I SEE, I SEE...
Meanwhile, installation of a new TV antenna proceeds at the top of the Gotham State Building.

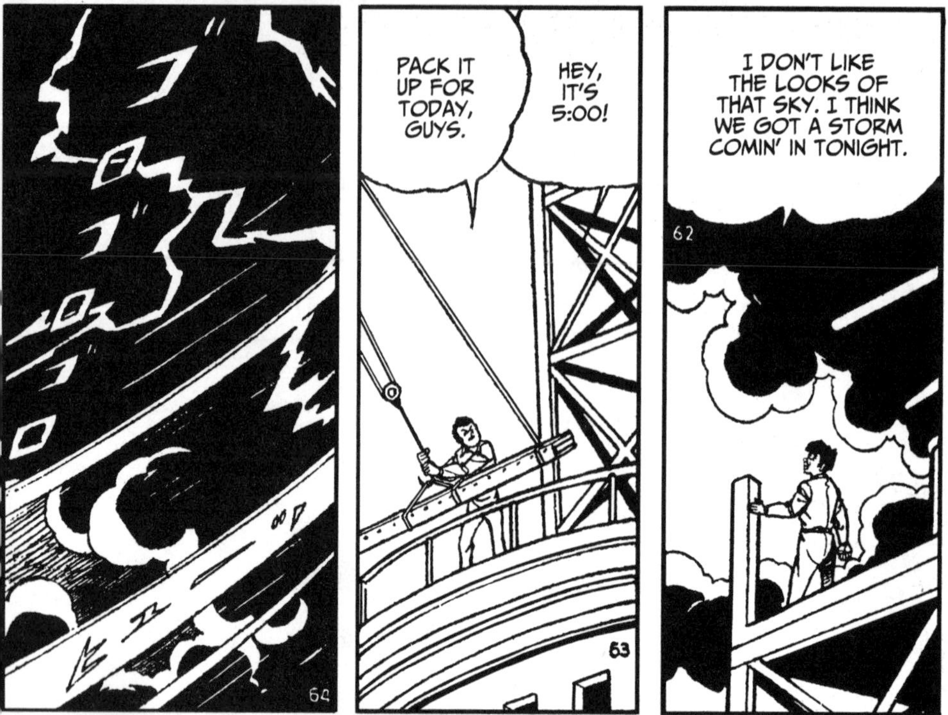
I DON'T LIKE THE LOOKS OF THAT SKY. I THINK WE GOT A STORM COMIN' IN TONIGHT.
HEY, IT'S 5:00!
PACK IT UP FOR TODAY, GUYS.

SFX: RUMBLE RUMBLE RUMBLE SFX: FWOOO

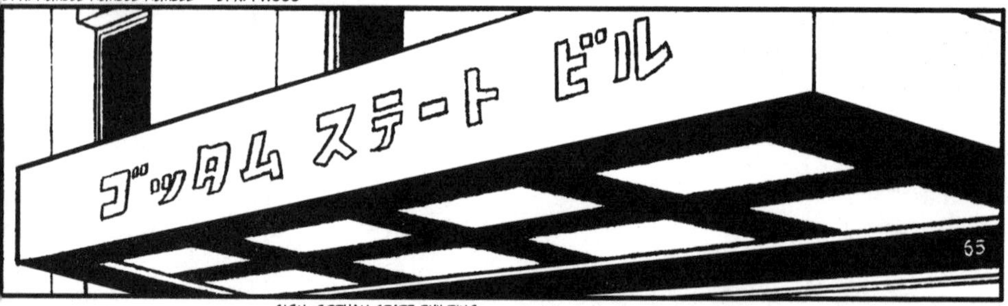
ゴッタム ステート ビル

SIGN: GOTHAM STATE BUILDING

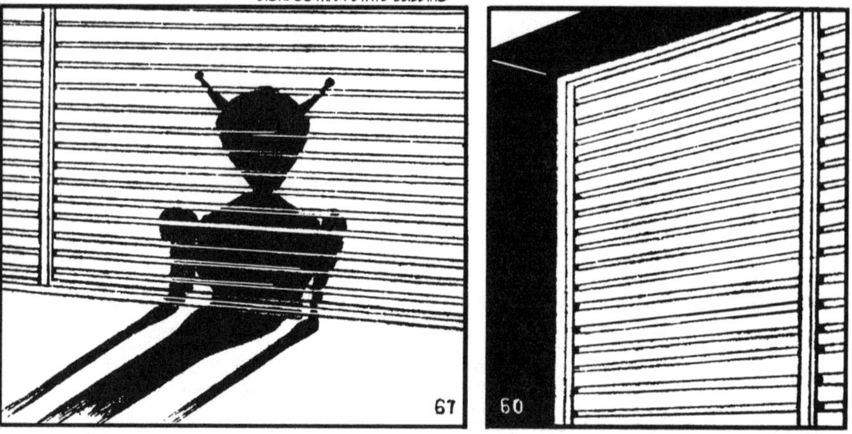

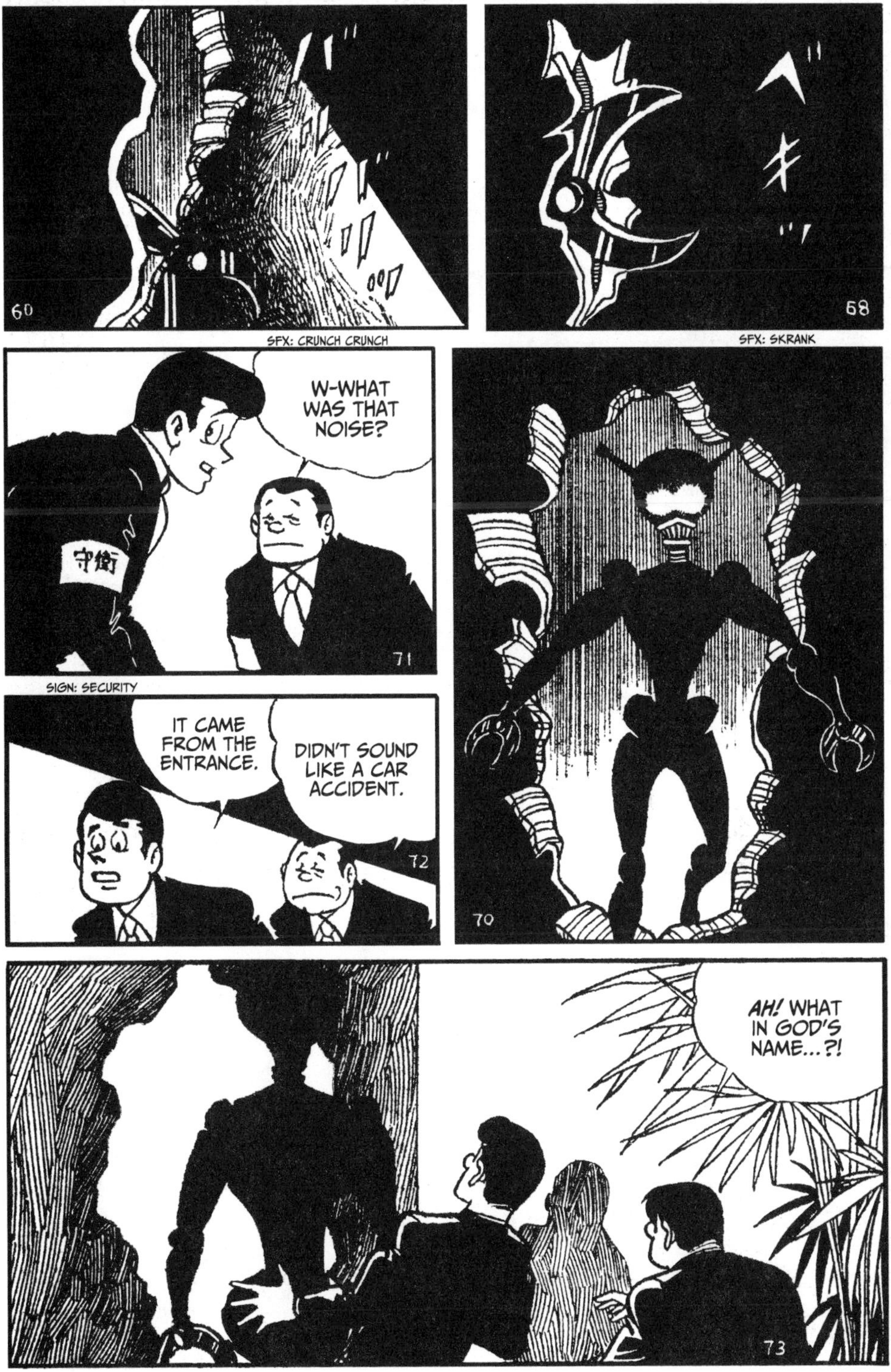
SFX: SKRANK
SFX: CRUNCH CRUNCH
W-WHAT WAS THAT NOISE?
守衛
SIGN: SECURITY
DIDN'T SOUND LIKE A CAR ACCIDENT.
IT CAME FROM THE ENTRANCE.
AH! WHAT IN GOD'S NAME...?!

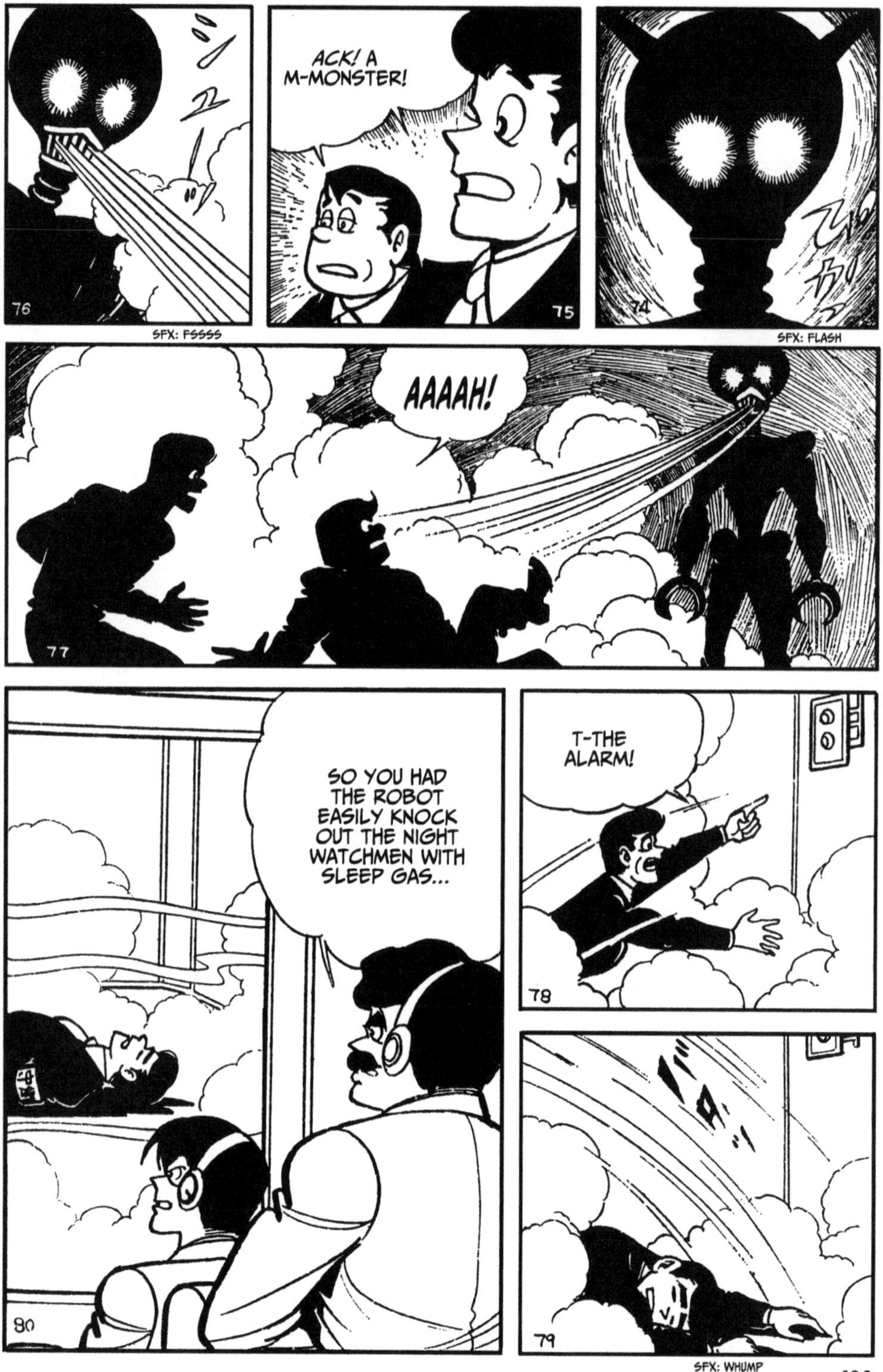
SFX: FLASH
ACK! A M-MONSTER!
SFX: FSSSS
AAAAH!
T-THE ALARM!
SFX: WHUMP
SO YOU HAD THE ROBOT EASILY KNOCK OUT THE NIGHT WATCHMEN WITH SLEEP GAS...

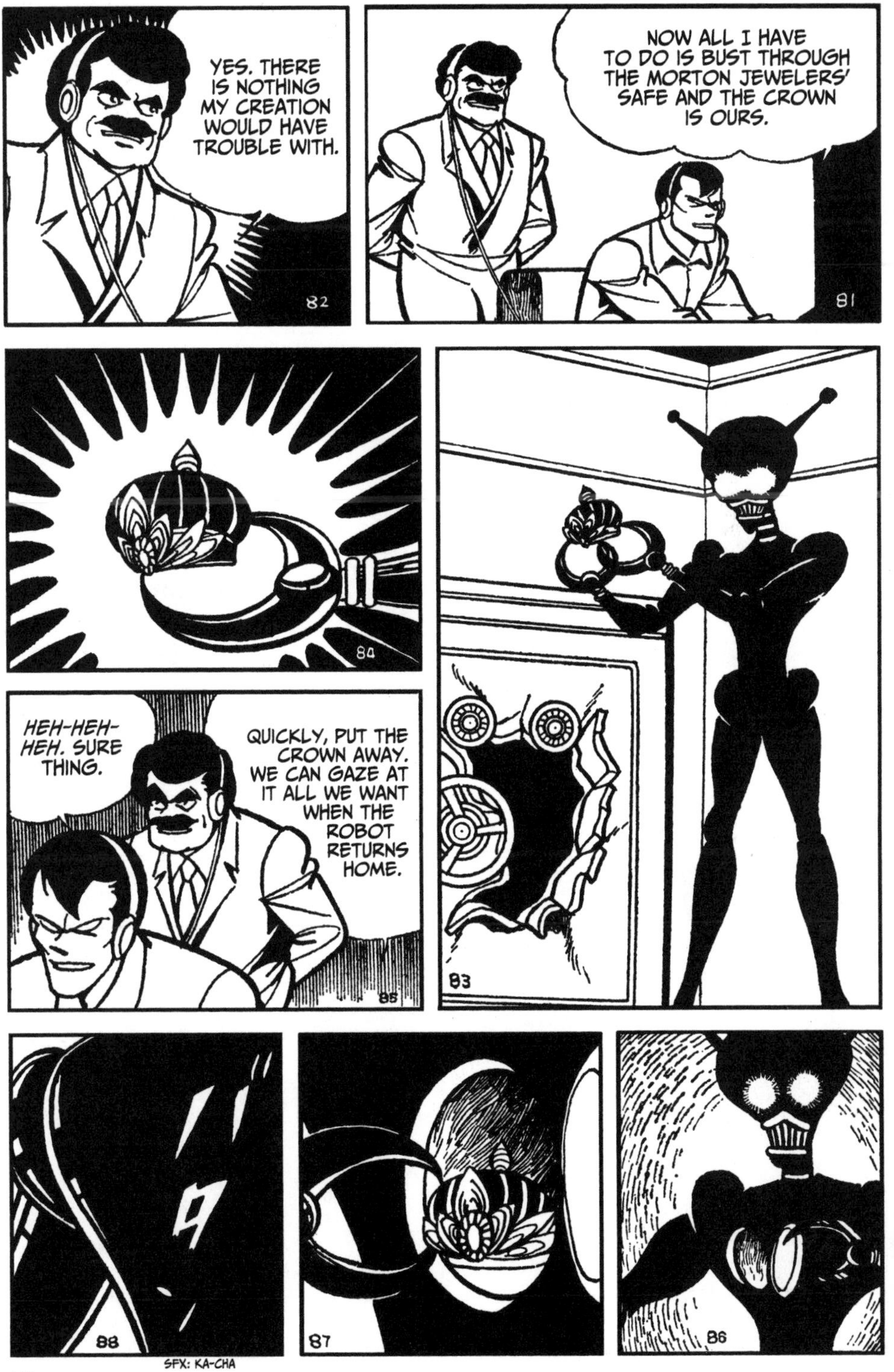
NOW ALL I HAVE TO DO IS BUST THROUGH THE MORTON JEWELERS' SAFE AND THE CROWN IS OURS.
YES. THERE IS NOTHING MY CREATION WOULD HAVE TROUBLE WITH.
QUICKLY, PUT THE CROWN AWAY. WE CAN GAZE AT IT ALL WE WANT WHEN THE ROBOT RETURNS HOME.
HEH-HEH-HEH. SURE THING.
SFX: KA-CHA

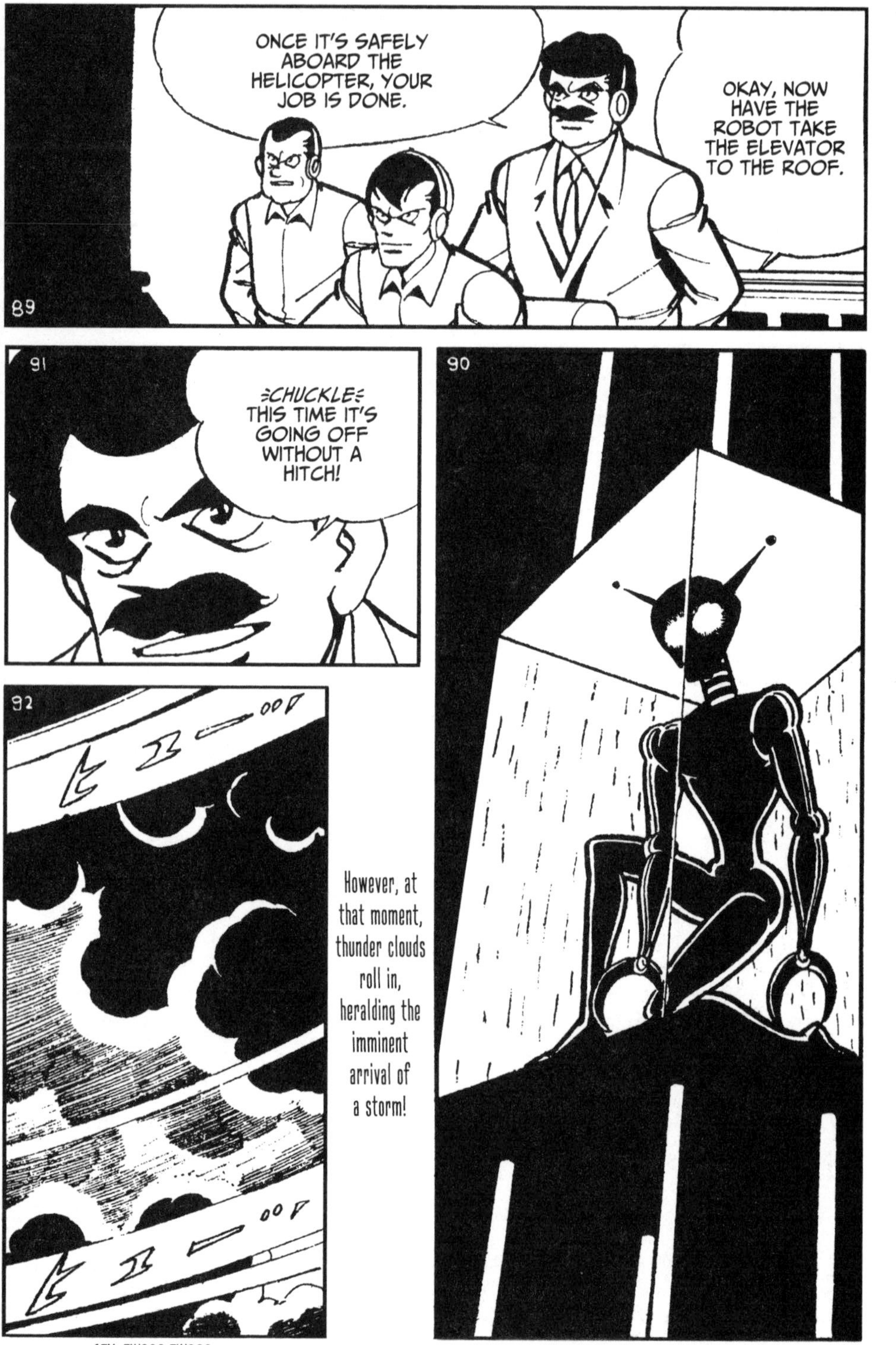
OKAY, NOW HAVE THE ROBOT TAKE THE ELEVATOR TO THE ROOF.
ONCE IT'S SAFELY ABOARD THE HELICOPTER, YOUR JOB IS DONE.
≡CHUCKLE≡ THIS TIME IT'S GOING OFF WITHOUT A HITCH!
However, at that moment, thunder clouds roll in, heralding the imminent arrival of a storm!

SFX: FWOOO FWOOO

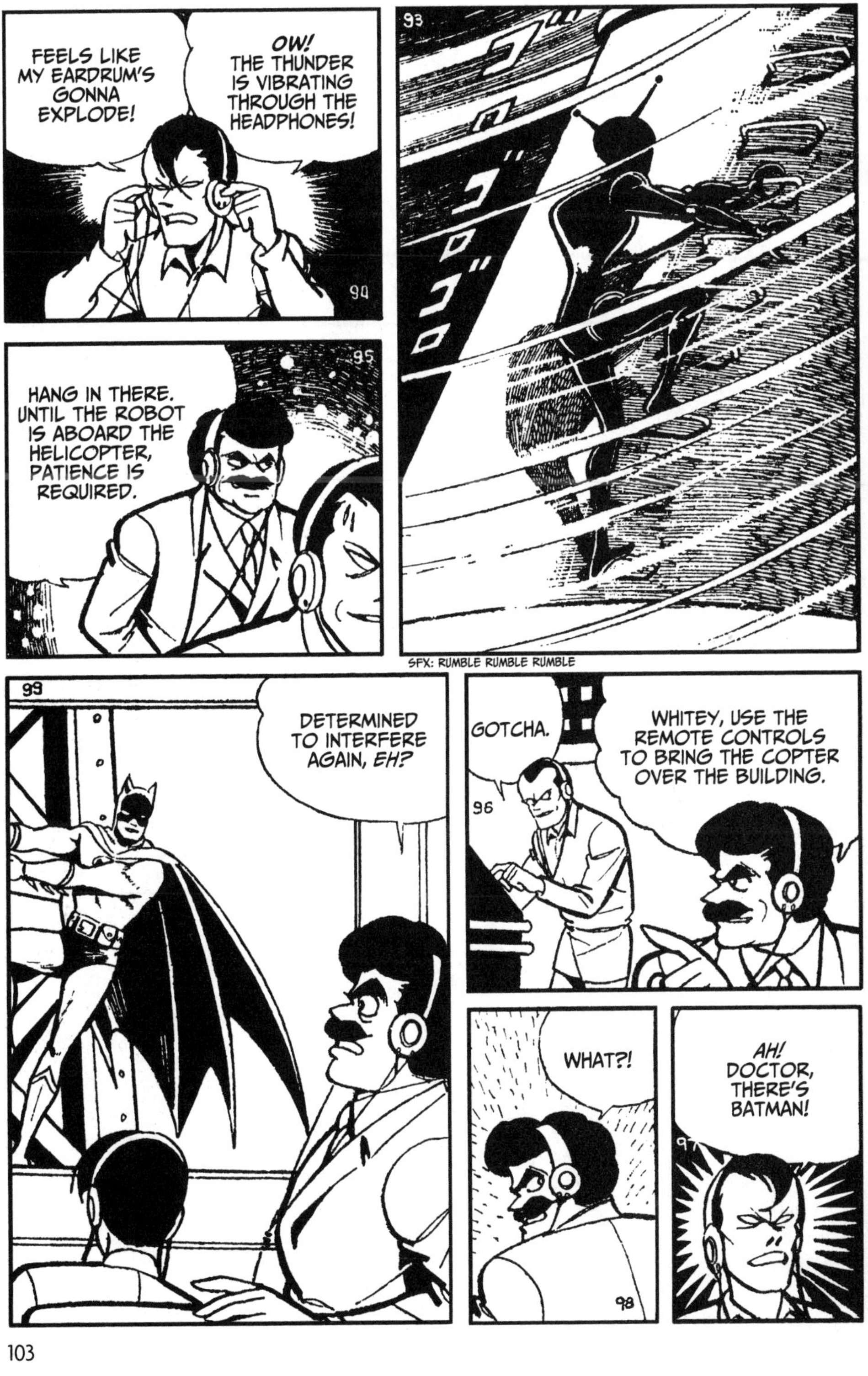
SFX: RUMBLE RUMBLE RUMBLE
OW! THE THUNDER IS VIBRATING THROUGH THE HEADPHONES!
FEELS LIKE MY EARDRUM'S GONNA EXPLODE!
HANG IN THERE. UNTIL THE ROBOT IS ABOARD THE HELICOPTER, PATIENCE IS REQUIRED.
WHITEY, USE THE REMOTE CONTROLS TO BRING THE COPTER OVER THE BUILDING.
GOTCHA.
AH! DOCTOR, THERE'S BATMAN!
WHAT?!
DETERMINED TO INTERFERE AGAIN, EH?

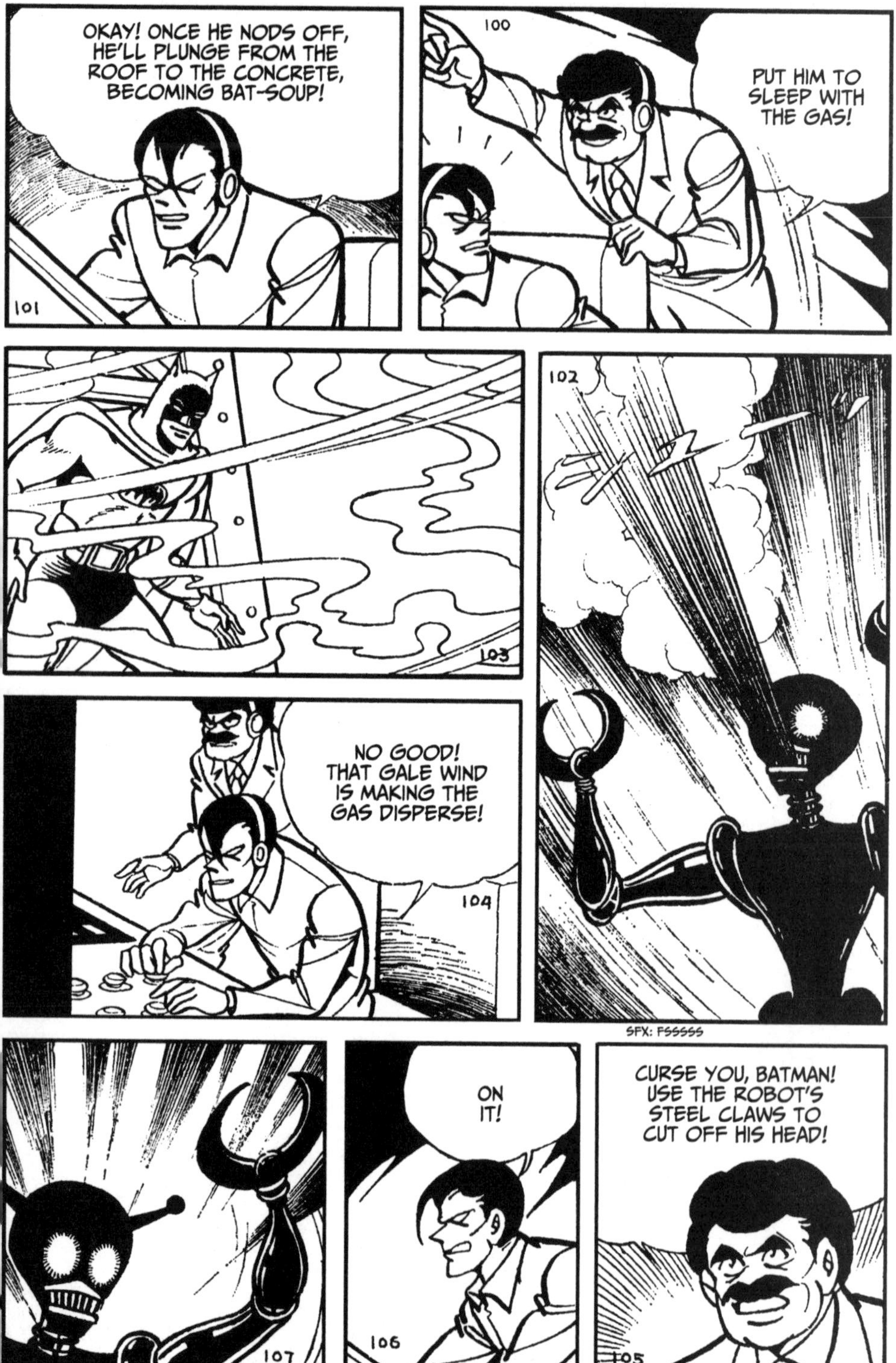
PUT HIM TO SLEEP WITH THE GAS!
OKAY! ONCE HE NODS OFF, HE'LL PLUNGE FROM THE ROOF TO THE CONCRETE, BECOMING BAT-SOUP!
SFX: FSSSSS
NO GOOD! THAT GALE WIND IS MAKING THE GAS DISPERSE!
CURSE YOU, BATMAN! USE THE ROBOT'S STEEL CLAWS TO CUT OFF HIS HEAD!
ON IT!

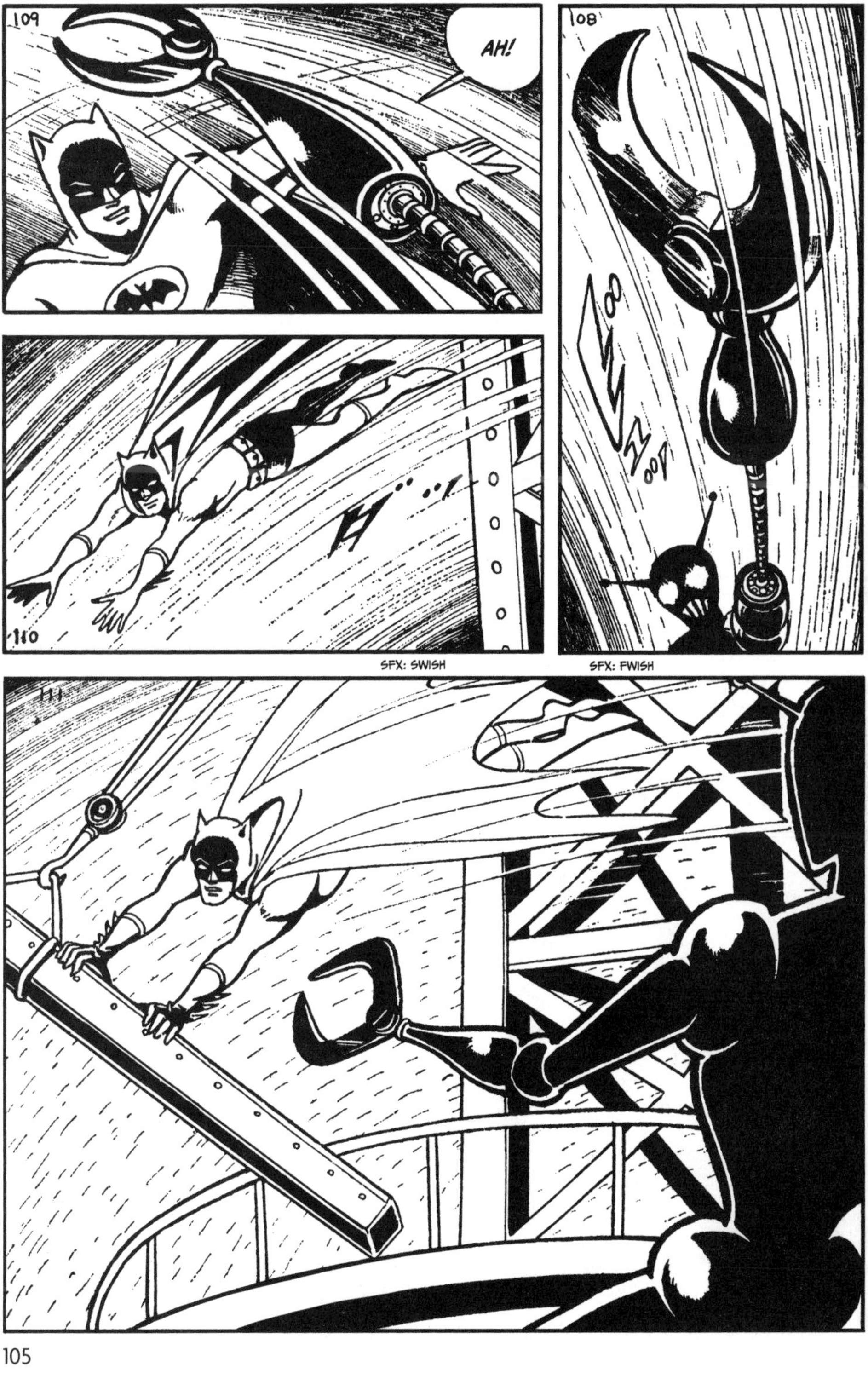
108
SFX: FWISH
109
AH!
110
SFX: SWISH
111

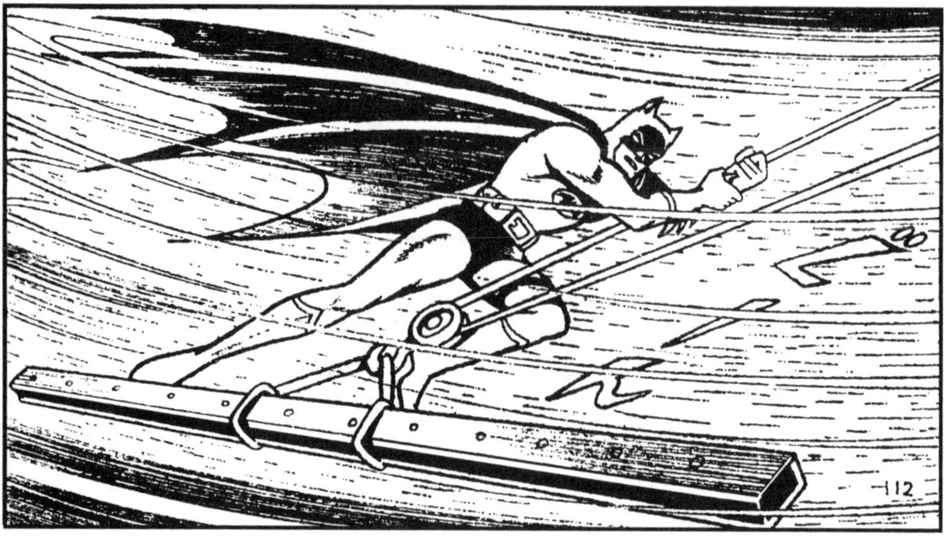
112

SFX: FWOOSH

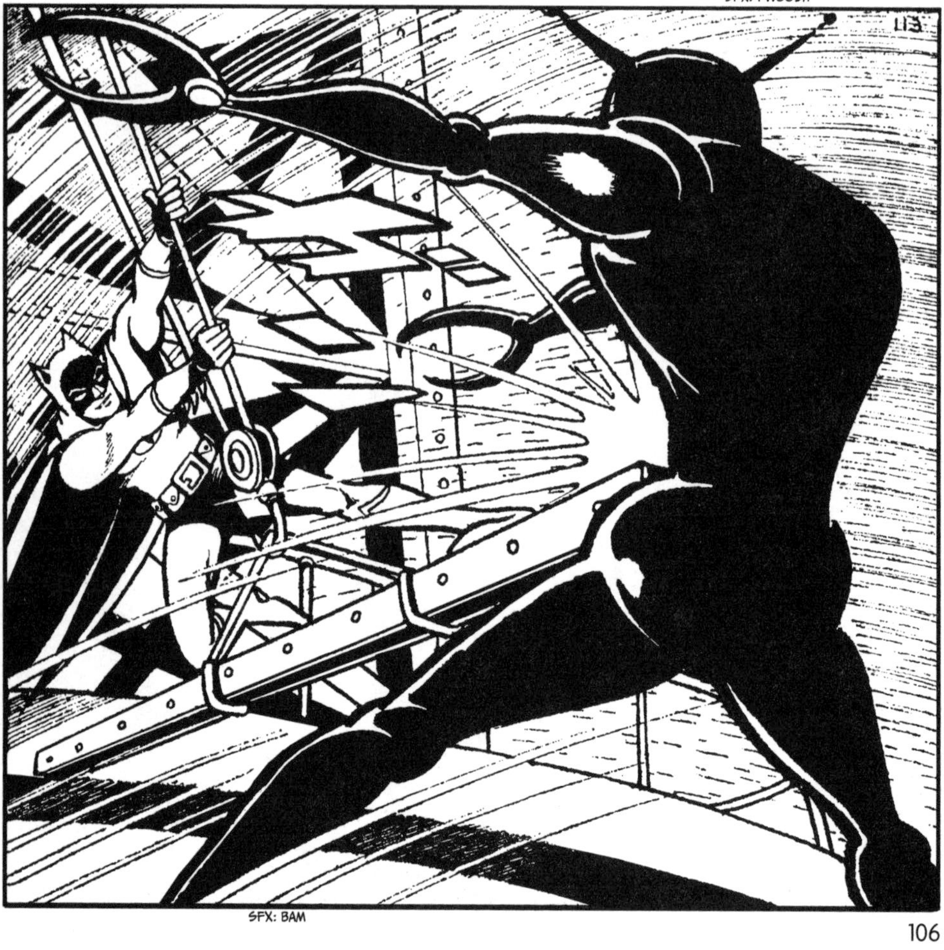
113

SFX: BAM

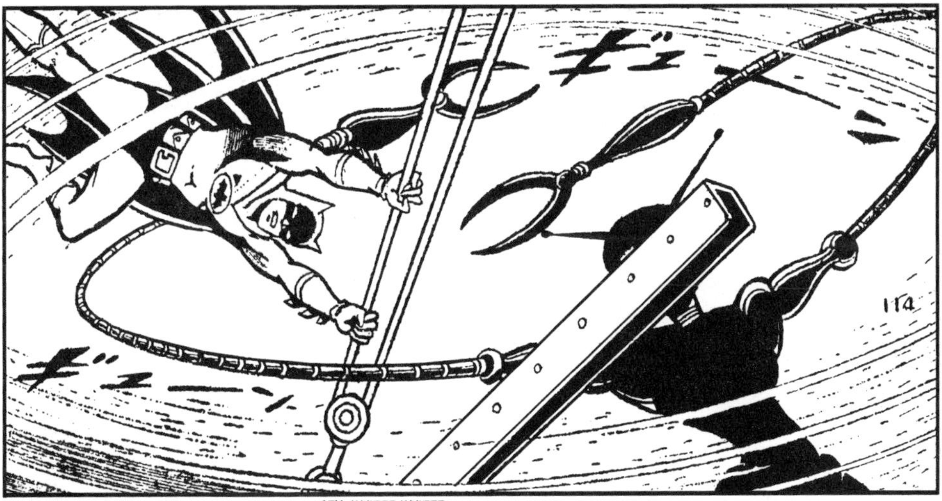

SFX: WHIZZZ WHIZZZ

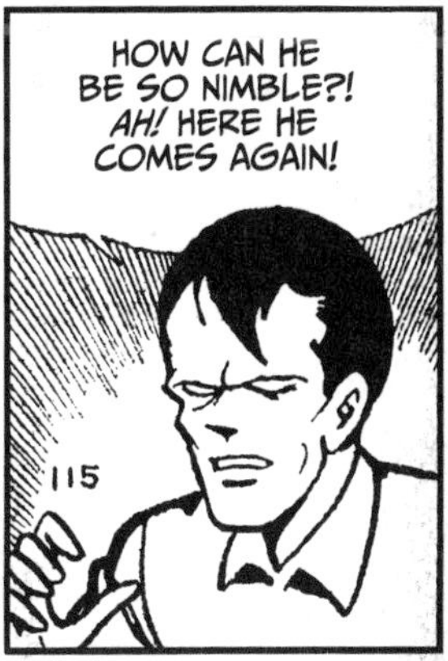
HOW CAN HE BE SO NIMBLE?! *AH!* HERE HE COMES AGAIN!

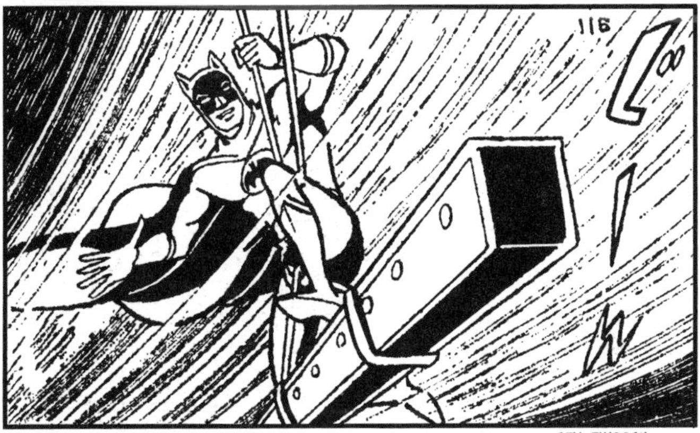

SFX: FWOOSH

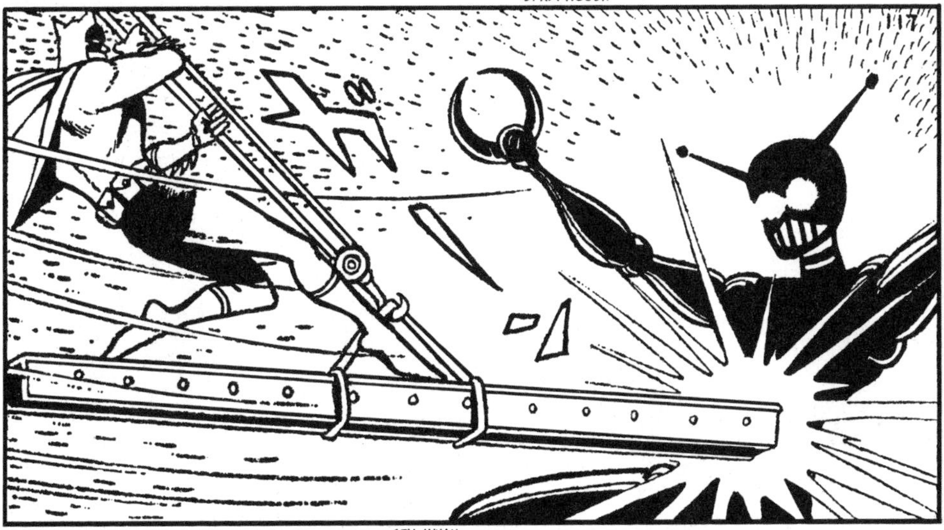

SFX: WHAM

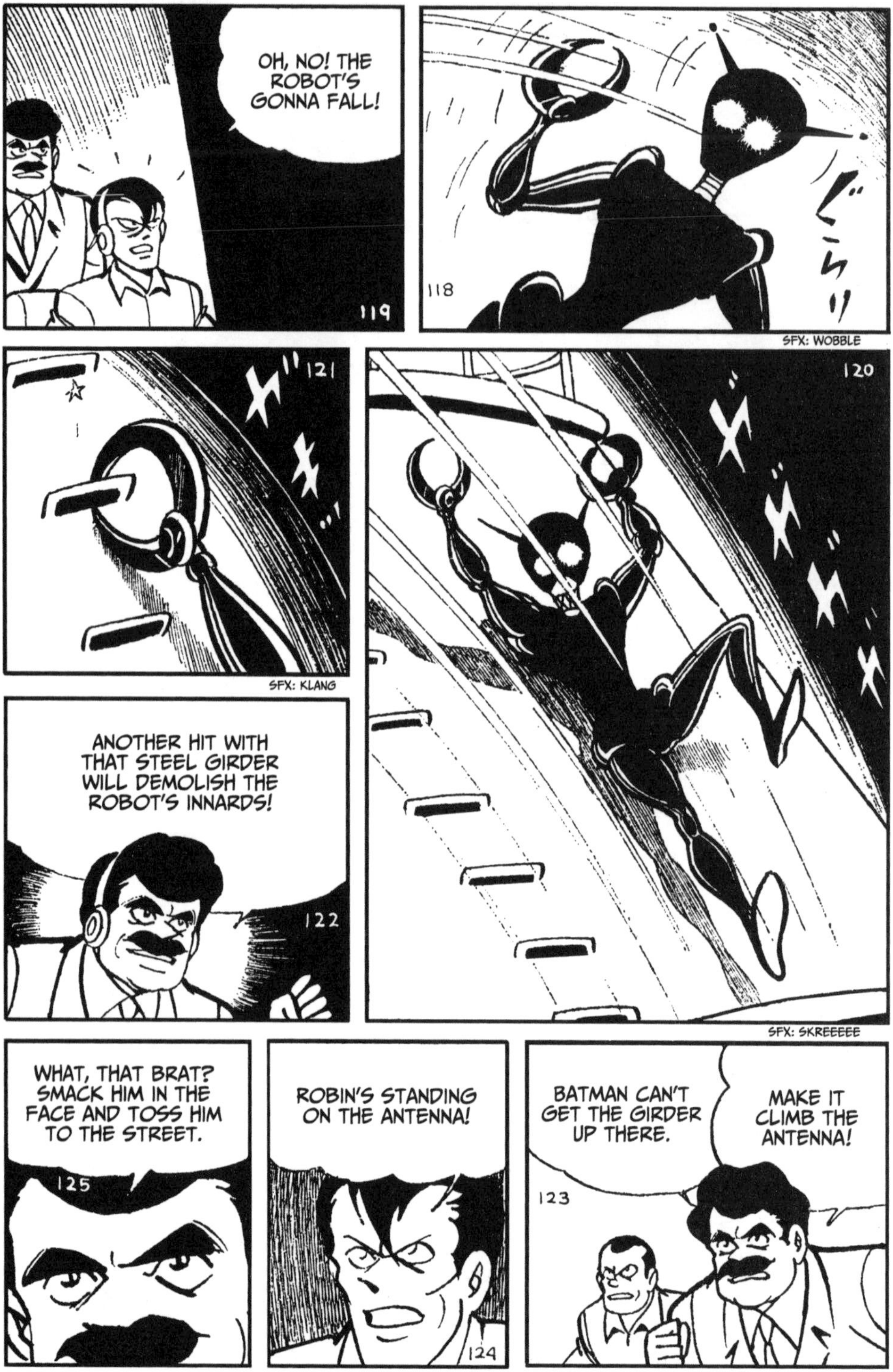
SFX: WOBBLE
OH, NO! THE ROBOT'S GONNA FALL!
SFX: SKREEEEE
SFX: KLANG
ANOTHER HIT WITH THAT STEEL GIRDER WILL DEMOLISH THE ROBOT'S INNARDS!
MAKE IT CLIMB THE ANTENNA!
BATMAN CAN'T GET THE GIRDER UP THERE.
ROBIN'S STANDING ON THE ANTENNA!
WHAT, THAT BRAT? SMACK HIM IN THE FACE AND TOSS HIM TO THE STREET.

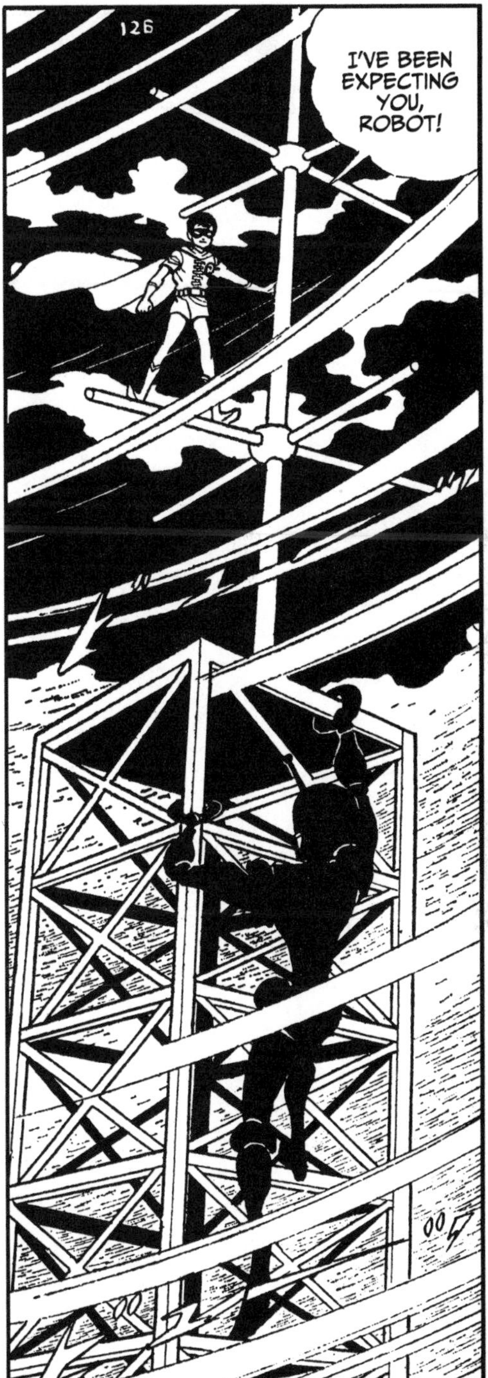
126
I'VE BEEN EXPECTING YOU, ROBOT!
SFX: FWOOO FWOOO

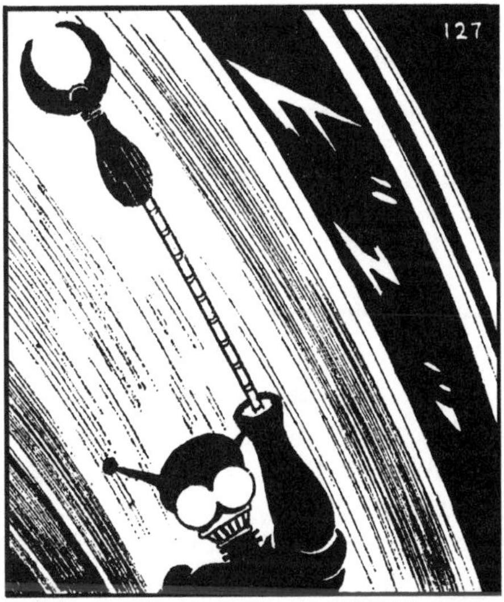
127
SFX: WHIZZZ

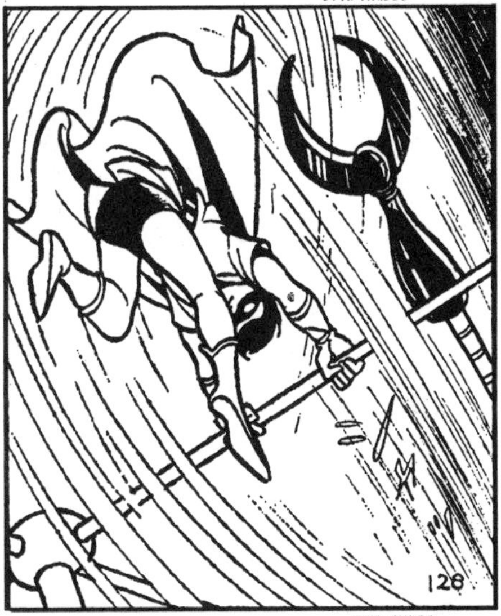
128
SFX: SWISH

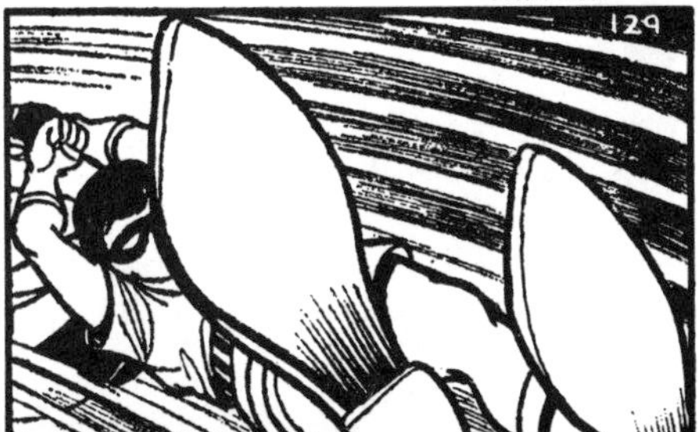
129

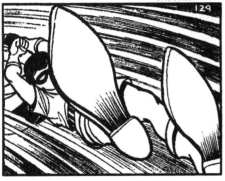

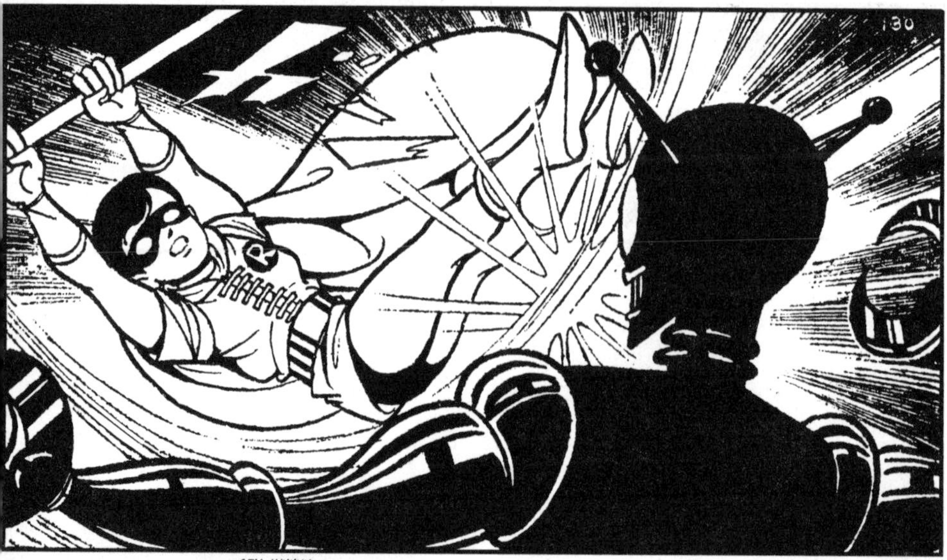
130
SFX: WHUNK

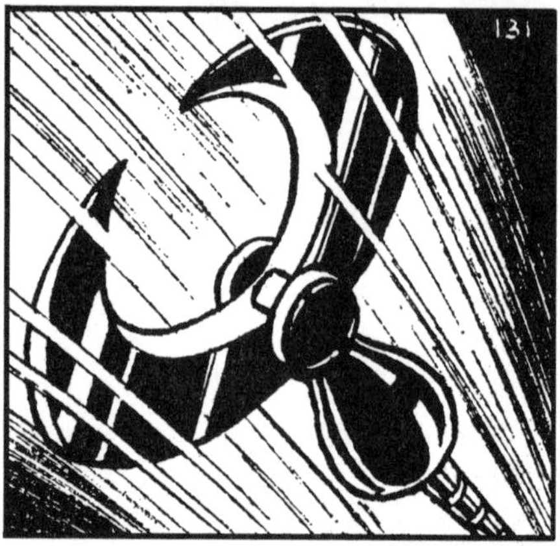
131

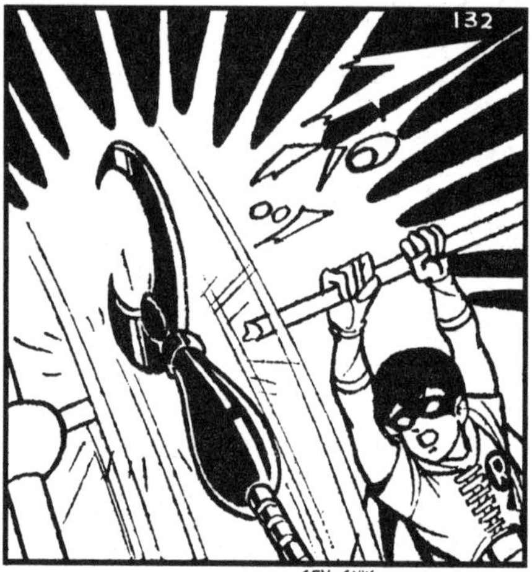
132
SFX: SNIK

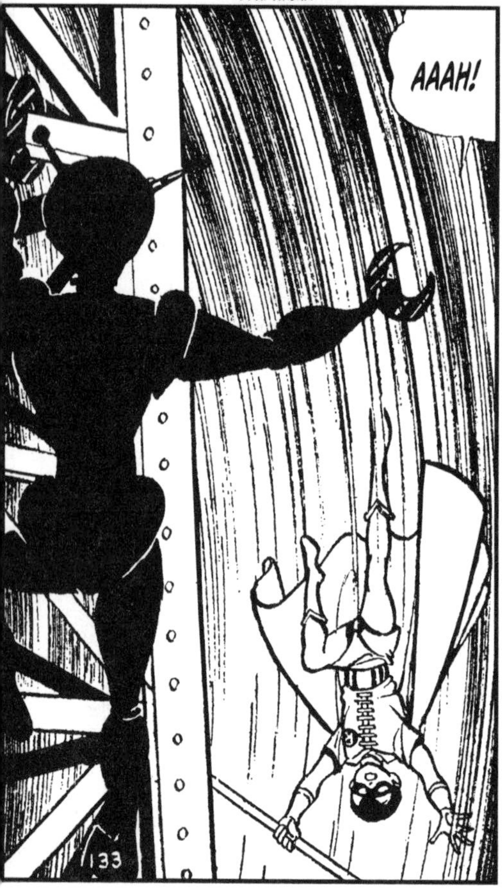
AAAH!
133

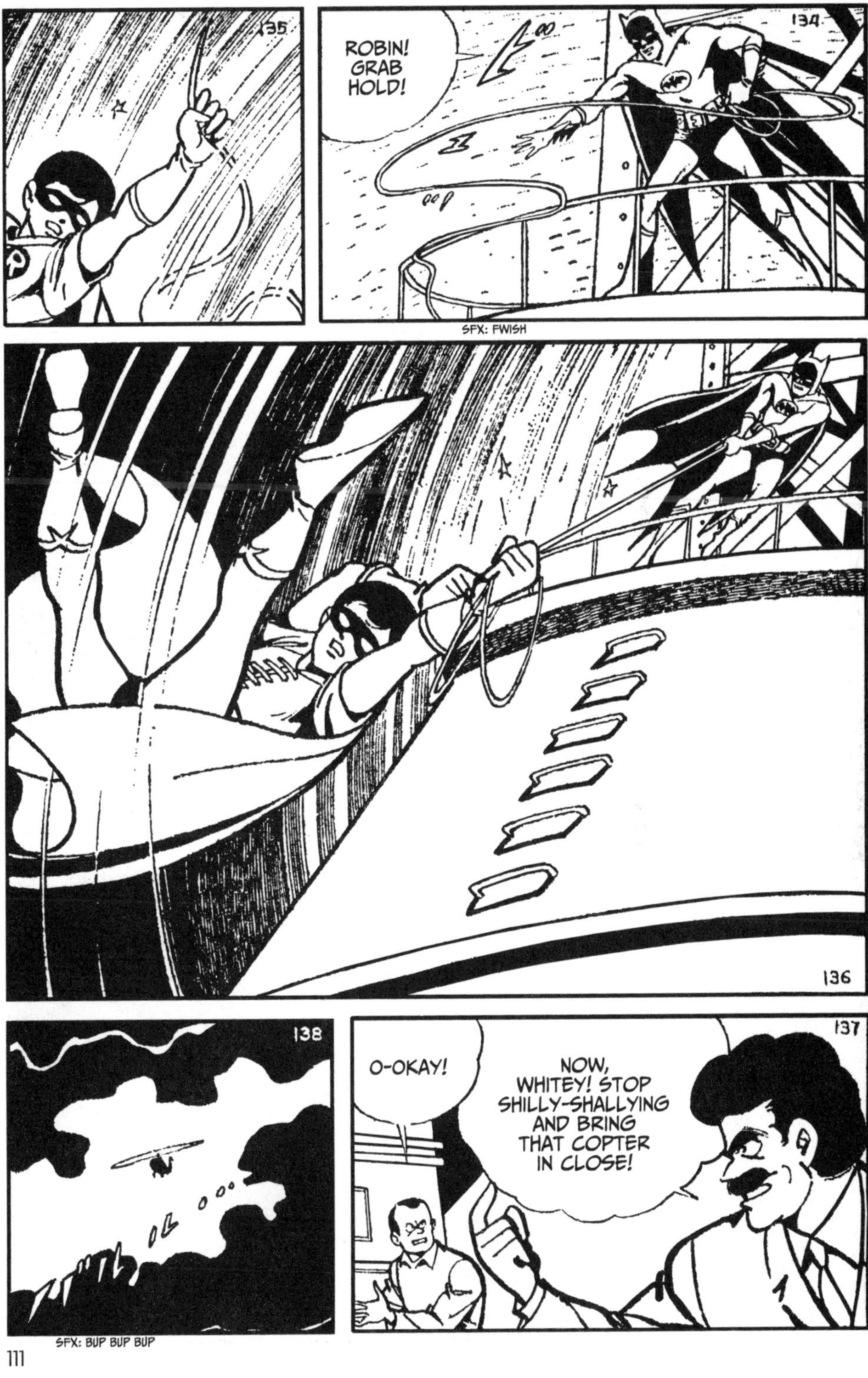
ROBIN! GRAB HOLD!
SFX: FWISH
NOW, WHITEY! STOP SHILLY-SHALLYING AND BRING THAT COPTER IN CLOSE!
O-OKAY!
SFX: BUP BUP BUP

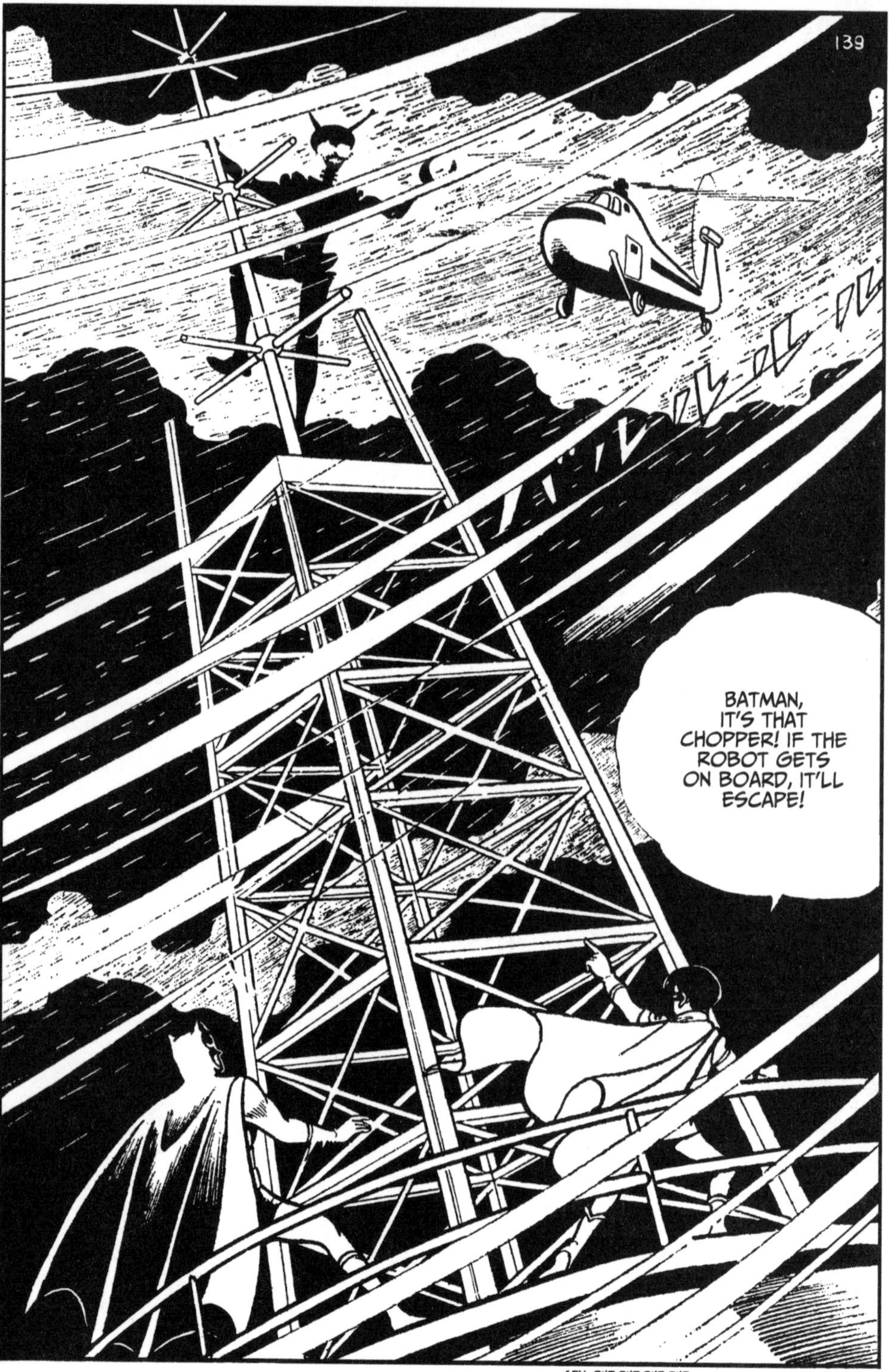
139
BATMAN, IT'S THAT CHOPPER! IF THE ROBOT GETS ON BOARD, IT'LL ESCAPE!

SFX: BUP BUP BUP BUP

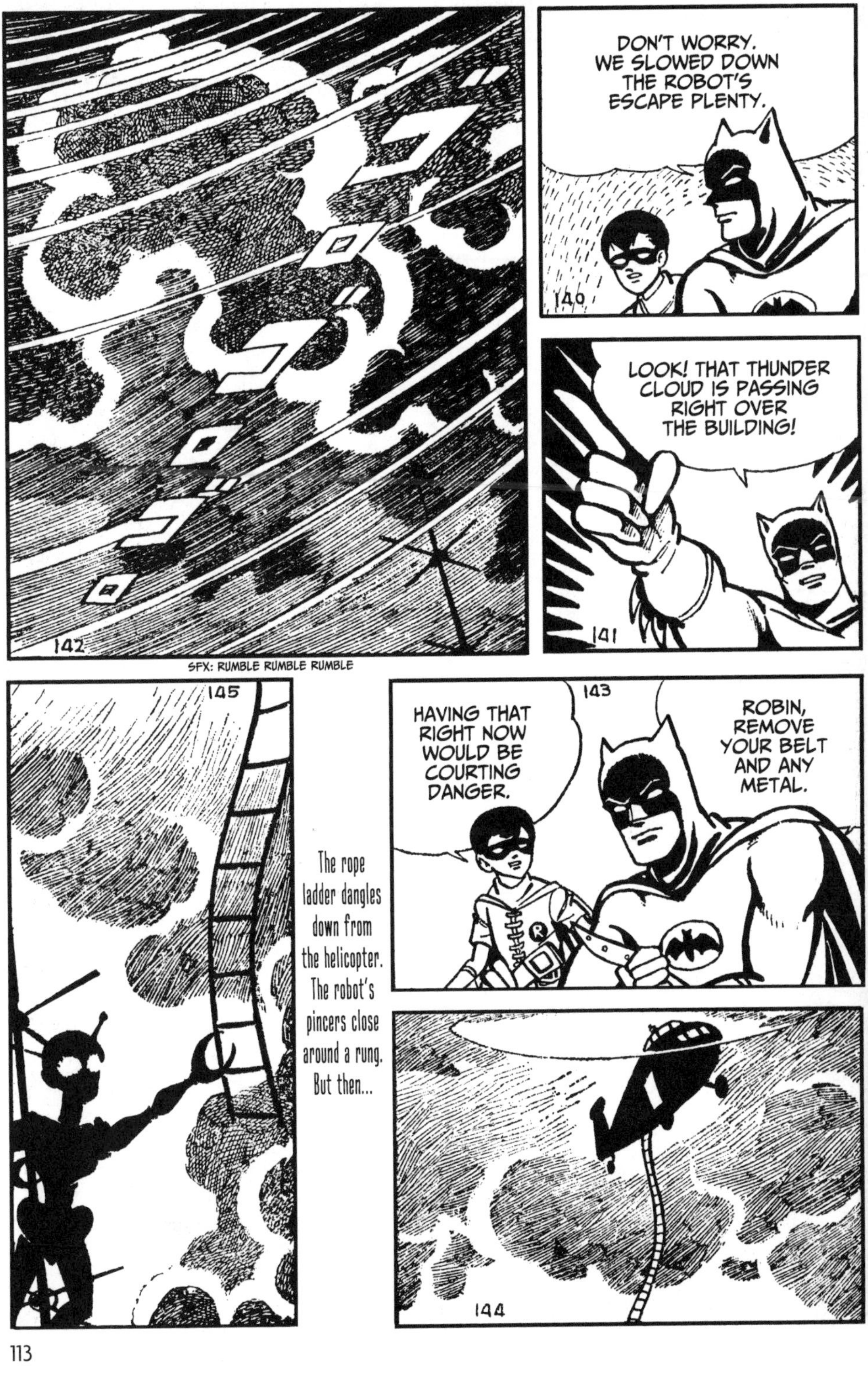
DON'T WORRY. WE SLOWED DOWN THE ROBOT'S ESCAPE PLENTY.
LOOK! THAT THUNDER CLOUD IS PASSING RIGHT OVER THE BUILDING!
SFX: RUMBLE RUMBLE RUMBLE
ROBIN, REMOVE YOUR BELT AND ANY METAL.
HAVING THAT RIGHT NOW WOULD BE COURTING DANGER.
The rope ladder dangles down from the helicopter. The robot's pincers close around a rung. But then...

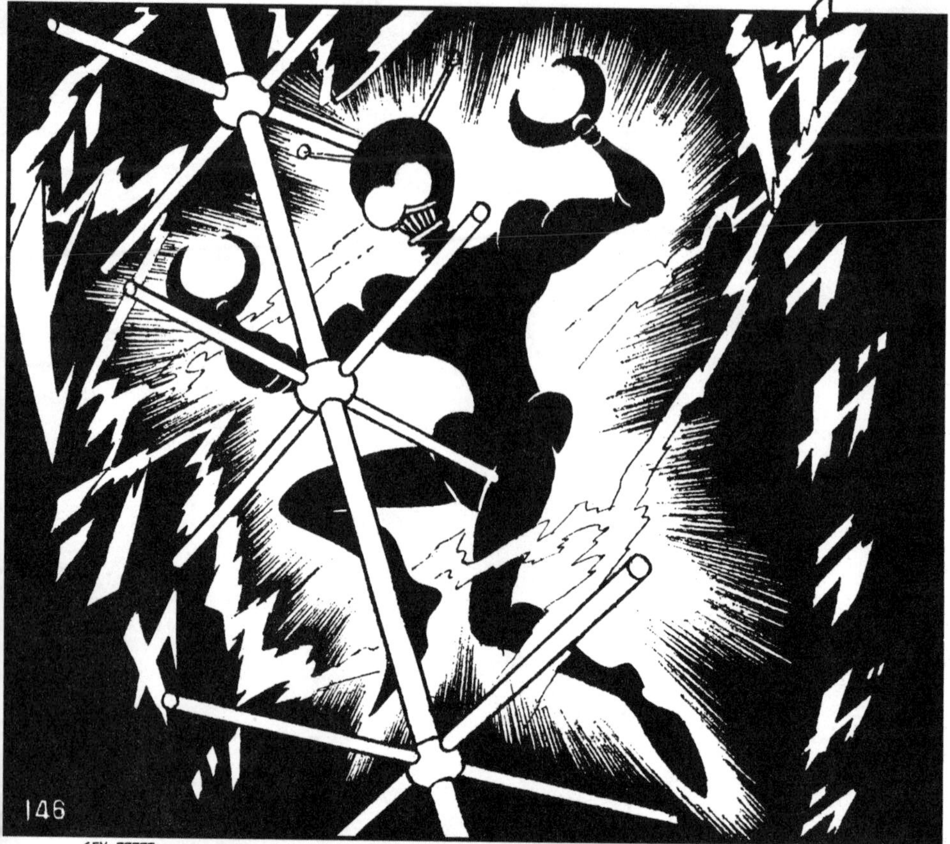
146

SFX: RATTLE RATTLE RATTLE

SFX: ZZZZT

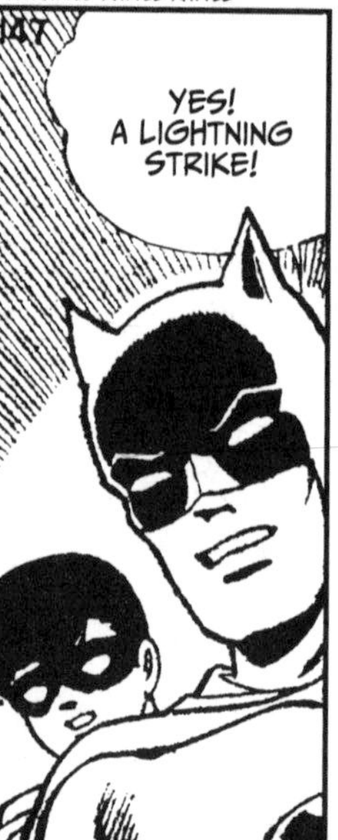
147
YES! A LIGHTNING STRIKE!

The electric shock travels through the headphones and into the three men in the hideout!

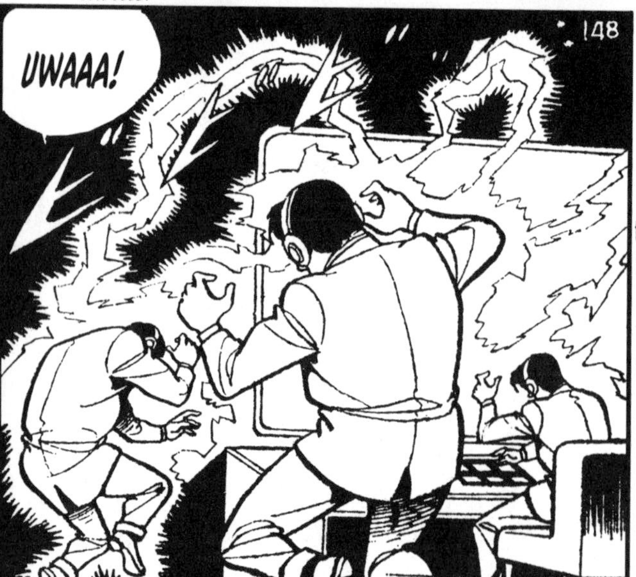
148
UWAAA!

SFX: BLINK

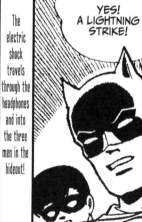

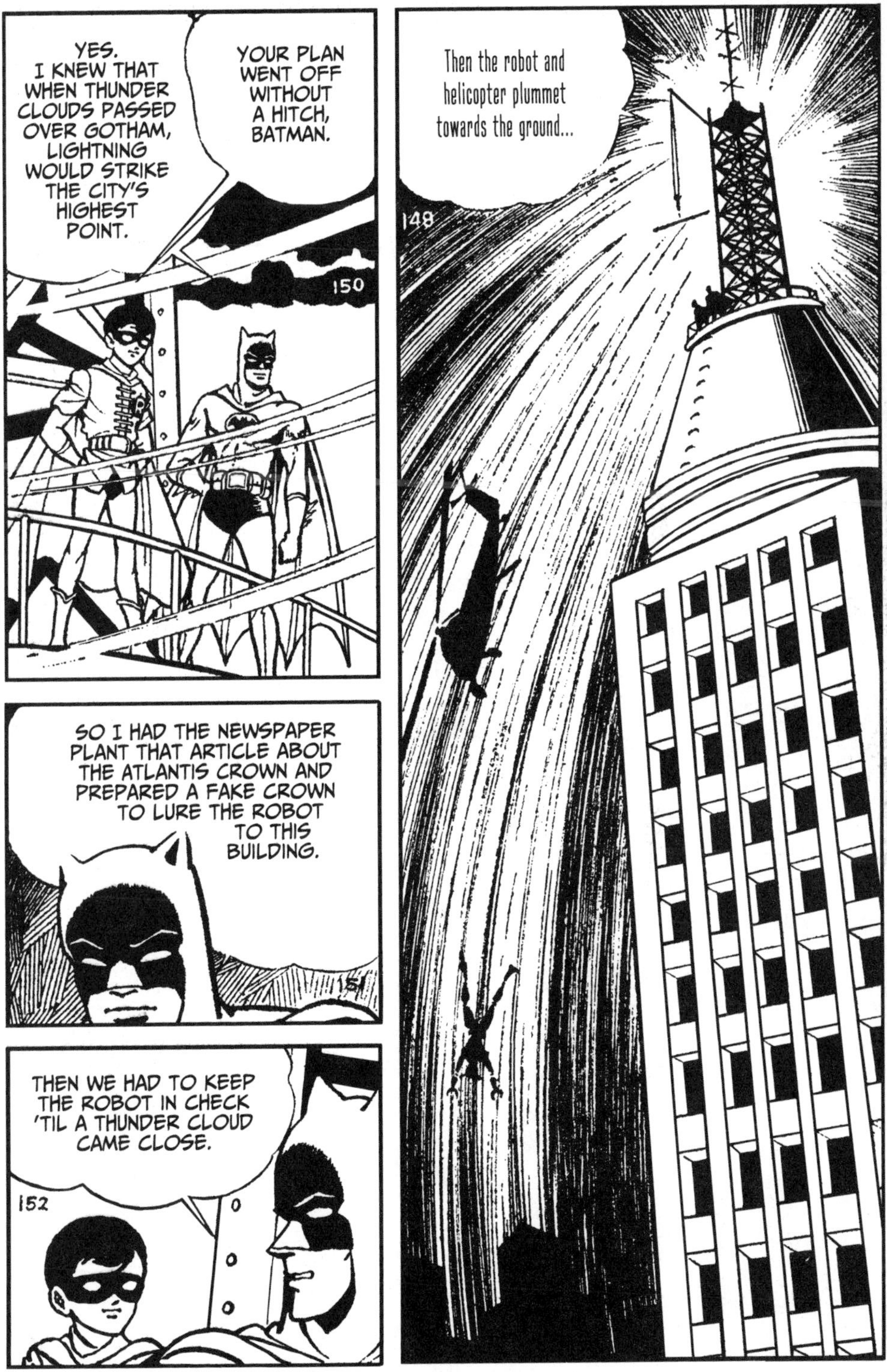
Then the robot and helicopter plummet towards the ground...
148
YOUR PLAN WENT OFF WITHOUT A HITCH, BATMAN.
YES. I KNEW THAT WHEN THUNDER CLOUDS PASSED OVER GOTHAM, LIGHTNING WOULD STRIKE THE CITY'S HIGHEST POINT.
150
SO I HAD THE NEWSPAPER PLANT THAT ARTICLE ABOUT THE ATLANTIS CROWN AND PREPARED A FAKE CROWN TO LURE THE ROBOT TO THIS BUILDING.
151
THEN WE HAD TO KEEP THE ROBOT IN CHECK 'TIL A THUNDER CLOUD CAME CLOSE.
152

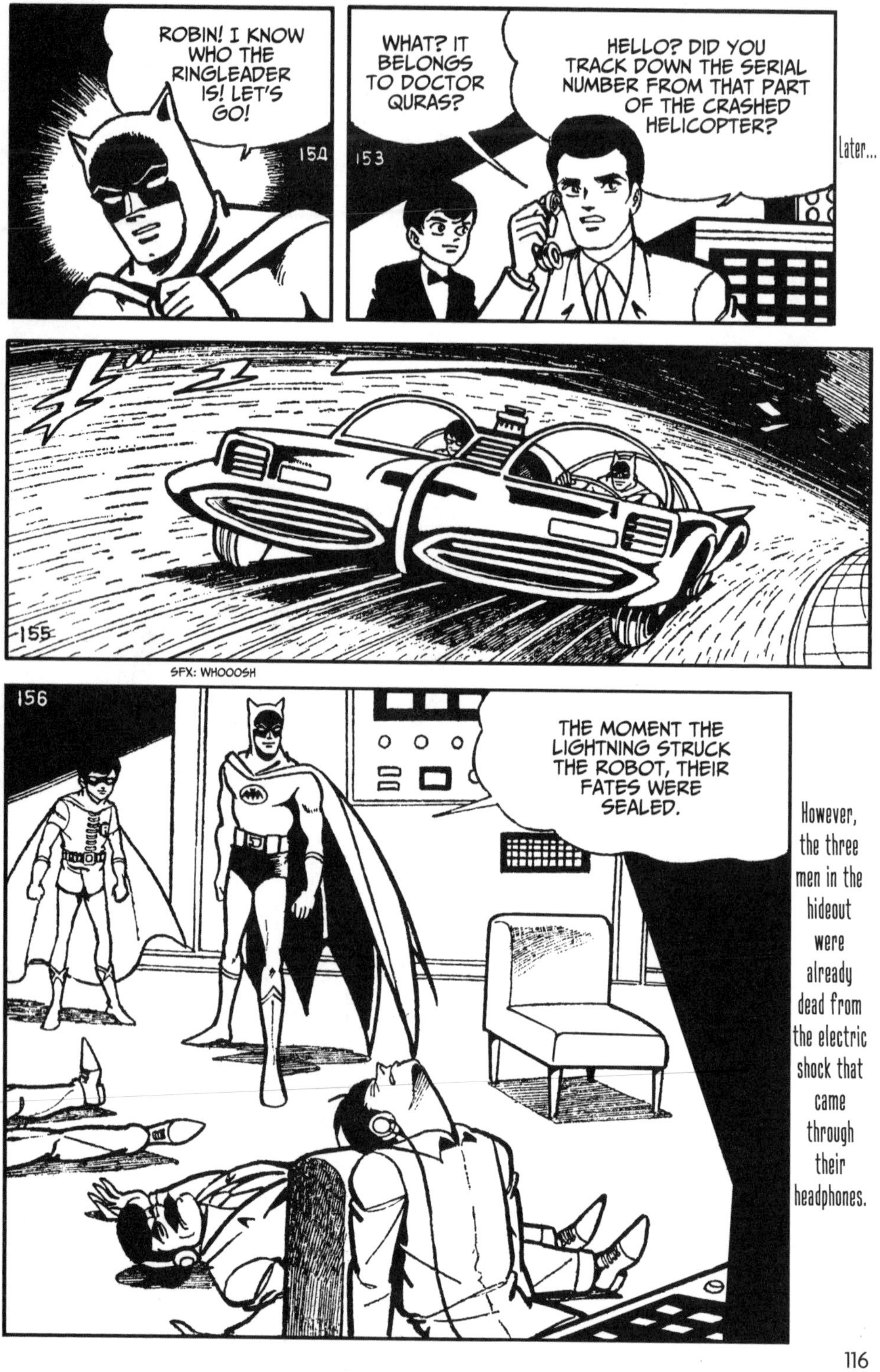
Later...
HELLO? DID YOU TRACK DOWN THE SERIAL NUMBER FROM THAT PART OF THE CRASHED HELICOPTER?
WHAT? IT BELONGS TO DOCTOR QURAS?
153
ROBIN! I KNOW WHO THE RINGLEADER IS! LET'S GO!
154
155
SFX: WHOOOSH
156
THE MOMENT THE LIGHTNING STRUCK THE ROBOT, THEIR FATES WERE SEALED.
However, the three men in the hideout were already dead from the electric shock that came through their headphones.

バットマン

BATMAN
EXCLUSIVE JAPANESE VERSION
SHONEN GAHOSHA

★ THE TERRIBLE CLAYFACE ENCOUNTER ★

Jiro Kuwata

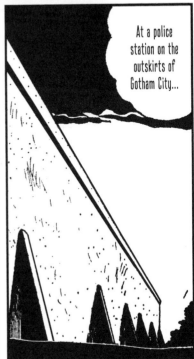

At a police station on the outskirts of Gotham City...

117

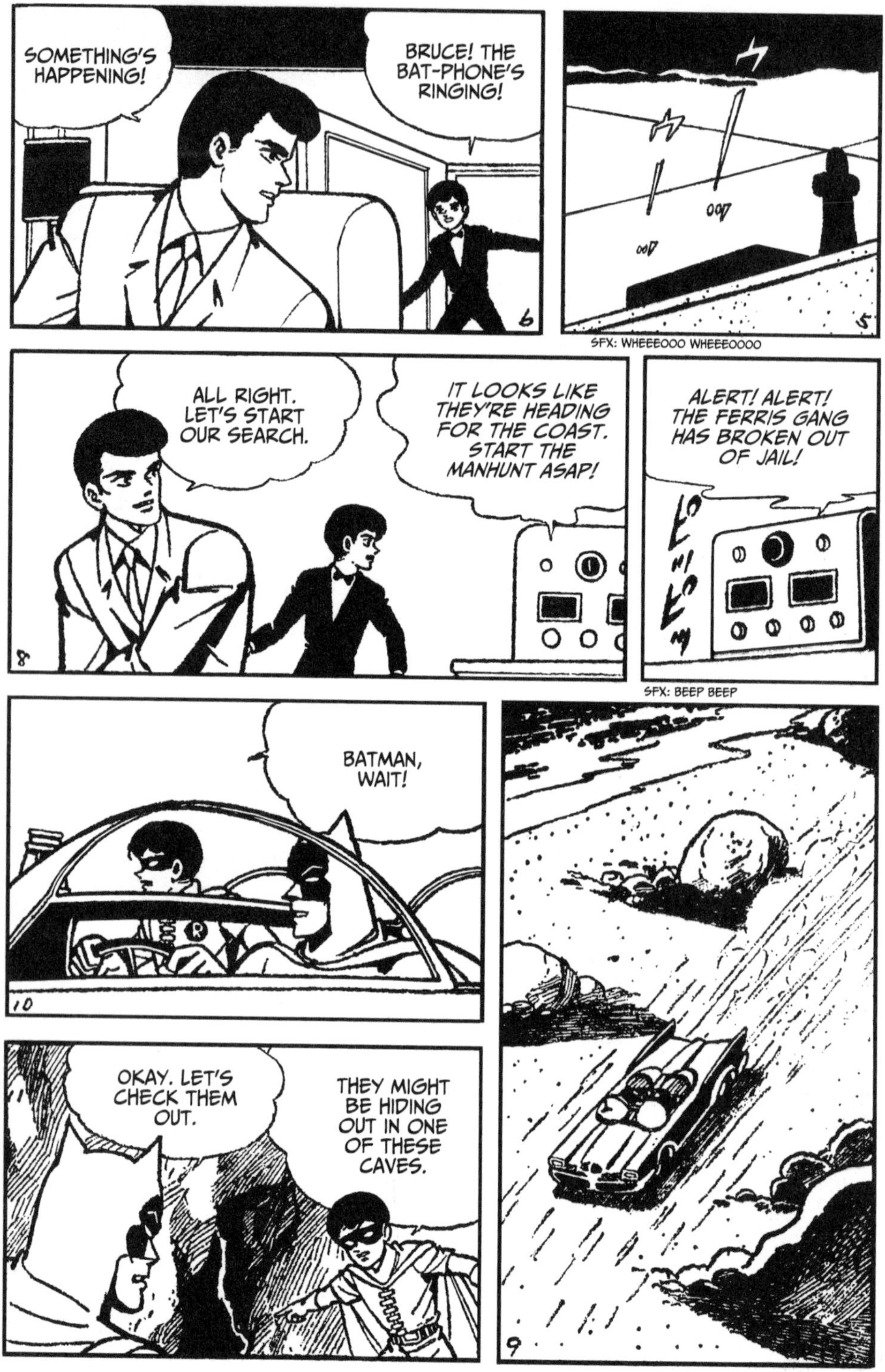
SFX: WHEEEOOO WHEEEOOOO
BRUCE! THE BAT-PHONE'S RINGING!
SOMETHING'S HAPPENING!
ALERT! ALERT! THE FERRIS GANG HAS BROKEN OUT OF JAIL!
SFX: BEEP BEEP
IT LOOKS LIKE THEY'RE HEADING FOR THE COAST. START THE MANHUNT ASAP!
ALL RIGHT. LET'S START OUR SEARCH.
BATMAN, WAIT!
THEY MIGHT BE HIDING OUT IN ONE OF THESE CAVES.
OKAY. LET'S CHECK THEM OUT.

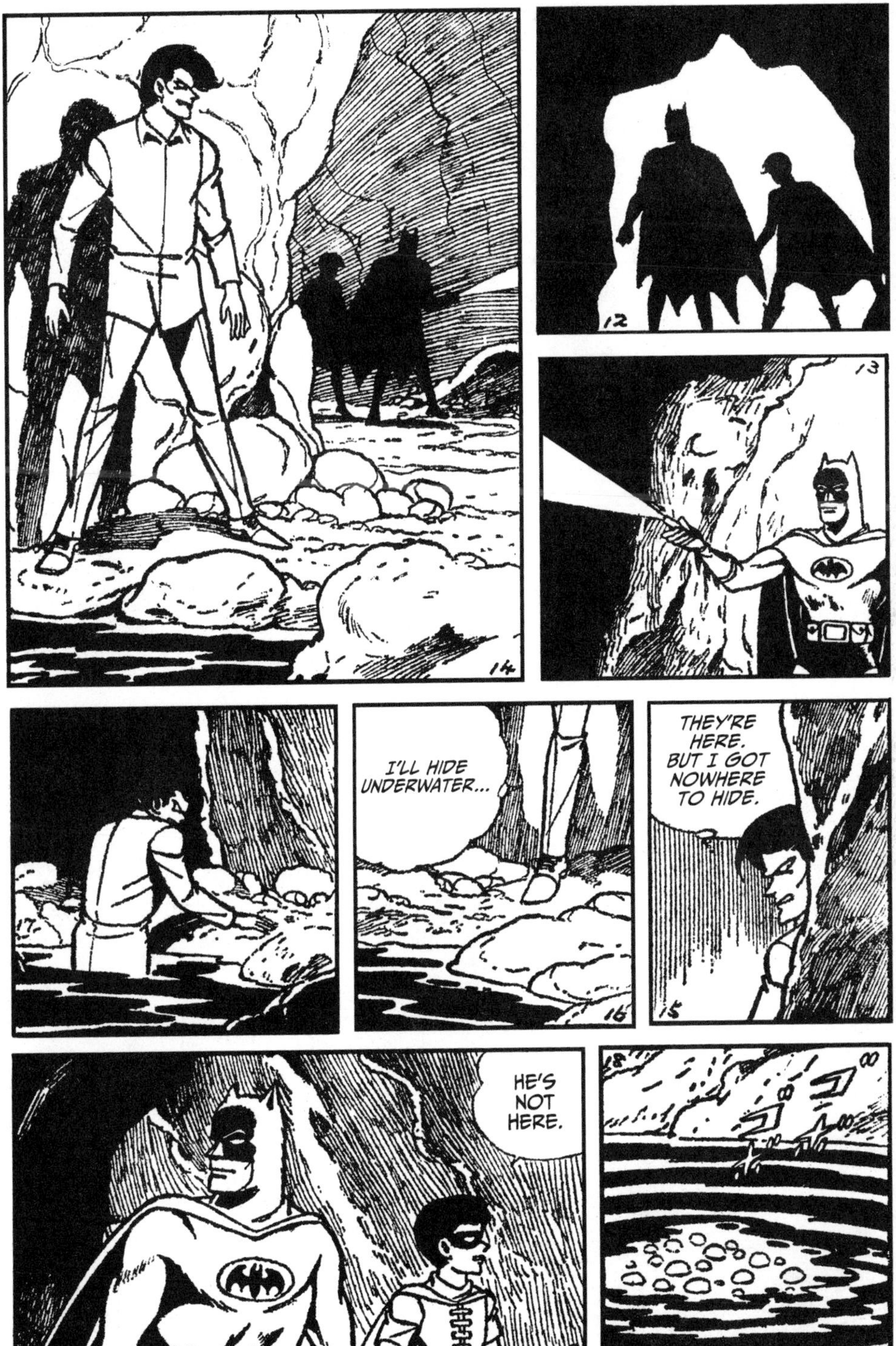
THEY'RE HERE. BUT I GOT NOWHERE TO HIDE.
I'LL HIDE UNDERWATER...
HE'S NOT HERE.

SFX: BLOOP BLOOP

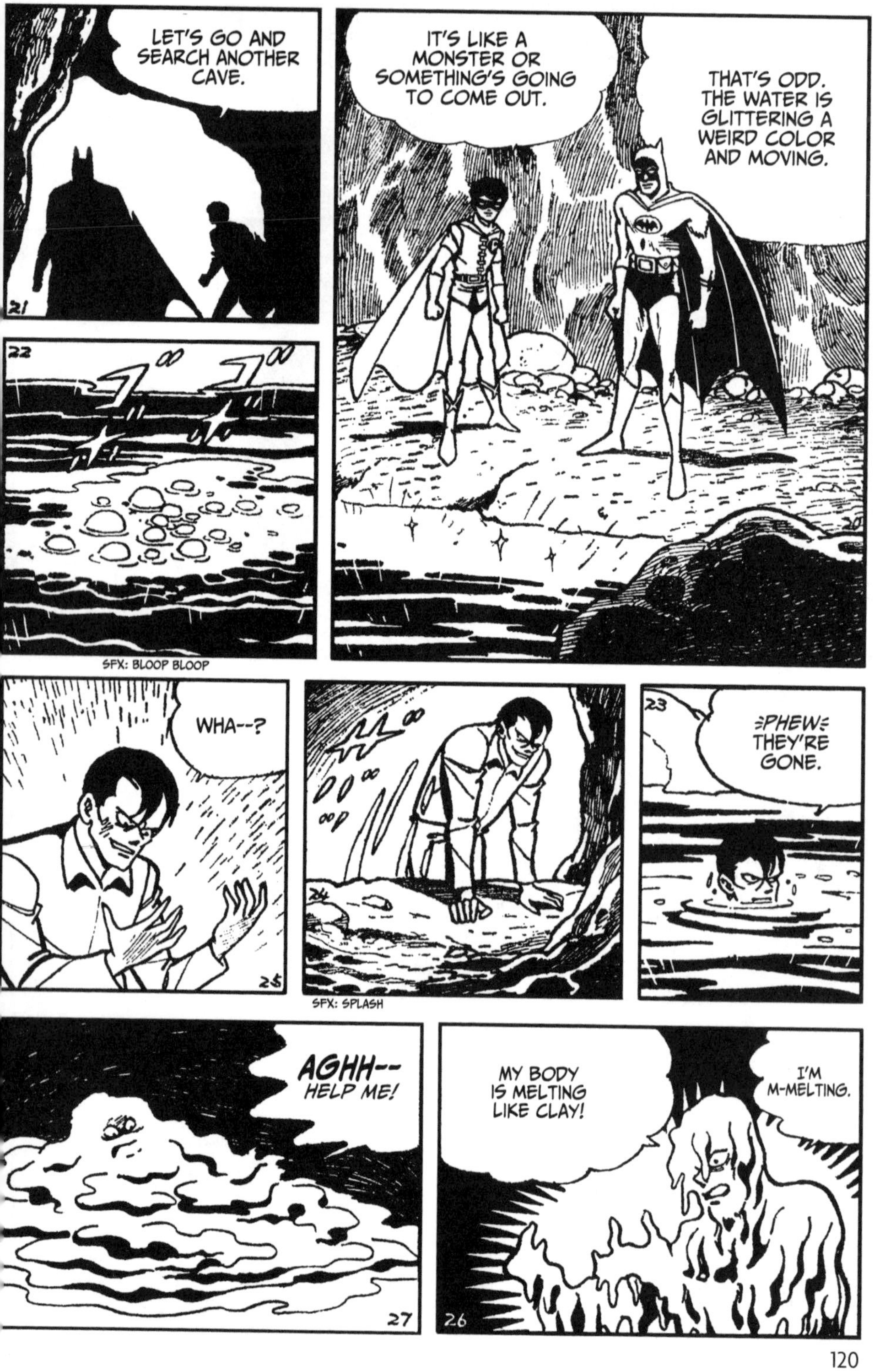
THAT'S ODD. THE WATER IS GLITTERING A WEIRD COLOR AND MOVING.
IT'S LIKE A MONSTER OR SOMETHING'S GOING TO COME OUT.
LET'S GO AND SEARCH ANOTHER CAVE.
SFX: BLOOP BLOOP
PHEW THEY'RE GONE.
SFX: SPLASH
WHA--?
I'M M-MELTING.
MY BODY IS MELTING LIKE CLAY!
AGHH-- HELP ME!

The bioplasm in the cave has turned Ferris, the escaped convict, into a clay-thing. And yet he has survived...

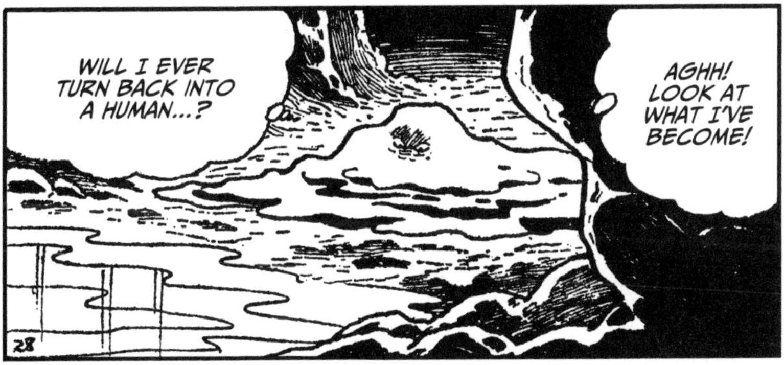
AGHH! LOOK AT WHAT I'VE BECOME!
WILL I EVER TURN BACK INTO A HUMAN...?

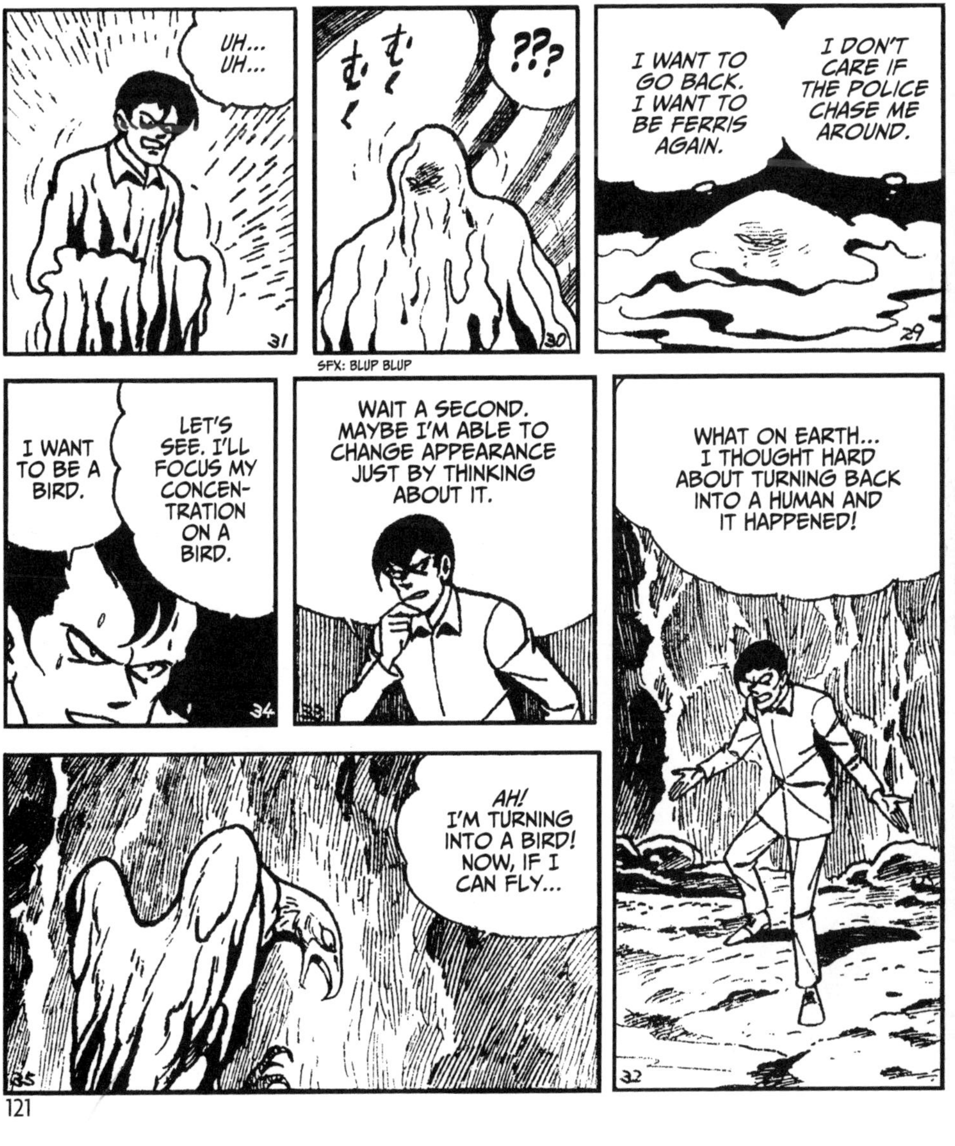
I DON'T CARE IF THE POLICE CHASE ME AROUND.
I WANT TO GO BACK. I WANT TO BE FERRIS AGAIN.
???
むくむく
SFX: BLUP BLUP
UH... UH...
WHAT ON EARTH... I THOUGHT HARD ABOUT TURNING BACK INTO A HUMAN AND IT HAPPENED!
WAIT A SECOND. MAYBE I'M ABLE TO CHANGE APPEARANCE JUST BY THINKING ABOUT IT.
LET'S SEE. I'LL FOCUS MY CONCEN-TRATION ON A BIRD.
I WANT TO BE A BIRD.
AH! I'M TURNING INTO A BIRD! NOW, IF I CAN FLY...

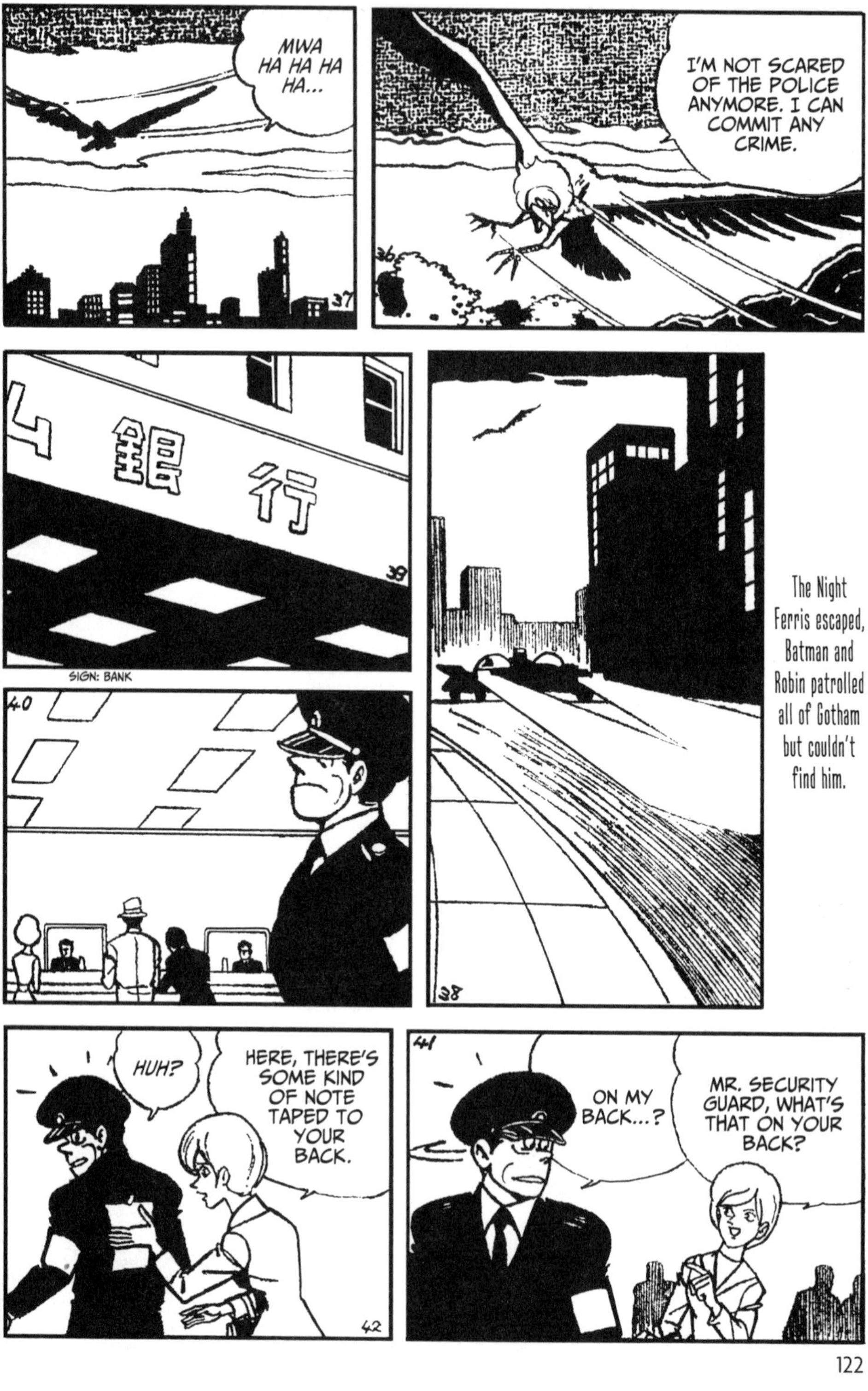

I'M NOT SCARED OF THE POLICE ANYMORE. I CAN COMMIT ANY CRIME.
MWA HA HA HA HA...
The Night Ferris escaped, Batman and Robin patrolled all of Gotham but couldn't find him.
SIGN: BANK
MR. SECURITY GUARD, WHAT'S THAT ON YOUR BACK?
ON MY BACK...?
HERE, THERE'S SOME KIND OF NOTE TAPED TO YOUR BACK.
HUH?

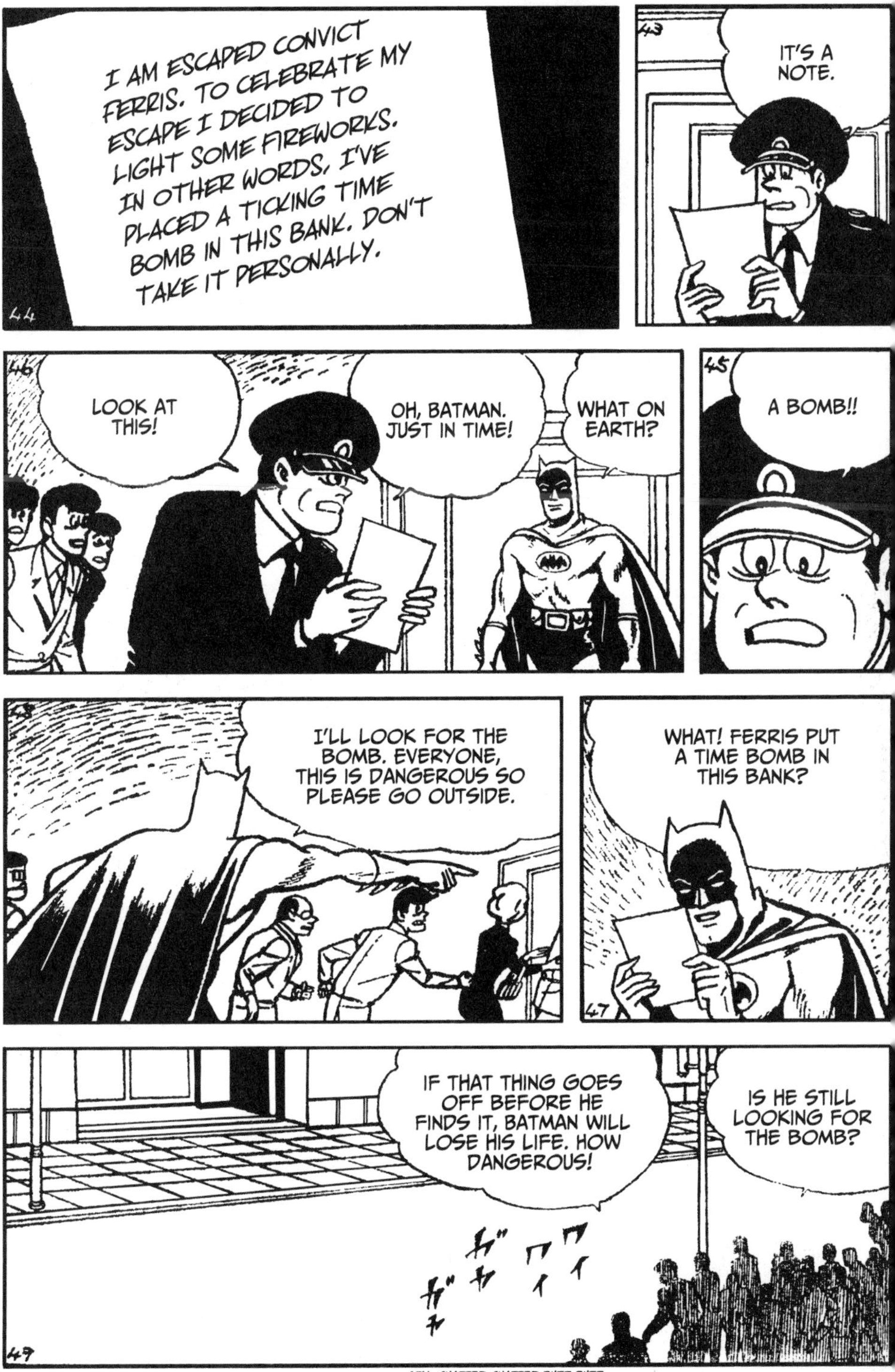
IT'S A NOTE.
I AM ESCAPED CONVICT FERRIS. TO CELEBRATE MY ESCAPE I DECIDED TO LIGHT SOME FIREWORKS. IN OTHER WORDS, I'VE PLACED A TICKING TIME BOMB IN THIS BANK. DON'T TAKE IT PERSONALLY.
A BOMB!!
WHAT ON EARTH?
OH, BATMAN. JUST IN TIME!
LOOK AT THIS!
WHAT! FERRIS PUT A TIME BOMB IN THIS BANK?
I'LL LOOK FOR THE BOMB. EVERYONE, THIS IS DANGEROUS SO PLEASE GO OUTSIDE.
IS HE STILL LOOKING FOR THE BOMB?
IF THAT THING GOES OFF BEFORE HE FINDS IT, BATMAN WILL LOSE HIS LIFE. HOW DANGEROUS!
ガヤガヤ
ワイワイ

SFX: CHATTER CHATTER BUZZ BUZZ

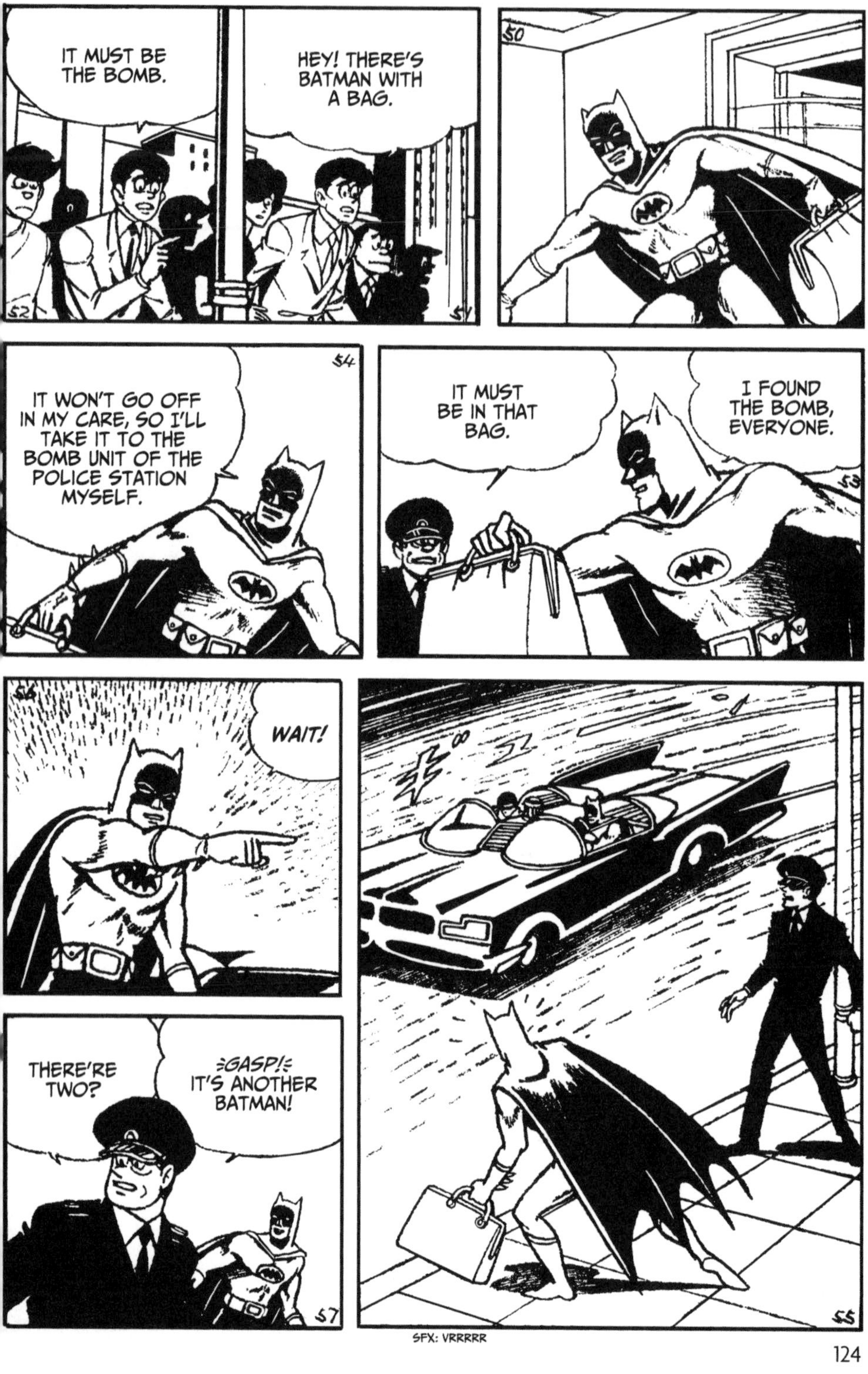
HEY! THERE'S BATMAN WITH A BAG.
IT MUST BE THE BOMB.
I FOUND THE BOMB, EVERYONE.
IT MUST BE IN THAT BAG.
IT WON'T GO OFF IN MY CARE, SO I'LL TAKE IT TO THE BOMB UNIT OF THE POLICE STATION MYSELF.
WAIT!
GASP! IT'S ANOTHER BATMAN!
THERE'RE TWO?

SFX: VRRRRR

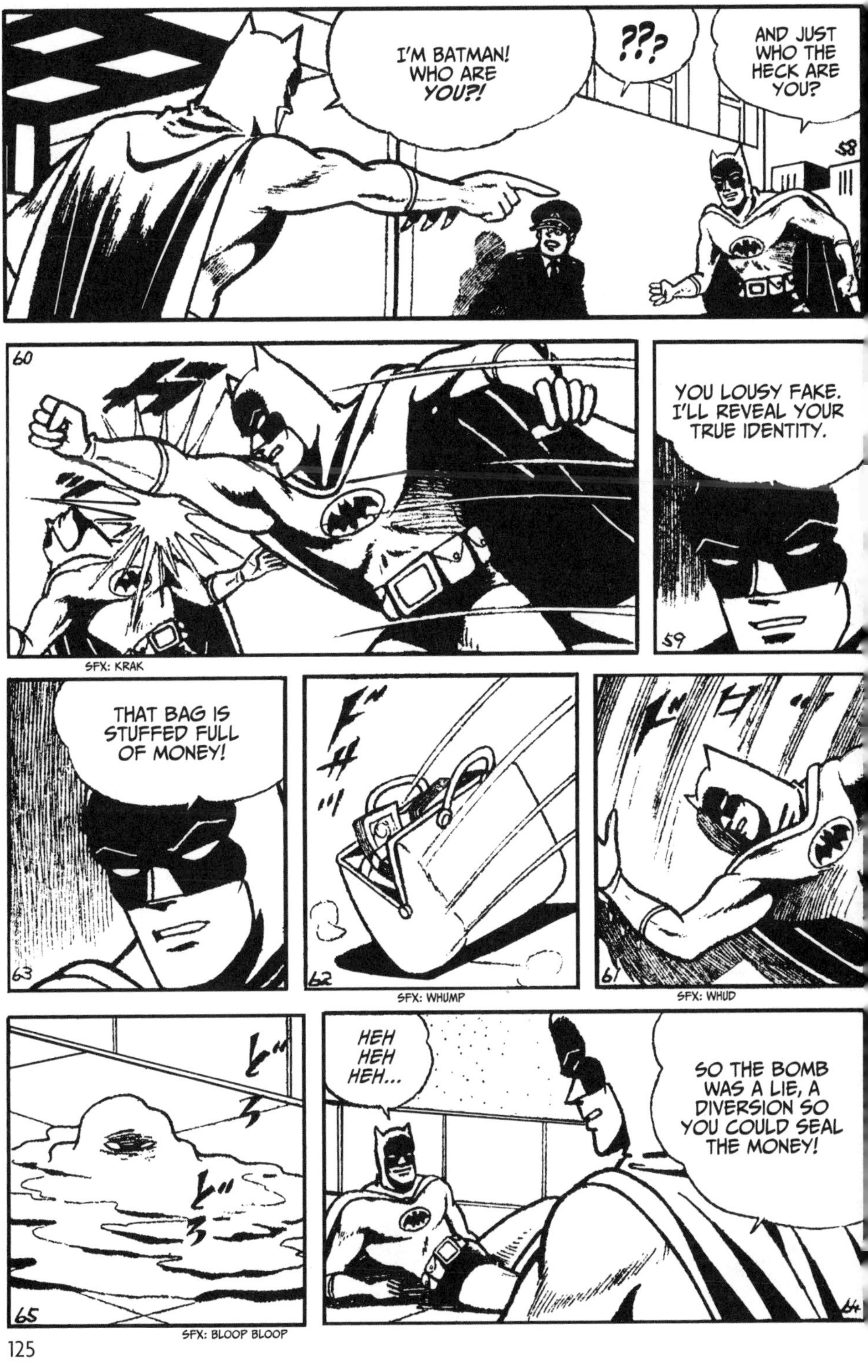
AND JUST WHO THE HECK ARE YOU?
???
I'M BATMAN! WHO ARE *YOU?!*
YOU LOUSY FAKE. I'LL REVEAL YOUR TRUE IDENTITY.
SFX: KRAK
SFX: WHUD
SFX: WHUMP
THAT BAG IS STUFFED FULL OF MONEY!
SO THE BOMB WAS A LIE, A DIVERSION SO YOU COULD SEAL THE MONEY!
HEH HEH HEH...
SFX: BLOOP BLOOP

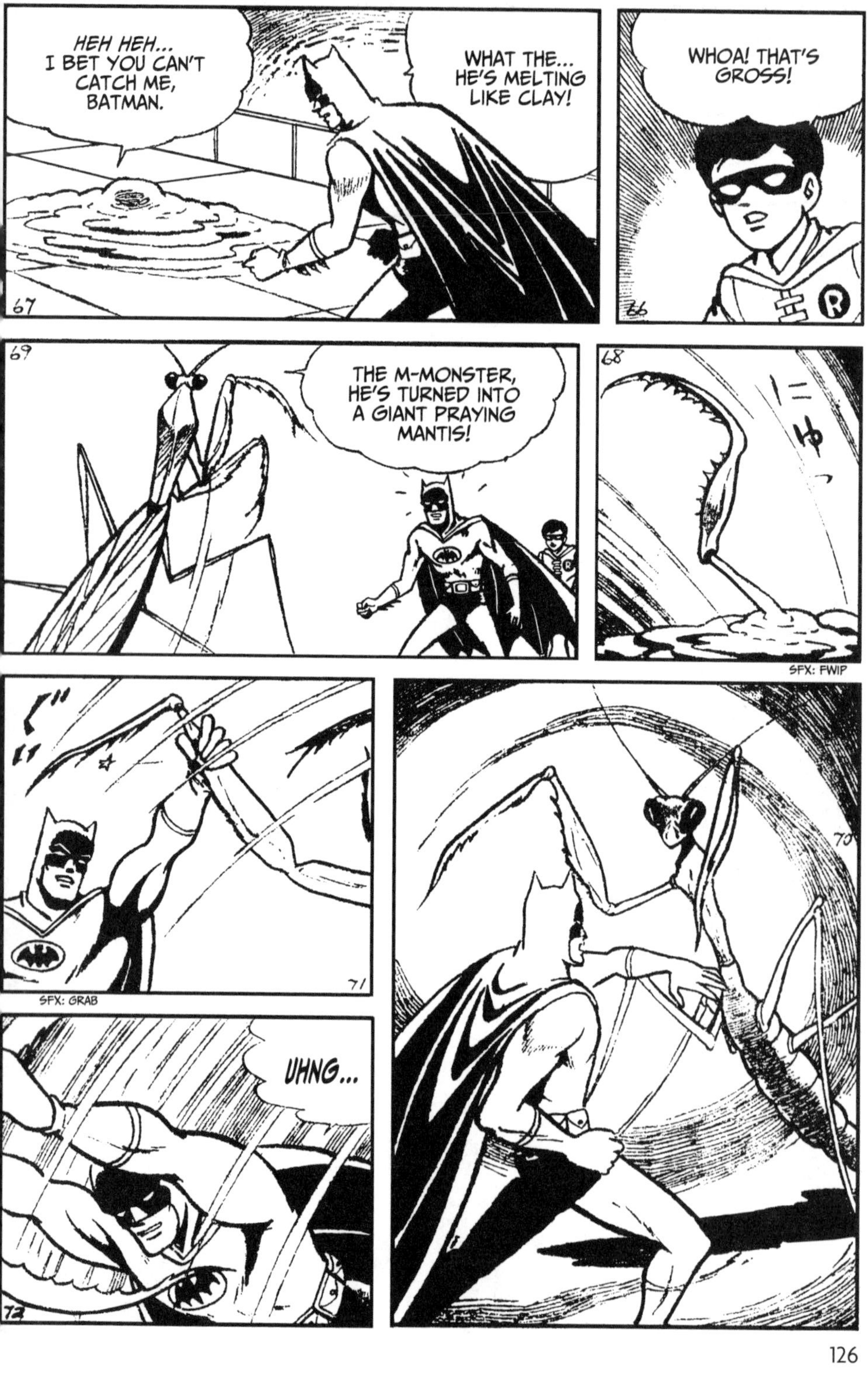
WHOA! THAT'S GROSS!
WHAT THE... HE'S MELTING LIKE CLAY!
HEH HEH... I BET YOU CAN'T CATCH ME, BATMAN.
SFX: FWIP
THE M-MONSTER, HE'S TURNED INTO A GIANT PRAYING MANTIS!
SFX: GRAB
UHNG...

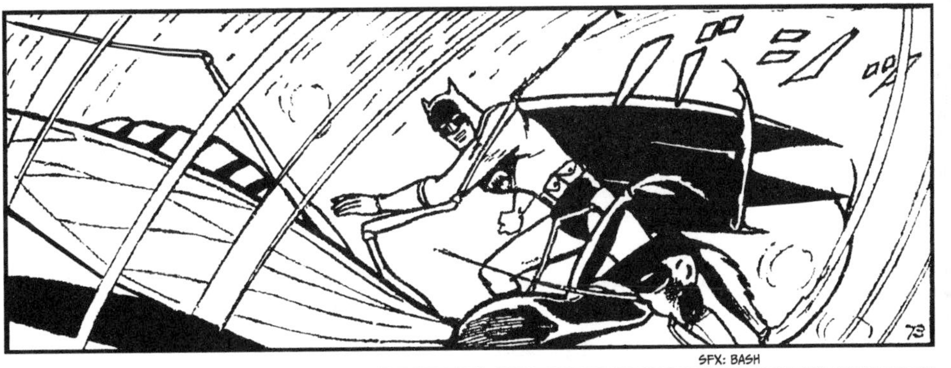

SFX: BASH

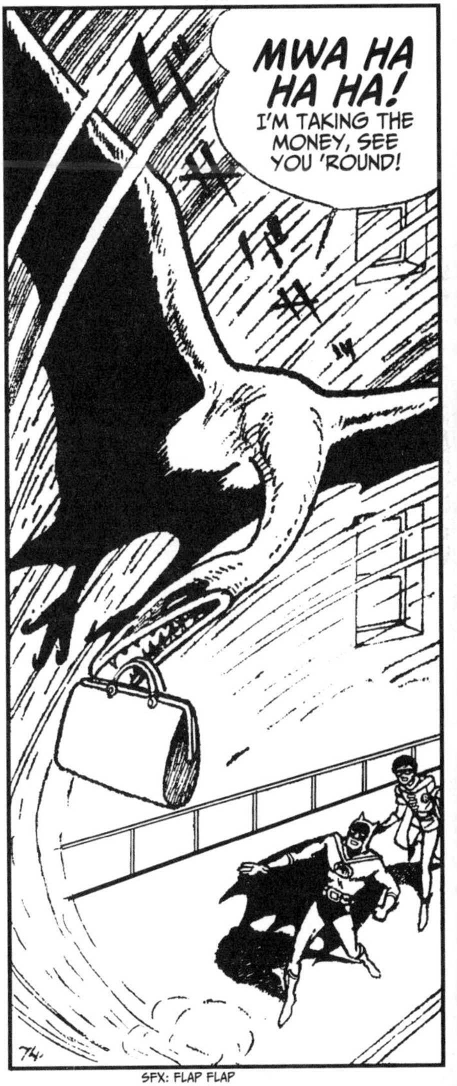
MWA HA HA HA! I'M TAKING THE MONEY, SEE YOU 'ROUND!

SFX: FLAP FLAP

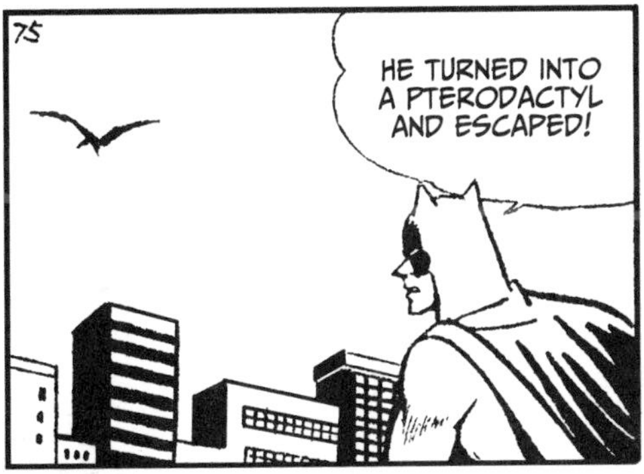
HE TURNED INTO A PTERODACTYL AND ESCAPED!

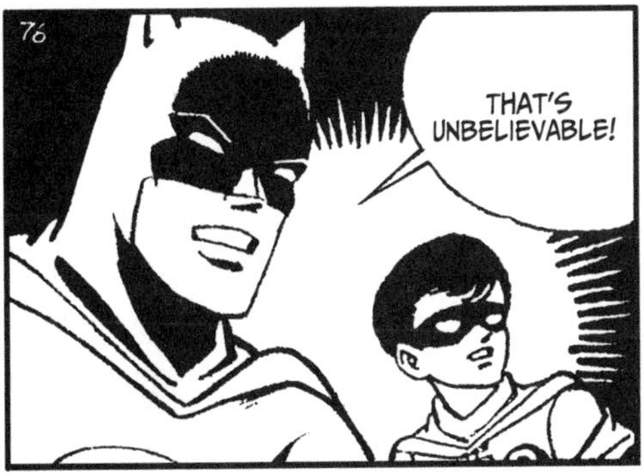
THAT'S UNBELIEVABLE!

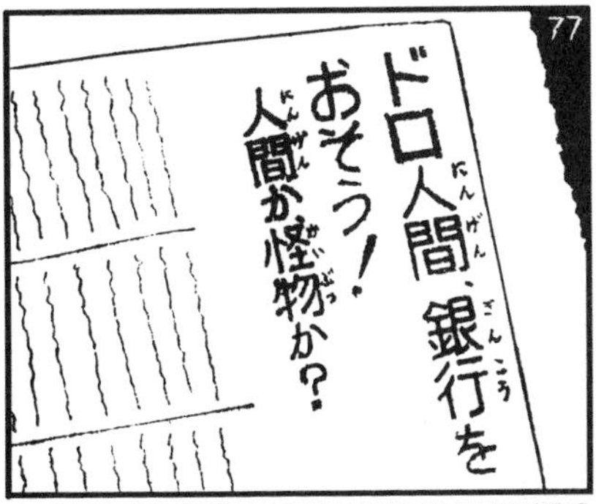
ドロ人間、銀行をおそう！
人間か怪物か？

NEWSPAPER TEXT: CLAYFACE ROBS BANK! HUMAN OR MONSTER?

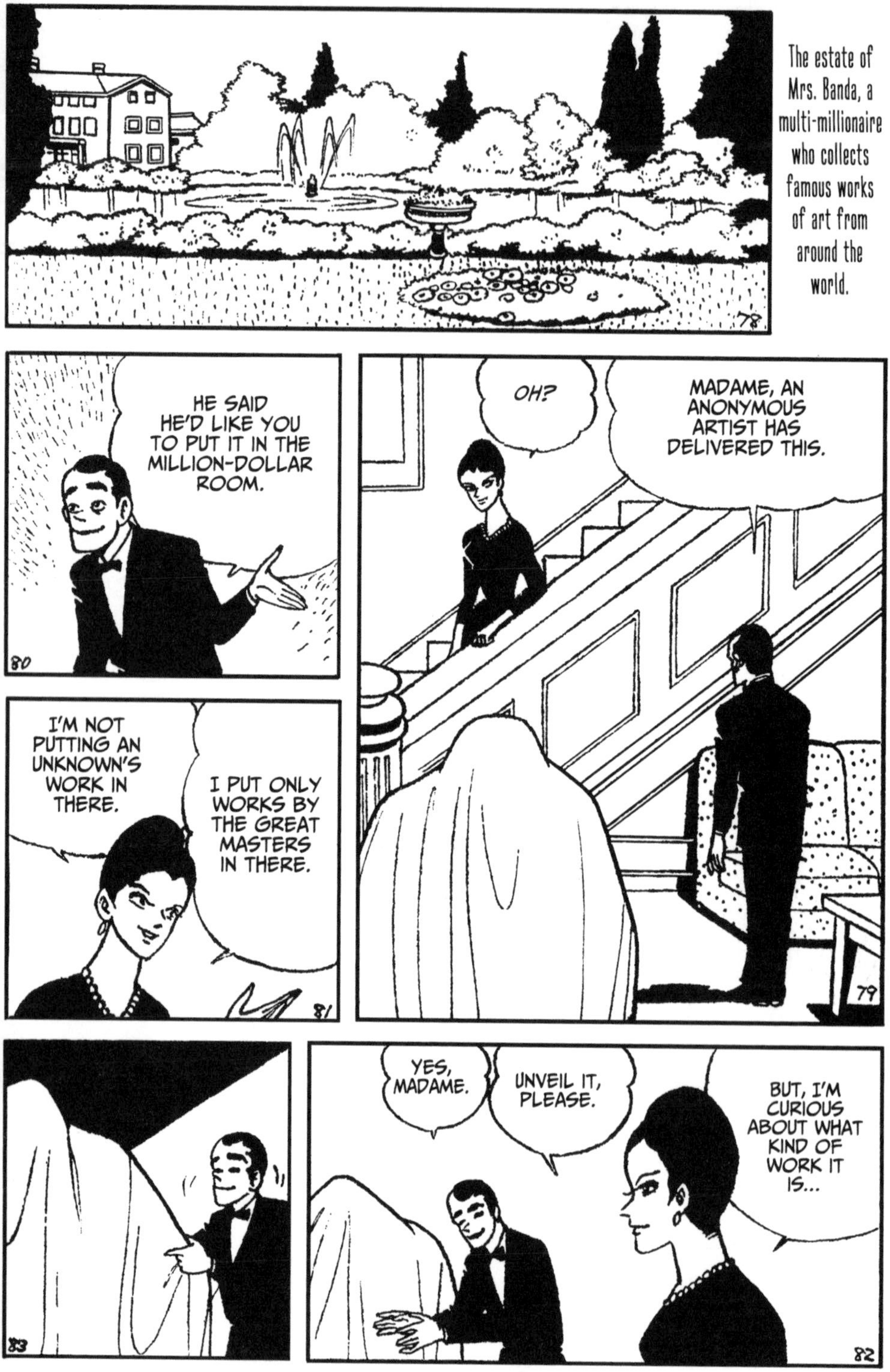
The estate of Mrs. Banda, a multi-millionaire who collects famous works of art from around the world.
MADAME, AN ANONYMOUS ARTIST HAS DELIVERED THIS.
OH?
HE SAID HE'D LIKE YOU TO PUT IT IN THE MILLION-DOLLAR ROOM.
I'M NOT PUTTING AN UNKNOWN'S WORK IN THERE.
I PUT ONLY WORKS BY THE GREAT MASTERS IN THERE.
BUT, I'M CURIOUS ABOUT WHAT KIND OF WORK IT IS...
UNVEIL IT, PLEASE.
YES, MADAME.

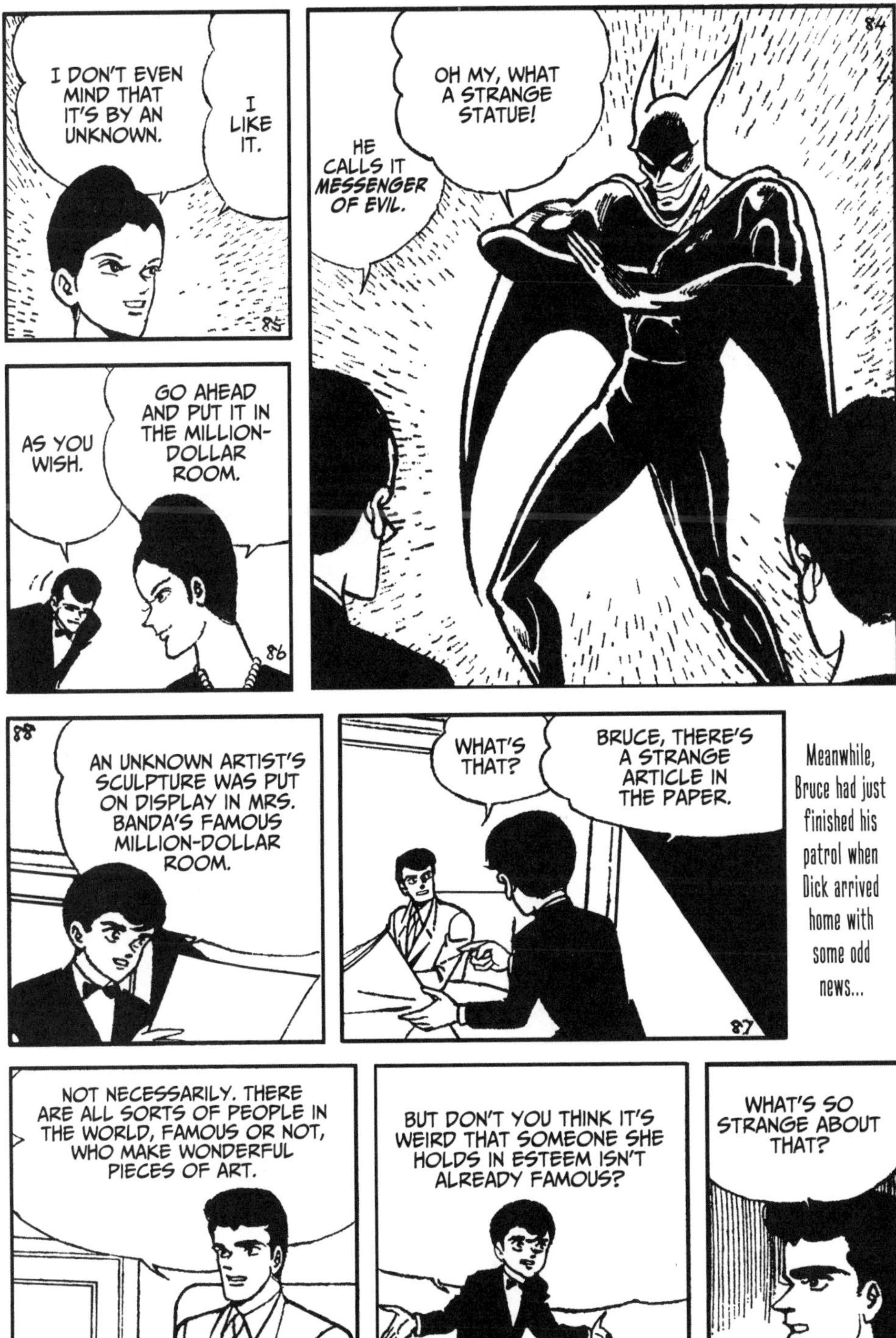
OH MY, WHAT A STRANGE STATUE!
HE CALLS IT *MESSENGER OF EVIL.*
I LIKE IT.
I DON'T EVEN MIND THAT IT'S BY AN UNKNOWN.
GO AHEAD AND PUT IT IN THE MILLION-DOLLAR ROOM.
AS YOU WISH.
Meanwhile, Bruce had just finished his patrol when Dick arrived home with some odd news...
BRUCE, THERE'S A STRANGE ARTICLE IN THE PAPER.
WHAT'S THAT?
AN UNKNOWN ARTIST'S SCULPTURE WAS PUT ON DISPLAY IN MRS. BANDA'S FAMOUS MILLION-DOLLAR ROOM.
WHAT'S SO STRANGE ABOUT THAT?
BUT DON'T YOU THINK IT'S WEIRD THAT SOMEONE SHE HOLDS IN ESTEEM ISN'T ALREADY FAMOUS?
NOT NECESSARILY. THERE ARE ALL SORTS OF PEOPLE IN THE WORLD, FAMOUS OR NOT, WHO MAKE WONDERFUL PIECES OF ART.

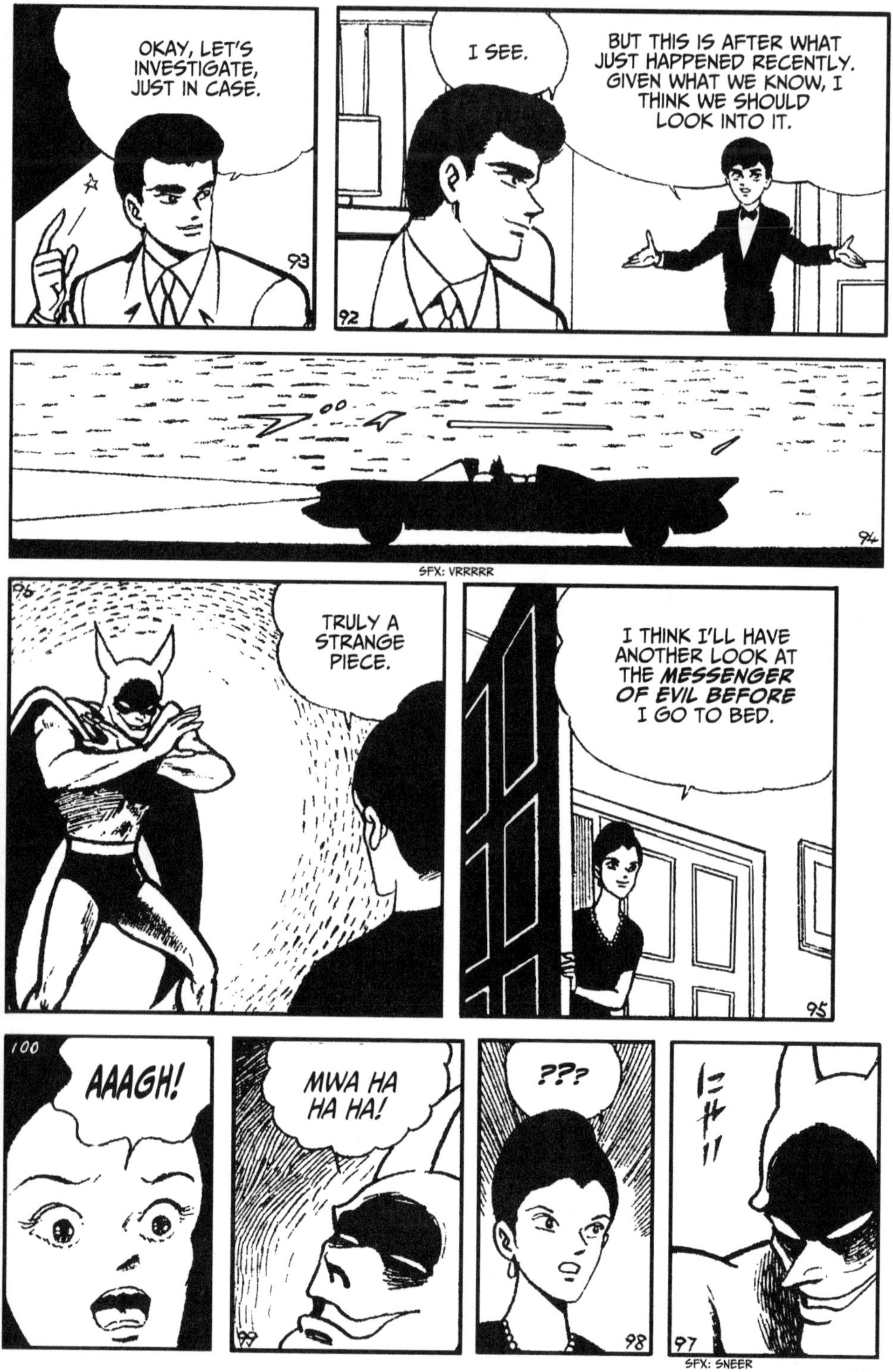
BUT THIS IS AFTER WHAT JUST HAPPENED RECENTLY. GIVEN WHAT WE KNOW, I THINK WE SHOULD LOOK INTO IT.
I SEE.
OKAY, LET'S INVESTIGATE, JUST IN CASE.
SFX: VRRRRR
I THINK I'LL HAVE ANOTHER LOOK AT THE *MESSENGER OF EVIL BEFORE* I GO TO BED.
TRULY A STRANGE PIECE.
SFX: SNEER
???
MWA HA HA HA!
AAAGH!

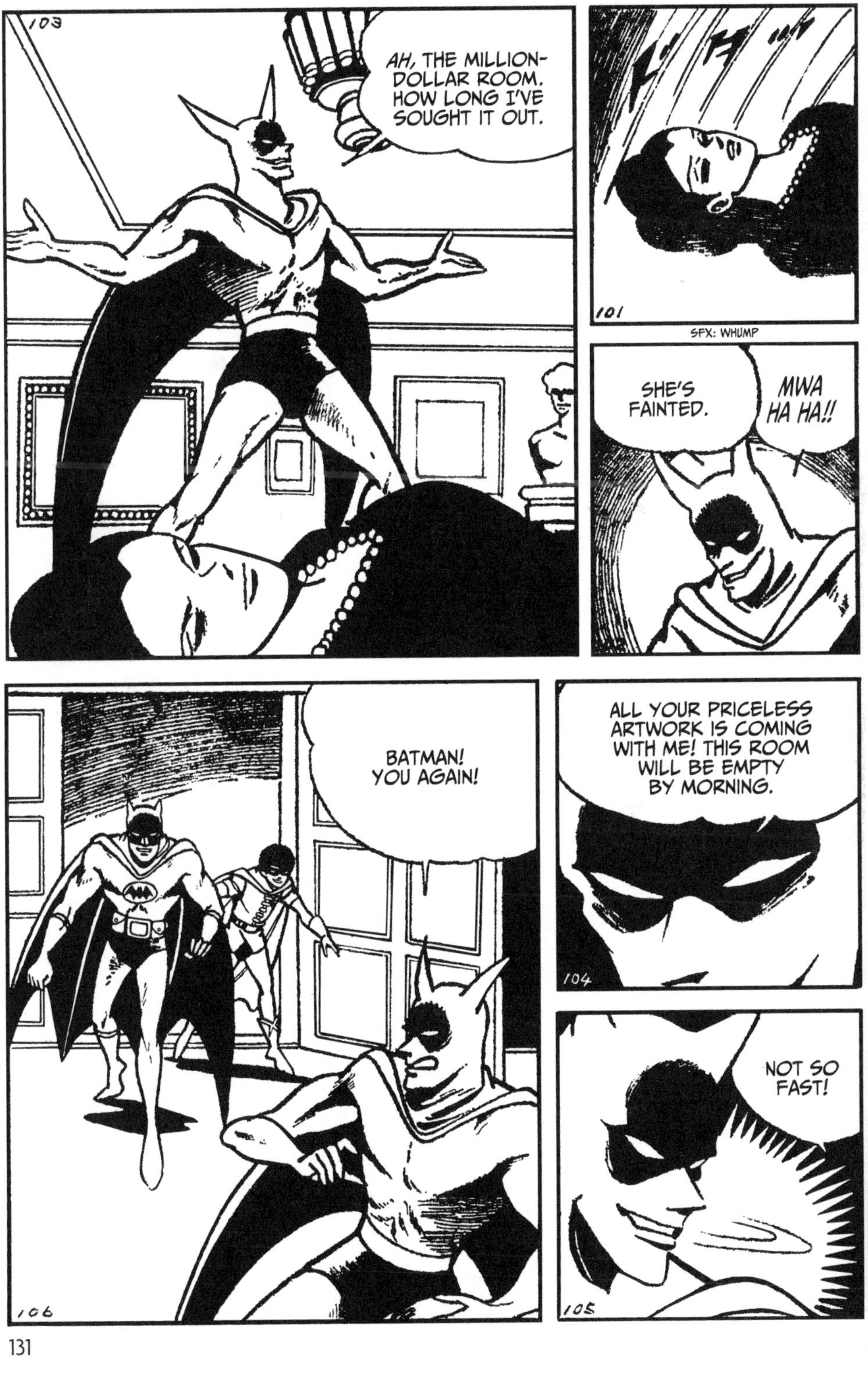
SFX: WHUMP
MWA HA HA!!
SHE'S FAINTED.
AH, THE MILLION-DOLLAR ROOM. HOW LONG I'VE SOUGHT IT OUT.
ALL YOUR PRICELESS ARTWORK IS COMING WITH ME! THIS ROOM WILL BE EMPTY BY MORNING.
NOT SO FAST!
BATMAN! YOU AGAIN!

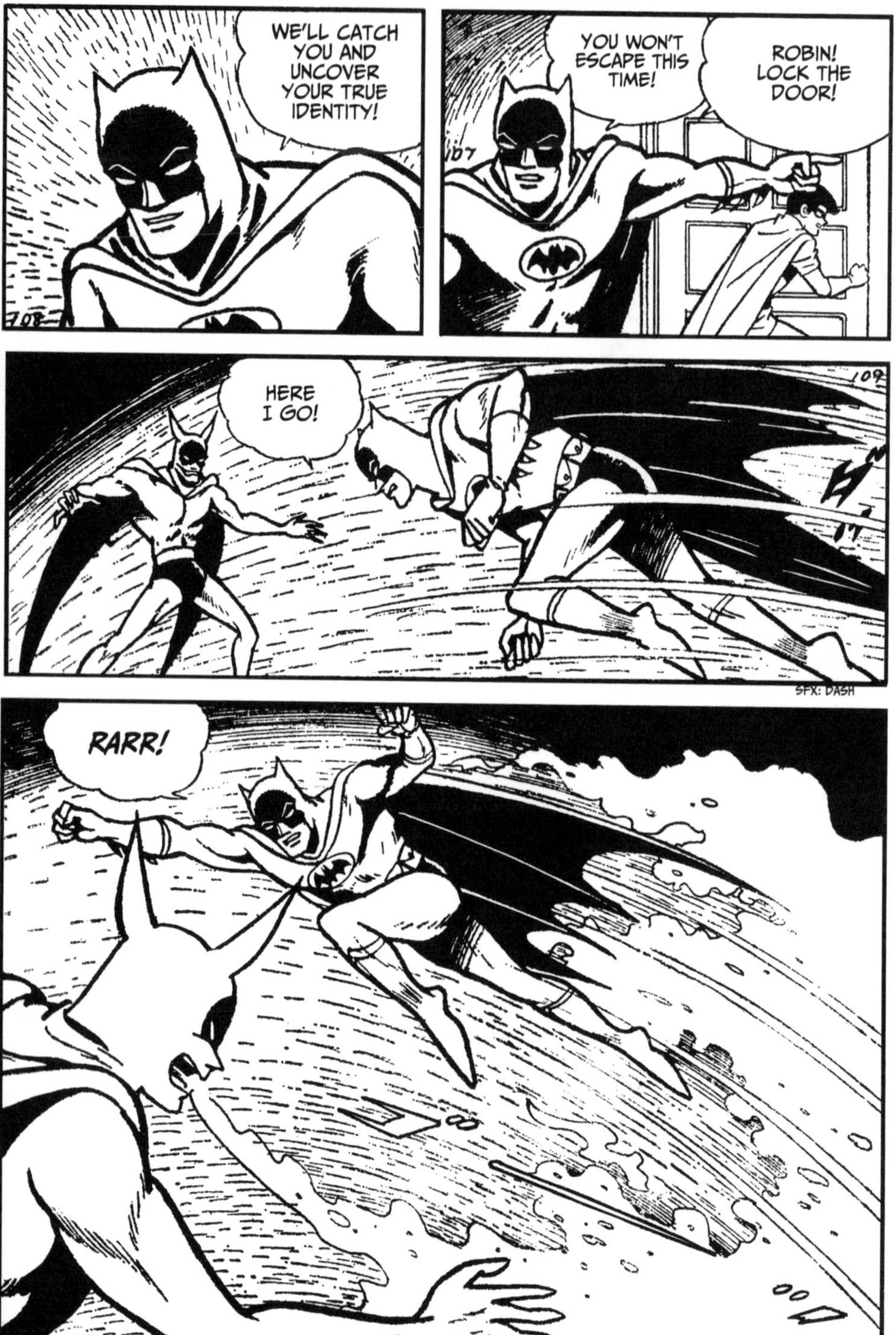
ROBIN! LOCK THE DOOR!
YOU WON'T ESCAPE THIS TIME!
WE'LL CATCH YOU AND UNCOVER YOUR TRUE IDENTITY!
HERE I GO!
SFX: DASH
RARR!
SFX: BLOOSH

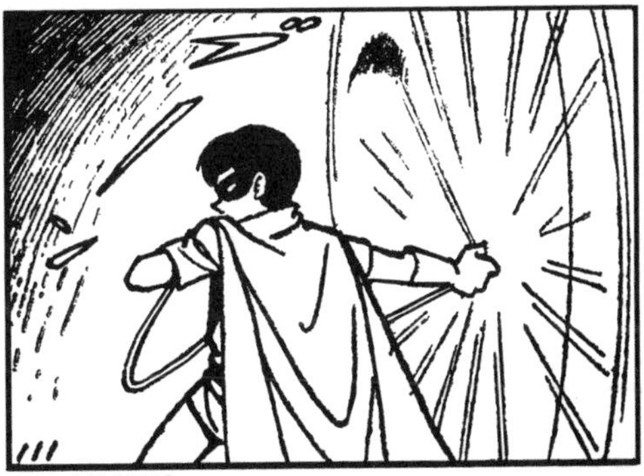

SFX: WHOOP

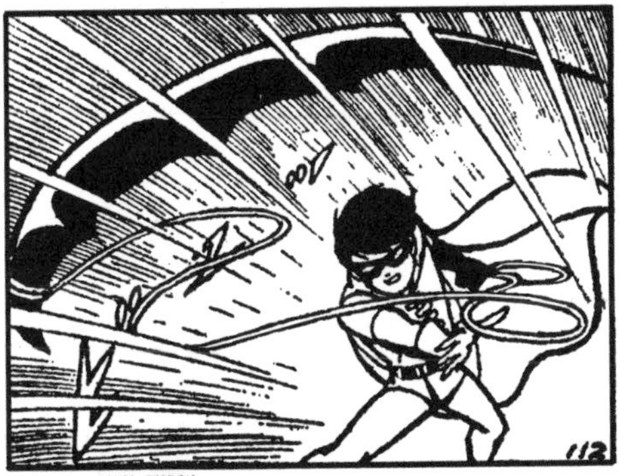

SFX: FWISH

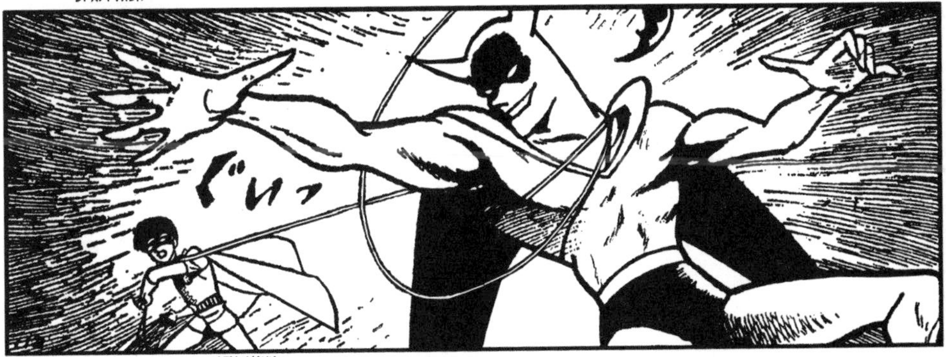

SFX: YANK

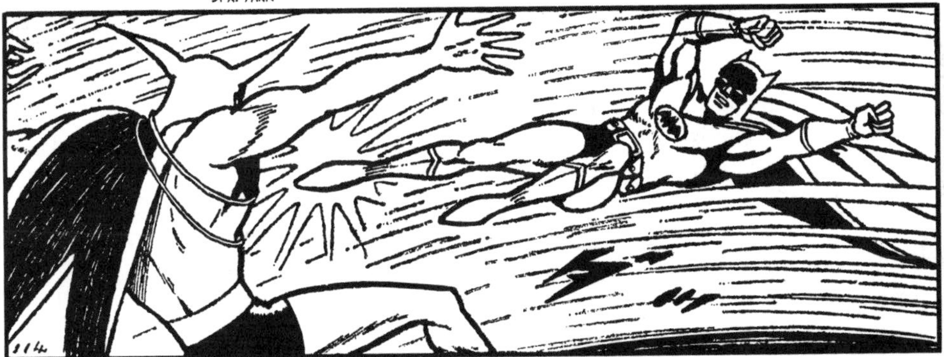

SFX: WHUD

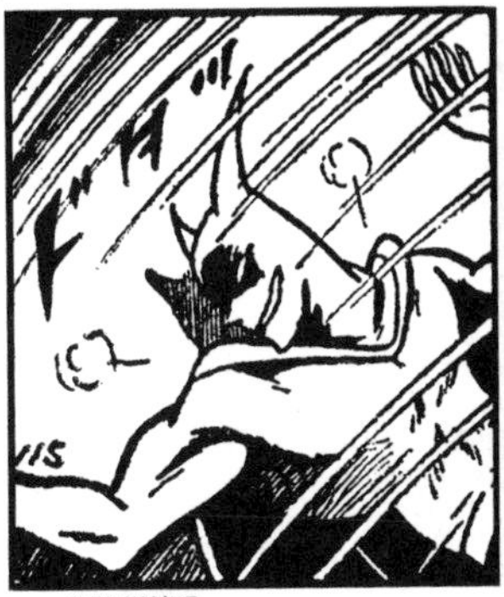

SFX: WHUMP

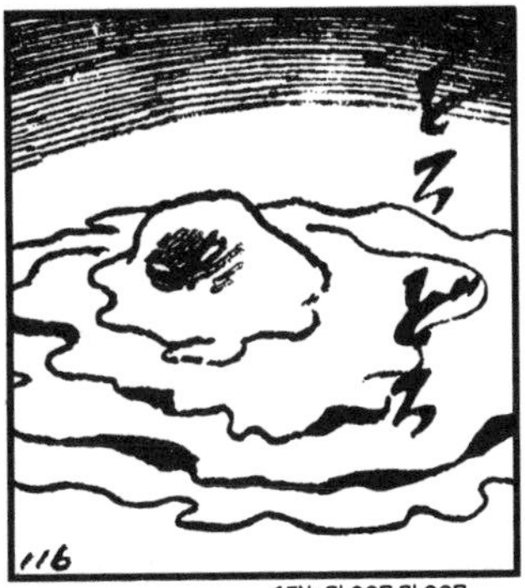

SFX: BLOOP BLOOP

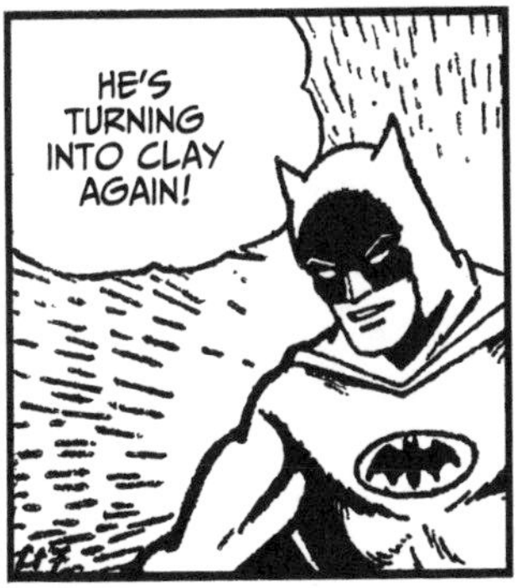
HE'S TURNING INTO CLAY AGAIN!

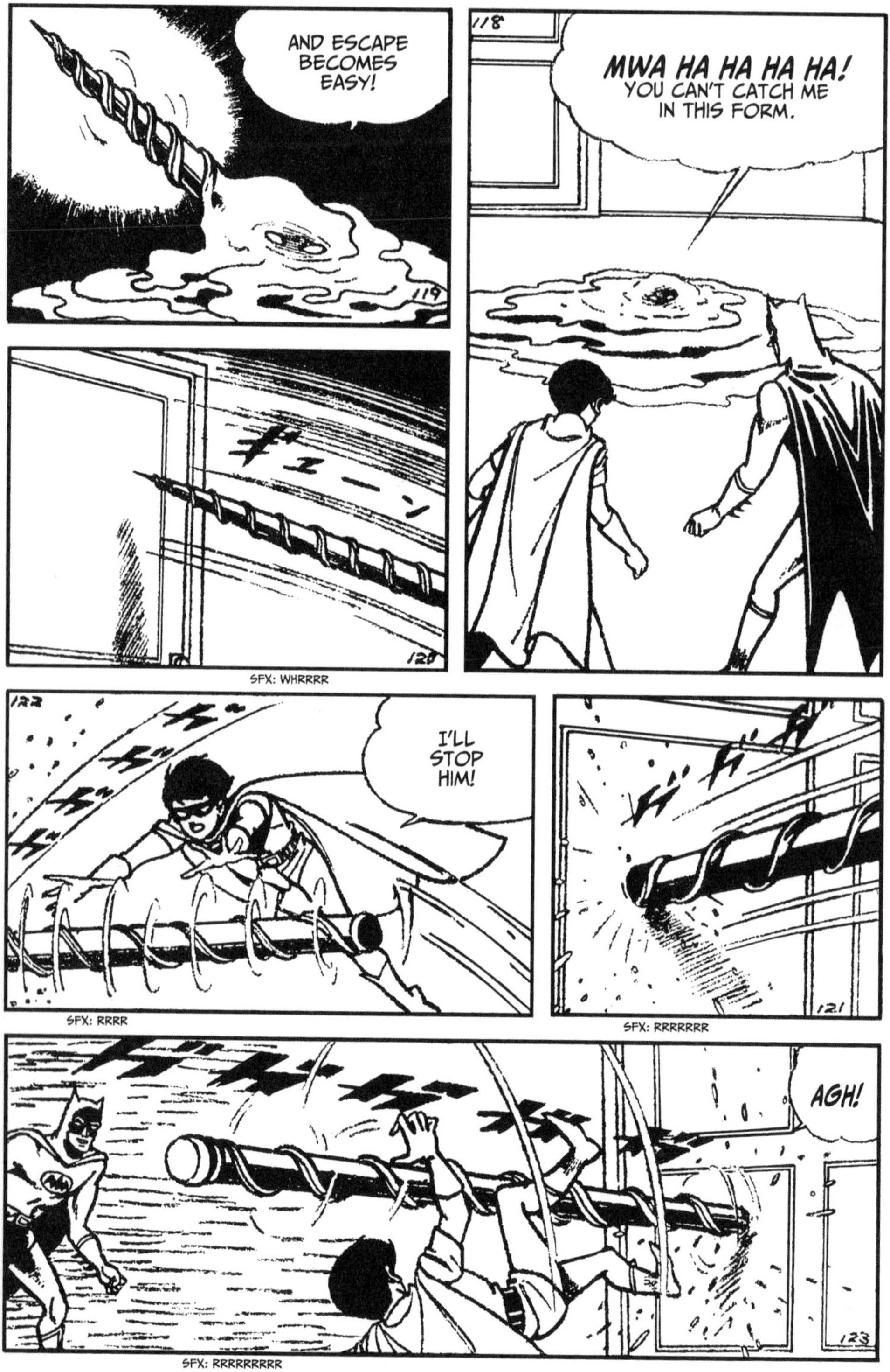
MWA HA HA HA HA! YOU CAN'T CATCH ME IN THIS FORM.
AND ESCAPE BECOMES EASY!
SFX: WHRRRR
SFX: RRRRRRR
I'LL STOP HIM!
SFX: RRRR
AGH!
SFX: RRRRRRRRR

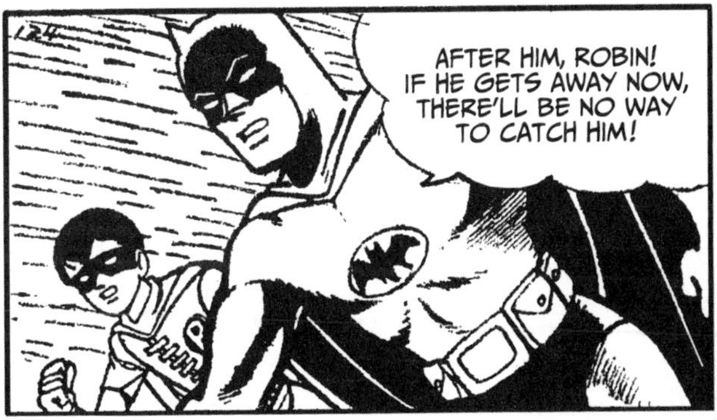
AFTER HIM, ROBIN! IF HE GETS AWAY NOW, THERE'LL BE NO WAY TO CATCH HIM!

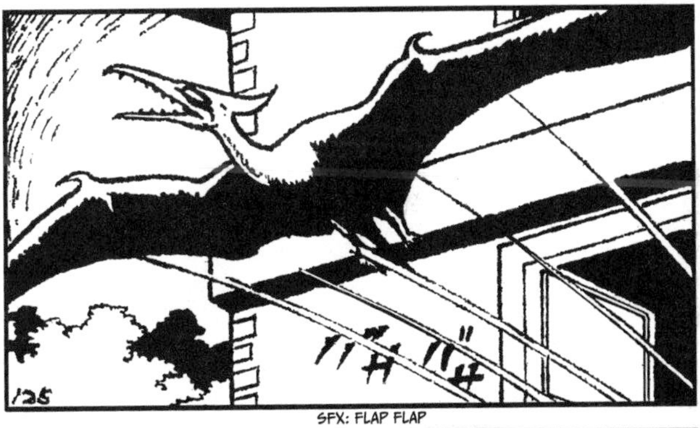

SFX: FLAP FLAP

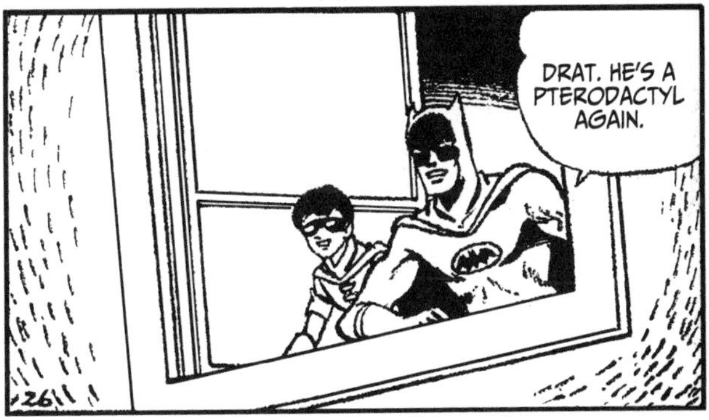
DRAT. HE'S A PTERODACTYL AGAIN.

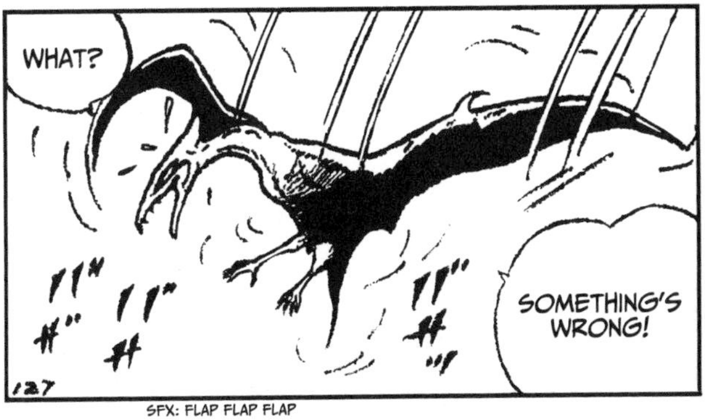
WHAT?
SOMETHING'S WRONG!

SFX: FLAP FLAP FLAP

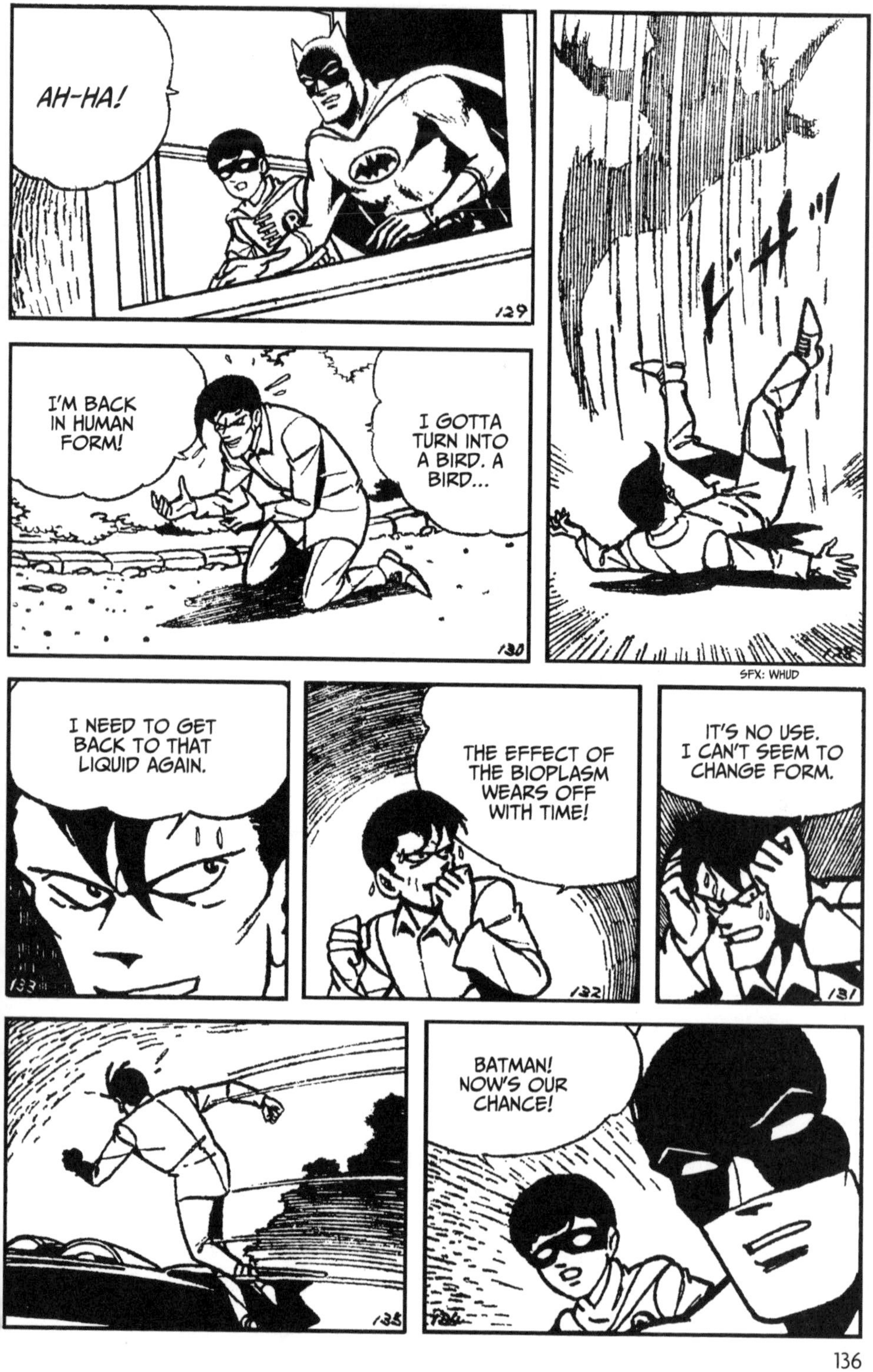
SFX: WHUD
AH-HA!
I GOTTA TURN INTO A BIRD. A BIRD...
I'M BACK IN HUMAN FORM!
IT'S NO USE. I CAN'T SEEM TO CHANGE FORM.
THE EFFECT OF THE BIOPLASM WEARS OFF WITH TIME!
I NEED TO GET BACK TO THAT LIQUID AGAIN.
BATMAN! NOW'S OUR CHANCE!

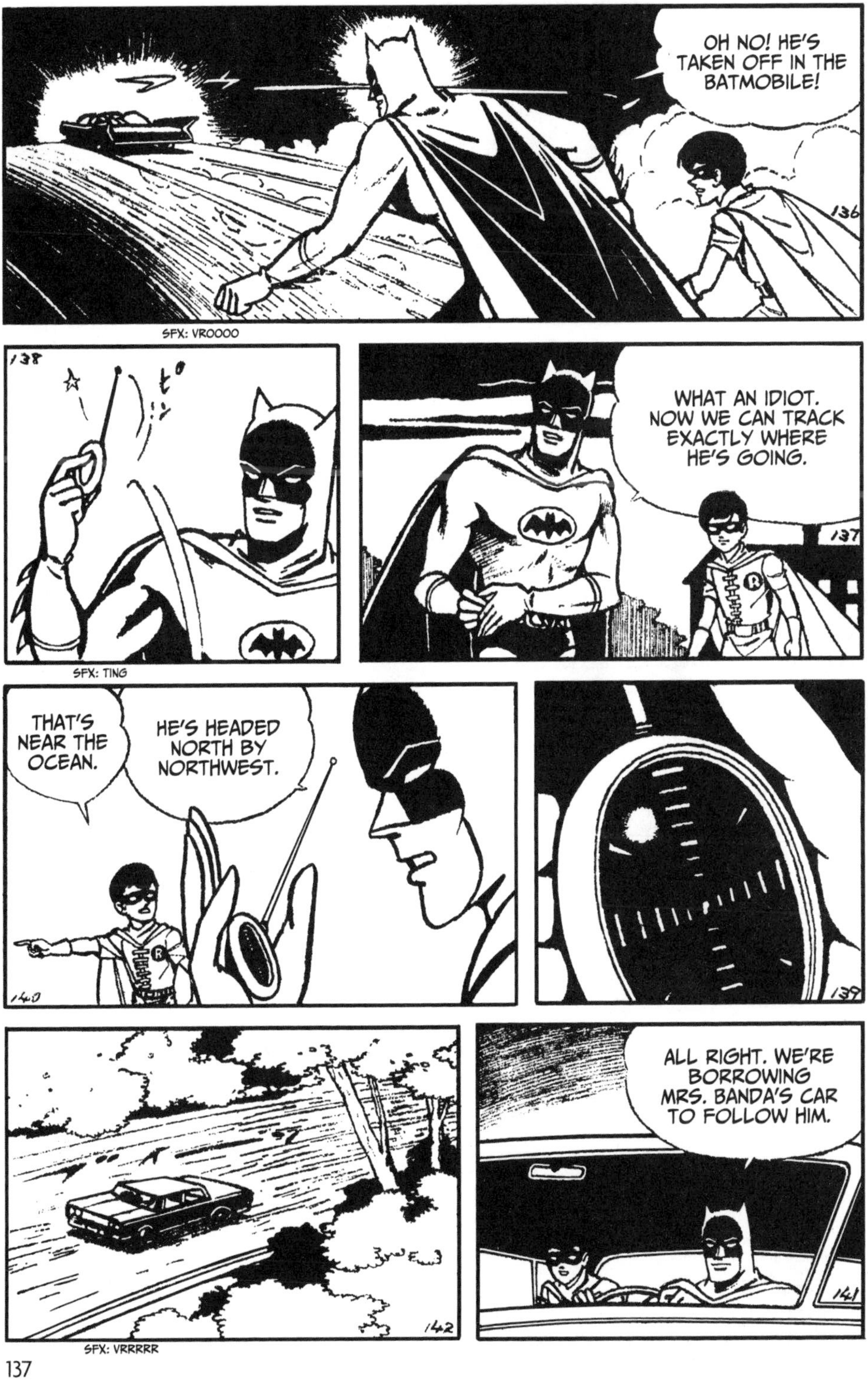
OH NO! HE'S TAKEN OFF IN THE BATMOBILE!
SFX: VROOOO
WHAT AN IDIOT. NOW WE CAN TRACK EXACTLY WHERE HE'S GOING.
SFX: TING
HE'S HEADED NORTH BY NORTHWEST.
THAT'S NEAR THE OCEAN.
ALL RIGHT. WE'RE BORROWING MRS. BANDA'S CAR TO FOLLOW HIM.
SFX: VRRRRR

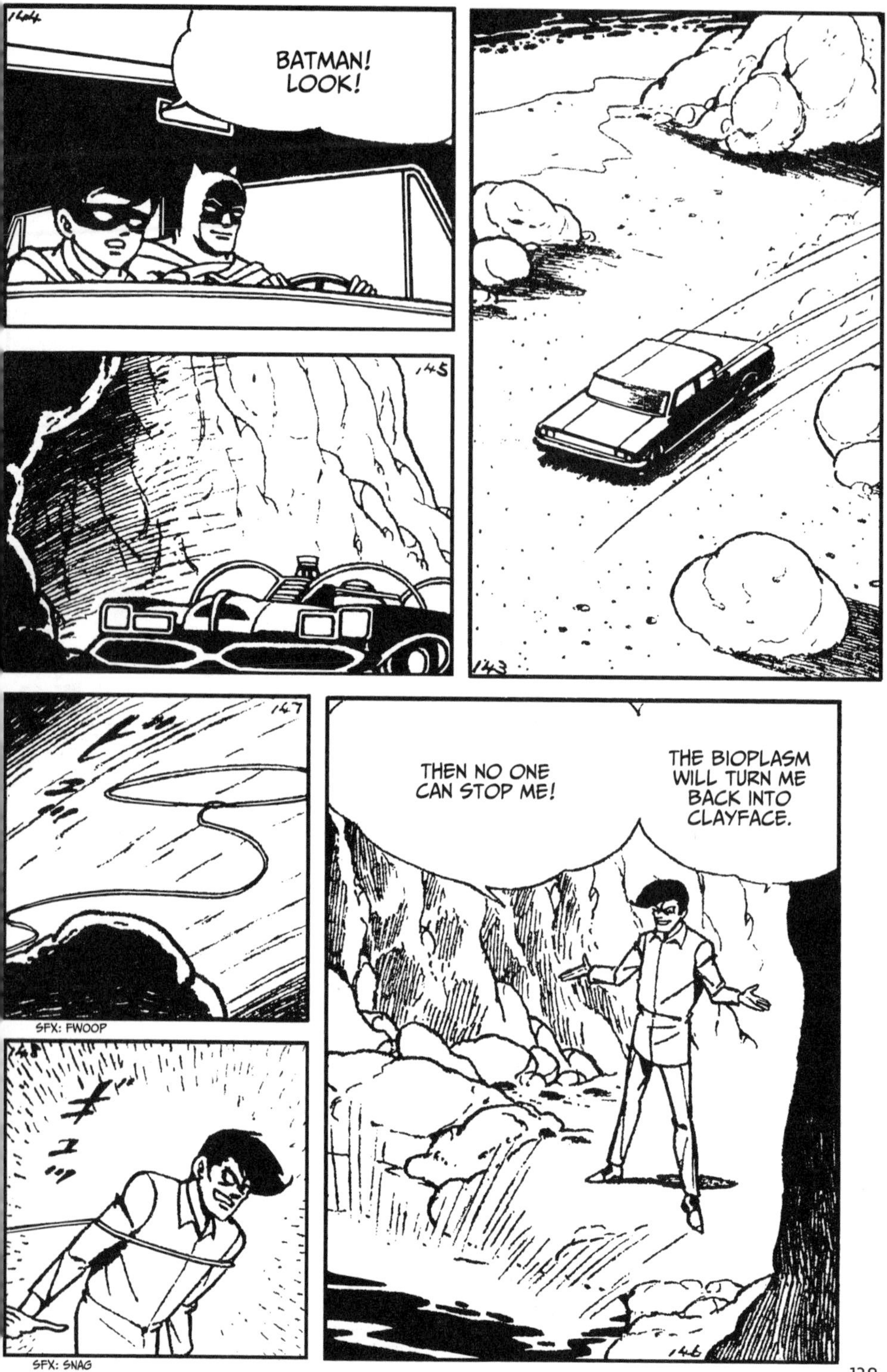
BATMAN! LOOK!
THE BIOPLASM WILL TURN ME BACK INTO CLAYFACE.
THEN NO ONE CAN STOP ME!
SFX: FWOOP
SFX: SNAG

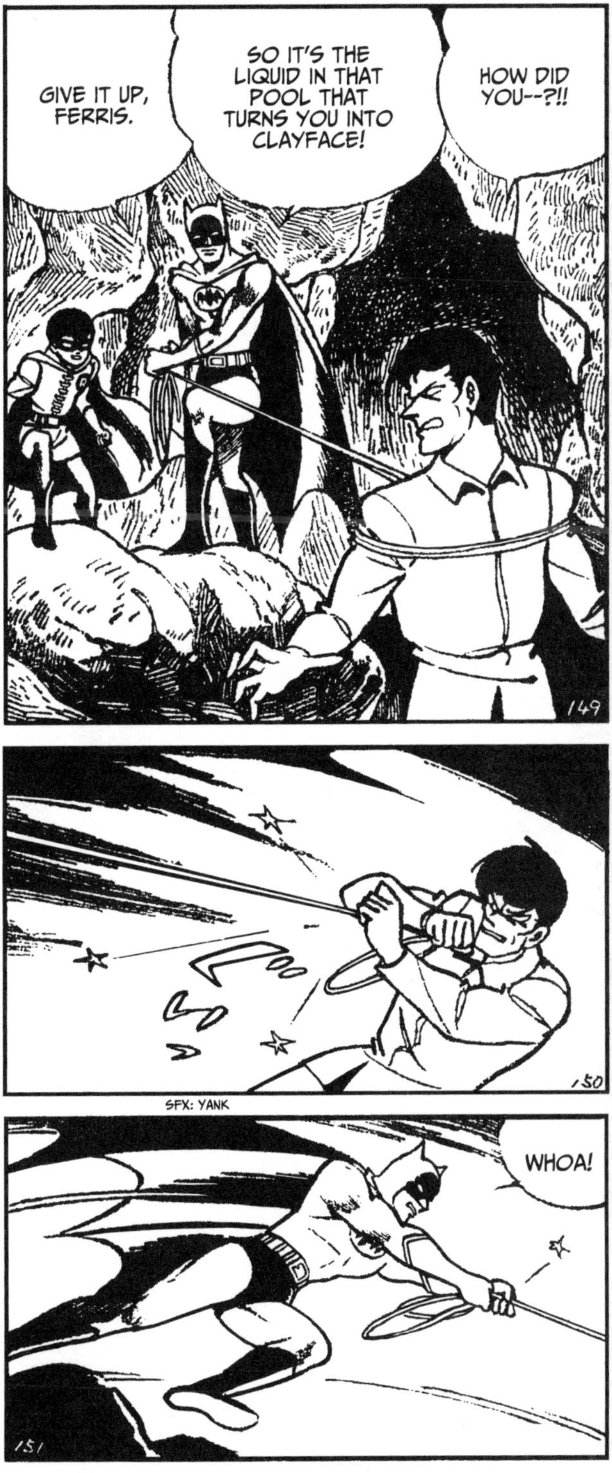
HOW DID YOU--?!!
SO IT'S THE LIQUID IN THAT POOL THAT TURNS YOU INTO CLAYFACE!
GIVE IT UP, FERRIS.
SFX: YANK
WHOA!

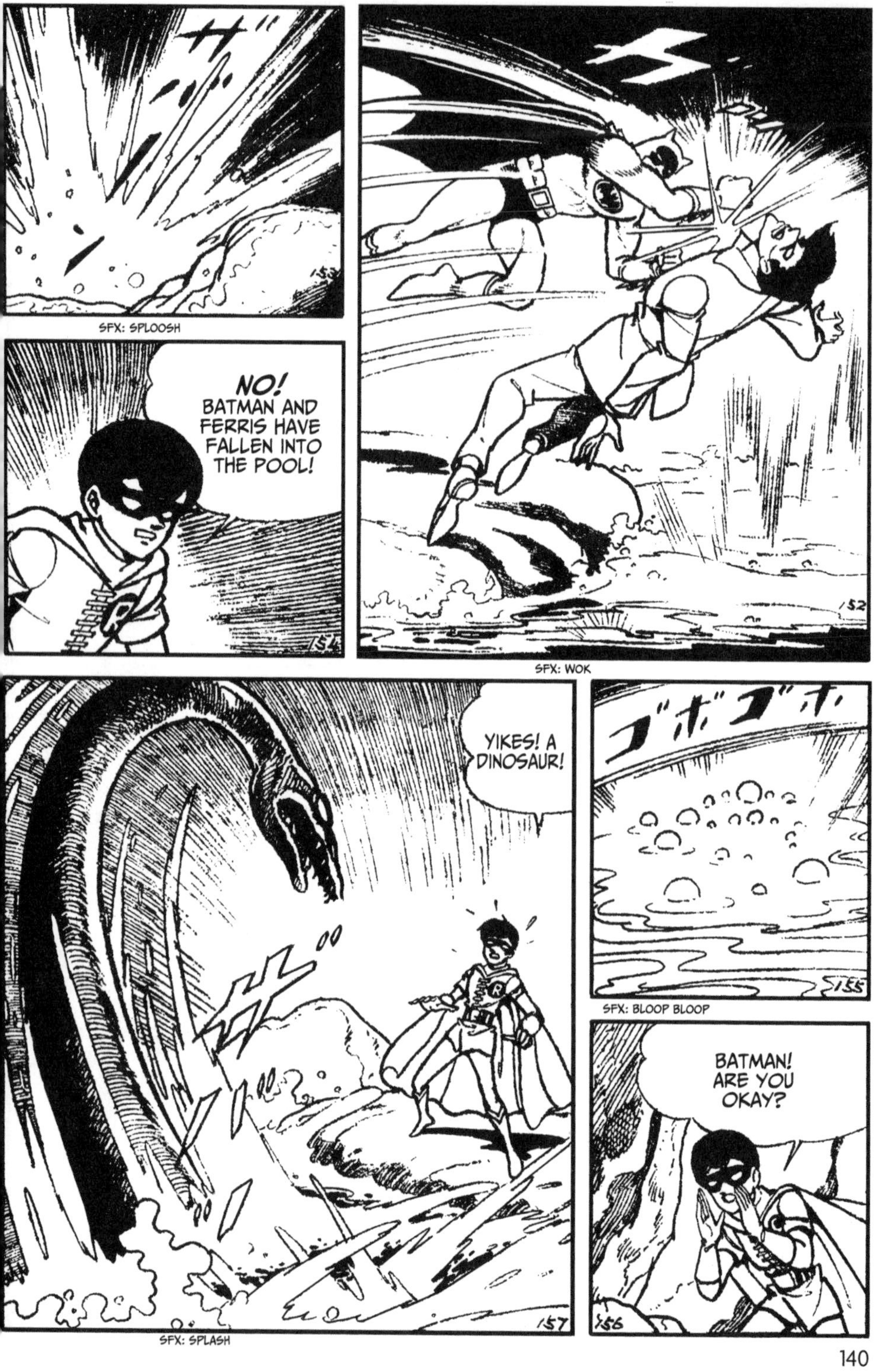
SFX: WOK
SFX: SPLOOSH
NO! BATMAN AND FERRIS HAVE FALLEN INTO THE POOL!
SFX: BLOOP BLOOP
BATMAN! ARE YOU OKAY?
YIKES! A DINOSAUR!
SFX: SPLASH

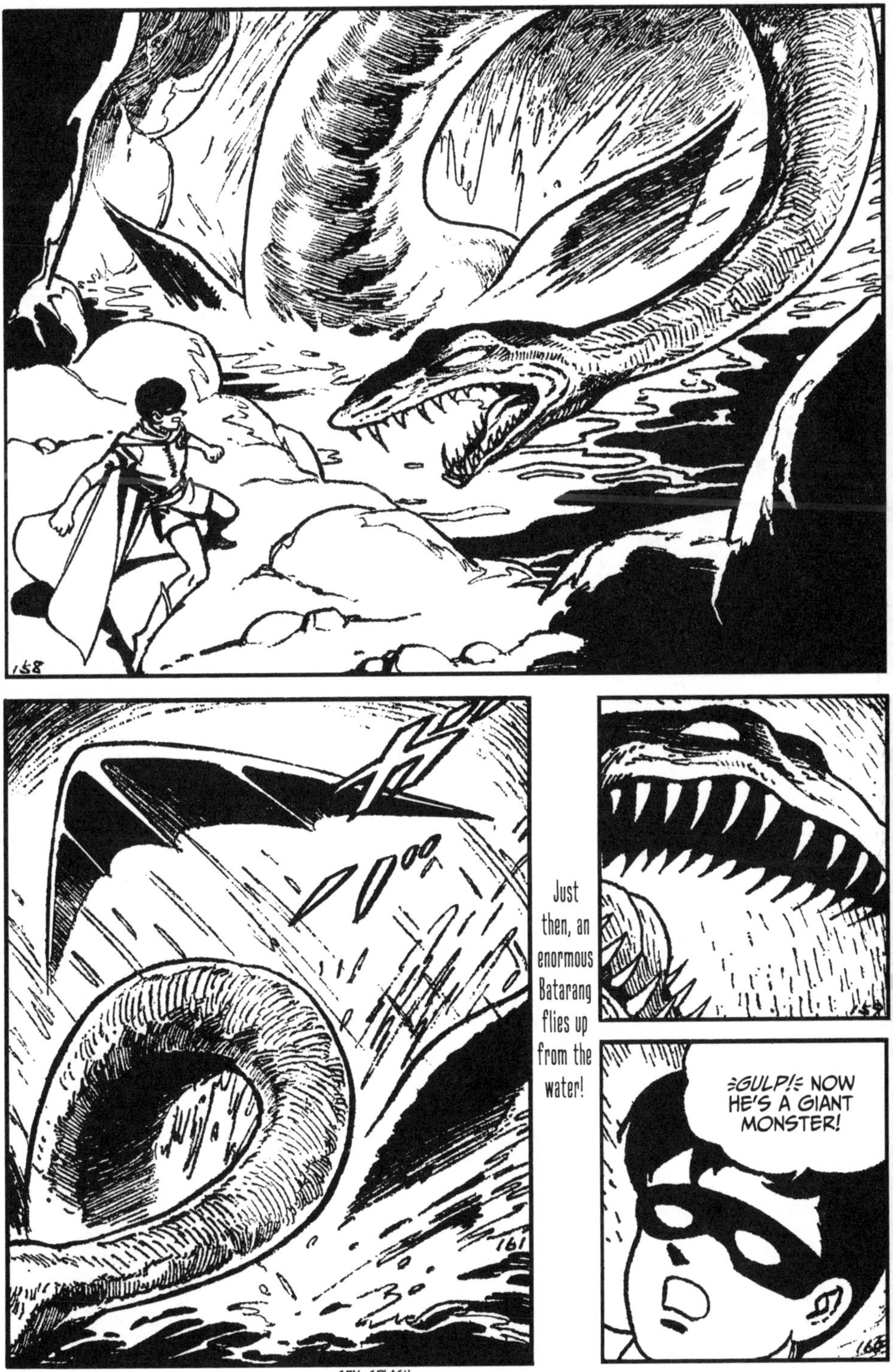
≈GULP!≈ NOW HE'S A GIANT MONSTER!
Just then, an enormous Batarang flies up from the water!

SFX: SPLASH

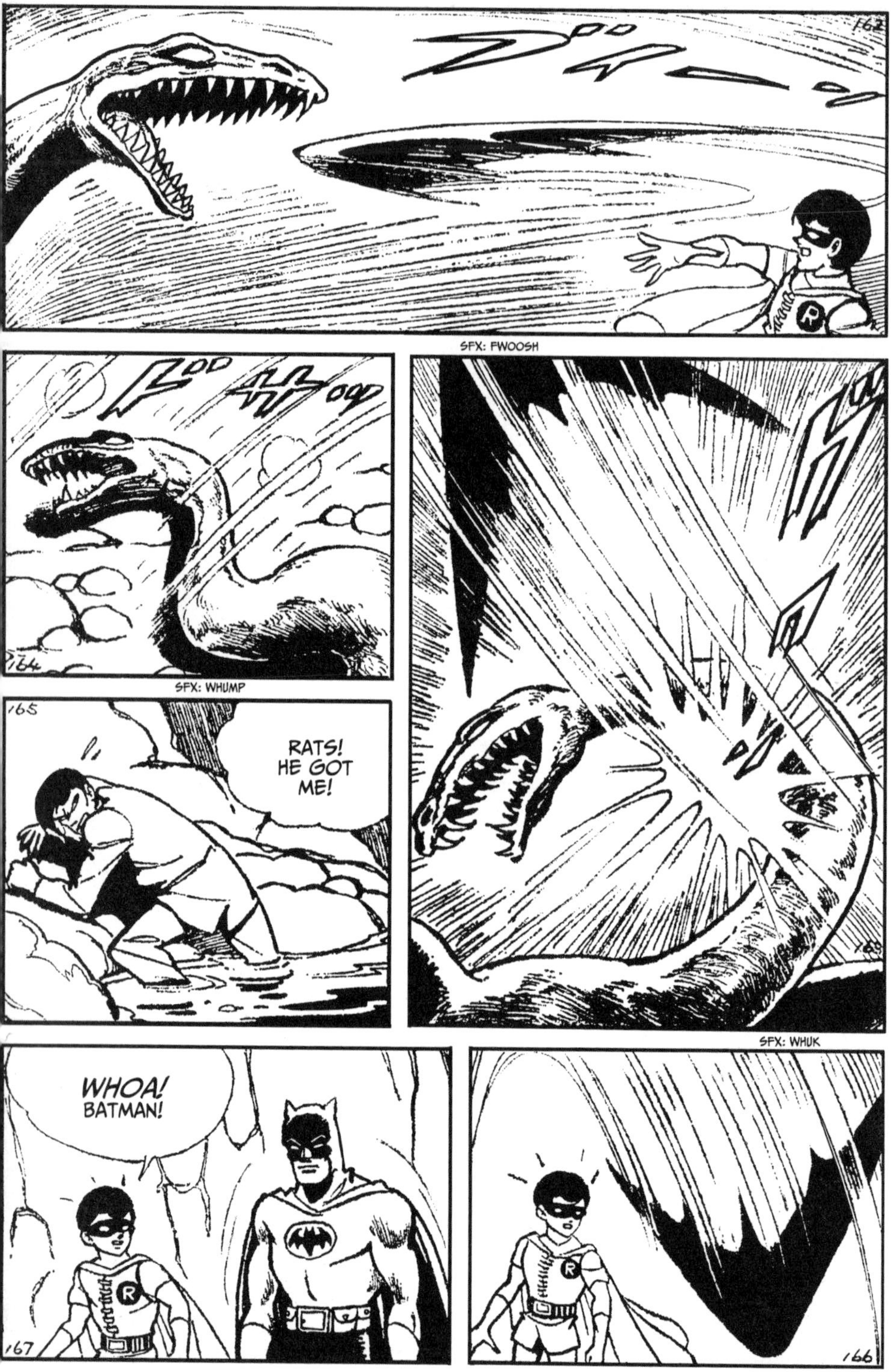
SFX: FWOOSH
SFX: WHUK
SFX: WHUMP
RATS! HE GOT ME!
WHOA! BATMAN!

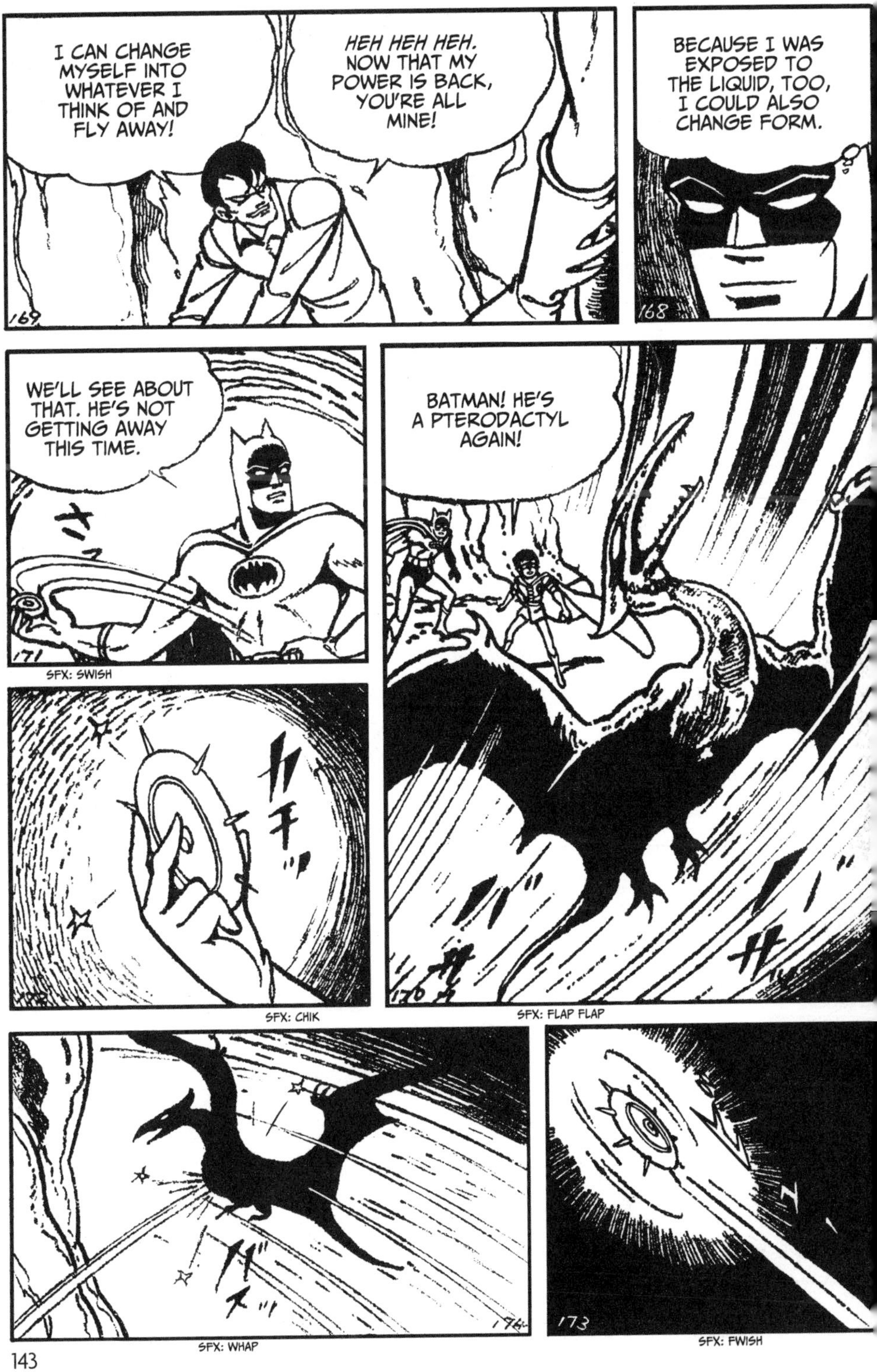
BECAUSE I WAS EXPOSED TO THE LIQUID, TOO, I COULD ALSO CHANGE FORM.
HEH HEH HEH. NOW THAT MY POWER IS BACK, YOU'RE ALL MINE!
I CAN CHANGE MYSELF INTO WHATEVER I THINK OF AND FLY AWAY!
BATMAN! HE'S A PTERODACTYL AGAIN!
SFX: FLAP FLAP
WE'LL SEE ABOUT THAT. HE'S NOT GETTING AWAY THIS TIME.
SFX: SWISH
SFX: CHIK
SFX: FWISH
SFX: WHAP

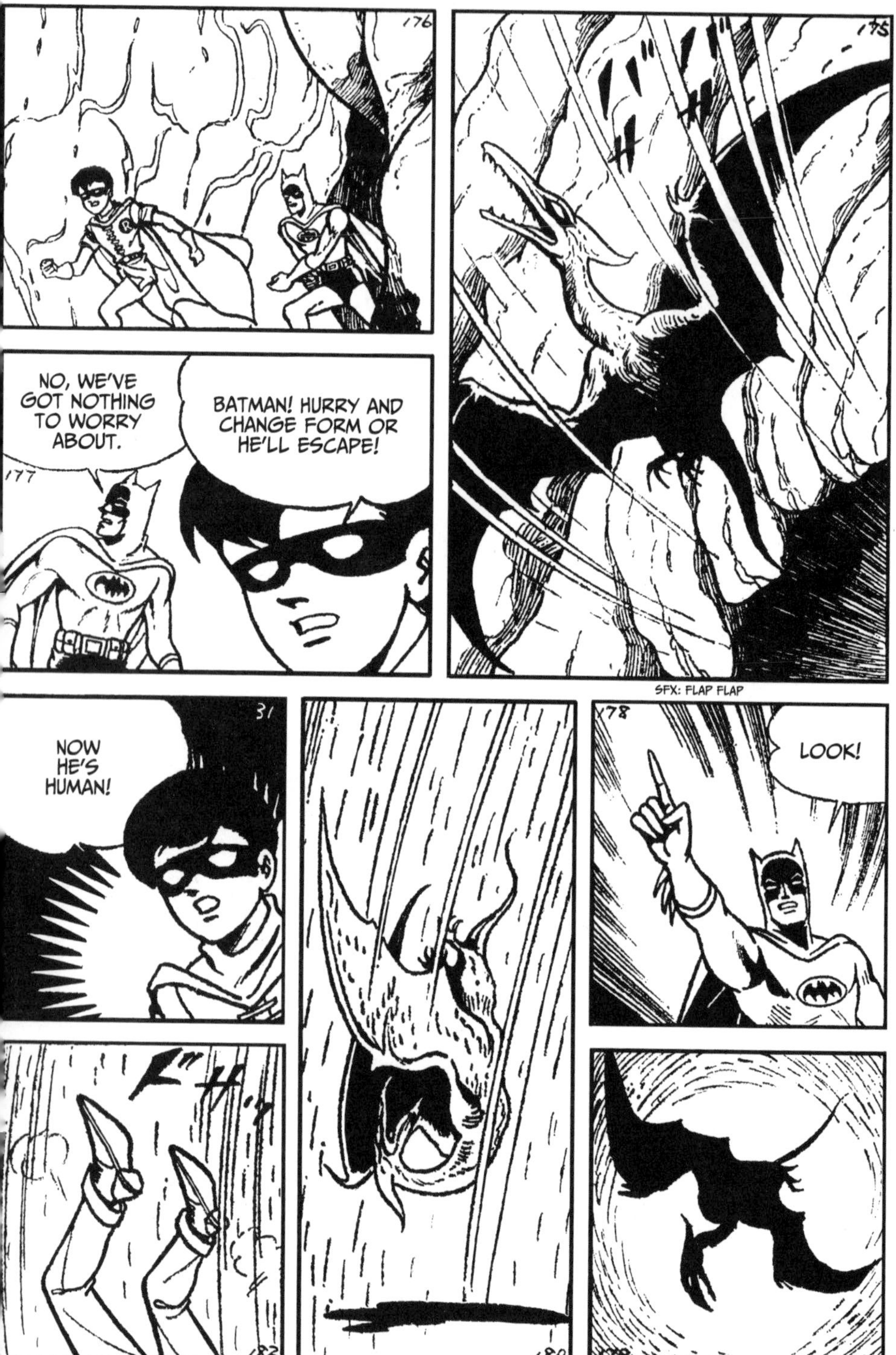
SFX: FLAP FLAP
BATMAN! HURRY AND CHANGE FORM OR HE'LL ESCAPE!
NO, WE'VE GOT NOTHING TO WORRY ABOUT.
LOOK!
NOW HE'S HUMAN!
SFX: WHUMP

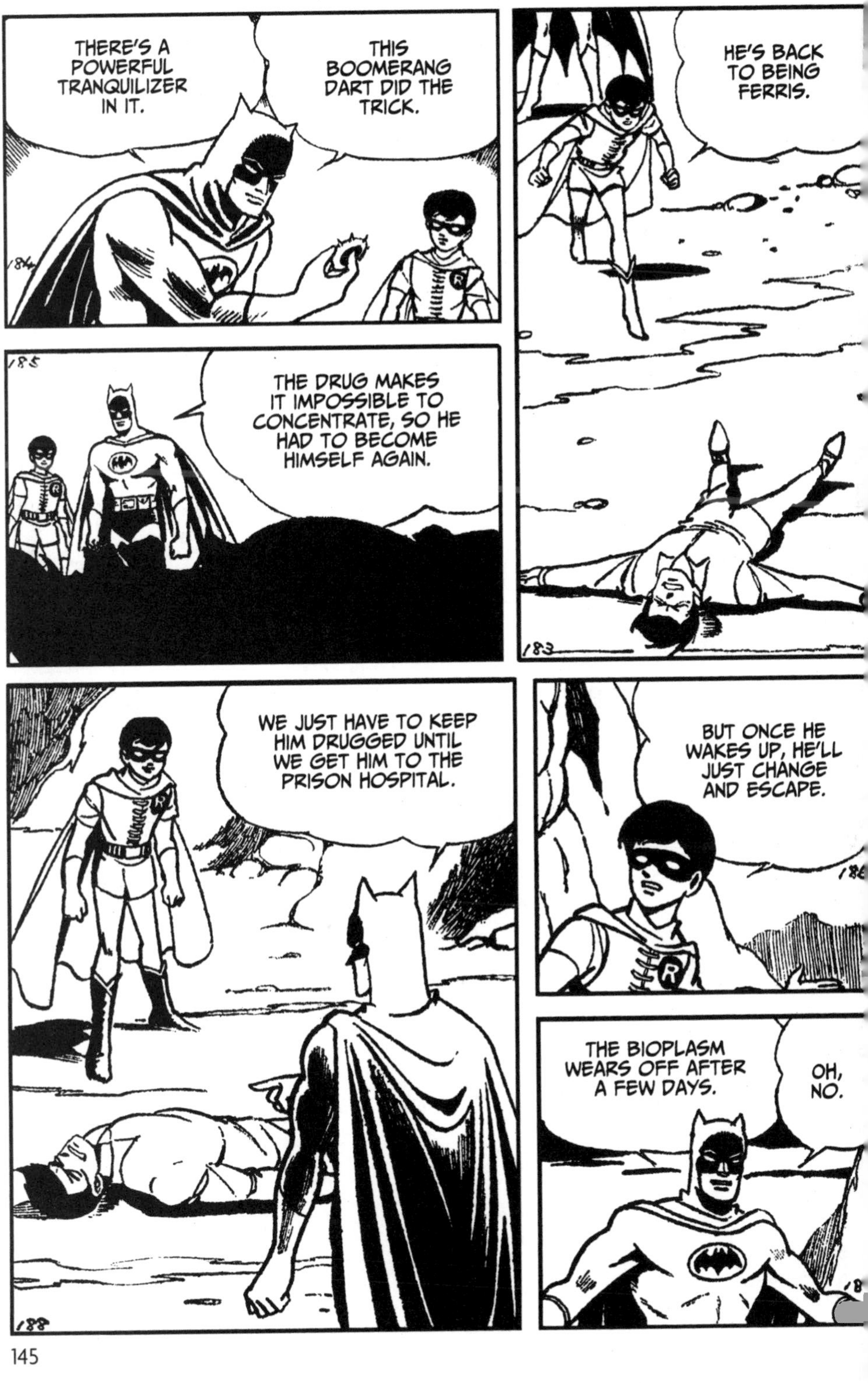
HE'S BACK TO BEING FERRIS.
THIS BOOMERANG DART DID THE TRICK.
THERE'S A POWERFUL TRANQUILIZER IN IT.
THE DRUG MAKES IT IMPOSSIBLE TO CONCENTRATE, SO HE HAD TO BECOME HIMSELF AGAIN.
BUT ONCE HE WAKES UP, HE'LL JUST CHANGE AND ESCAPE.
OH, NO.
THE BIOPLASM WEARS OFF AFTER A FEW DAYS.
WE JUST HAVE TO KEEP HIM DRUGGED UNTIL WE GET HIM TO THE PRISON HOSPITAL.

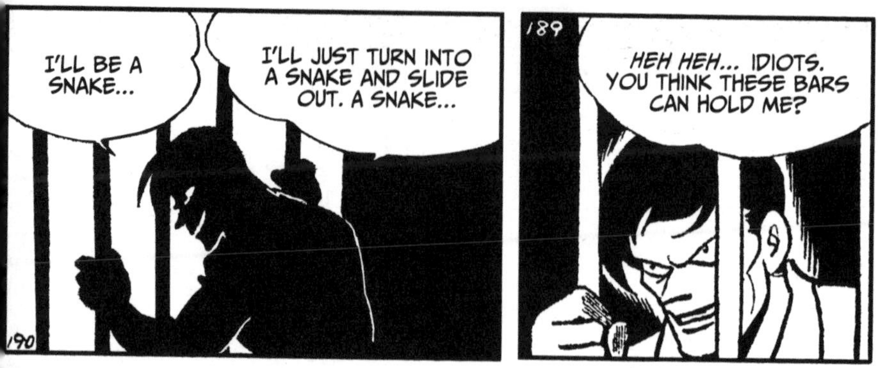
189
HEH HEH... IDIOTS. YOU THINK THESE BARS CAN HOLD ME?
I'LL JUST TURN INTO A SNAKE AND SLIDE OUT. A SNAKE...
I'LL BE A SNAKE...
190

Eventually, Ferris wakes up in a jail cell...

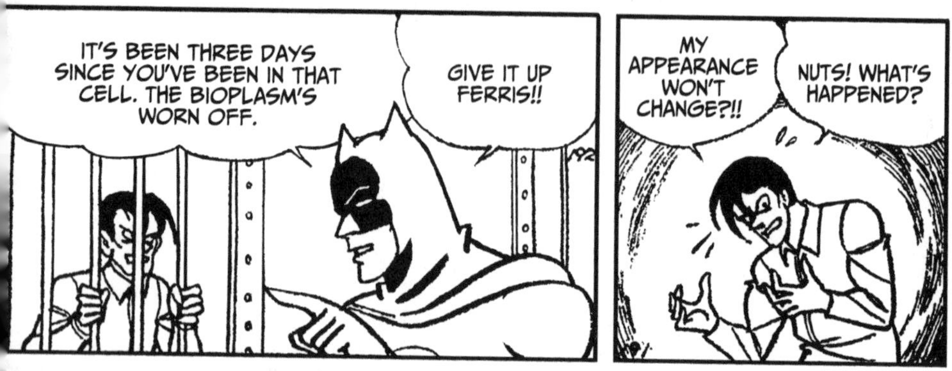
NUTS! WHAT'S HAPPENED?
MY APPEARANCE WON'T CHANGE?!!
GIVE IT UP FERRIS!!
IT'S BEEN THREE DAYS SINCE YOU'VE BEEN IN THAT CELL. THE BIOPLASM'S WORN OFF.
192

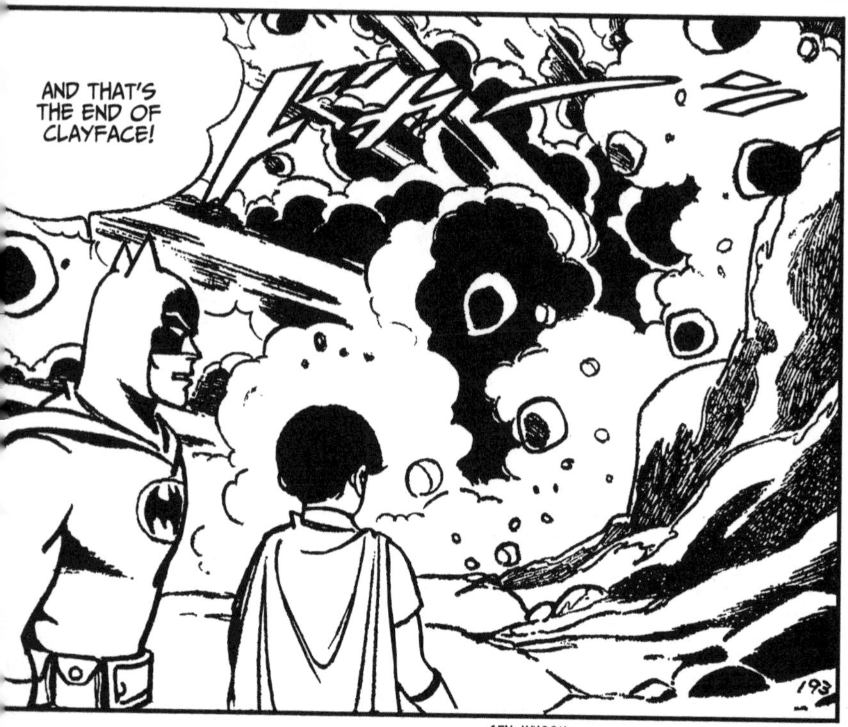
AND THAT'S THE END OF CLAYFACE!
193

SFX: WHOOM

And so, Batman and Robin destroyed the cave by the mysterious lake, and its water evaporated like fog.

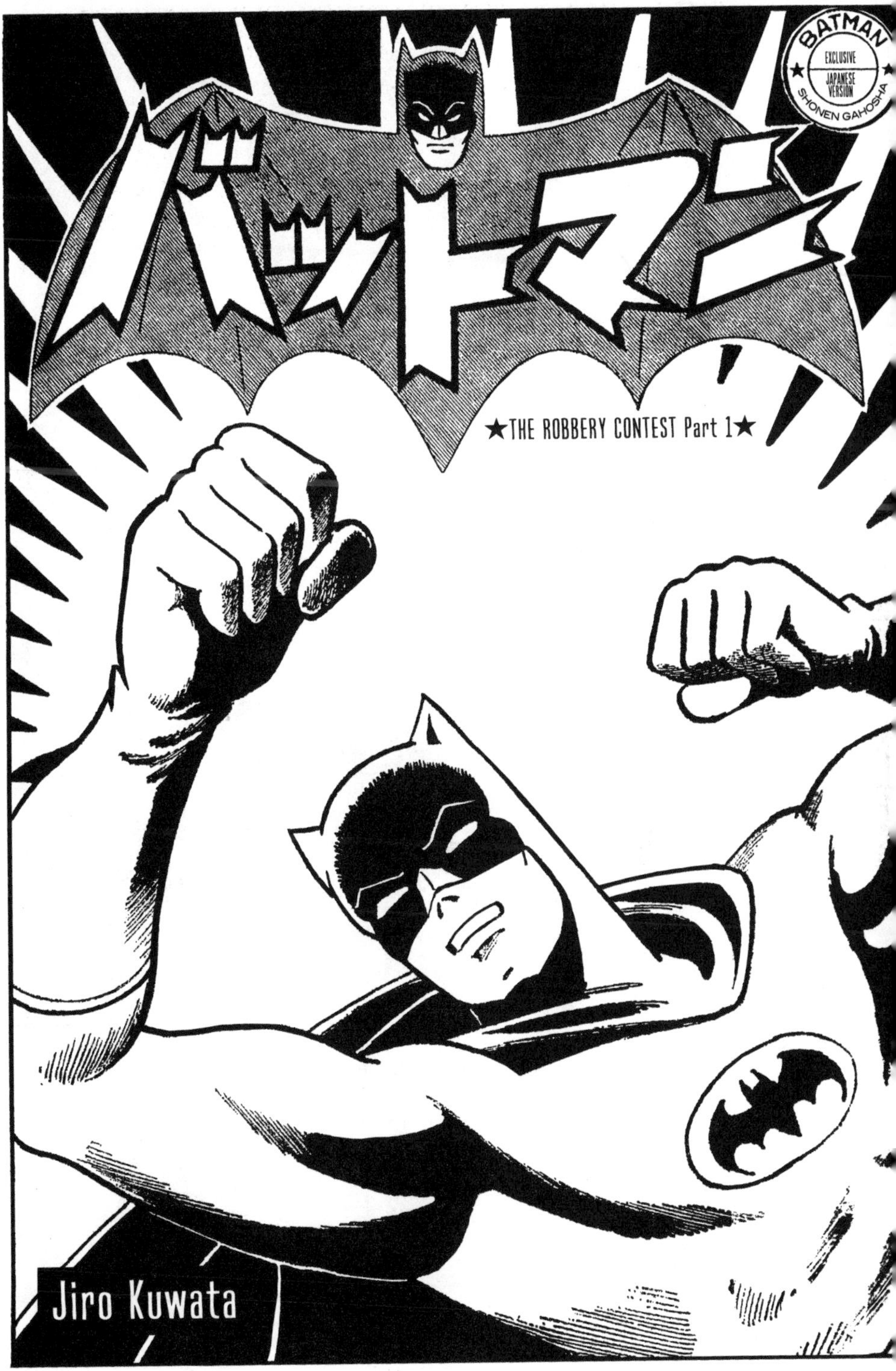

BATMAN
EXCLUSIVE
JAPANESE VERSION
SHONEN GAHOSHA
バットマン
★THE ROBBERY CONTEST Part 1★
Jiro Kuwata

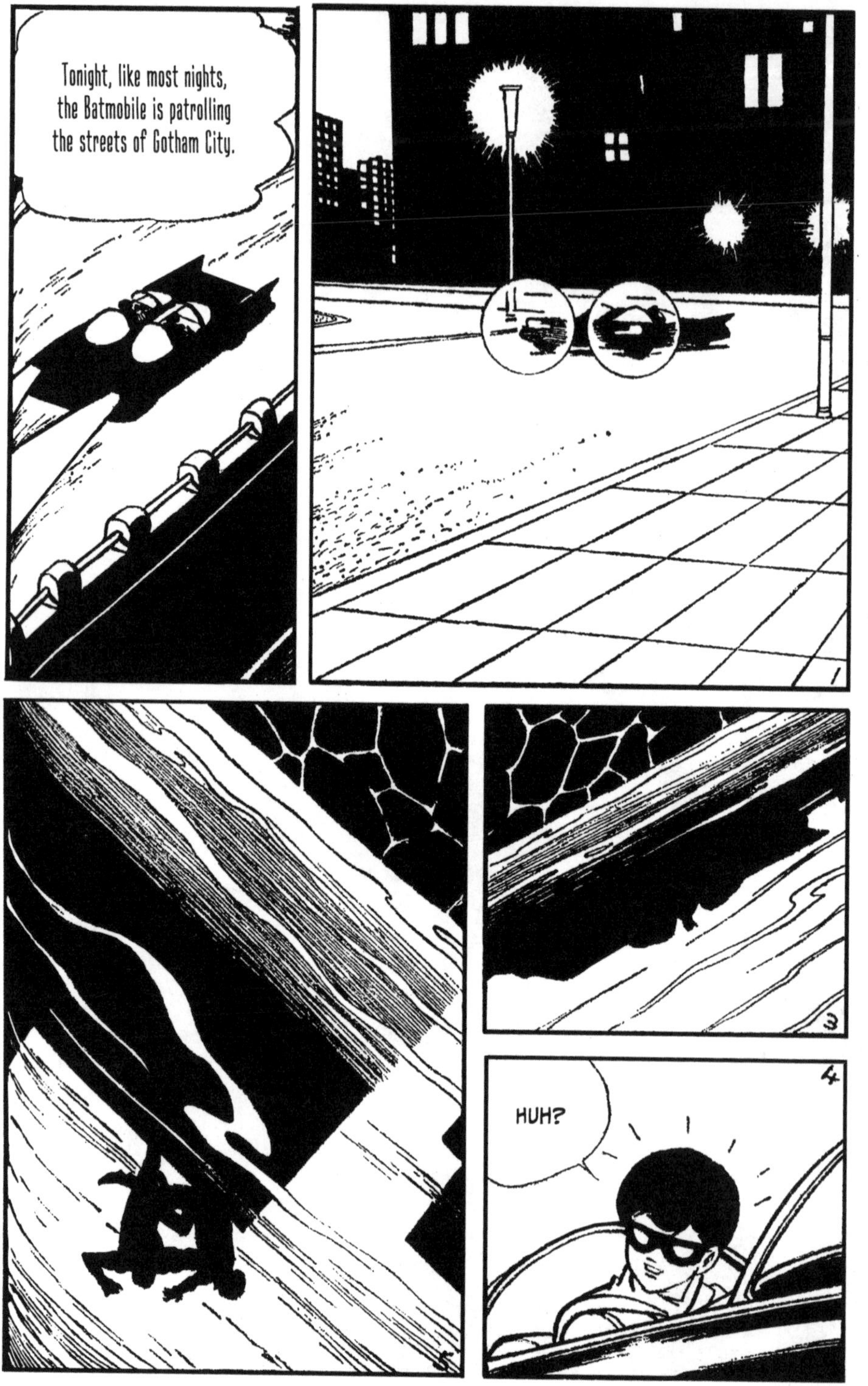
Tonight, like most nights, the Batmobile is patrolling the streets of Gotham City.
HUH?

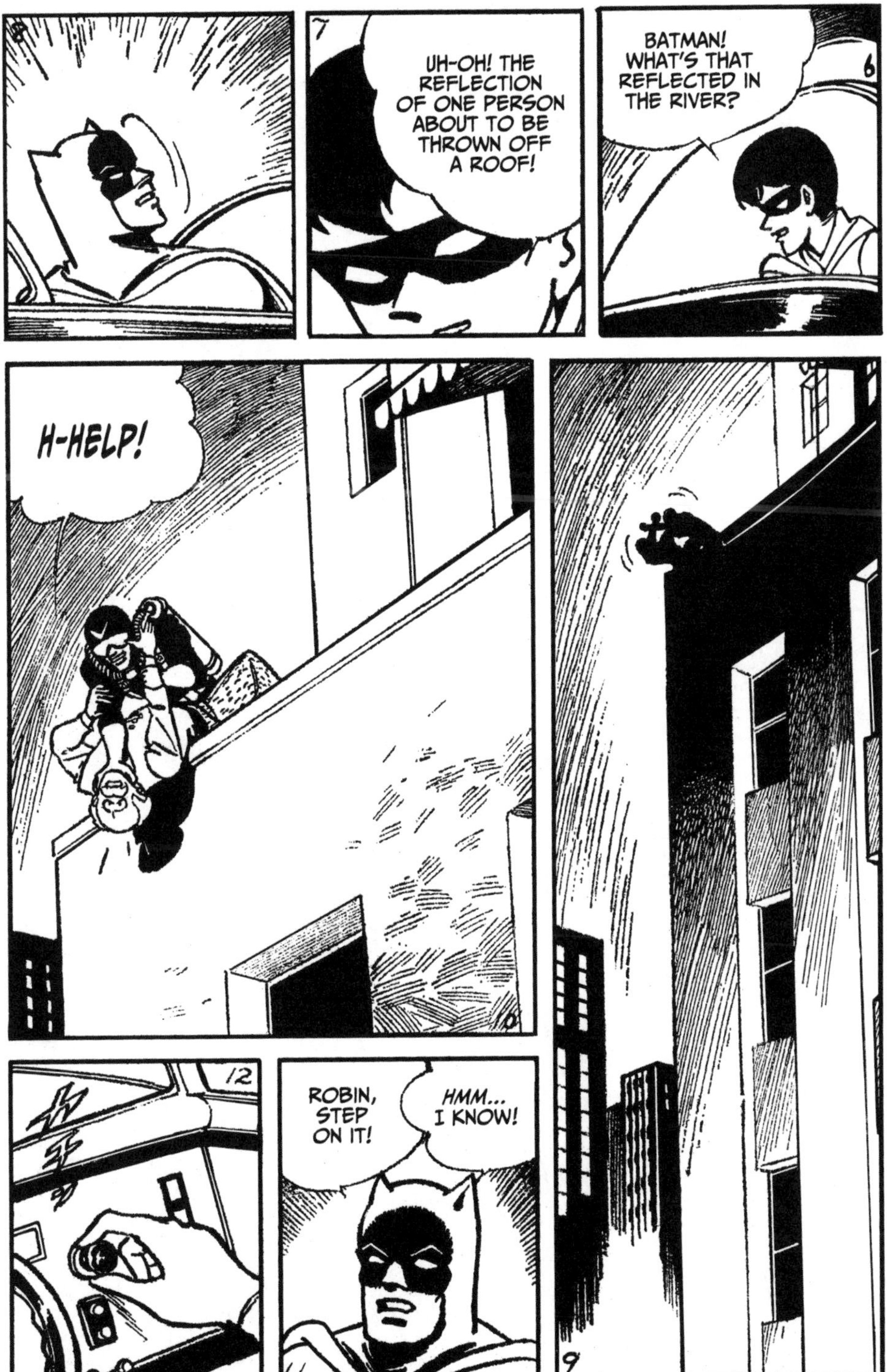
BATMAN! WHAT'S THAT REFLECTED IN THE RIVER?
UH-OH! THE REFLECTION OF ONE PERSON ABOUT TO BE THROWN OFF A ROOF!
H-HELP!
HMM... I KNOW!
ROBIN, STEP ON IT!

SFX: KLIK

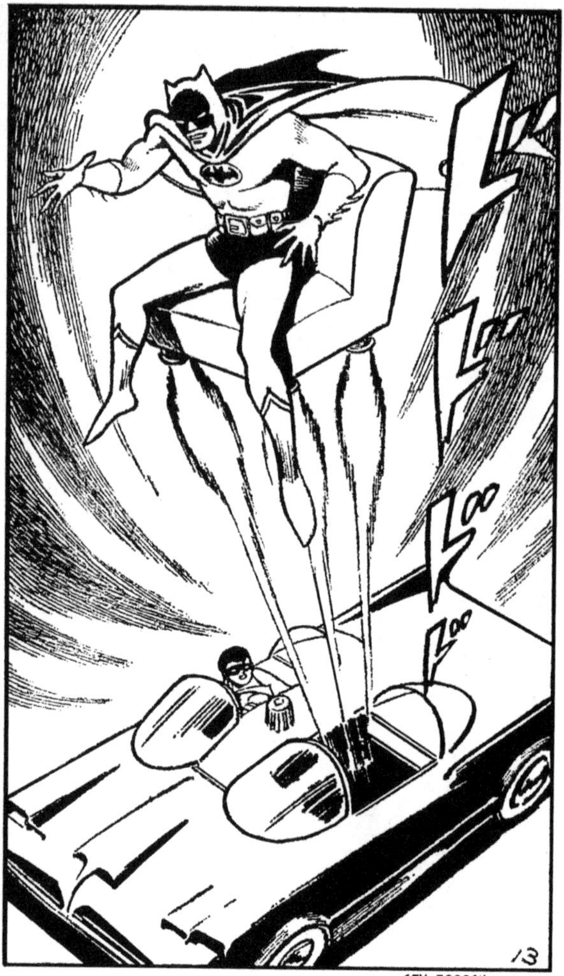

SFX: FOOOSH

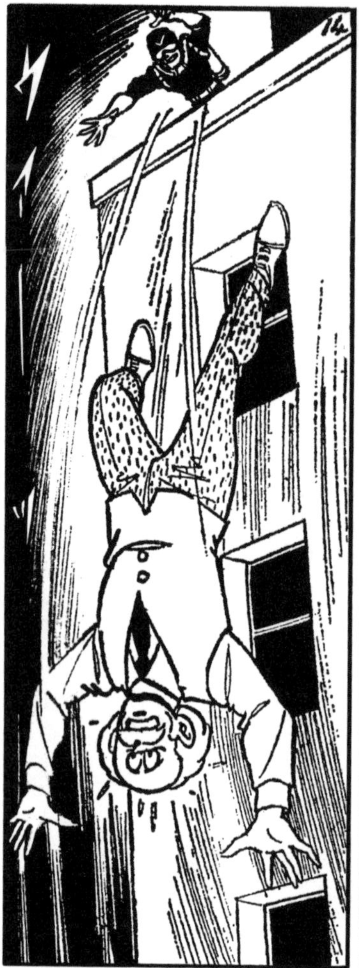

SFX: FOOOO

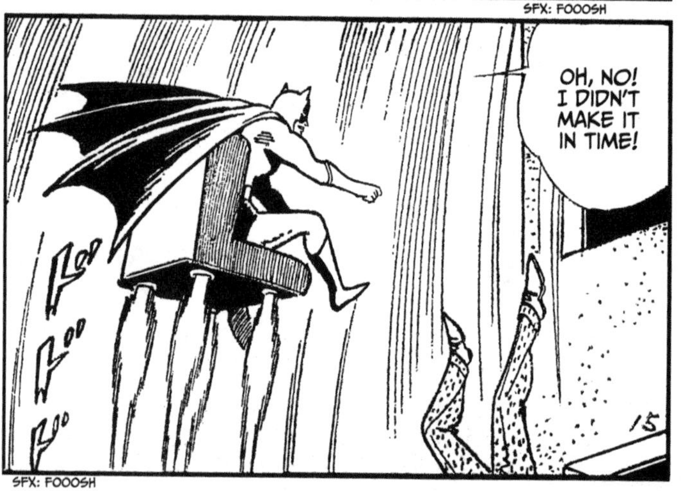
OH, NO! I DIDN'T MAKE IT IN TIME!

SFX: FOOOSH

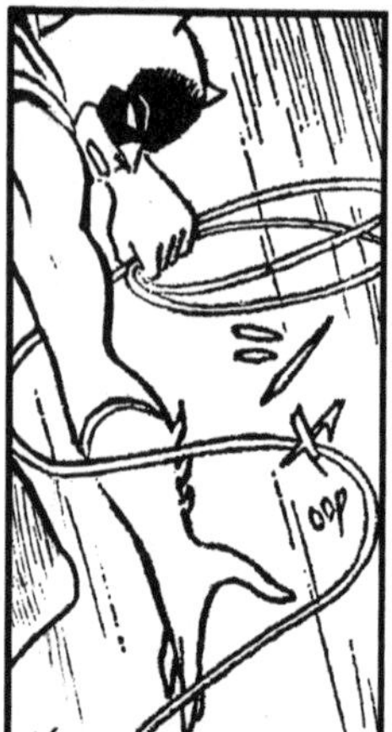

SFX: SWISH

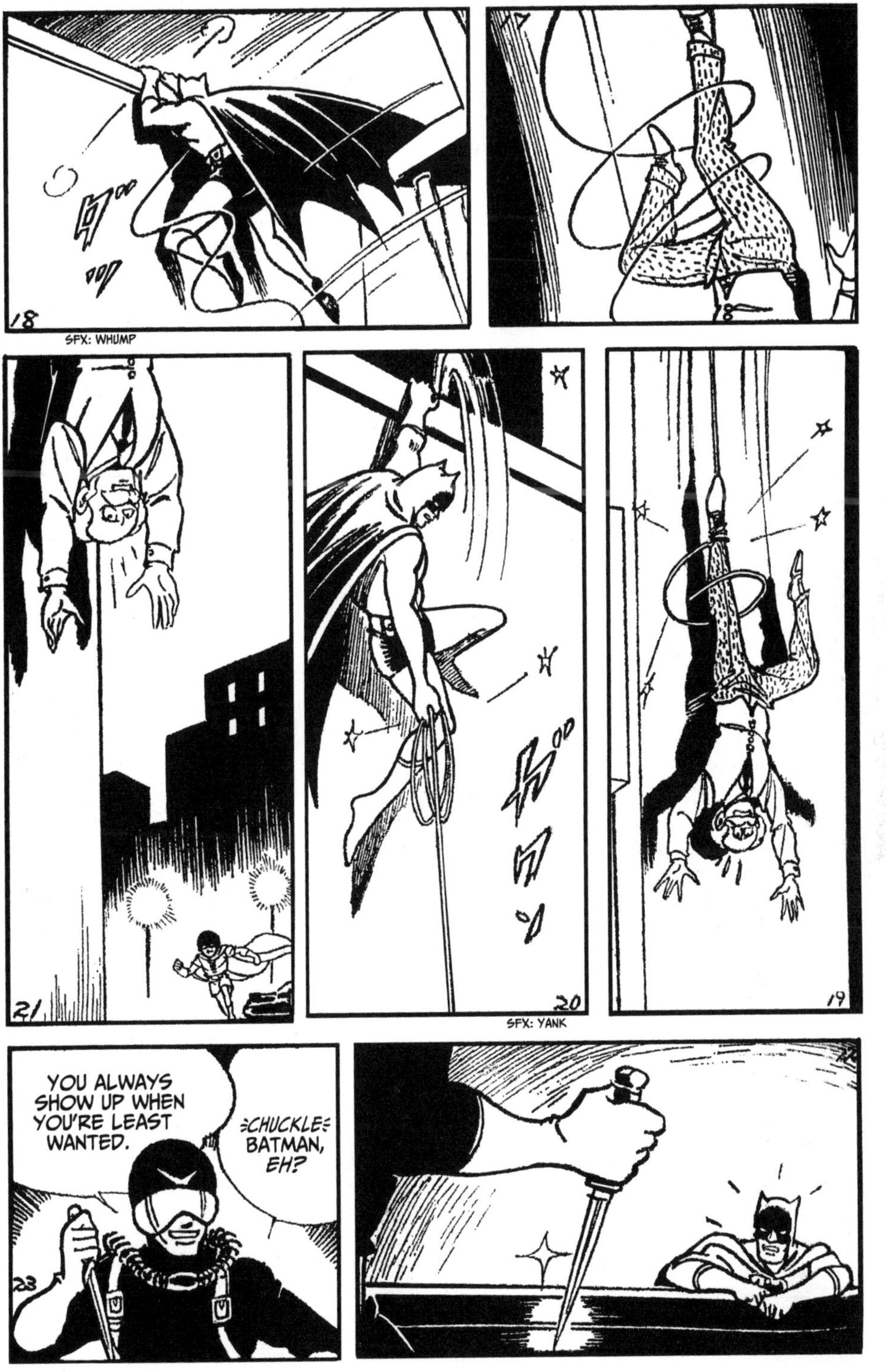
SFX: WHUMP
SFX: YANK
CHUCKLE
BATMAN, EH?
YOU ALWAYS SHOW UP WHEN YOU'RE LEAST WANTED.

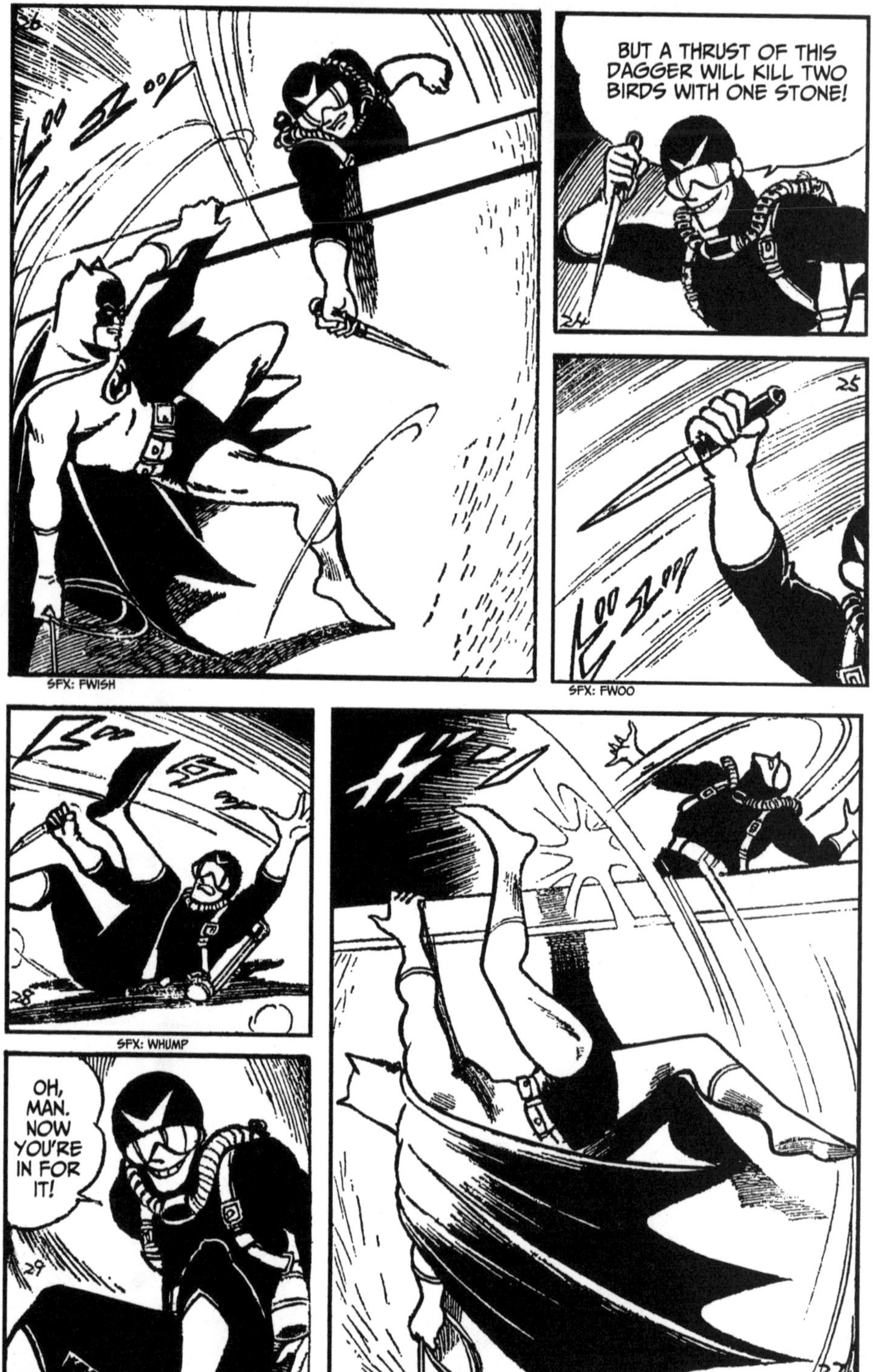
BUT A THRUST OF THIS DAGGER WILL KILL TWO BIRDS WITH ONE STONE!
SFX: FWOO
SFX: FWISH
SFX: KRAK
SFX: WHUMP
OH, MAN. NOW YOU'RE IN FOR IT!

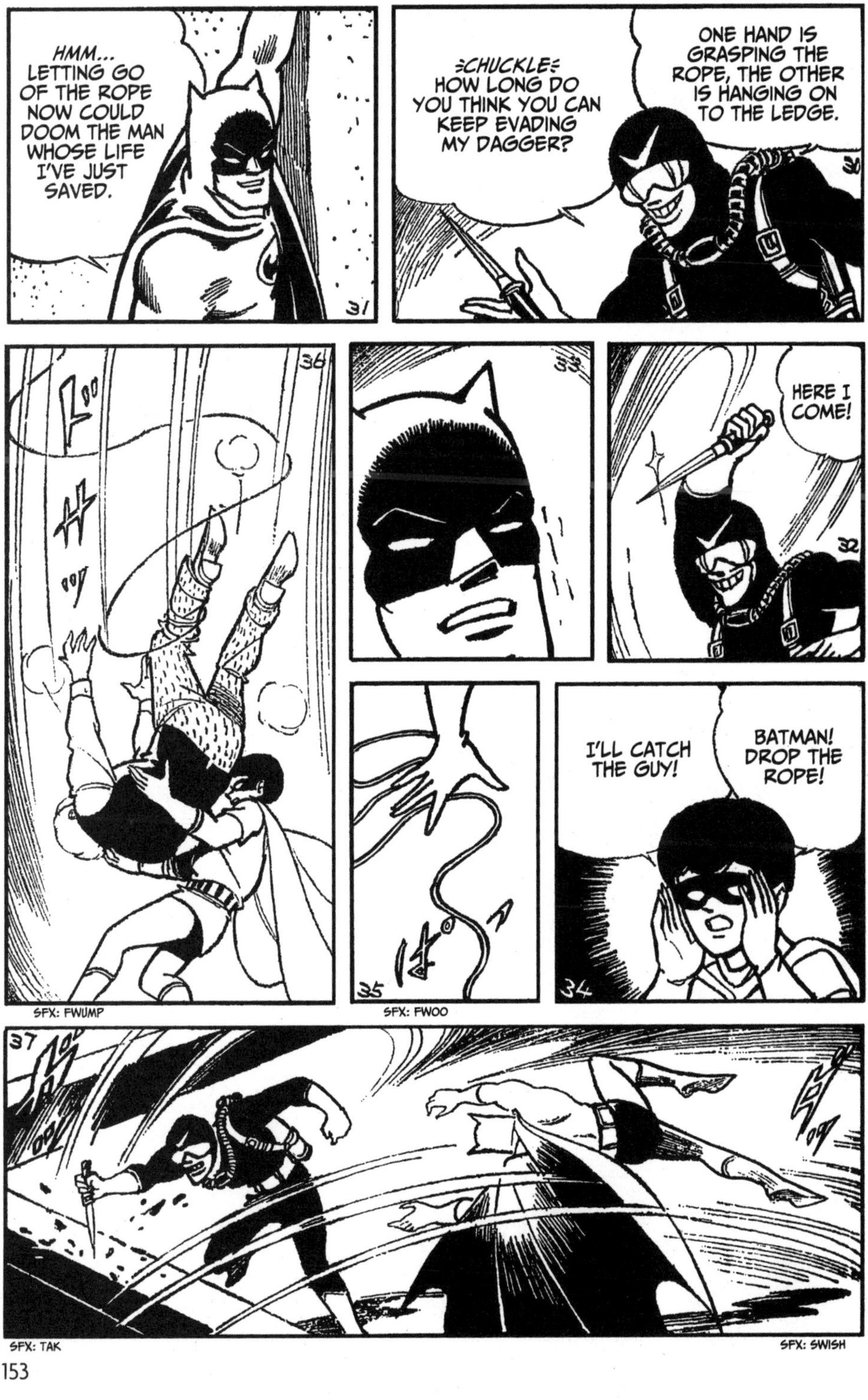
ONE HAND IS GRASPING THE ROPE, THE OTHER IS HANGING ON TO THE LEDGE.
≈CHUCKLE≈ HOW LONG DO YOU THINK YOU CAN KEEP EVADING MY DAGGER?
HMM... LETTING GO OF THE ROPE NOW COULD DOOM THE MAN WHOSE LIFE I'VE JUST SAVED.
HERE I COME!
BATMAN! DROP THE ROPE!
I'LL CATCH THE GUY!
SFX: FWOO
SFX: FWUMP
SFX: SWISH
SFX: TAK

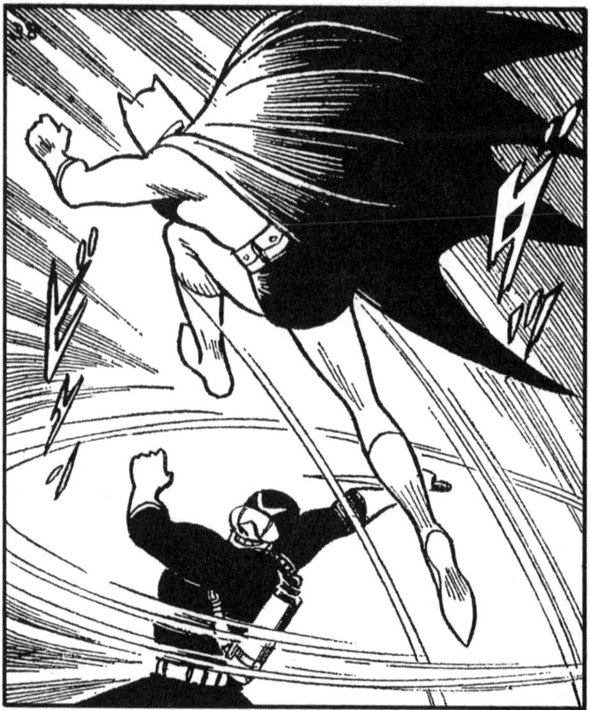

SFX: SLASH

SFX: SWISH

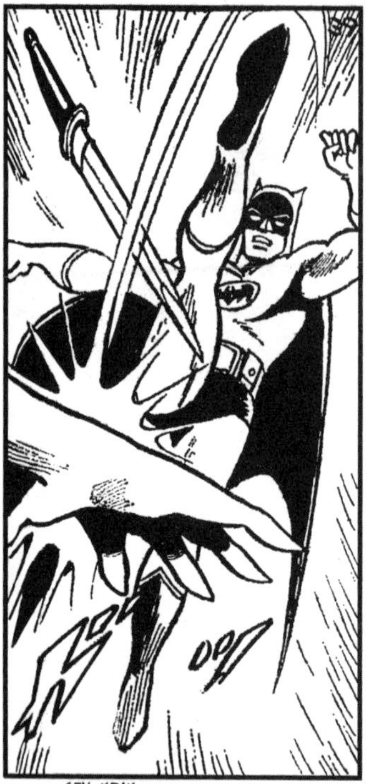

SFX: KRAK

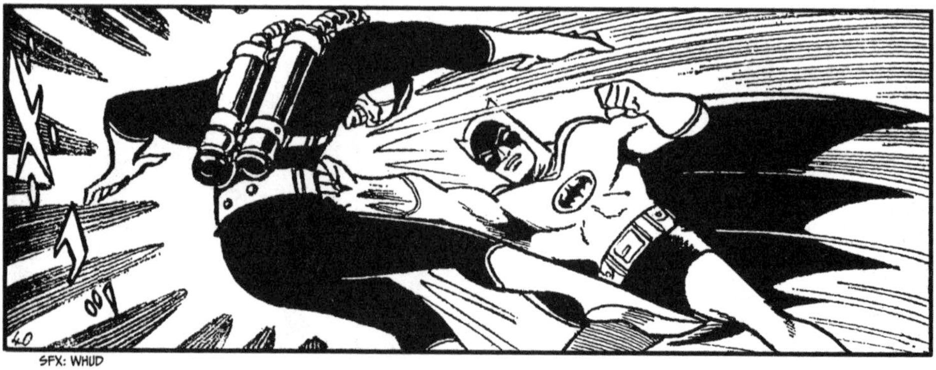

SFX: WHUD

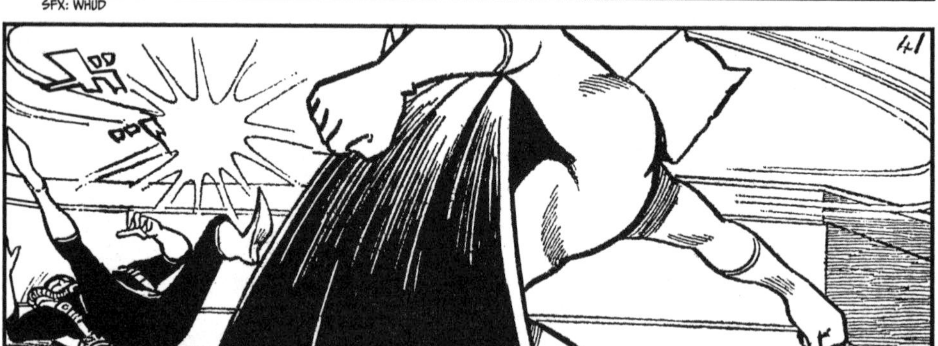

SFX: CHOK

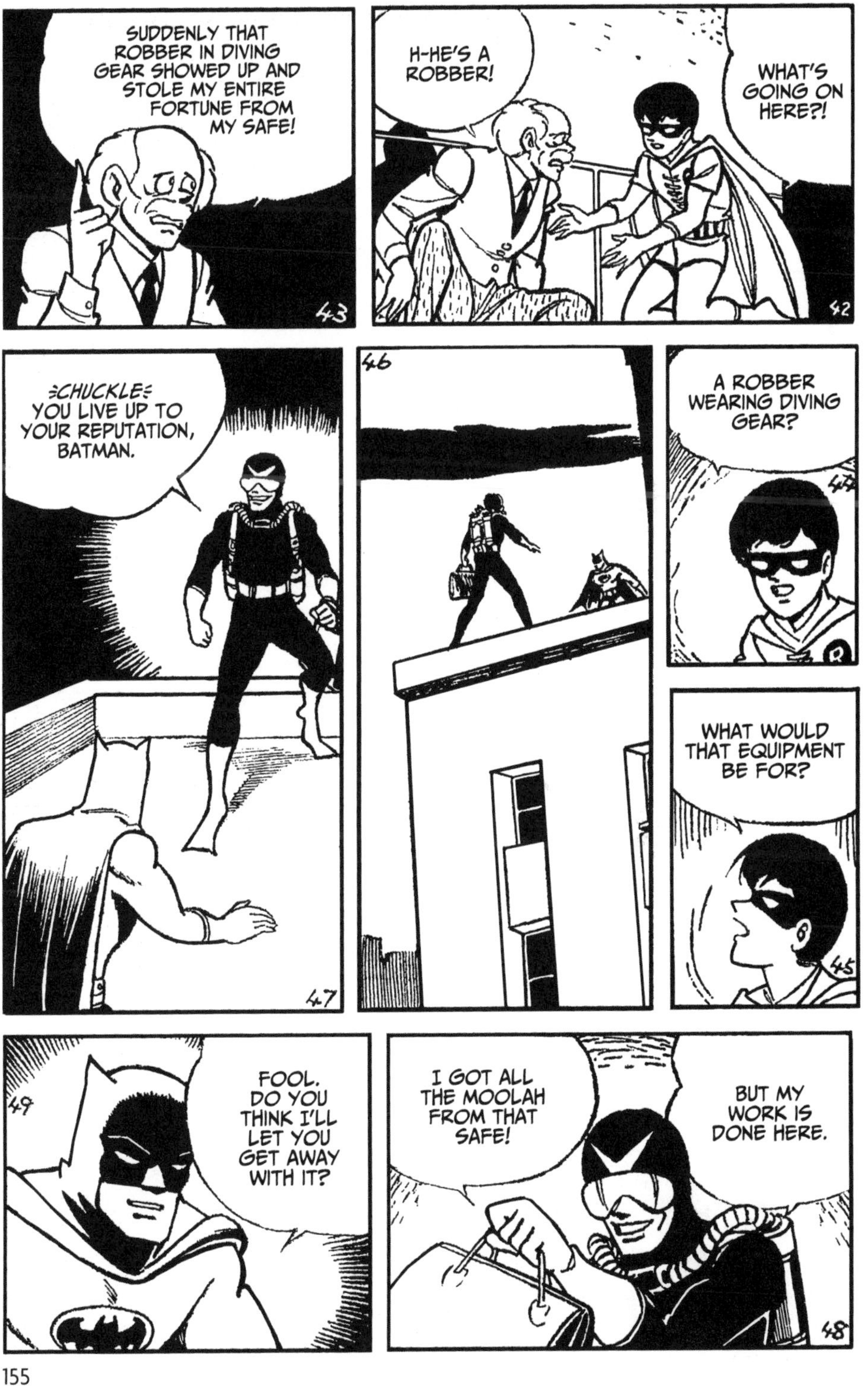
WHAT'S GOING ON HERE?!
H-HE'S A ROBBER!
SUDDENLY THAT ROBBER IN DIVING GEAR SHOWED UP AND STOLE MY ENTIRE FORTUNE FROM MY SAFE!
A ROBBER WEARING DIVING GEAR?
WHAT WOULD THAT EQUIPMENT BE FOR?
=CHUCKLE= YOU LIVE UP TO YOUR REPUTATION, BATMAN.
BUT MY WORK IS DONE HERE.
I GOT ALL THE MOOLAH FROM THAT SAFE!
FOOL. DO YOU THINK I'LL LET YOU GET AWAY WITH IT?

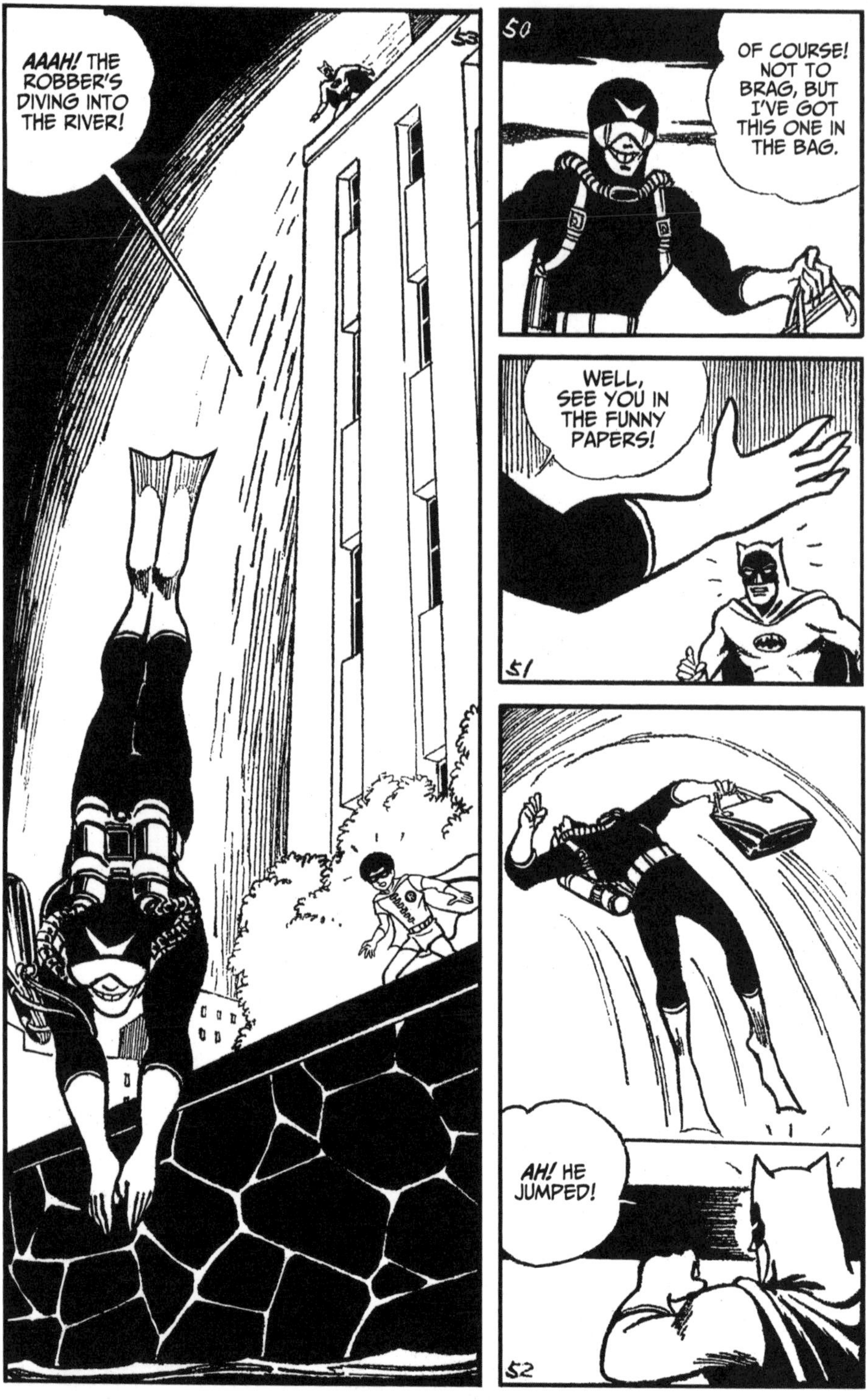
OF COURSE! NOT TO BRAG, BUT I'VE GOT THIS ONE IN THE BAG.
WELL, SEE YOU IN THE FUNNY PAPERS!
AH! HE JUMPED!
AAAH! THE ROBBER'S DIVING INTO THE RIVER!

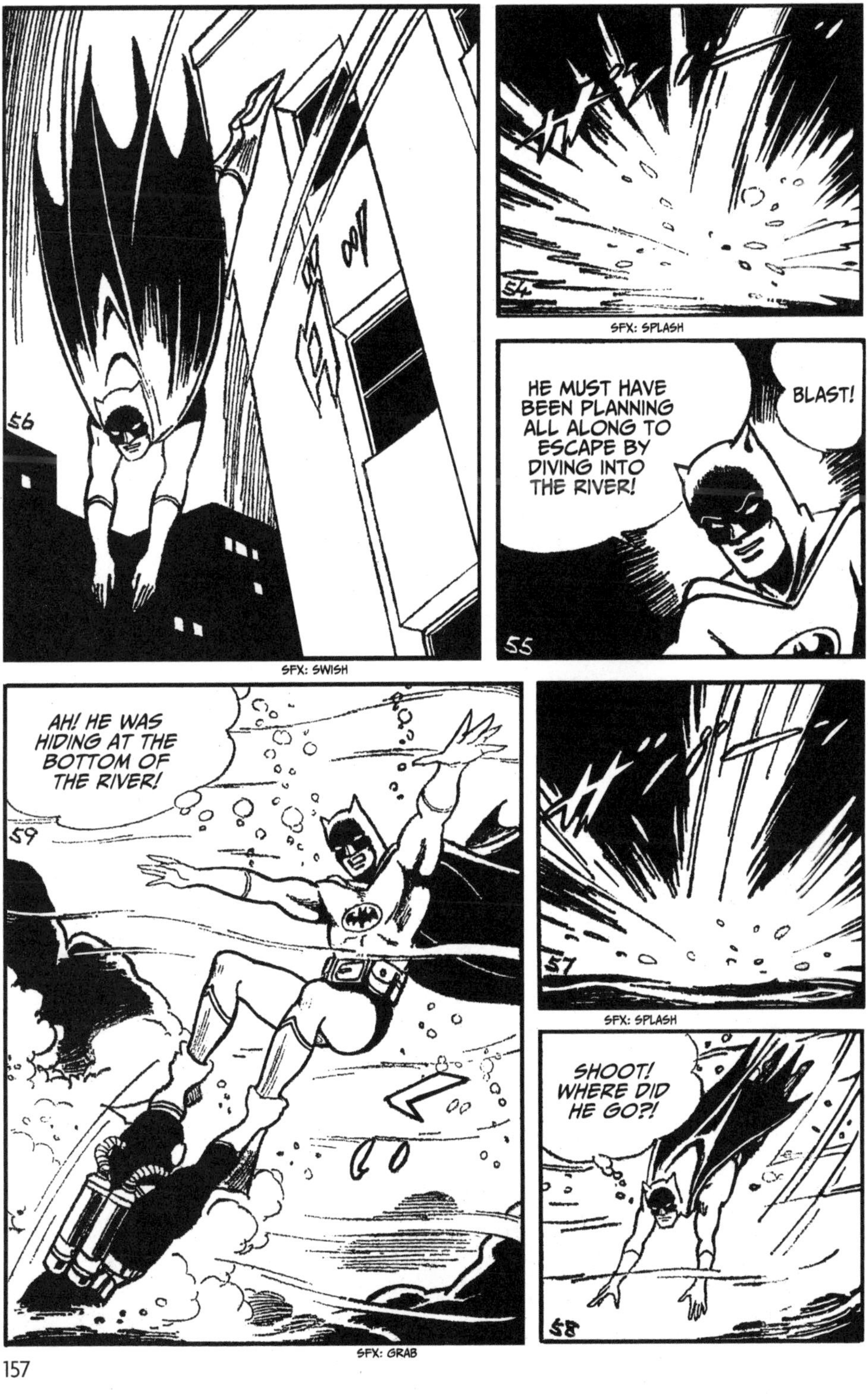
SFX: SPLASH
BLAST!
HE MUST HAVE BEEN PLANNING ALL ALONG TO ESCAPE BY DIVING INTO THE RIVER!
SFX: SWISH
SFX: SPLASH
SHOOT! WHERE DID HE GO?!
AH! HE WAS HIDING AT THE BOTTOM OF THE RIVER!
SFX: GRAB

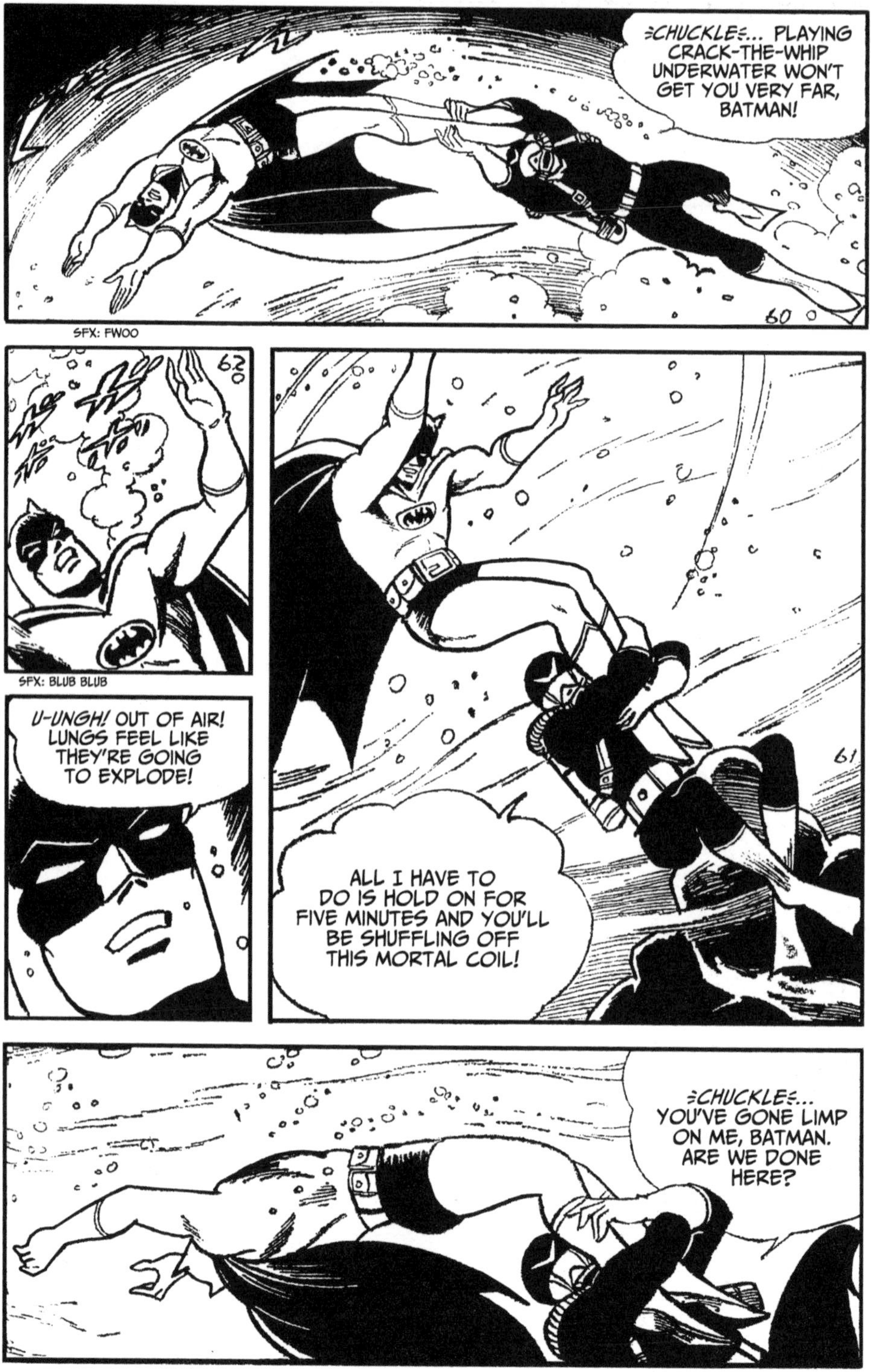
≈CHUCKLE≈... PLAYING CRACK-THE-WHIP UNDERWATER WON'T GET YOU VERY FAR, BATMAN!
SFX: FWOO
ALL I HAVE TO DO IS HOLD ON FOR FIVE MINUTES AND YOU'LL BE SHUFFLING OFF THIS MORTAL COIL!
SFX: BLUB BLUB
U-UNGH! OUT OF AIR! LUNGS FEEL LIKE THEY'RE GOING TO EXPLODE!
≈CHUCKLE≈... YOU'VE GONE LIMP ON ME, BATMAN. ARE WE DONE HERE?

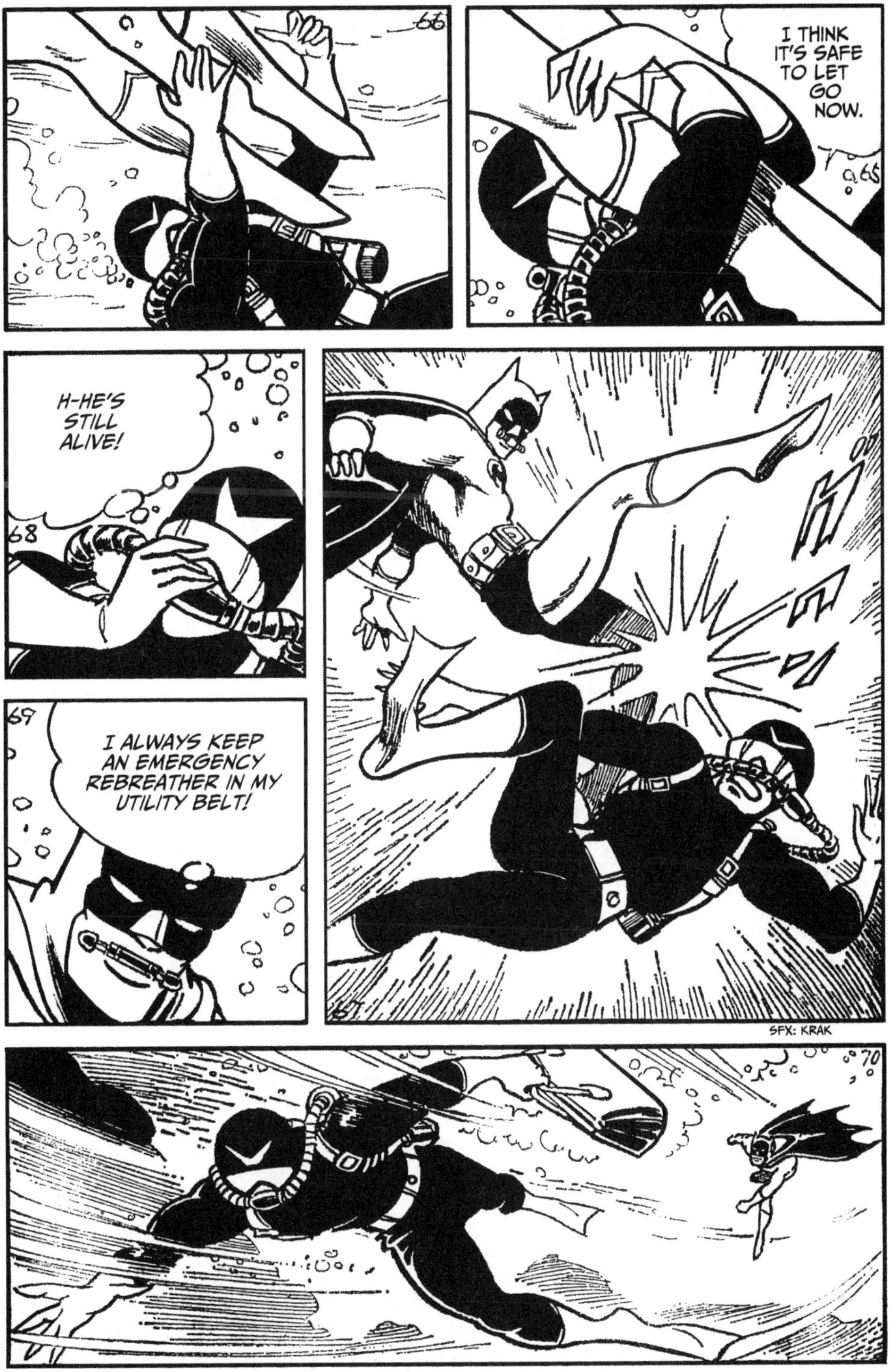
I THINK IT'S SAFE TO LET GO NOW.
SFX: KRAK
H-HE'S STILL ALIVE!
I ALWAYS KEEP AN EMERGENCY REBREATHER IN MY UTILITY BELT!

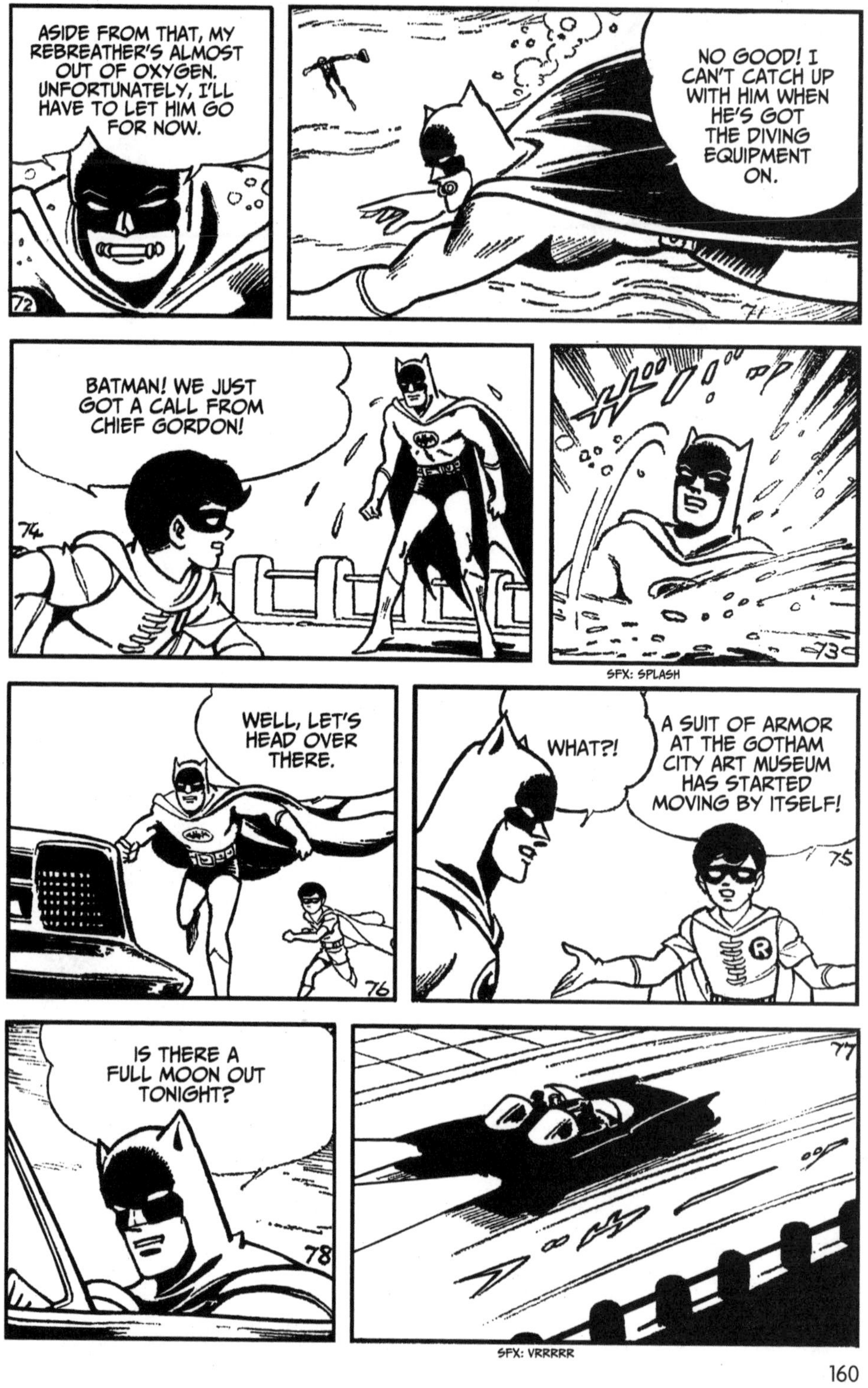
NO GOOD! I CAN'T CATCH UP WITH HIM WHEN HE'S GOT THE DIVING EQUIPMENT ON.
ASIDE FROM THAT, MY REBREATHER'S ALMOST OUT OF OXYGEN. UNFORTUNATELY, I'LL HAVE TO LET HIM GO FOR NOW.
SFX: SPLASH
BATMAN! WE JUST GOT A CALL FROM CHIEF GORDON!
A SUIT OF ARMOR AT THE GOTHAM CITY ART MUSEUM HAS STARTED MOVING BY ITSELF!
WHAT?!
WELL, LET'S HEAD OVER THERE.
SFX: VRRRRR
IS THERE A FULL MOON OUT TONIGHT?

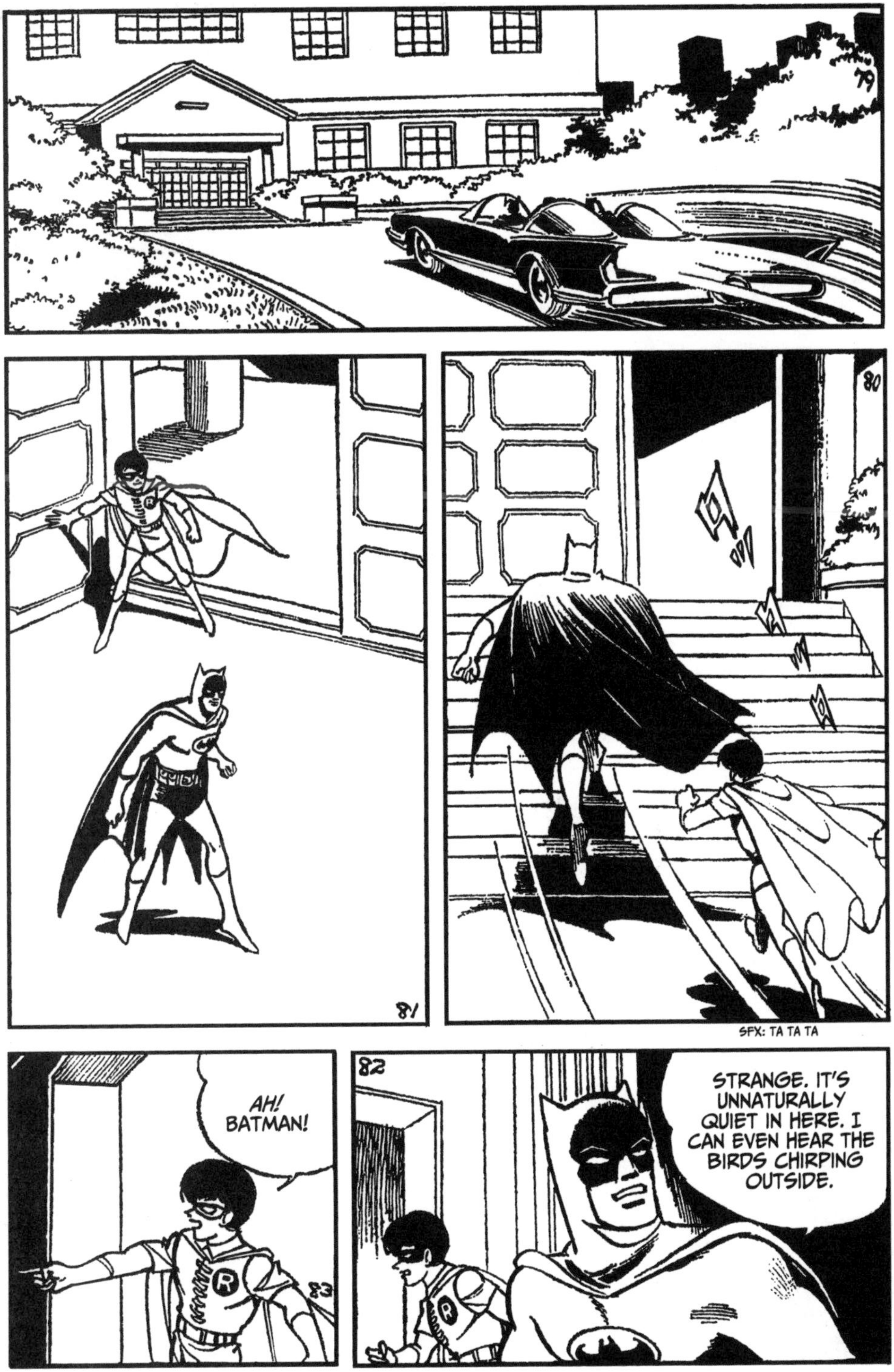
SFX: TA TA TA
STRANGE. IT'S UNNATURALLY QUIET IN HERE. I CAN EVEN HEAR THE BIRDS CHIRPING OUTSIDE.
AH! BATMAN!

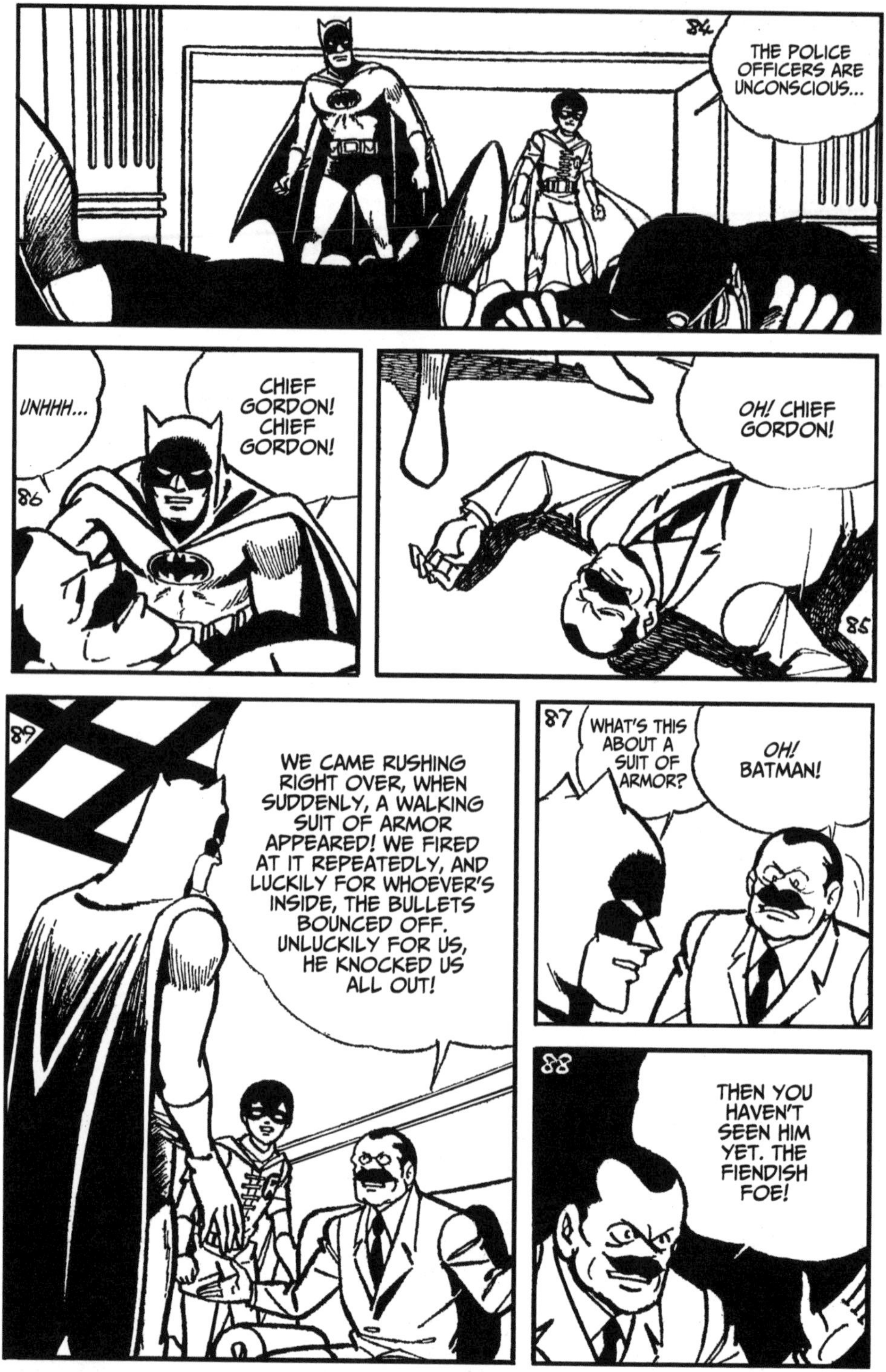
THE POLICE OFFICERS ARE UNCONSCIOUS...
OH! CHIEF GORDON!
CHIEF GORDON! CHIEF GORDON!
UNHHH...
OH! BATMAN!
WHAT'S THIS ABOUT A SUIT OF ARMOR?
THEN YOU HAVEN'T SEEN HIM YET. THE FIENDISH FOE!
WE CAME RUSHING RIGHT OVER, WHEN SUDDENLY, A WALKING SUIT OF ARMOR APPEARED! WE FIRED AT IT REPEATEDLY, AND LUCKILY FOR WHOEVER'S INSIDE, THE BULLETS BOUNCED OFF. UNLUCKILY FOR US, HE KNOCKED US ALL OUT!

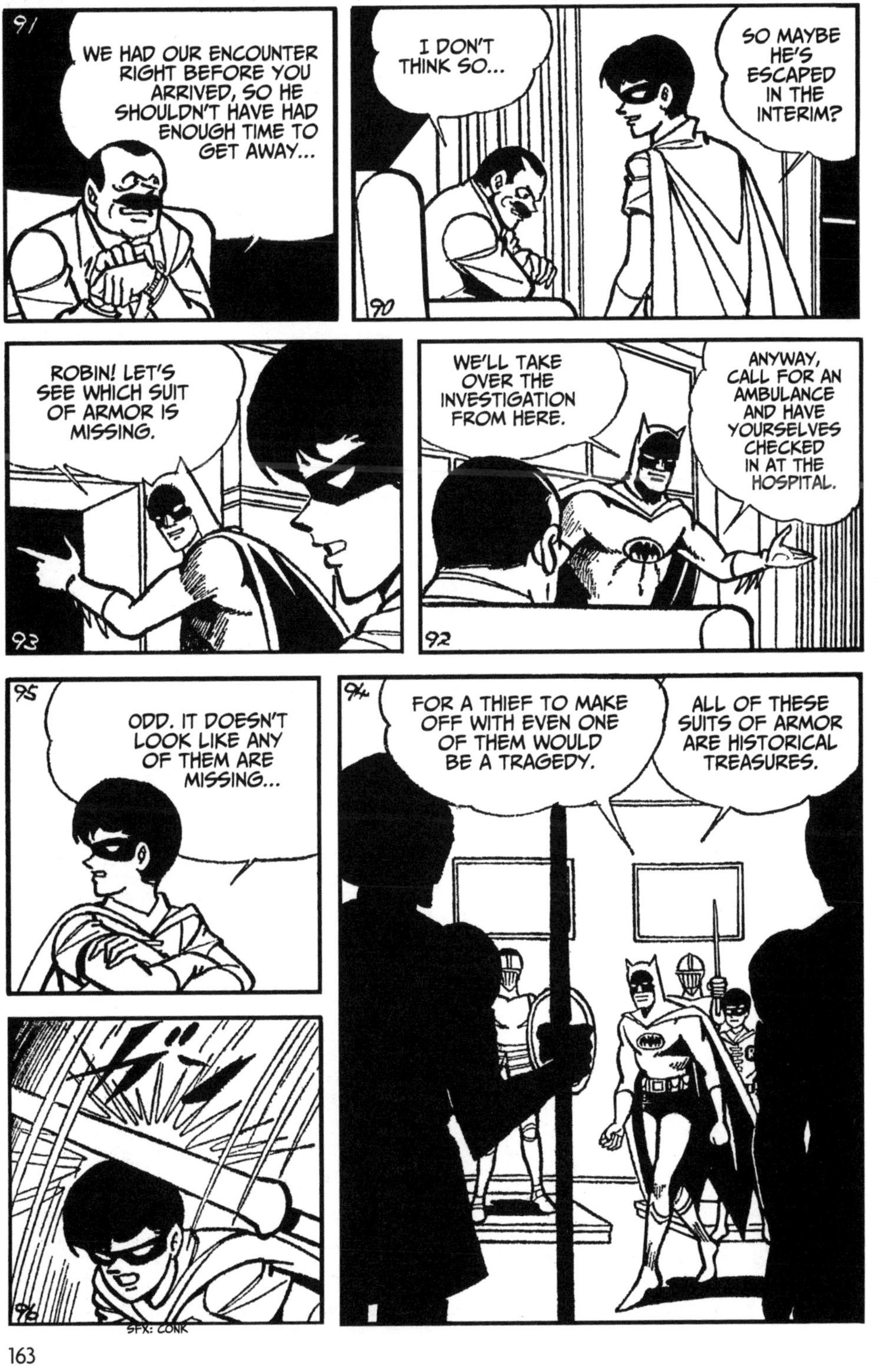
90
SO MAYBE HE'S ESCAPED IN THE INTERIM?
I DON'T THINK SO...
91
WE HAD OUR ENCOUNTER RIGHT BEFORE YOU ARRIVED, SO HE SHOULDN'T HAVE HAD ENOUGH TIME TO GET AWAY...
92
ANYWAY, CALL FOR AN AMBULANCE AND HAVE YOURSELVES CHECKED IN AT THE HOSPITAL.
WE'LL TAKE OVER THE INVESTIGATION FROM HERE.
93
ROBIN! LET'S SEE WHICH SUIT OF ARMOR IS MISSING.
94
ALL OF THESE SUITS OF ARMOR ARE HISTORICAL TREASURES.
FOR A THIEF TO MAKE OFF WITH EVEN ONE OF THEM WOULD BE A TRAGEDY.
95
ODD. IT DOESN'T LOOK LIKE ANY OF THEM ARE MISSING...
96
SFX: CONK

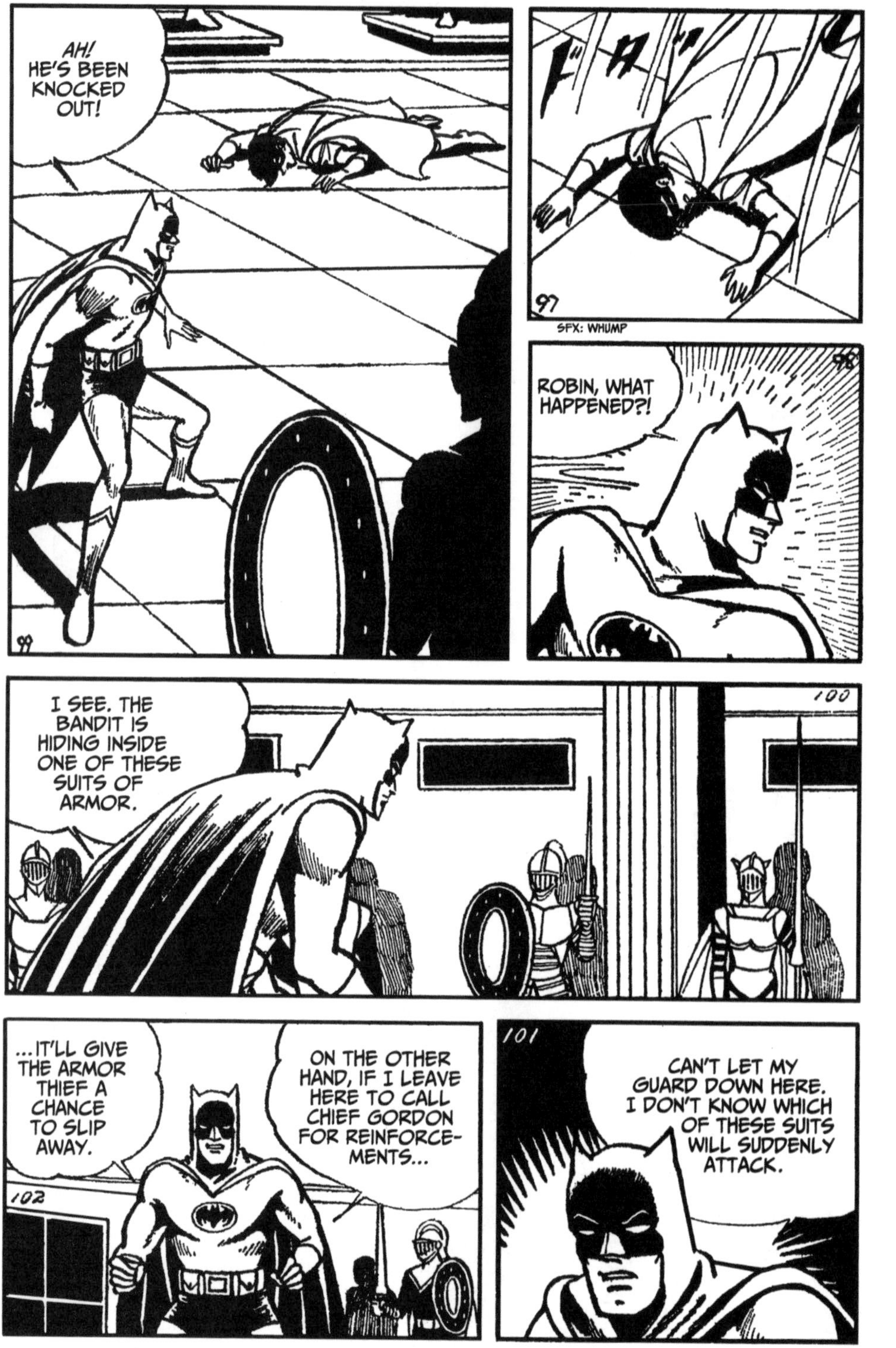
SFX: WHUMP
ROBIN, WHAT HAPPENED?!
AH! HE'S BEEN KNOCKED OUT!
I SEE. THE BANDIT IS HIDING INSIDE ONE OF THESE SUITS OF ARMOR.
CAN'T LET MY GUARD DOWN HERE. I DON'T KNOW WHICH OF THESE SUITS WILL SUDDENLY ATTACK.
ON THE OTHER HAND, IF I LEAVE HERE TO CALL CHIEF GORDON FOR REINFORCE-MENTS...
...IT'LL GIVE THE ARMOR THIEF A CHANCE TO SLIP AWAY.

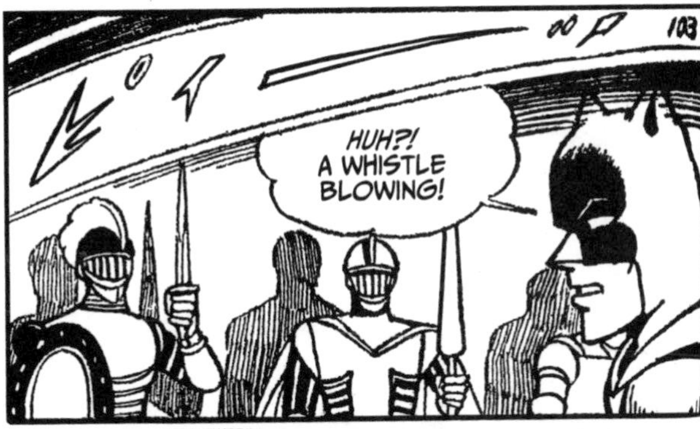
HUH?! A WHISTLE BLOWING!
SFX: TWEEET

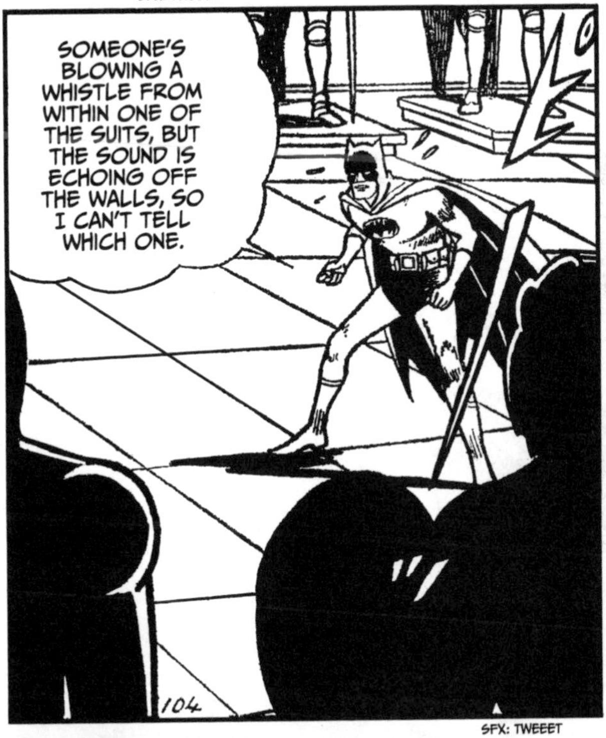
SOMEONE'S BLOWING A WHISTLE FROM WITHIN ONE OF THE SUITS, BUT THE SOUND IS ECHOING OFF THE WALLS, SO I CAN'T TELL WHICH ONE.
SFX: TWEEET

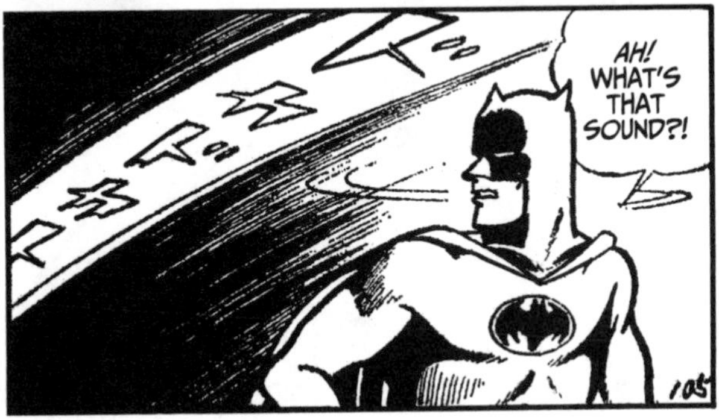
AH! WHAT'S THAT SOUND?!
SFX: CLOP CLOP CLOP

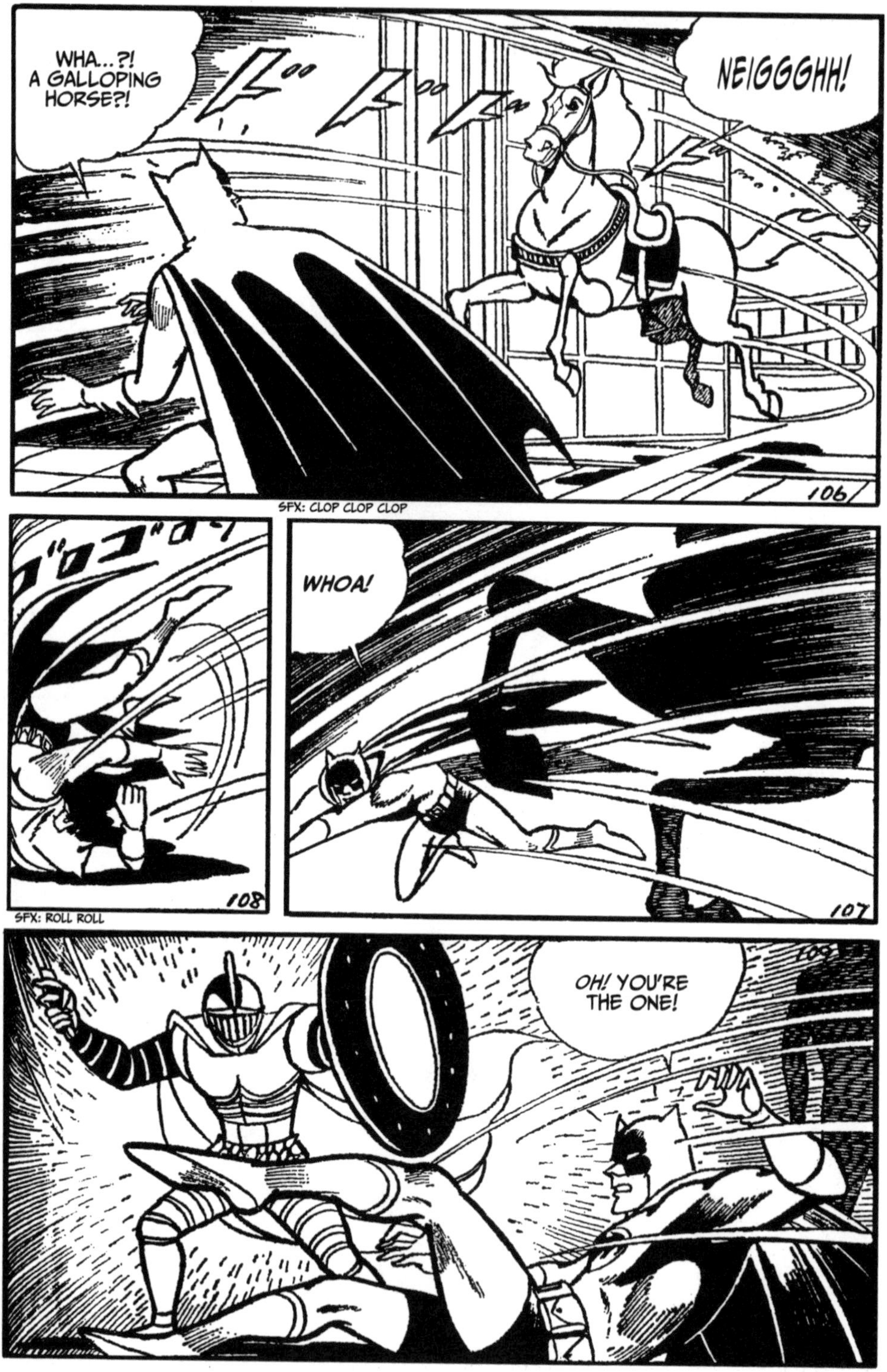
NEIGGGHH!
WHA...?! A GALLOPING HORSE?!
SFX: CLOP CLOP CLOP
WHOA!
SFX: ROLL ROLL
OH! YOU'RE THE ONE!

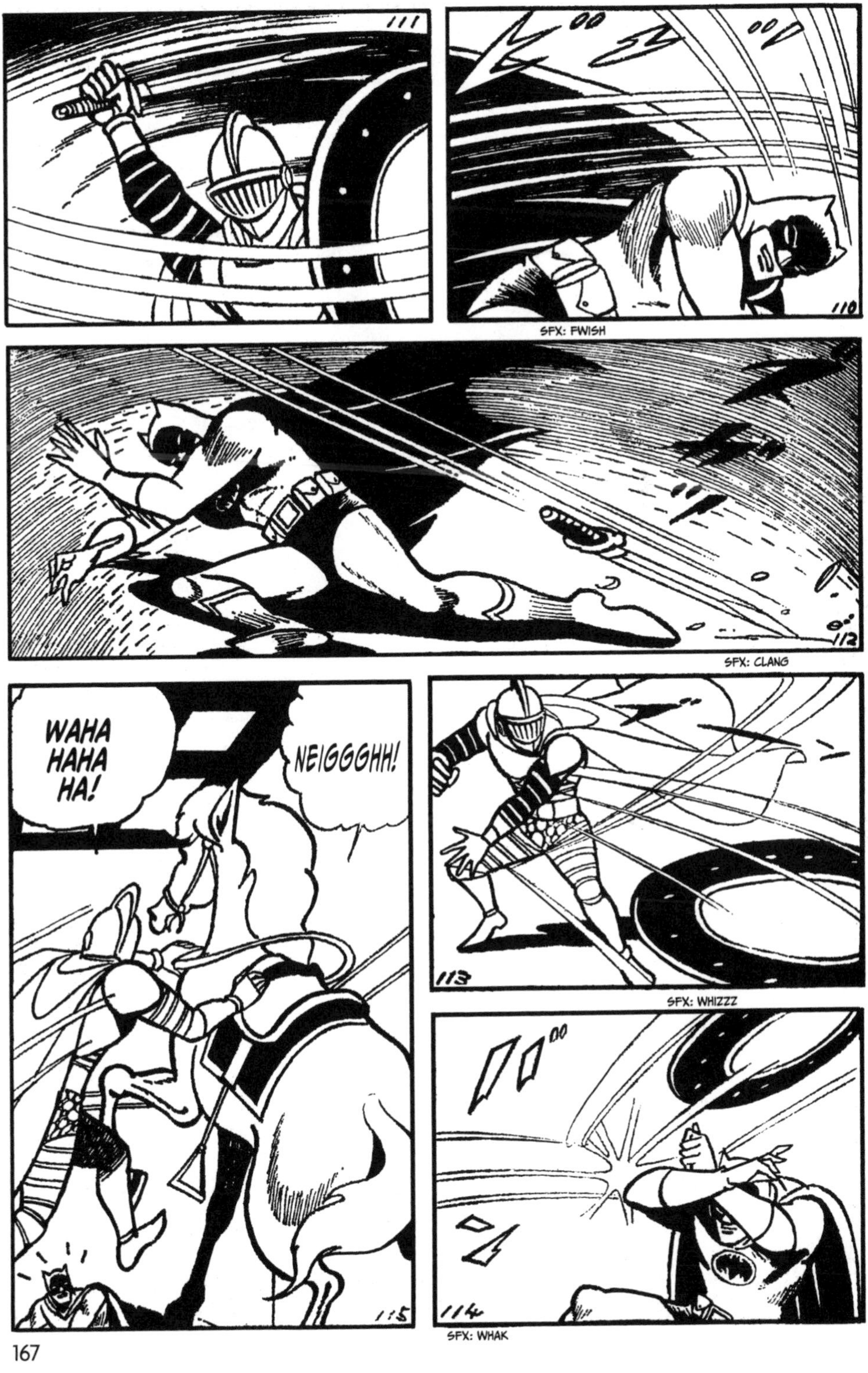
SFX: FWISH
SFX: CLANG
SFX: WHIZZZ
SFX: WHAK
NEIGGGHH!
WAHA HAHA HA!

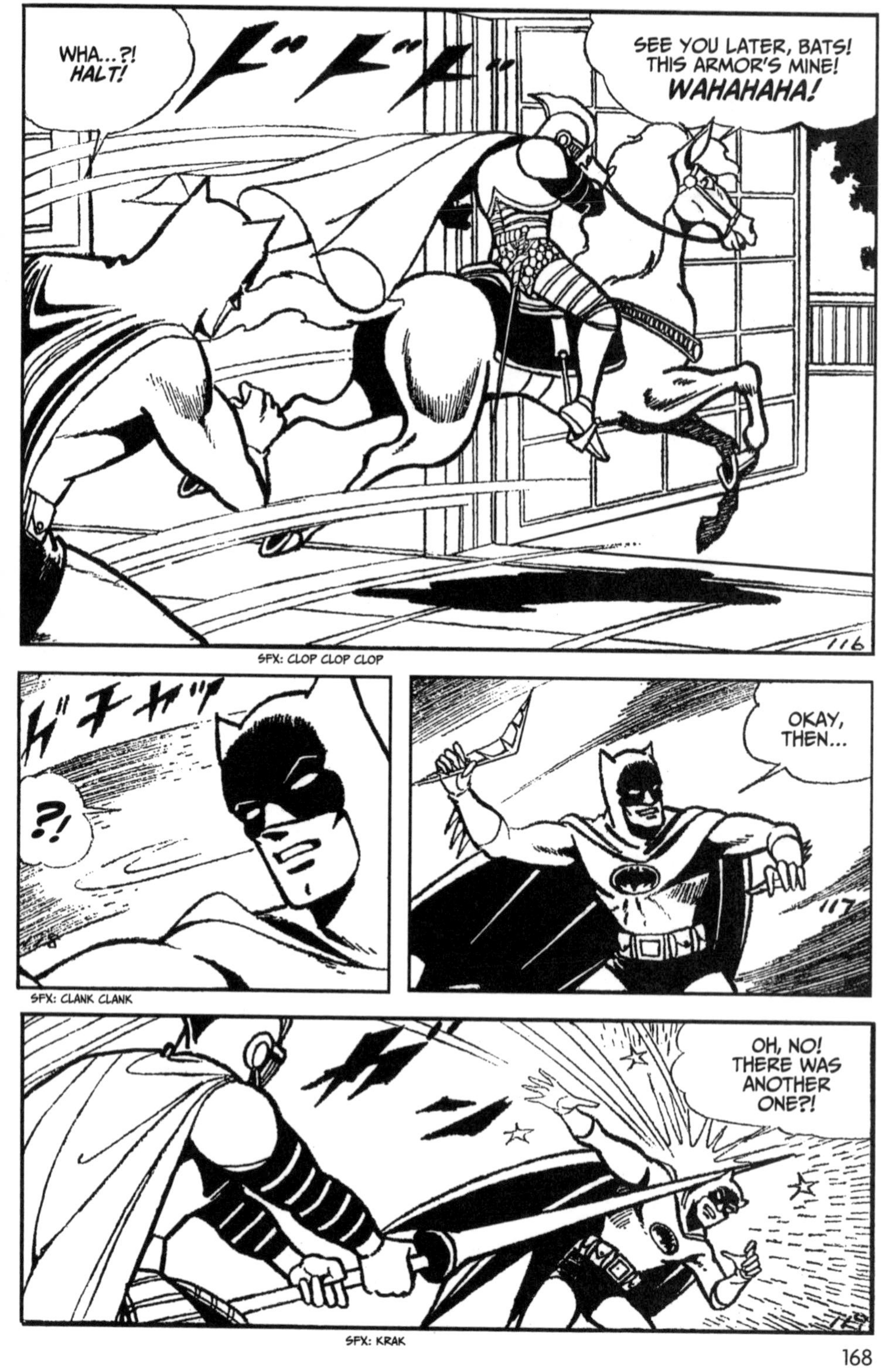
SEE YOU LATER, BATS! THIS ARMOR'S MINE! WAHAHAHA!
WHA...?! HALT!
SFX: CLOP CLOP CLOP
OKAY, THEN...
?!
SFX: CLANK CLANK
OH, NO! THERE WAS ANOTHER ONE?!
SFX: KRAK

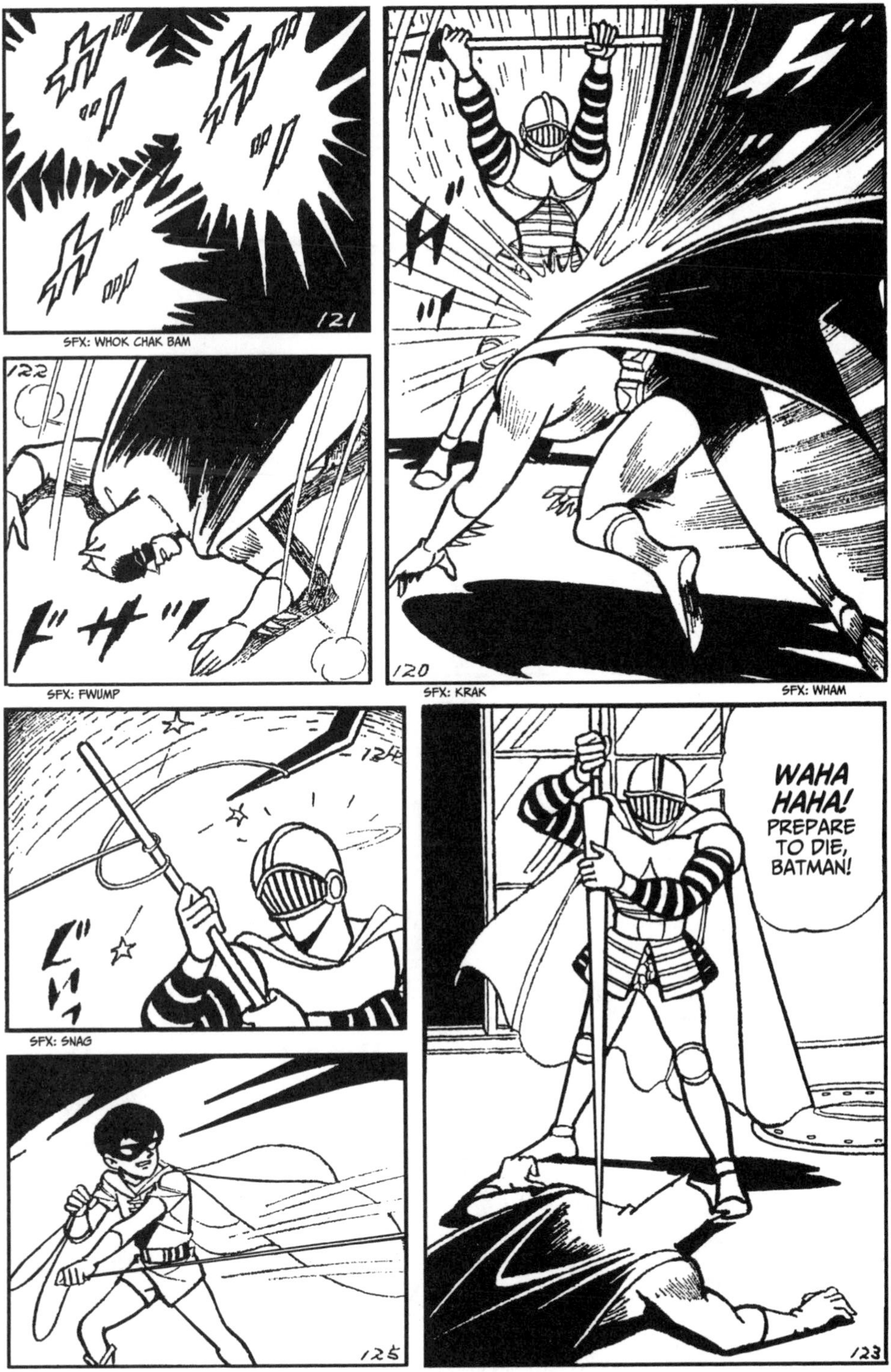
SFX: WHAM
SFX: KRAK
SFX: WHOK CHAK BAM
SFX: FWUMP
WAHA HAHA! PREPARE TO DIE, BATMAN!
SFX: SNAG

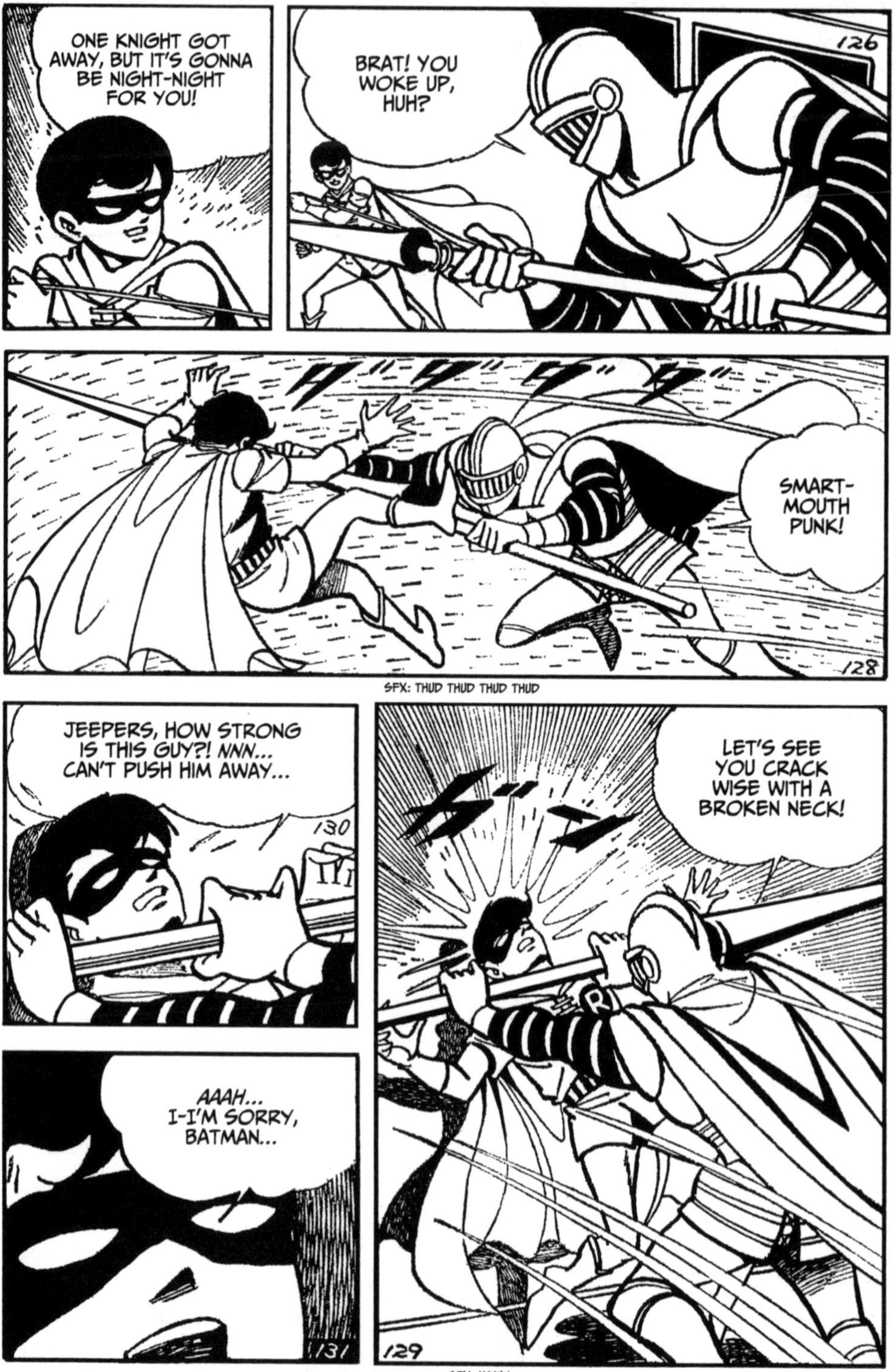
BRAT! YOU WOKE UP, HUH?
ONE KNIGHT GOT AWAY, BUT IT'S GONNA BE NIGHT-NIGHT FOR YOU!
SMART-MOUTH PUNK!
SFX: THUD THUD THUD THUD
LET'S SEE YOU CRACK WISE WITH A BROKEN NECK!
JEEPERS, HOW STRONG IS THIS GUY?! *NNN...* CAN'T PUSH HIM AWAY...
AAAH... I-I'M SORRY, BATMAN...
SFX: WHUK

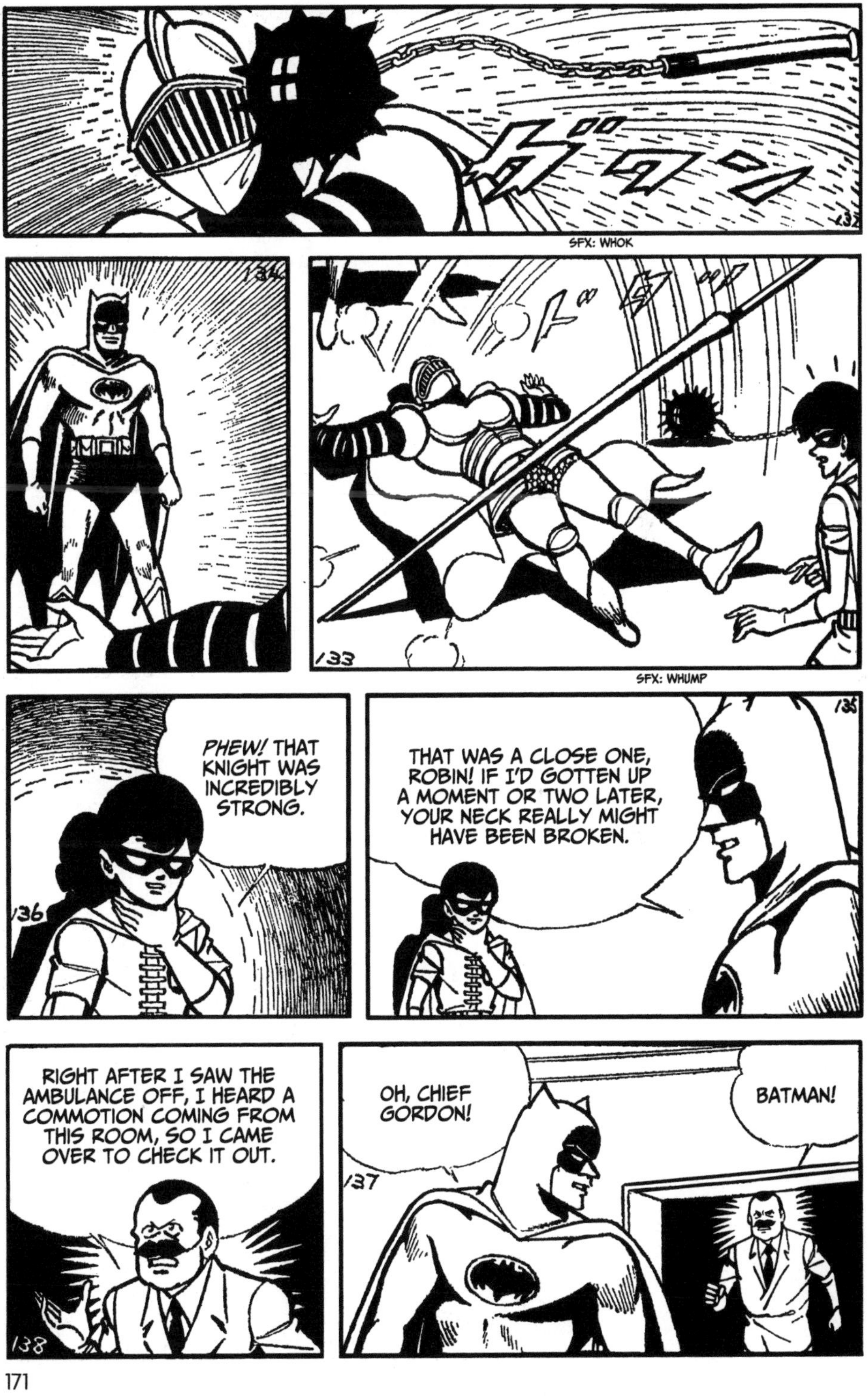
SFX: WHOK
SFX: WHUMP
THAT WAS A CLOSE ONE, ROBIN! IF I'D GOTTEN UP A MOMENT OR TWO LATER, YOUR NECK REALLY MIGHT HAVE BEEN BROKEN.
PHEW! THAT KNIGHT WAS INCREDIBLY STRONG.
BATMAN!
OH, CHIEF GORDON!
RIGHT AFTER I SAW THE AMBULANCE OFF, I HEARD A COMMOTION COMING FROM THIS ROOM, SO I CAME OVER TO CHECK IT OUT.

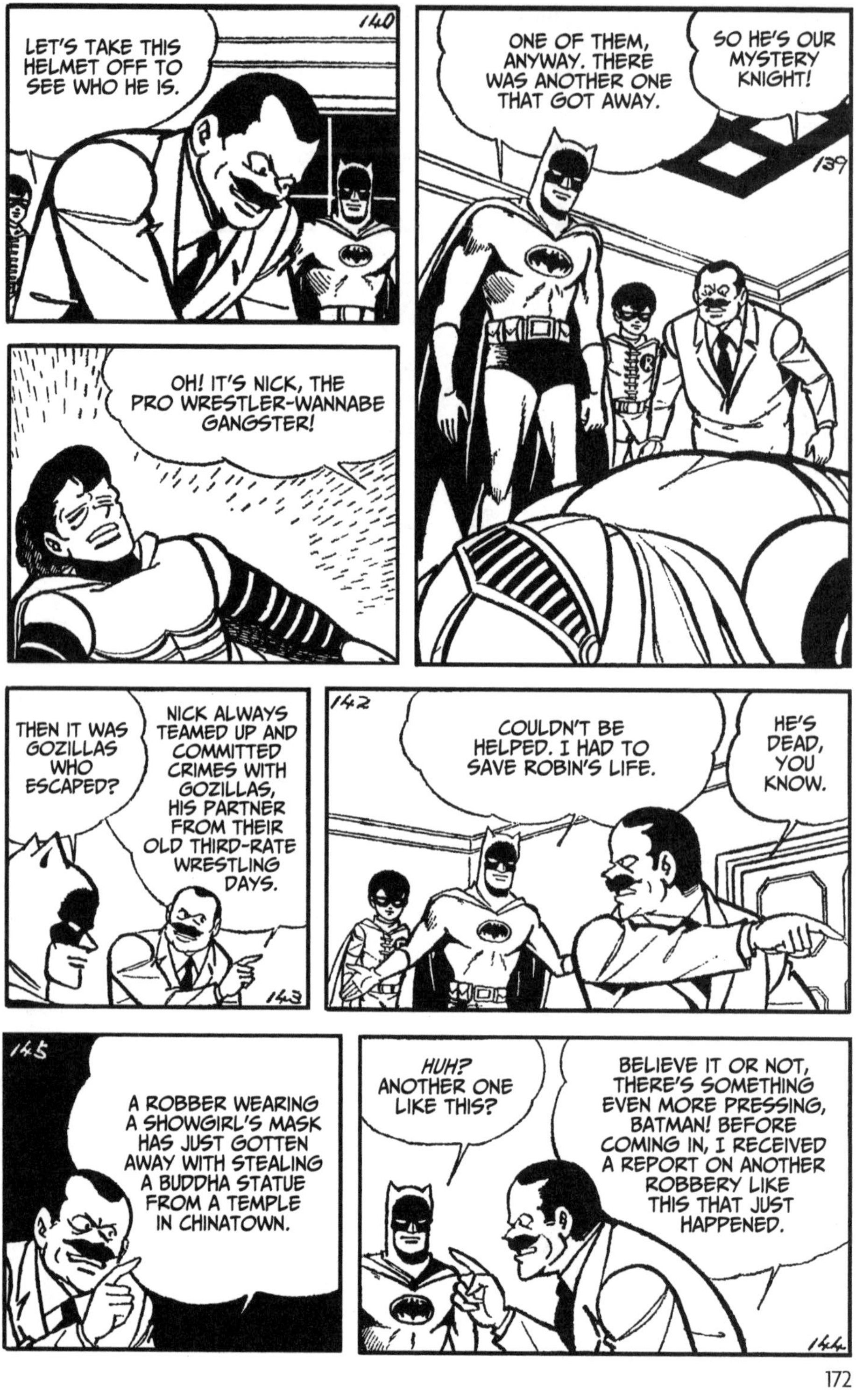
SO HE'S OUR MYSTERY KNIGHT!
ONE OF THEM, ANYWAY. THERE WAS ANOTHER ONE THAT GOT AWAY.
LET'S TAKE THIS HELMET OFF TO SEE WHO HE IS.
OH! IT'S NICK, THE PRO WRESTLER-WANNABE GANGSTER!
HE'S DEAD, YOU KNOW.
COULDN'T BE HELPED. I HAD TO SAVE ROBIN'S LIFE.
NICK ALWAYS TEAMED UP AND COMMITTED CRIMES WITH GOZILLAS, HIS PARTNER FROM THEIR OLD THIRD-RATE WRESTLING DAYS.
THEN IT WAS GOZILLAS WHO ESCAPED?
BELIEVE IT OR NOT, THERE'S SOMETHING EVEN MORE PRESSING, BATMAN! BEFORE COMING IN, I RECEIVED A REPORT ON ANOTHER ROBBERY LIKE THIS THAT JUST HAPPENED.
HUH? ANOTHER ONE LIKE THIS?
A ROBBER WEARING A SHOWGIRL'S MASK HAS JUST GOTTEN AWAY WITH STEALING A BUDDHA STATUE FROM A TEMPLE IN CHINATOWN.

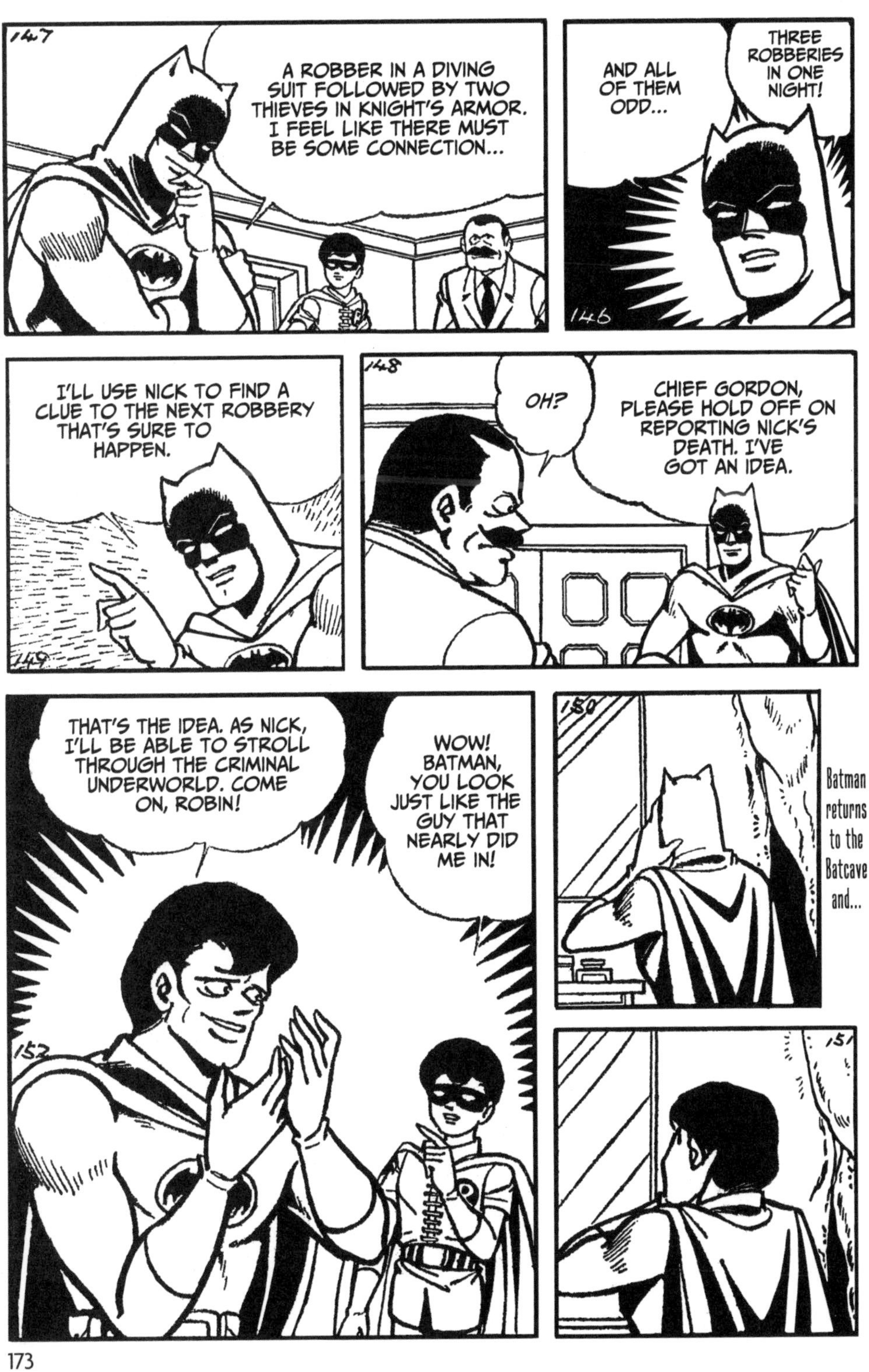
THREE ROBBERIES IN ONE NIGHT!
AND ALL OF THEM ODD...
A ROBBER IN A DIVING SUIT FOLLOWED BY TWO THIEVES IN KNIGHT'S ARMOR. I FEEL LIKE THERE MUST BE SOME CONNECTION...
CHIEF GORDON, PLEASE HOLD OFF ON REPORTING NICK'S DEATH. I'VE GOT AN IDEA.
OH?
I'LL USE NICK TO FIND A CLUE TO THE NEXT ROBBERY THAT'S SURE TO HAPPEN.
Batman returns to the Batcave and...
WOW! BATMAN, YOU LOOK JUST LIKE THE GUY THAT NEARLY DID ME IN!
THAT'S THE IDEA. AS NICK, I'LL BE ABLE TO STROLL THROUGH THE CRIMINAL UNDERWORLD. COME ON, ROBIN!

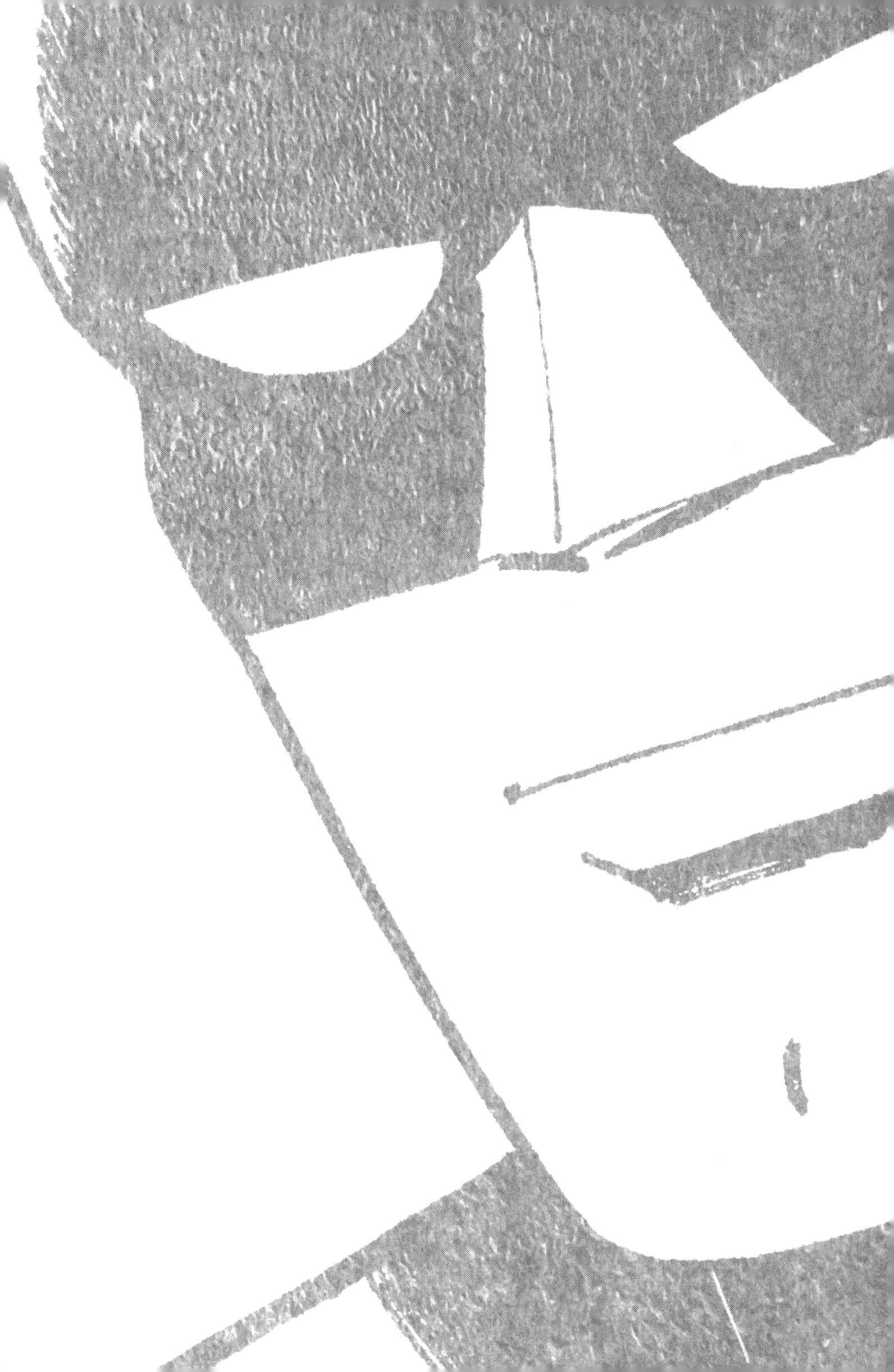

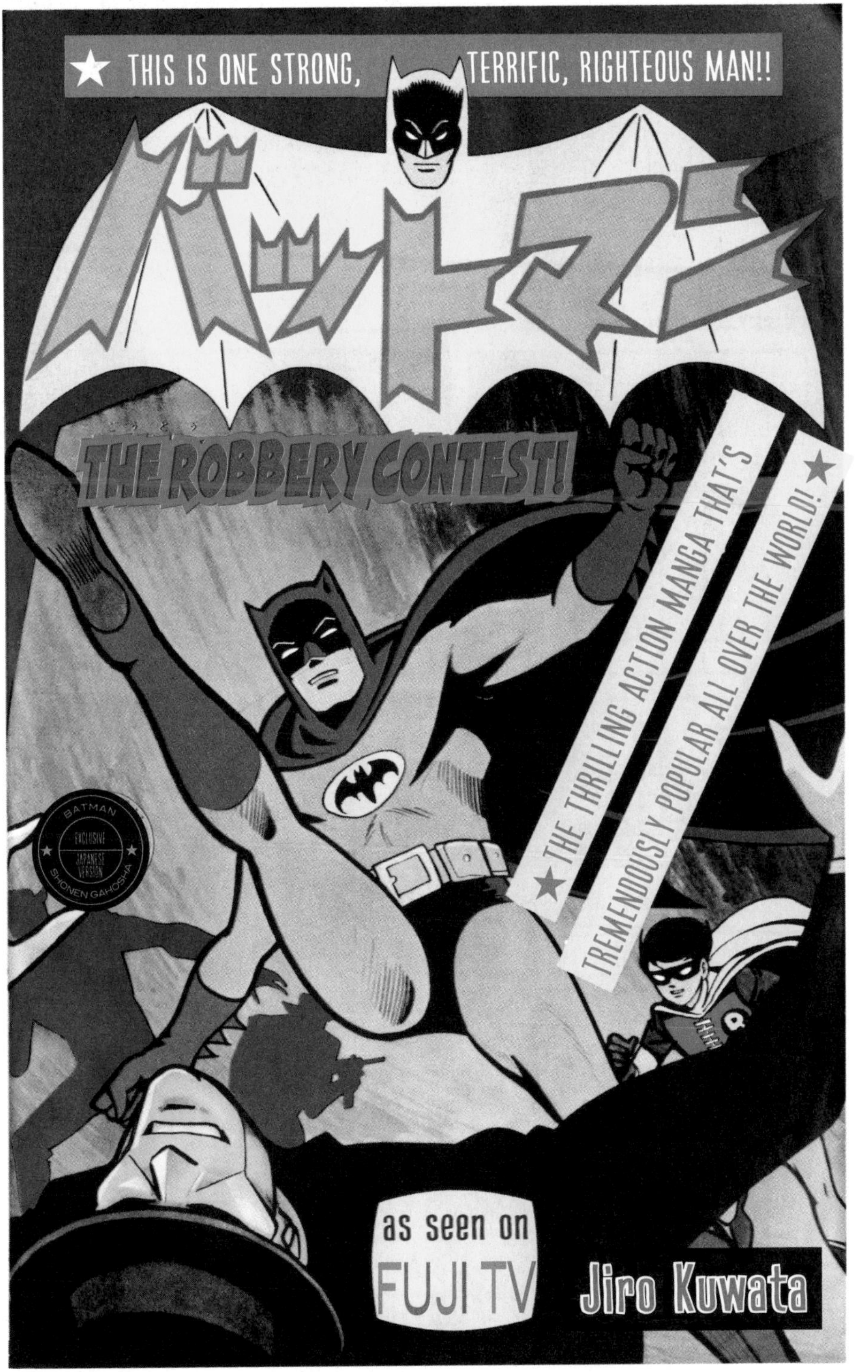
★ THIS IS ONE STRONG, TERRIFIC, RIGHTEOUS MAN!!
バットマン
THE ROBBERY CONTEST!
★ THE THRILLING ACTION MANGA THAT'S TREMENDOUSLY POPULAR ALL OVER THE WORLD! ★
BATMAN EXCLUSIVE JAPANESE VERSION SHONEN GAHOSHA
as seen on FUJI TV
Jiro Kuwata

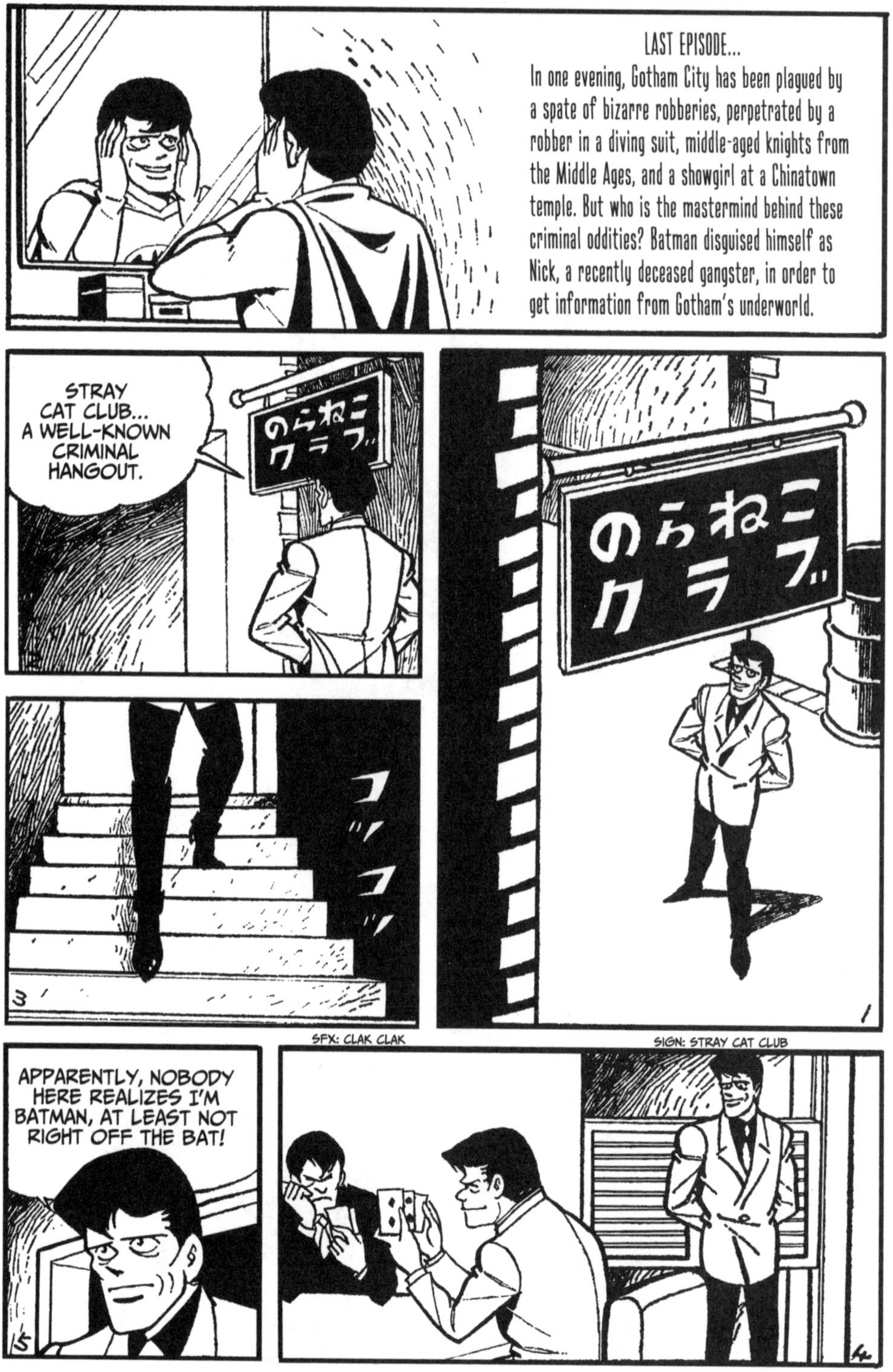
LAST EPISODE...
In one evening, Gotham City has been plagued by a spate of bizarre robberies, perpetrated by a robber in a diving suit, middle-aged knights from the Middle Ages, and a showgirl at a Chinatown temple. But who is the mastermind behind these criminal oddities? Batman disguised himself as Nick, a recently deceased gangster, in order to get information from Gotham's underworld.
のらねこクラブ
SIGN: STRAY CAT CLUB
STRAY CAT CLUB... A WELL-KNOWN CRIMINAL HANGOUT.
のらねこクラブ
コツコツ
SFX: CLAK CLAK
APPARENTLY, NOBODY HERE REALIZES I'M BATMAN, AT LEAST NOT RIGHT OFF THE BAT!

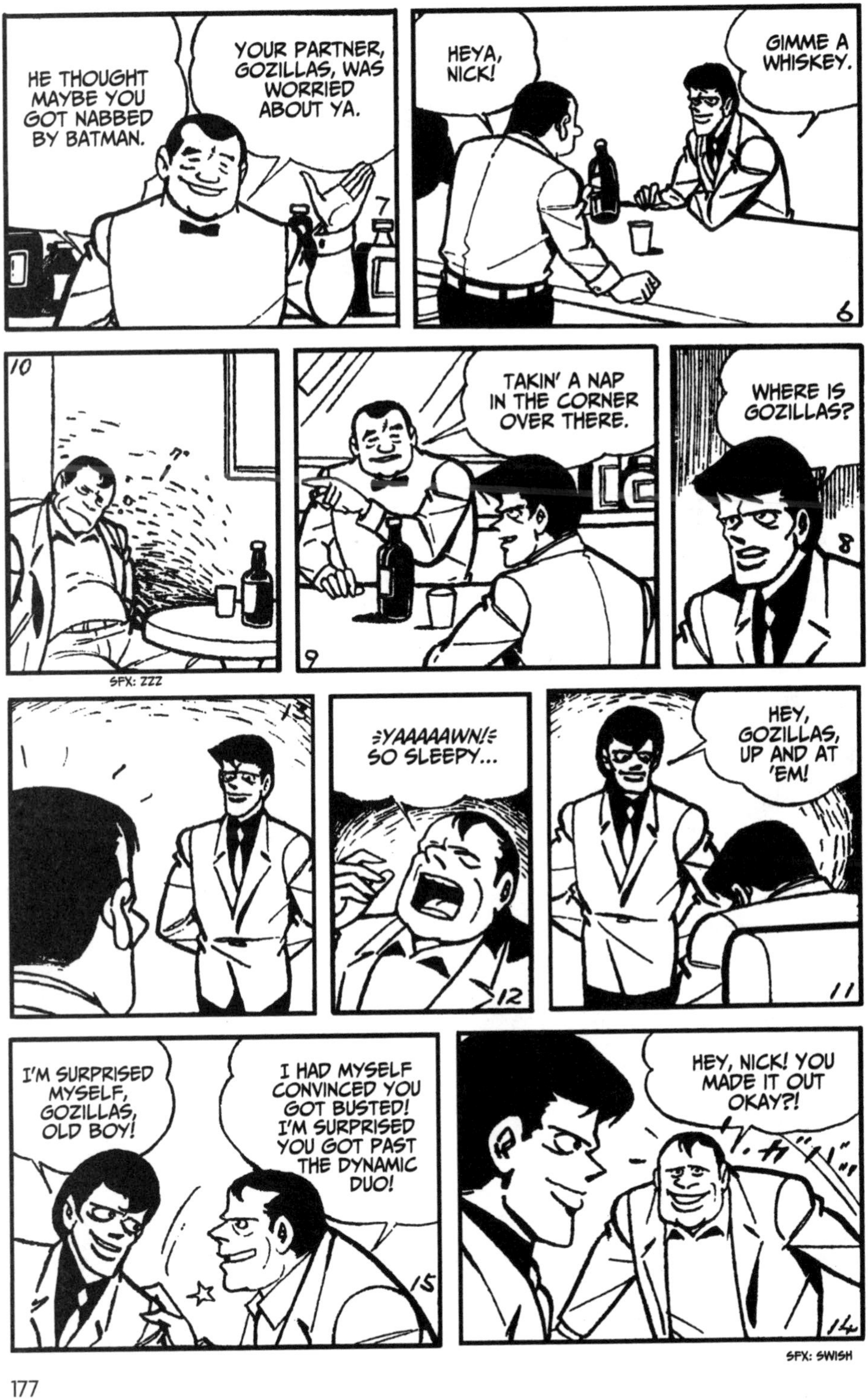
GIMME A WHISKEY.
HEYA, NICK!
YOUR PARTNER, GOZILLAS, WAS WORRIED ABOUT YA.
HE THOUGHT MAYBE YOU GOT NABBED BY BATMAN.
WHERE IS GOZILLAS?
TAKIN' A NAP IN THE CORNER OVER THERE.
SFX: ZZZ
HEY, GOZILLAS, UP AND AT 'EM!
YAAAAAWN! SO SLEEPY...
HEY, NICK! YOU MADE IT OUT OKAY?!
SFX: SWISH
I HAD MYSELF CONVINCED YOU GOT BUSTED! I'M SURPRISED YOU GOT PAST THE DYNAMIC DUO!
I'M SURPRISED MYSELF, GOZILLAS, OLD BOY!

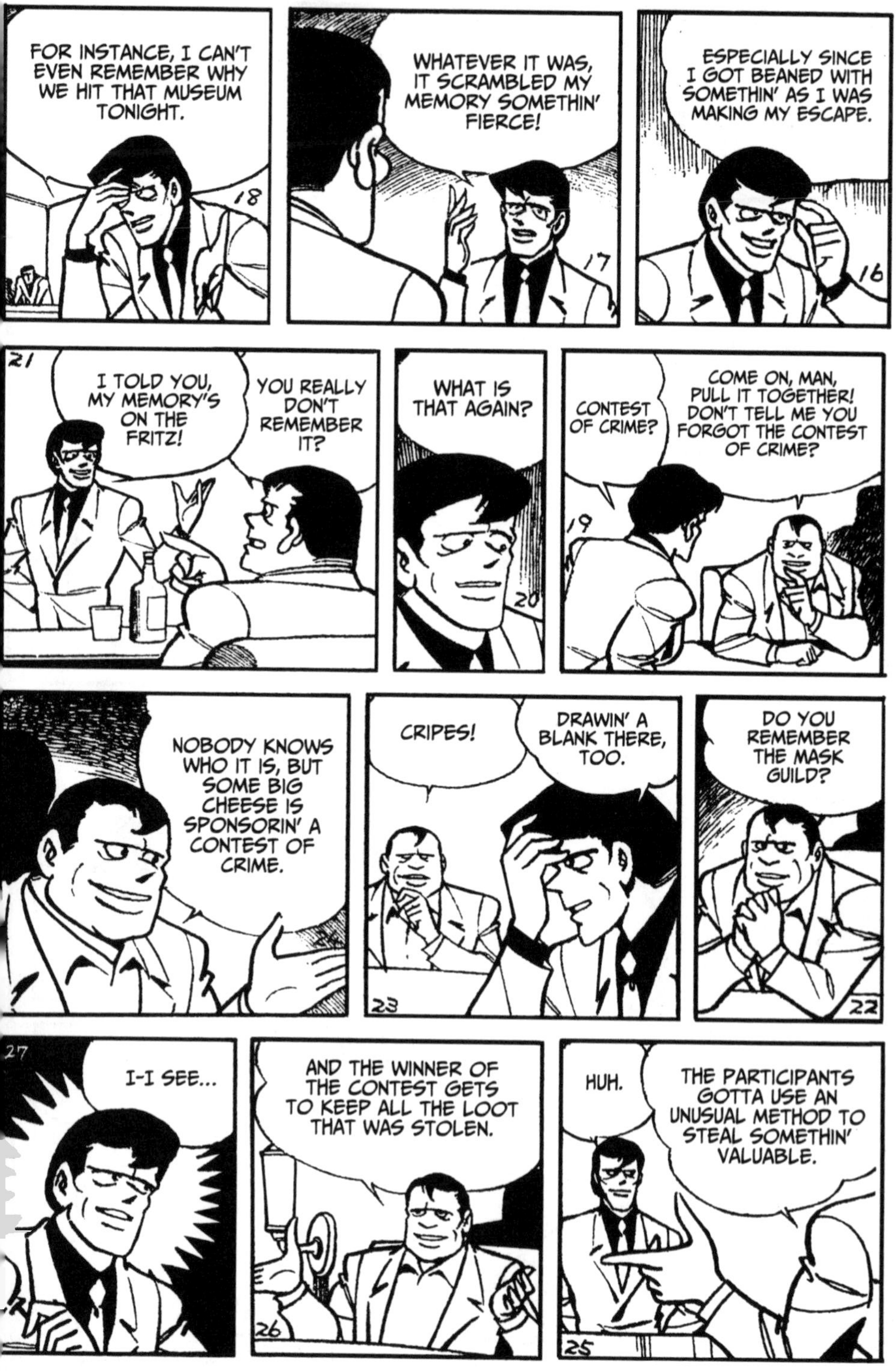
ESPECIALLY SINCE I GOT BEANED WITH SOMETHIN' AS I WAS MAKING MY ESCAPE.
WHATEVER IT WAS, IT SCRAMBLED MY MEMORY SOMETHIN' FIERCE!
FOR INSTANCE, I CAN'T EVEN REMEMBER WHY WE HIT THAT MUSEUM TONIGHT.
COME ON, MAN, PULL IT TOGETHER! DON'T TELL ME YOU FORGOT THE CONTEST OF CRIME?
CONTEST OF CRIME?
WHAT IS THAT AGAIN?
YOU REALLY DON'T REMEMBER IT?
I TOLD YOU, MY MEMORY'S ON THE FRITZ!
DO YOU REMEMBER THE MASK GUILD?
DRAWIN' A BLANK THERE, TOO.
CRIPES!
NOBODY KNOWS WHO IT IS, BUT SOME BIG CHEESE IS SPONSORIN' A CONTEST OF CRIME.
THE PARTICIPANTS GOTTA USE AN UNUSUAL METHOD TO STEAL SOMETHIN' VALUABLE.
HUH.
AND THE WINNER OF THE CONTEST GETS TO KEEP ALL THE LOOT THAT WAS STOLEN.
I-I SEE...

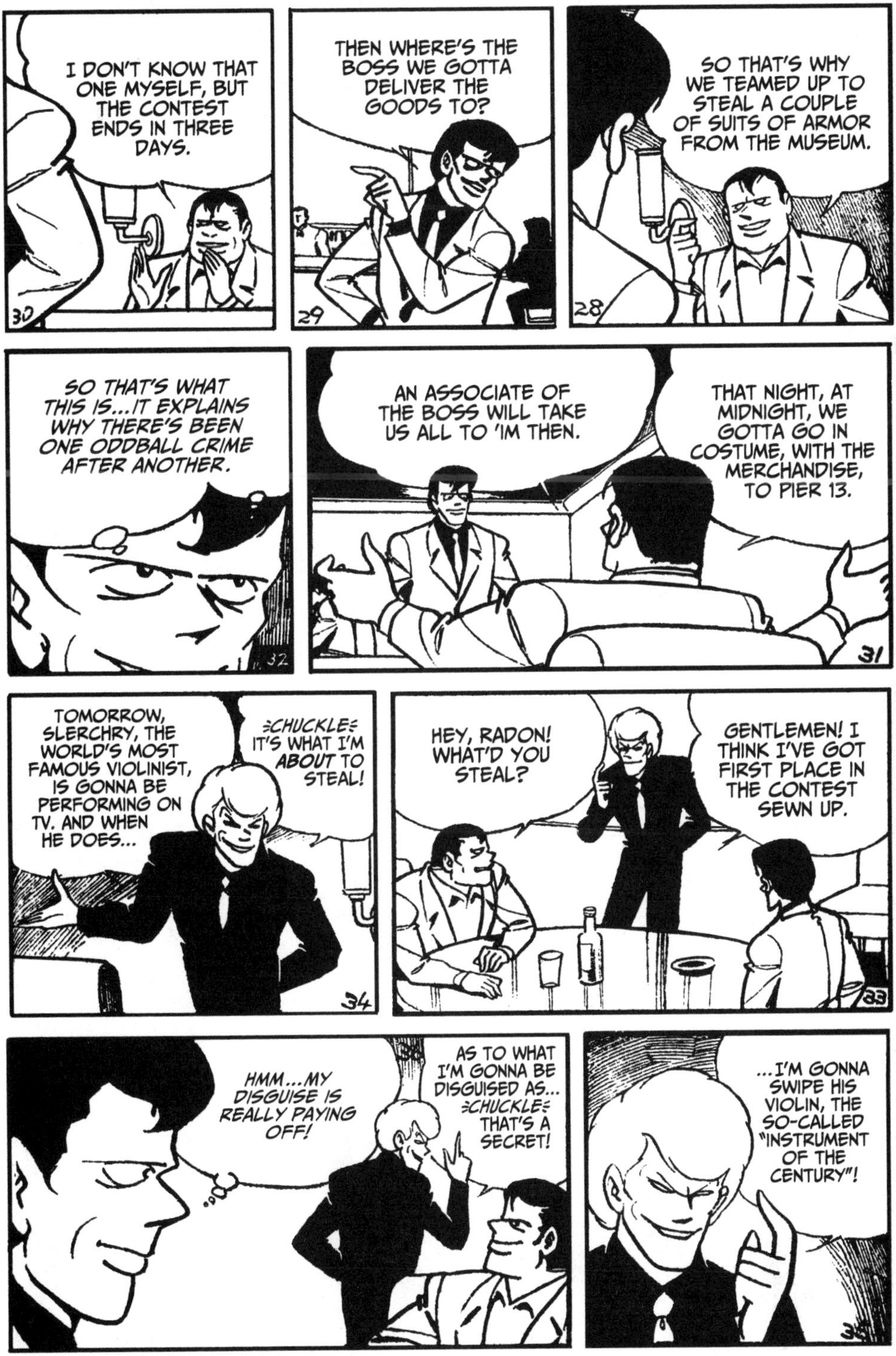
SO THAT'S WHY WE TEAMED UP TO STEAL A COUPLE OF SUITS OF ARMOR FROM THE MUSEUM.
THEN WHERE'S THE BOSS WE GOTTA DELIVER THE GOODS TO?
I DON'T KNOW THAT ONE MYSELF, BUT THE CONTEST ENDS IN THREE DAYS.
THAT NIGHT, AT MIDNIGHT, WE GOTTA GO IN COSTUME, WITH THE MERCHANDISE, TO PIER 13.
AN ASSOCIATE OF THE BOSS WILL TAKE US ALL TO 'IM THEN.
SO THAT'S WHAT THIS IS...IT EXPLAINS WHY THERE'S BEEN ONE ODDBALL CRIME AFTER ANOTHER.
GENTLEMEN! I THINK I'VE GOT FIRST PLACE IN THE CONTEST SEWN UP.
HEY, RADON! WHAT'D YOU STEAL?
≈CHUCKLE≈ IT'S WHAT I'M *ABOUT* TO STEAL!
TOMORROW, SLERCHRY, THE WORLD'S MOST FAMOUS VIOLINIST, IS GONNA BE PERFORMING ON TV. AND WHEN HE DOES...
...I'M GONNA SWIPE HIS VIOLIN, THE SO-CALLED "INSTRUMENT OF THE CENTURY"!
AS TO WHAT I'M GONNA BE DISGUISED AS... ≈CHUCKLE≈ THAT'S A SECRET!
HMM...MY DISGUISE IS REALLY PAYING OFF!

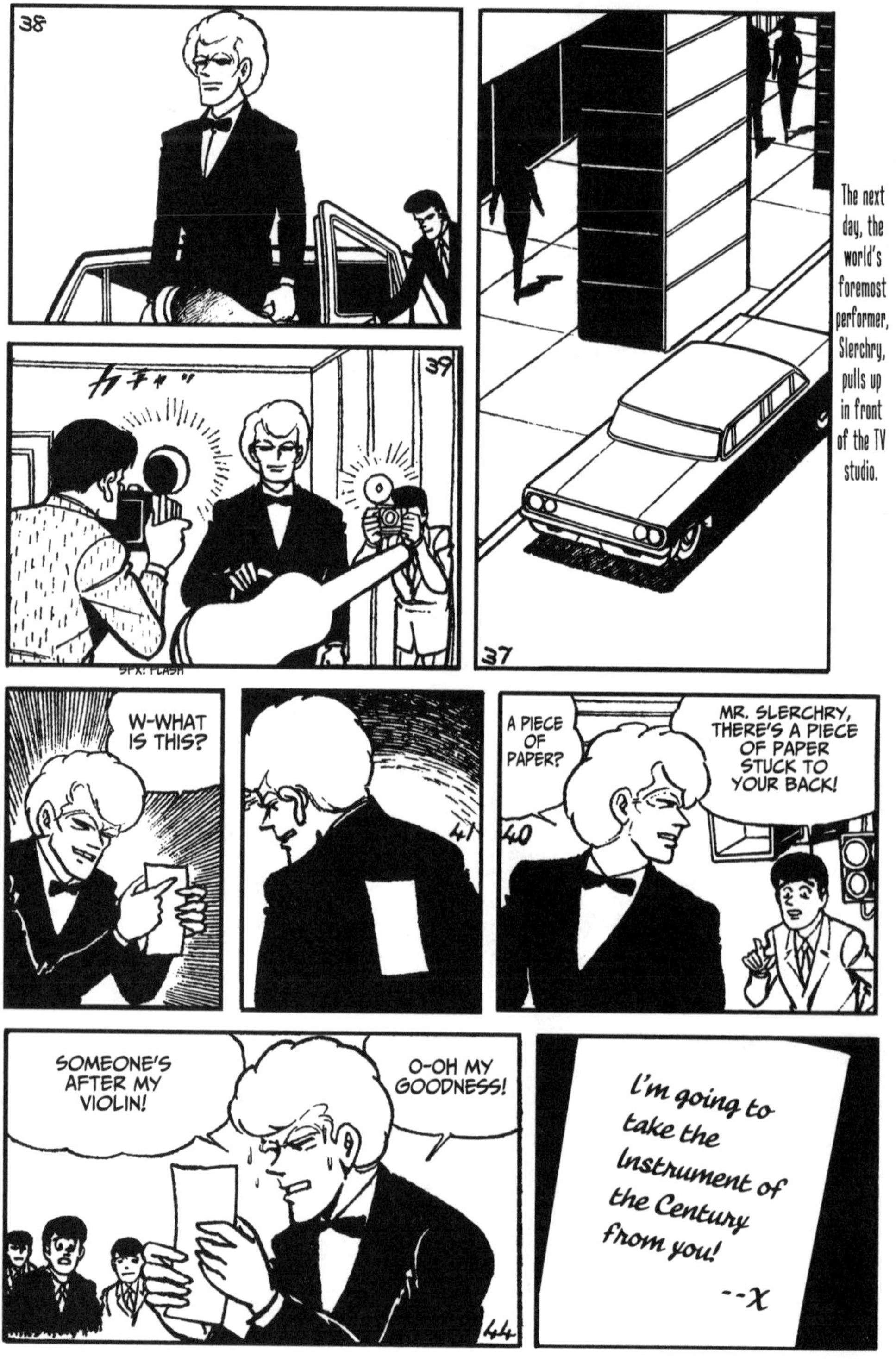
The next day, the world's foremost performer, Slerchry, pulls up in front of the TV studio.
SFX: FLASH
MR. SLERCHRY, THERE'S A PIECE OF PAPER STUCK TO YOUR BACK!
A PIECE OF PAPER?
W-WHAT IS THIS?
I'm going to take the Instrument of the Century from you!
--X
O-OH MY GOODNESS!
SOMEONE'S AFTER MY VIOLIN!

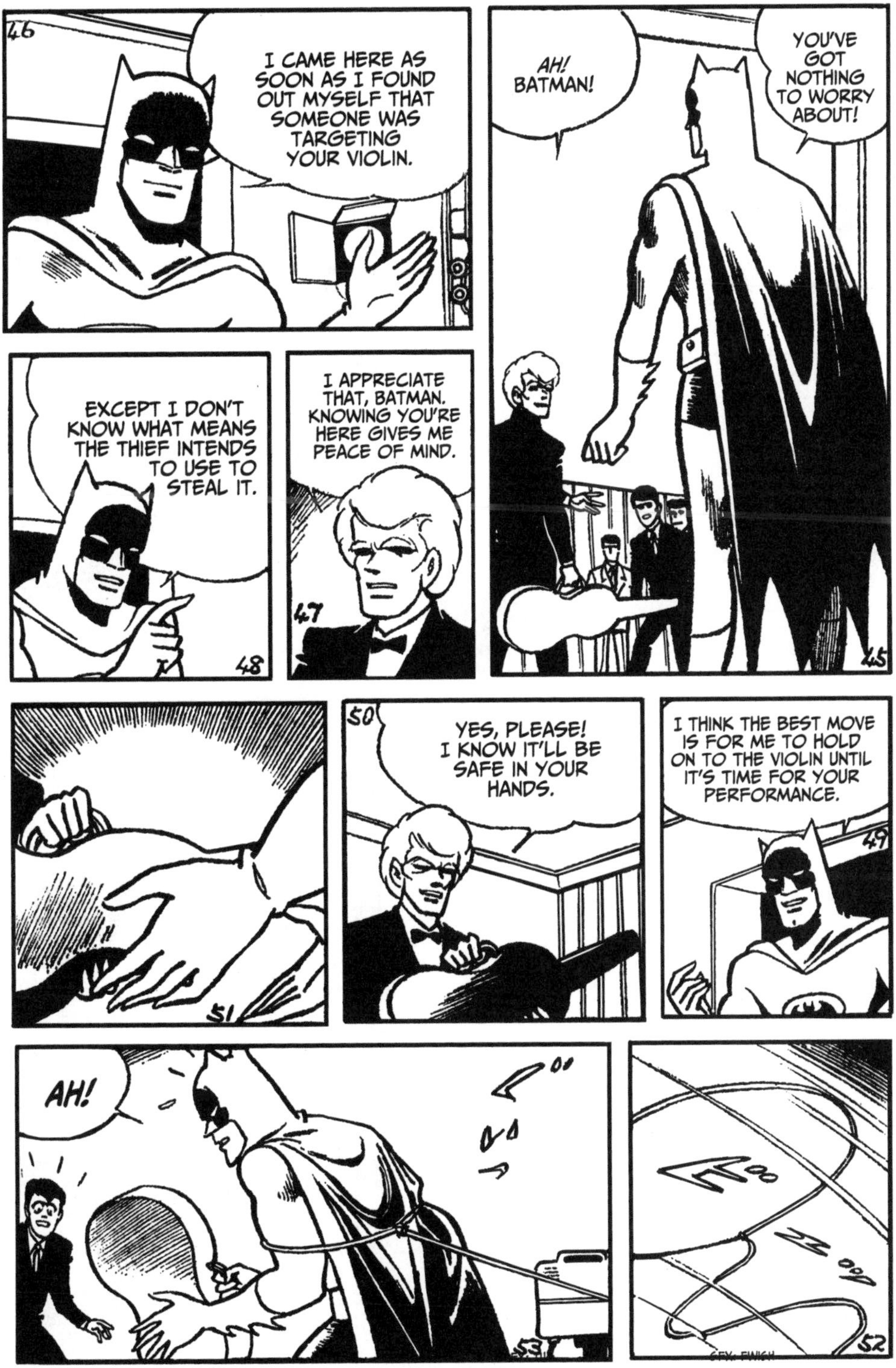
YOU'VE GOT NOTHING TO WORRY ABOUT!
AH! BATMAN!
I CAME HERE AS SOON AS I FOUND OUT MYSELF THAT SOMEONE WAS TARGETING YOUR VIOLIN.
I APPRECIATE THAT, BATMAN. KNOWING YOU'RE HERE GIVES ME PEACE OF MIND.
EXCEPT I DON'T KNOW WHAT MEANS THE THIEF INTENDS TO USE TO STEAL IT.
I THINK THE BEST MOVE IS FOR ME TO HOLD ON TO THE VIOLIN UNTIL IT'S TIME FOR YOUR PERFORMANCE.
YES, PLEASE! I KNOW IT'LL BE SAFE IN YOUR HANDS.
AH!

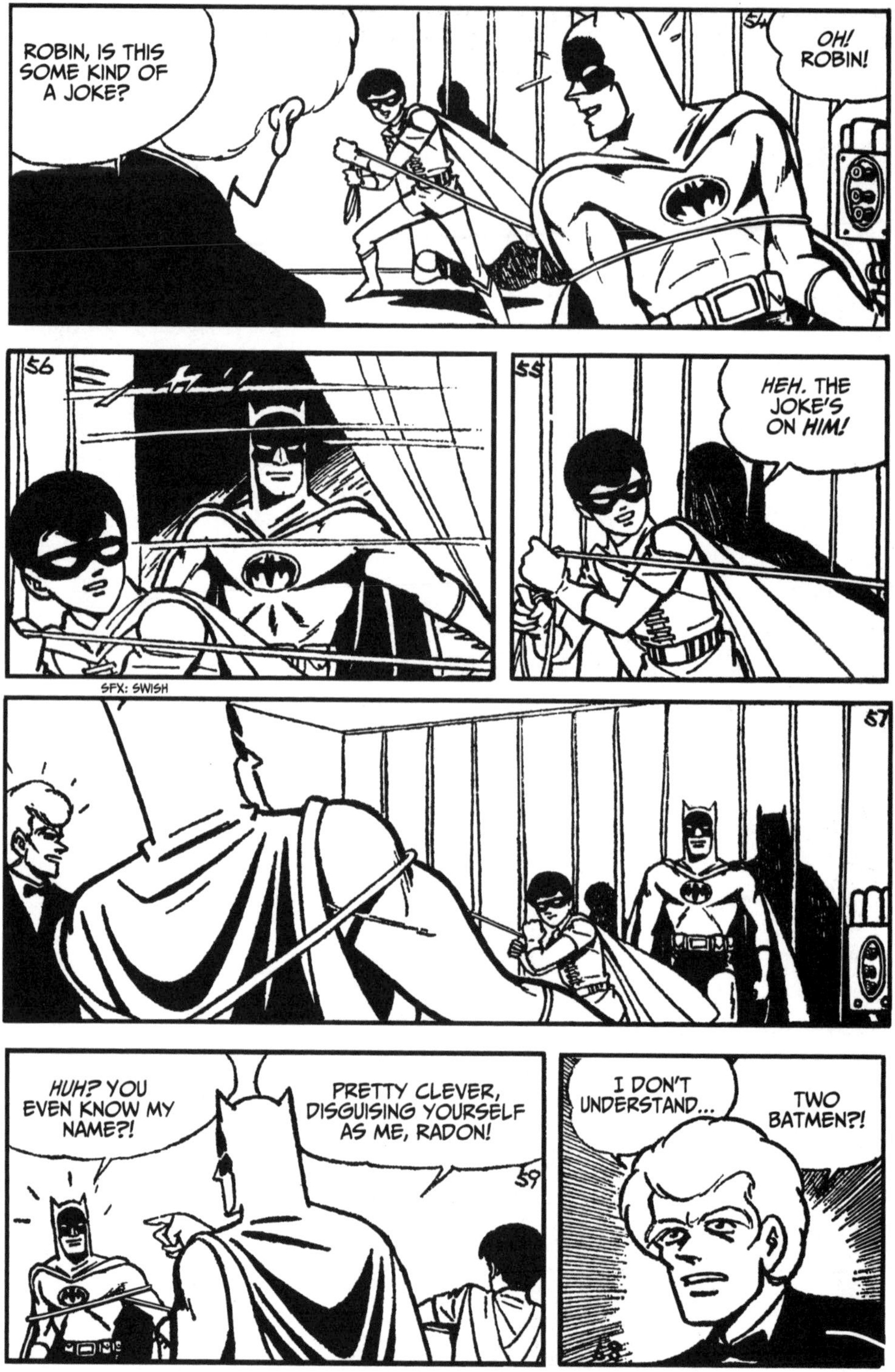
OH! ROBIN!
ROBIN, IS THIS SOME KIND OF A JOKE?
HEH. THE JOKE'S ON HIM!
SFX: SWISH
TWO BATMEN?!
I DON'T UNDERSTAND...
PRETTY CLEVER, DISGUISING YOURSELF AS ME, RADON!
HUH? YOU EVEN KNOW MY NAME?!

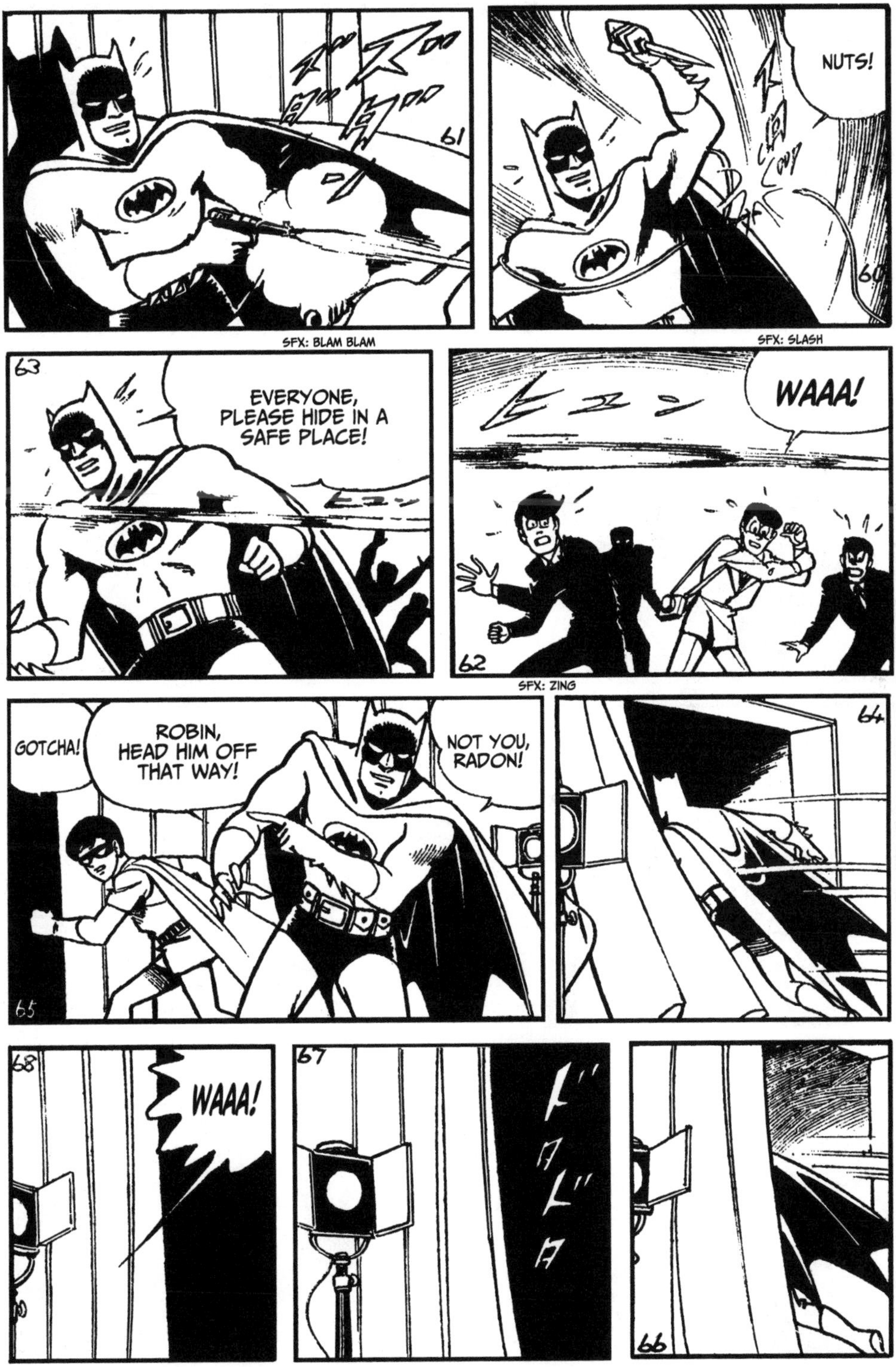
NUTS!
SFX: SLASH
SFX: BLAM BLAM
WAAA!
SFX: ZING
EVERYONE, PLEASE HIDE IN A SAFE PLACE!
NOT YOU, RADON!
ROBIN, HEAD HIM OFF THAT WAY!
GOTCHA!
SFX: CRASH SLAM
WAAA!

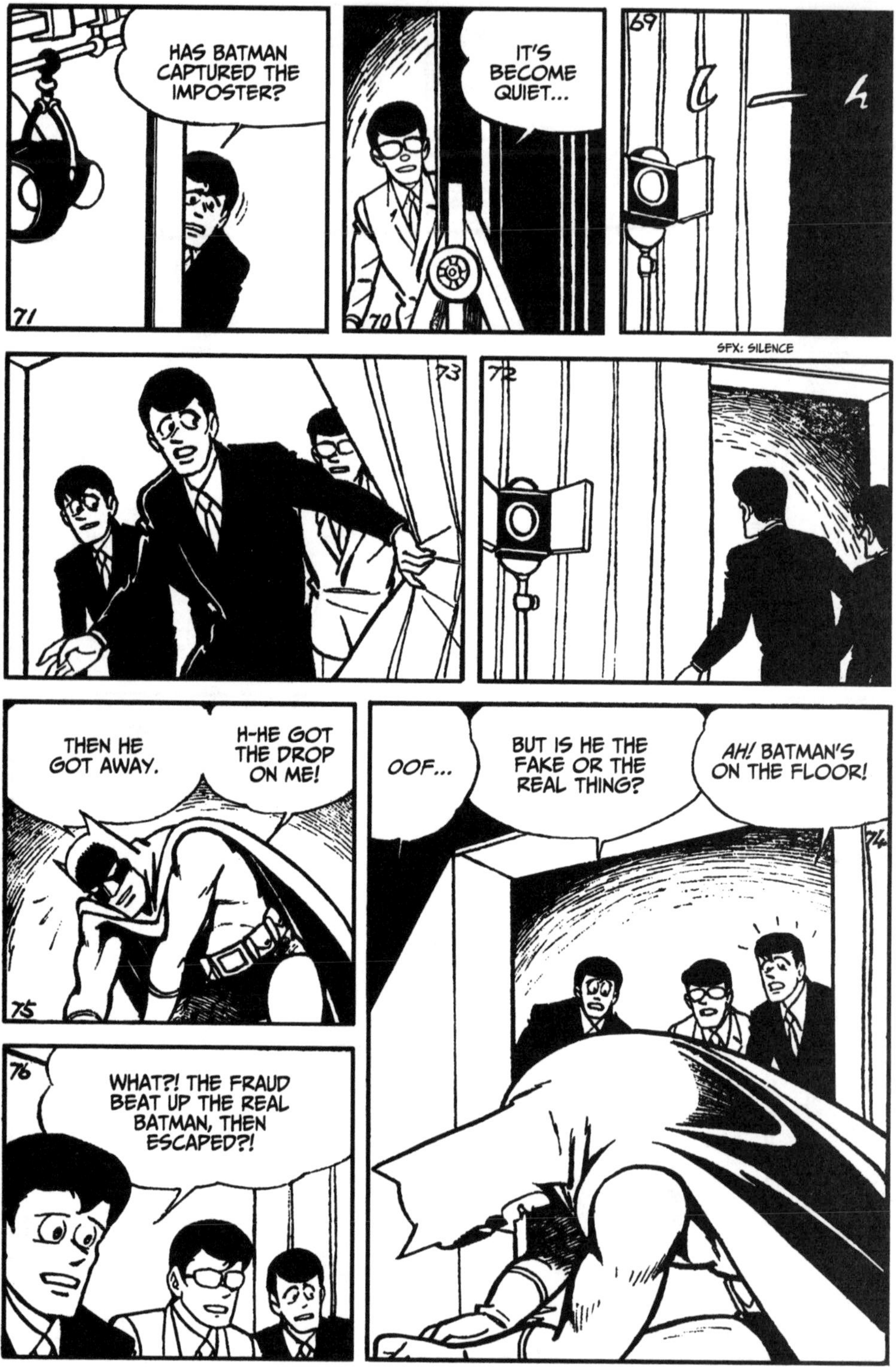
SFX: SILENCE
IT'S BECOME QUIET...
HAS BATMAN CAPTURED THE IMPOSTER?
AH! BATMAN'S ON THE FLOOR!
BUT IS HE THE FAKE OR THE REAL THING?
OOF...
H-HE GOT THE DROP ON ME!
THEN HE GOT AWAY.
WHAT?! THE FRAUD BEAT UP THE REAL BATMAN, THEN ESCAPED?!

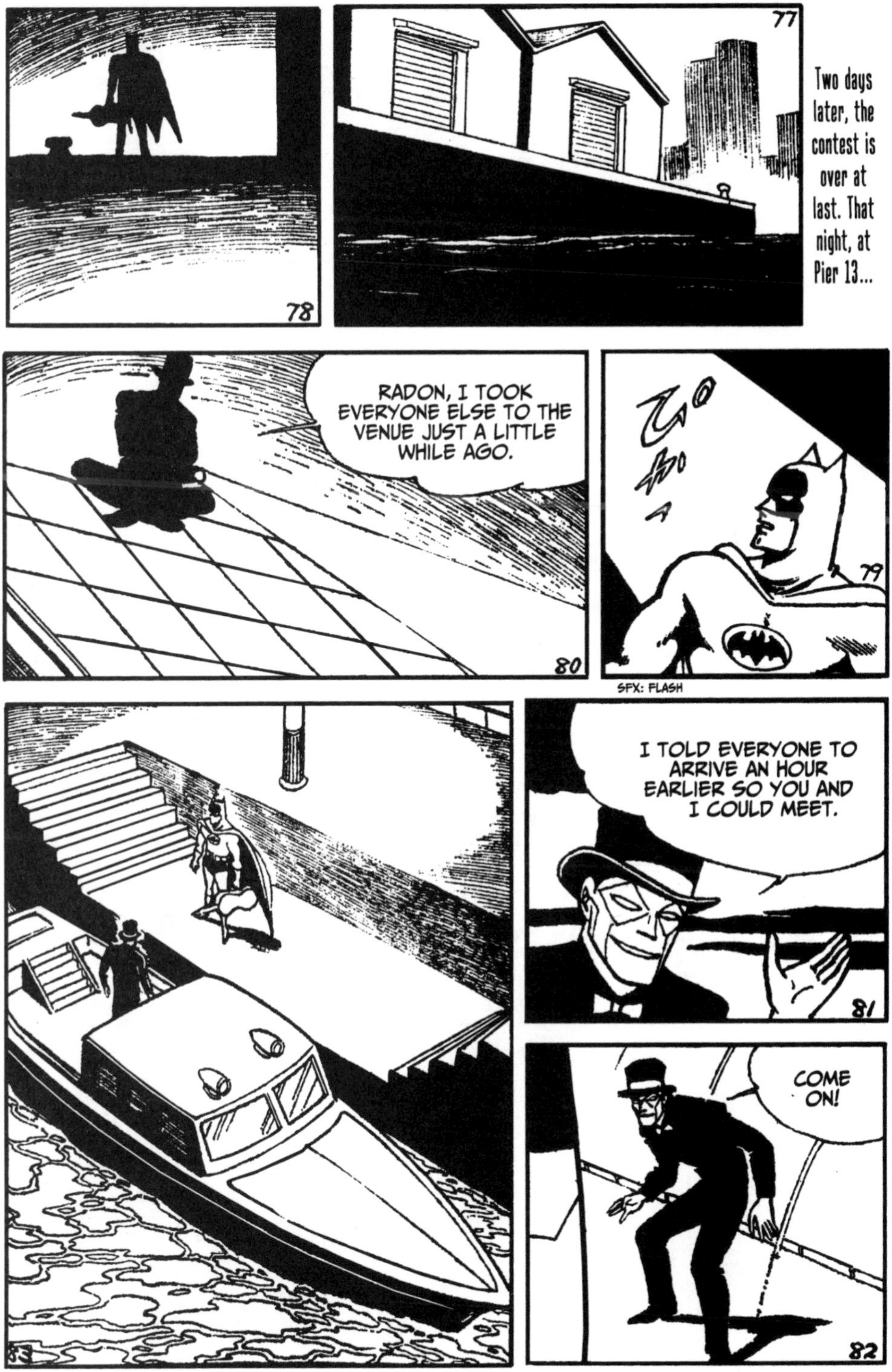
Two days later, the contest is over at last. That night, at Pier 13...
SFX: FLASH
RADON, I TOOK EVERYONE ELSE TO THE VENUE JUST A LITTLE WHILE AGO.
I TOLD EVERYONE TO ARRIVE AN HOUR EARLIER SO YOU AND I COULD MEET.
COME ON!

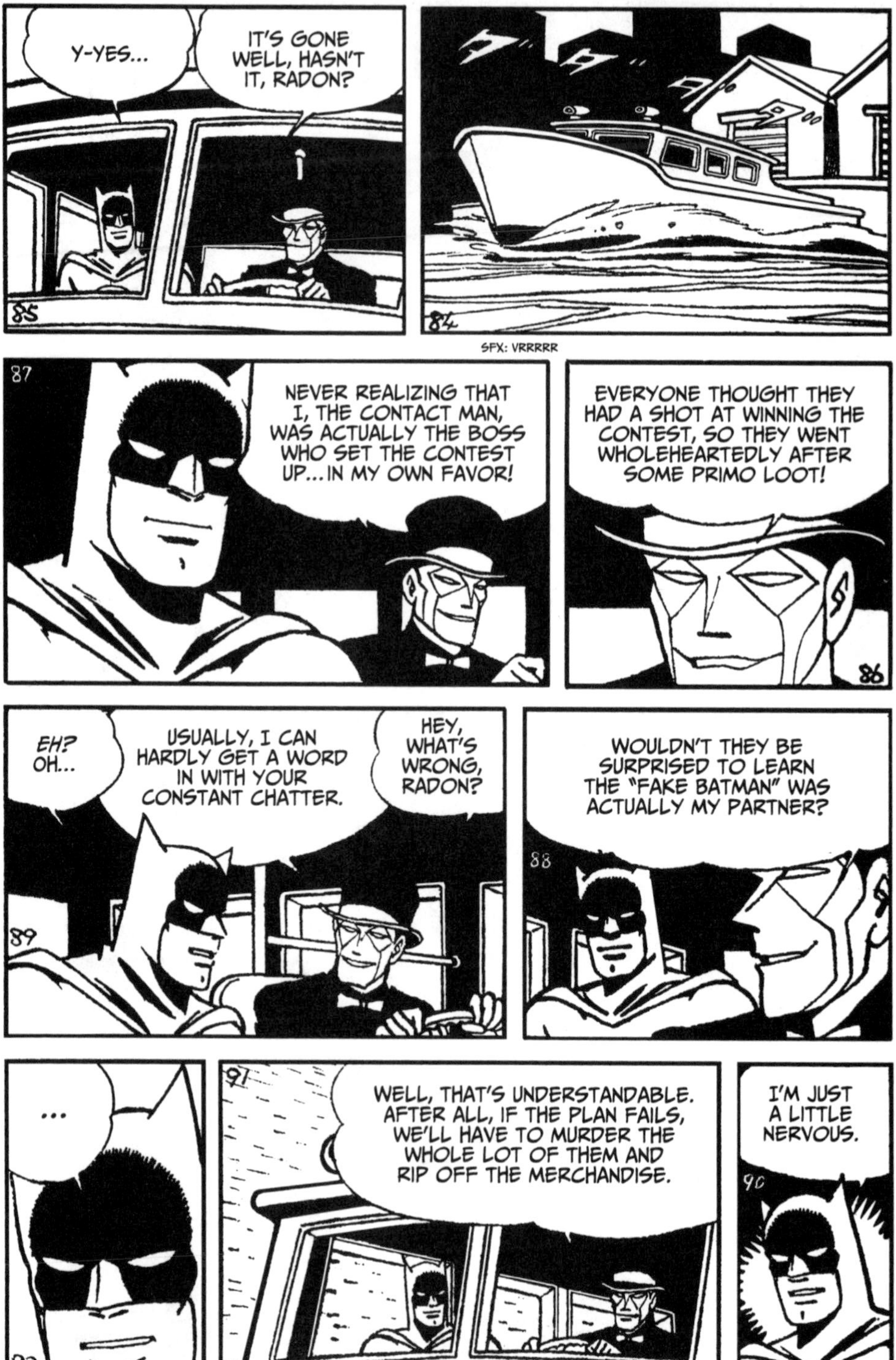
SFX: VRRRRR
IT'S GONE WELL, HASN'T IT, RADON?
Y-YES...
EVERYONE THOUGHT THEY HAD A SHOT AT WINNING THE CONTEST, SO THEY WENT WHOLEHEARTEDLY AFTER SOME PRIMO LOOT!
NEVER REALIZING THAT I, THE CONTACT MAN, WAS ACTUALLY THE BOSS WHO SET THE CONTEST UP...IN MY OWN FAVOR!
WOULDN'T THEY BE SURPRISED TO LEARN THE "FAKE BATMAN" WAS ACTUALLY MY PARTNER?
HEY, WHAT'S WRONG, RADON?
USUALLY, I CAN HARDLY GET A WORD IN WITH YOUR CONSTANT CHATTER.
EH? OH...
I'M JUST A LITTLE NERVOUS.
WELL, THAT'S UNDERSTANDABLE. AFTER ALL, IF THE PLAN FAILS, WE'LL HAVE TO MURDER THE WHOLE LOT OF THEM AND RIP OFF THE MERCHANDISE.
...

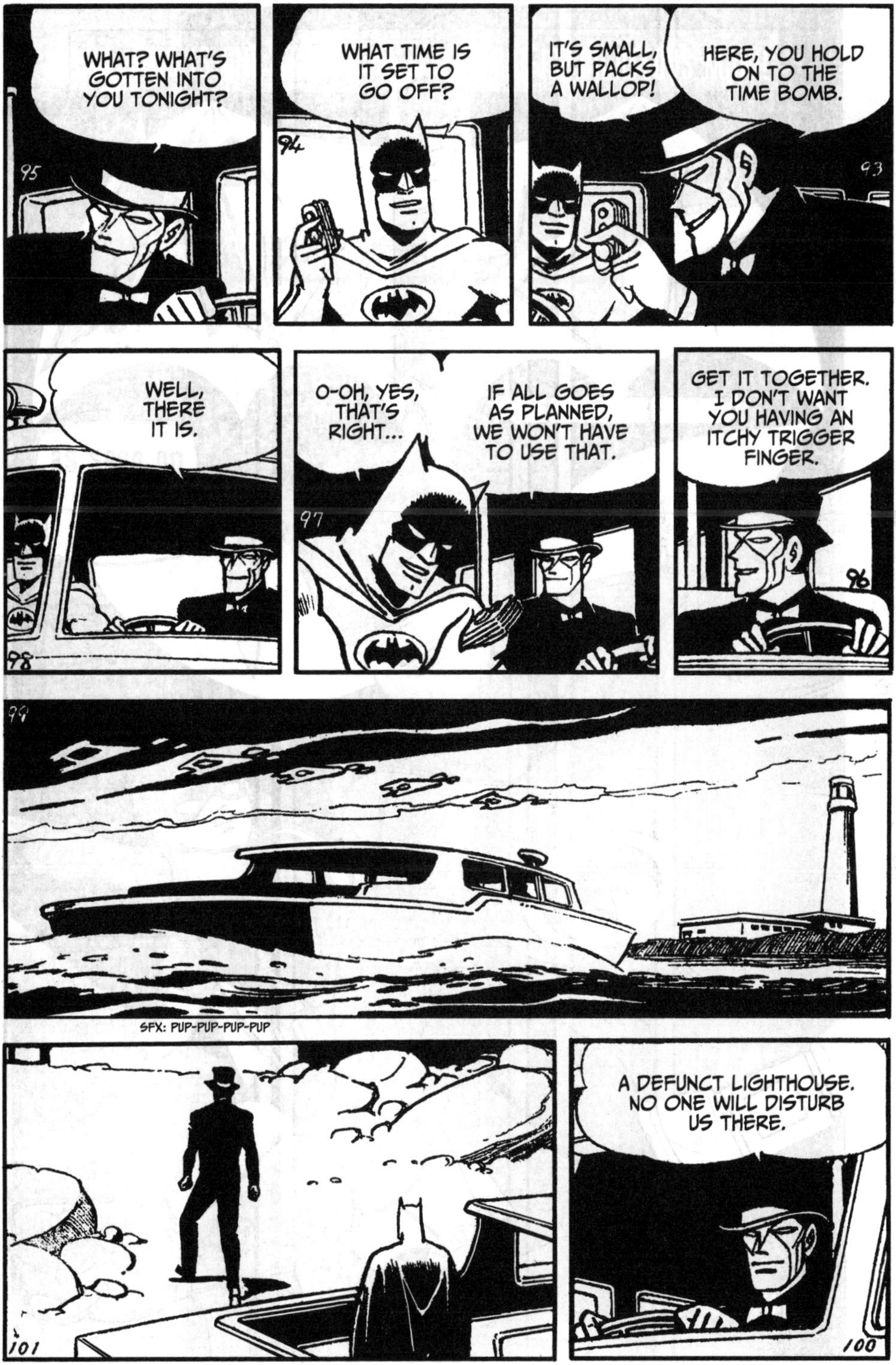
HERE, YOU HOLD ON TO THE TIME BOMB.
IT'S SMALL, BUT PACKS A WALLOP!
WHAT TIME IS IT SET TO GO OFF?
WHAT? WHAT'S GOTTEN INTO YOU TONIGHT?
GET IT TOGETHER. I DON'T WANT YOU HAVING AN ITCHY TRIGGER FINGER.
IF ALL GOES AS PLANNED, WE WON'T HAVE TO USE THAT.
O-OH, YES, THAT'S RIGHT...
WELL, THERE IT IS.
SFX: PUP-PUP-PUP-PUP
A DEFUNCT LIGHTHOUSE. NO ONE WILL DISTURB US THERE.

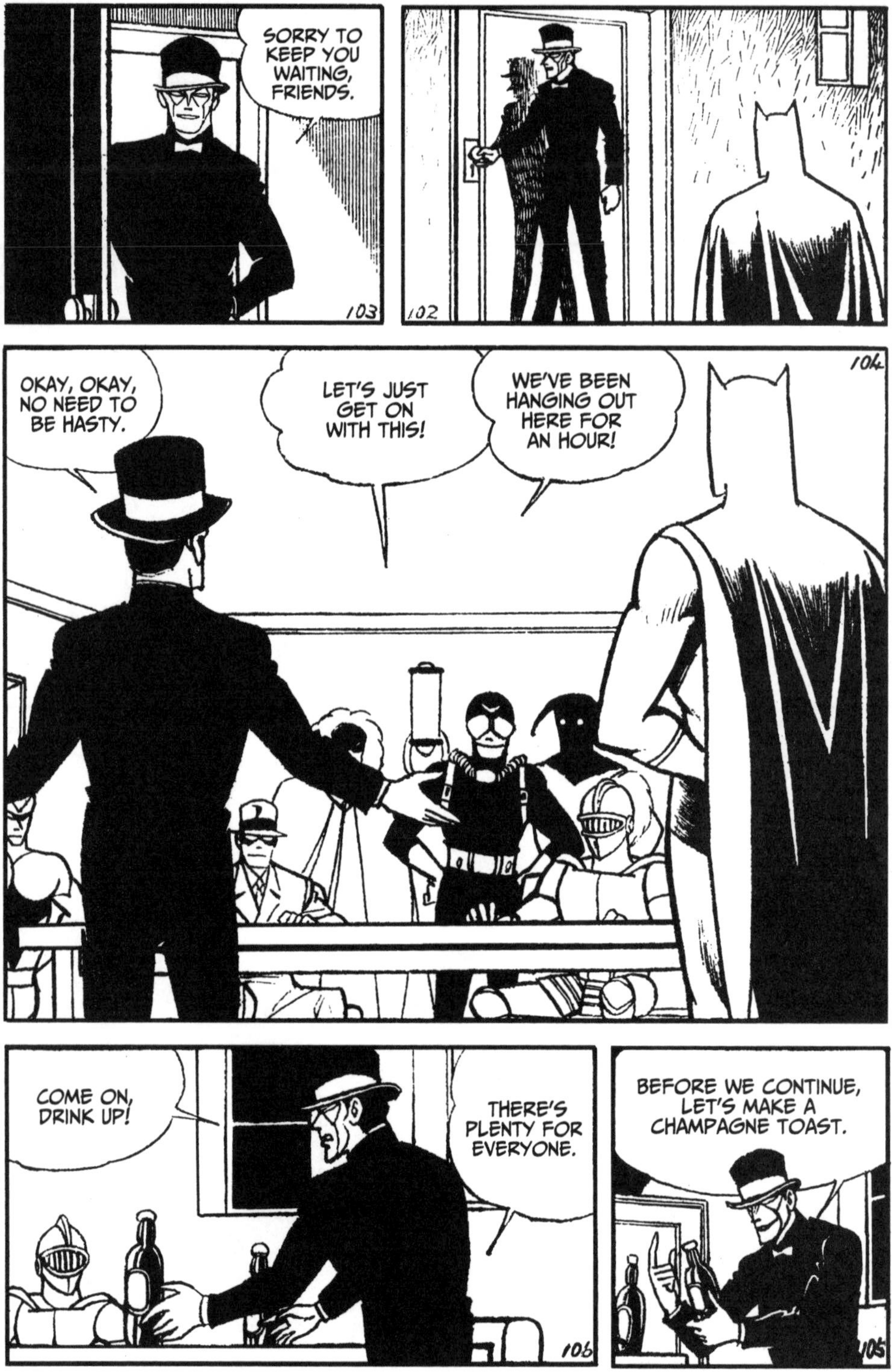
SORRY TO KEEP YOU WAITING, FRIENDS.
WE'VE BEEN HANGING OUT HERE FOR AN HOUR!
LET'S JUST GET ON WITH THIS!
OKAY, OKAY, NO NEED TO BE HASTY.
BEFORE WE CONTINUE, LET'S MAKE A CHAMPAGNE TOAST.
THERE'S PLENTY FOR EVERYONE.
COME ON, DRINK UP!

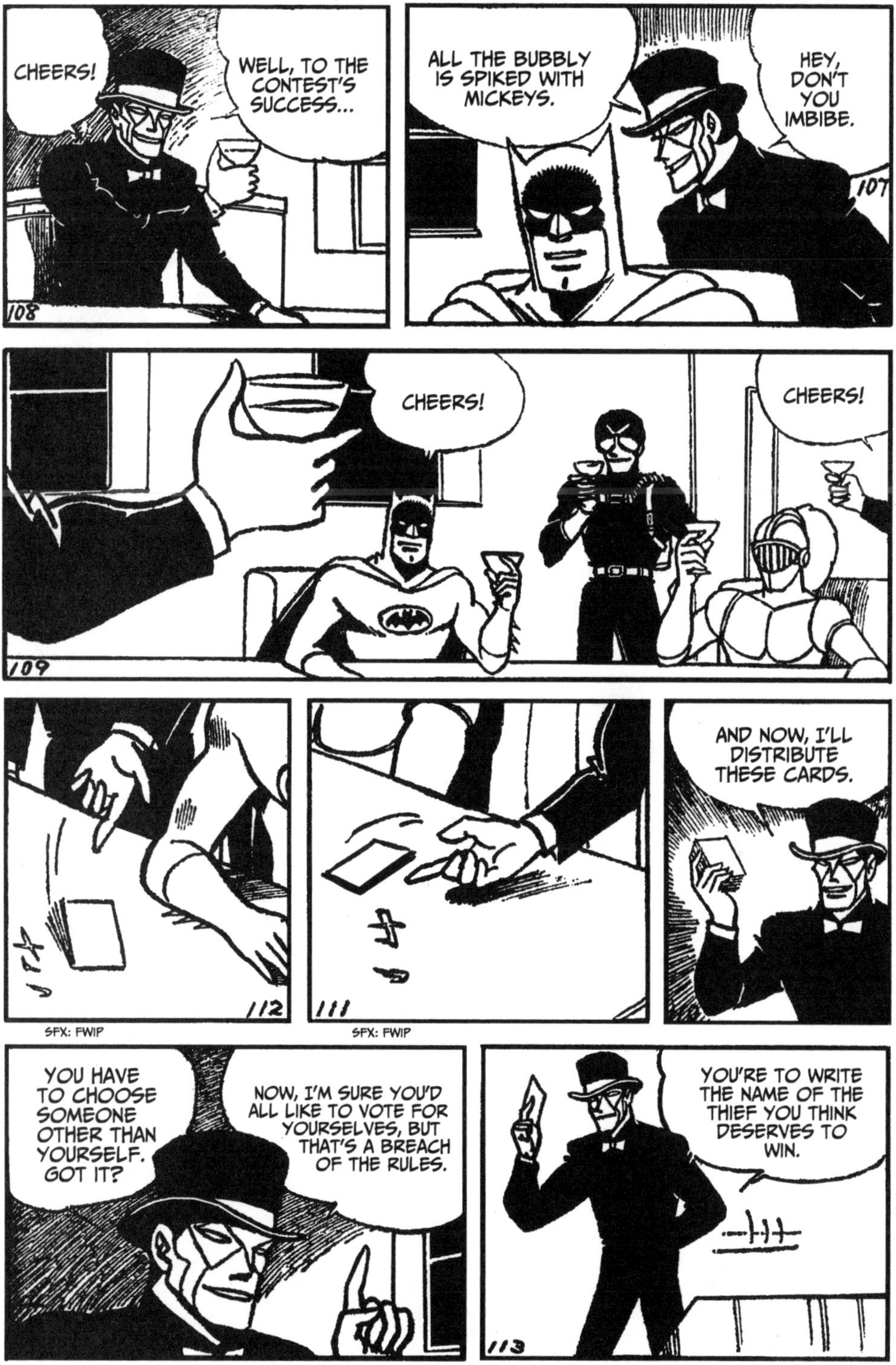
HEY, DON'T YOU IMBIBE.
ALL THE BUBBLY IS SPIKED WITH MICKEYS.
WELL, TO THE CONTEST'S SUCCESS...
CHEERS!
CHEERS!
CHEERS!
AND NOW, I'LL DISTRIBUTE THESE CARDS.
YOU'RE TO WRITE THE NAME OF THE THIEF YOU THINK DESERVES TO WIN.
NOW, I'M SURE YOU'D ALL LIKE TO VOTE FOR YOURSELVES, BUT THAT'S A BREACH OF THE RULES.
YOU HAVE TO CHOOSE SOMEONE OTHER THAN YOURSELF. GOT IT?

SFX: FWIP

SFX: FWIP

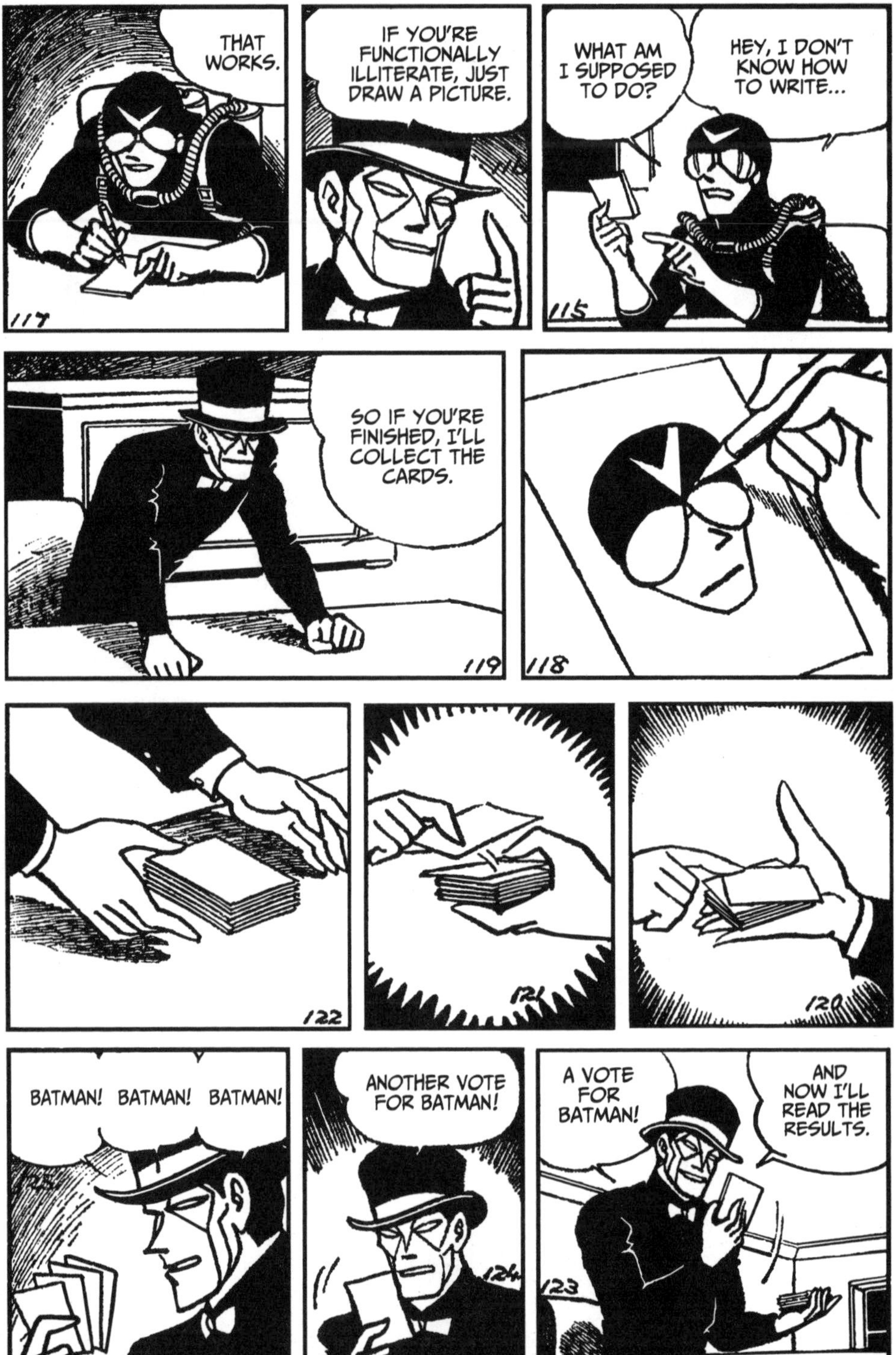
HEY, I DON'T KNOW HOW TO WRITE...
WHAT AM I SUPPOSED TO DO?
IF YOU'RE FUNCTIONALLY ILLITERATE, JUST DRAW A PICTURE.
THAT WORKS.
SO IF YOU'RE FINISHED, I'LL COLLECT THE CARDS.
AND NOW I'LL READ THE RESULTS.
A VOTE FOR BATMAN!
ANOTHER VOTE FOR BATMAN!
BATMAN! BATMAN! BATMAN!

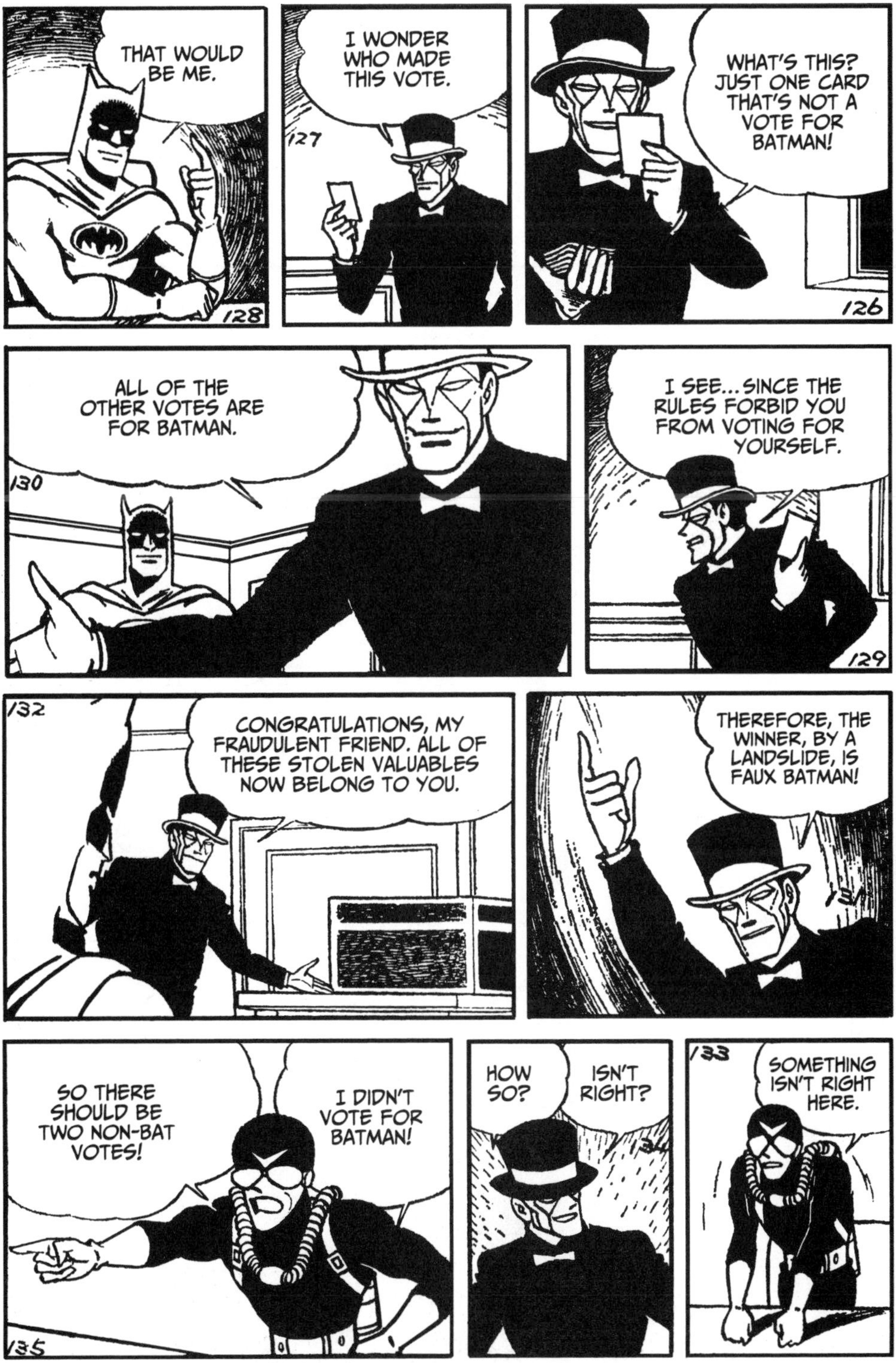
WHAT'S THIS? JUST ONE CARD THAT'S NOT A VOTE FOR BATMAN!
I WONDER WHO MADE THIS VOTE.
THAT WOULD BE ME.
I SEE... SINCE THE RULES FORBID YOU FROM VOTING FOR YOURSELF.
ALL OF THE OTHER VOTES ARE FOR BATMAN.
THEREFORE, THE WINNER, BY A LANDSLIDE, IS FAUX BATMAN!
CONGRATULATIONS, MY FRAUDULENT FRIEND. ALL OF THESE STOLEN VALUABLES NOW BELONG TO YOU.
SOMETHING ISN'T RIGHT HERE.
ISN'T RIGHT?
HOW SO?
I DIDN'T VOTE FOR BATMAN!
SO THERE SHOULD BE TWO NON-BAT VOTES!

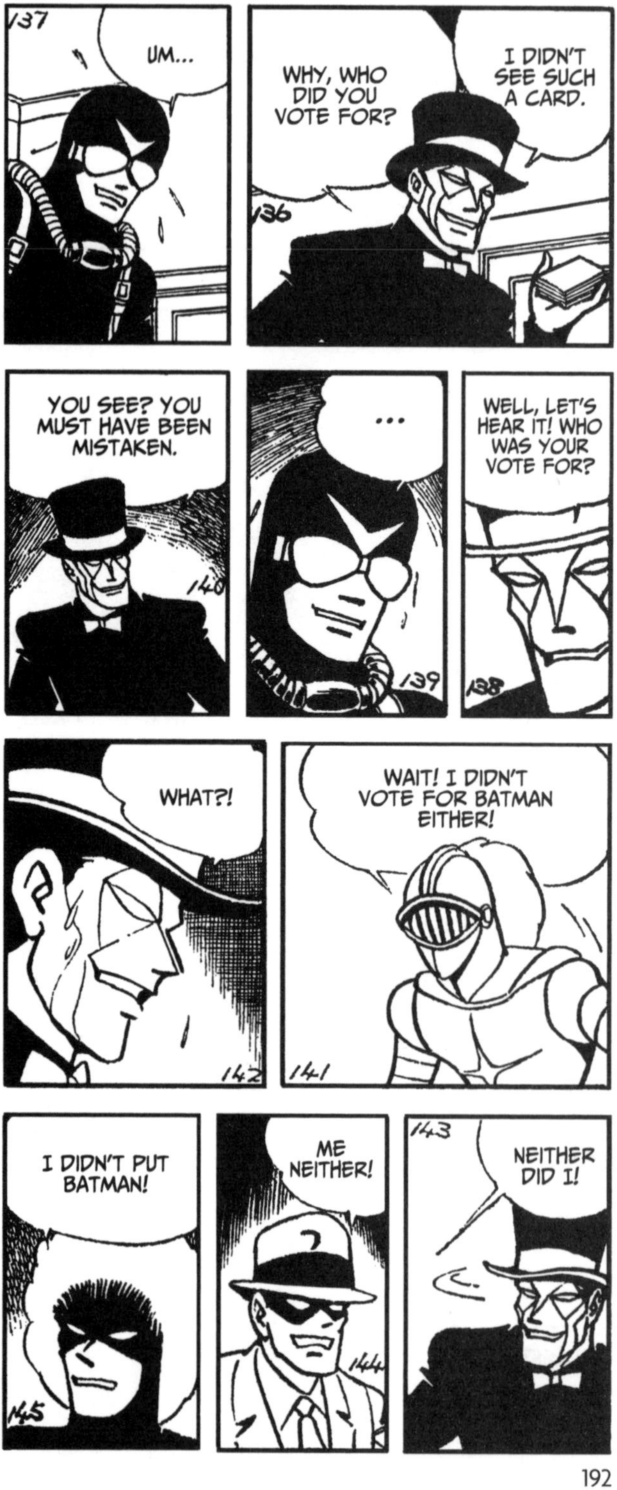
I DIDN'T SEE SUCH A CARD.
WHY, WHO DID YOU VOTE FOR?
UM...
WELL, LET'S HEAR IT! WHO WAS YOUR VOTE FOR?
...
YOU SEE? YOU MUST HAVE BEEN MISTAKEN.
WAIT! I DIDN'T VOTE FOR BATMAN EITHER!
WHAT?!
NEITHER DID I!
ME NEITHER!
I DIDN'T PUT BATMAN!

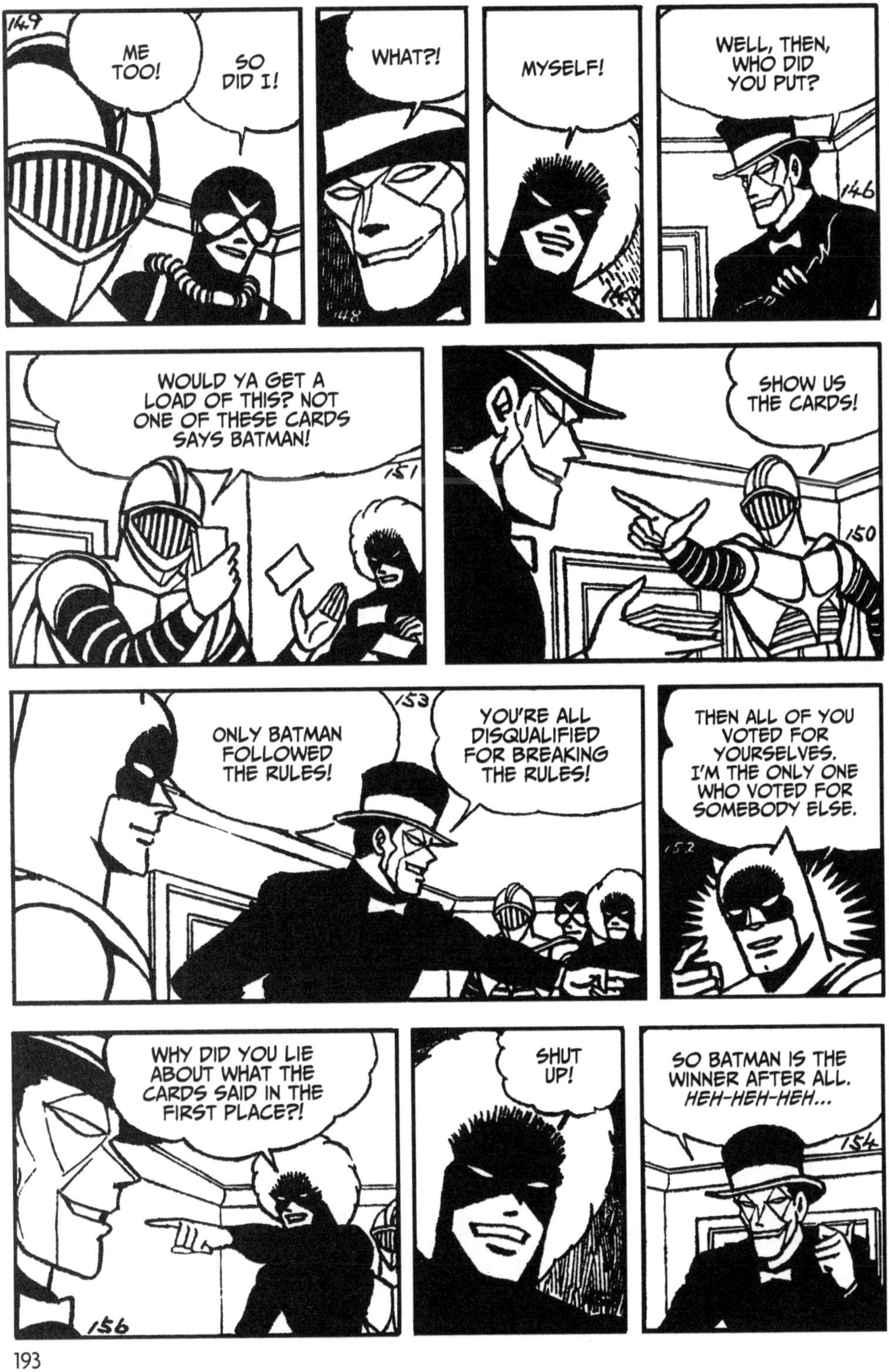

WELL, THEN, WHO DID YOU PUT?
MYSELF!
WHAT?!
SO DID I!
ME TOO!
SHOW US THE CARDS!
WOULD YA GET A LOAD OF THIS? NOT ONE OF THESE CARDS SAYS BATMAN!
THEN ALL OF YOU VOTED FOR YOURSELVES. I'M THE ONLY ONE WHO VOTED FOR SOMEBODY ELSE.
YOU'RE ALL DISQUALIFIED FOR BREAKING THE RULES!
ONLY BATMAN FOLLOWED THE RULES!
SO BATMAN IS THE WINNER AFTER ALL. *HEH-HEH-HEH...*
SHUT UP!
WHY DID YOU LIE ABOUT WHAT THE CARDS SAID IN THE FIRST PLACE?!

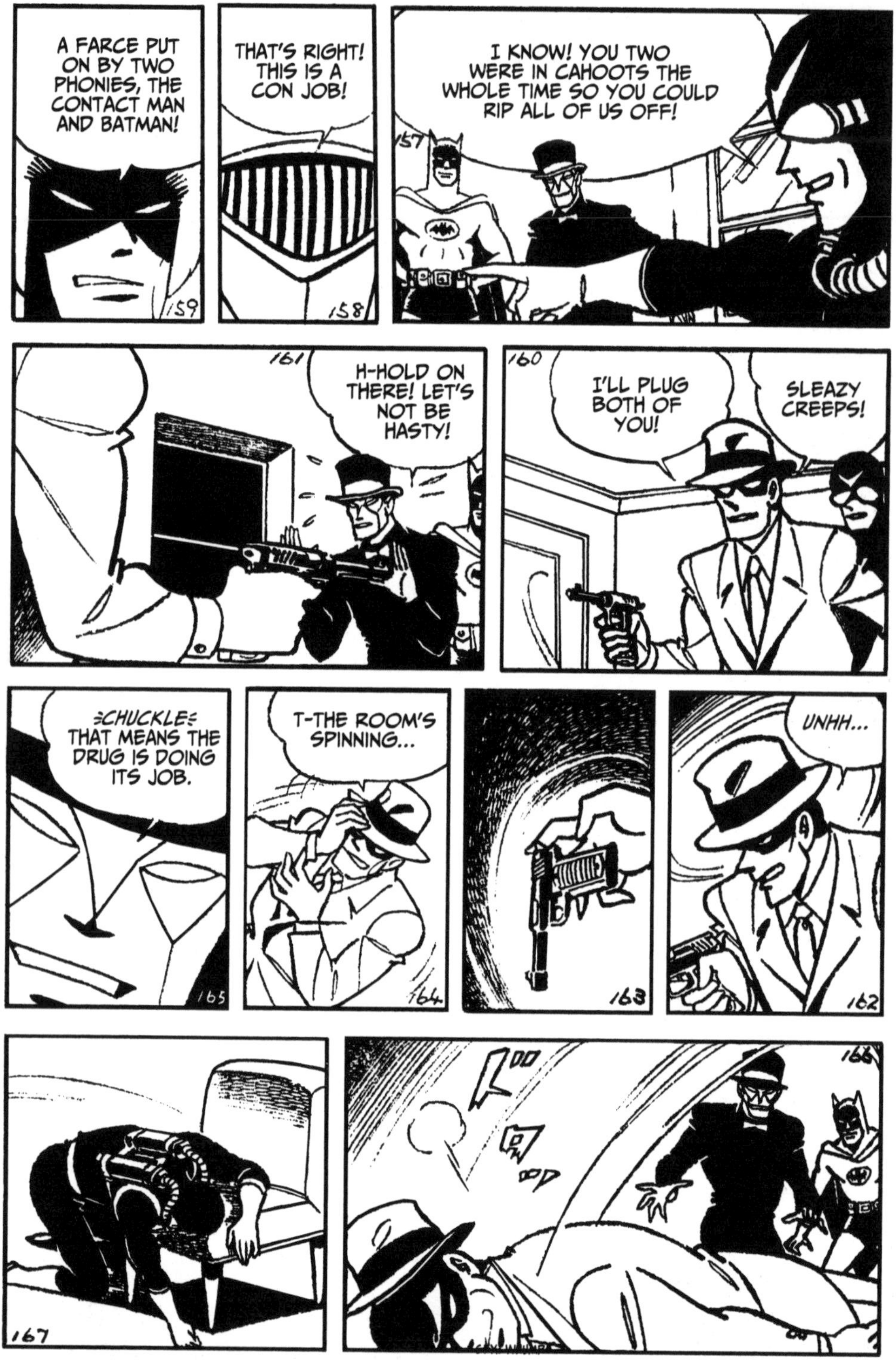
I KNOW! YOU TWO WERE IN CAHOOTS THE WHOLE TIME SO YOU COULD RIP ALL OF US OFF!
THAT'S RIGHT! THIS IS A CON JOB!
A FARCE PUT ON BY TWO PHONIES, THE CONTACT MAN AND BATMAN!
SLEAZY CREEPS!
I'LL PLUG BOTH OF YOU!
H-HOLD ON THERE! LET'S NOT BE HASTY!
UNHH...
T-THE ROOM'S SPINNING...
=CHUCKLE= THAT MEANS THE DRUG IS DOING ITS JOB.

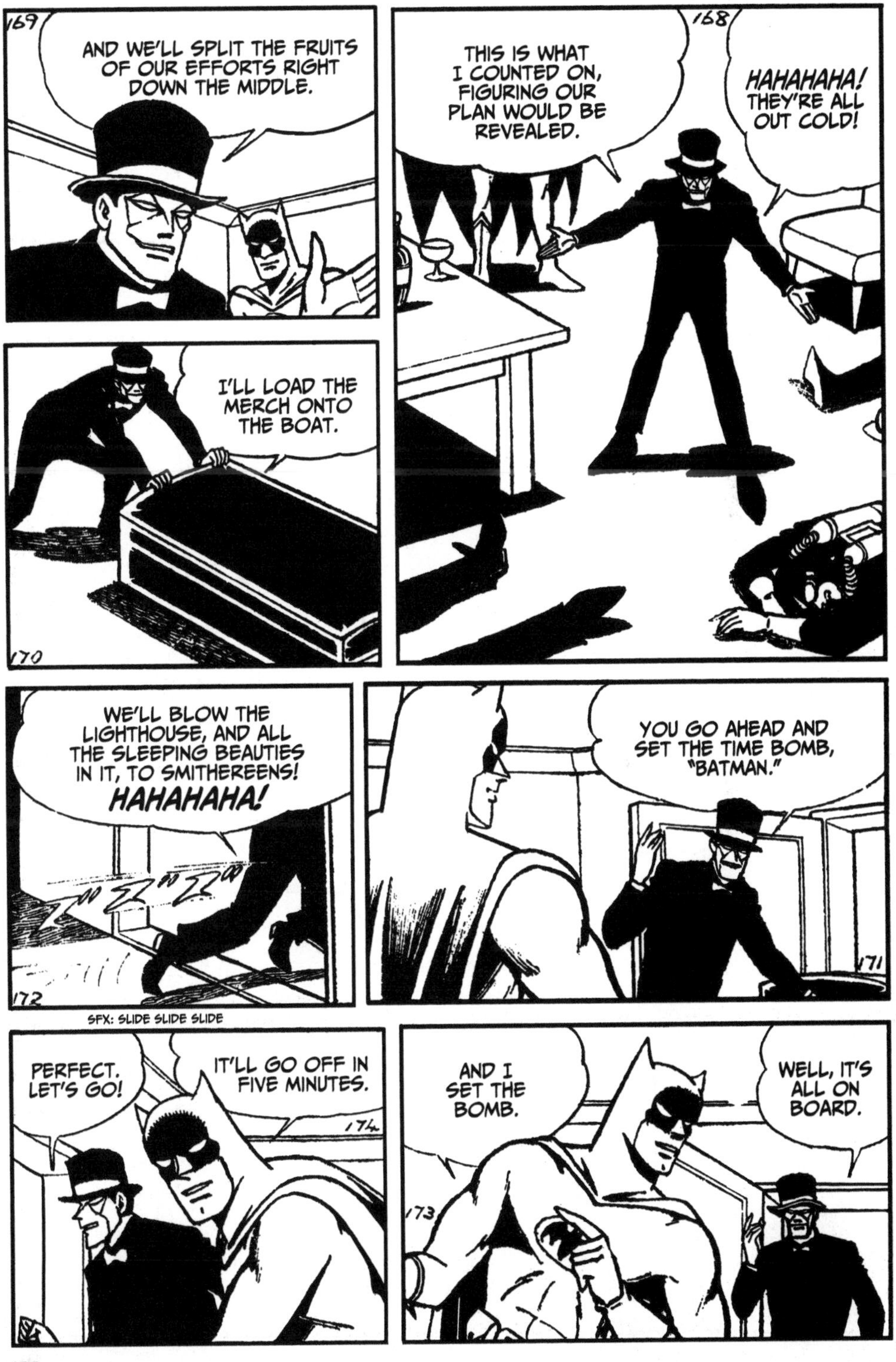
HAHAHAHA! THEY'RE ALL OUT COLD!
THIS IS WHAT I COUNTED ON, FIGURING OUR PLAN WOULD BE REVEALED.
AND WE'LL SPLIT THE FRUITS OF OUR EFFORTS RIGHT DOWN THE MIDDLE.
I'LL LOAD THE MERCH ONTO THE BOAT.
YOU GO AHEAD AND SET THE TIME BOMB, "BATMAN."
WE'LL BLOW THE LIGHTHOUSE, AND ALL THE SLEEPING BEAUTIES IN IT, TO SMITHEREENS! HAHAHAHA!
SFX: SLIDE SLIDE SLIDE
WELL, IT'S ALL ON BOARD.
AND I SET THE BOMB.
IT'LL GO OFF IN FIVE MINUTES.
PERFECT. LET'S GO!

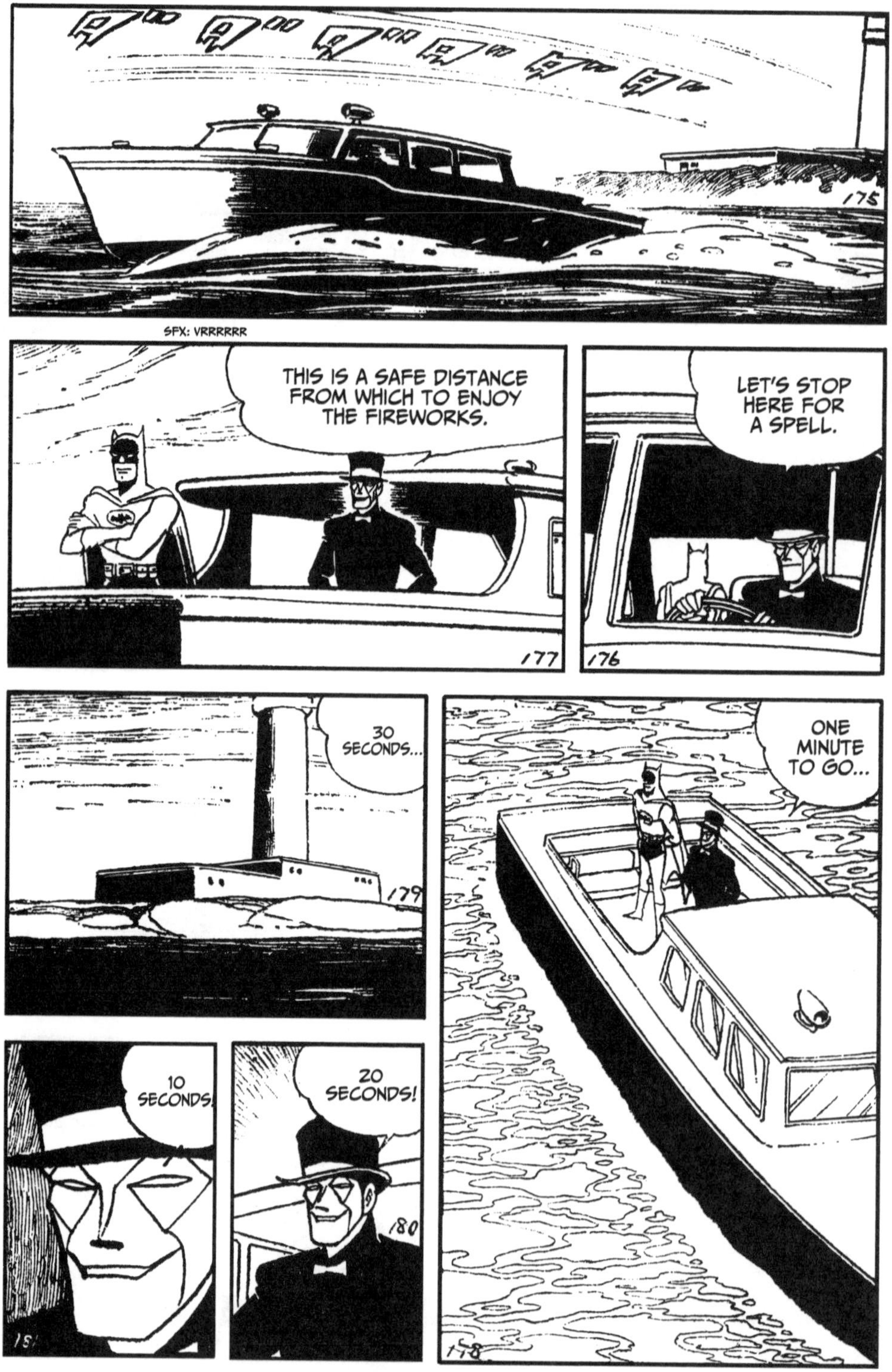
SFX: VRRRRRR
LET'S STOP HERE FOR A SPELL.
THIS IS A SAFE DISTANCE FROM WHICH TO ENJOY THE FIREWORKS.
ONE MINUTE TO GO...
30 SECONDS...
20 SECONDS!
10 SECONDS!

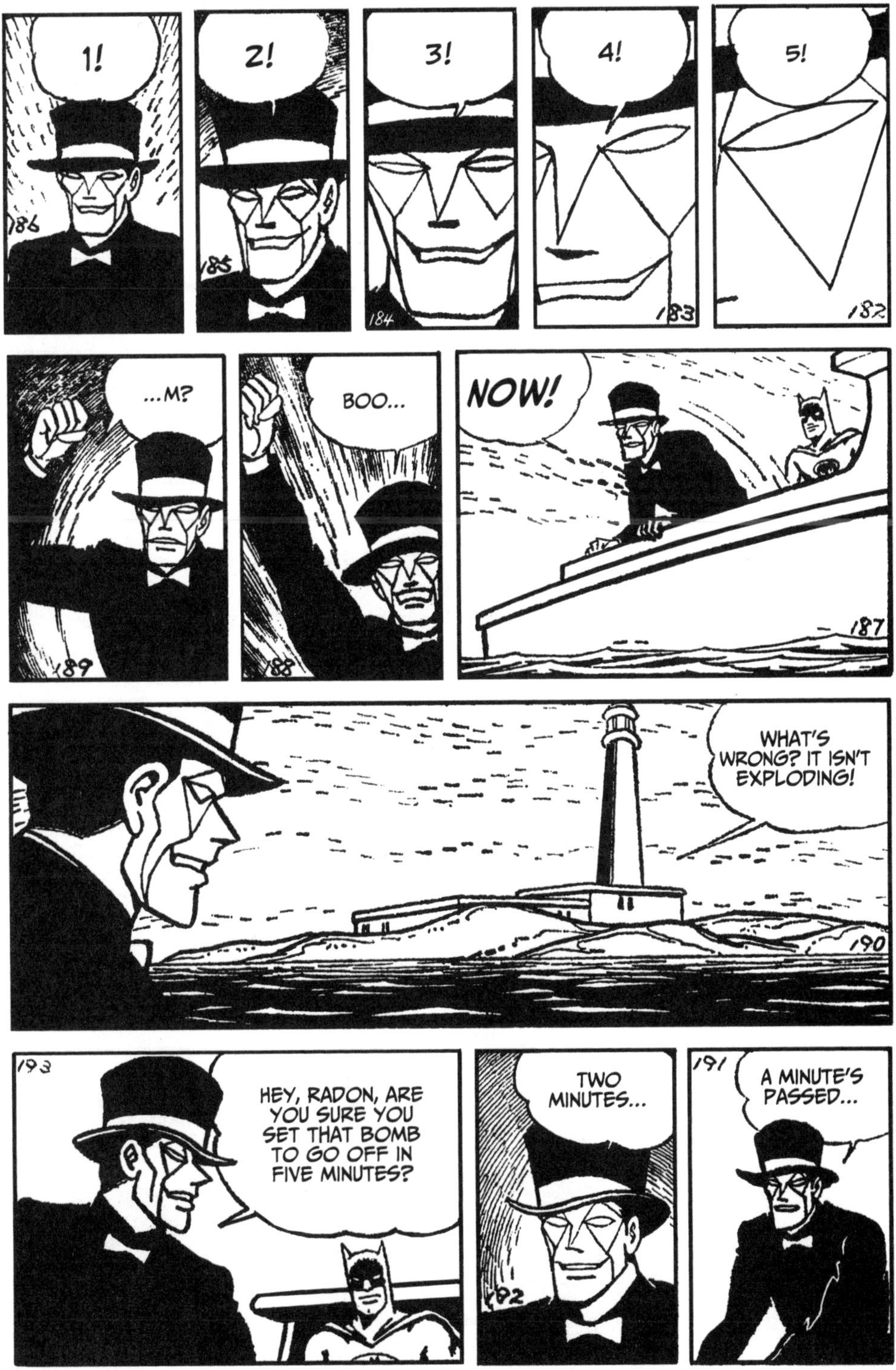
5!
4!
3!
2!
1!
NOW!
BOO...
...M?
WHAT'S WRONG? IT ISN'T EXPLODING!
A MINUTE'S PASSED...
TWO MINUTES...
HEY, RADON, ARE YOU SURE YOU SET THAT BOMB TO GO OFF IN FIVE MINUTES?

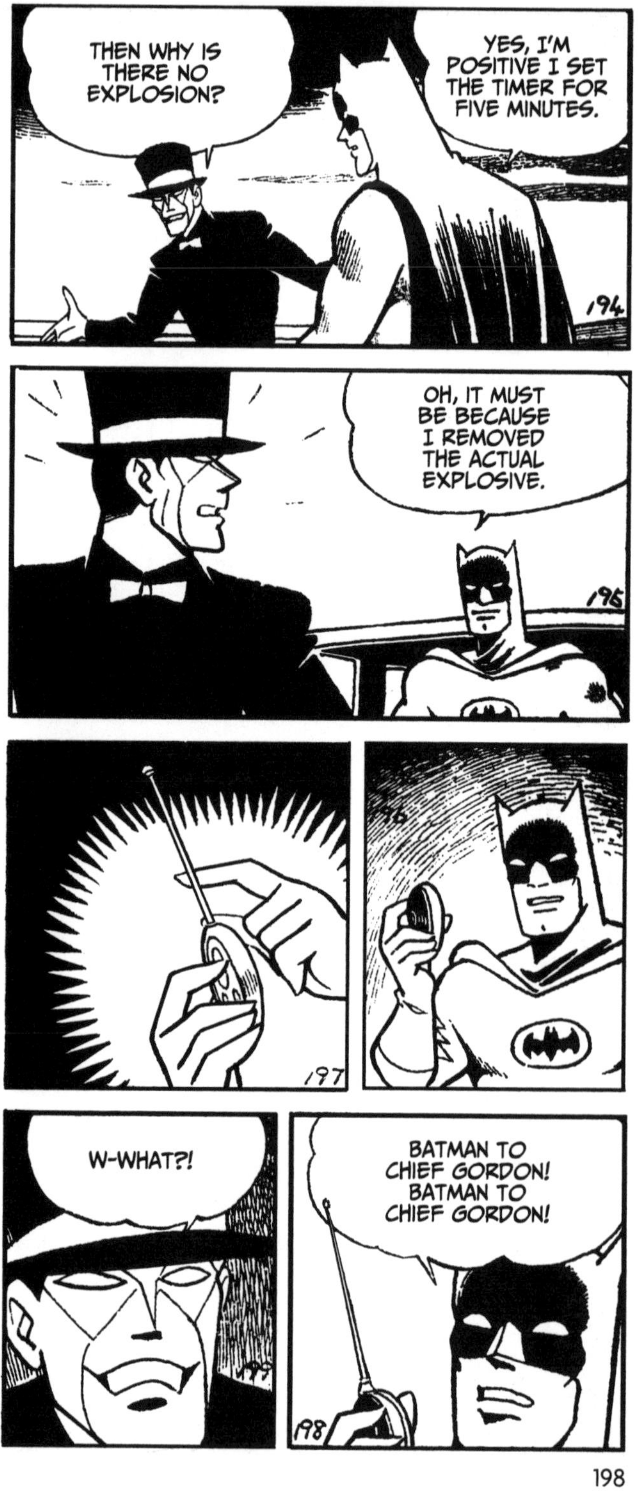
YES, I'M POSITIVE I SET THE TIMER FOR FIVE MINUTES.
THEN WHY IS THERE NO EXPLOSION?
OH, IT MUST BE BECAUSE I REMOVED THE ACTUAL EXPLOSIVE.
BATMAN TO CHIEF GORDON! BATMAN TO CHIEF GORDON!
W-WHAT?!

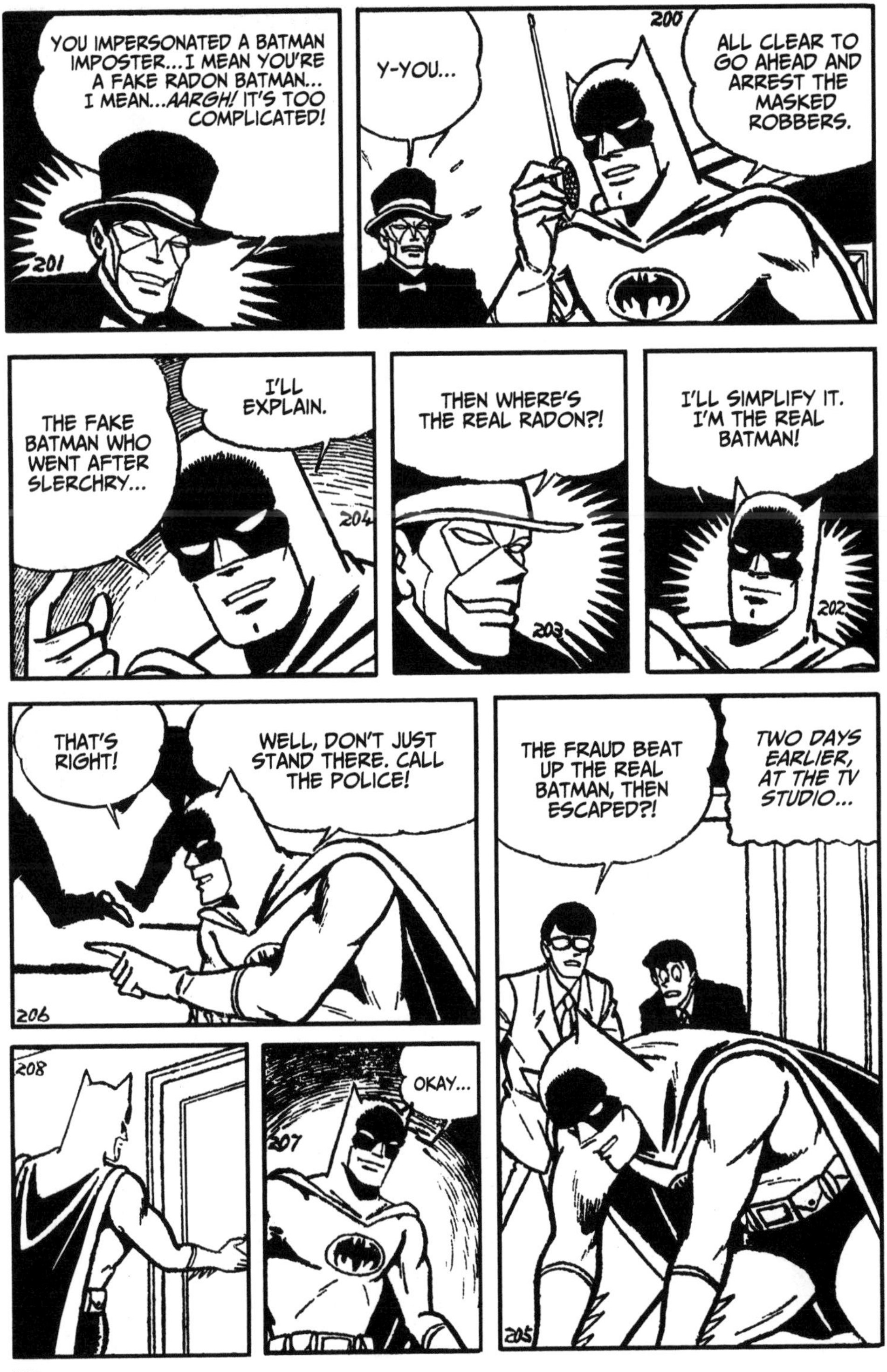
ALL CLEAR TO GO AHEAD AND ARREST THE MASKED ROBBERS.
Y-YOU...
YOU IMPERSONATED A BATMAN IMPOSTER...I MEAN YOU'RE A FAKE RADON BATMAN... I MEAN...*AARGH!* IT'S TOO COMPLICATED!
I'LL SIMPLIFY IT. I'M THE REAL BATMAN!
THEN WHERE'S THE REAL RADON?!
I'LL EXPLAIN.
THE FAKE BATMAN WHO WENT AFTER SLERCHRY...
TWO DAYS EARLIER, AT THE TV STUDIO...
THE FRAUD BEAT UP THE REAL BATMAN, THEN ESCAPED?!
WELL, DON'T JUST STAND THERE. CALL THE POLICE!
THAT'S RIGHT!
OKAY...

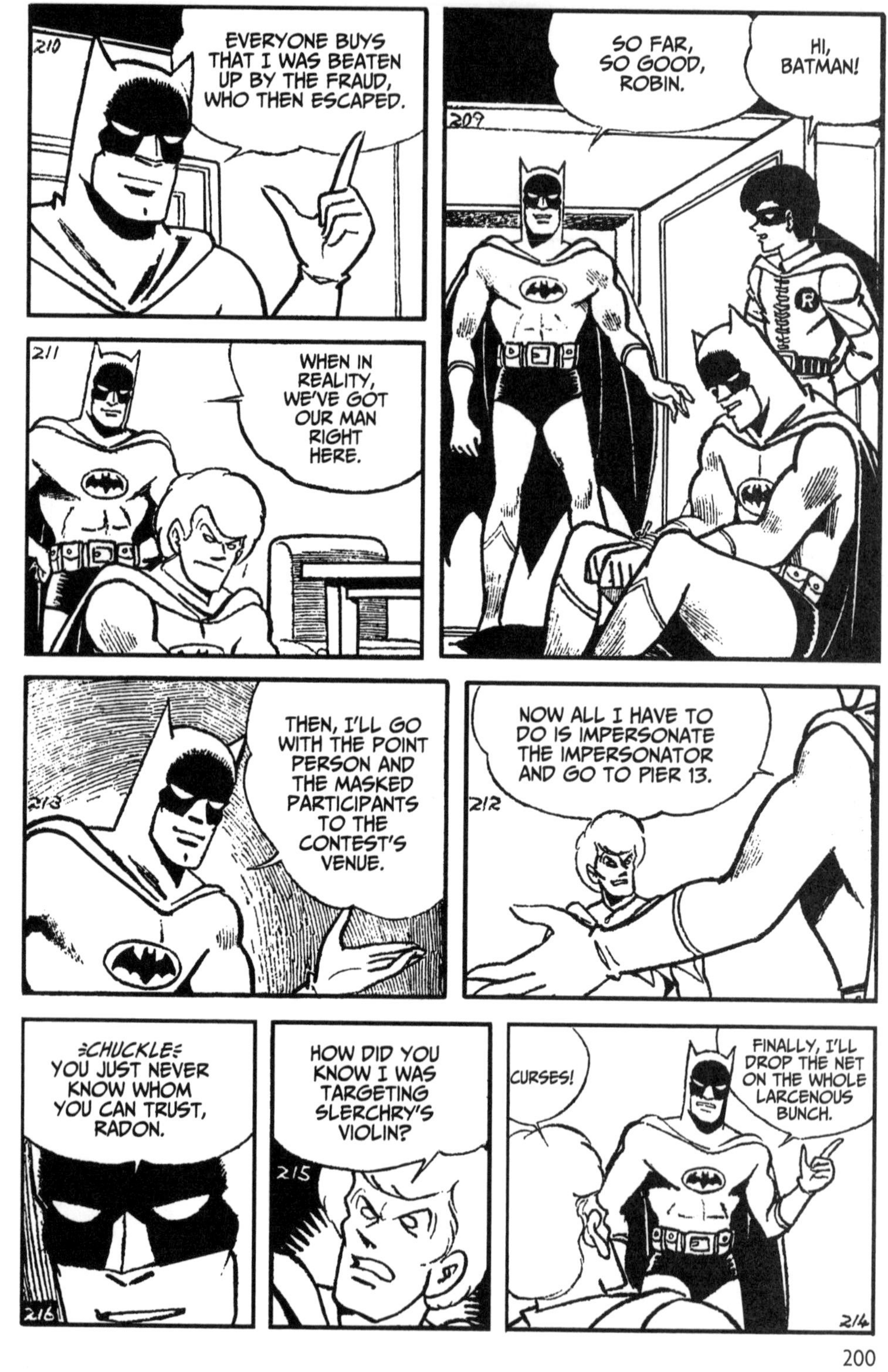
HI, BATMAN!
SO FAR, SO GOOD, ROBIN.
EVERYONE BUYS THAT I WAS BEATEN UP BY THE FRAUD, WHO THEN ESCAPED.
WHEN IN REALITY, WE'VE GOT OUR MAN RIGHT HERE.
NOW ALL I HAVE TO DO IS IMPERSONATE THE IMPERSONATOR AND GO TO PIER 13.
THEN, I'LL GO WITH THE POINT PERSON AND THE MASKED PARTICIPANTS TO THE CONTEST'S VENUE.
FINALLY, I'LL DROP THE NET ON THE WHOLE LARCENOUS BUNCH.
CURSES!
HOW DID YOU KNOW I WAS TARGETING SLERCHRY'S VIOLIN?
CHUCKLE
YOU JUST NEVER KNOW WHOM YOU CAN TRUST, RADON.

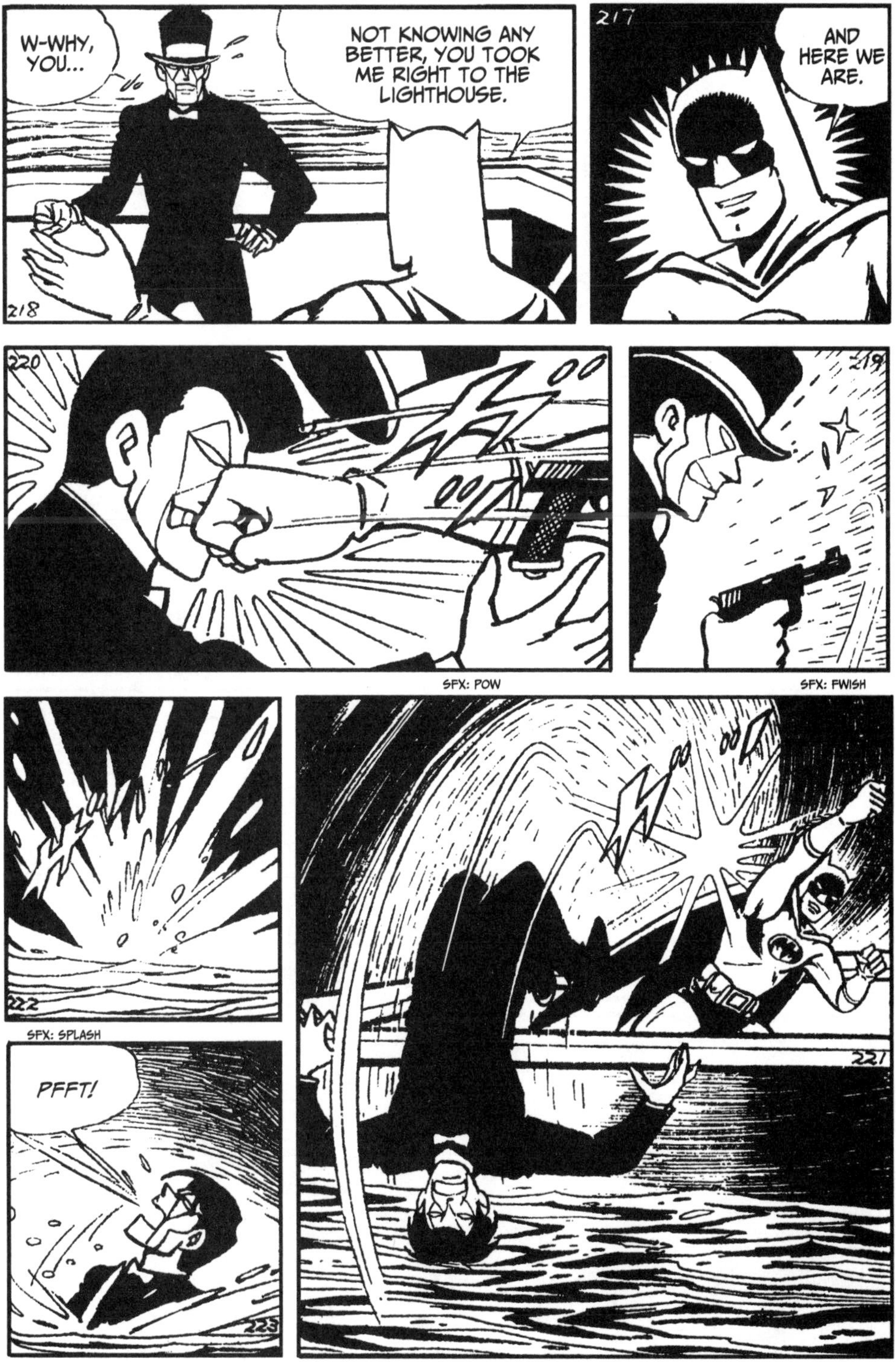
AND HERE WE ARE.
NOT KNOWING ANY BETTER, YOU TOOK ME RIGHT TO THE LIGHTHOUSE.
W-WHY, YOU...
SFX: FWISH
SFX: POW
SFX: KRAK
SFX: SPLASH
PFFT!

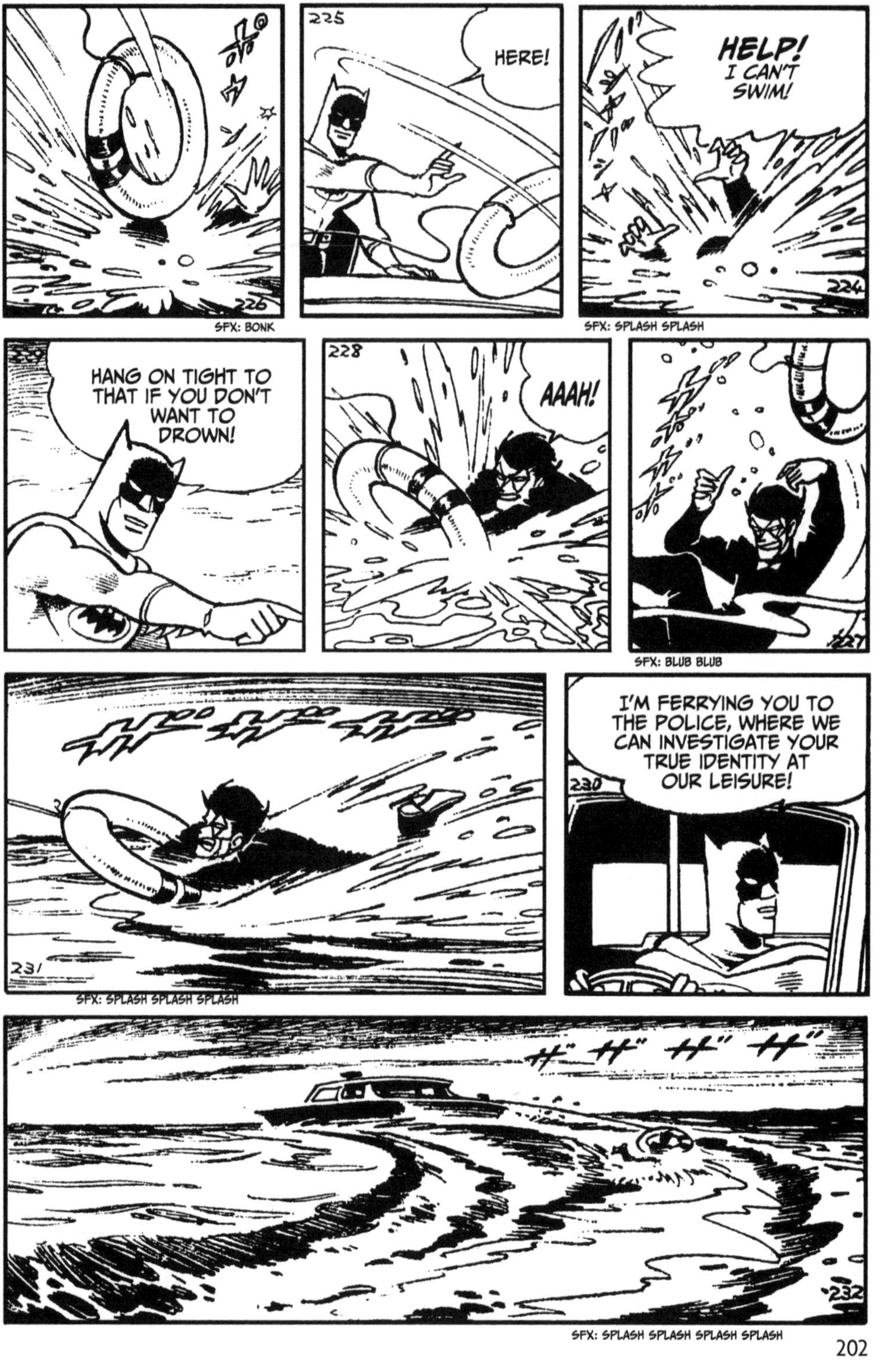
HELP! I CAN'T SWIM!
SFX: SPLASH SPLASH
HERE!
SFX: BONK
SFX: BLUB BLUB
AAAH!
HANG ON TIGHT TO THAT IF YOU DON'T WANT TO DROWN!
I'M FERRYING YOU TO THE POLICE, WHERE WE CAN INVESTIGATE YOUR TRUE IDENTITY AT OUR LEISURE!
SFX: SPLASH SPLASH SPLASH
SFX: SPLASH SPLASH SPLASH SPLASH

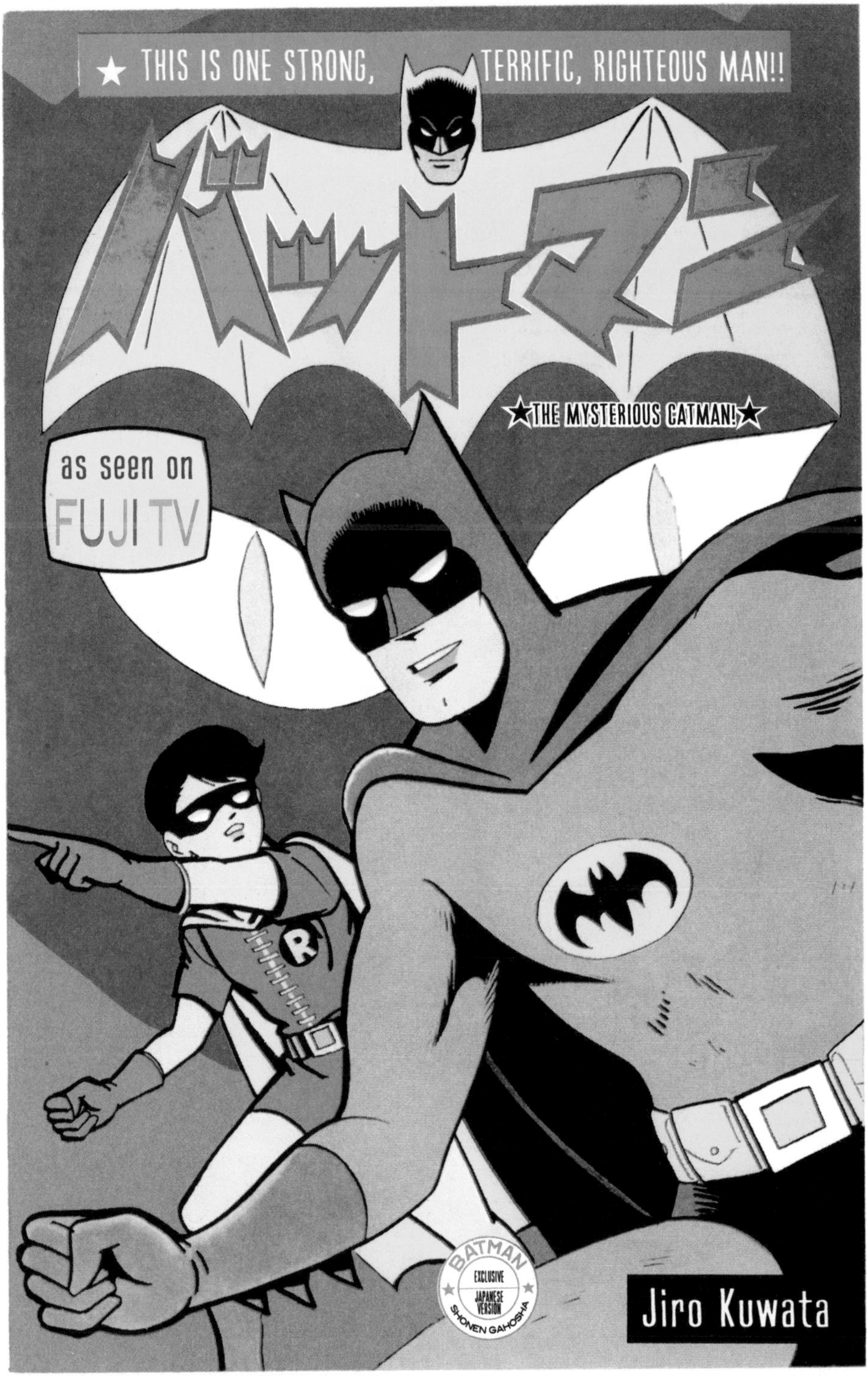
★ THIS IS ONE STRONG, TERRIFIC, RIGHTEOUS MAN!!
バットマン
★THE MYSTERIOUS CATMAN!★
as seen on FUJI TV
BATMAN EXCLUSIVE JAPANESE VERSION SHONEN GAHOSHA
R
Jiro Kuwata

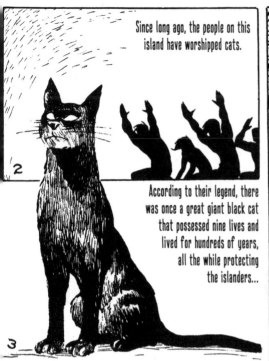

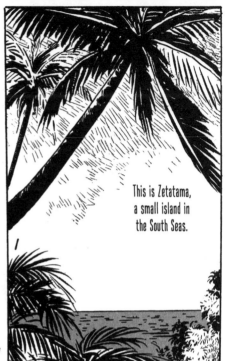

This is Zetatama, a small island in the South Seas.
Since long ago, the people on this island have worshipped cats.
According to their legend, there was once a great giant black cat that possessed nine lives and lived for hundreds of years, all the while protecting the islanders...

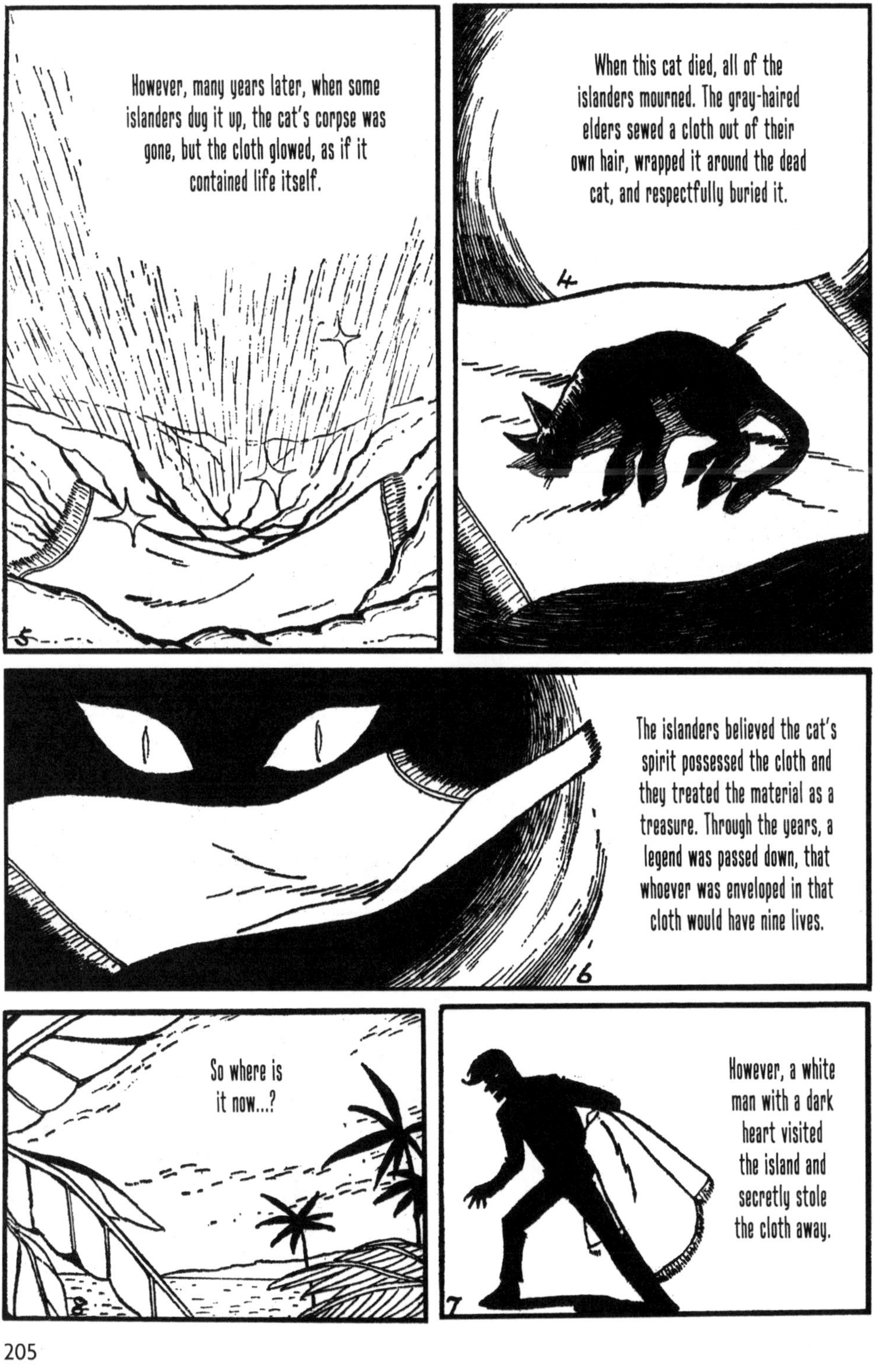
When this cat died, all of the islanders mourned. The gray-haired elders sewed a cloth out of their own hair, wrapped it around the dead cat, and respectfully buried it.
However, many years later, when some islanders dug it up, the cat's corpse was gone, but the cloth glowed, as if it contained life itself.
The islanders believed the cat's spirit possessed the cloth and they treated the material as a treasure. Through the years, a legend was passed down, that whoever was enveloped in that cloth would have nine lives.
However, a white man with a dark heart visited the island and secretly stole the cloth away.
So where is it now...?

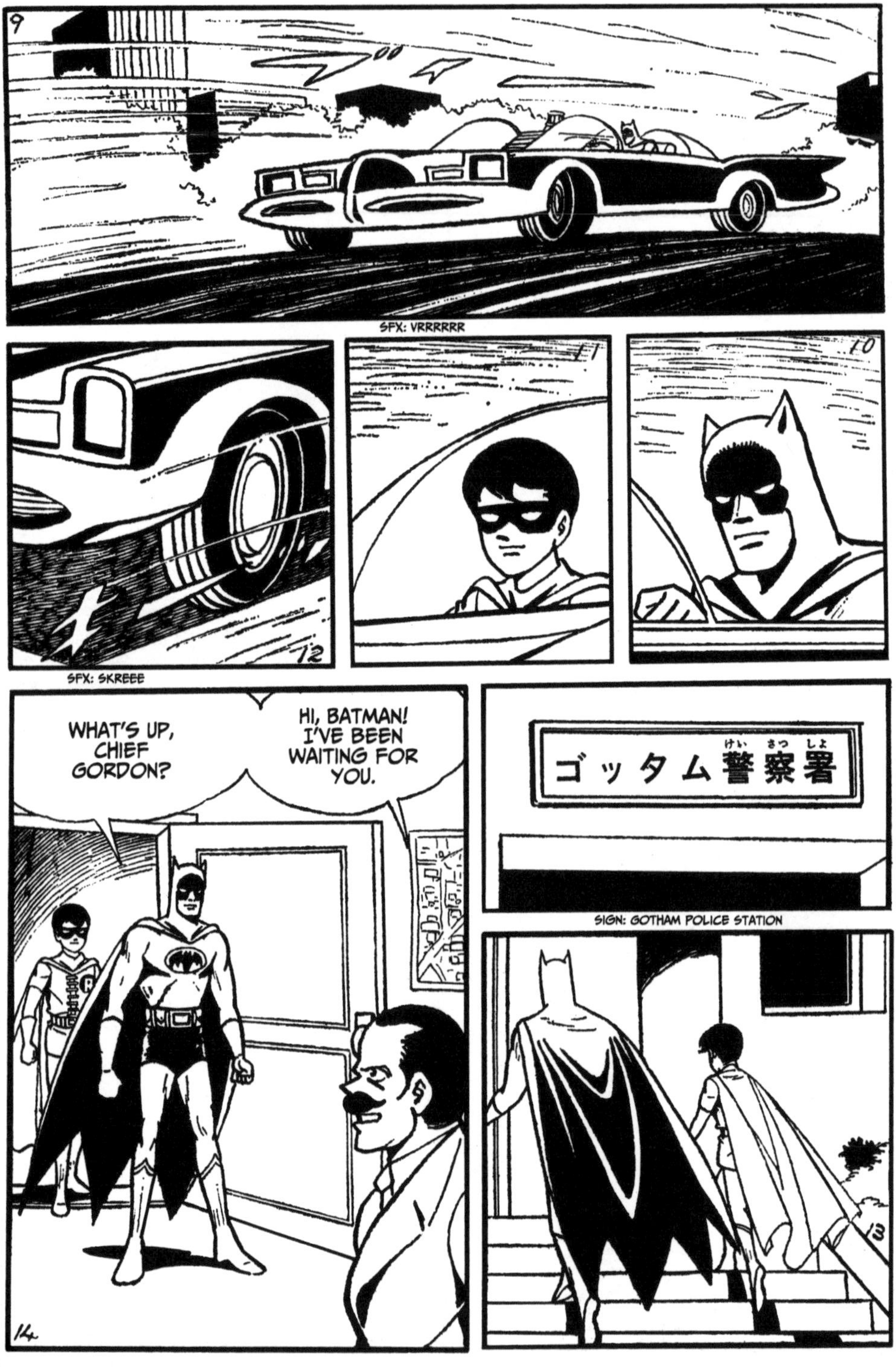
SFX: VRRRRRR
SFX: SKREEE
ゴッタム警察署
けいさつしょ
SIGN: GOTHAM POLICE STATION
HI, BATMAN! I'VE BEEN WAITING FOR YOU.
WHAT'S UP, CHIEF GORDON?

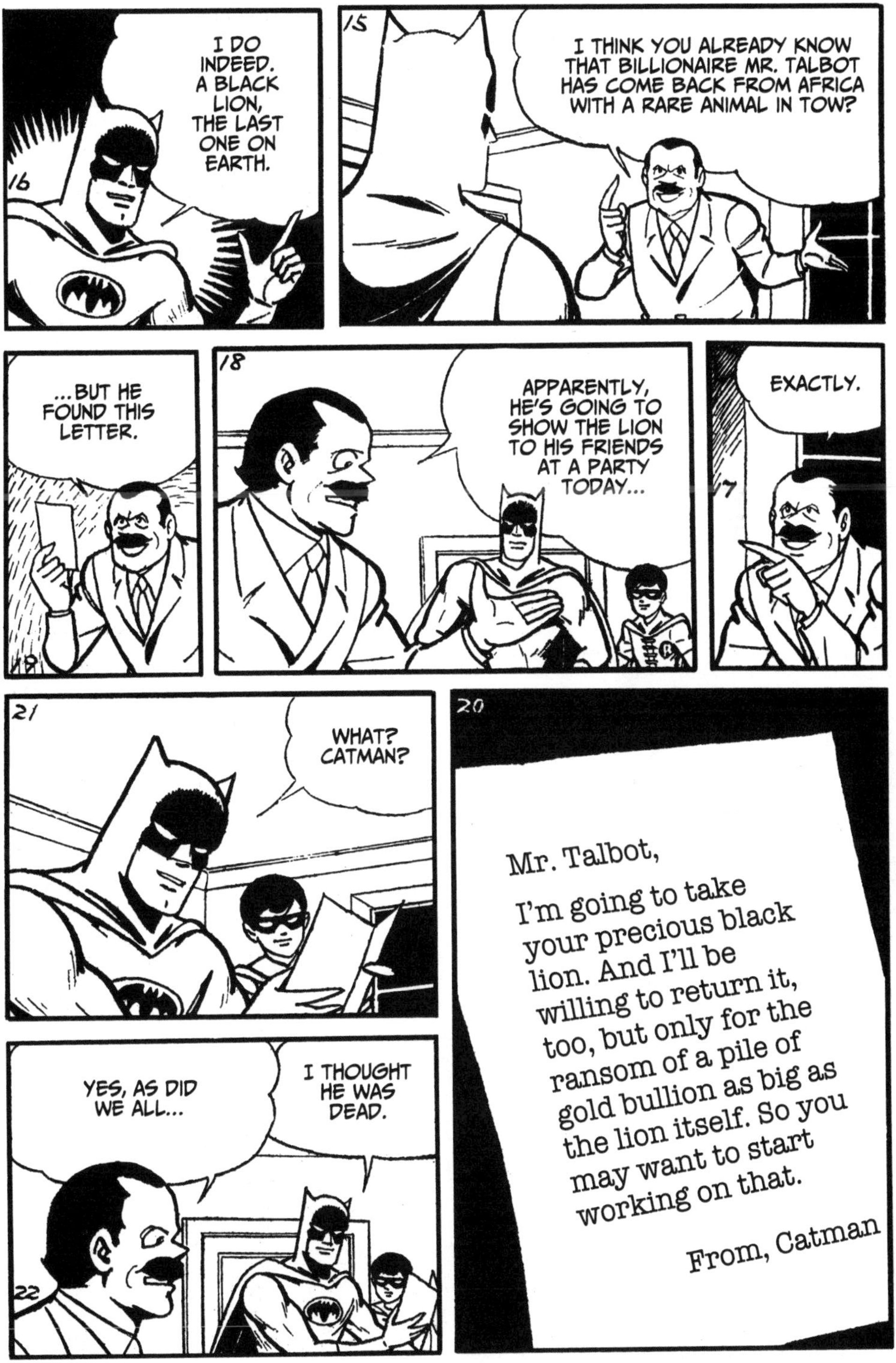

I THINK YOU ALREADY KNOW THAT BILLIONAIRE MR. TALBOT HAS COME BACK FROM AFRICA WITH A RARE ANIMAL IN TOW?
I DO INDEED. A BLACK LION, THE LAST ONE ON EARTH.
EXACTLY.
APPARENTLY, HE'S GOING TO SHOW THE LION TO HIS FRIENDS AT A PARTY TODAY...
...BUT HE FOUND THIS LETTER.
Mr. Talbot,
I'm going to take your precious black lion. And I'll be willing to return it, too, but only for the ransom of a pile of gold bullion as big as the lion itself. So you may want to start working on that.
From, Catman
WHAT? CATMAN?
I THOUGHT HE WAS DEAD.
YES, AS DID WE ALL...

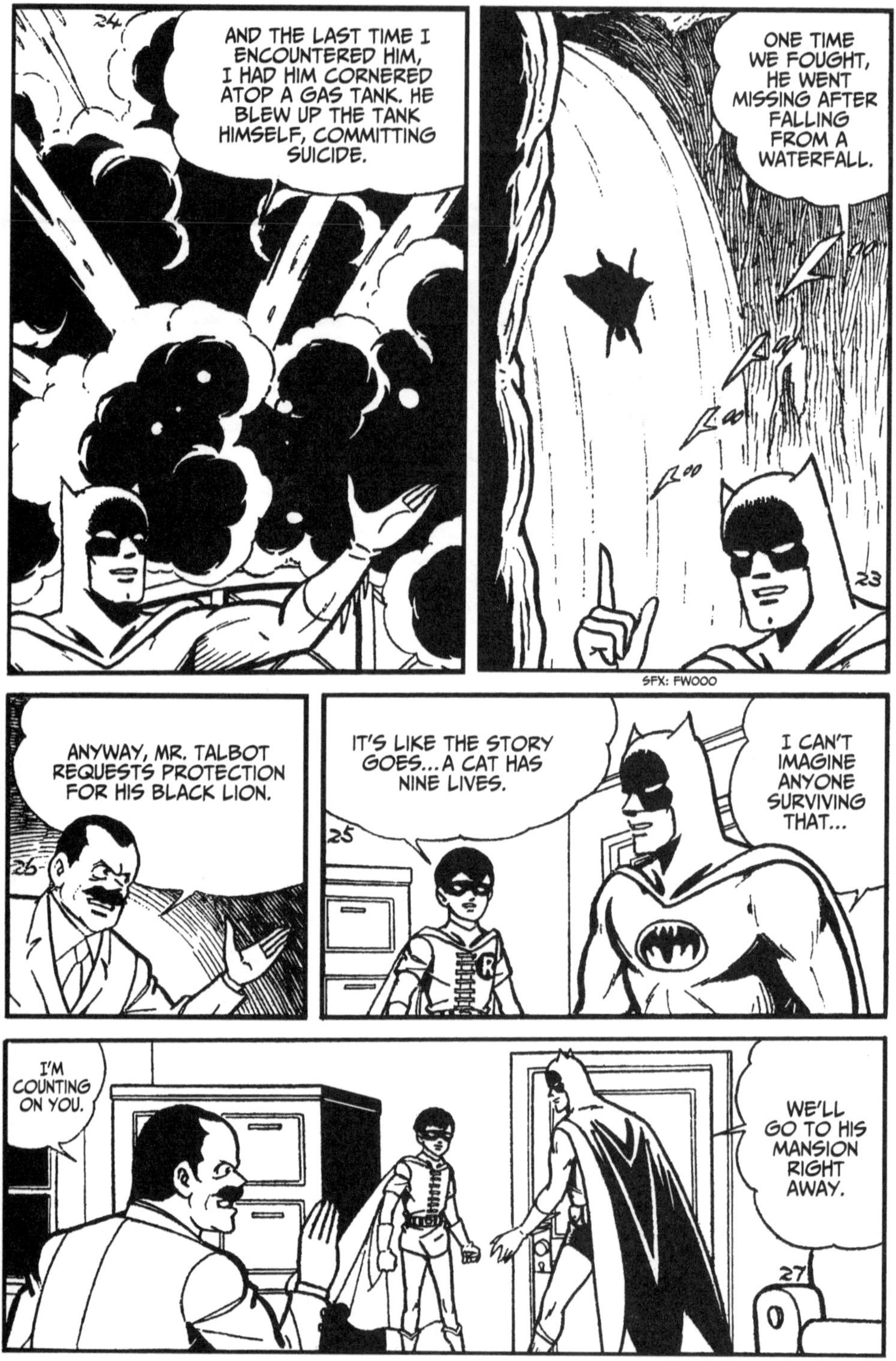
ONE TIME WE FOUGHT, HE WENT MISSING AFTER FALLING FROM A WATERFALL.
SFX: FWOOO
AND THE LAST TIME I ENCOUNTERED HIM, I HAD HIM CORNERED ATOP A GAS TANK. HE BLEW UP THE TANK HIMSELF, COMMITTING SUICIDE.
I CAN'T IMAGINE ANYONE SURVIVING THAT...
IT'S LIKE THE STORY GOES...A CAT HAS NINE LIVES.
ANYWAY, MR. TALBOT REQUESTS PROTECTION FOR HIS BLACK LION.
WE'LL GO TO HIS MANSION RIGHT AWAY.
I'M COUNTING ON YOU.

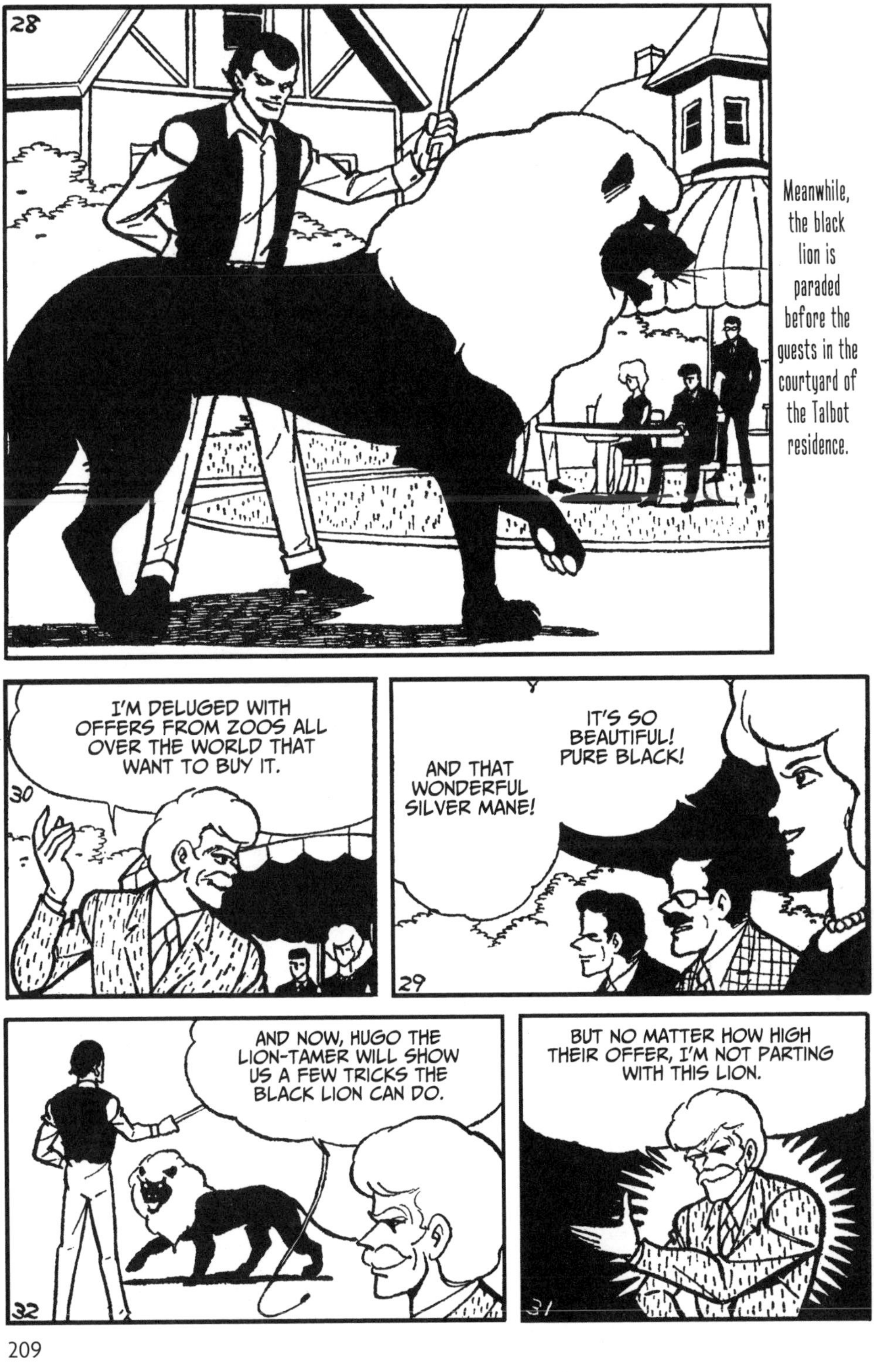
Meanwhile, the black lion is paraded before the guests in the courtyard of the Talbot residence.
IT'S SO BEAUTIFUL! PURE BLACK!
AND THAT WONDERFUL SILVER MANE!
I'M DELUGED WITH OFFERS FROM ZOOS ALL OVER THE WORLD THAT WANT TO BUY IT.
BUT NO MATTER HOW HIGH THEIR OFFER, I'M NOT PARTING WITH THIS LION.
AND NOW, HUGO THE LION-TAMER WILL SHOW US A FEW TRICKS THE BLACK LION CAN DO.

SFX: VRRRR

HUH! IT'S AS OBEDIENT AS A PET CAT!

SFX: VROOOO

AH! LOOK OUT!

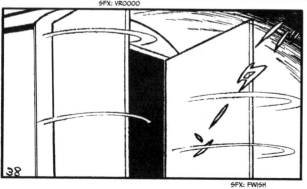

SFX: FWISH

WHO DARES DRIVE A TRUCK INTO MY COURTYARD?!

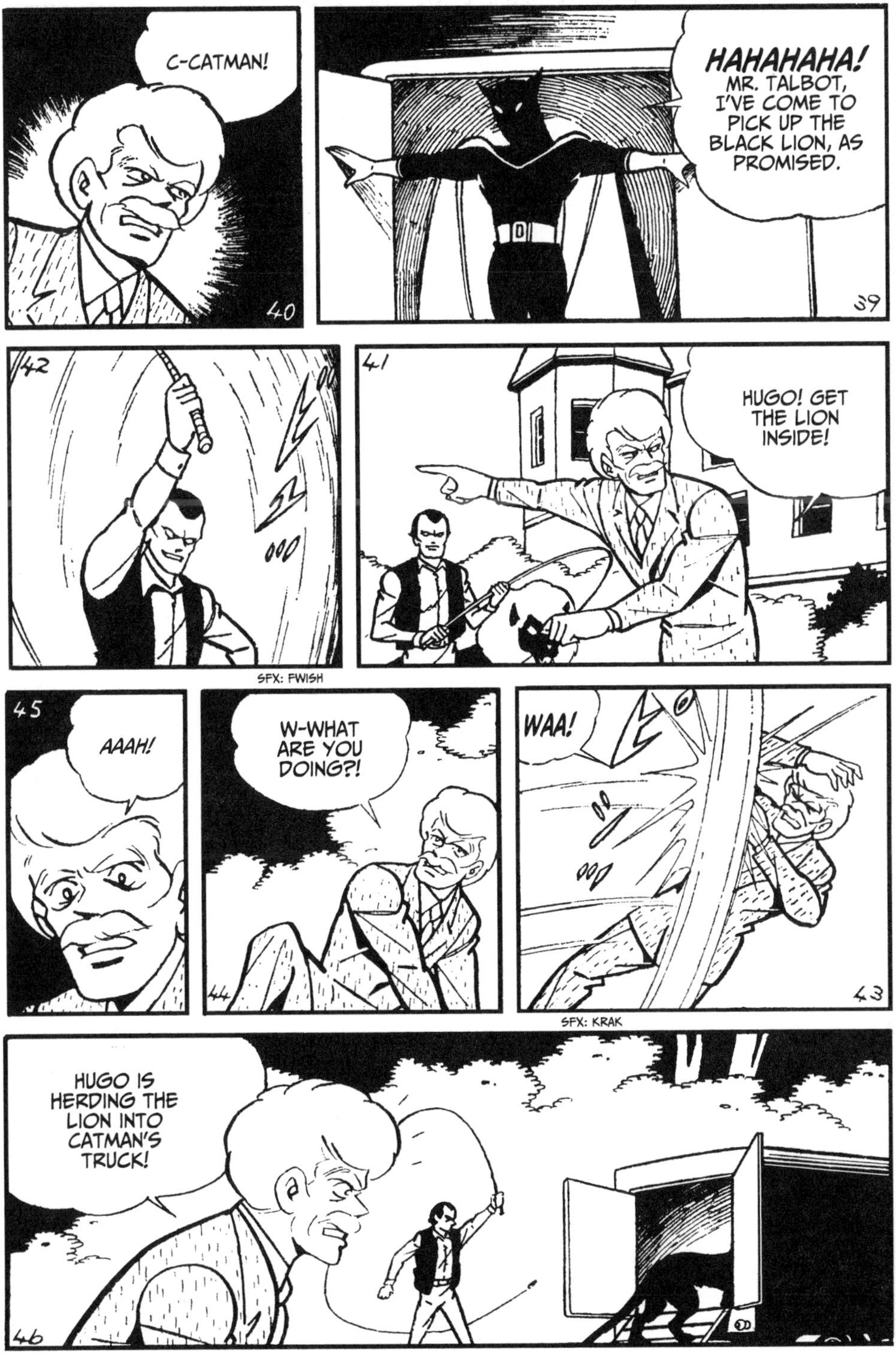
HAHAHAHA! MR. TALBOT, I'VE COME TO PICK UP THE BLACK LION, AS PROMISED.
C-CATMAN!
HUGO! GET THE LION INSIDE!
SFX: FWISH
WAA!
SFX: KRAK
W-WHAT ARE YOU DOING?!
AAAH!
HUGO IS HERDING THE LION INTO CATMAN'S TRUCK!

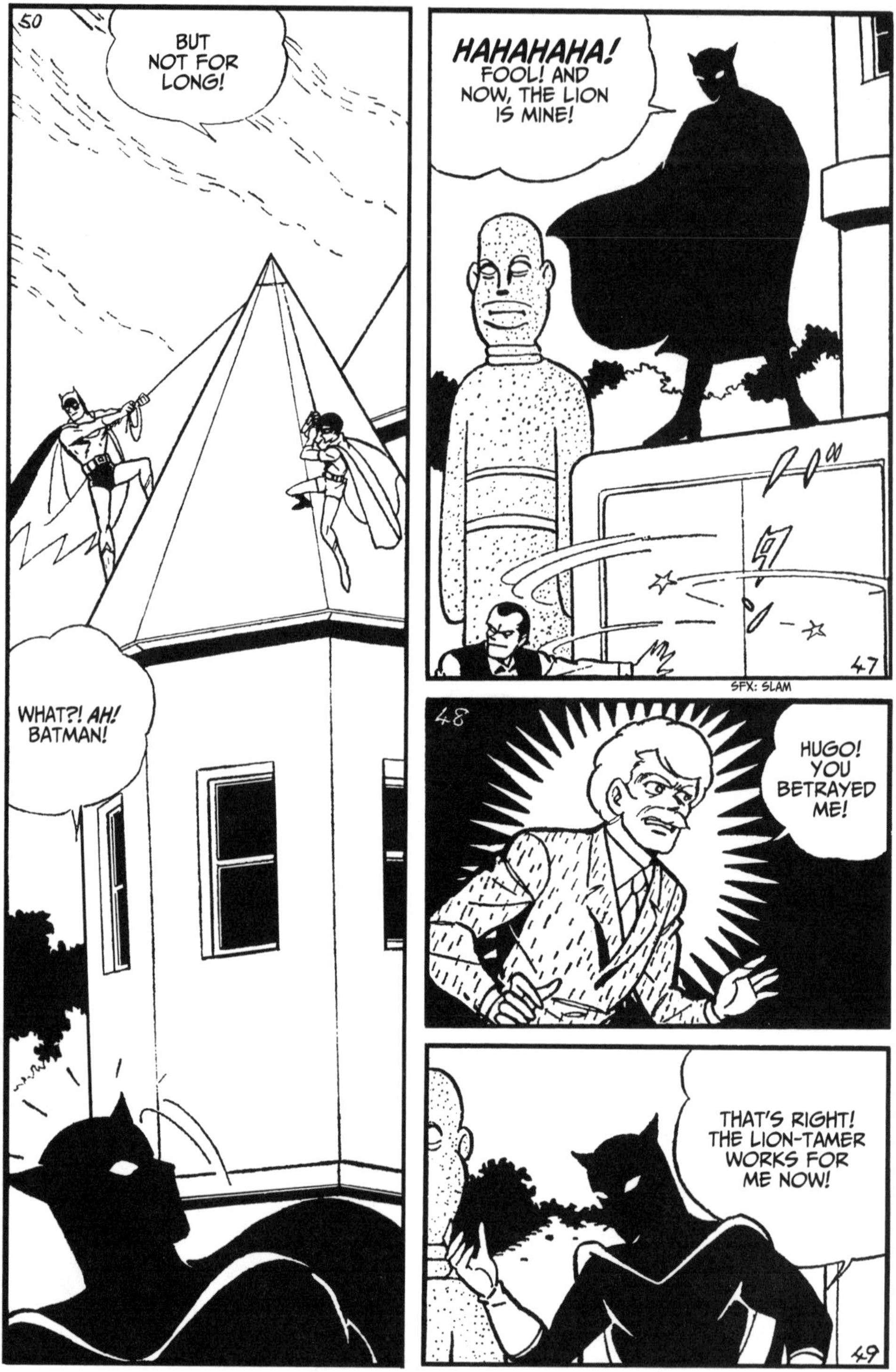
HAHAHAHA! FOOL! AND NOW, THE LION IS MINE!
SFX: SLAM
HUGO! YOU BETRAYED ME!
THAT'S RIGHT! THE LION-TAMER WORKS FOR ME NOW!
BUT NOT FOR LONG!
WHAT?! AH! BATMAN!

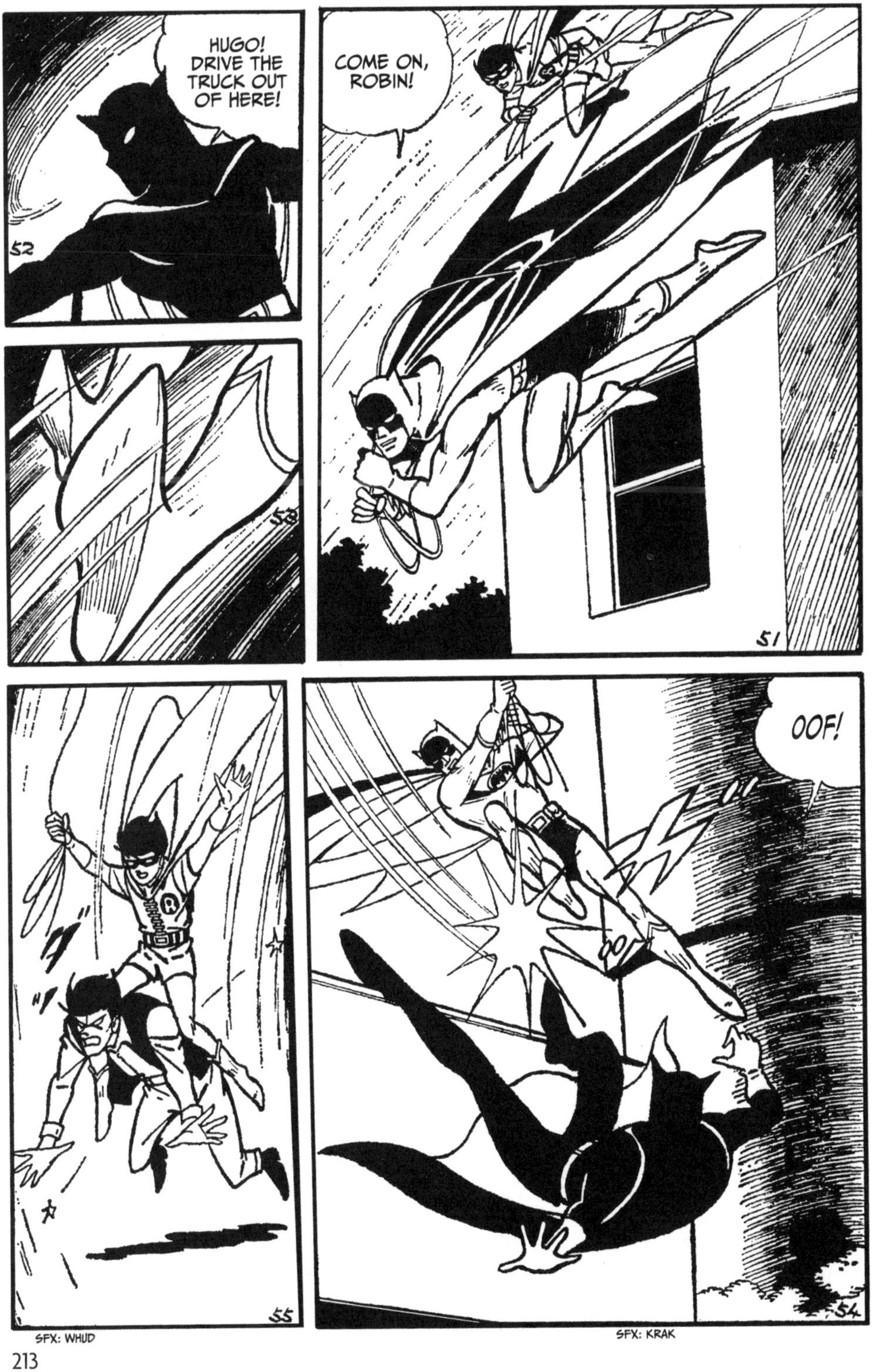
COME ON, ROBIN!
HUGO! DRIVE THE TRUCK OUT OF HERE!
OOF!

SFX: KRAK

SFX: WHUD

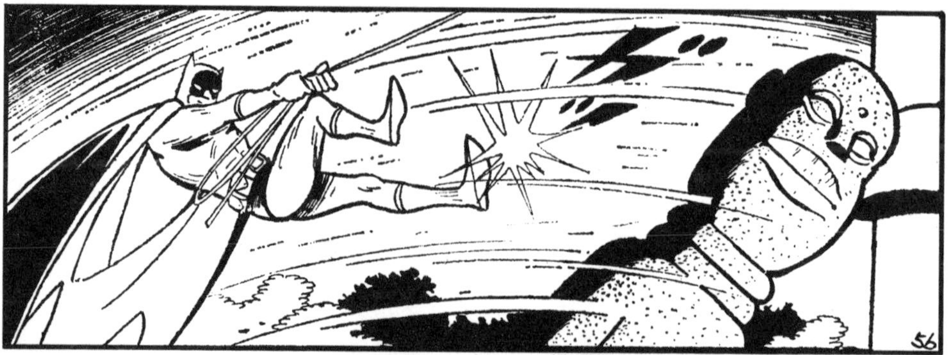

SFX: WHAK

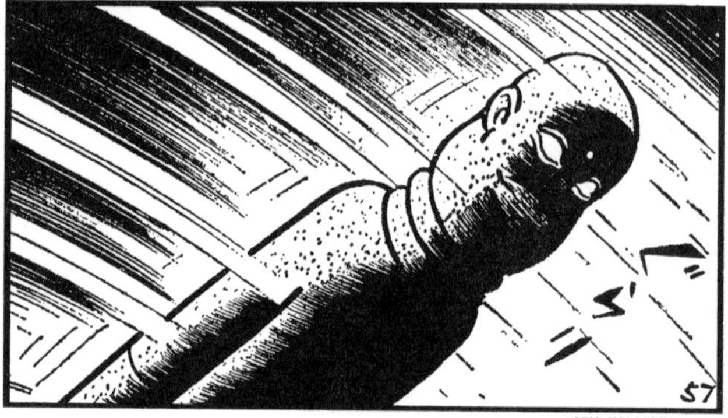

SFX: WOBBLE

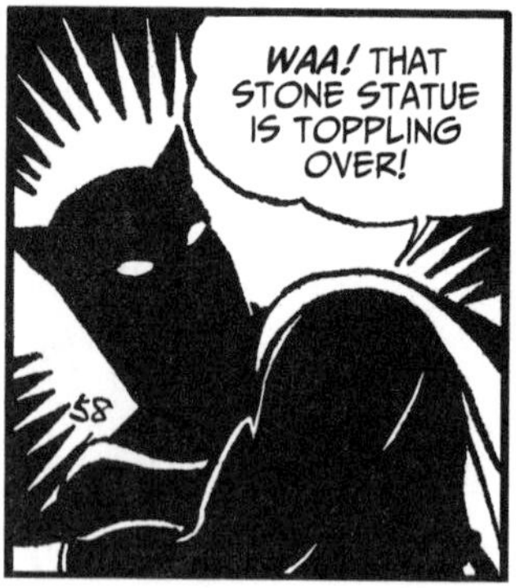
WAA! THAT STONE STATUE IS TOPPLING OVER!

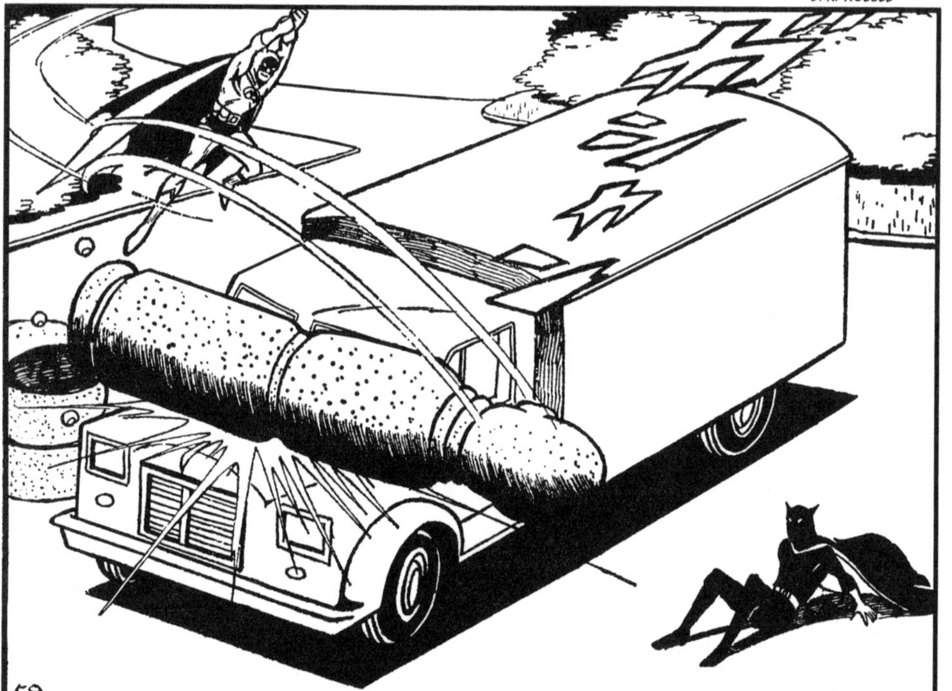

SFX: CRASH

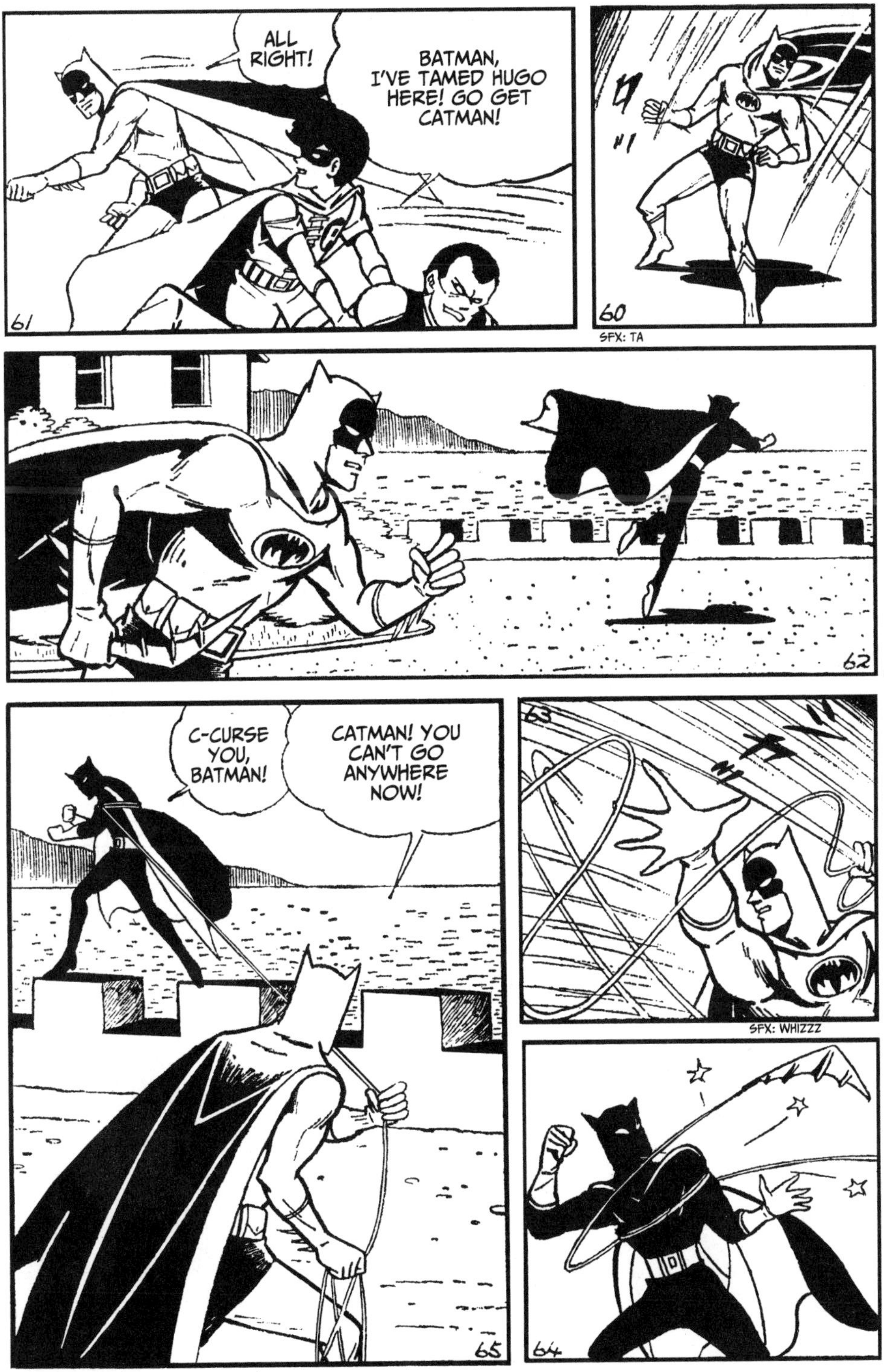
SFX: TA
BATMAN, I'VE TAMED HUGO HERE! GO GET CATMAN!
ALL RIGHT!
SFX: WHIZZZ
CATMAN! YOU CAN'T GO ANYWHERE NOW!
C-CURSE YOU, BATMAN!

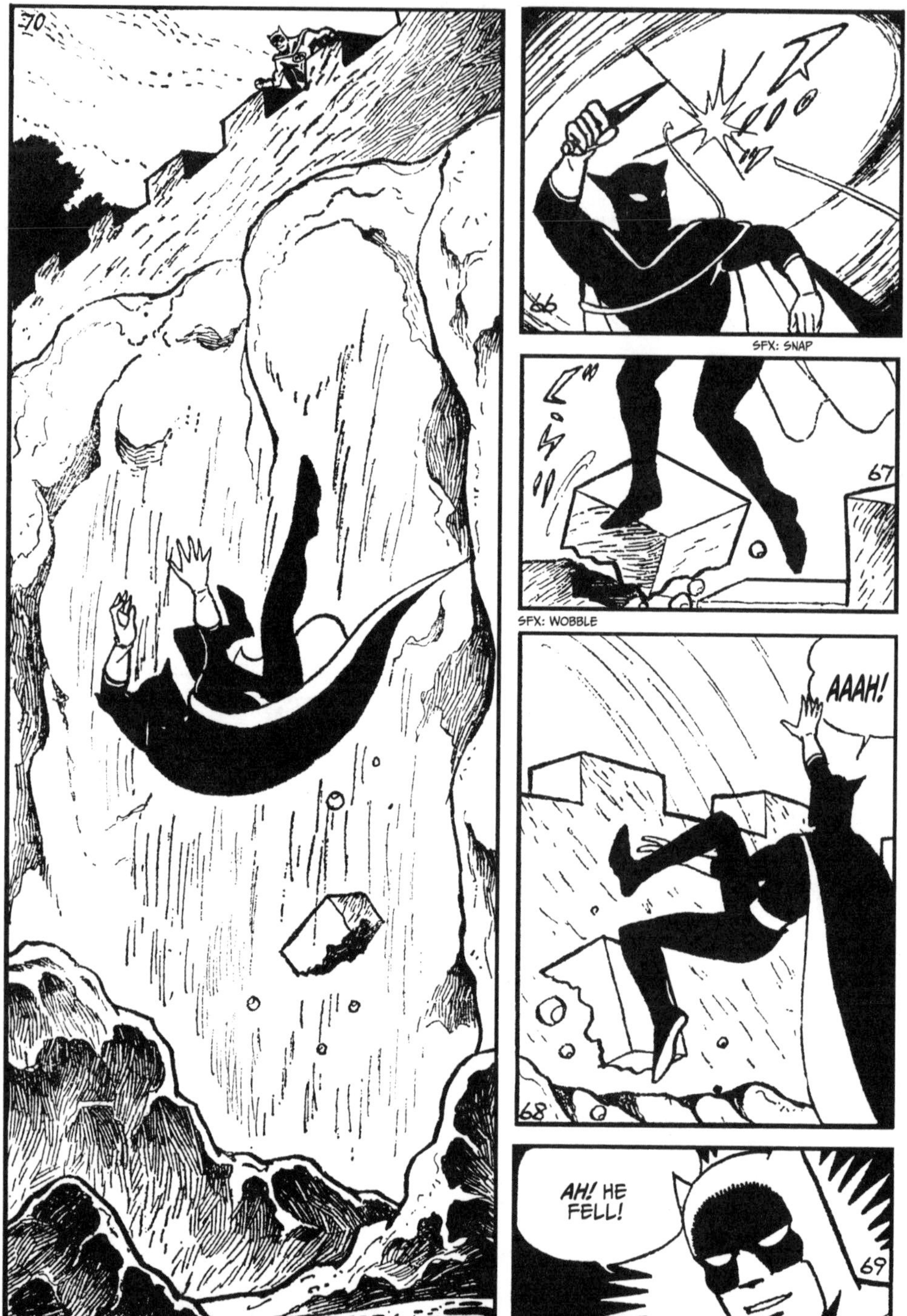
SFX: SNAP
SFX: WOBBLE
AAAH!
AH! HE FELL!

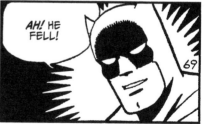

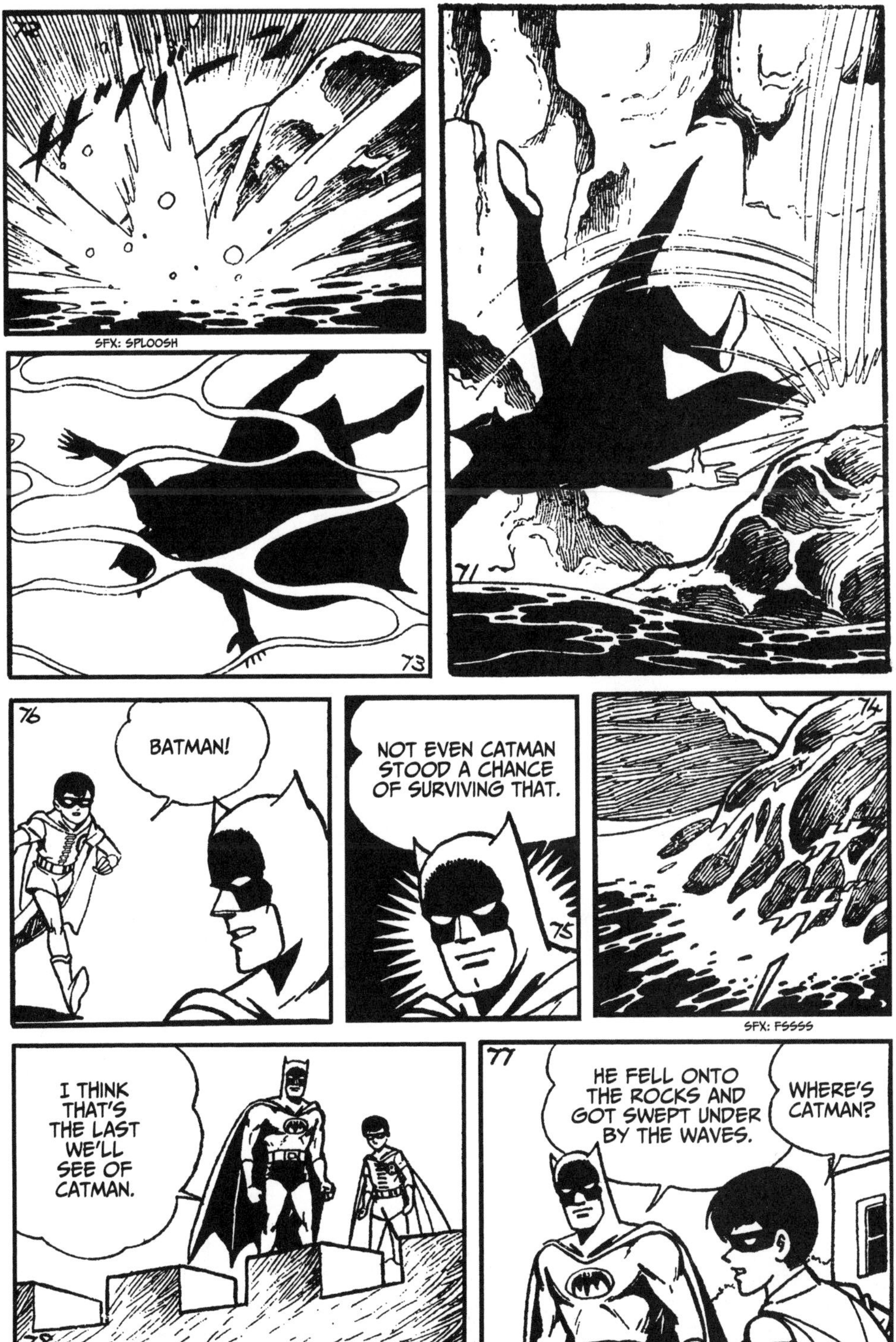
SFX: SPLOOSH
SFX: FSSSS
NOT EVEN CATMAN STOOD A CHANCE OF SURVIVING THAT.
BATMAN!
WHERE'S CATMAN?
HE FELL ONTO THE ROCKS AND GOT SWEPT UNDER BY THE WAVES.
I THINK THAT'S THE LAST WE'LL SEE OF CATMAN.

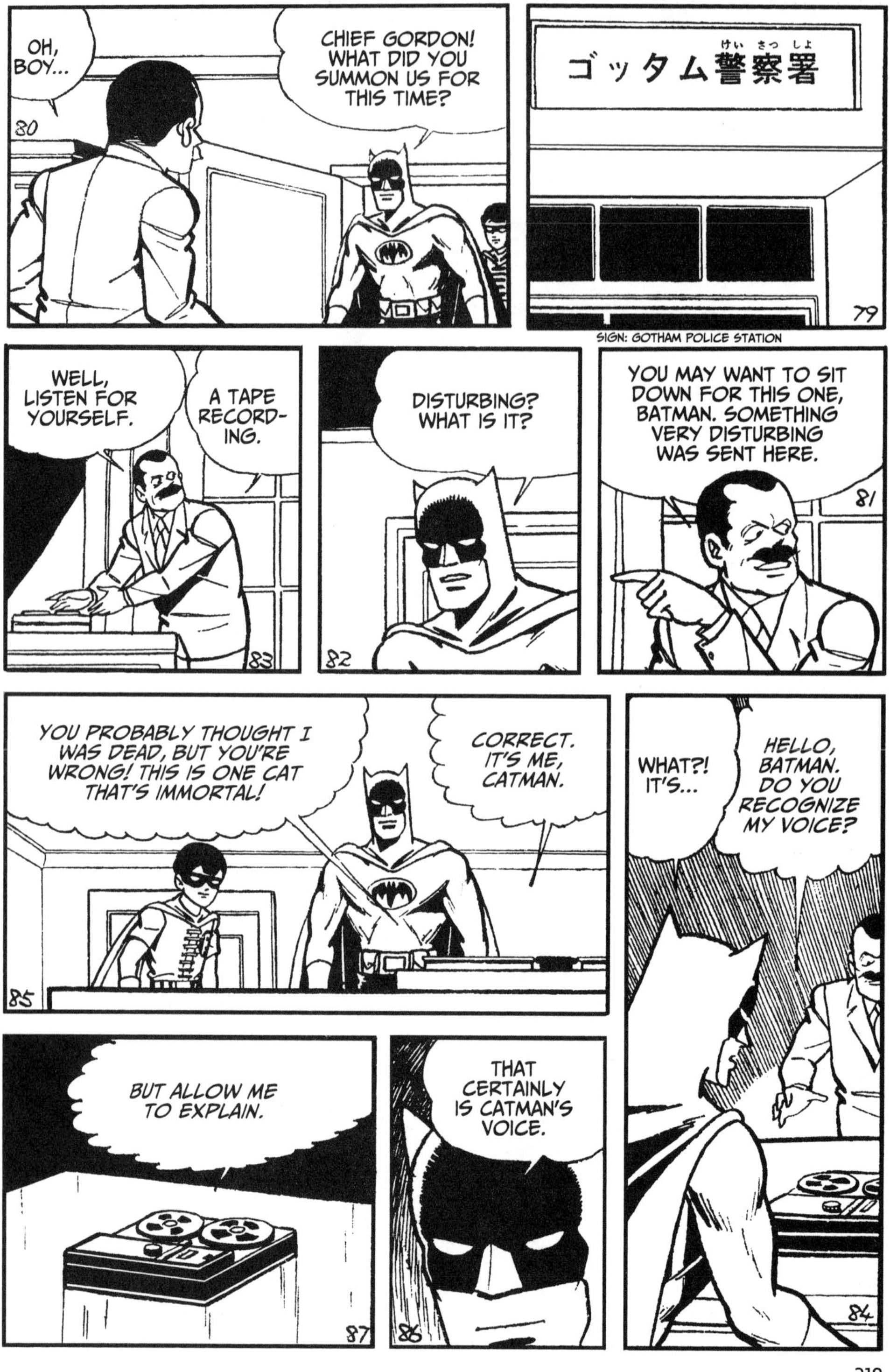
ゴッタム警察署
けいさつしょ
SIGN: GOTHAM POLICE STATION
CHIEF GORDON! WHAT DID YOU SUMMON US FOR THIS TIME?
OH, BOY...
YOU MAY WANT TO SIT DOWN FOR THIS ONE, BATMAN. SOMETHING VERY DISTURBING WAS SENT HERE.
DISTURBING? WHAT IS IT?
A TAPE RECORD-ING.
WELL, LISTEN FOR YOURSELF.
HELLO, BATMAN. DO YOU RECOGNIZE MY VOICE?
WHAT?! IT'S...
CORRECT. IT'S ME, CATMAN.
YOU PROBABLY THOUGHT I WAS DEAD, BUT YOU'RE WRONG! THIS IS ONE CAT THAT'S IMMORTAL!
THAT CERTAINLY IS CATMAN'S VOICE.
BUT ALLOW ME TO EXPLAIN.

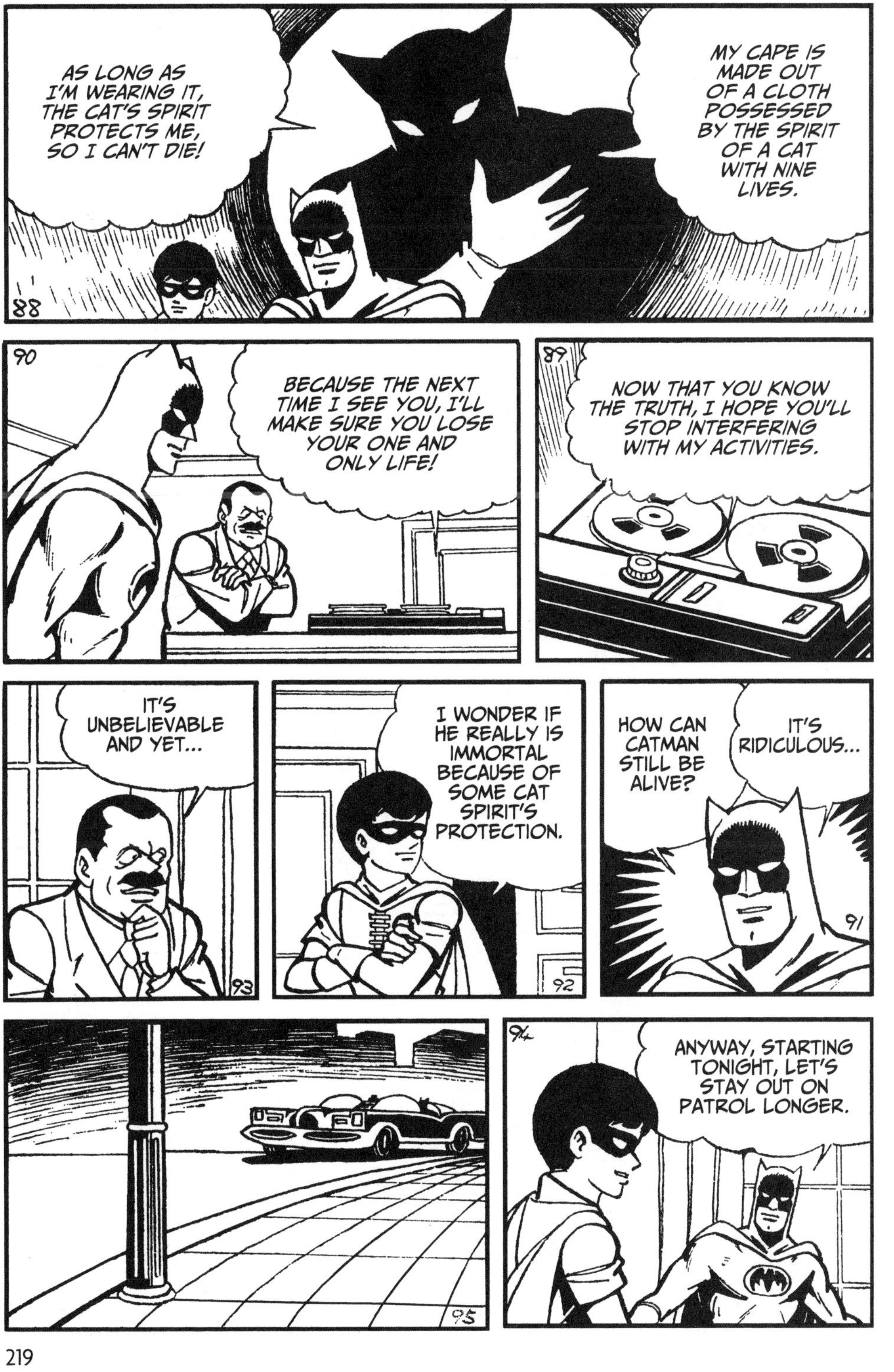
MY CAPE IS MADE OUT OF A CLOTH POSSESSED BY THE SPIRIT OF A CAT WITH NINE LIVES.
AS LONG AS I'M WEARING IT, THE CAT'S SPIRIT PROTECTS ME, SO I CAN'T DIE!
88
89
NOW THAT YOU KNOW THE TRUTH, I HOPE YOU'LL STOP INTERFERING WITH MY ACTIVITIES.
90
BECAUSE THE NEXT TIME I SEE YOU, I'LL MAKE SURE YOU LOSE YOUR ONE AND ONLY LIFE!
IT'S RIDICULOUS...
HOW CAN CATMAN STILL BE ALIVE?
91
I WONDER IF HE REALLY IS IMMORTAL BECAUSE OF SOME CAT SPIRIT'S PROTECTION.
92
IT'S UNBELIEVABLE AND YET...
93
94
ANYWAY, STARTING TONIGHT, LET'S STAY OUT ON PATROL LONGER.
95

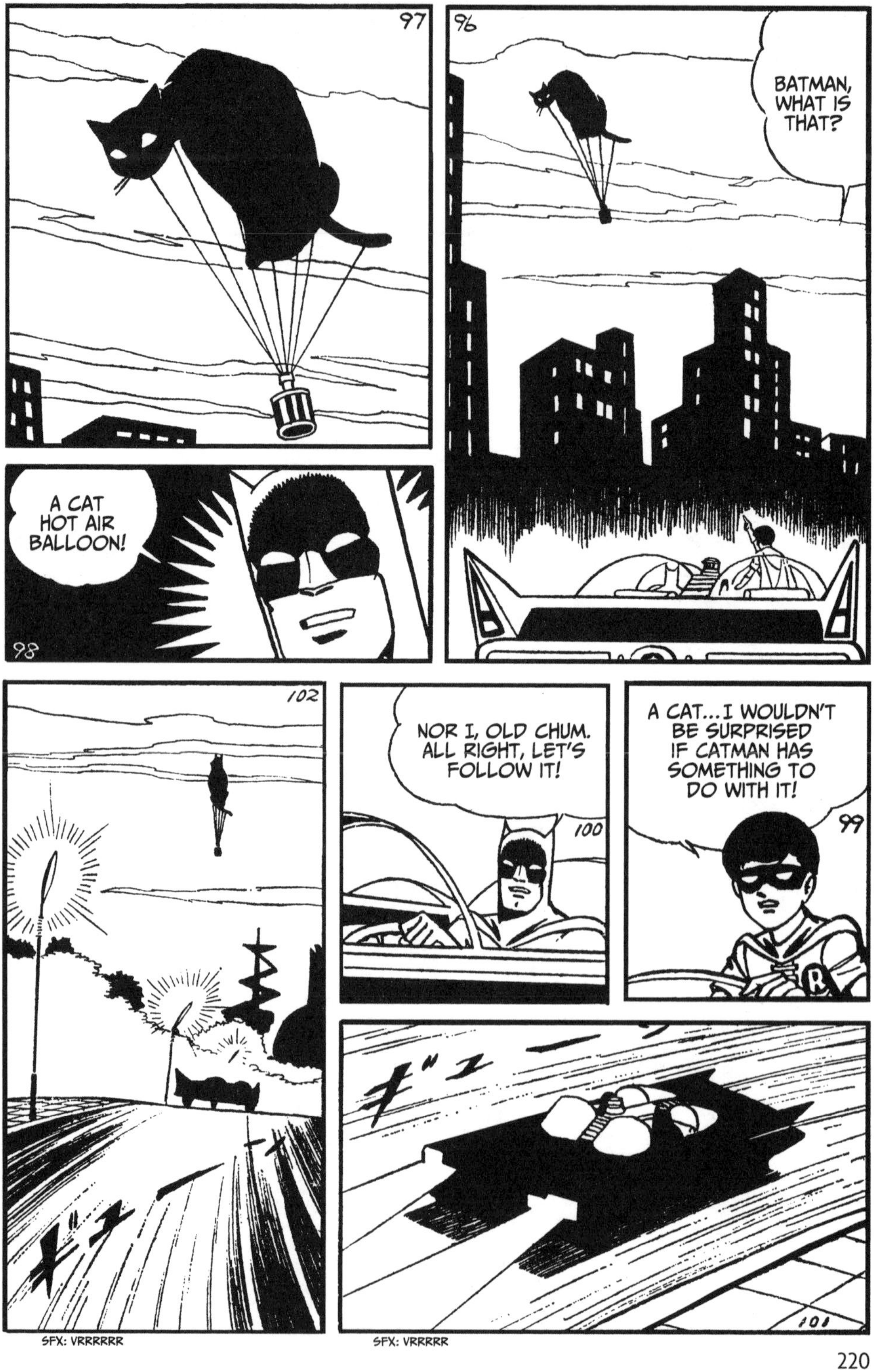
BATMAN, WHAT IS THAT?
A CAT HOT AIR BALLOON!
A CAT...I WOULDN'T BE SURPRISED IF CATMAN HAS SOMETHING TO DO WITH IT!
NOR I, OLD CHUM. ALL RIGHT, LET'S FOLLOW IT!

SFX: VRRRRR

SFX: VRRRRRR

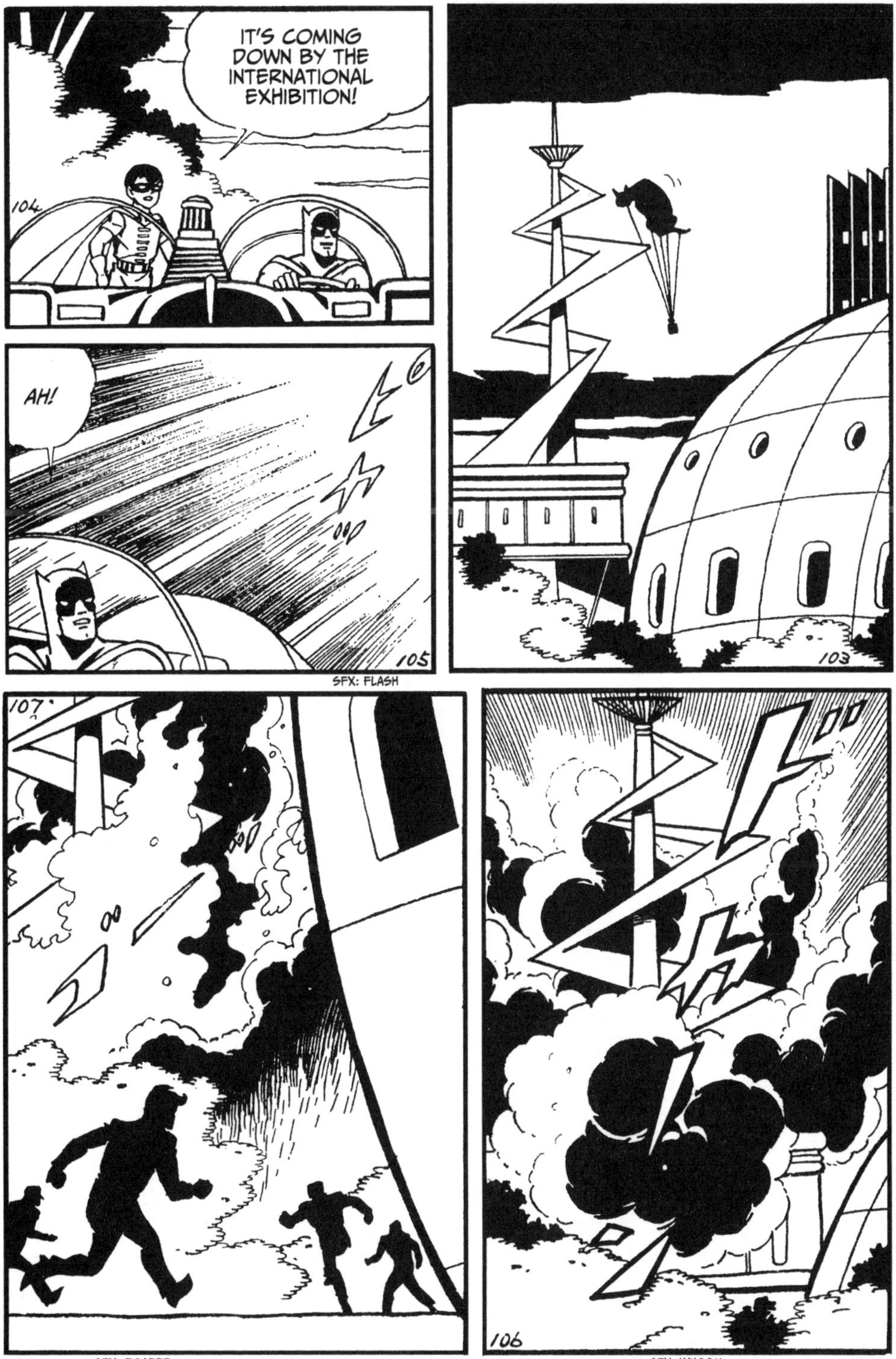
IT'S COMING DOWN BY THE INTERNATIONAL EXHIBITION!
AH!
SFX: FLASH
SFX: WHOOM
SFX: ROARRR

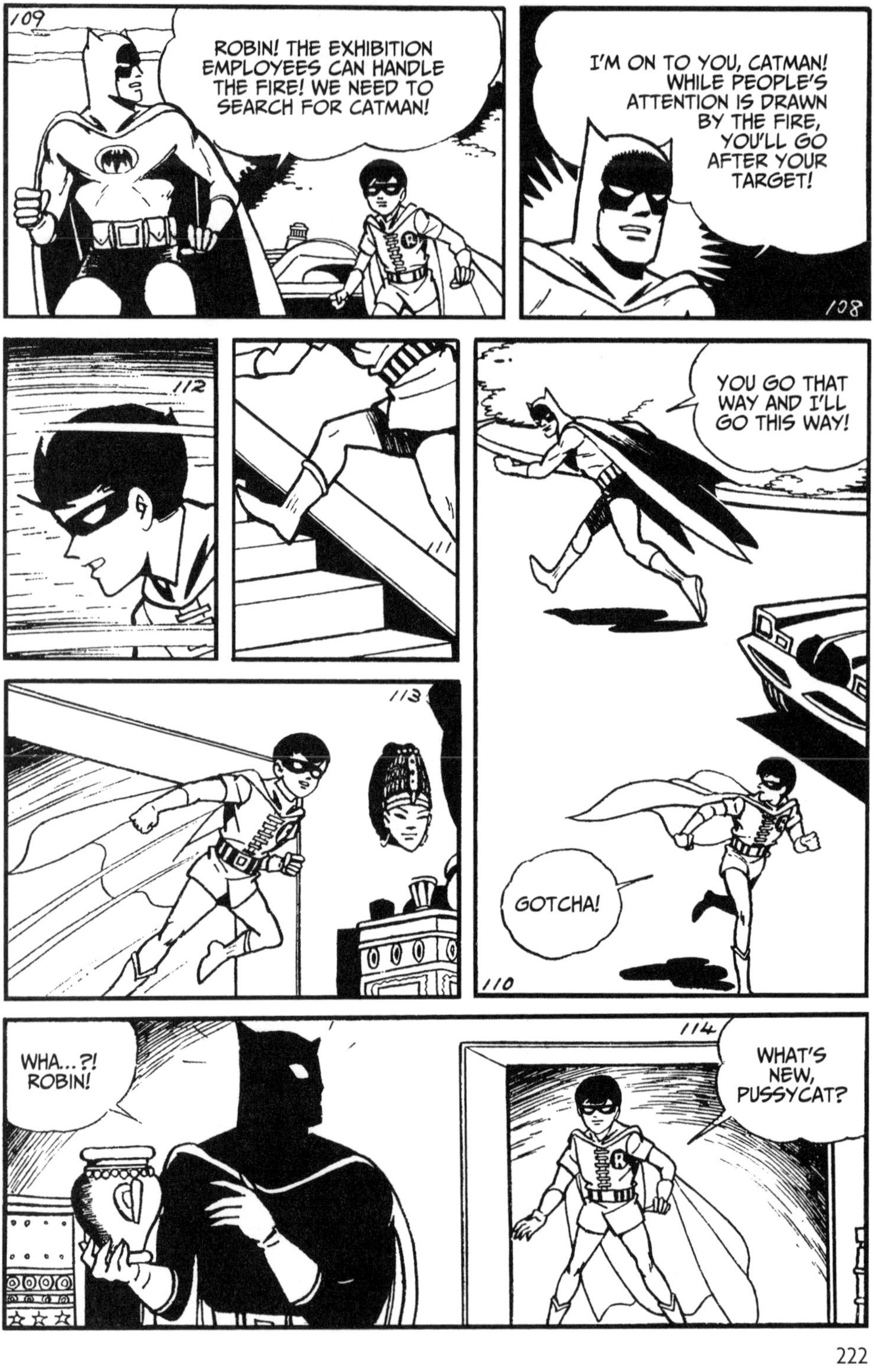
I'M ON TO YOU, CATMAN! WHILE PEOPLE'S ATTENTION IS DRAWN BY THE FIRE, YOU'LL GO AFTER YOUR TARGET!
ROBIN! THE EXHIBITION EMPLOYEES CAN HANDLE THE FIRE! WE NEED TO SEARCH FOR CATMAN!
YOU GO THAT WAY AND I'LL GO THIS WAY!
GOTCHA!
WHAT'S NEW, PUSSYCAT?
WHA...?! ROBIN!

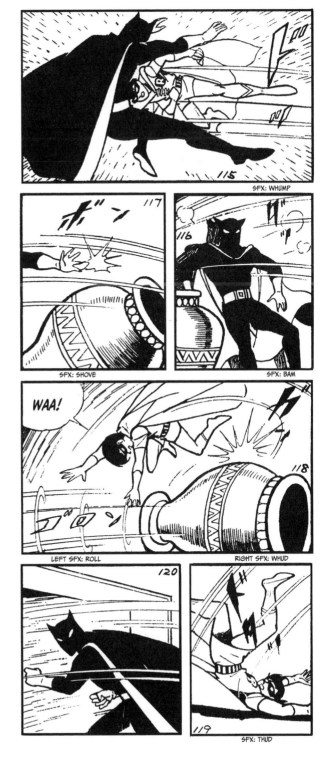

SFX: WHUMP

SFX: SHOVE

SFX: BAM

WAA!

LEFT SFX: ROLL

RIGHT SFX: WHUD

SFX: THUD

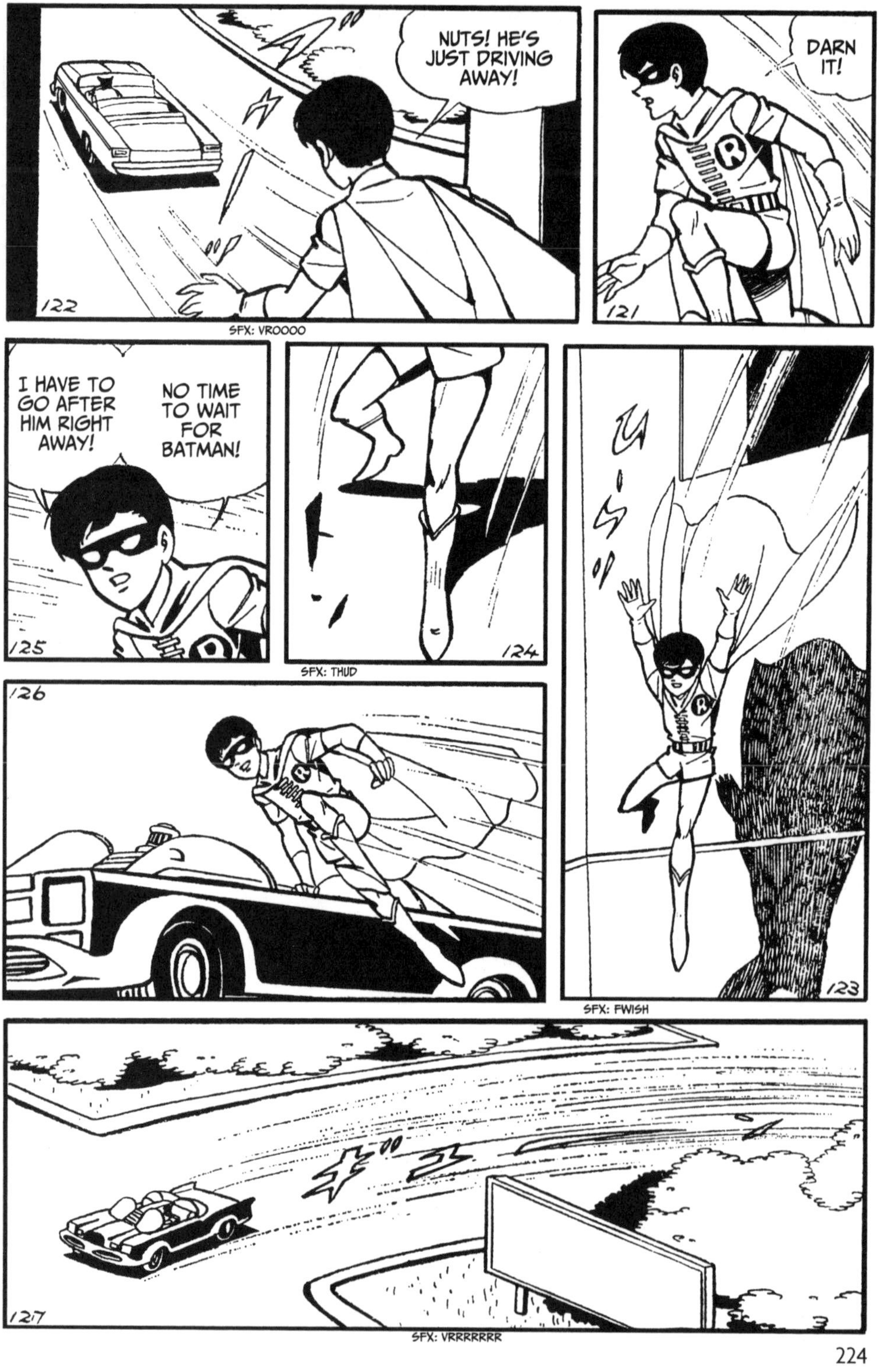
DARN IT!
NUTS! HE'S JUST DRIVING AWAY!
SFX: VROOOO
SFX: FWISH
SFX: THUD
NO TIME TO WAIT FOR BATMAN!
I HAVE TO GO AFTER HIM RIGHT AWAY!
SFX: VRRRRRRR

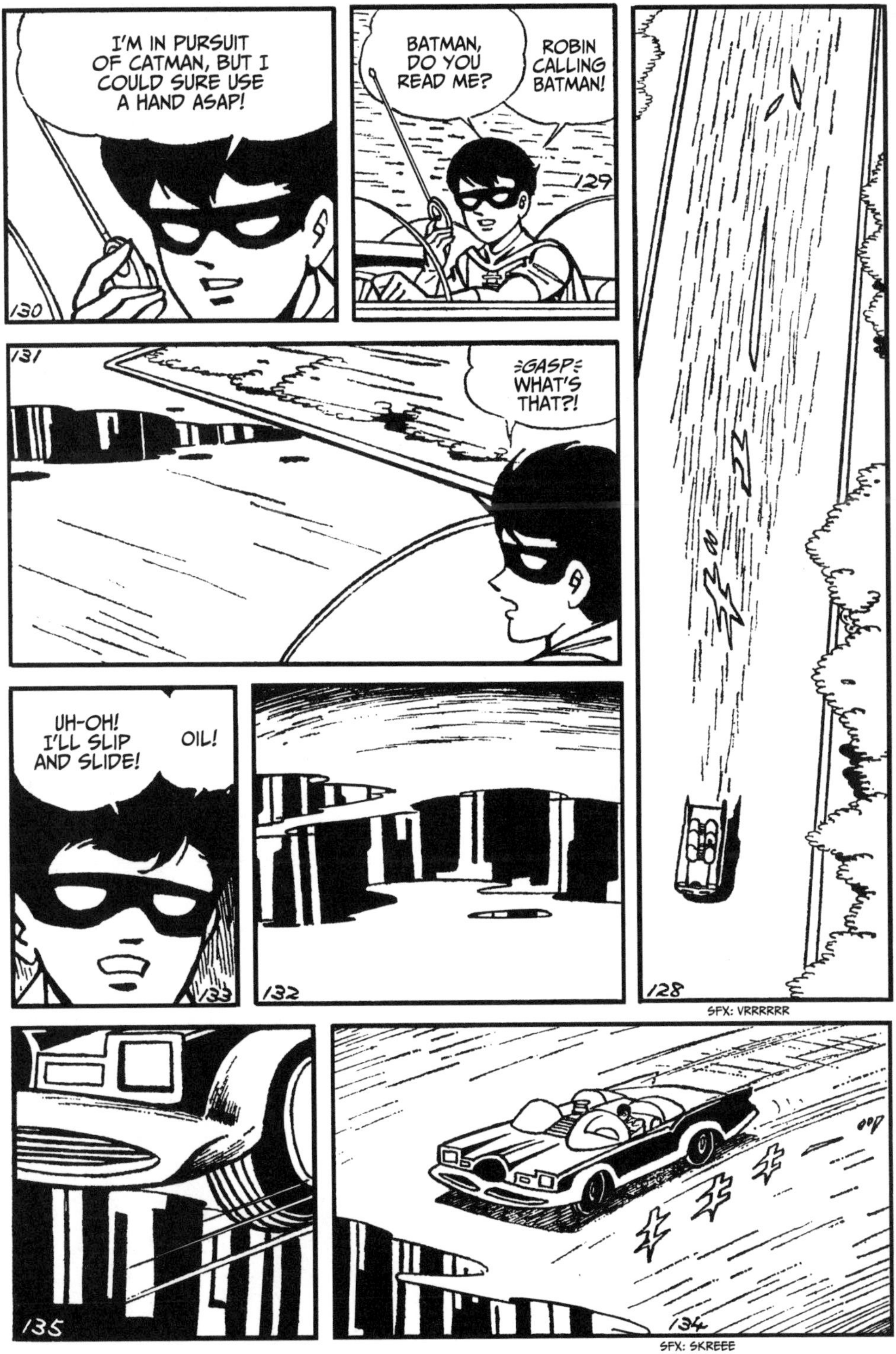
SFX: VRRRRRR
ROBIN CALLING BATMAN!
BATMAN, DO YOU READ ME?
I'M IN PURSUIT OF CATMAN, BUT I COULD SURE USE A HAND ASAP!
=GASP= WHAT'S THAT?!
OIL!
UH-OH! I'LL SLIP AND SLIDE!
SFX: SKREEE

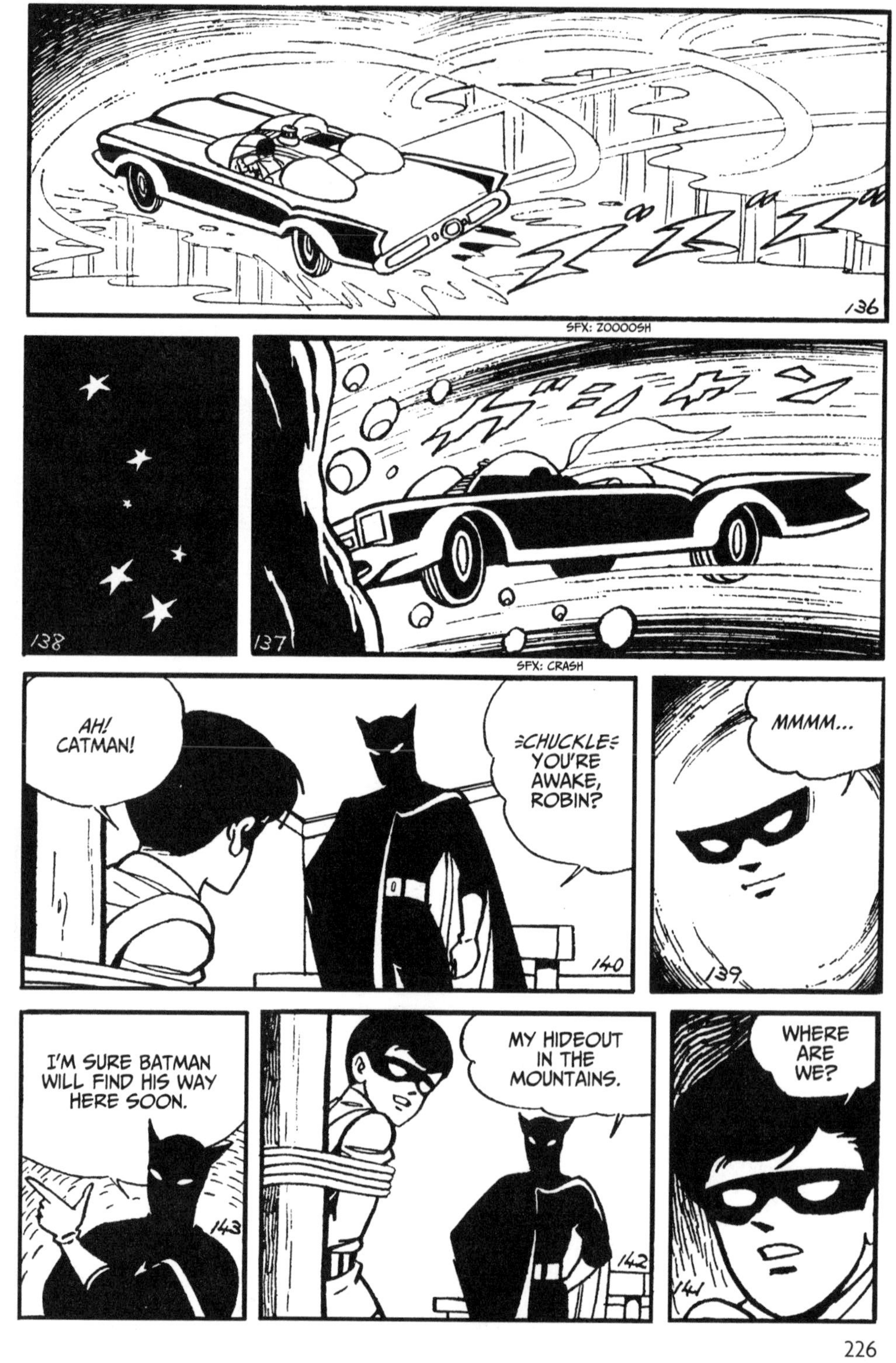
SFX: ZOOOOSH
SFX: CRASH
MMMM...
≈CHUCKLE≈ YOU'RE AWAKE, ROBIN?
AH! CATMAN!
WHERE ARE WE?
MY HIDEOUT IN THE MOUNTAINS.
I'M SURE BATMAN WILL FIND HIS WAY HERE SOON.

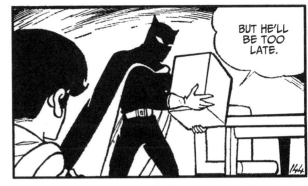

BUT HE'LL BE TOO LATE.
BY THEN, YOU AND THIS COTTAGE WILL BE ASHES.
SFX: SPLASH SPLASH
WHAT ARE YOU GOING TO DO?
ISN'T IT OBVIOUS?
I'M STARTING ANOTHER FIRE!
AS THIS PLACE BURNS DOWN, I'LL BE ON MY WAY TO ANOTHER HIDEOUT.
SFX: FWOOO

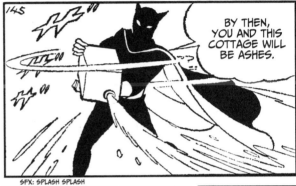

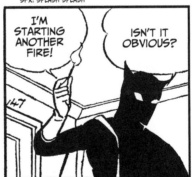

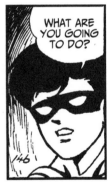

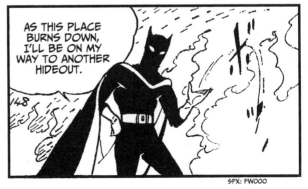

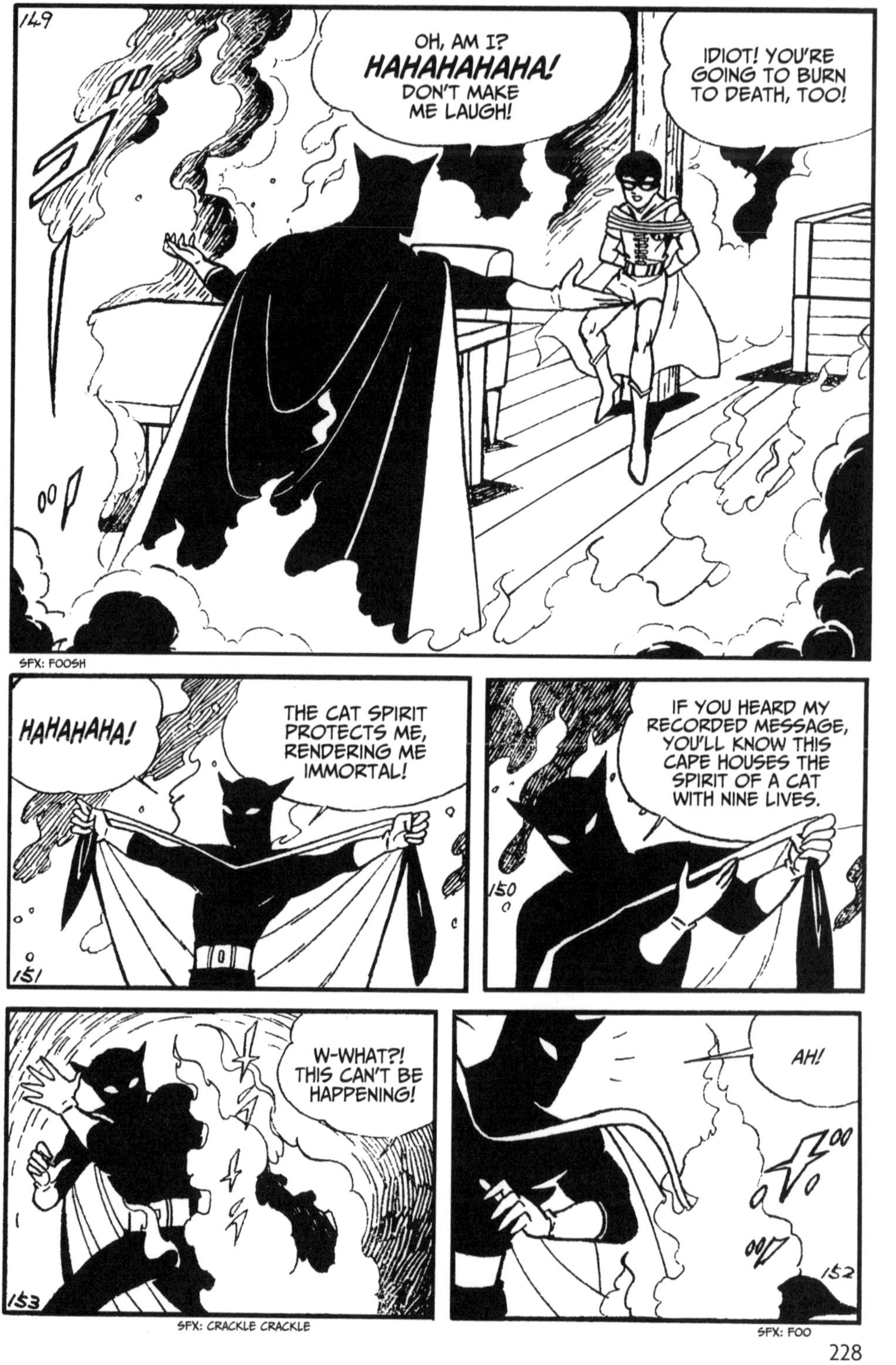
IDIOT! YOU'RE GOING TO BURN TO DEATH, TOO!
OH, AM I? **HAHAHAHAHA!** DON'T MAKE ME LAUGH!
SFX: FOOSH
IF YOU HEARD MY RECORDED MESSAGE, YOU'LL KNOW THIS CAPE HOUSES THE SPIRIT OF A CAT WITH NINE LIVES.
THE CAT SPIRIT PROTECTS ME, RENDERING ME IMMORTAL!
HAHAHAHA!
AH!
SFX: FOO
W-WHAT?! THIS CAN'T BE HAPPENING!
SFX: CRACKLE CRACKLE

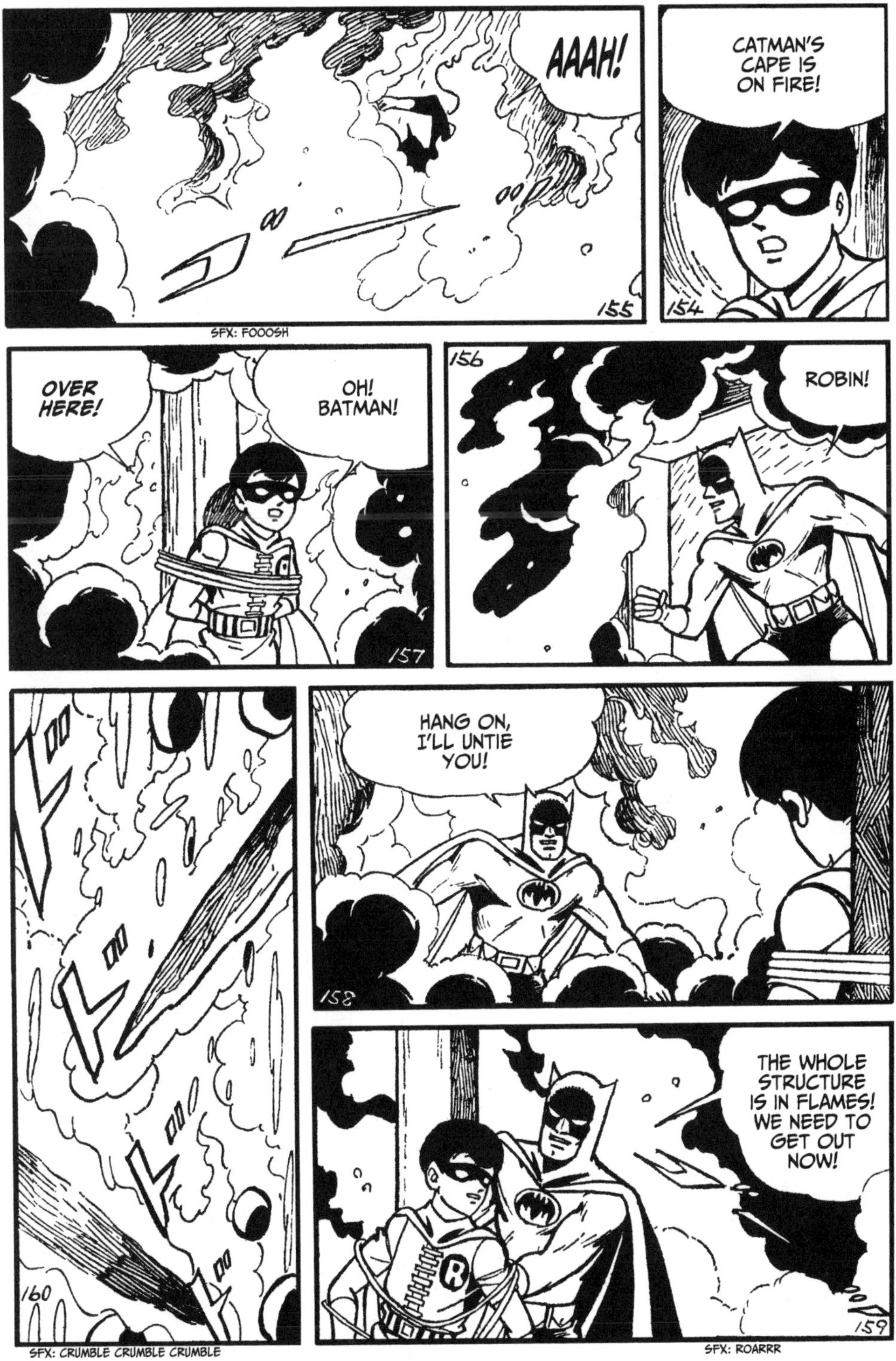
CATMAN'S CAPE IS ON FIRE!
154
AAAH!
155
SFX: FOOOSH
ROBIN!
156
OH! BATMAN!
OVER HERE!
157
HANG ON, I'LL UNTIE YOU!
158
THE WHOLE STRUCTURE IS IN FLAMES! WE NEED TO GET OUT NOW!
159
SFX: ROARRR
160
SFX: CRUMBLE CRUMBLE CRUMBLE

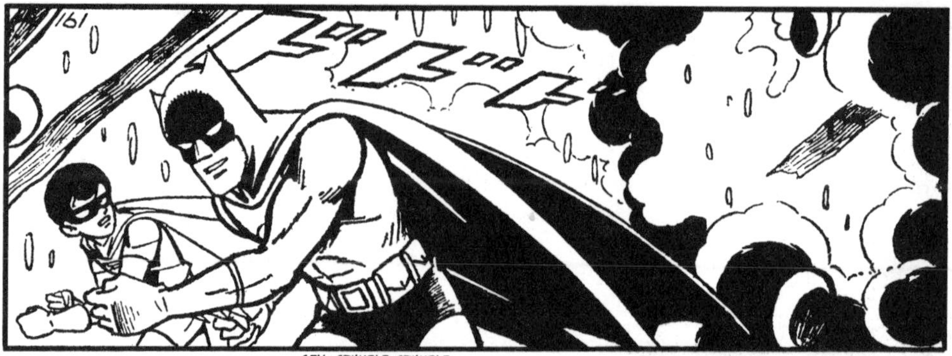

SFX: CRUMBLE CRUMBLE

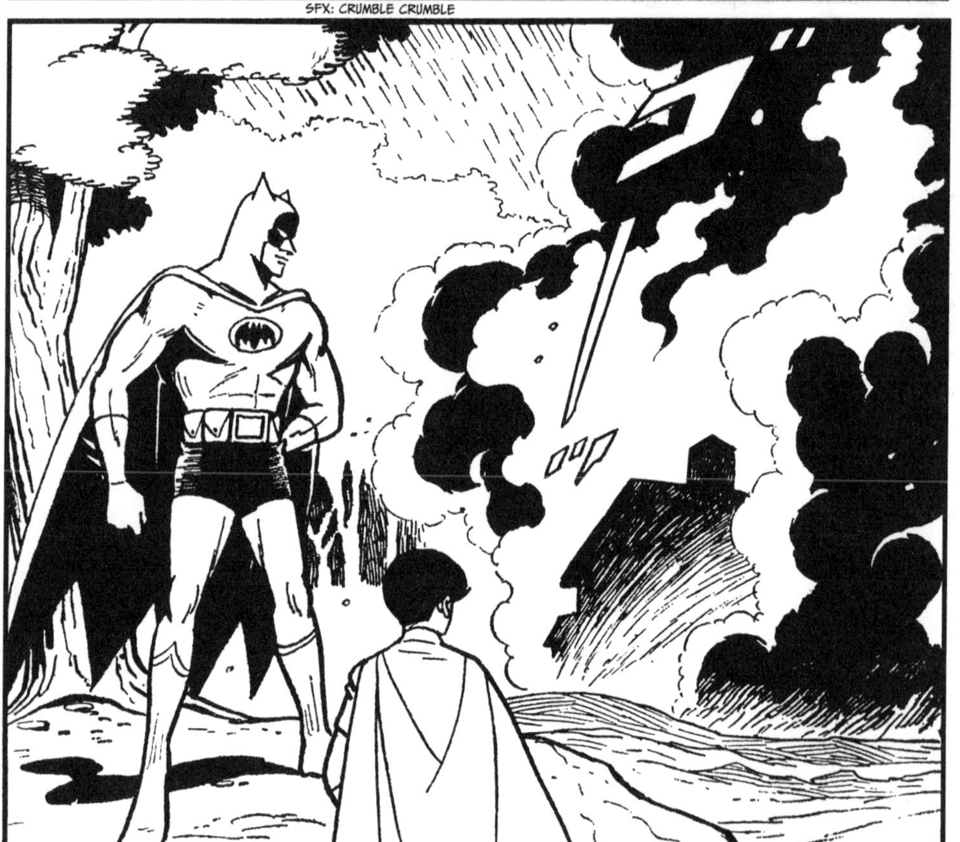

SFX: ROARRRR

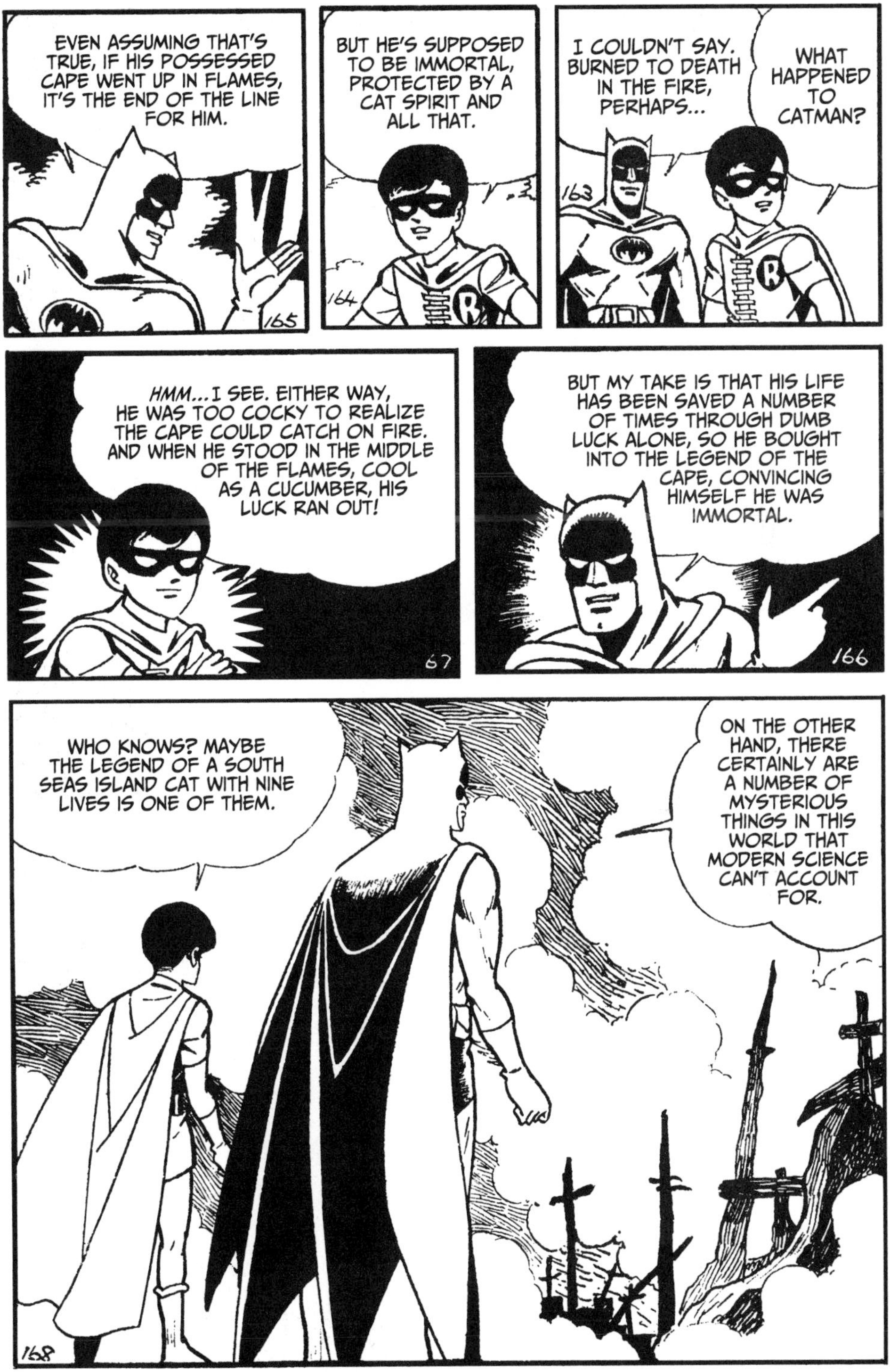
WHAT HAPPENED TO CATMAN?
I COULDN'T SAY. BURNED TO DEATH IN THE FIRE, PERHAPS...
BUT HE'S SUPPOSED TO BE IMMORTAL, PROTECTED BY A CAT SPIRIT AND ALL THAT.
EVEN ASSUMING THAT'S TRUE, IF HIS POSSESSED CAPE WENT UP IN FLAMES, IT'S THE END OF THE LINE FOR HIM.
BUT MY TAKE IS THAT HIS LIFE HAS BEEN SAVED A NUMBER OF TIMES THROUGH DUMB LUCK ALONE, SO HE BOUGHT INTO THE LEGEND OF THE CAPE, CONVINCING HIMSELF HE WAS IMMORTAL.
HMM...I SEE. EITHER WAY, HE WAS TOO COCKY TO REALIZE THE CAPE COULD CATCH ON FIRE. AND WHEN HE STOOD IN THE MIDDLE OF THE FLAMES, COOL AS A CUCUMBER, HIS LUCK RAN OUT!
ON THE OTHER HAND, THERE CERTAINLY ARE A NUMBER OF MYSTERIOUS THINGS IN THIS WORLD THAT MODERN SCIENCE CAN'T ACCOUNT FOR.
WHO KNOWS? MAYBE THE LEGEND OF A SOUTH SEAS ISLAND CAT WITH NINE LIVES IS ONE OF THEM.

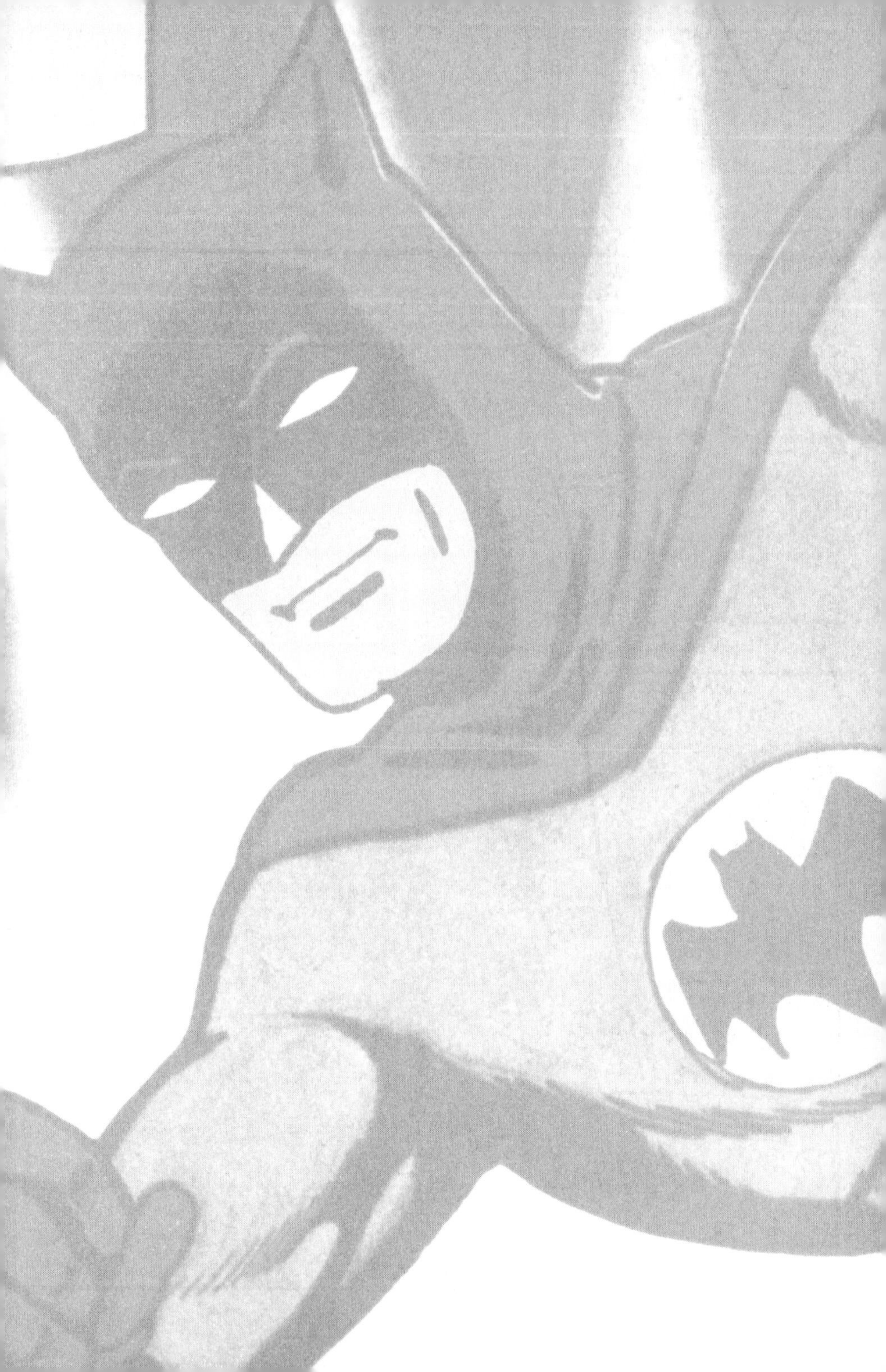

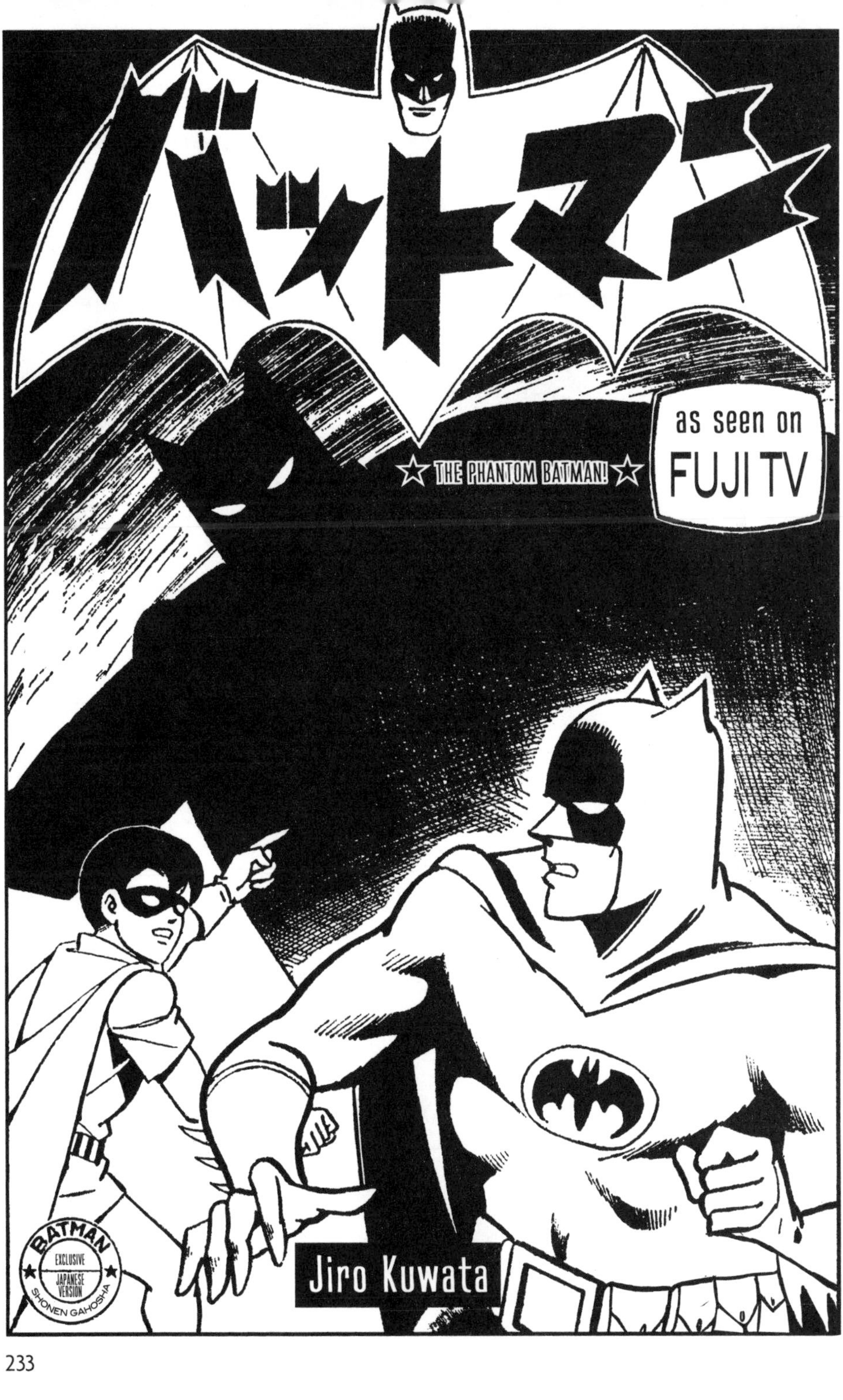
バットマン
☆THE PHANTOM BATMAN!☆
as seen on
FUJI TV
BATMAN
EXCLUSIVE
JAPANESE VERSION
SHONEN GAHOSHA
Jiro Kuwata

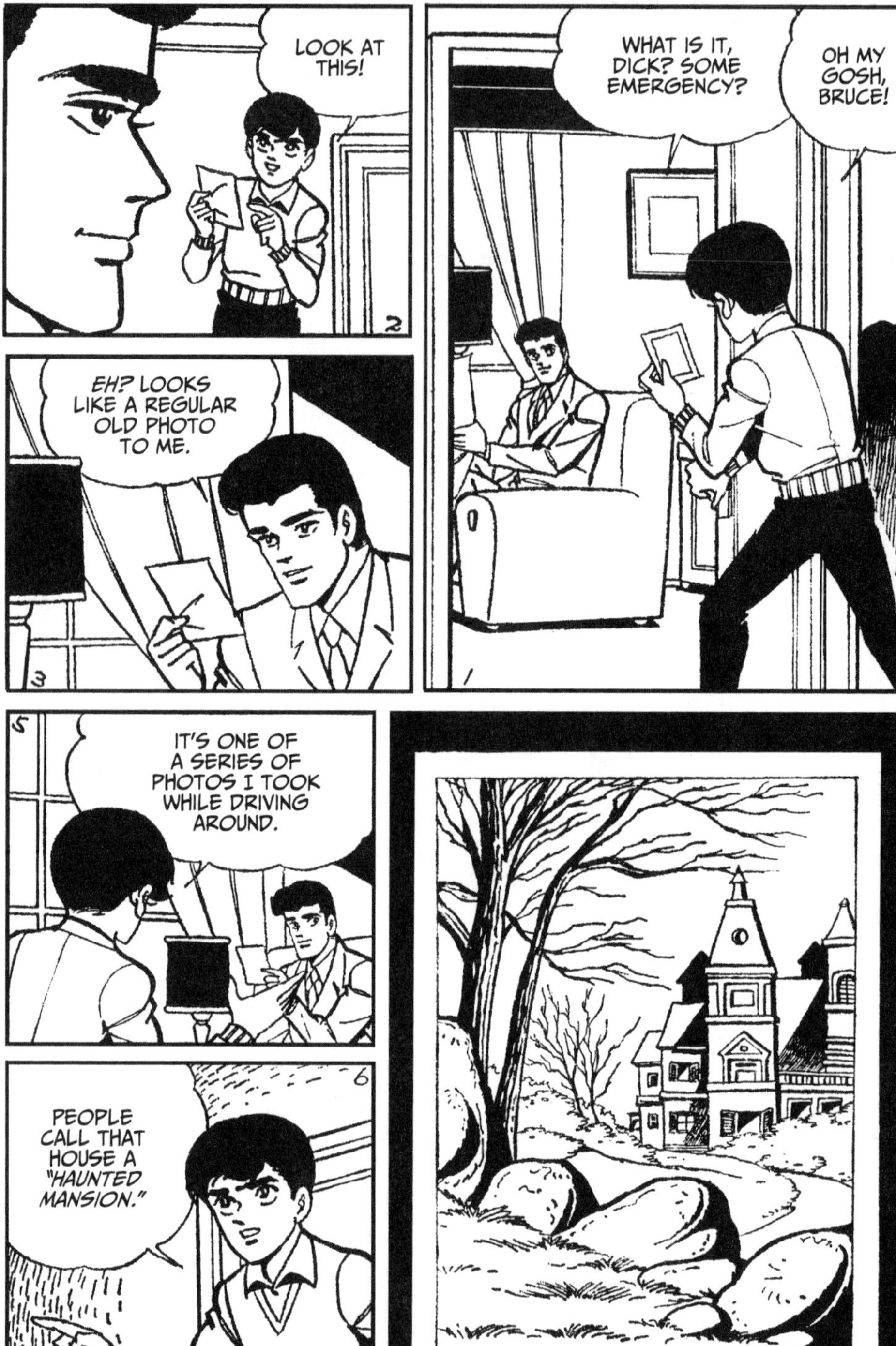
OH MY GOSH, BRUCE!
WHAT IS IT, DICK? SOME EMERGENCY?
LOOK AT THIS!
EH? LOOKS LIKE A REGULAR OLD PHOTO TO ME.
IT'S ONE OF A SERIES OF PHOTOS I TOOK WHILE DRIVING AROUND.
PEOPLE CALL THAT HOUSE A *"HAUNTED MANSION."*

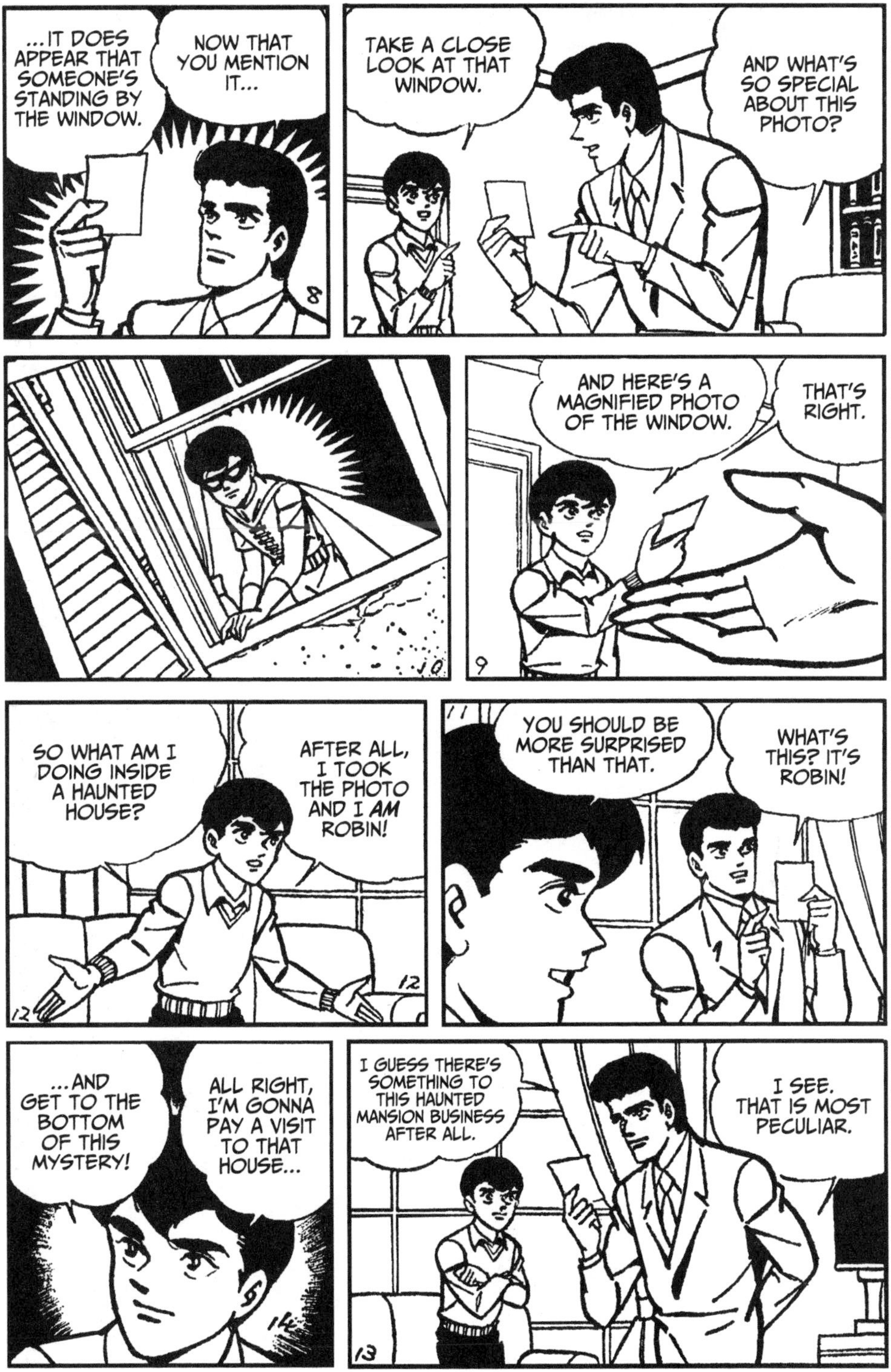
AND WHAT'S SO SPECIAL ABOUT THIS PHOTO?
TAKE A CLOSE LOOK AT THAT WINDOW.
NOW THAT YOU MENTION IT...
...IT DOES APPEAR THAT SOMEONE'S STANDING BY THE WINDOW.
THAT'S RIGHT.
AND HERE'S A MAGNIFIED PHOTO OF THE WINDOW.
WHAT'S THIS? IT'S ROBIN!
YOU SHOULD BE MORE SURPRISED THAN THAT.
AFTER ALL, I TOOK THE PHOTO AND I *AM* ROBIN!
SO WHAT AM I DOING INSIDE A HAUNTED HOUSE?
I SEE. THAT IS MOST PECULIAR.
I GUESS THERE'S SOMETHING TO THIS HAUNTED MANSION BUSINESS AFTER ALL.
ALL RIGHT, I'M GONNA PAY A VISIT TO THAT HOUSE...
...AND GET TO THE BOTTOM OF THIS MYSTERY!

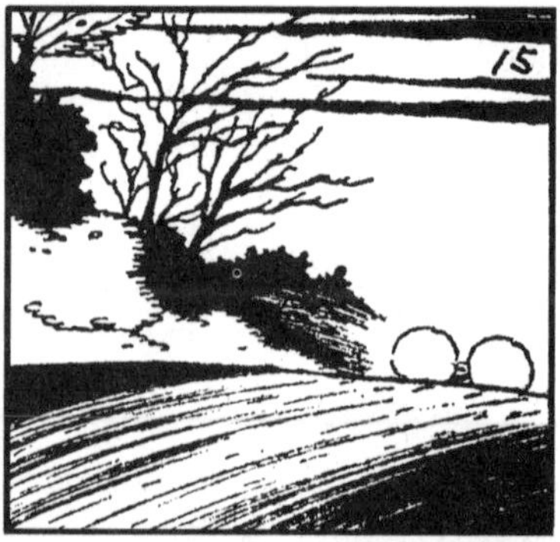

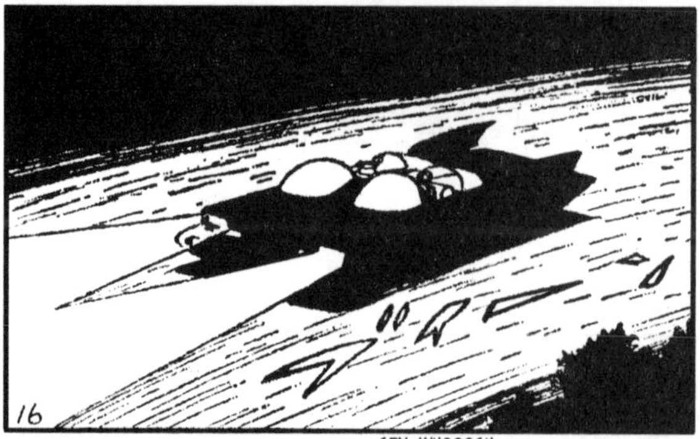

SFX: WHOOOSH

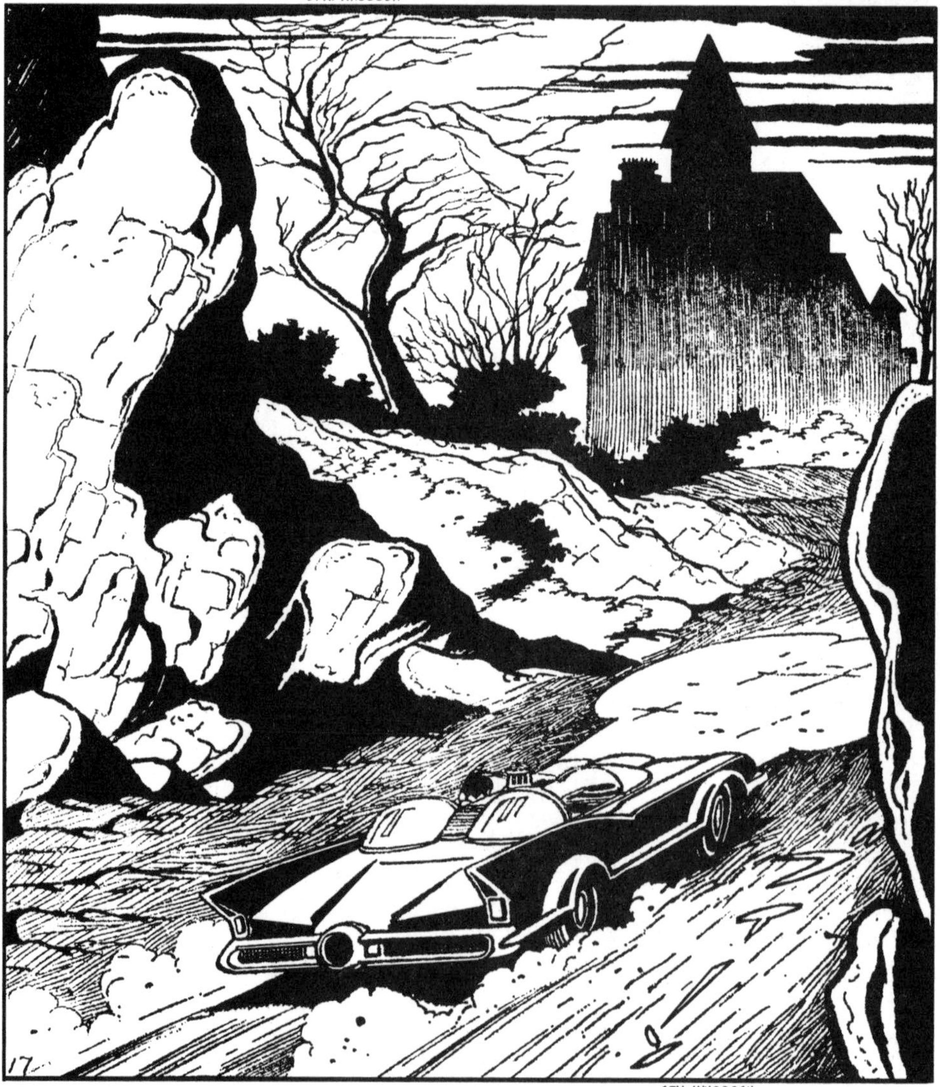

SFX: WHOOOSH

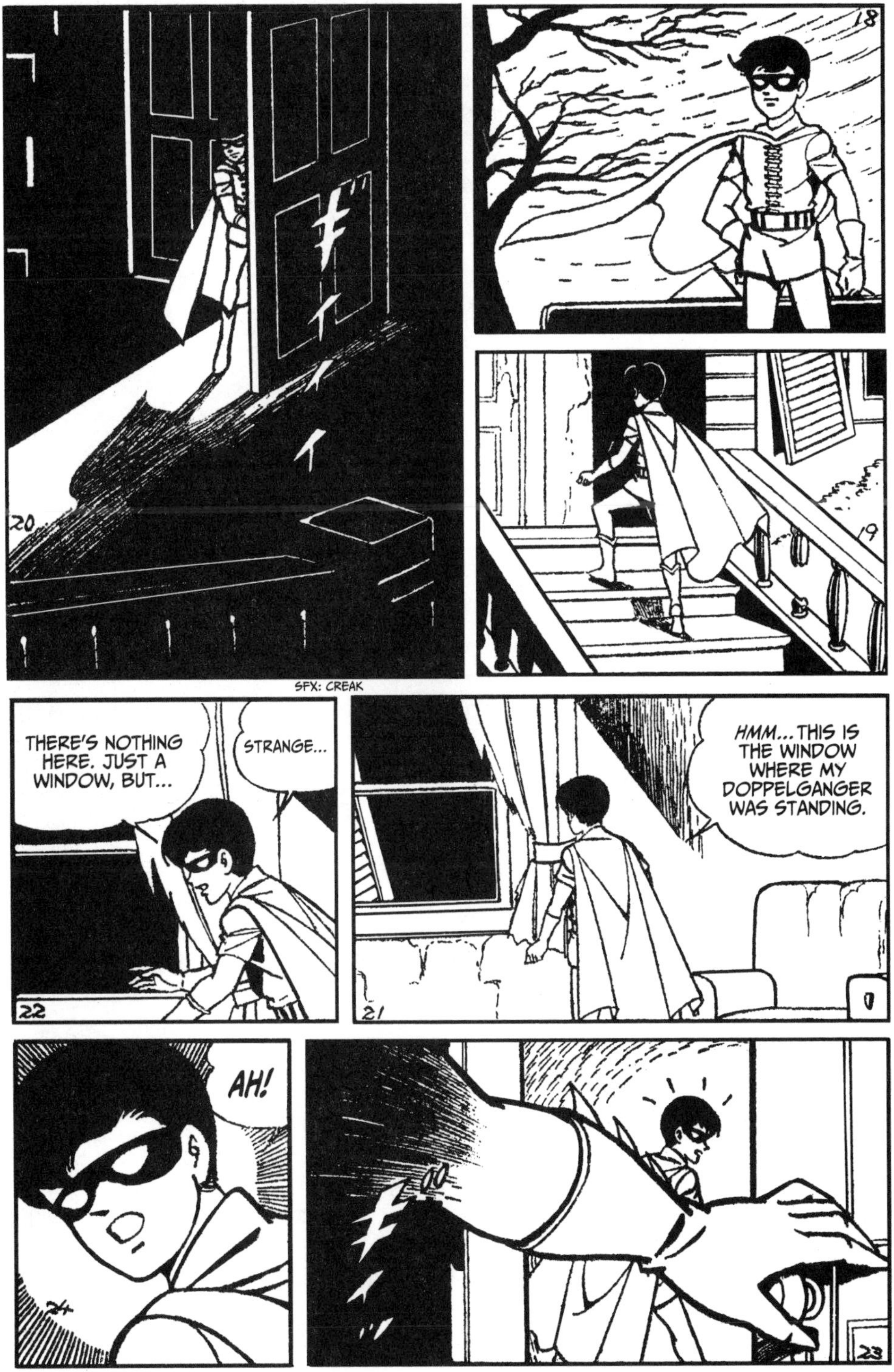
SFX: CREAK
HMM... THIS IS THE WINDOW WHERE MY DOPPELGANGER WAS STANDING.
STRANGE...
THERE'S NOTHING HERE. JUST A WINDOW, BUT...
SFX: CREAK
AH!

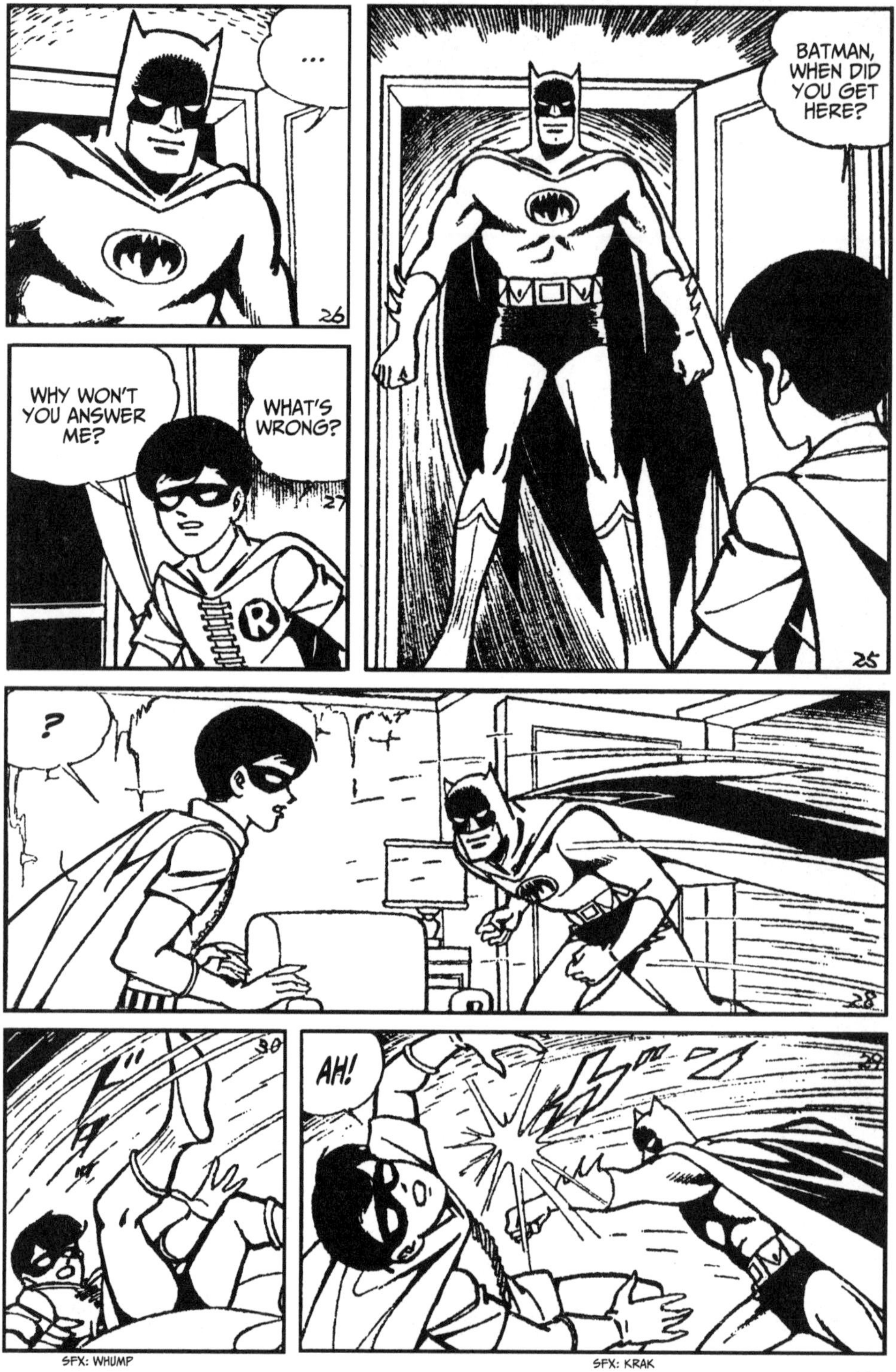
BATMAN, WHEN DID YOU GET HERE?
...
WHAT'S WRONG?
WHY WON'T YOU ANSWER ME?
?
AH!
SFX: KRAK
SFX: WHUMP

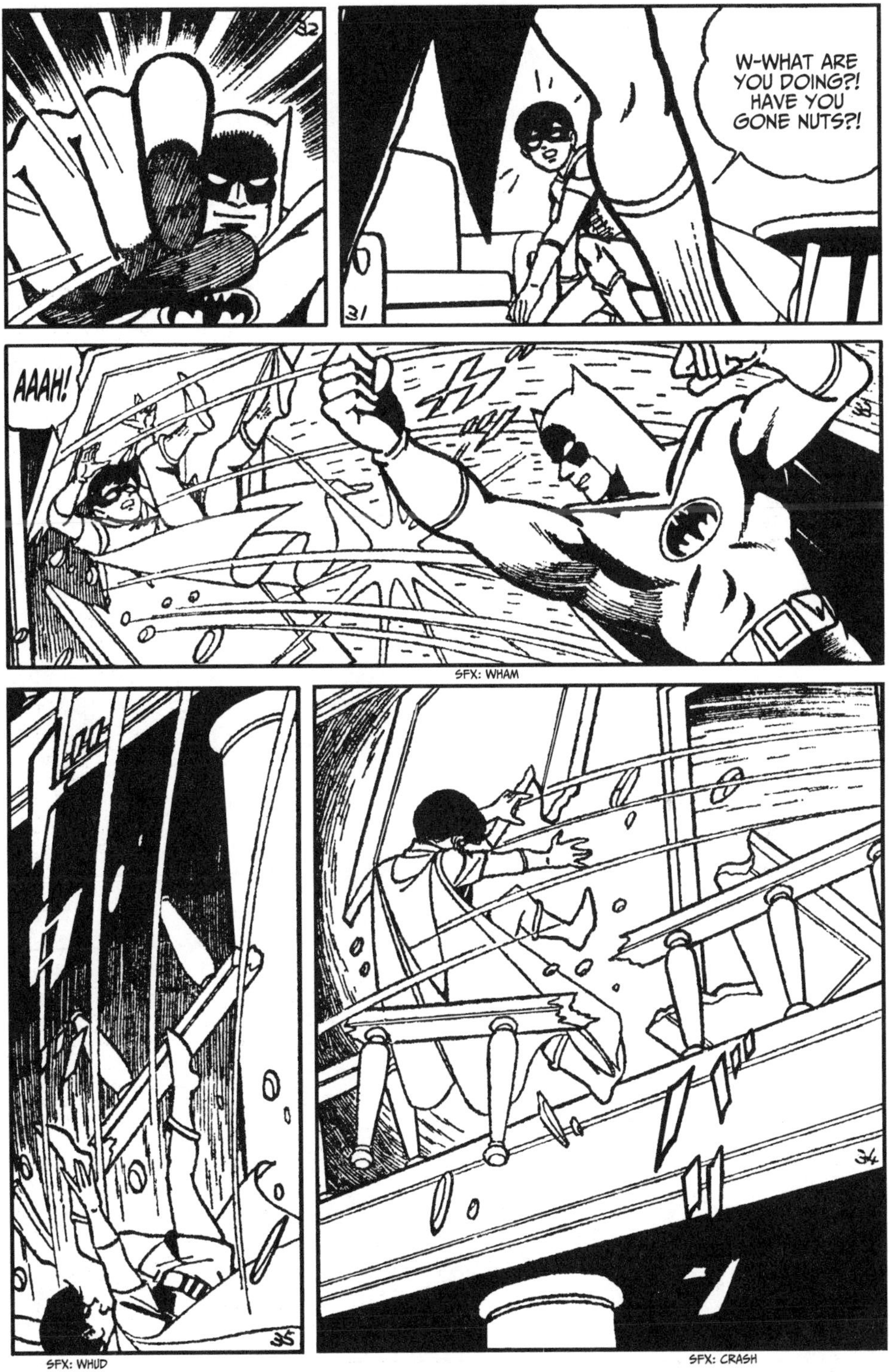
W-WHAT ARE YOU DOING?! HAVE YOU GONE NUTS?!
AAAH!
SFX: WHAM
SFX: CRASH
SFX: WHUD

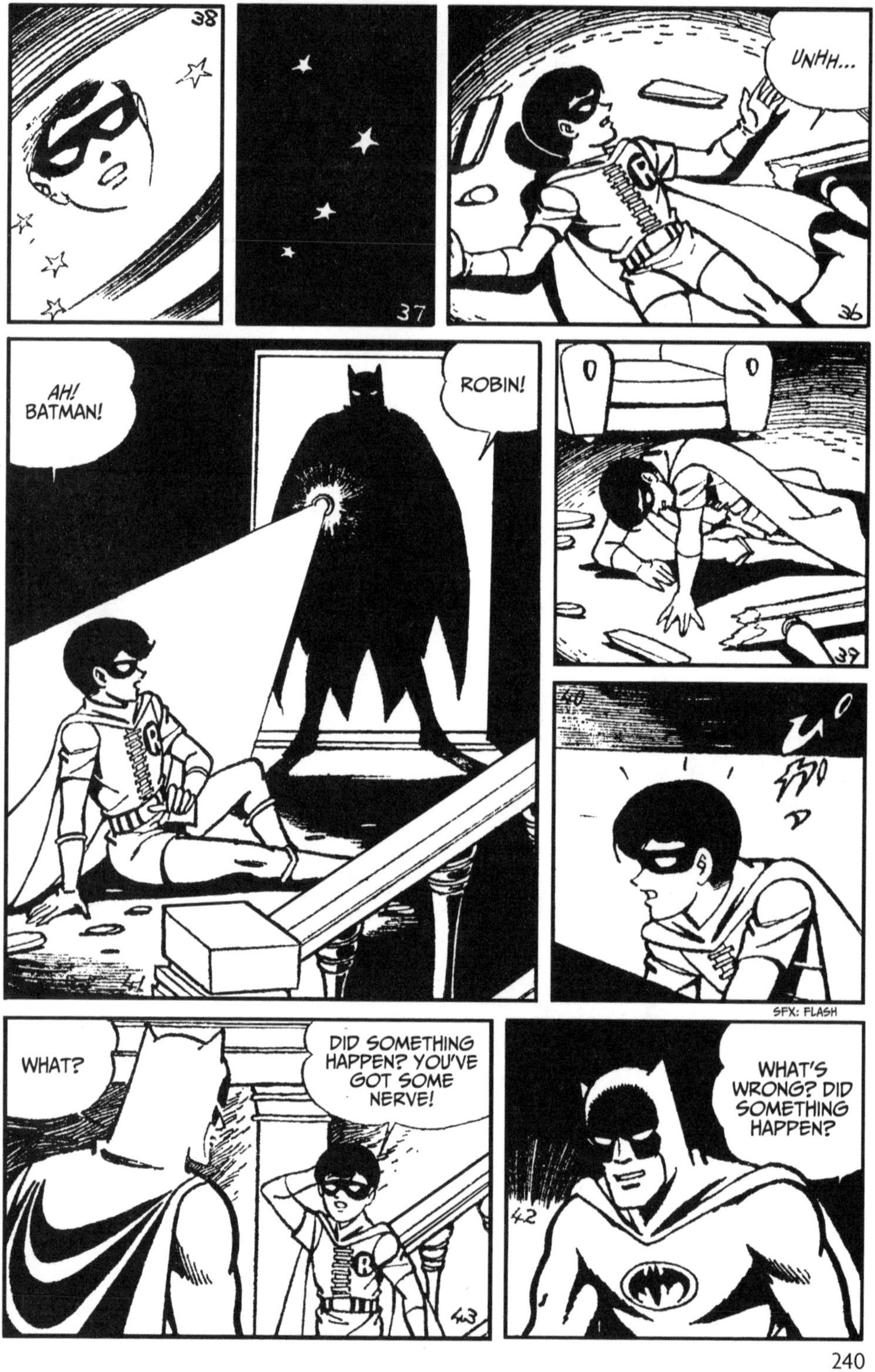
UNHH...
SFX: FLASH
ROBIN!
AH! BATMAN!
WHAT'S WRONG? DID SOMETHING HAPPEN?
DID SOMETHING HAPPEN? YOU'VE GOT SOME NERVE!
WHAT?

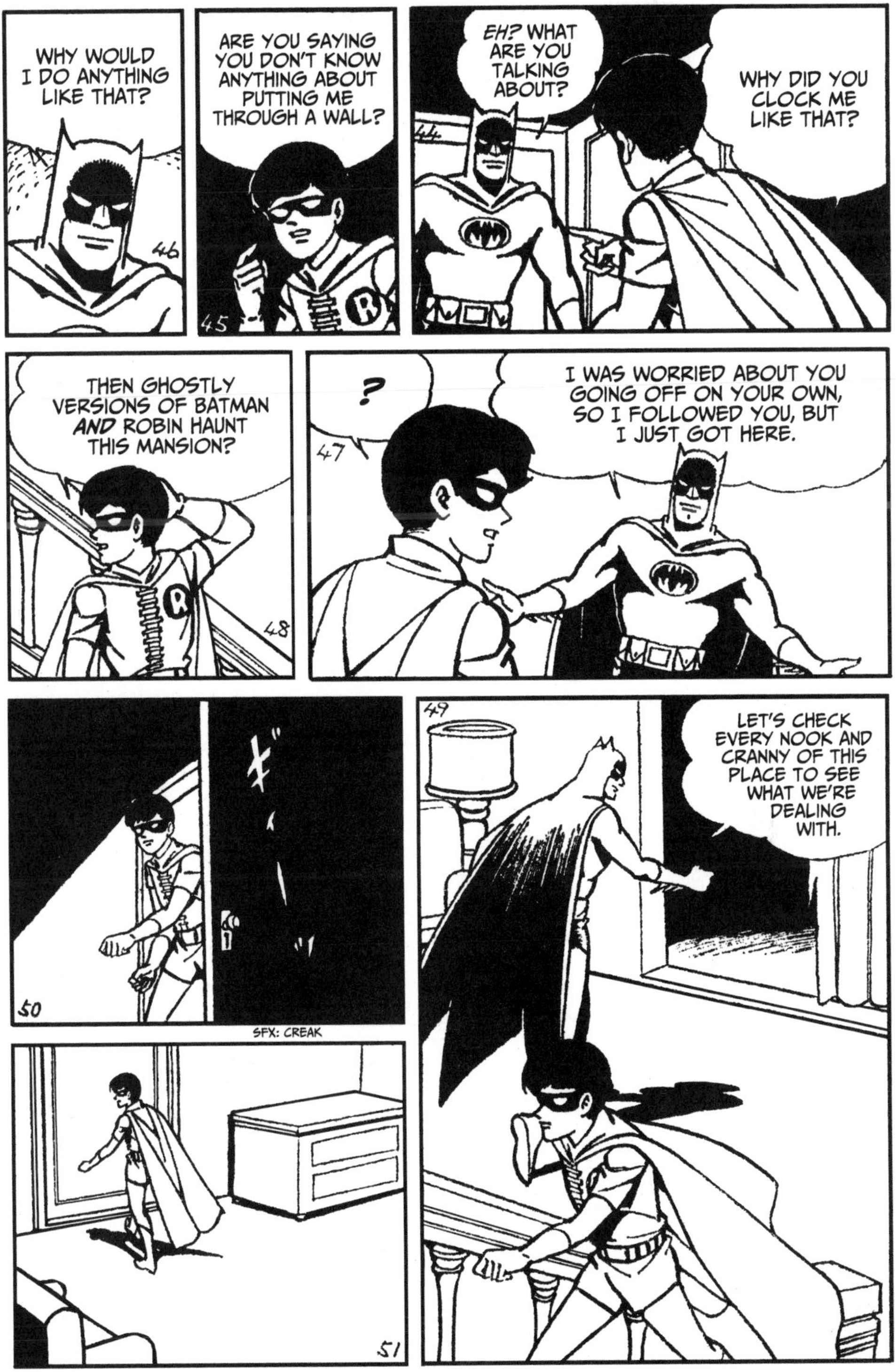
WHY DID YOU CLOCK ME LIKE THAT?
EH? WHAT ARE YOU TALKING ABOUT?
ARE YOU SAYING YOU DON'T KNOW ANYTHING ABOUT PUTTING ME THROUGH A WALL?
WHY WOULD I DO ANYTHING LIKE THAT?
I WAS WORRIED ABOUT YOU GOING OFF ON YOUR OWN, SO I FOLLOWED YOU, BUT I JUST GOT HERE.
?
THEN GHOSTLY VERSIONS OF BATMAN AND ROBIN HAUNT THIS MANSION?
LET'S CHECK EVERY NOOK AND CRANNY OF THIS PLACE TO SEE WHAT WE'RE DEALING WITH.
SFX: CREAK

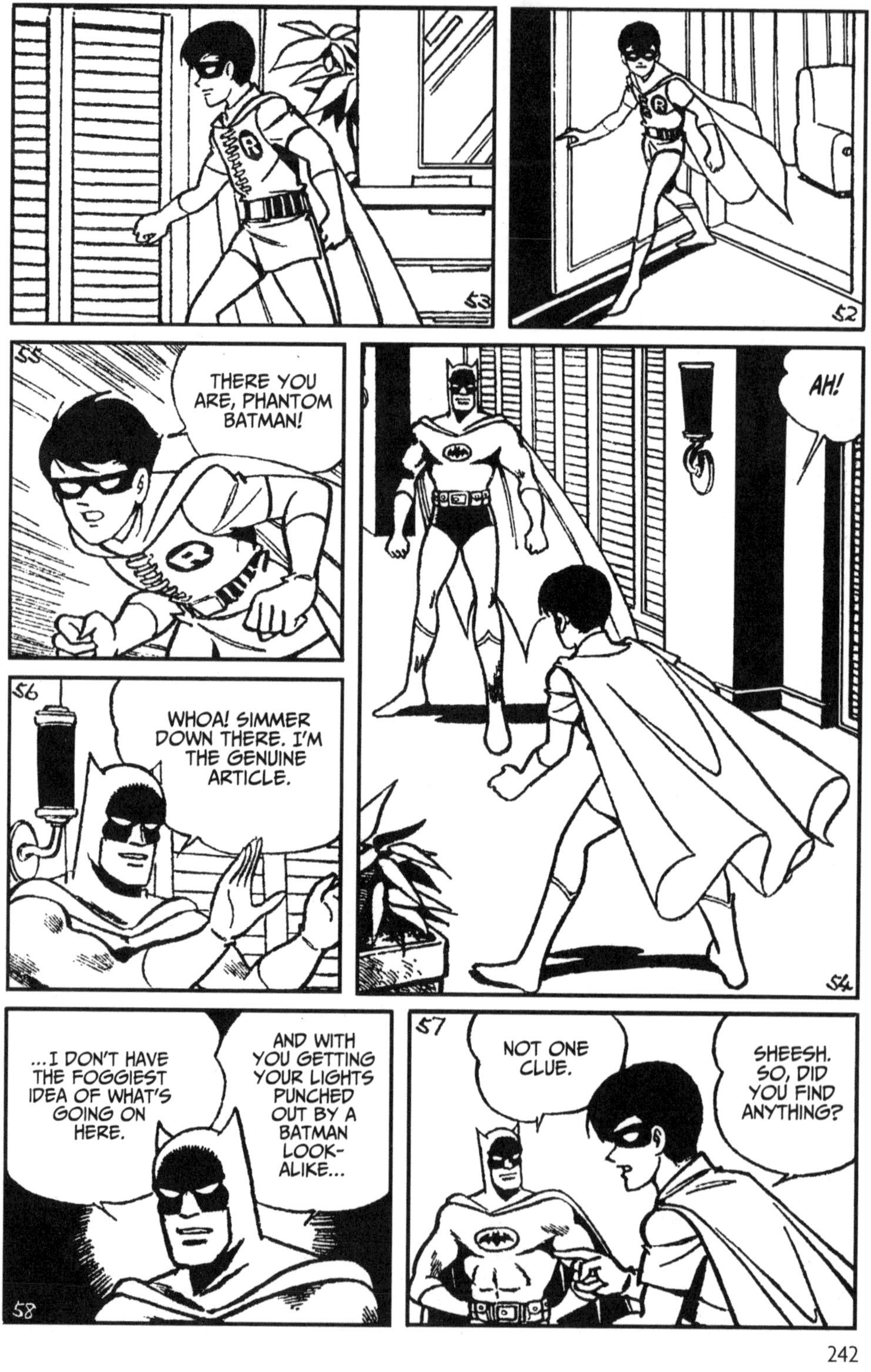
AH!
THERE YOU ARE, PHANTOM BATMAN!
WHOA! SIMMER DOWN THERE. I'M THE GENUINE ARTICLE.
SHEESH. SO, DID YOU FIND ANYTHING?
NOT ONE CLUE.
AND WITH YOU GETTING YOUR LIGHTS PUNCHED OUT BY A BATMAN LOOK-ALIKE...
...I DON'T HAVE THE FOGGIEST IDEA OF WHAT'S GOING ON HERE.

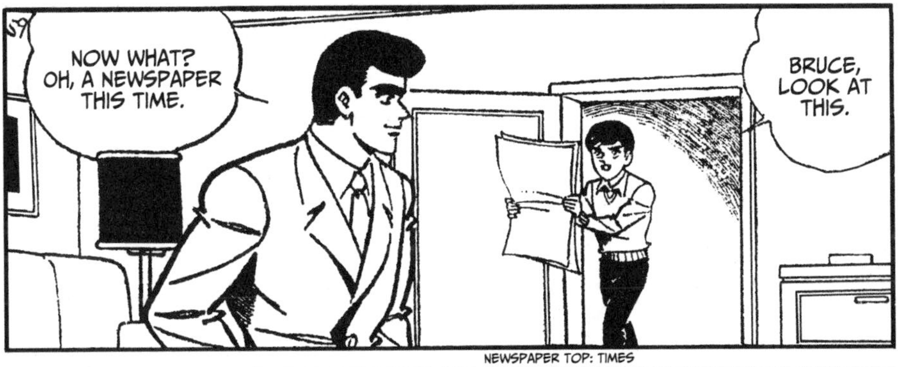
The next day...
BRUCE, LOOK AT THIS.
NOW WHAT? OH, A NEWSPAPER THIS TIME.

NEWSPAPER TOP: TIMES

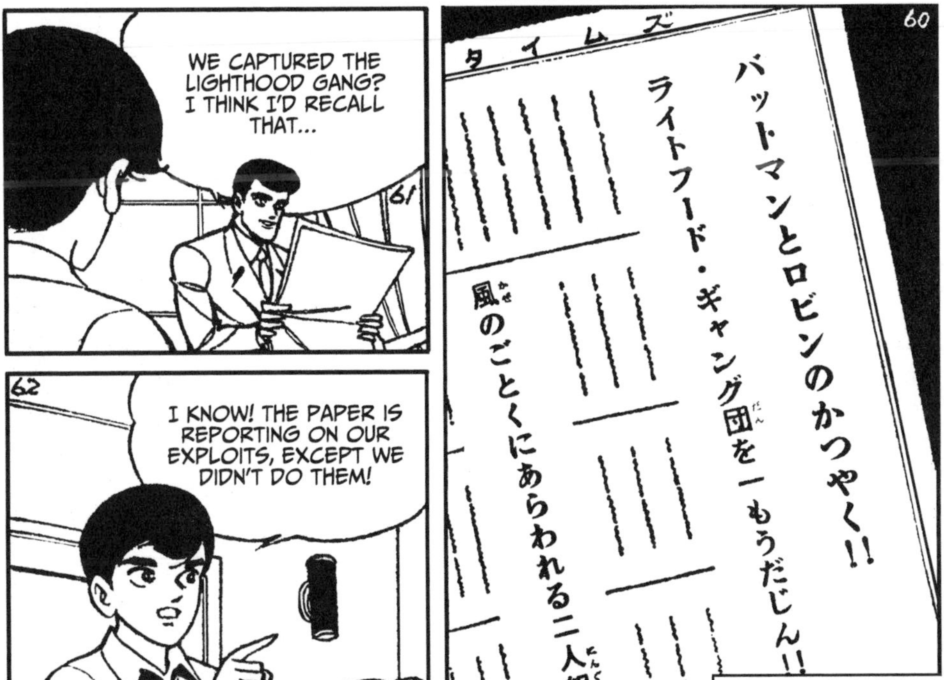
タイムズ
バットマンとロビンのかつやく!!
ライトフード・ギャング団を一もうだじん!!
風のごとくにあらわれる二人組
WE CAPTURED THE LIGHTHOOD GANG? I THINK I'D RECALL THAT...
I KNOW! THE PAPER IS REPORTING ON OUR EXPLOITS, EXCEPT WE DIDN'T DO THEM!

RIGHT HEADLINE: BATMAN AND ROBIN ROUND UP THE LIGHTHOOD GANG!

LEFT HEADLINE: THE DYNAMIC DUO APPEAR LIKE THE WIND

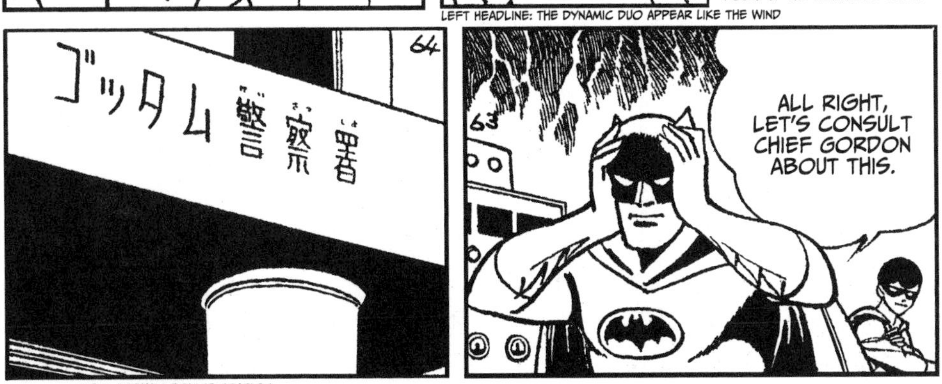
ALL RIGHT, LET'S CONSULT CHIEF GORDON ABOUT THIS.
ゴッタム警察署

SIGN: GOTHAM POLICE STATION

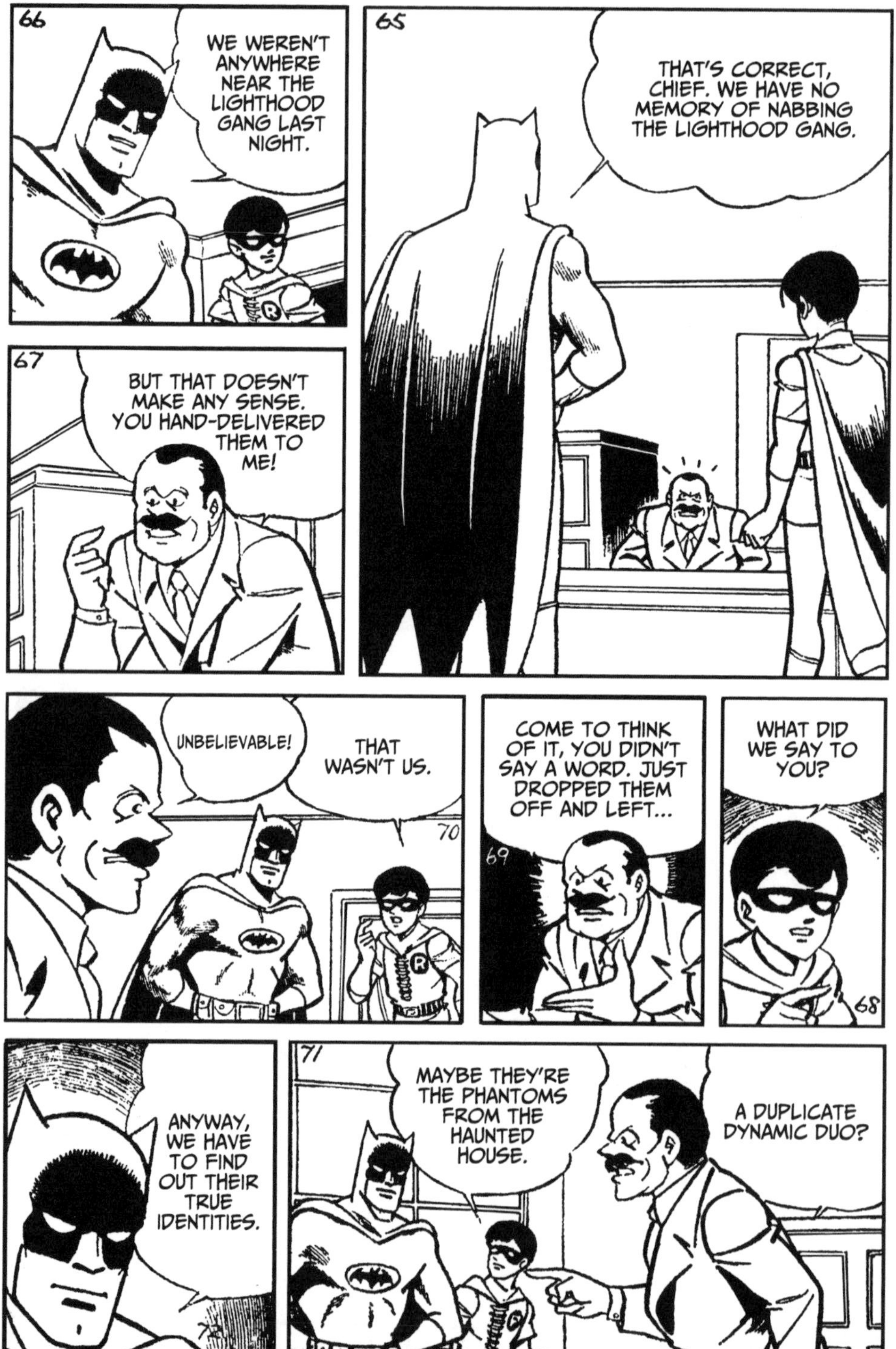
THAT'S CORRECT, CHIEF. WE HAVE NO MEMORY OF NABBING THE LIGHTHOOD GANG.
WE WEREN'T ANYWHERE NEAR THE LIGHTHOOD GANG LAST NIGHT.
BUT THAT DOESN'T MAKE ANY SENSE. YOU HAND-DELIVERED THEM TO ME!
WHAT DID WE SAY TO YOU?
COME TO THINK OF IT, YOU DIDN'T SAY A WORD. JUST DROPPED THEM OFF AND LEFT...
THAT WASN'T US.
UNBELIEVABLE!
A DUPLICATE DYNAMIC DUO?
MAYBE THEY'RE THE PHANTOMS FROM THE HAUNTED HOUSE.
ANYWAY, WE HAVE TO FIND OUT THEIR TRUE IDENTITIES.

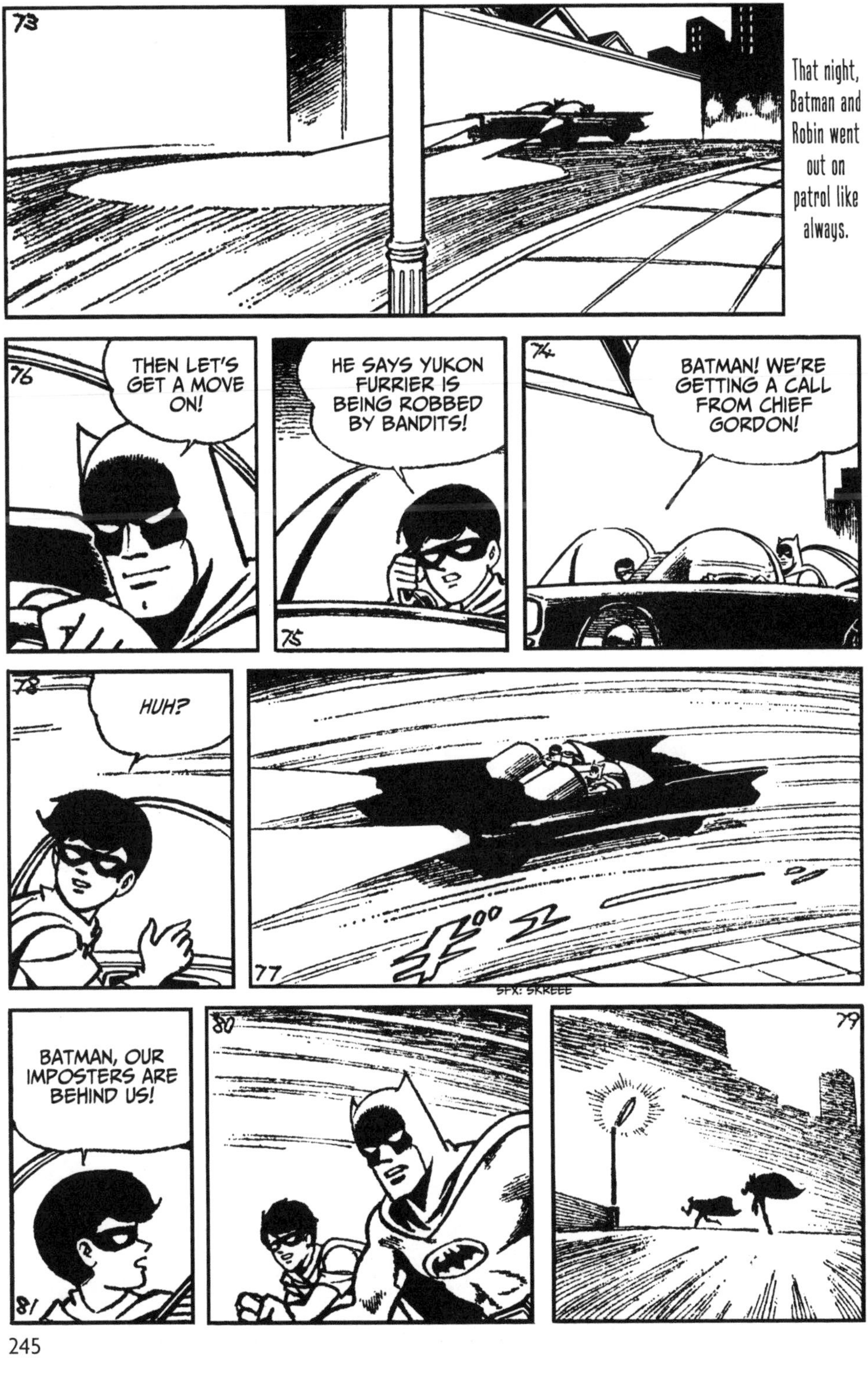
That night, Batman and Robin went out on patrol like always.
BATMAN! WE'RE GETTING A CALL FROM CHIEF GORDON!
HE SAYS YUKON FURRIER IS BEING ROBBED BY BANDITS!
THEN LET'S GET A MOVE ON!
SFX: SKREEE
HUH?
BATMAN, OUR IMPOSTERS ARE BEHIND US!

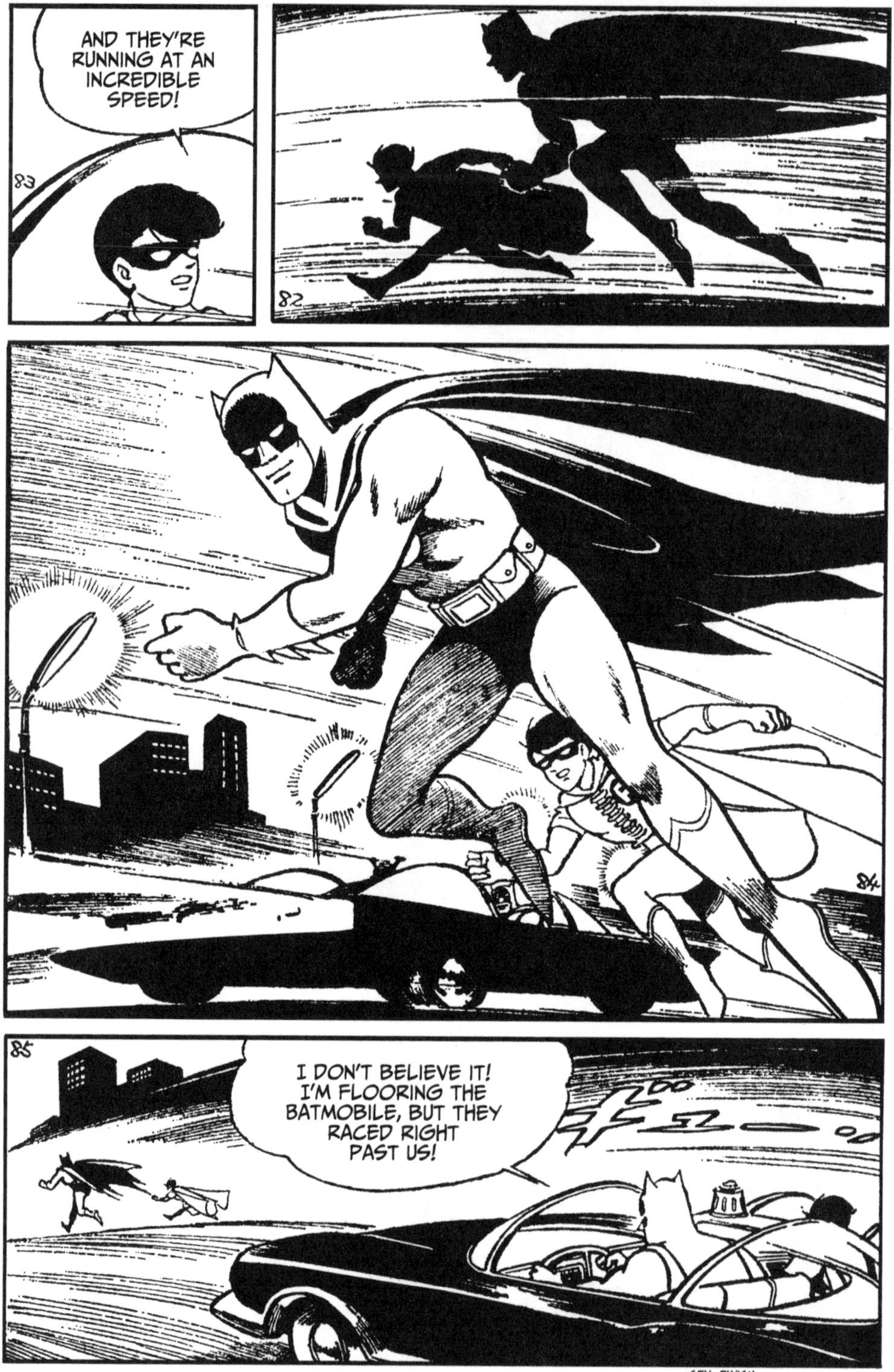
AND THEY'RE RUNNING AT AN INCREDIBLE SPEED!
I DON'T BELIEVE IT! I'M FLOORING THE BATMOBILE, BUT THEY RACED RIGHT PAST US!

SFX: FWISH

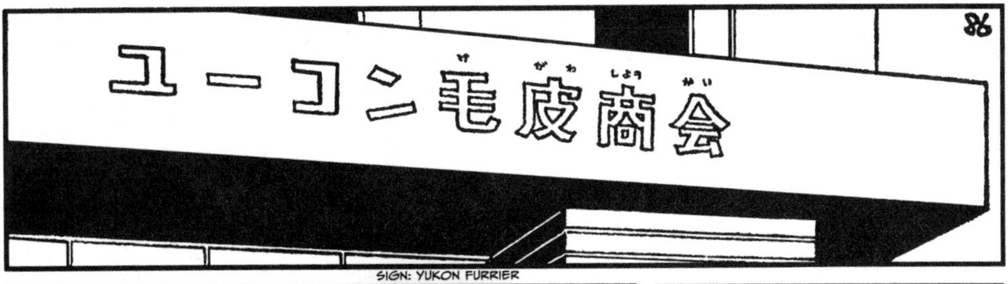
86
ユーコン毛皮商会
SIGN: YUKON FURRIER

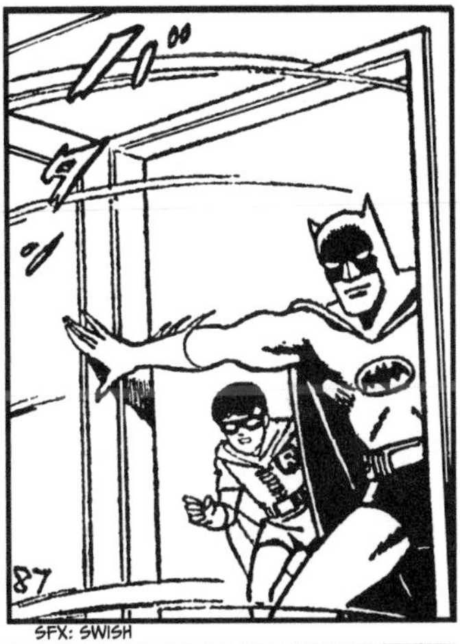
87
SFX: SWISH

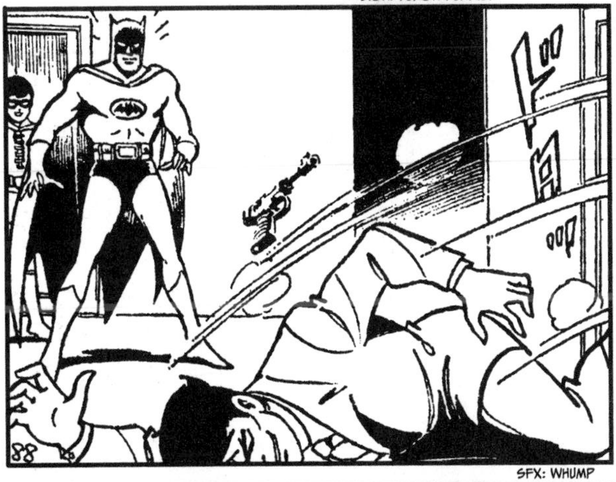
88
SFX: WHUMP

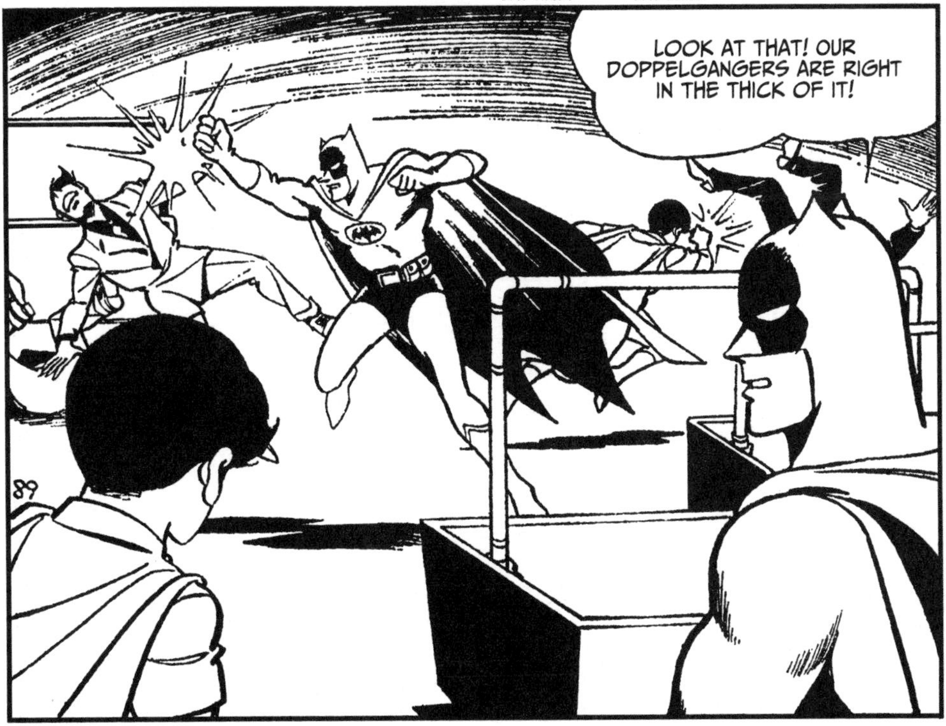
89
LOOK AT THAT! OUR DOPPELGANGERS ARE RIGHT IN THE THICK OF IT!

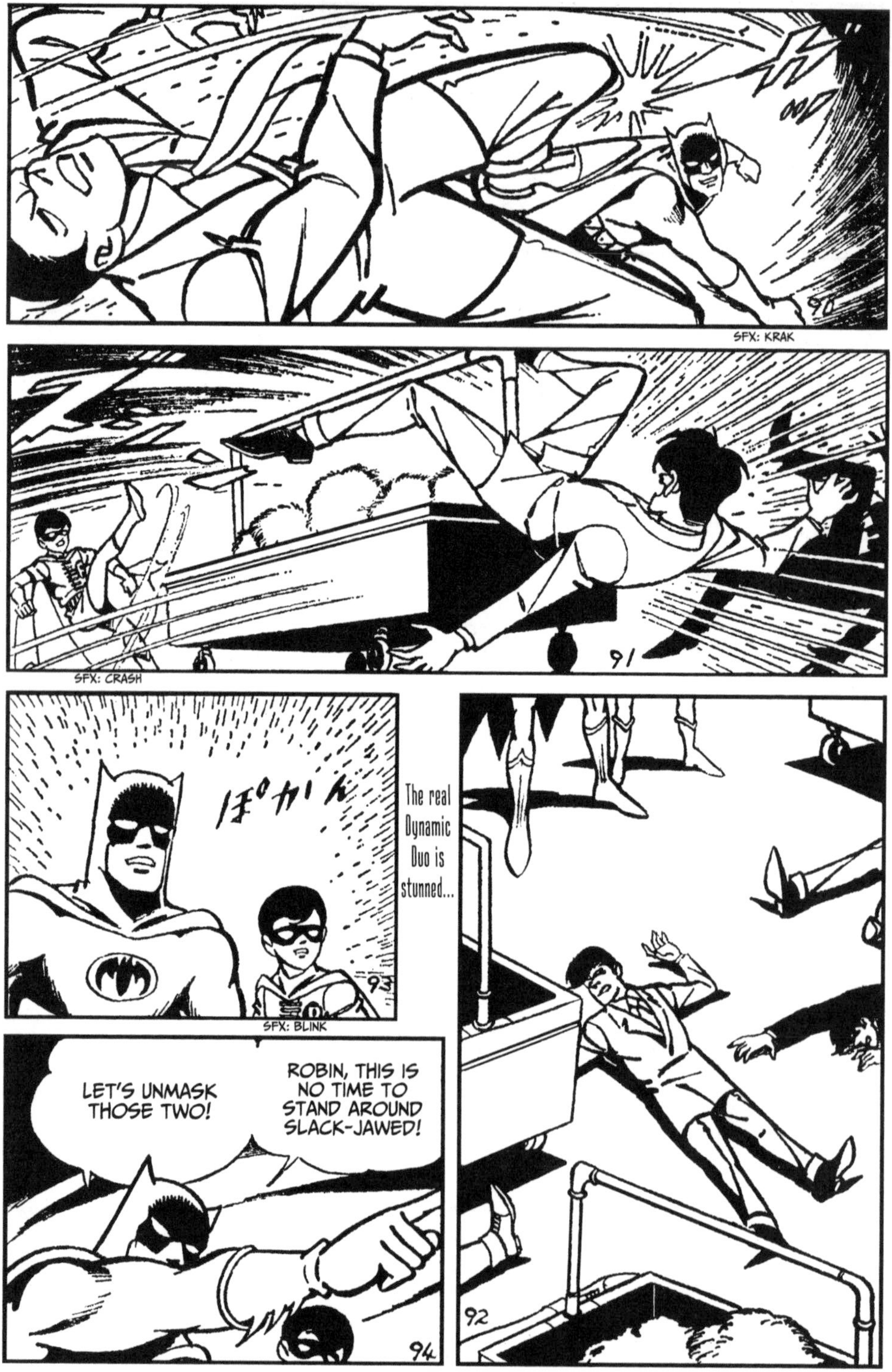
SFX: KRAK
SFX: CRASH
The real Dynamic Duo is stunned...
ぽかん
SFX: BLINK
ROBIN, THIS IS NO TIME TO STAND AROUND SLACK-JAWED!
LET'S UNMASK THOSE TWO!

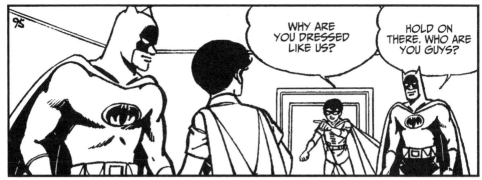

HOLD ON THERE. WHO ARE YOU GUYS?
WHY ARE YOU DRESSED LIKE US?
SFX: FWOO FWOO
AH...
T-THEY DISAPPEARED?!
UNBELIEVABLE... WAS IT SOME KIND OF OPTICAL ILLUSION?
BUT THESE ROBBERS ARE STILL HERE, KNOCKED OUT AND IN THE FLESH.
?

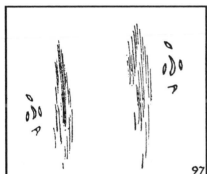

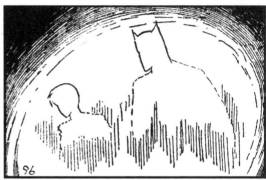

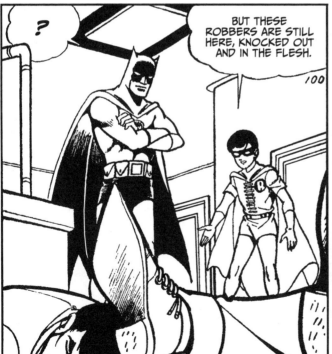

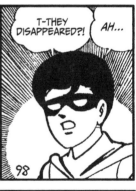

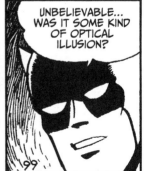

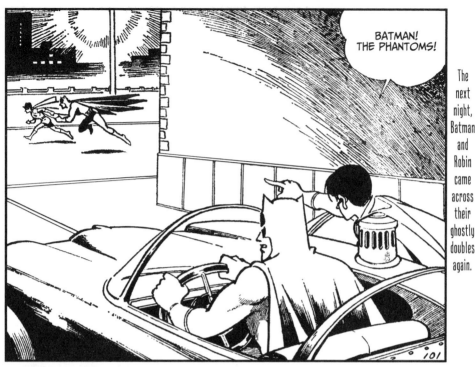

The next night, Batman and Robin came across their ghostly doubles again.
BATMAN! THE PHANTOMS!
ALL RIGHT! YOU GO AFTER ROBIN, I'LL CATCH BATMAN!
WE'LL NAB 'EM TONIGHT FOR SURE!
MM! HE DUCKED INTO THAT BUILDING!
SFX: CREAK

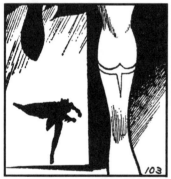

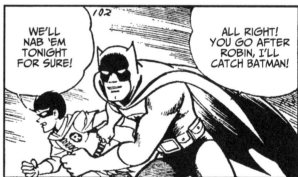

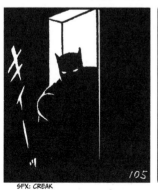

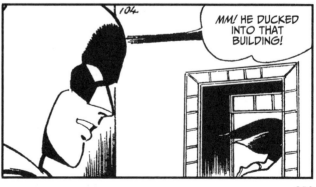

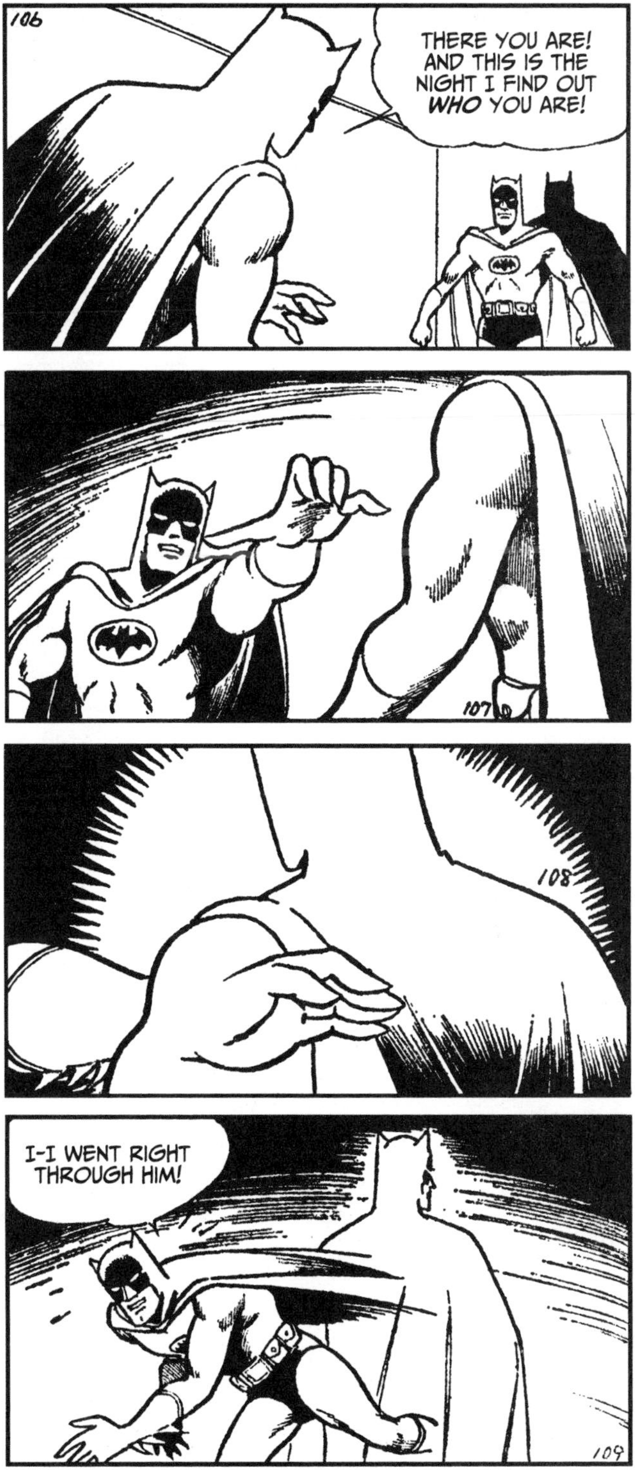
THERE YOU ARE! AND THIS IS THE NIGHT I FIND OUT **WHO** YOU ARE!
I-I WENT RIGHT THROUGH HIM!

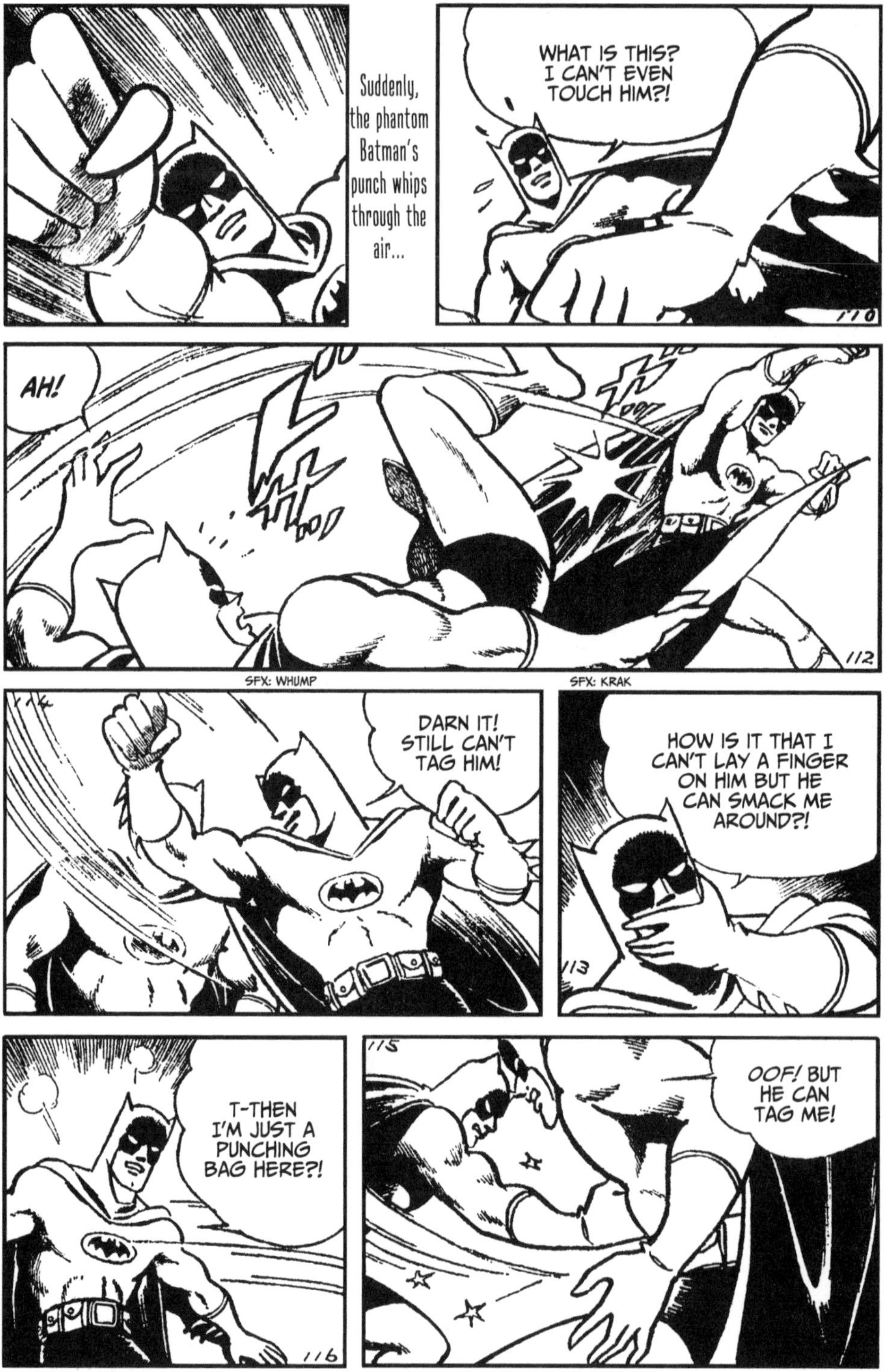
WHAT IS THIS? I CAN'T EVEN TOUCH HIM?!
Suddenly, the phantom Batman's punch whips through the air...
AH!
SFX: KRAK
SFX: WHUMP
HOW IS IT THAT I CAN'T LAY A FINGER ON HIM BUT HE CAN SMACK ME AROUND?!
DARN IT! STILL CAN'T TAG HIM!
OOF! BUT HE CAN TAG ME!
T-THEN I'M JUST A PUNCHING BAG HERE?!

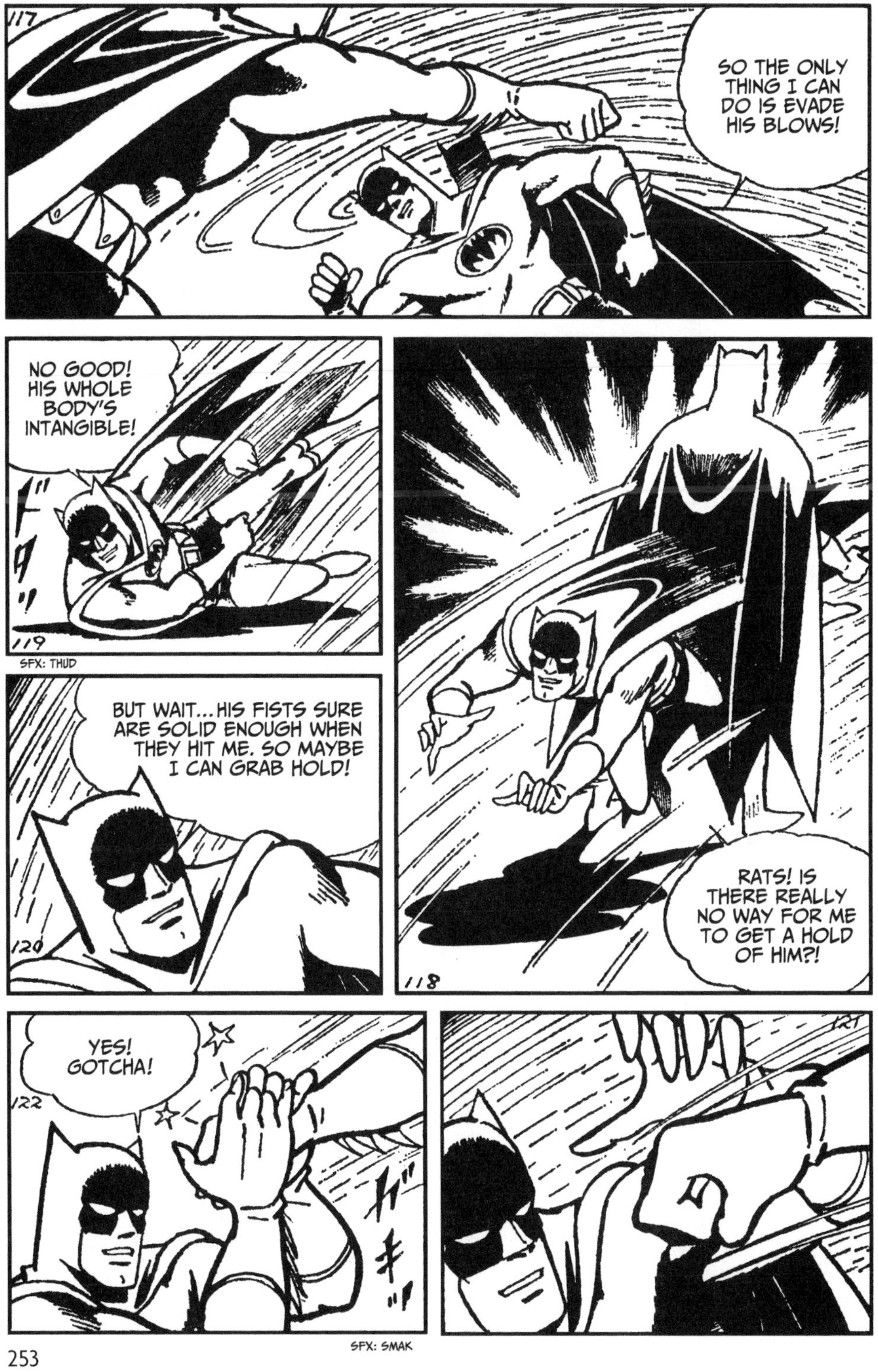
SO THE ONLY THING I CAN DO IS EVADE HIS BLOWS!
RATS! IS THERE REALLY NO WAY FOR ME TO GET A HOLD OF HIM?!
NO GOOD! HIS WHOLE BODY'S INTANGIBLE!
BUT WAIT...HIS FISTS SURE ARE SOLID ENOUGH WHEN THEY HIT ME. SO MAYBE I CAN GRAB HOLD!
YES! GOTCHA!

SFX: THUD

SFX: SMAK

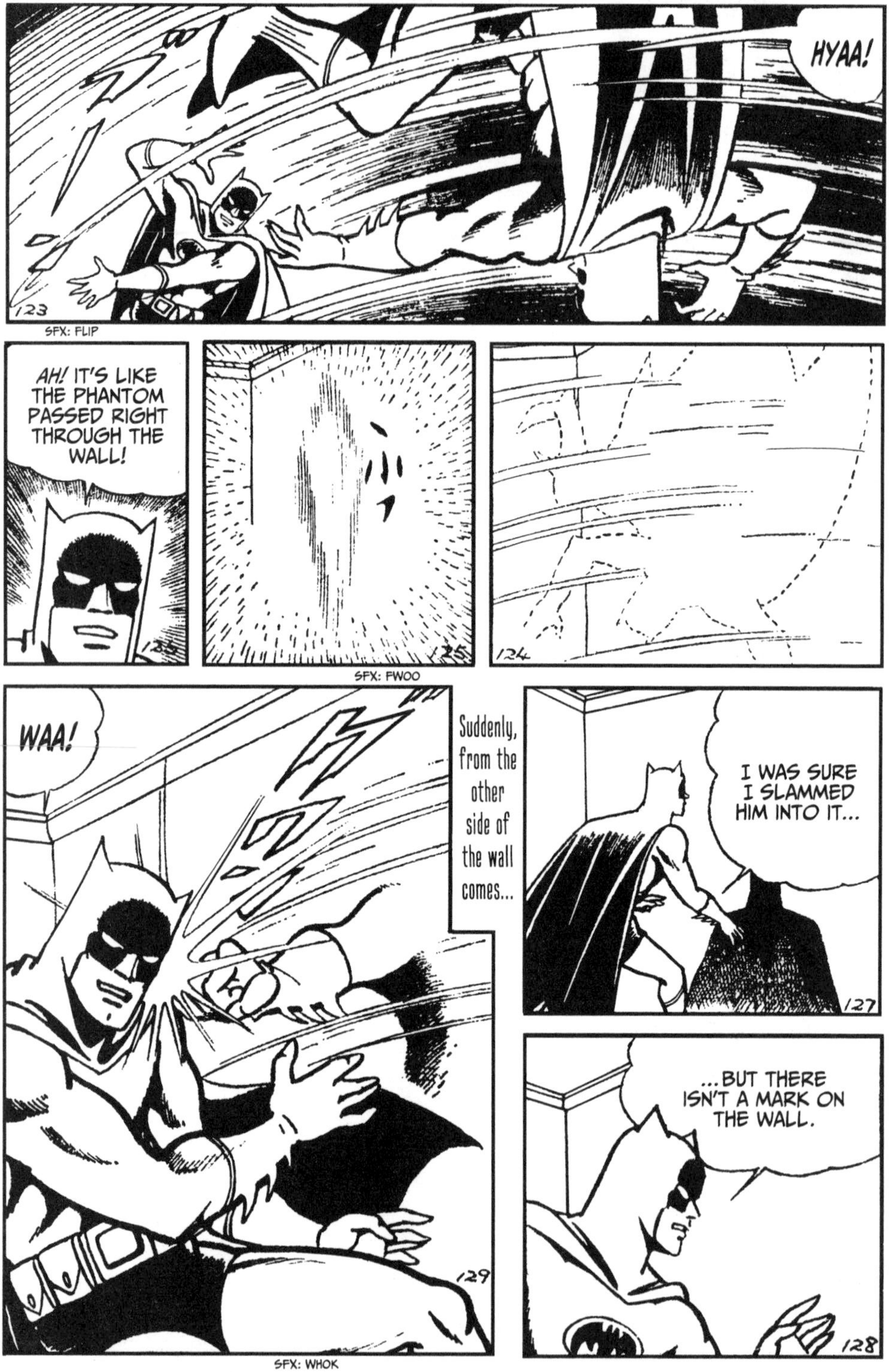
HYAA!
SFX: FLIP
SFX: FWOO
AH! IT'S LIKE THE PHANTOM PASSED RIGHT THROUGH THE WALL!
I WAS SURE I SLAMMED HIM INTO IT...
...BUT THERE ISN'T A MARK ON THE WALL.
Suddenly, from the other side of the wall comes...
WAA!
SFX: WHOK

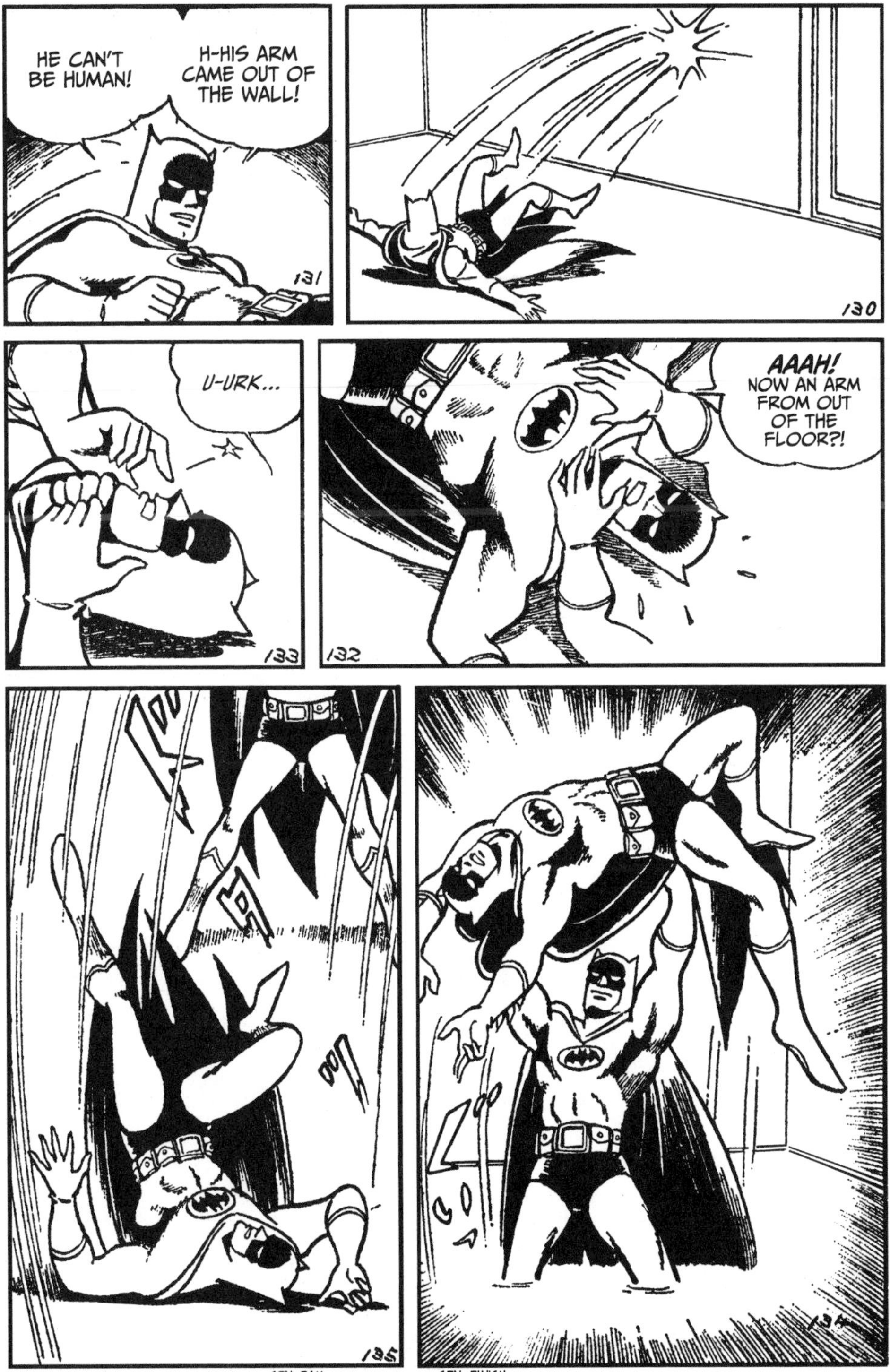
H-HIS ARM CAME OUT OF THE WALL!
HE CAN'T BE HUMAN!
AAAH! NOW AN ARM FROM OUT OF THE FLOOR?!
U-URK...

SFX: FWISH

SFX: BAM

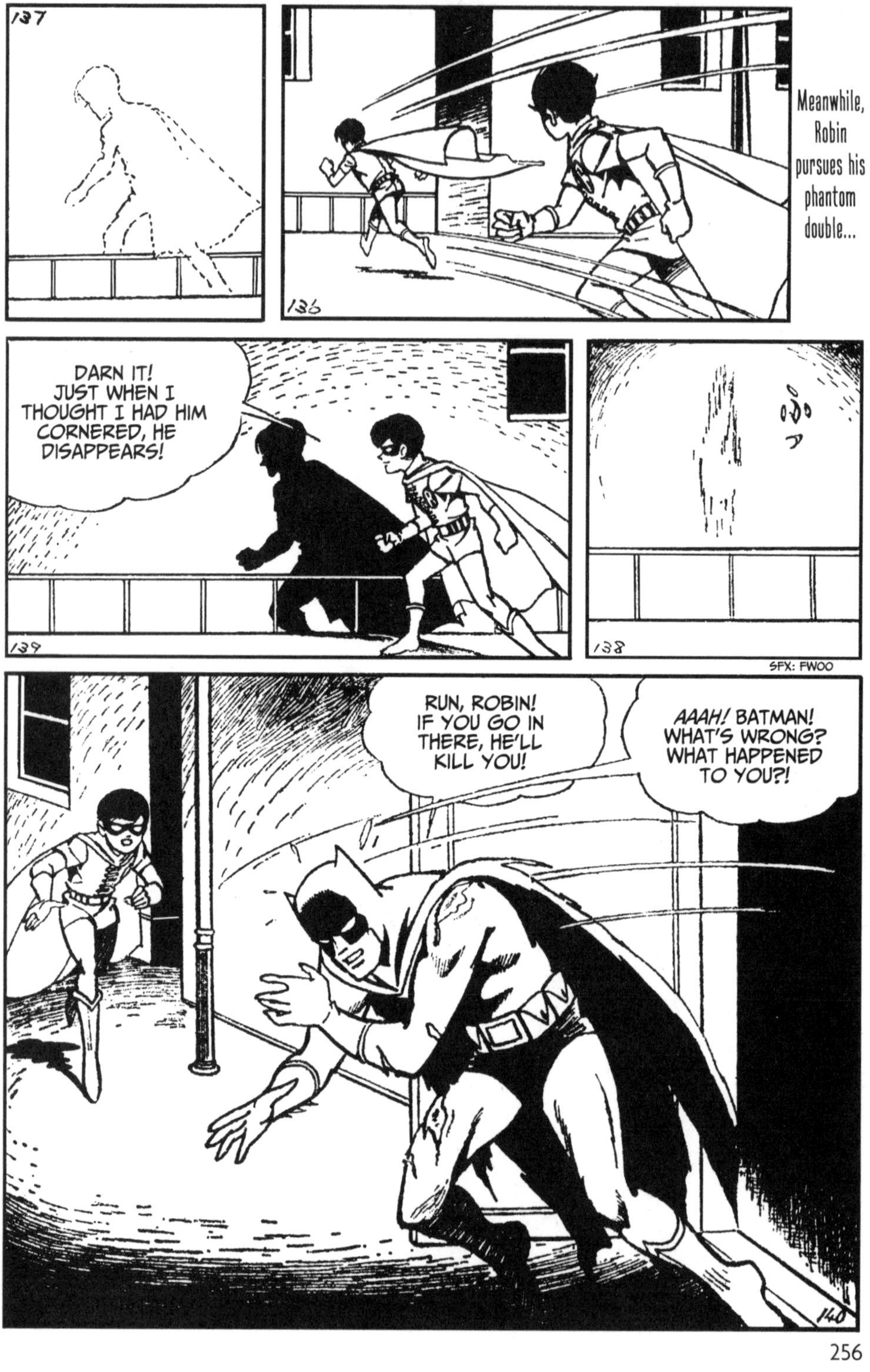
Meanwhile, Robin pursues his phantom double...
136
137
138
SFX: FWOO
DARN IT! JUST WHEN I THOUGHT I HAD HIM CORNERED, HE DISAPPEARS!
139
AAAH! BATMAN! WHAT'S WRONG? WHAT HAPPENED TO YOU?!
RUN, ROBIN! IF YOU GO IN THERE, HE'LL KILL YOU!
140

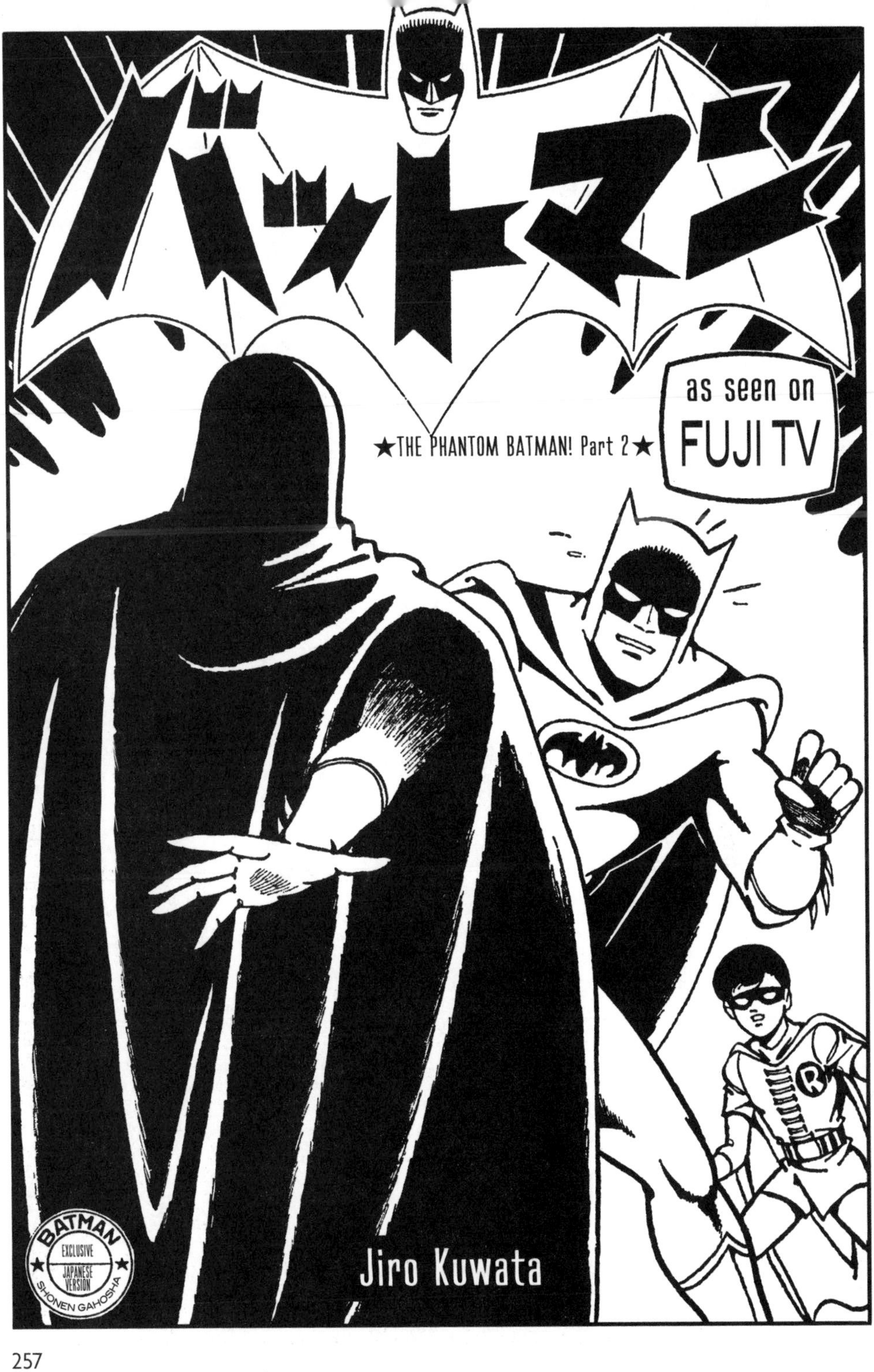
バットマン
as seen on
FUJI TV
★THE PHANTOM BATMAN! Part 2★
BATMAN
EXCLUSIVE
JAPANESE VERSION
SHONEN GAHOSHA
Jiro Kuwata

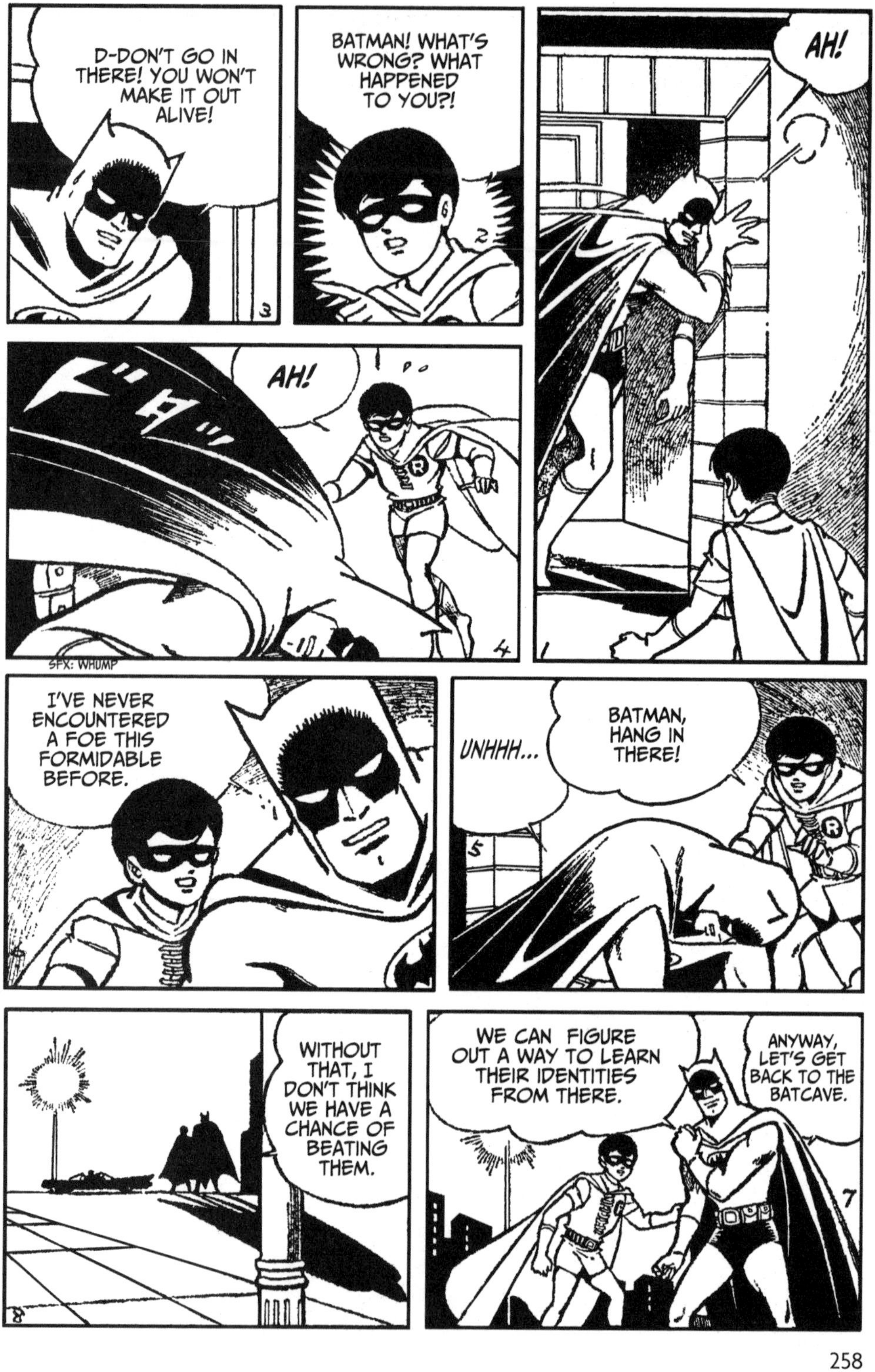
AH!
BATMAN! WHAT'S WRONG? WHAT HAPPENED TO YOU?!
D-DON'T GO IN THERE! YOU WON'T MAKE IT OUT ALIVE!
AH!
SFX: WHUMP
BATMAN, HANG IN THERE!
UNHHH...
I'VE NEVER ENCOUNTERED A FOE THIS FORMIDABLE BEFORE.
ANYWAY, LET'S GET BACK TO THE BATCAVE.
WE CAN FIGURE OUT A WAY TO LEARN THEIR IDENTITIES FROM THERE.
WITHOUT THAT, I DON'T THINK WE HAVE A CHANCE OF BEATING THEM.

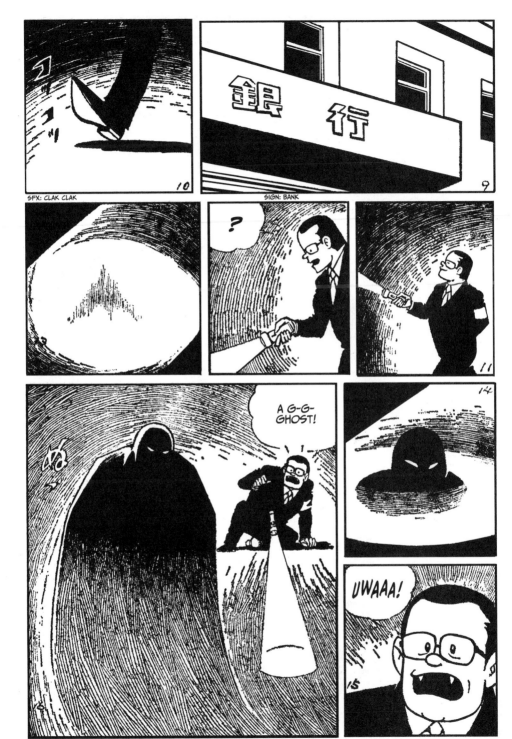

SFX: CLAK CLAK

SIGN: BANK

A G-G-GHOST!

UWAAA!

SFX: FOO

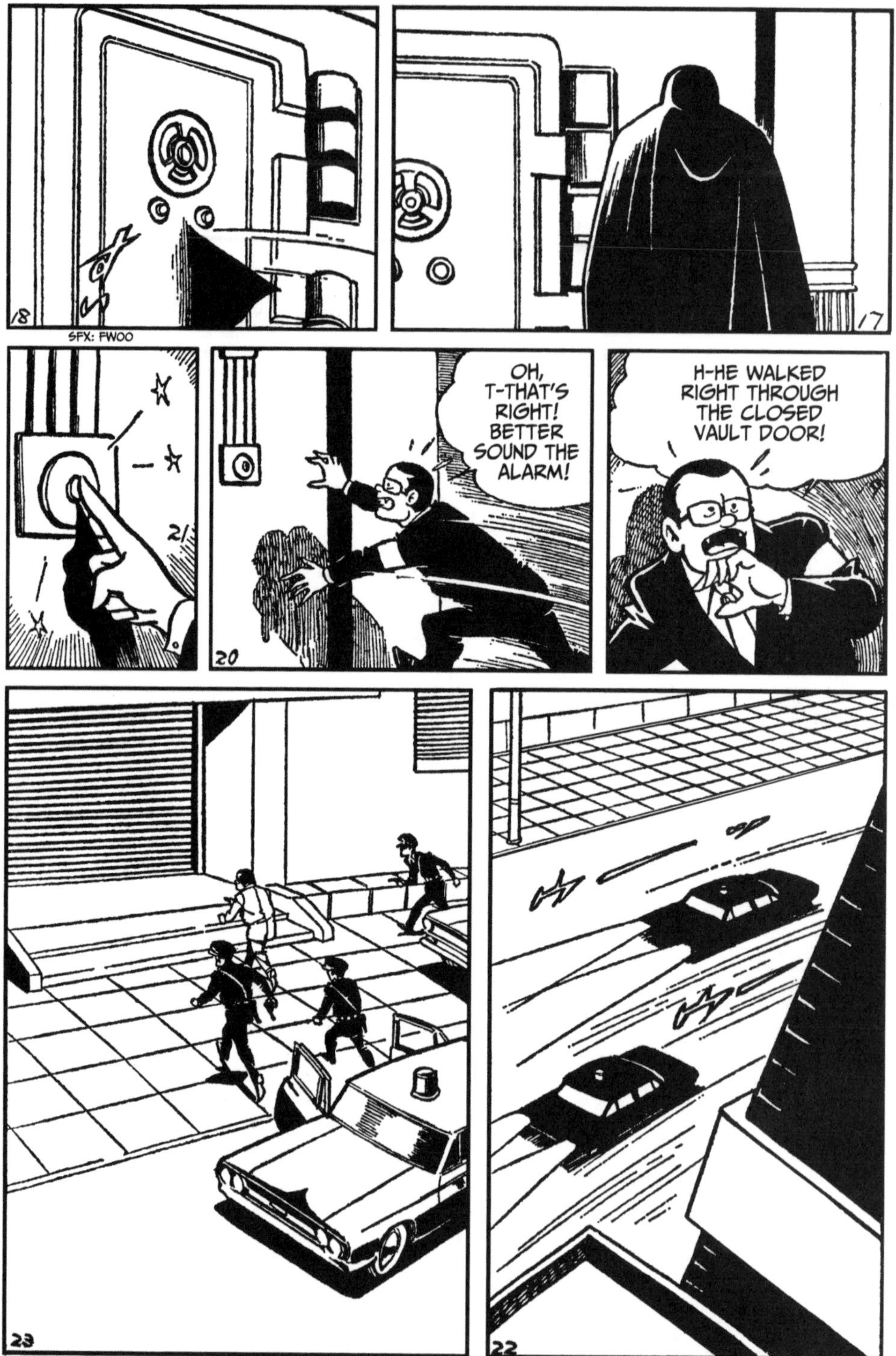
SFX: FWOO
H-HE WALKED RIGHT THROUGH THE CLOSED VAULT DOOR!
OH, T-THAT'S RIGHT! BETTER SOUND THE ALARM!
SFX: WHEEEOOO WHEEOOO

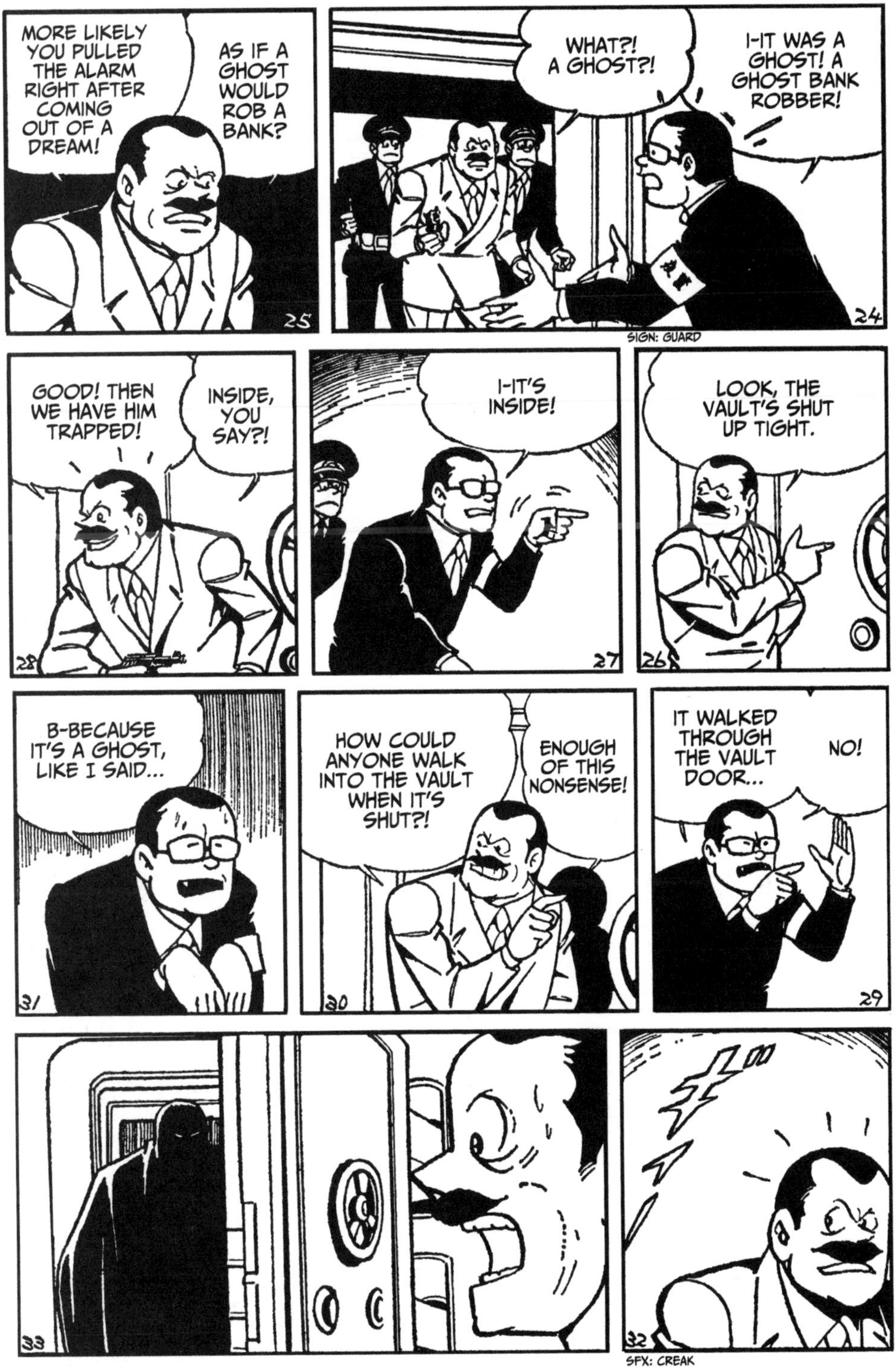
I-IT WAS A GHOST! A GHOST BANK ROBBER!
WHAT?! A GHOST?!
SIGN: GUARD
AS IF A GHOST WOULD ROB A BANK?
MORE LIKELY YOU PULLED THE ALARM RIGHT AFTER COMING OUT OF A DREAM!
LOOK, THE VAULT'S SHUT UP TIGHT.
I-IT'S INSIDE!
INSIDE, YOU SAY?!
GOOD! THEN WE HAVE HIM TRAPPED!
NO!
IT WALKED THROUGH THE VAULT DOOR...
ENOUGH OF THIS NONSENSE!
HOW COULD ANYONE WALK INTO THE VAULT WHEN IT'S SHUT?!
B-BECAUSE IT'S A GHOST, LIKE I SAID...
SFX: CREAK

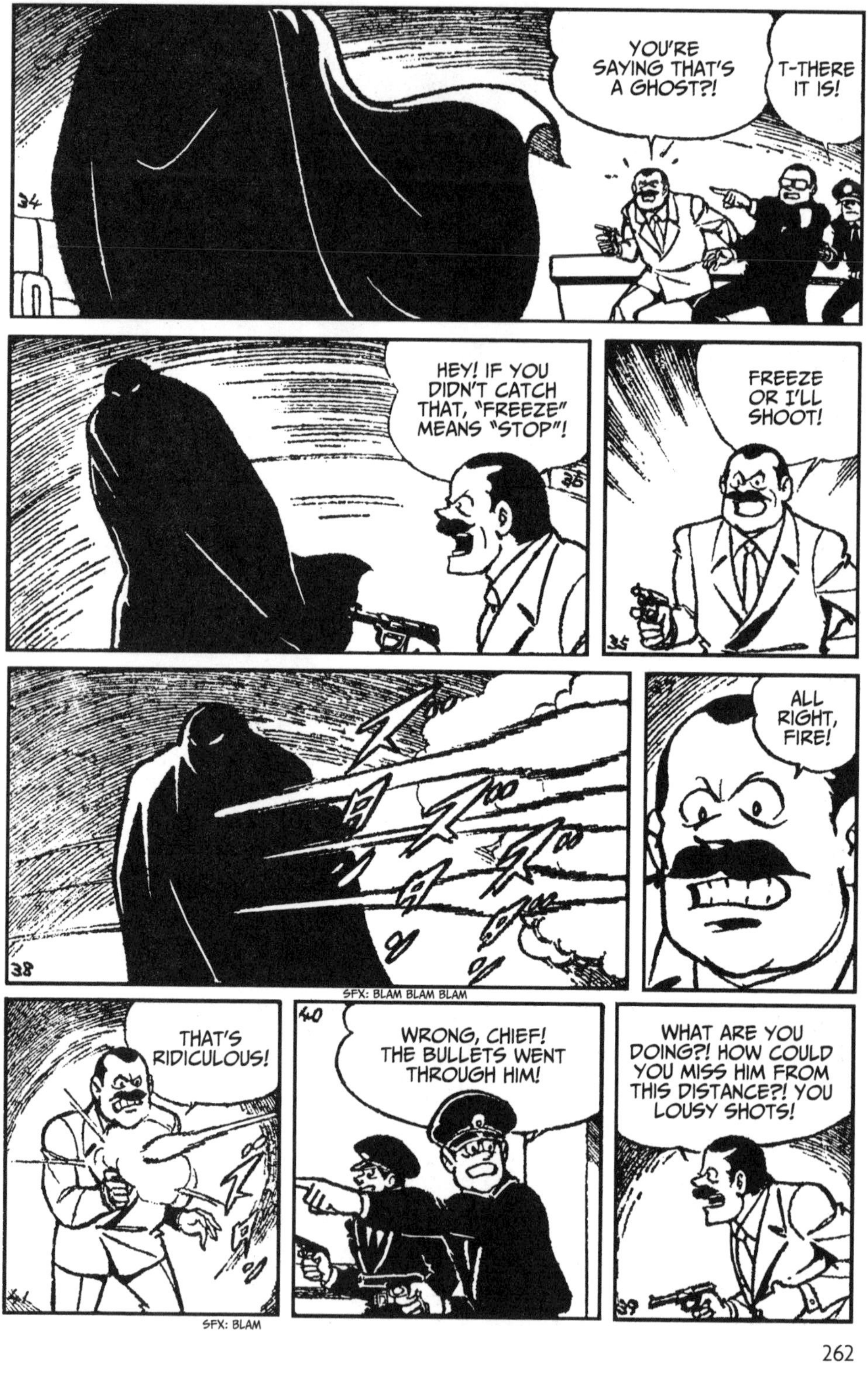
T-THERE IT IS!
YOU'RE SAYING THAT'S A GHOST?!
FREEZE OR I'LL SHOOT!
HEY! IF YOU DIDN'T CATCH THAT, "FREEZE" MEANS "STOP"!
ALL RIGHT, FIRE!
SFX: BLAM BLAM BLAM
WHAT ARE YOU DOING?! HOW COULD YOU MISS HIM FROM THIS DISTANCE?! YOU LOUSY SHOTS!
WRONG, CHIEF! THE BULLETS WENT THROUGH HIM!
THAT'S RIDICULOUS!
SFX: BLAM

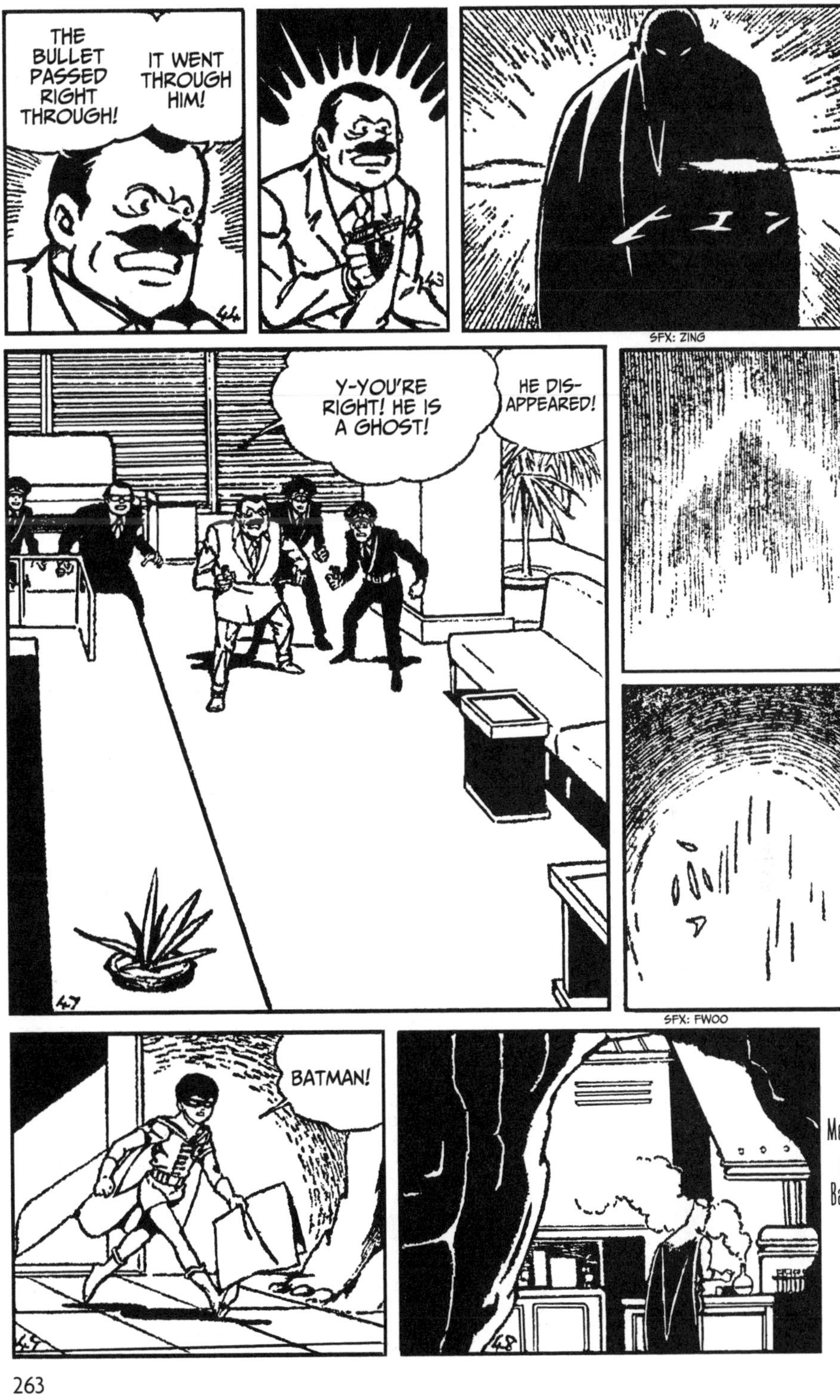
SFX: ZING
IT WENT THROUGH HIM!
THE BULLET PASSED RIGHT THROUGH!
SFX: FWOO
HE DIS-APPEARED!
Y-YOU'RE RIGHT! HE IS A GHOST!
BATMAN!

Meanwhile, at the Batcave...

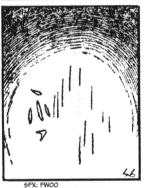

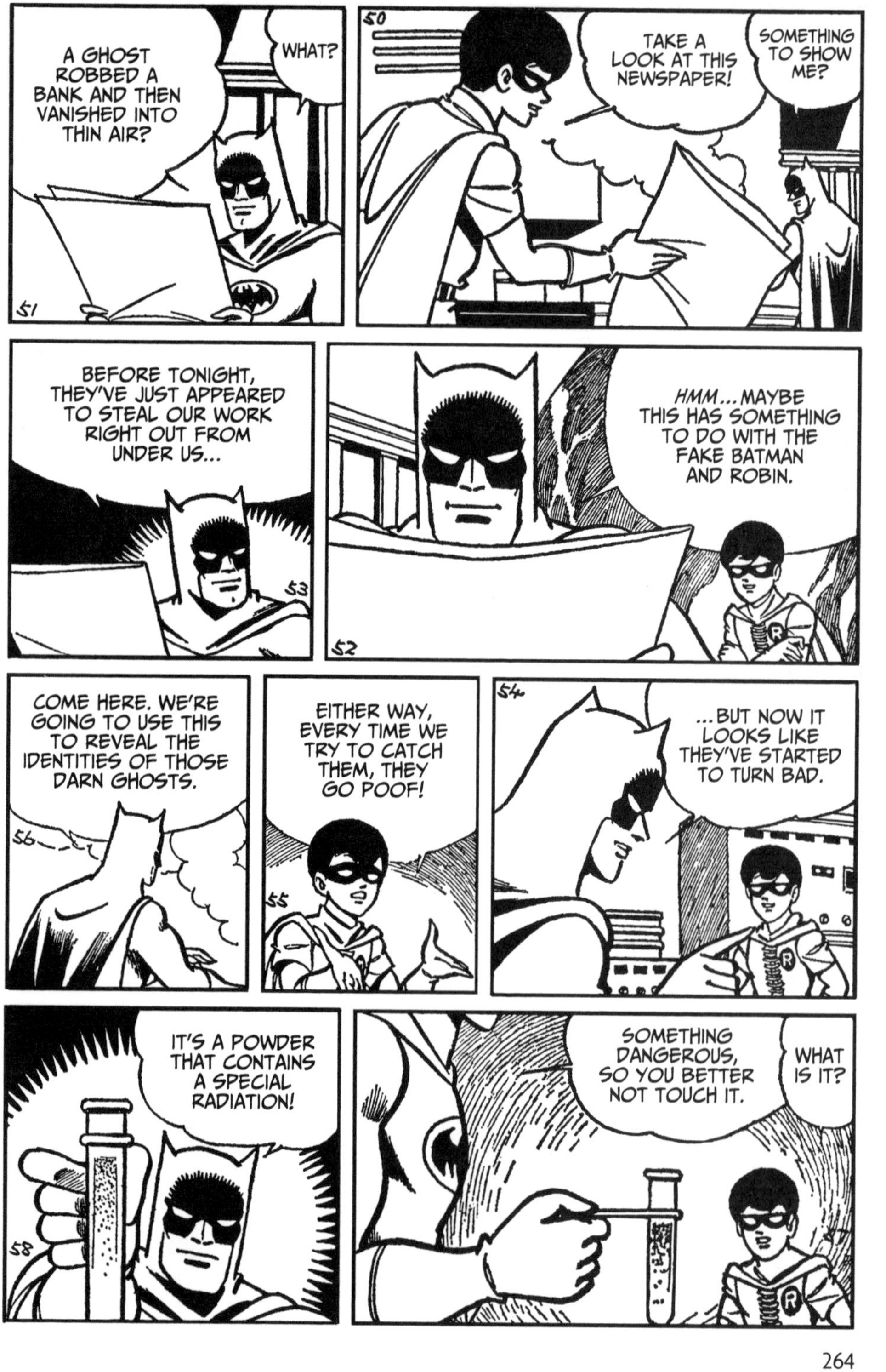
SOMETHING TO SHOW ME?
TAKE A LOOK AT THIS NEWSPAPER!
WHAT?
A GHOST ROBBED A BANK AND THEN VANISHED INTO THIN AIR?
HMM... MAYBE THIS HAS SOMETHING TO DO WITH THE FAKE BATMAN AND ROBIN.
BEFORE TONIGHT, THEY'VE JUST APPEARED TO STEAL OUR WORK RIGHT OUT FROM UNDER US...
...BUT NOW IT LOOKS LIKE THEY'VE STARTED TO TURN BAD.
EITHER WAY, EVERY TIME WE TRY TO CATCH THEM, THEY GO POOF!
COME HERE. WE'RE GOING TO USE THIS TO REVEAL THE IDENTITIES OF THOSE DARN GHOSTS.
WHAT IS IT?
SOMETHING DANGEROUS, SO YOU BETTER NOT TOUCH IT.
IT'S A POWDER THAT CONTAINS A SPECIAL RADIATION!

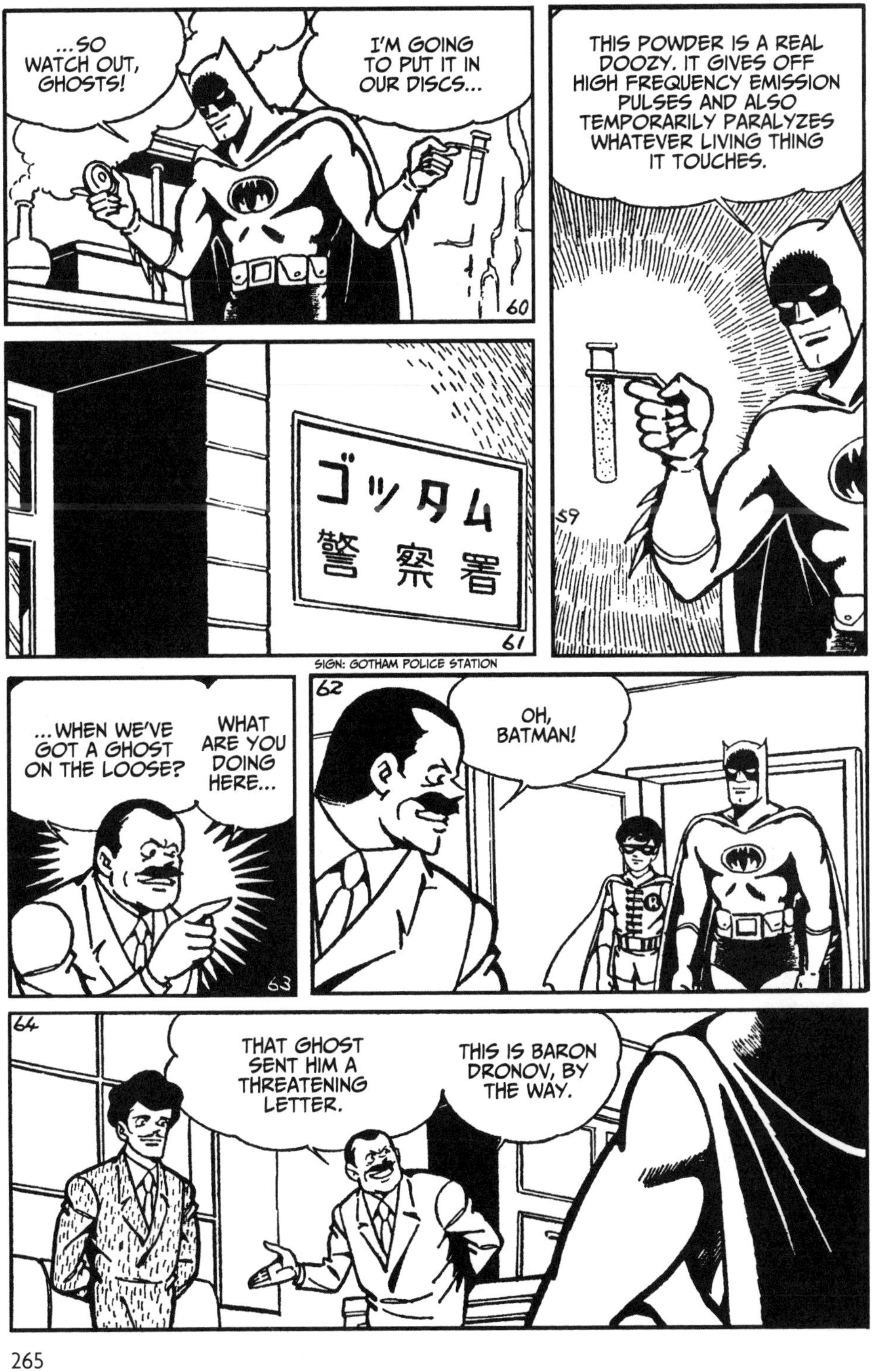
THIS POWDER IS A REAL DOOZY. IT GIVES OFF HIGH FREQUENCY EMISSION PULSES AND ALSO TEMPORARILY PARALYZES WHATEVER LIVING THING IT TOUCHES.
59
I'M GOING TO PUT IT IN OUR DISCS...
...SO WATCH OUT, GHOSTS!
60
ゴッタム
警察署
61
SIGN: GOTHAM POLICE STATION
62
OH, BATMAN!
WHAT ARE YOU DOING HERE...
...WHEN WE'VE GOT A GHOST ON THE LOOSE?
63
64
THIS IS BARON DRONOV, BY THE WAY.
THAT GHOST SENT HIM A THREATENING LETTER.

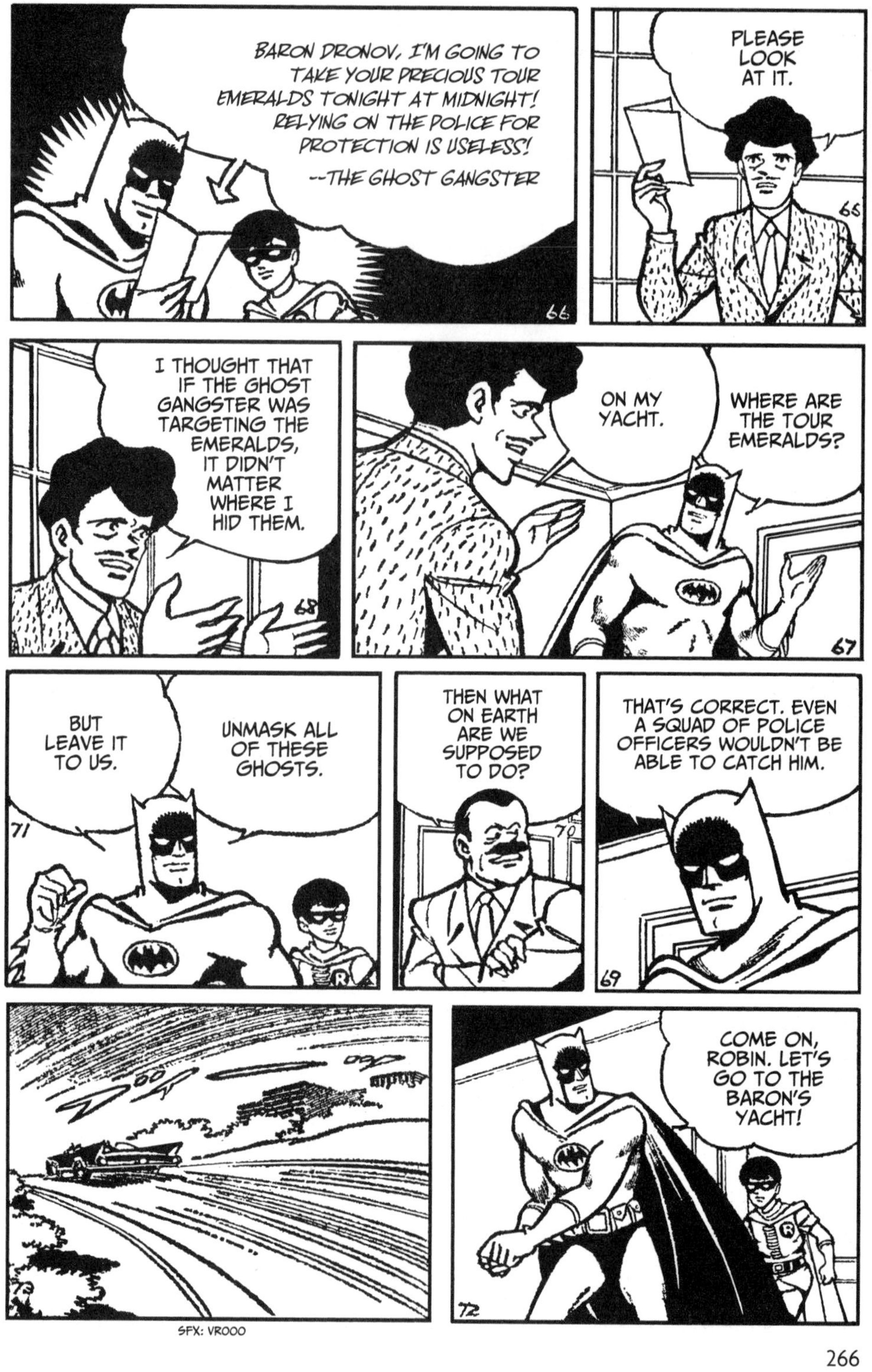
PLEASE LOOK AT IT.
BARON DRONOV, I'M GOING TO TAKE YOUR PRECIOUS TOUR EMERALDS TONIGHT AT MIDNIGHT! RELYING ON THE POLICE FOR PROTECTION IS USELESS!
--THE GHOST GANGSTER
WHERE ARE THE TOUR EMERALDS?
ON MY YACHT.
I THOUGHT THAT IF THE GHOST GANGSTER WAS TARGETING THE EMERALDS, IT DIDN'T MATTER WHERE I HID THEM.
THAT'S CORRECT. EVEN A SQUAD OF POLICE OFFICERS WOULDN'T BE ABLE TO CATCH HIM.
THEN WHAT ON EARTH ARE WE SUPPOSED TO DO?
UNMASK ALL OF THESE GHOSTS.
BUT LEAVE IT TO US.
COME ON, ROBIN. LET'S GO TO THE BARON'S YACHT!

SFX: VROOO

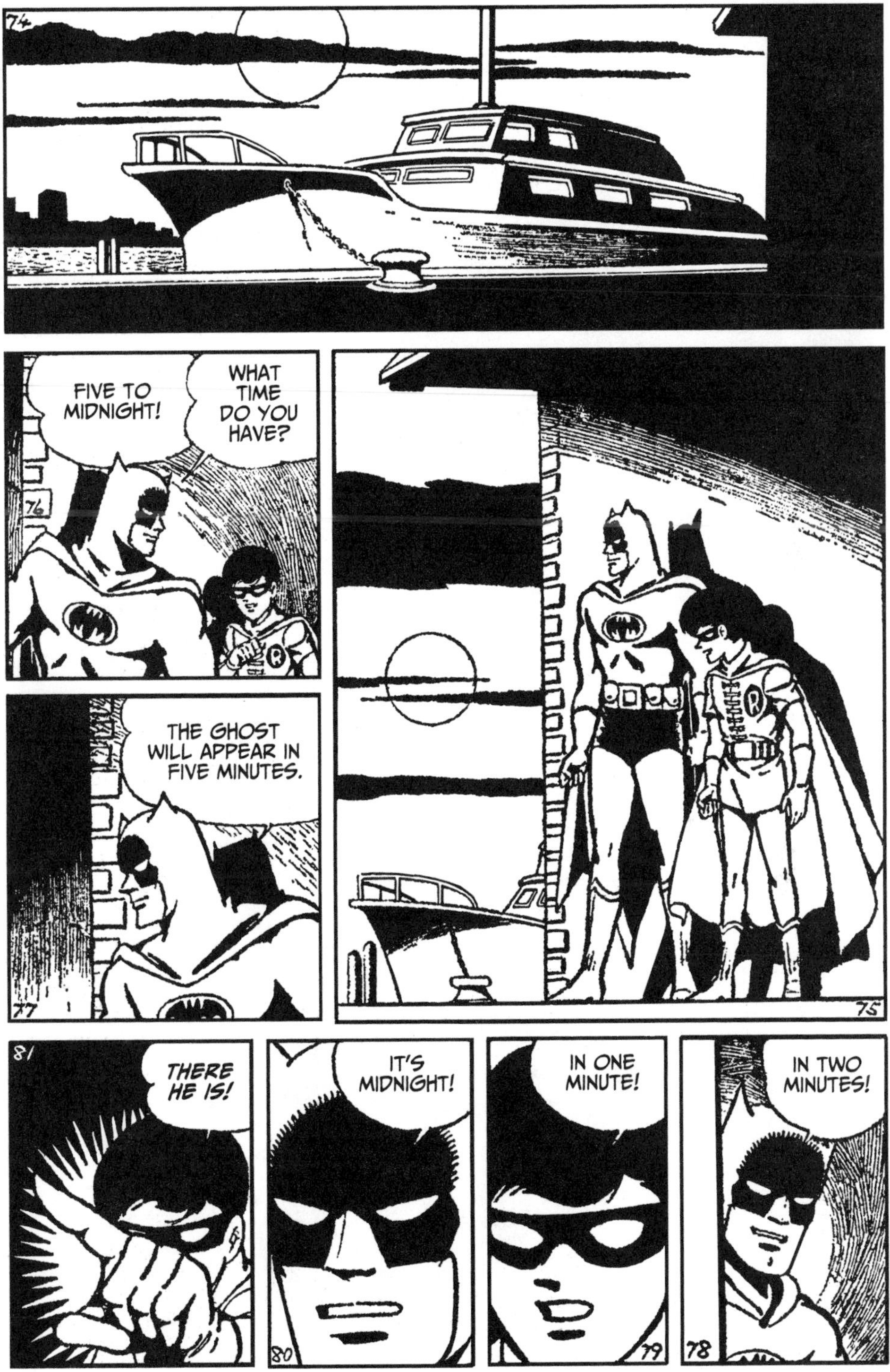
WHAT TIME DO YOU HAVE?
FIVE TO MIDNIGHT!
THE GHOST WILL APPEAR IN FIVE MINUTES.
IN TWO MINUTES!
IN ONE MINUTE!
IT'S MIDNIGHT!
THERE HE IS!

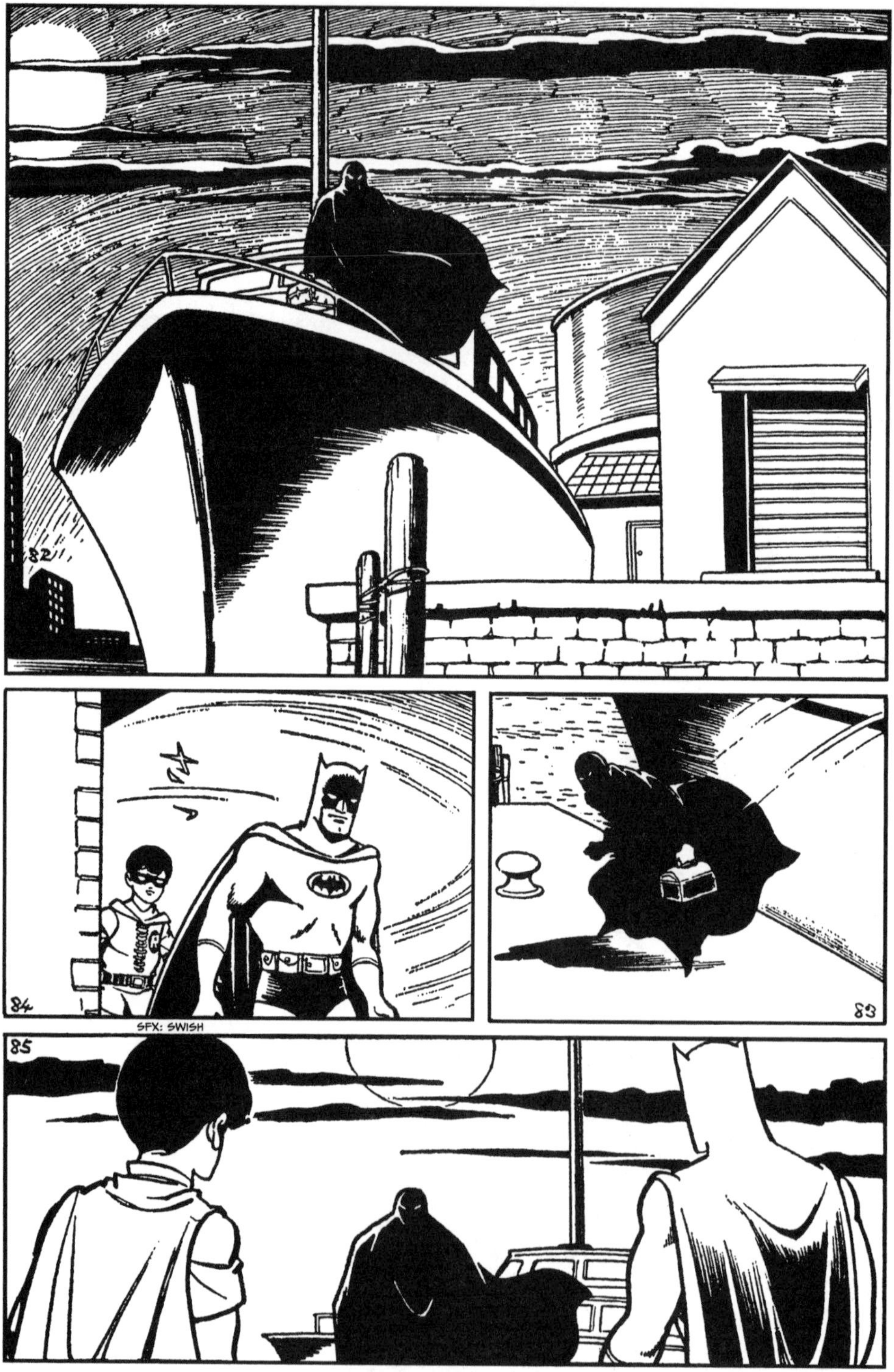
SFX: SWISH

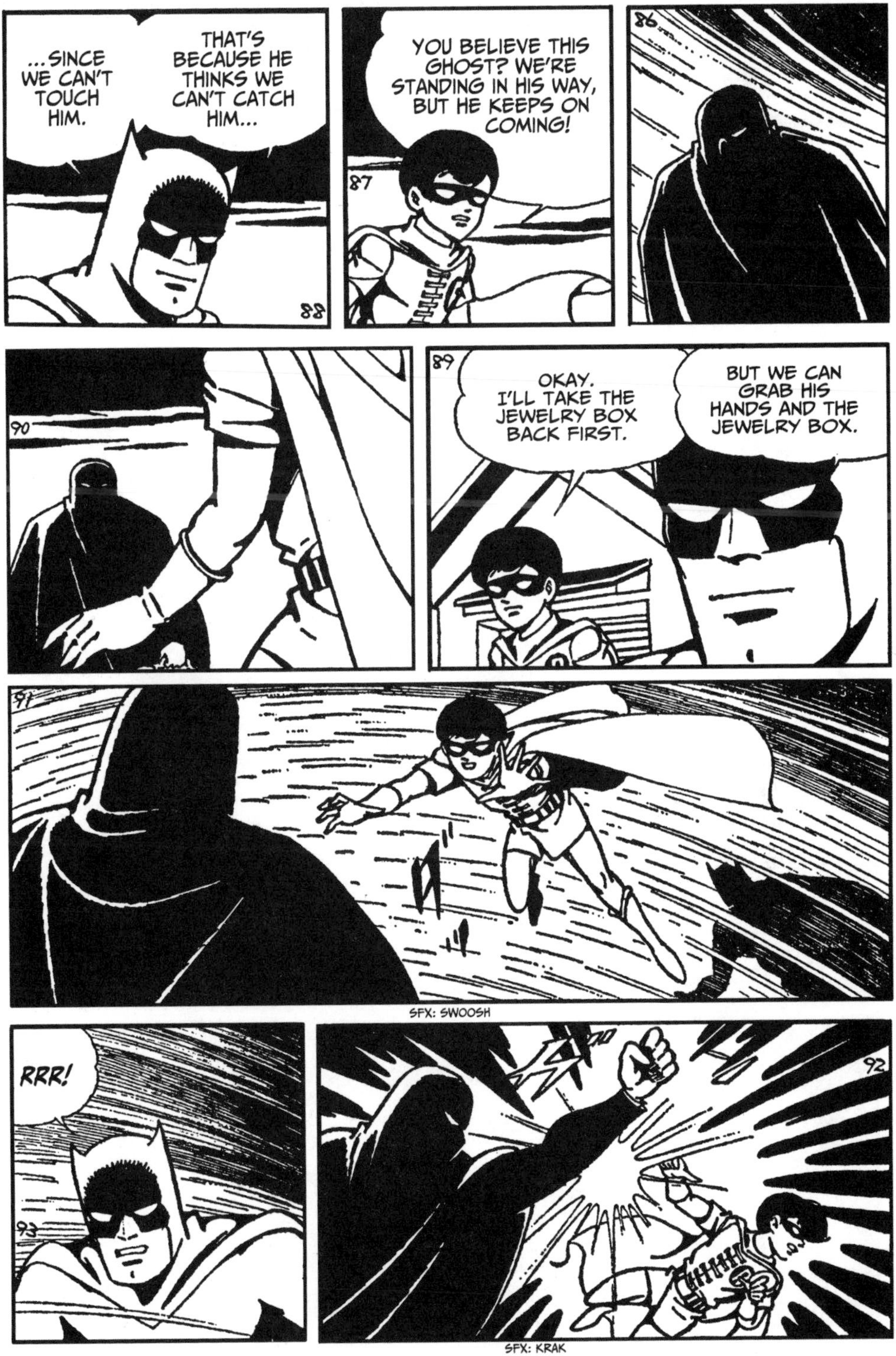
YOU BELIEVE THIS GHOST? WE'RE STANDING IN HIS WAY, BUT HE KEEPS ON COMING!
THAT'S BECAUSE HE THINKS WE CAN'T CATCH HIM...
...SINCE WE CAN'T TOUCH HIM.
BUT WE CAN GRAB HIS HANDS AND THE JEWELRY BOX.
OKAY. I'LL TAKE THE JEWELRY BOX BACK FIRST.
SFX: SWOOSH
SFX: KRAK
RRR!

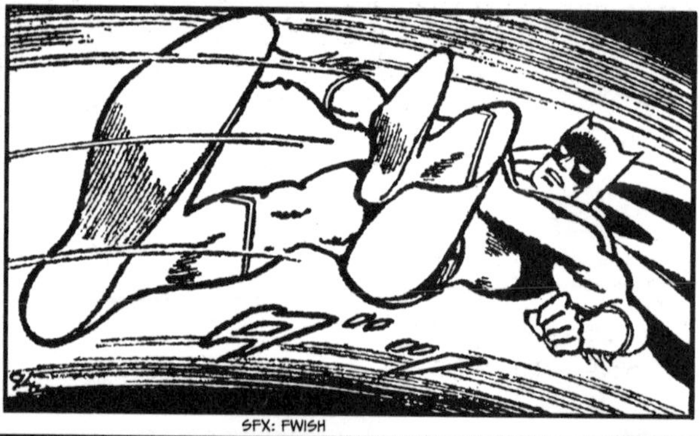

SFX: FWISH

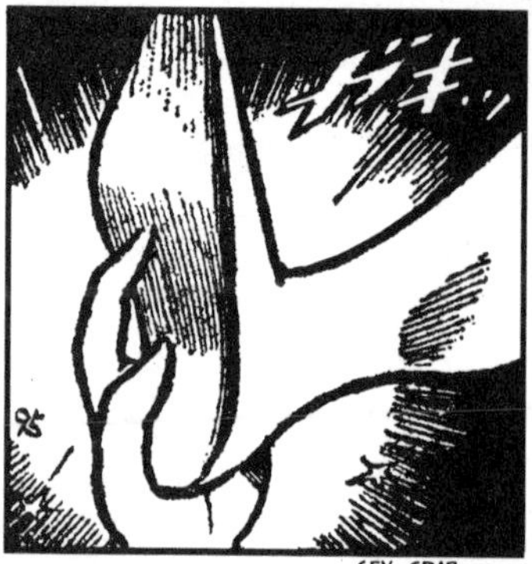

SFX: GRAB

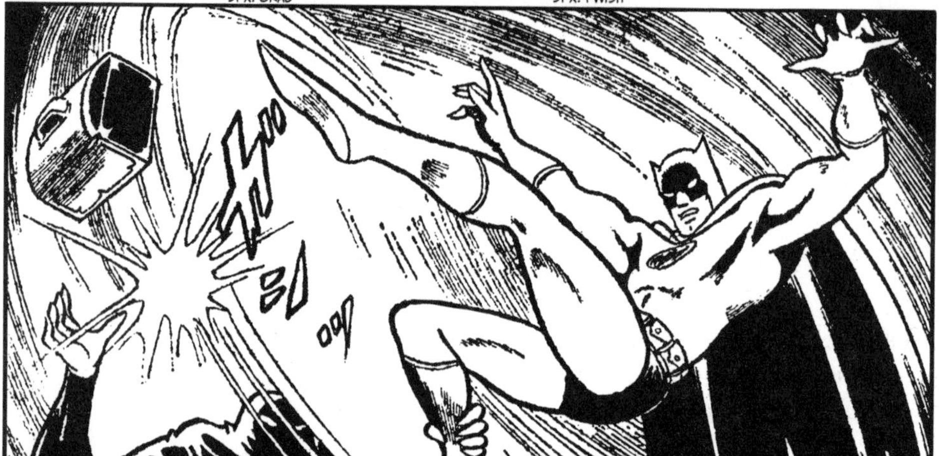

SFX: WHAK

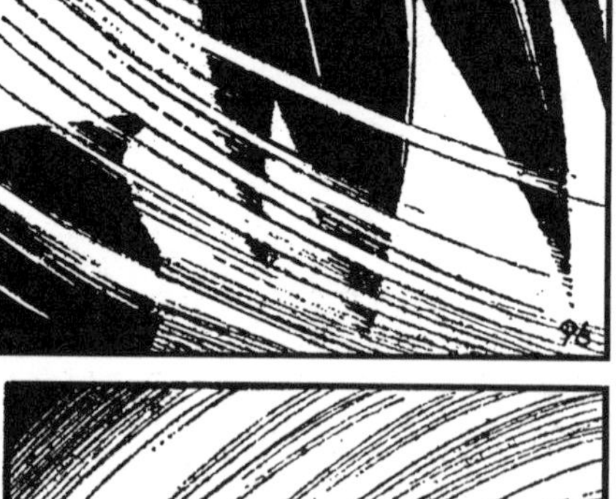

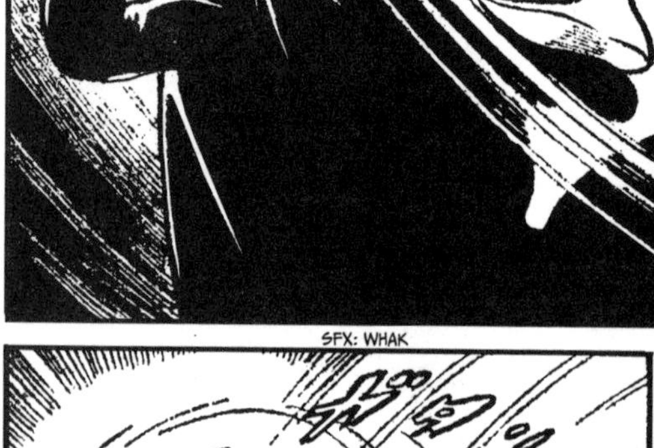

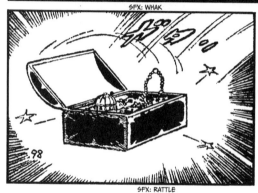

SFX: RATTLE

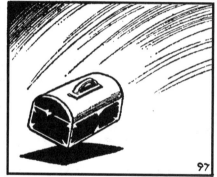

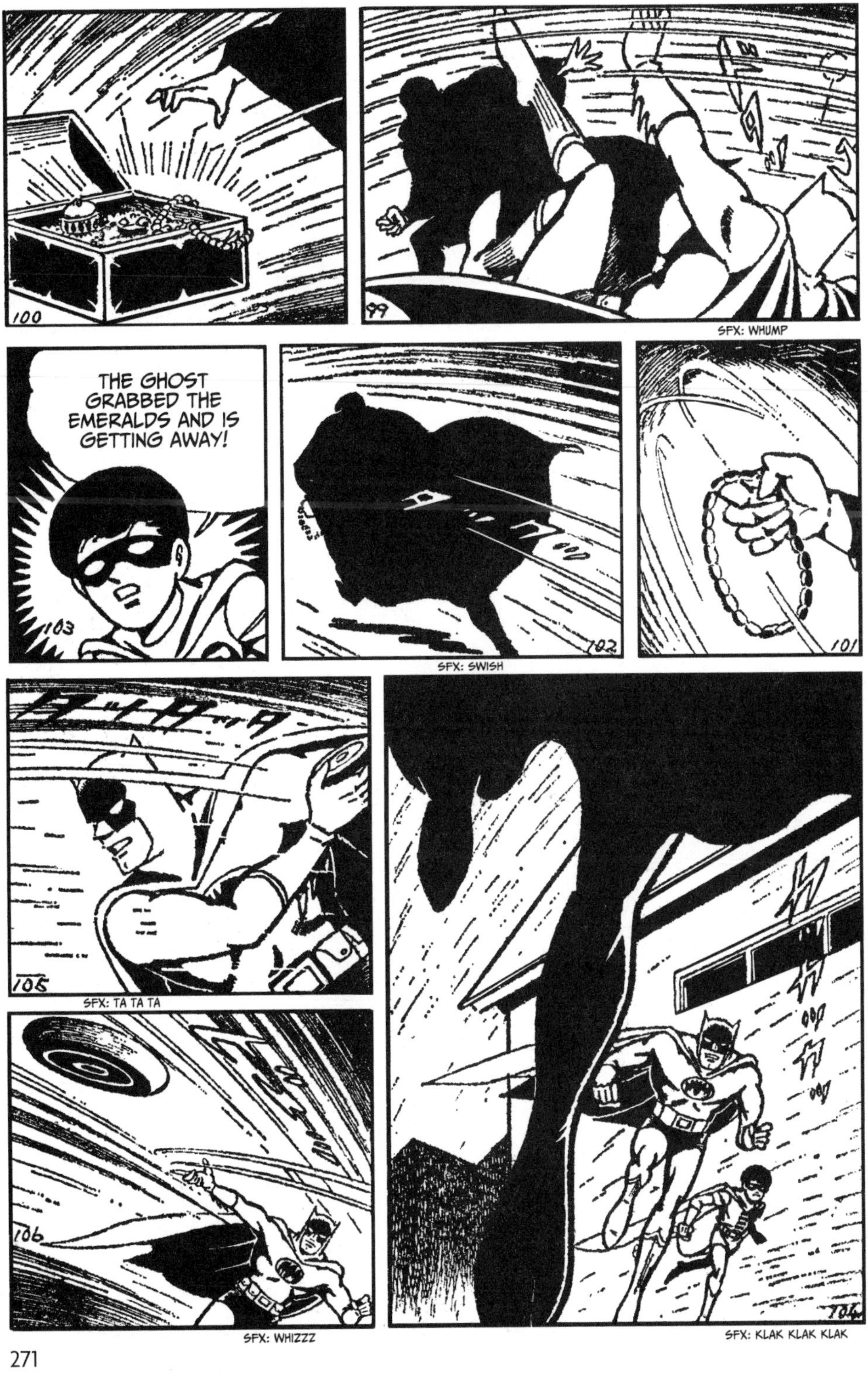
SFX: WHUMP
SFX: SWISH
THE GHOST GRABBED THE EMERALDS AND IS GETTING AWAY!
SFX: KLAK KLAK KLAK
SFX: TA TA TA
SFX: WHIZZZ

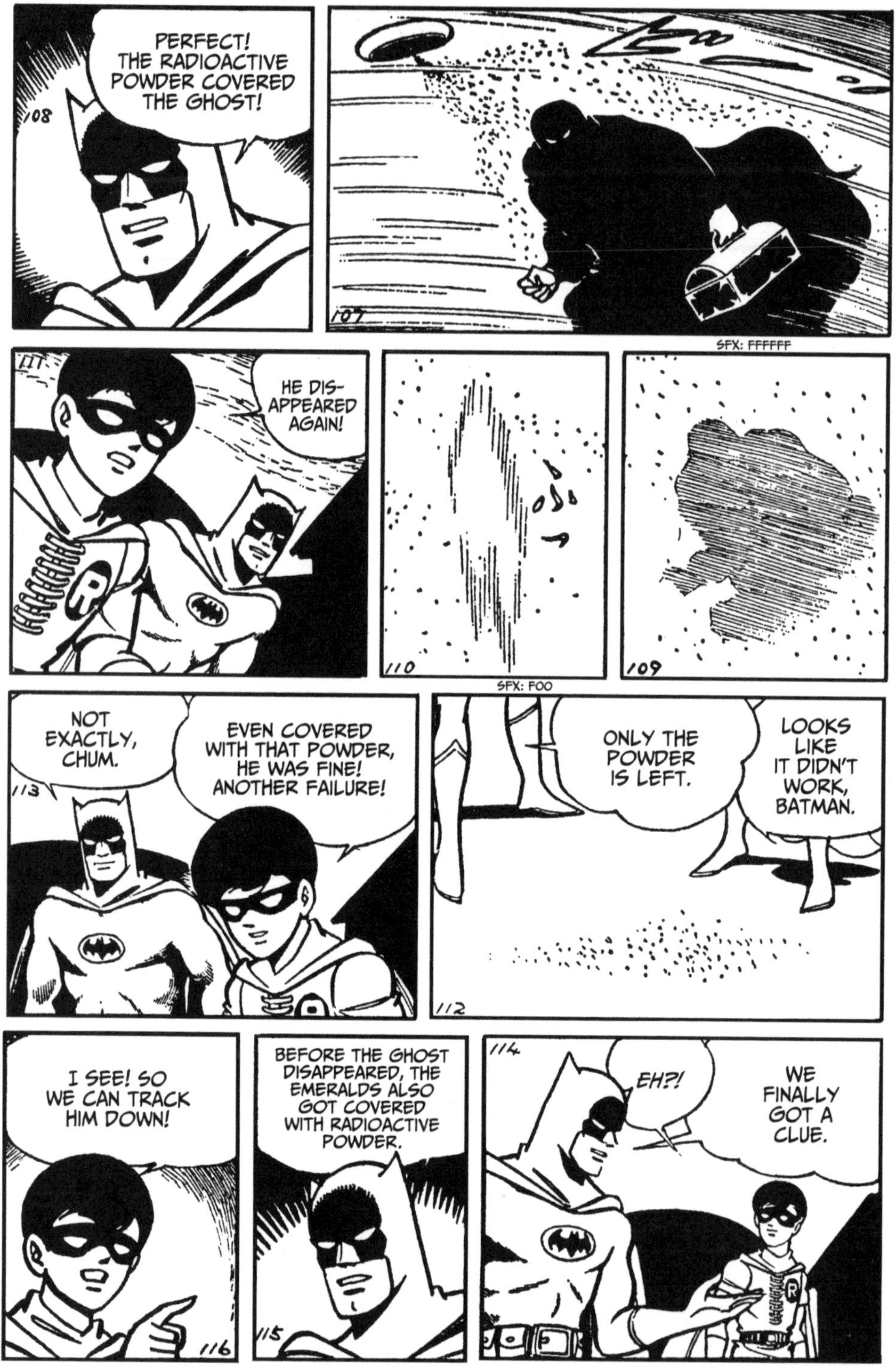
SFX: FFFFFF
PERFECT! THE RADIOACTIVE POWDER COVERED THE GHOST!
SFX: FOO
HE DIS-APPEARED AGAIN!
LOOKS LIKE IT DIDN'T WORK, BATMAN.
ONLY THE POWDER IS LEFT.
EVEN COVERED WITH THAT POWDER, HE WAS FINE! ANOTHER FAILURE!
NOT EXACTLY, CHUM.
WE FINALLY GOT A CLUE.
EH?!
BEFORE THE GHOST DISAPPEARED, THE EMERALDS ALSO GOT COVERED WITH RADIOACTIVE POWDER.
I SEE! SO WE CAN TRACK HIM DOWN!

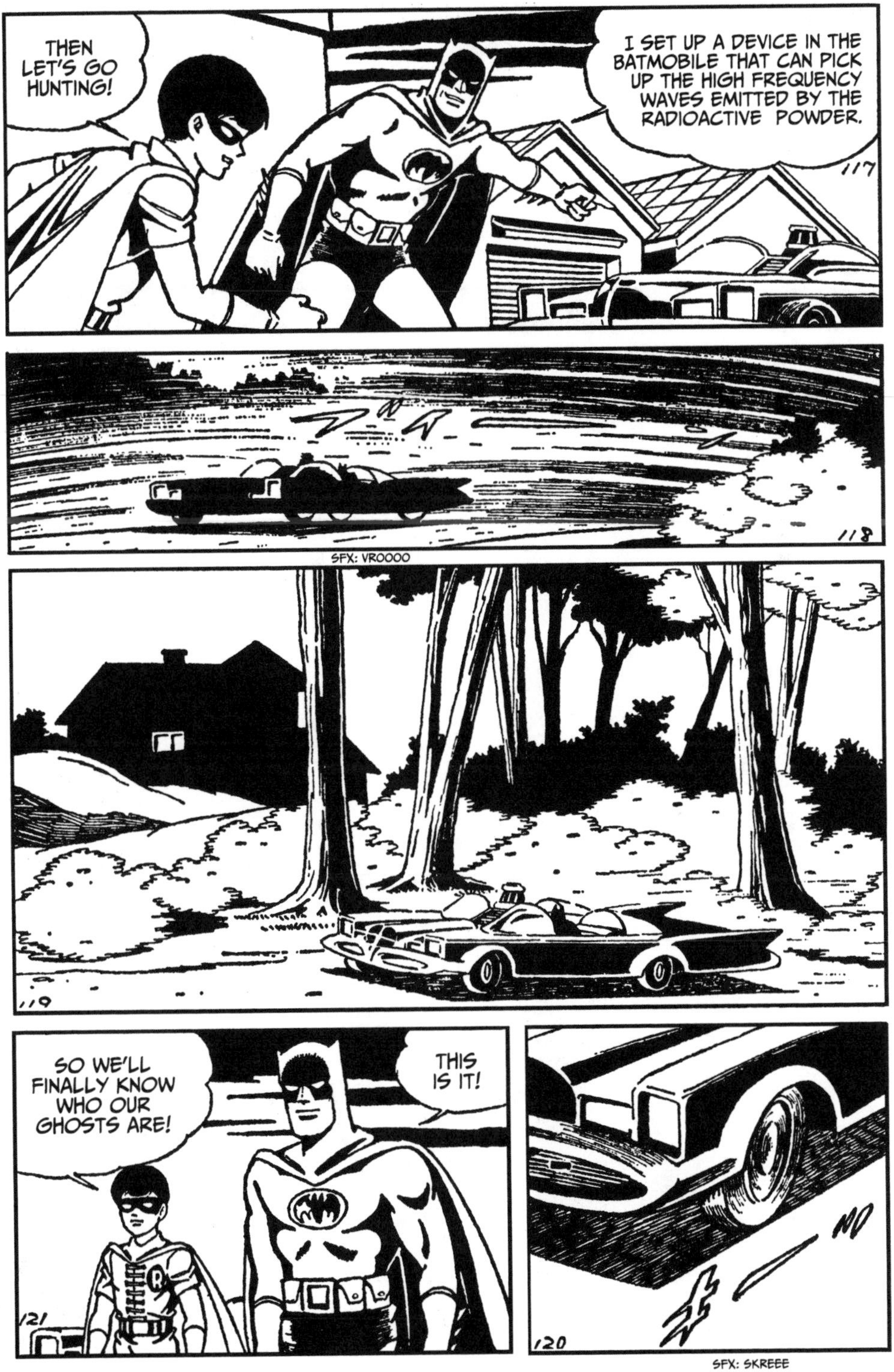
I SET UP A DEVICE IN THE BATMOBILE THAT CAN PICK UP THE HIGH FREQUENCY WAVES EMITTED BY THE RADIOACTIVE POWDER.
THEN LET'S GO HUNTING!
SFX: VROOOO
SFX: SKREEE
THIS IS IT!
SO WE'LL FINALLY KNOW WHO OUR GHOSTS ARE!

AH!

123

122

SFX: CREAK

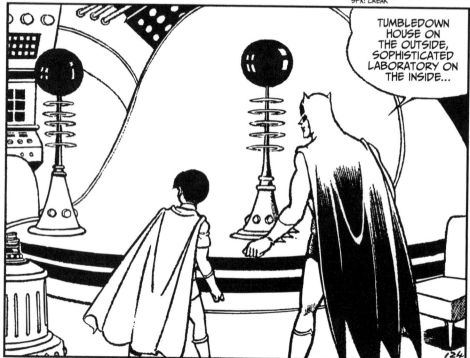

TUMBLEDOWN HOUSE ON THE OUTSIDE, SOPHISTICATED LABORATORY ON THE INSIDE...

124

126

EH?!

BATMAN AND ROBIN, HOW NICE OF YOU TO COME.

125

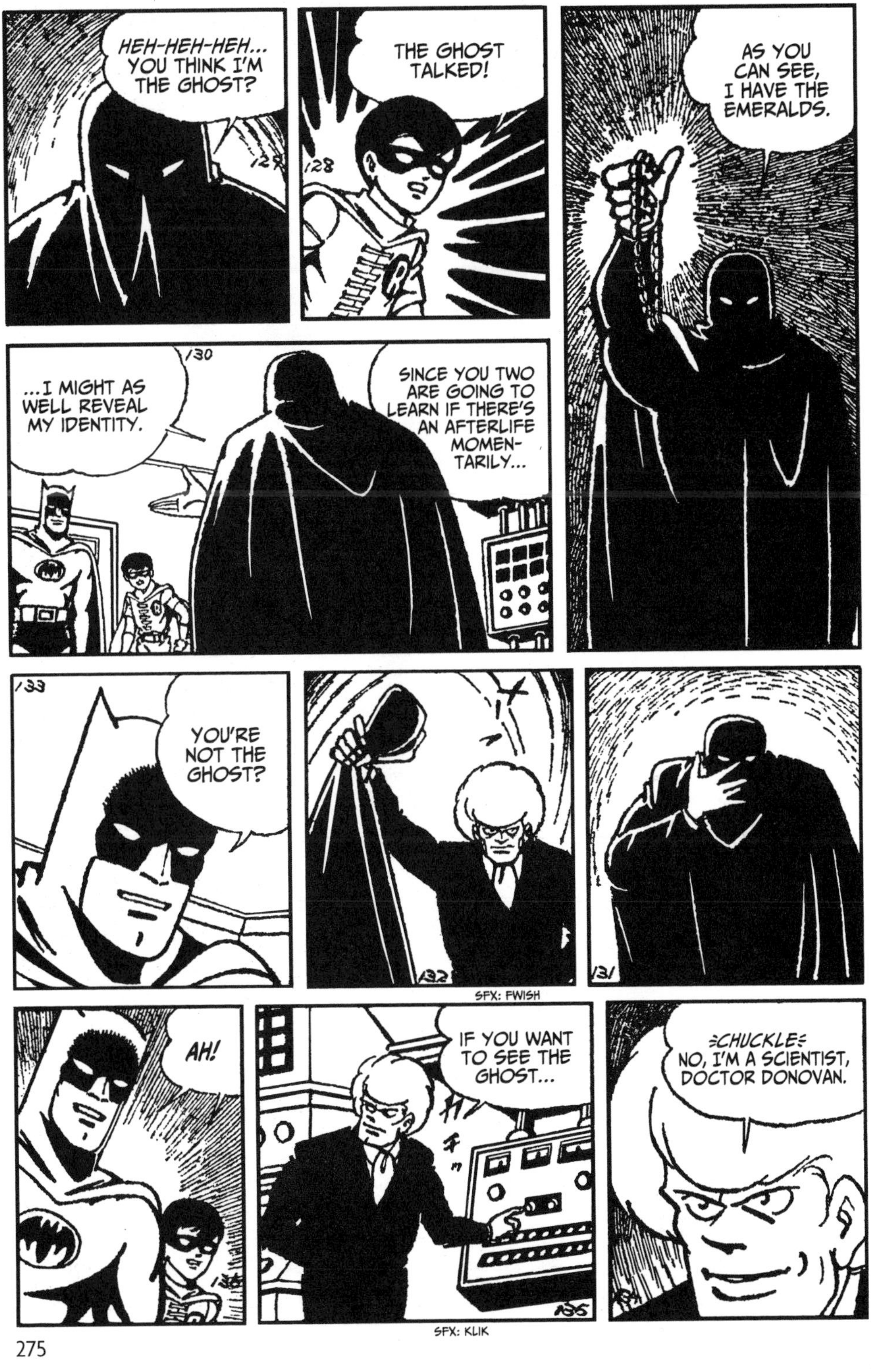
AS YOU CAN SEE, I HAVE THE EMERALDS.
THE GHOST TALKED!
HEH-HEH-HEH... YOU THINK I'M THE GHOST?
SINCE YOU TWO ARE GOING TO LEARN IF THERE'S AN AFTERLIFE MOMENTARILY...
...I MIGHT AS WELL REVEAL MY IDENTITY.
SFX: FWISH
YOU'RE NOT THE GHOST?
≈CHUCKLE≈ NO, I'M A SCIENTIST, DOCTOR DONOVAN.
IF YOU WANT TO SEE THE GHOST...
SFX: KLIK
AH!

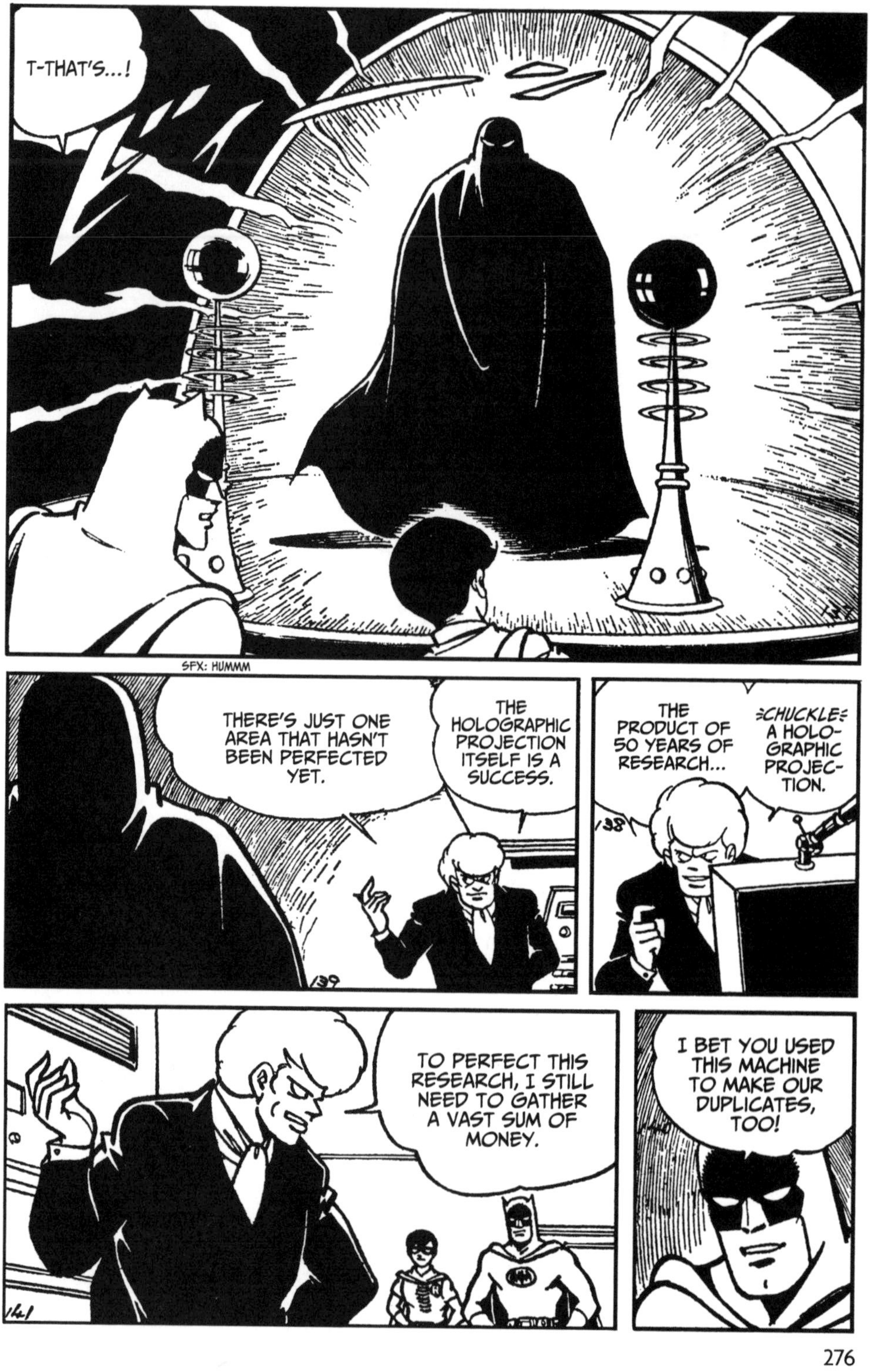
T-THAT'S...!
SFX: HUMMM
≡CHUCKLE≡ A HOLO-GRAPHIC PROJEC-TION.
THE PRODUCT OF 50 YEARS OF RESEARCH...
THE HOLOGRAPHIC PROJECTION ITSELF IS A SUCCESS.
THERE'S JUST ONE AREA THAT HASN'T BEEN PERFECTED YET.
I BET YOU USED THIS MACHINE TO MAKE OUR DUPLICATES, TOO!
TO PERFECT THIS RESEARCH, I STILL NEED TO GATHER A VAST SUM OF MONEY.

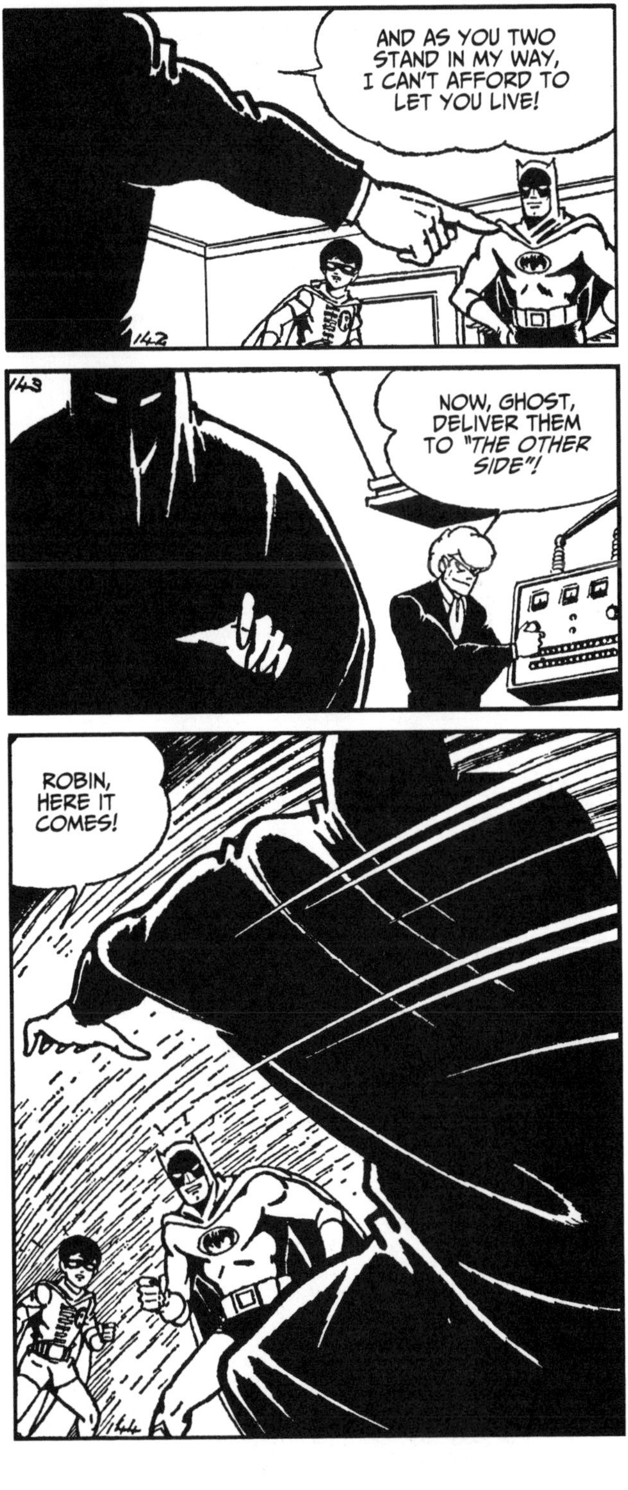
AND AS YOU TWO STAND IN MY WAY, I CAN'T AFFORD TO LET YOU LIVE!
NOW, GHOST, DELIVER THEM TO "THE OTHER SIDE"!
ROBIN, HERE IT COMES!

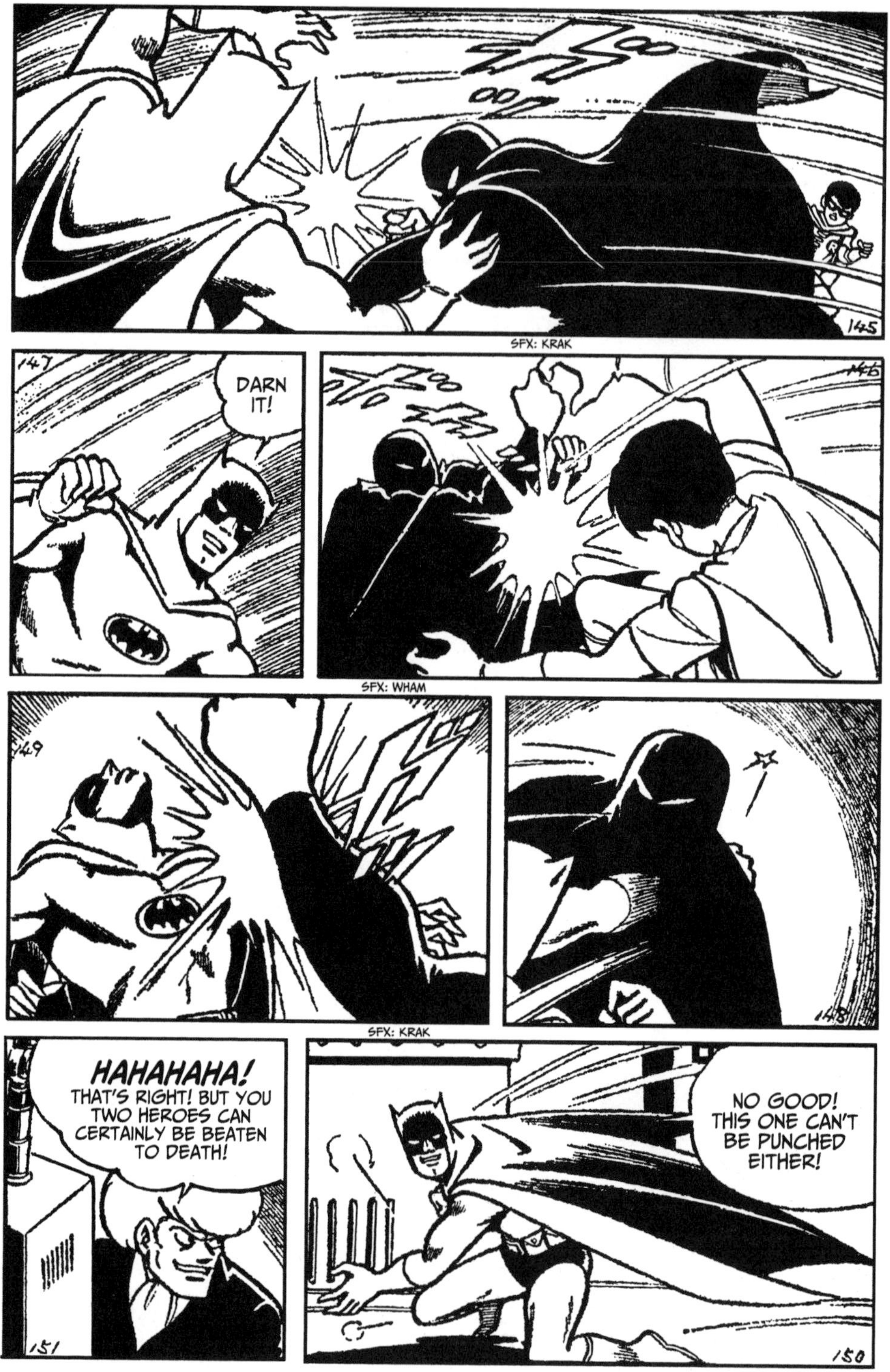
SFX: KRAK
DARN IT!
SFX: WHAM
SFX: KRAK
NO GOOD! THIS ONE CAN'T BE PUNCHED EITHER!
HAHAHAHA! THAT'S RIGHT! BUT YOU TWO HEROES CAN CERTAINLY BE BEATEN TO DEATH!

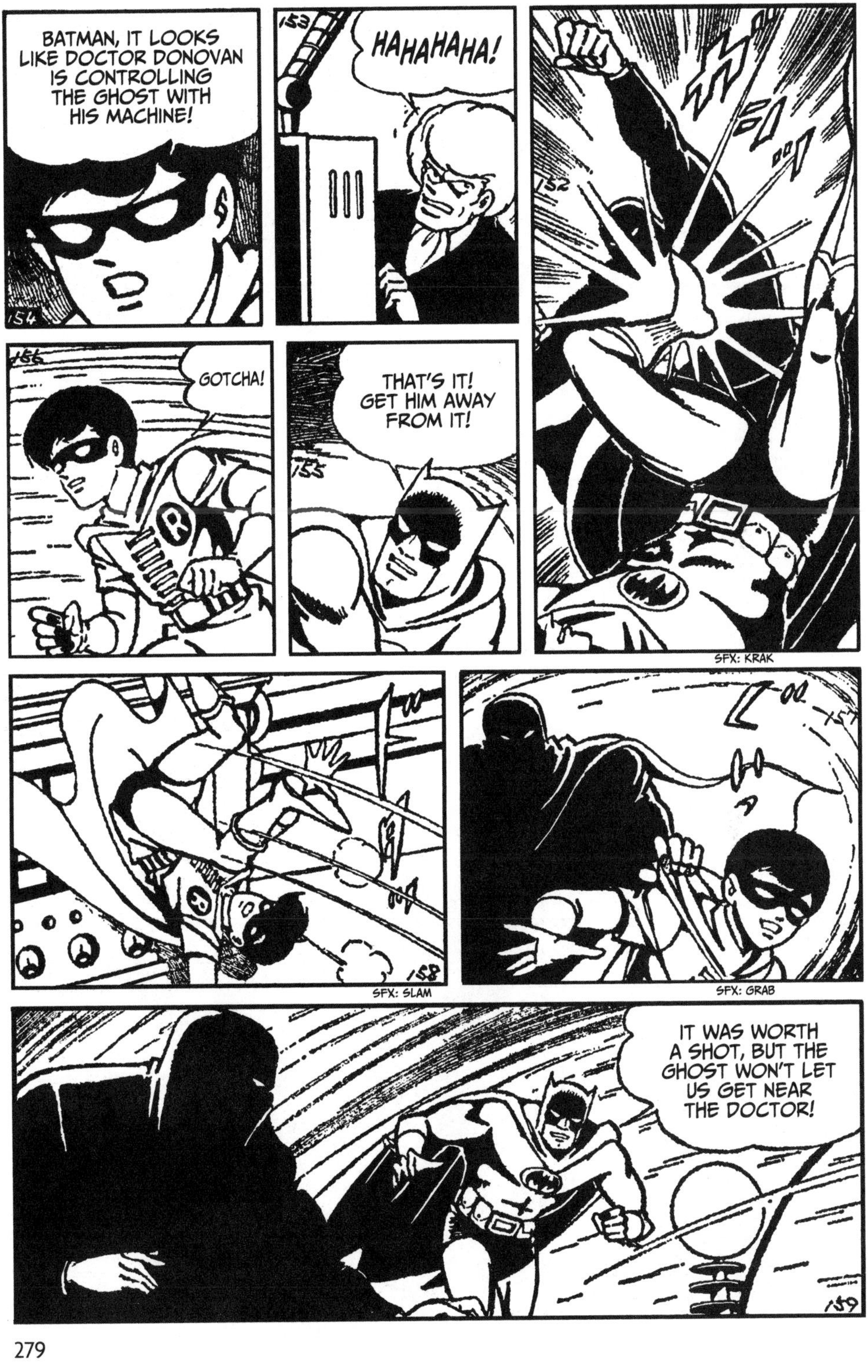
SFX: KRAK
HAHAHAHA!
BATMAN, IT LOOKS LIKE DOCTOR DONOVAN IS CONTROLLING THE GHOST WITH HIS MACHINE!
THAT'S IT! GET HIM AWAY FROM IT!
GOTCHA!
SFX: GRAB
SFX: SLAM
IT WAS WORTH A SHOT, BUT THE GHOST WON'T LET US GET NEAR THE DOCTOR!

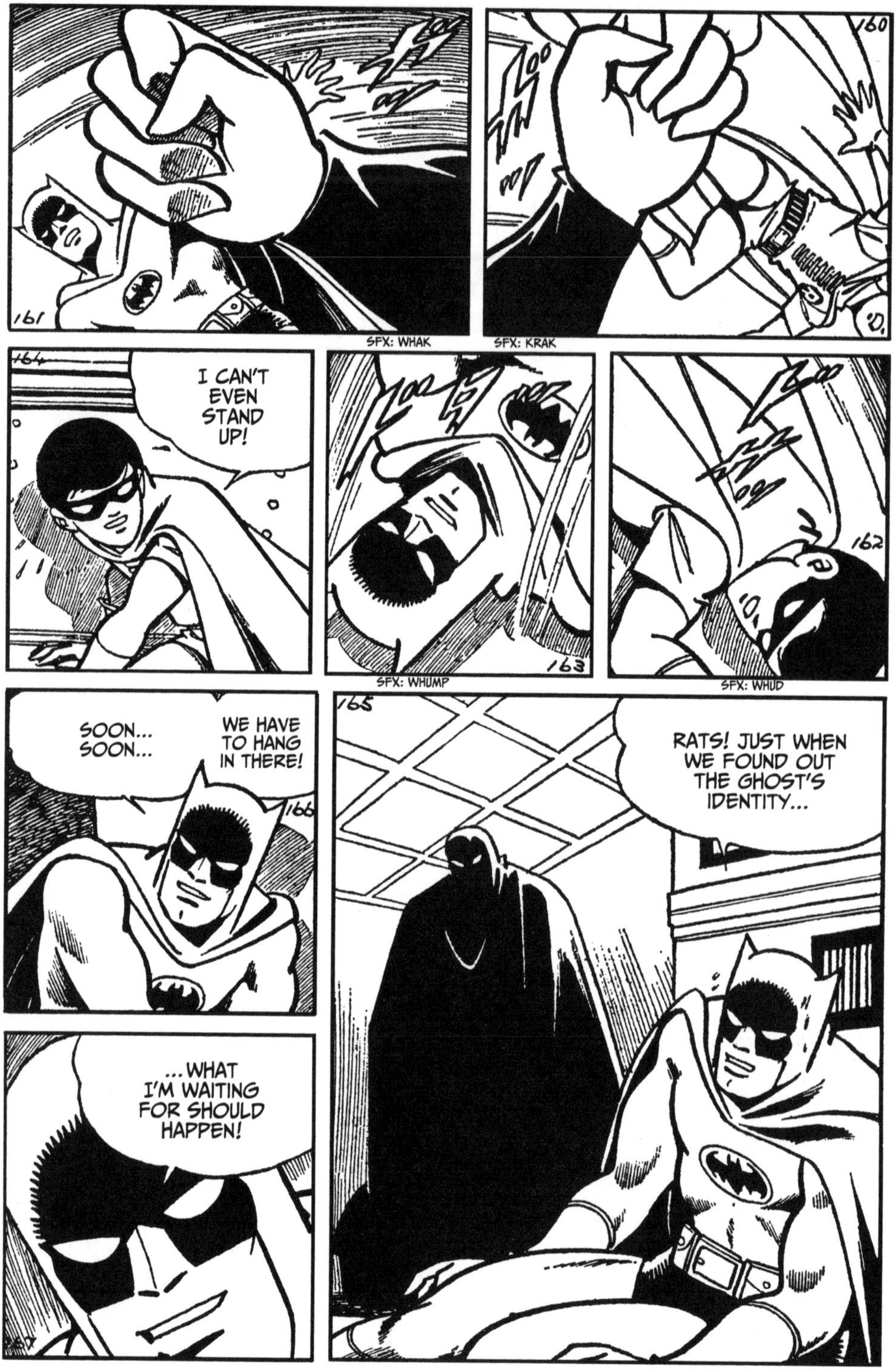
SFX: KRAK
SFX: WHAK
SFX: WHUD
SFX: WHUMP
I CAN'T EVEN STAND UP!
RATS! JUST WHEN WE FOUND OUT THE GHOST'S IDENTITY...
WE HAVE TO HANG IN THERE!
SOON... SOON...
...WHAT I'M WAITING FOR SHOULD HAPPEN!

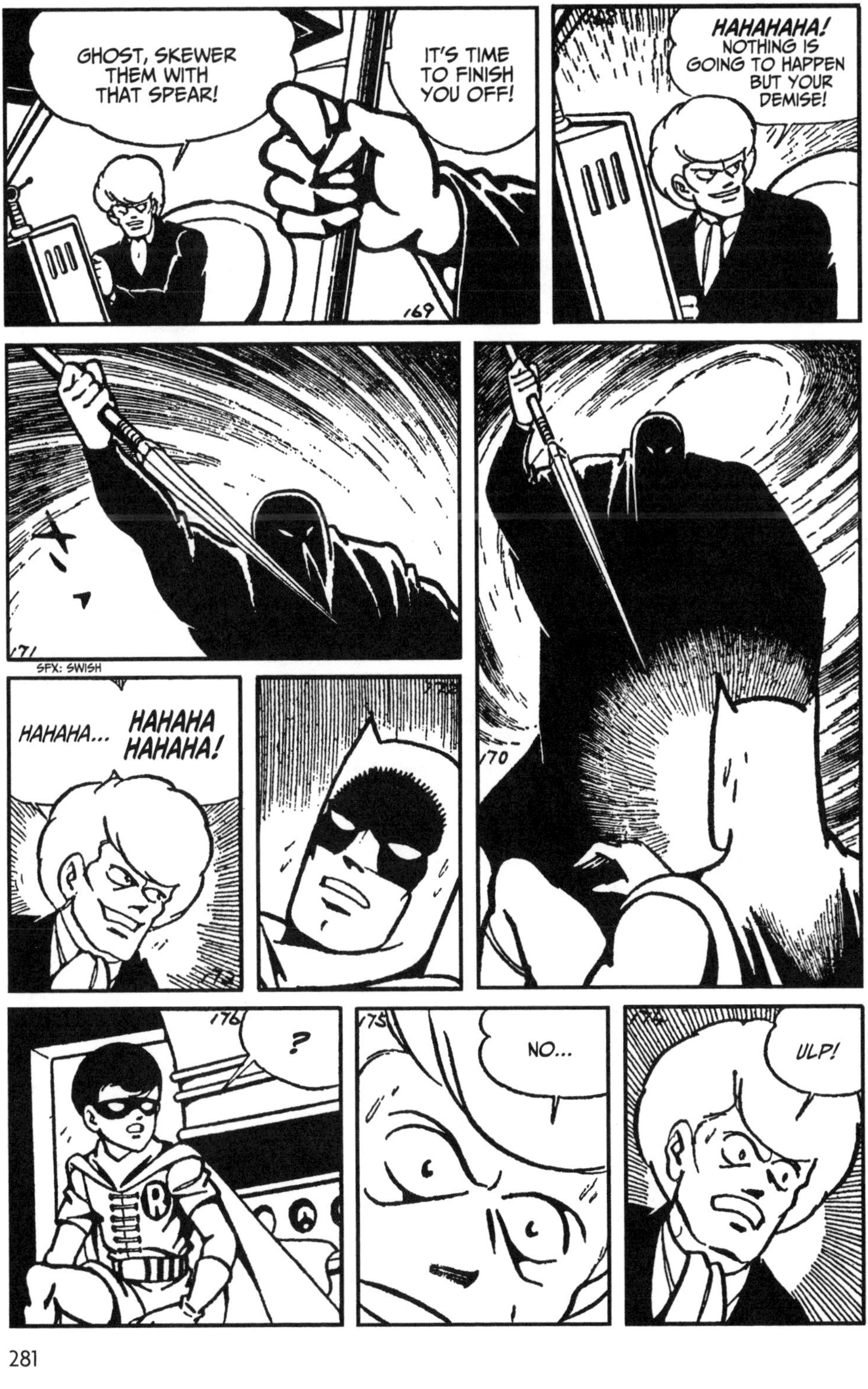
HAHAHAHA! NOTHING IS GOING TO HAPPEN BUT YOUR DEMISE!
IT'S TIME TO FINISH YOU OFF!
GHOST, SKEWER THEM WITH THAT SPEAR!
SFX: SWISH
HAHAHA... HAHAHA HAHAHA!
ULP!
NO...
?

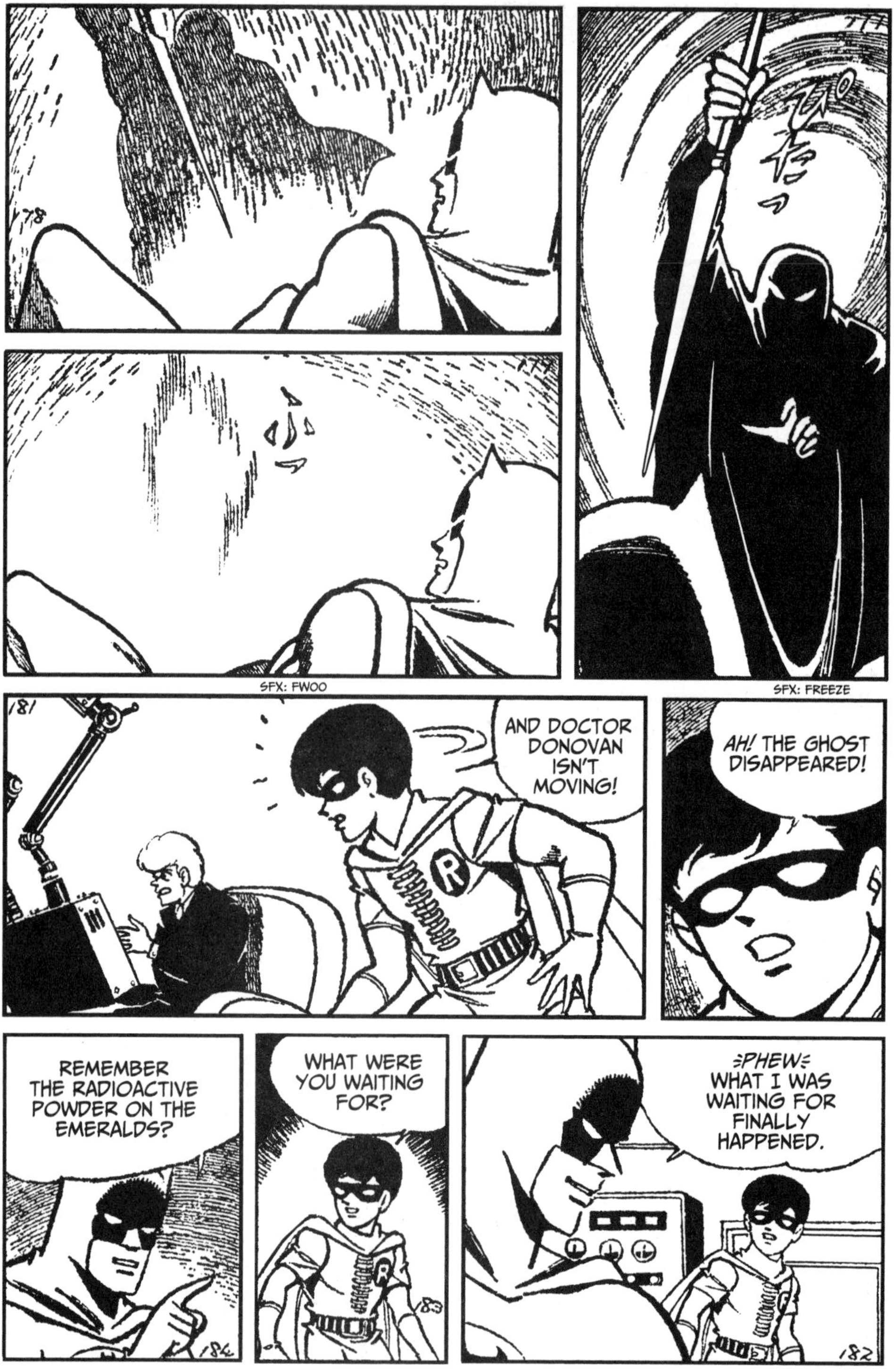
SFX: FREEZE
SFX: FWOO
AH! THE GHOST DISAPPEARED!
AND DOCTOR DONOVAN ISN'T MOVING!
≈PHEW≈ WHAT I WAS WAITING FOR FINALLY HAPPENED.
WHAT WERE YOU WAITING FOR?
REMEMBER THE RADIOACTIVE POWDER ON THE EMERALDS?

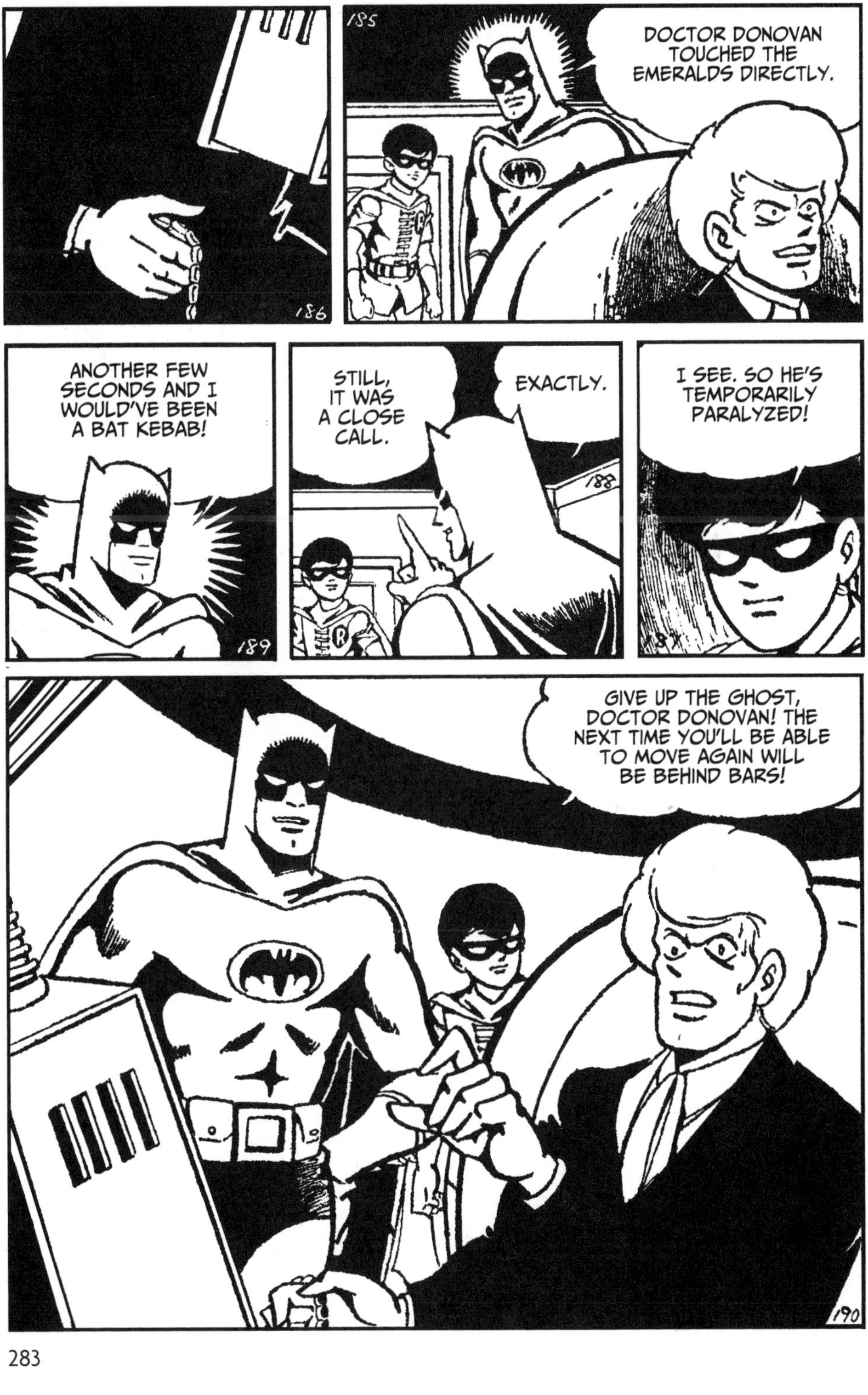
DOCTOR DONOVAN TOUCHED THE EMERALDS DIRECTLY.
I SEE. SO HE'S TEMPORARILY PARALYZED!
EXACTLY.
STILL, IT WAS A CLOSE CALL.
ANOTHER FEW SECONDS AND I WOULD'VE BEEN A BAT KEBAB!
GIVE UP THE GHOST, DOCTOR DONOVAN! THE NEXT TIME YOU'LL BE ABLE TO MOVE AGAIN WILL BE BEHIND BARS!

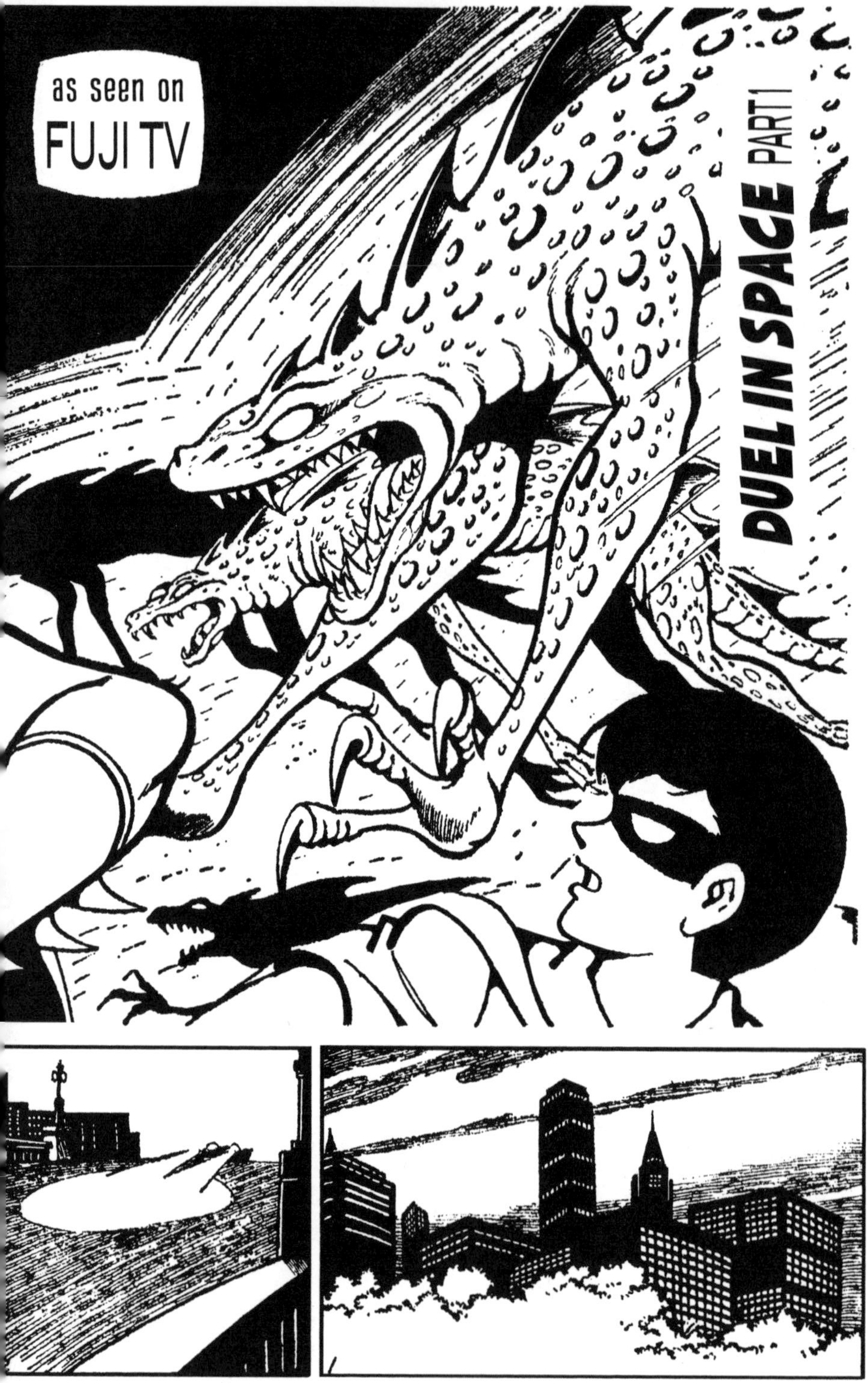
as seen on
FUJI TV
DUEL IN SPACE PART 1

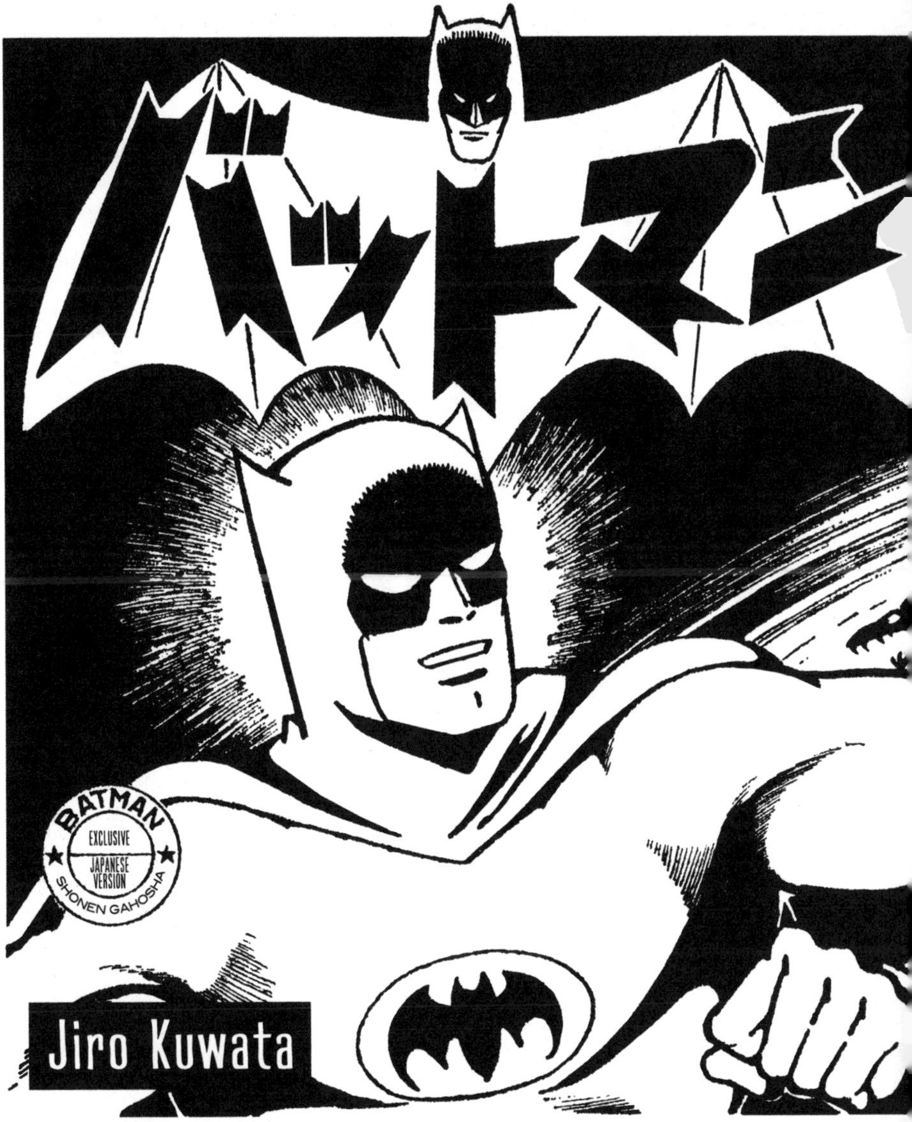
バットマ
BATMAN
EXCLUSIVE
JAPANESE VERSION
SHONEN GAHOSHA
Jiro Kuwata

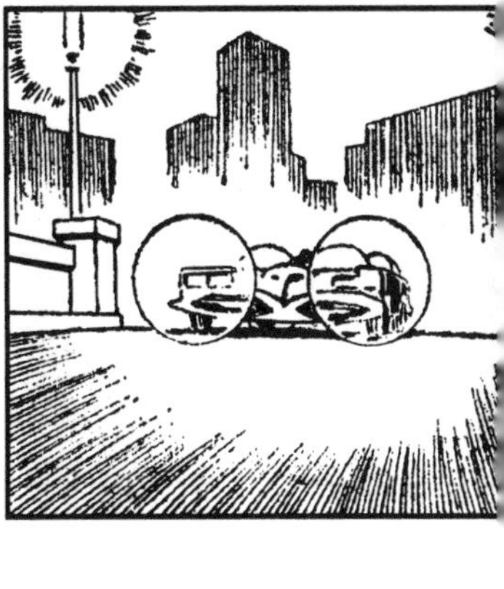

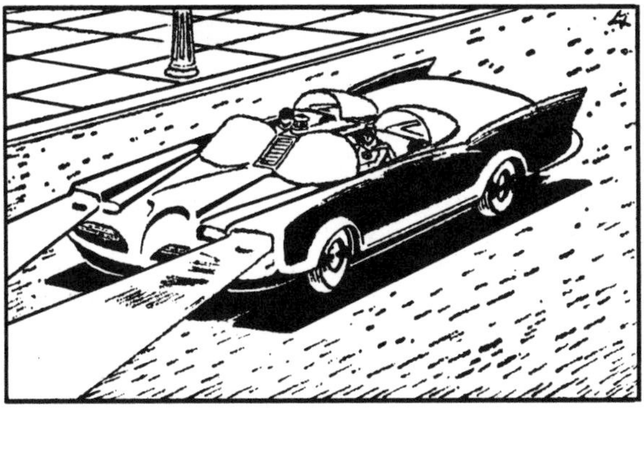

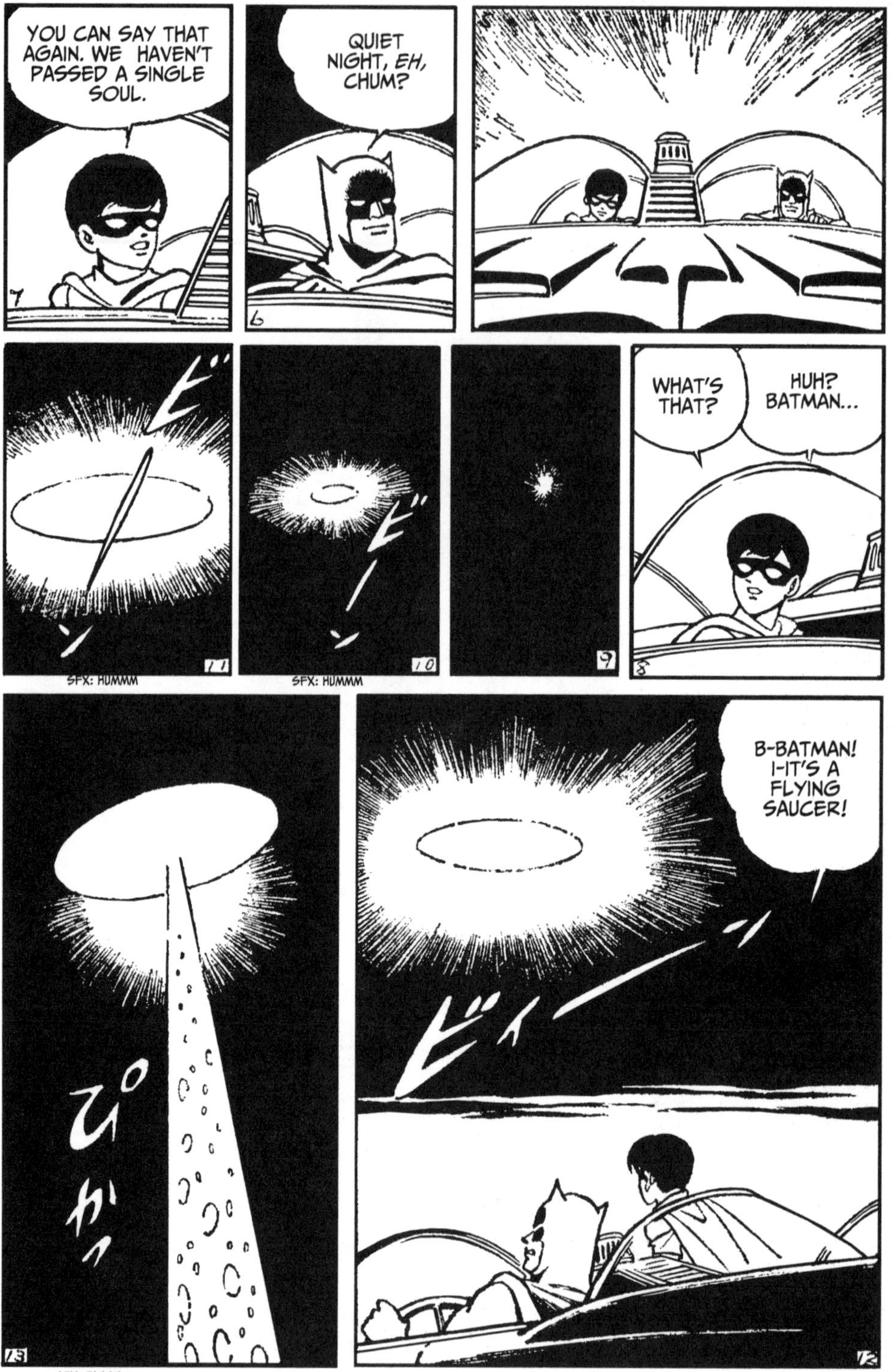
QUIET NIGHT, *EH*, CHUM?
YOU CAN SAY THAT AGAIN. WE HAVEN'T PASSED A SINGLE SOUL.
HUH? BATMAN...
WHAT'S THAT?
SFX: HUMMM
SFX: HUMMM
B-BATMAN! I-IT'S A FLYING SAUCER!
SFX: HUMMM
SFX: FLASH

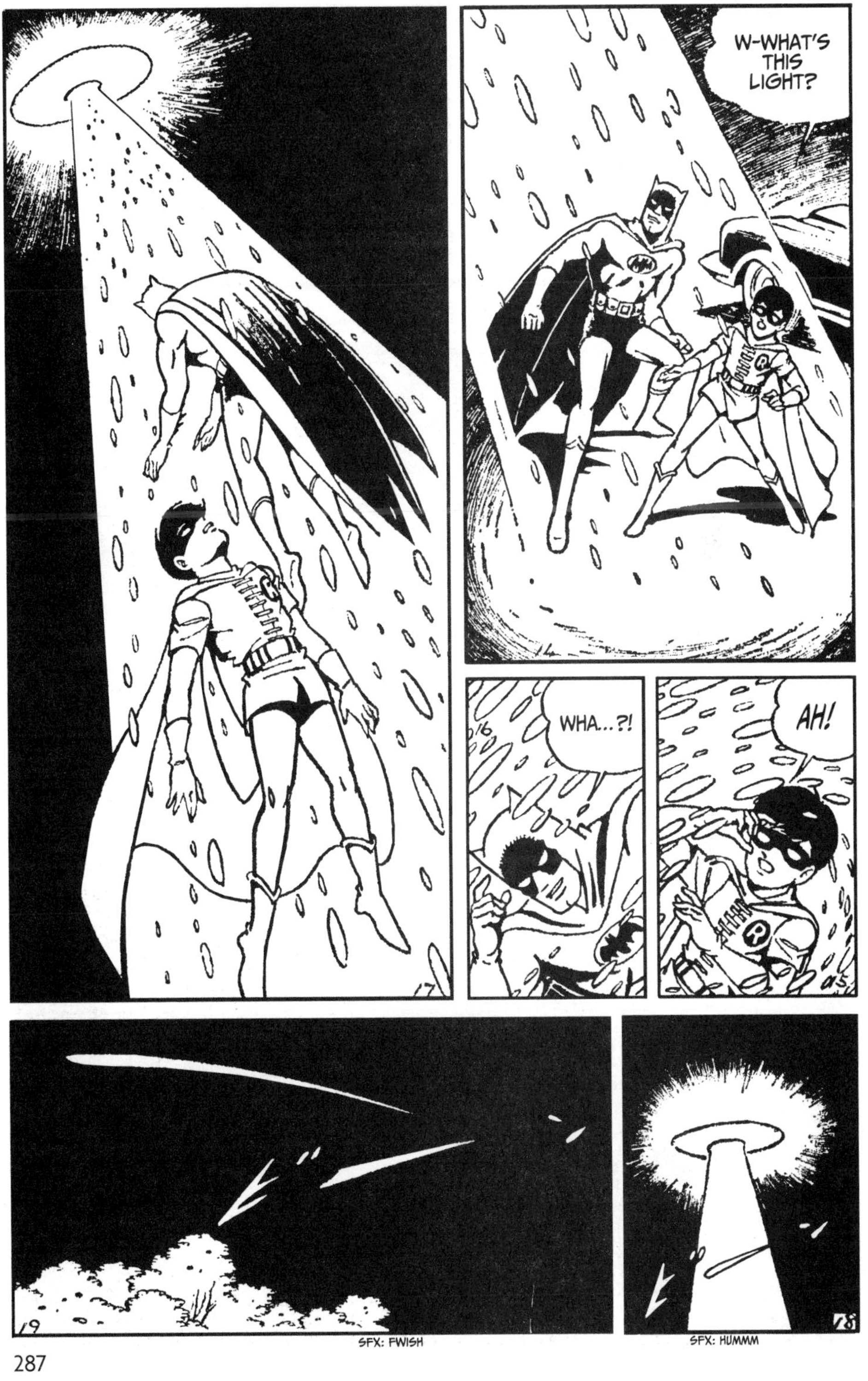
W-WHAT'S THIS LIGHT?
AH!
WHA...?!
SFX: HUMMM
SFX: FWISH

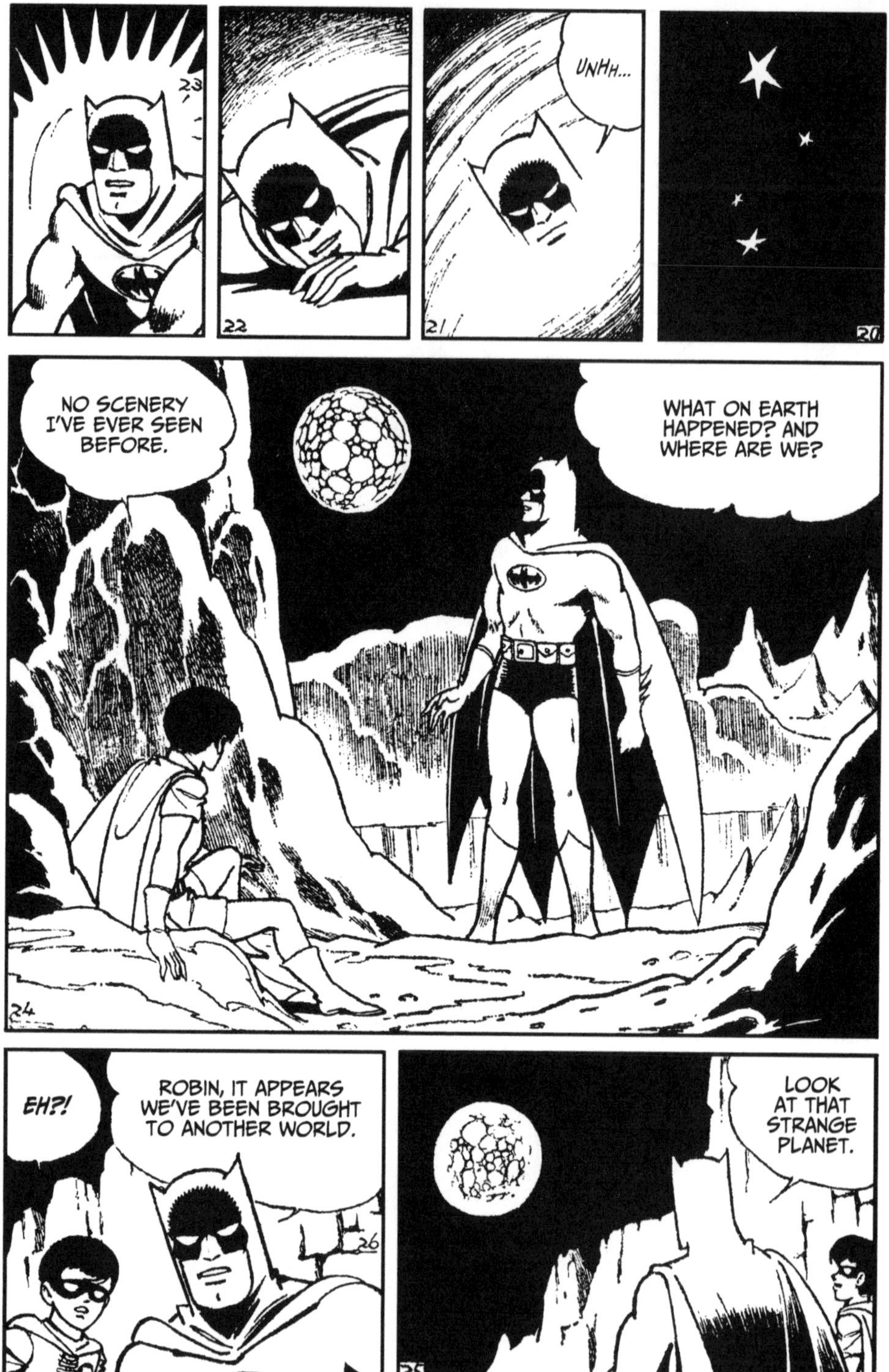
UNHH...
WHAT ON EARTH HAPPENED? AND WHERE ARE WE?
NO SCENERY I'VE EVER SEEN BEFORE.
LOOK AT THAT STRANGE PLANET.
ROBIN, IT APPEARS WE'VE BEEN BROUGHT TO ANOTHER WORLD.
EH?!

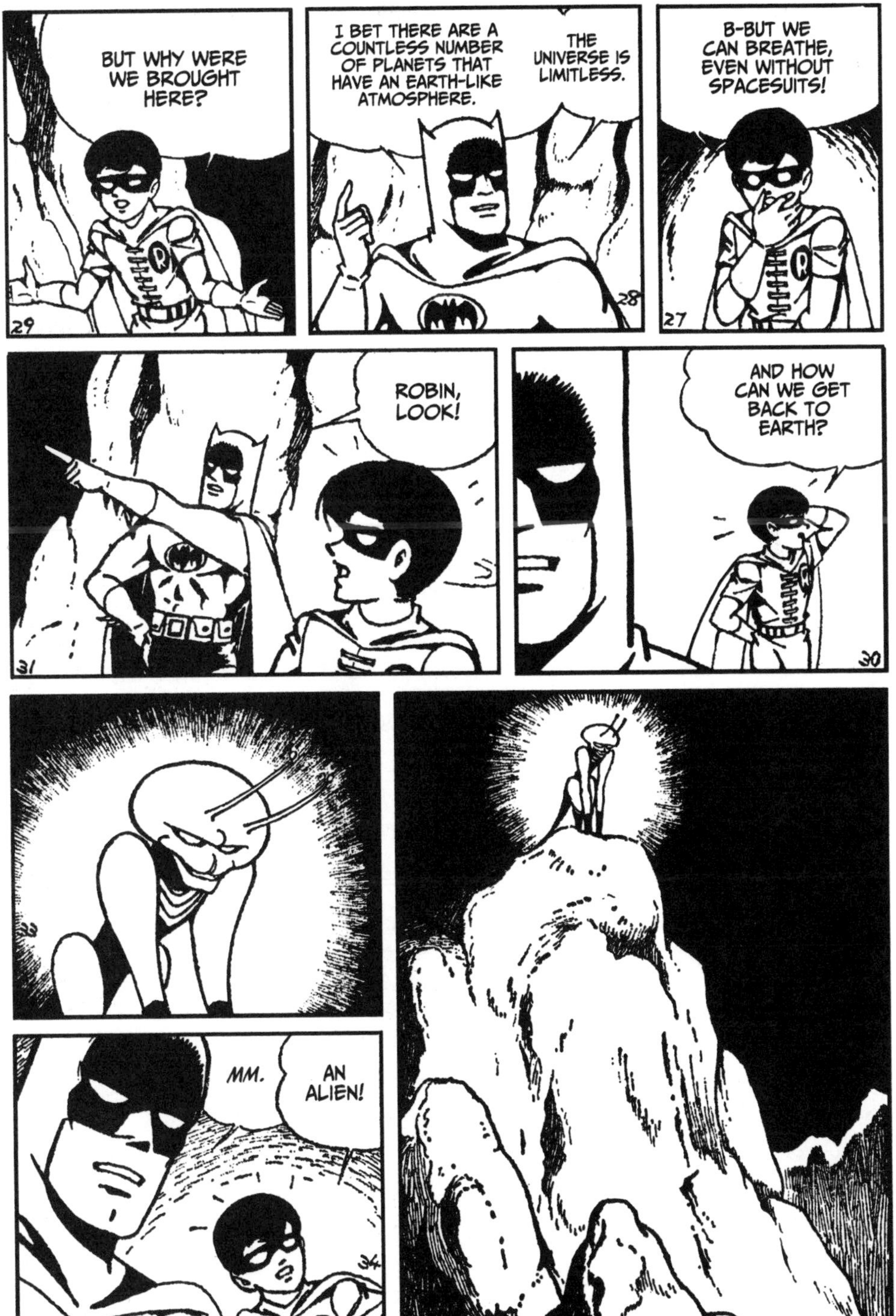
B-BUT WE CAN BREATHE, EVEN WITHOUT SPACESUITS!
THE UNIVERSE IS LIMITLESS.
I BET THERE ARE A COUNTLESS NUMBER OF PLANETS THAT HAVE AN EARTH-LIKE ATMOSPHERE.
BUT WHY WERE WE BROUGHT HERE?
AND HOW CAN WE GET BACK TO EARTH?
ROBIN, LOOK!
AN ALIEN!
MM.

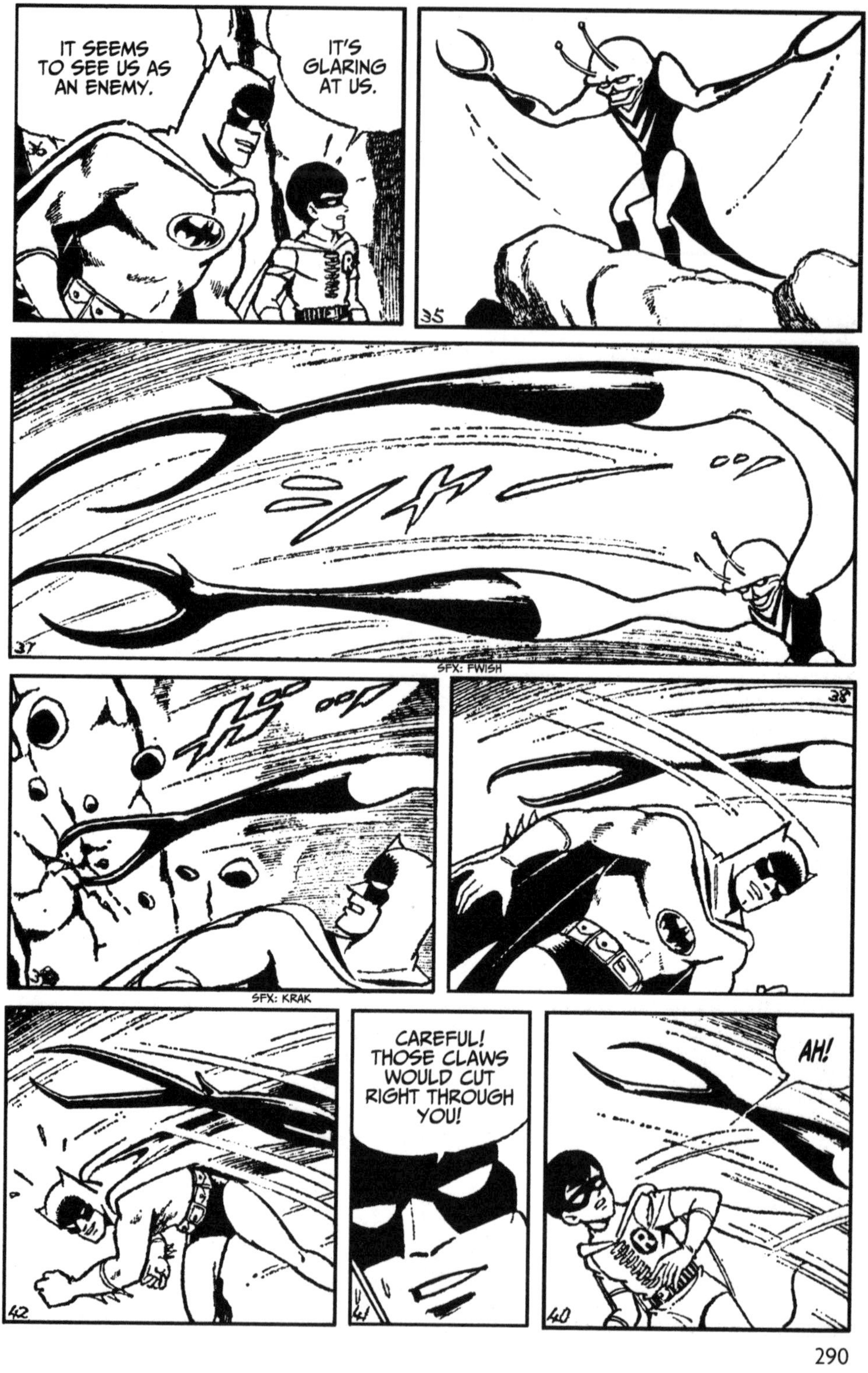
IT'S GLARING AT US.
IT SEEMS TO SEE US AS AN ENEMY.
SFX: FWISH
SFX: KRAK
AH!
CAREFUL! THOSE CLAWS WOULD CUT RIGHT THROUGH YOU!

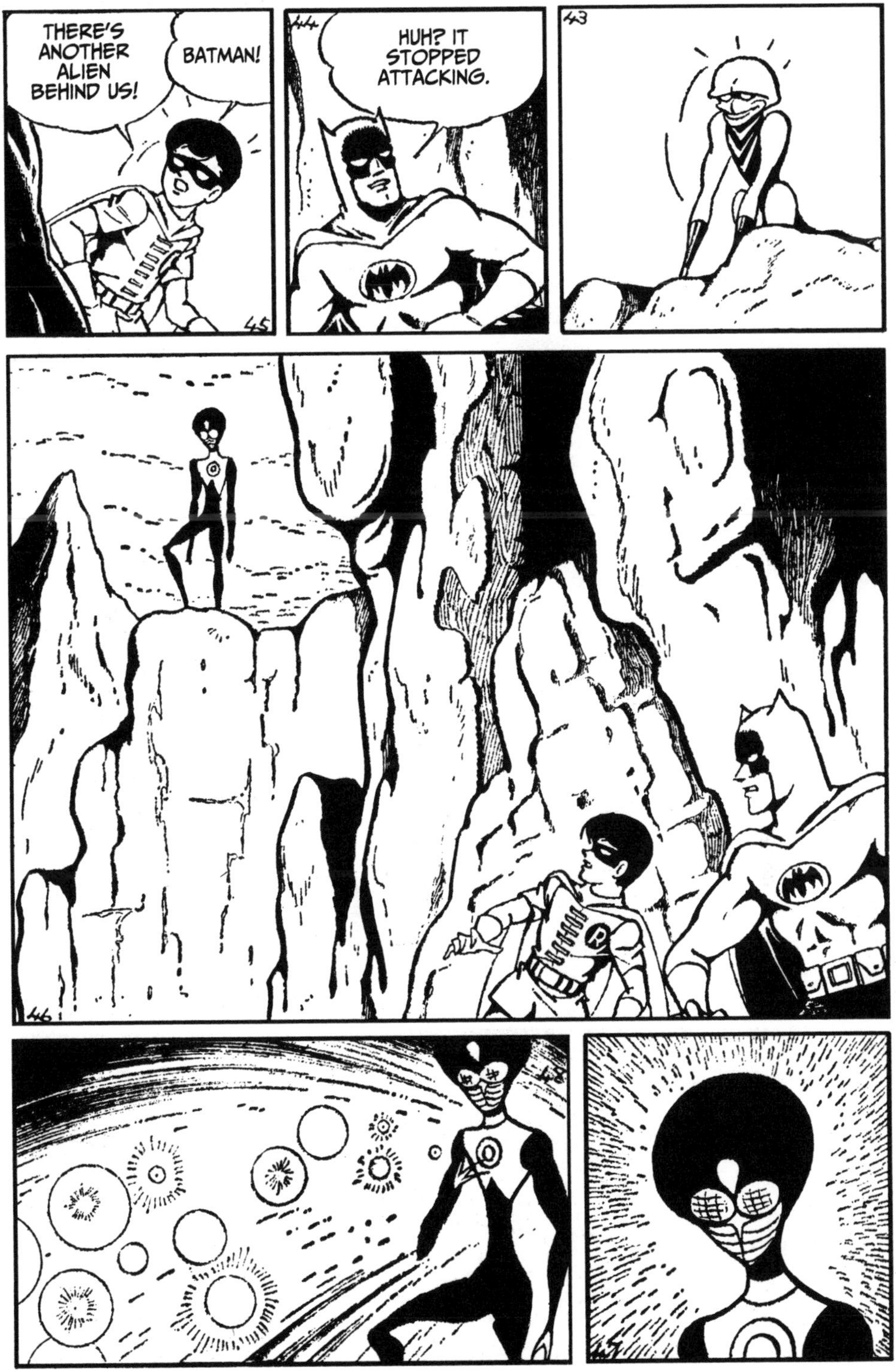
HUH? IT STOPPED ATTACKING.
BATMAN!
THERE'S ANOTHER ALIEN BEHIND US!

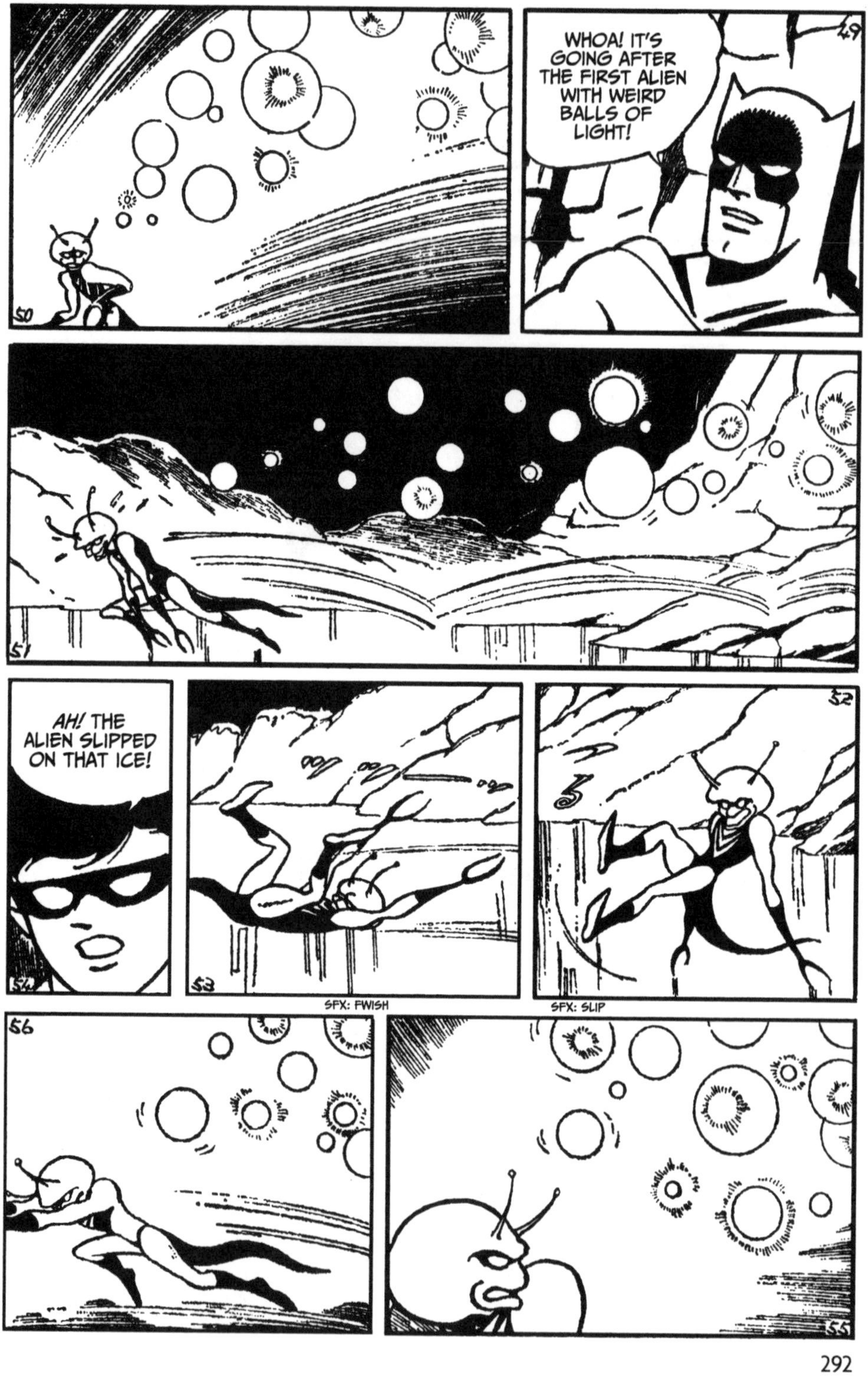
WHOA! IT'S GOING AFTER THE FIRST ALIEN WITH WEIRD BALLS OF LIGHT!
SFX: SLIP
SFX: FWISH
AH! THE ALIEN SLIPPED ON THAT ICE!

THE HOSTILE ALIEN MADE IT ACROSS THE ICE. WONDER IF IT'LL ESCAPE.

UH-OH. THOSE BALLS ARE SUDDENLY PICKING UP SPEED!

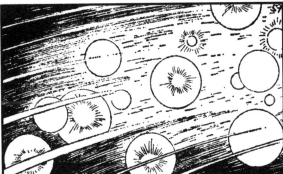

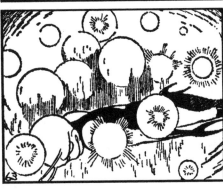

SKRAKK!

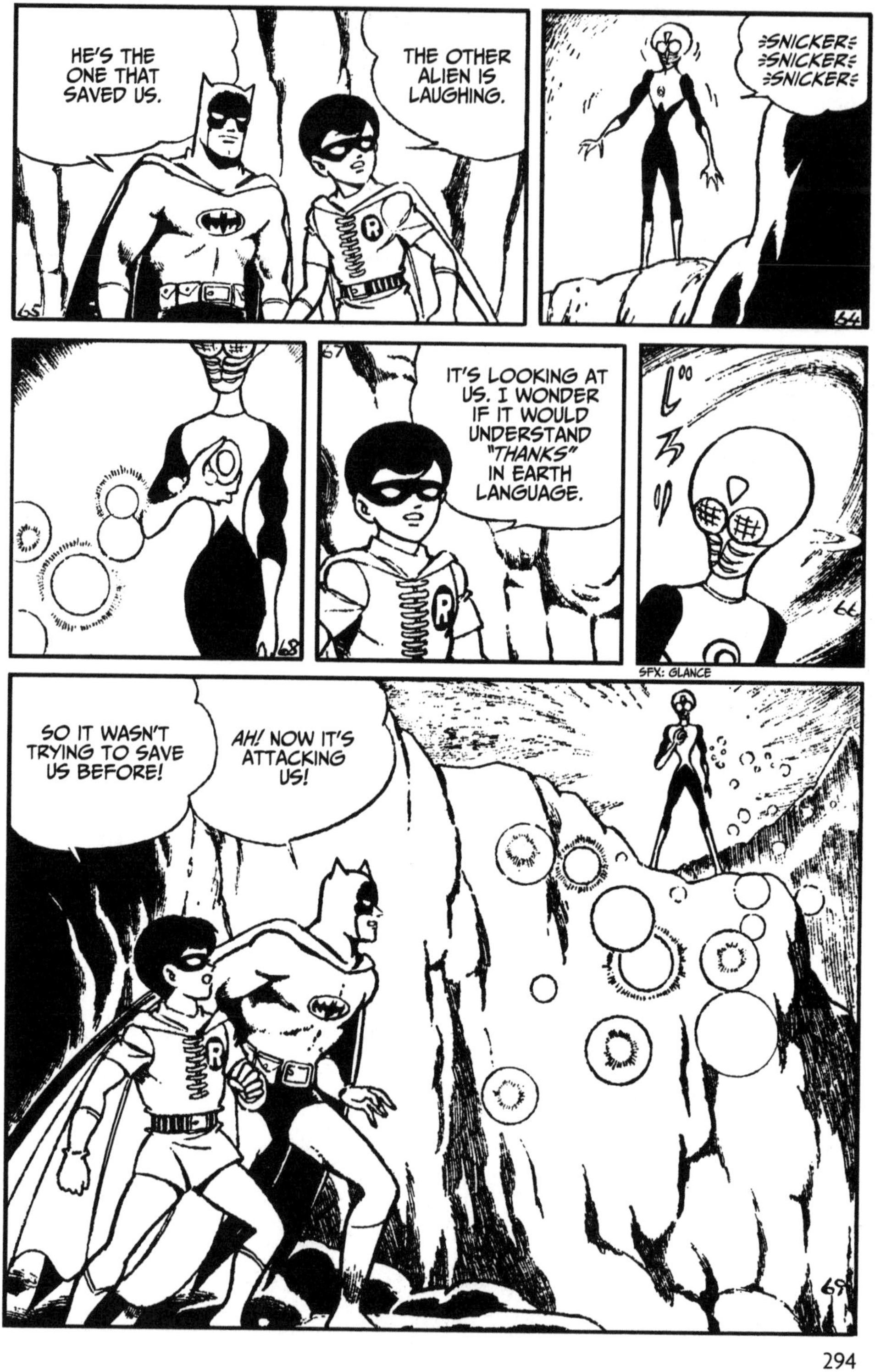

SNICKER SNICKER SNICKER
THE OTHER ALIEN IS LAUGHING.
HE'S THE ONE THAT SAVED US.
SFX: GLANCE
IT'S LOOKING AT US. I WONDER IF IT WOULD UNDERSTAND *"THANKS"* IN EARTH LANGUAGE.
AH! NOW IT'S ATTACKING US!
SO IT WASN'T TRYING TO SAVE US BEFORE!

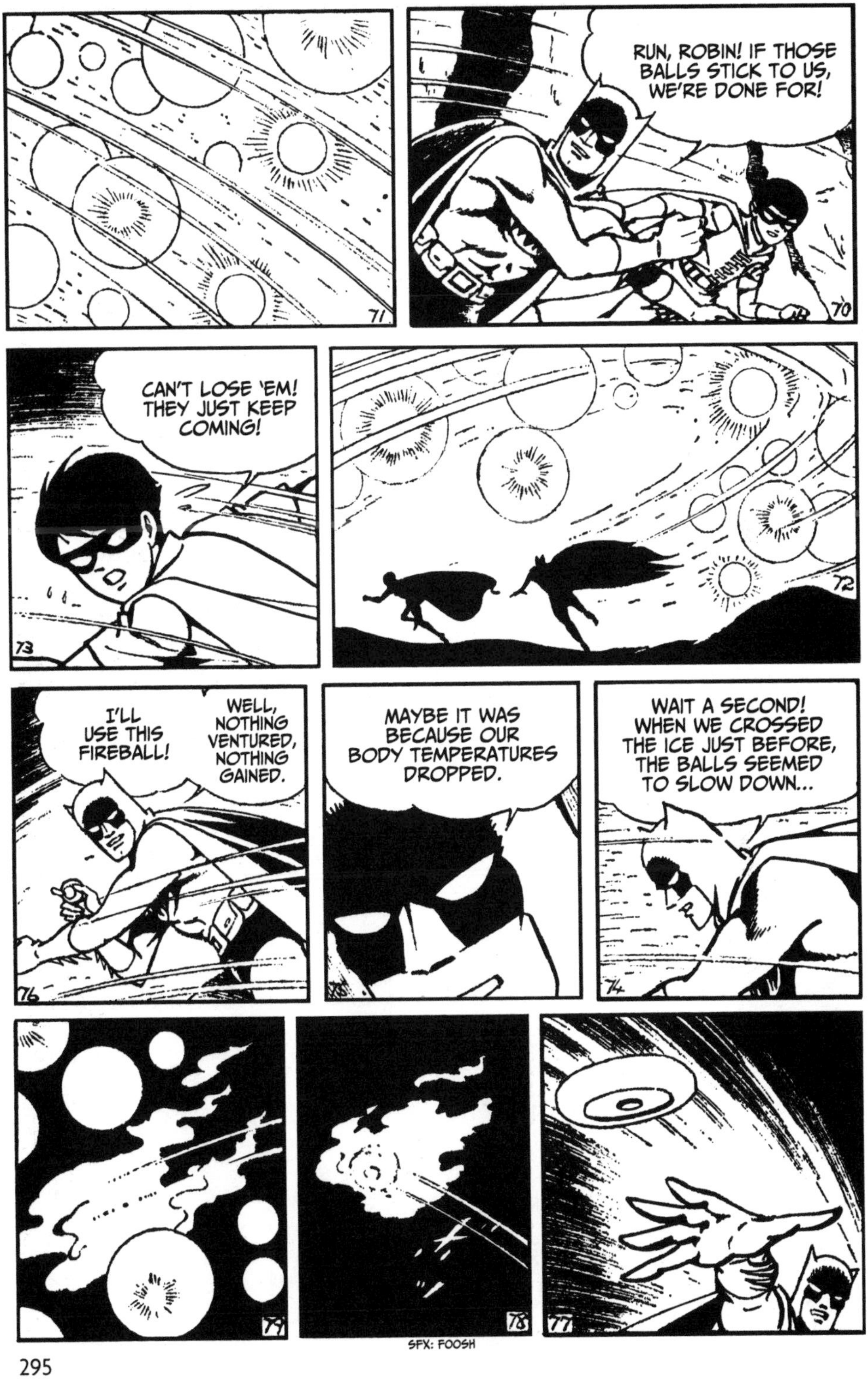
RUN, ROBIN! IF THOSE BALLS STICK TO US, WE'RE DONE FOR!
CAN'T LOSE 'EM! THEY JUST KEEP COMING!
WAIT A SECOND! WHEN WE CROSSED THE ICE JUST BEFORE, THE BALLS SEEMED TO SLOW DOWN...
MAYBE IT WAS BECAUSE OUR BODY TEMPERATURES DROPPED.
WELL, NOTHING VENTURED, NOTHING GAINED.
I'LL USE THIS FIREBALL!
SFX: FOOSH

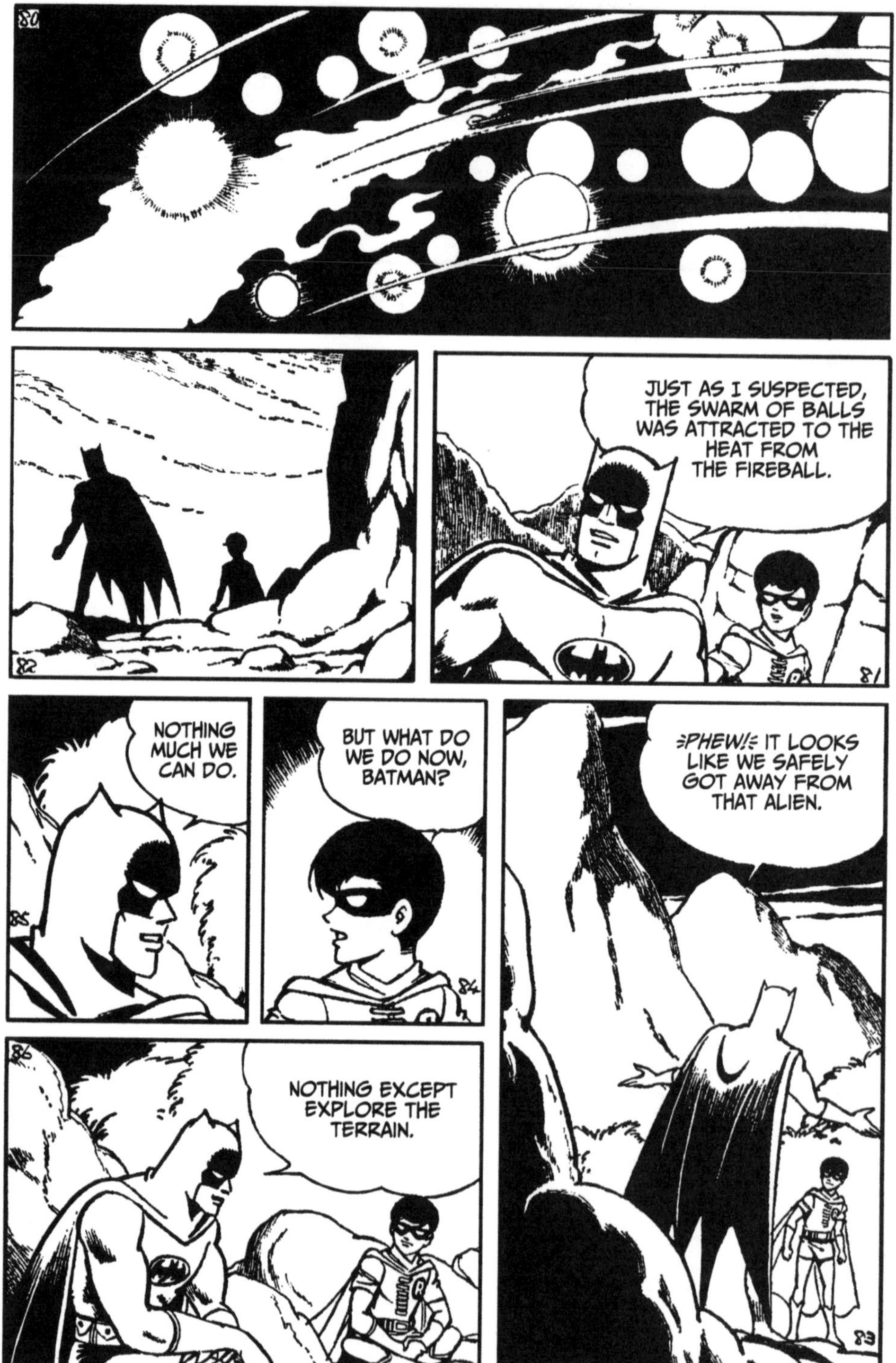
JUST AS I SUSPECTED, THE SWARM OF BALLS WAS ATTRACTED TO THE HEAT FROM THE FIREBALL.
PHEW! IT LOOKS LIKE WE SAFELY GOT AWAY FROM THAT ALIEN.
BUT WHAT DO WE DO NOW, BATMAN?
NOTHING MUCH WE CAN DO.
NOTHING EXCEPT EXPLORE THE TERRAIN.

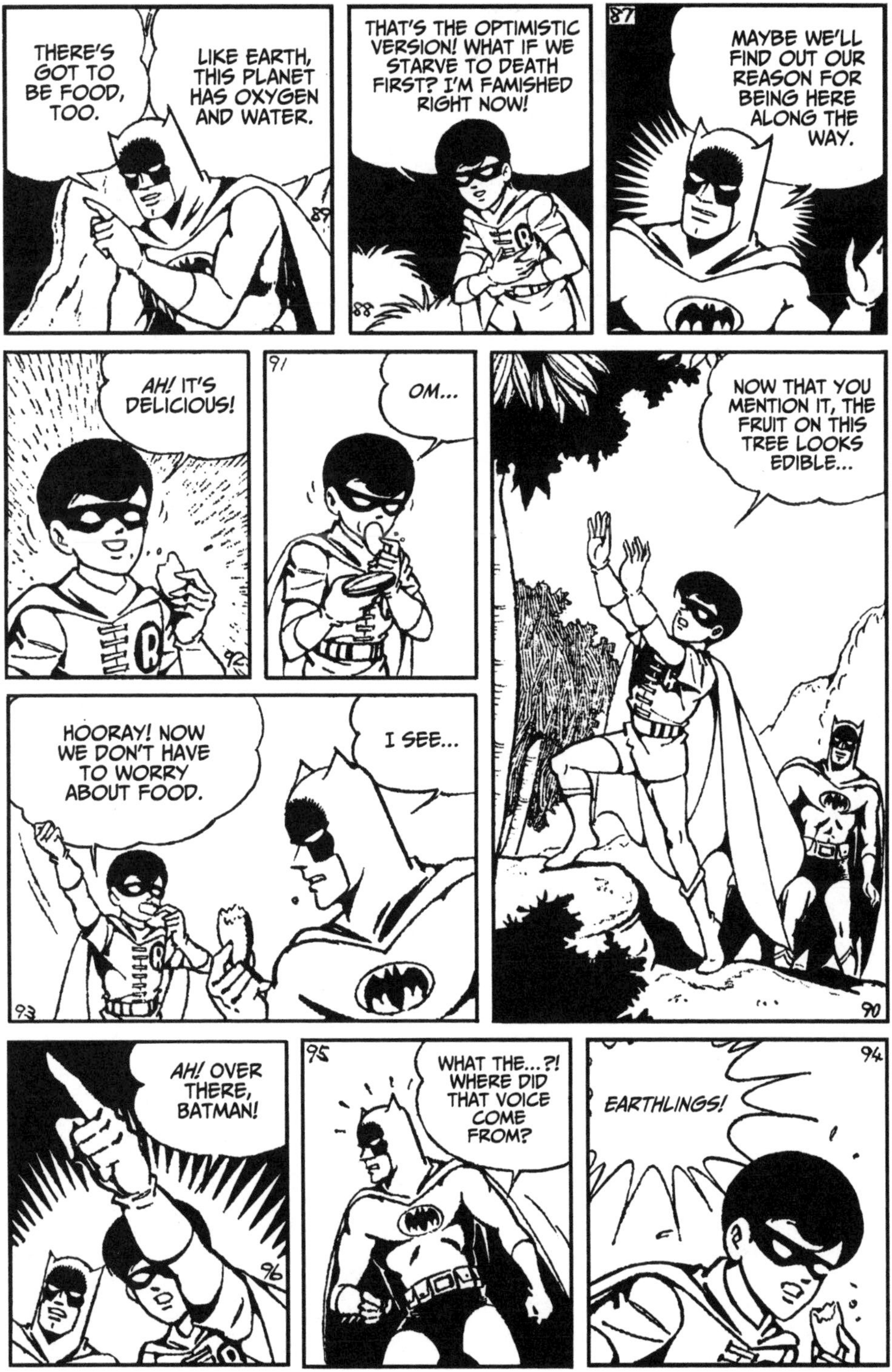
MAYBE WE'LL FIND OUT OUR REASON FOR BEING HERE ALONG THE WAY.
THAT'S THE OPTIMISTIC VERSION! WHAT IF WE STARVE TO DEATH FIRST? I'M FAMISHED RIGHT NOW!
LIKE EARTH, THIS PLANET HAS OXYGEN AND WATER.
THERE'S GOT TO BE FOOD, TOO.
NOW THAT YOU MENTION IT, THE FRUIT ON THIS TREE LOOKS EDIBLE...
OM...
AH! IT'S DELICIOUS!
I SEE...
HOORAY! NOW WE DON'T HAVE TO WORRY ABOUT FOOD.
EARTHLINGS!
WHAT THE...?! WHERE DID THAT VOICE COME FROM?
AH! OVER THERE, BATMAN!

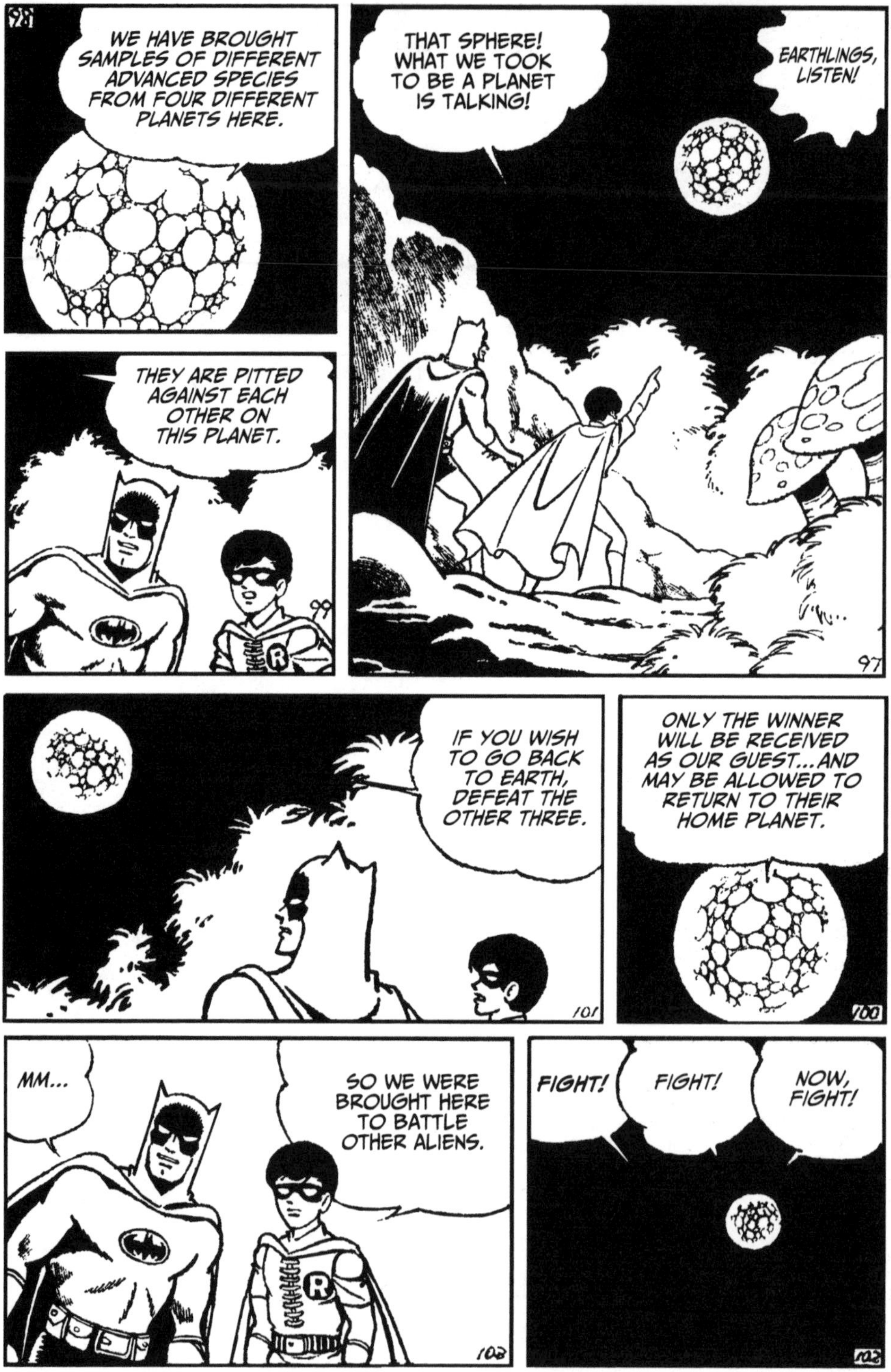
EARTHLINGS, LISTEN!
THAT SPHERE! WHAT WE TOOK TO BE A PLANET IS TALKING!
WE HAVE BROUGHT SAMPLES OF DIFFERENT ADVANCED SPECIES FROM FOUR DIFFERENT PLANETS HERE.
THEY ARE PITTED AGAINST EACH OTHER ON THIS PLANET.
ONLY THE WINNER WILL BE RECEIVED AS OUR GUEST...AND MAY BE ALLOWED TO RETURN TO THEIR HOME PLANET.
IF YOU WISH TO GO BACK TO EARTH, DEFEAT THE OTHER THREE.
NOW, FIGHT!
FIGHT!
FIGHT!
SO WE WERE BROUGHT HERE TO BATTLE OTHER ALIENS.
MM...

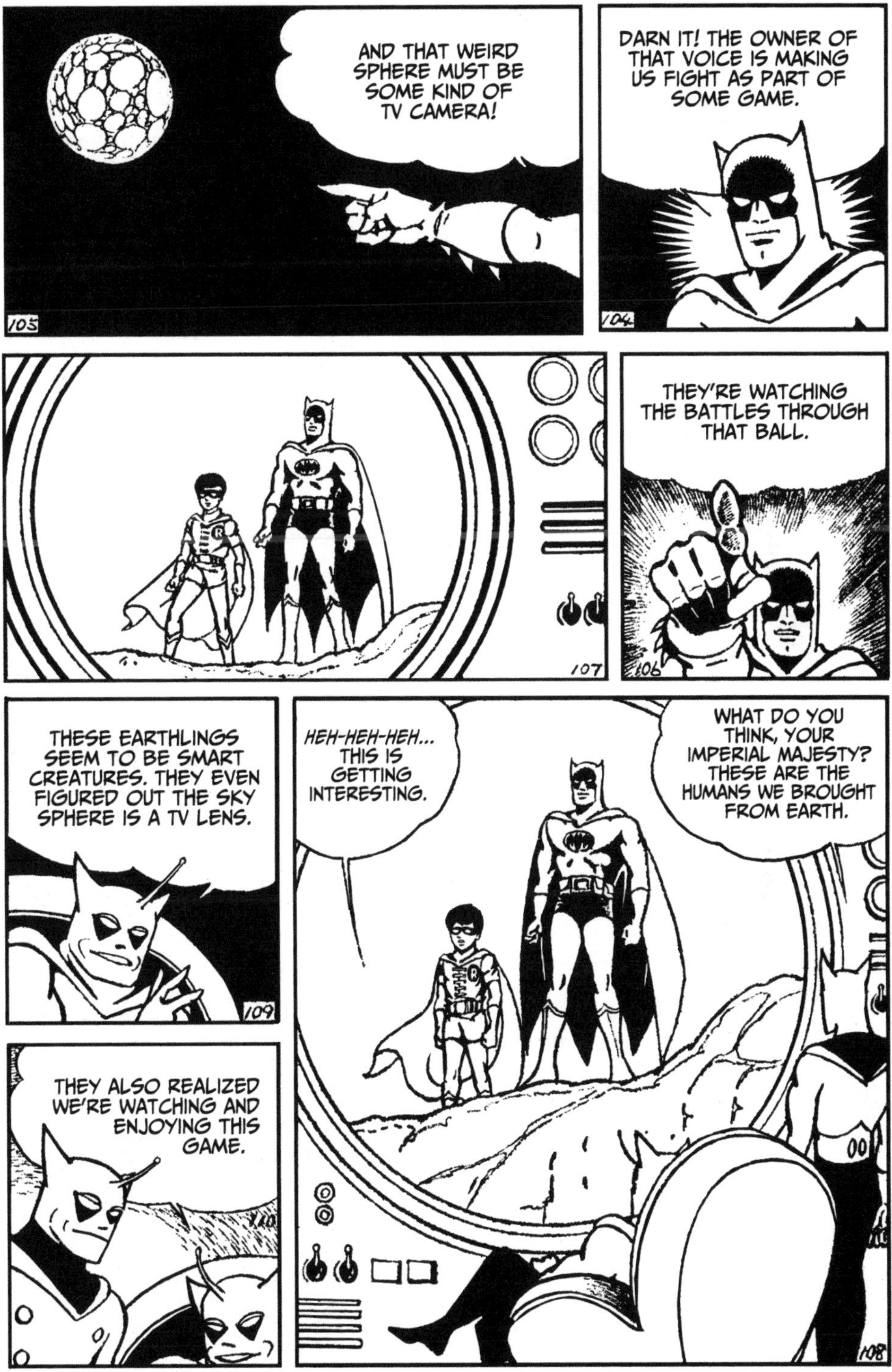
DARN IT! THE OWNER OF THAT VOICE IS MAKING US FIGHT AS PART OF SOME GAME.
AND THAT WEIRD SPHERE MUST BE SOME KIND OF TV CAMERA!
THEY'RE WATCHING THE BATTLES THROUGH THAT BALL.
WHAT DO YOU THINK, YOUR IMPERIAL MAJESTY? THESE ARE THE HUMANS WE BROUGHT FROM EARTH.
HEH-HEH-HEH... THIS IS GETTING INTERESTING.
THESE EARTHLINGS SEEM TO BE SMART CREATURES. THEY EVEN FIGURED OUT THE SKY SPHERE IS A TV LENS.
THEY ALSO REALIZED WE'RE WATCHING AND ENJOYING THIS GAME.

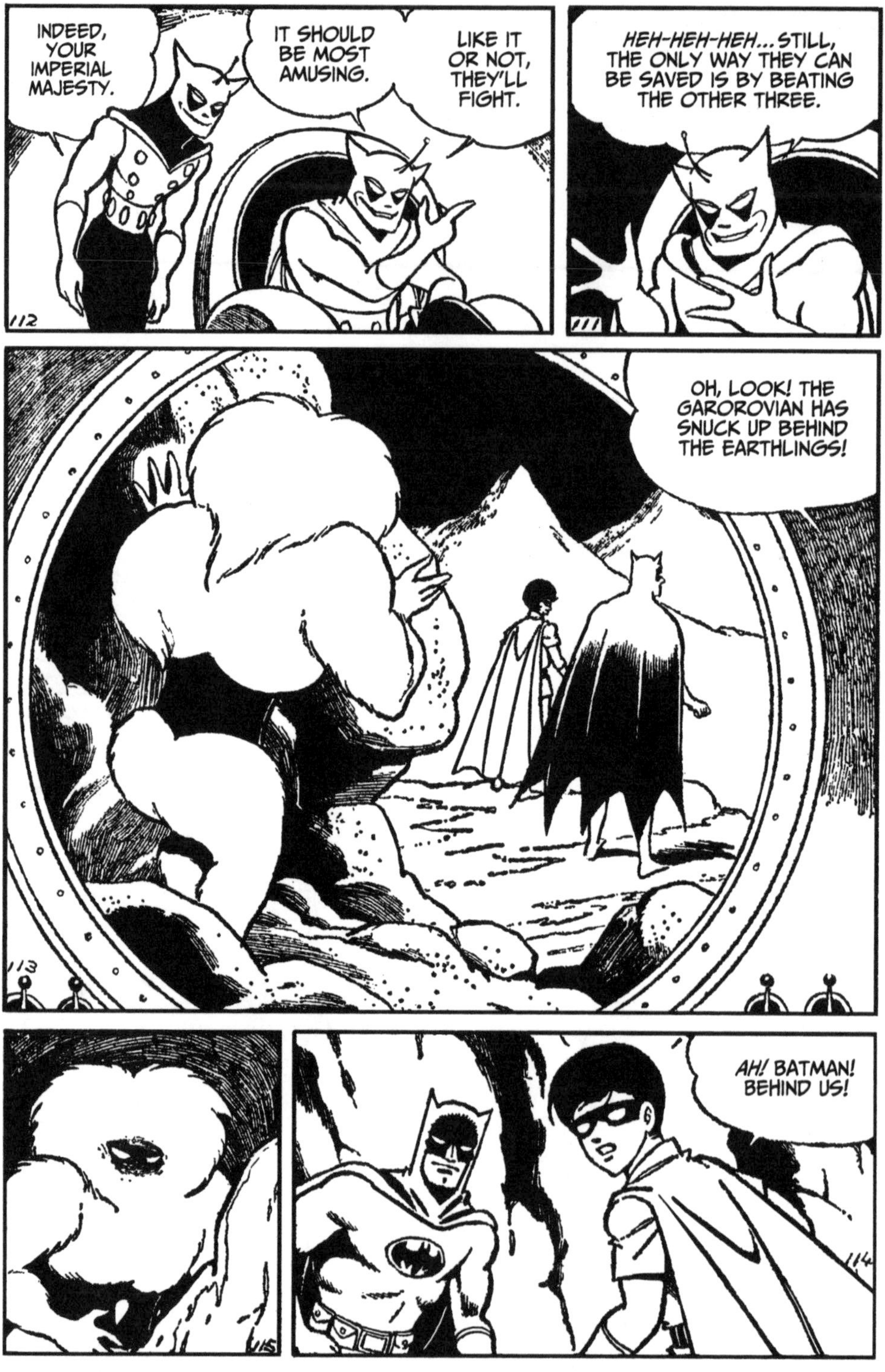

HEH-HEH-HEH...STILL, THE ONLY WAY THEY CAN BE SAVED IS BY BEATING THE OTHER THREE.
IT SHOULD BE MOST AMUSING.
LIKE IT OR NOT, THEY'LL FIGHT.
INDEED, YOUR IMPERIAL MAJESTY.
OH, LOOK! THE GAROROVIAN HAS SNUCK UP BEHIND THE EARTHLINGS!
AH! BATMAN! BEHIND US!

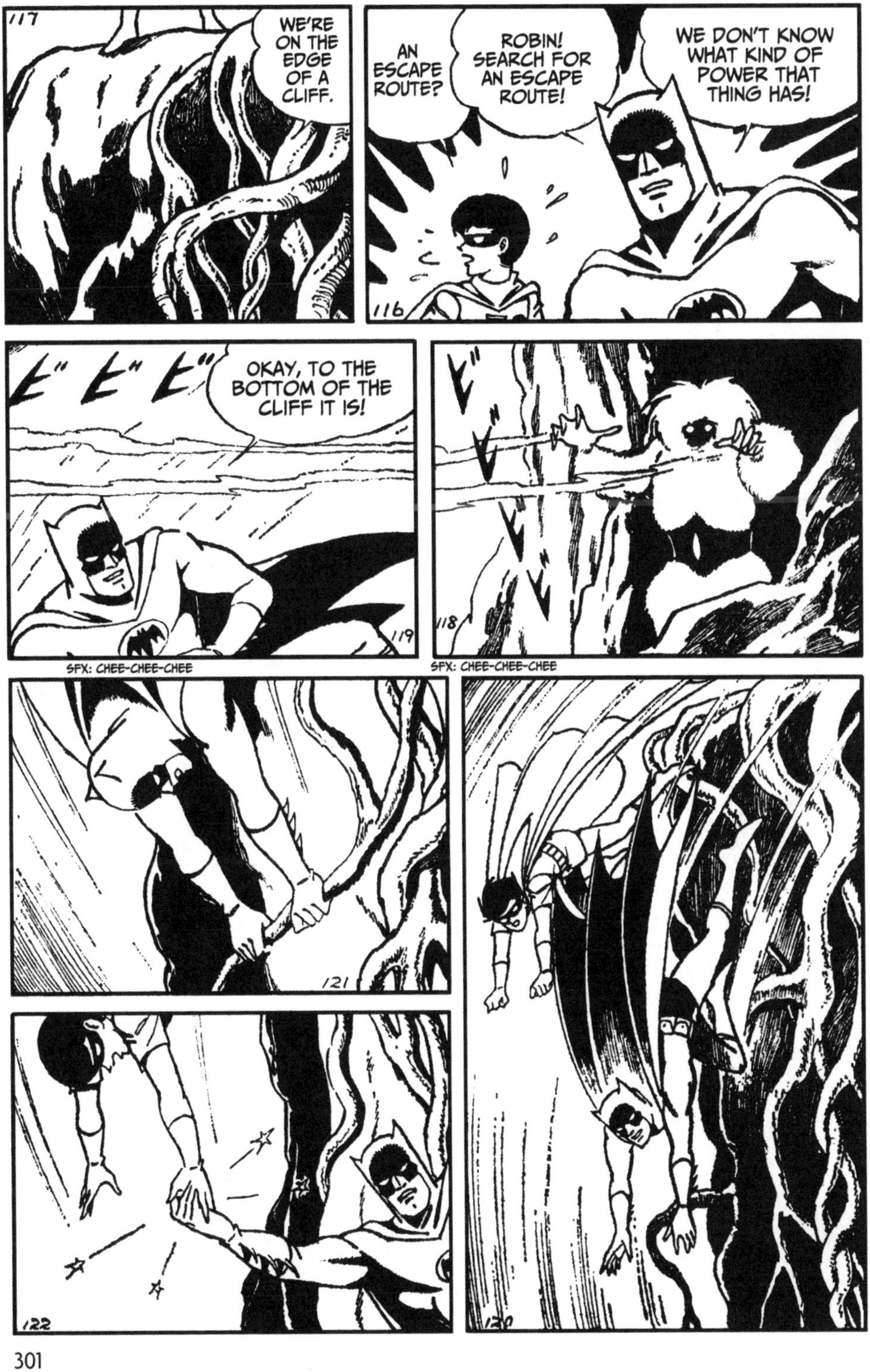
WE DON'T KNOW WHAT KIND OF POWER THAT THING HAS!
ROBIN! SEARCH FOR AN ESCAPE ROUTE!
AN ESCAPE ROUTE?
WE'RE ON THE EDGE OF A CLIFF.
SFX: CHEE-CHEE-CHEE
OKAY, TO THE BOTTOM OF THE CLIFF IT IS!
SFX: CHEE-CHEE-CHEE

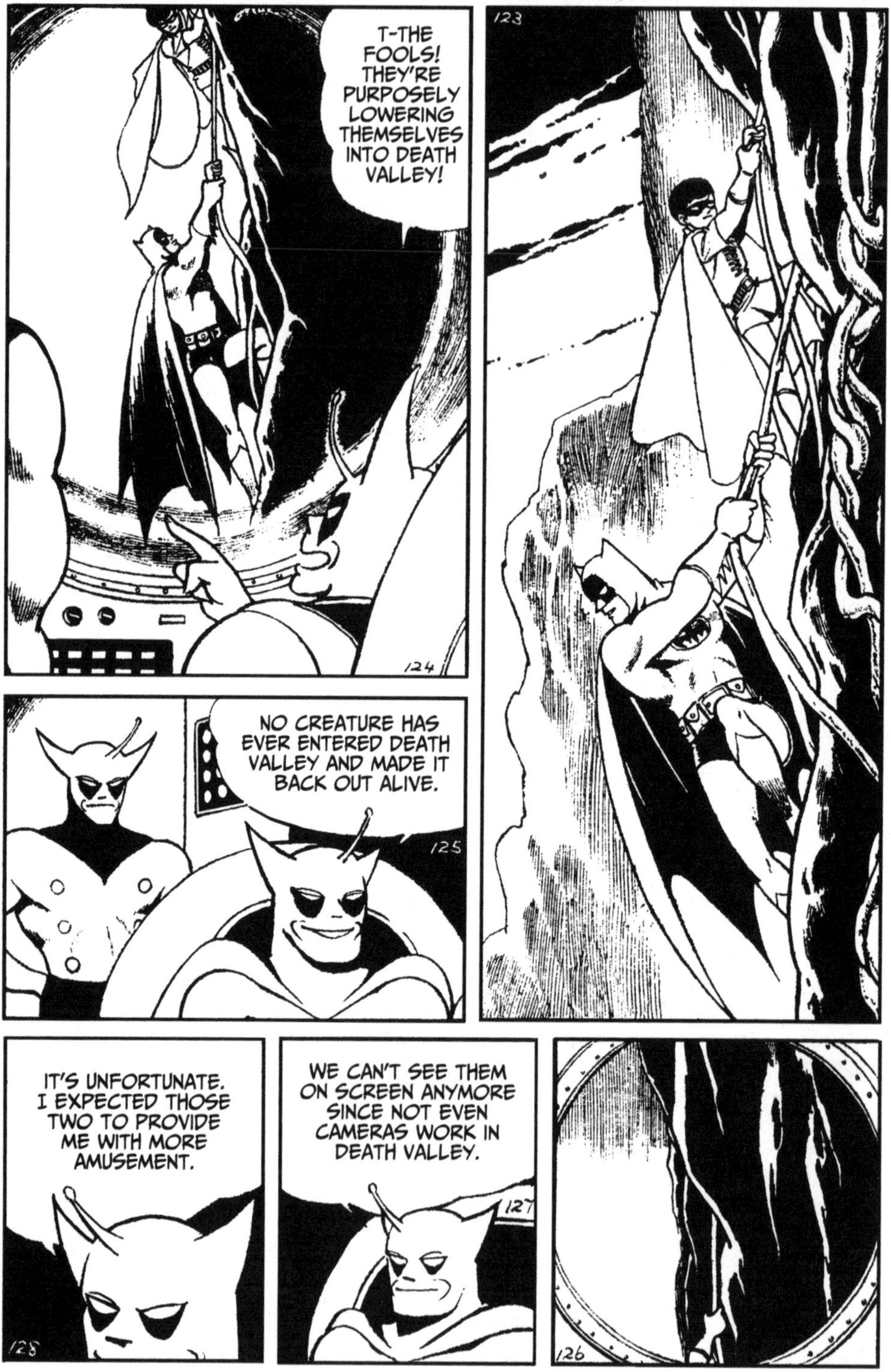
T-THE FOOLS! THEY'RE PURPOSELY LOWERING THEMSELVES INTO DEATH VALLEY!
NO CREATURE HAS EVER ENTERED DEATH VALLEY AND MADE IT BACK OUT ALIVE.
WE CAN'T SEE THEM ON SCREEN ANYMORE SINCE NOT EVEN CAMERAS WORK IN DEATH VALLEY.
IT'S UNFORTUNATE. I EXPECTED THOSE TWO TO PROVIDE ME WITH MORE AMUSEMENT.

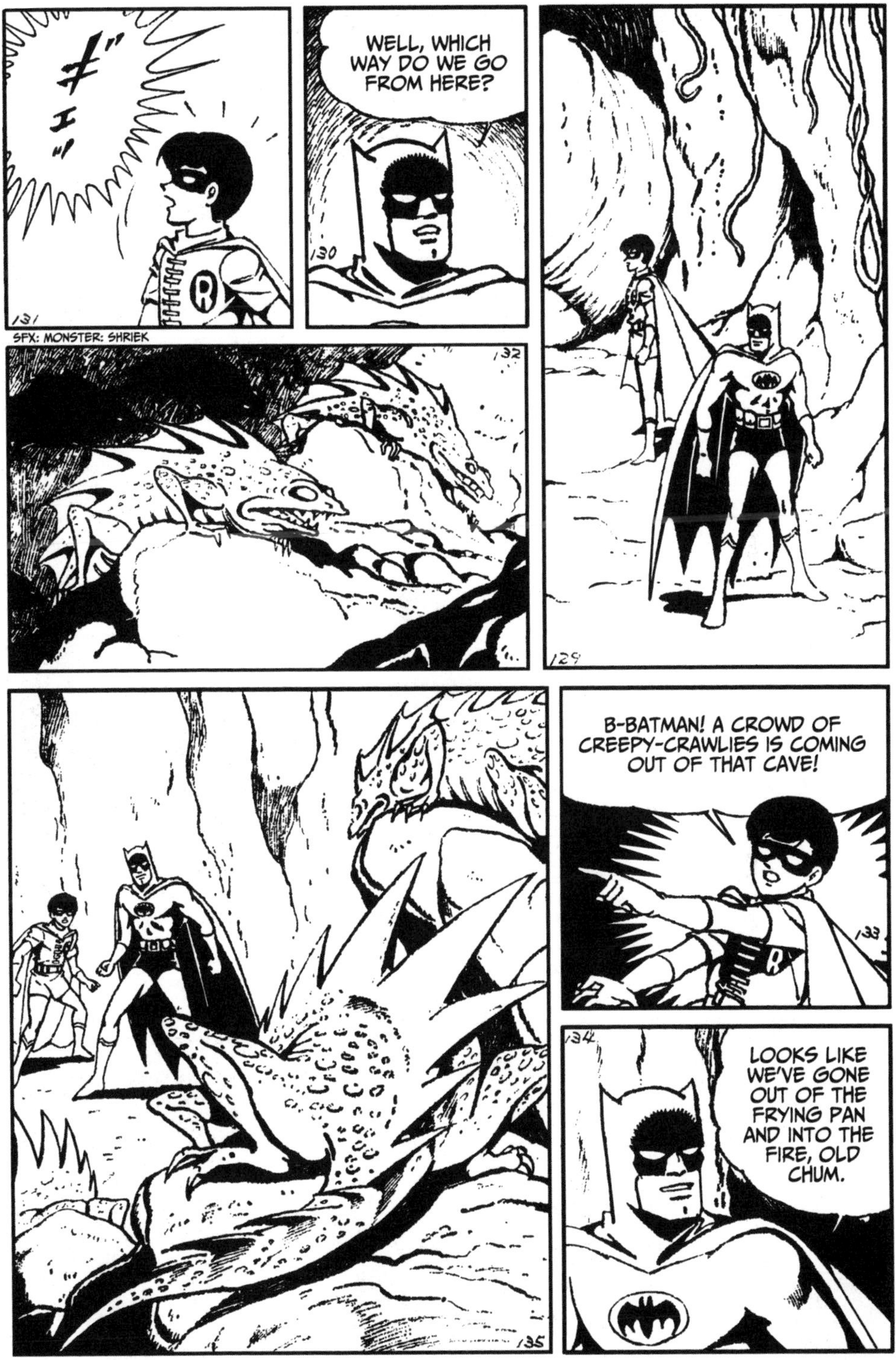
WELL, WHICH WAY DO WE GO FROM HERE?
ギエッ
SFX: MONSTER: SHRIEK
B-BATMAN! A CROWD OF CREEPY-CRAWLIES IS COMING OUT OF THAT CAVE!
LOOKS LIKE WE'VE GONE OUT OF THE FRYING PAN AND INTO THE FIRE, OLD CHUM.

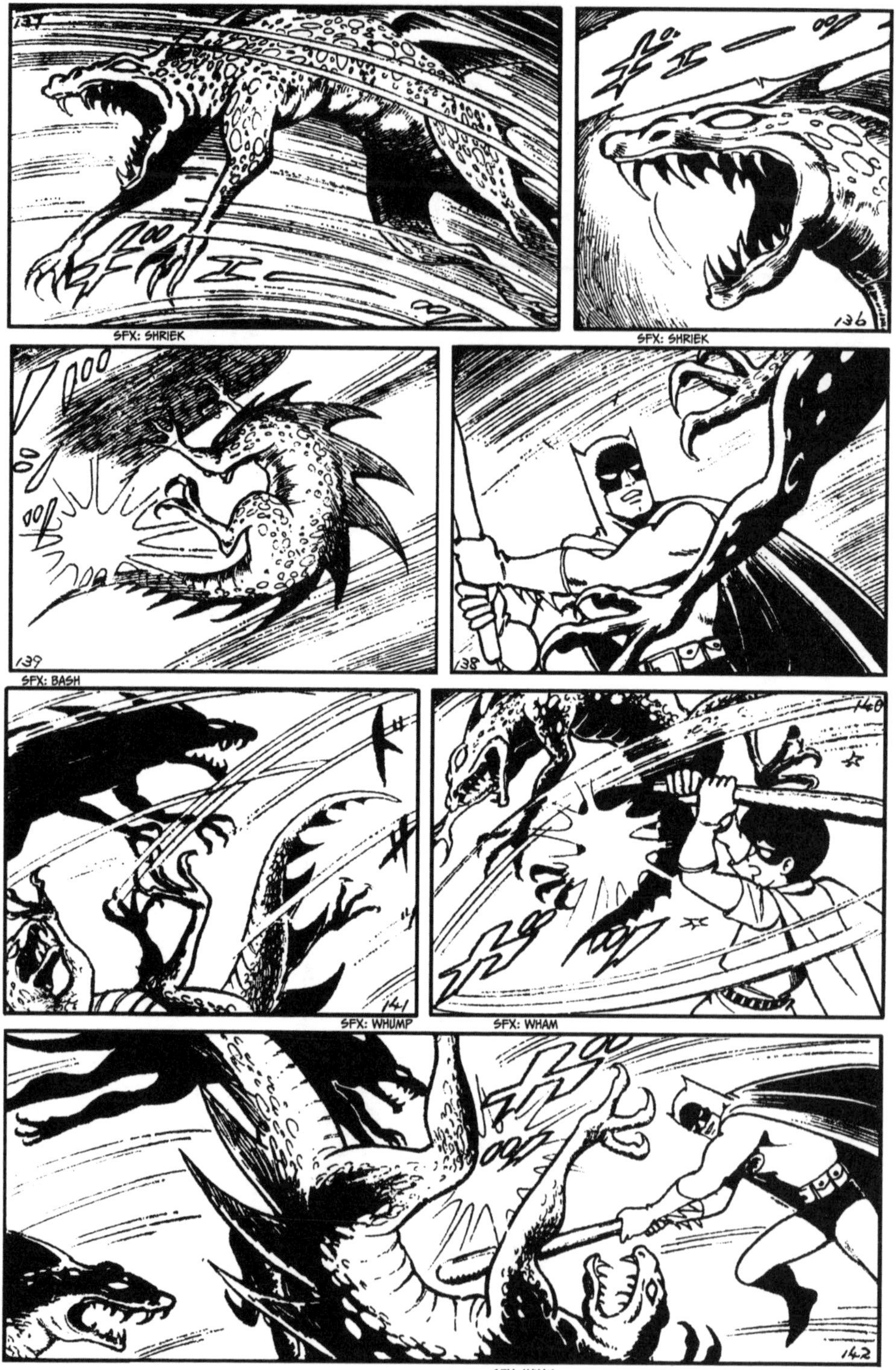
SFX: SHRIEK
SFX: SHRIEK
SFX: BASH
SFX: WHAM
SFX: WHUMP
SFX: WHAK

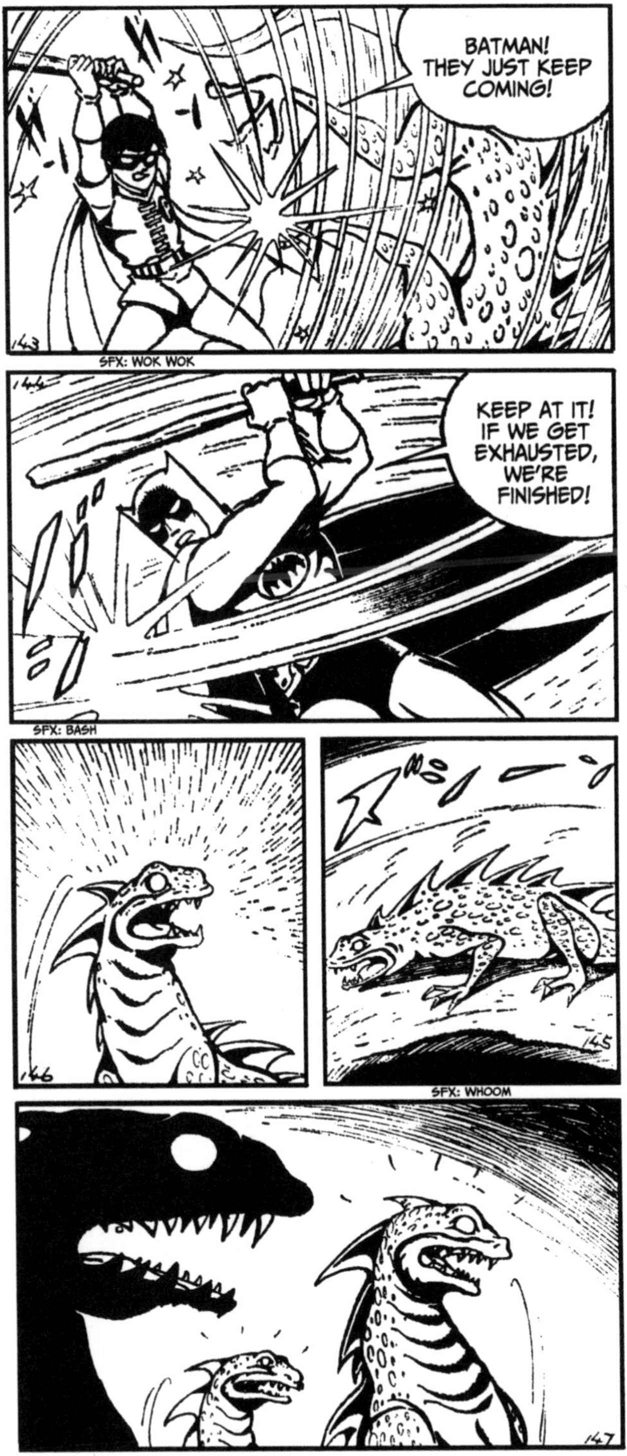
BATMAN! THEY JUST KEEP COMING!
SFX: WOK WOK
KEEP AT IT! IF WE GET EXHAUSTED, WE'RE FINISHED!
SFX: BASH
SFX: WHOOM

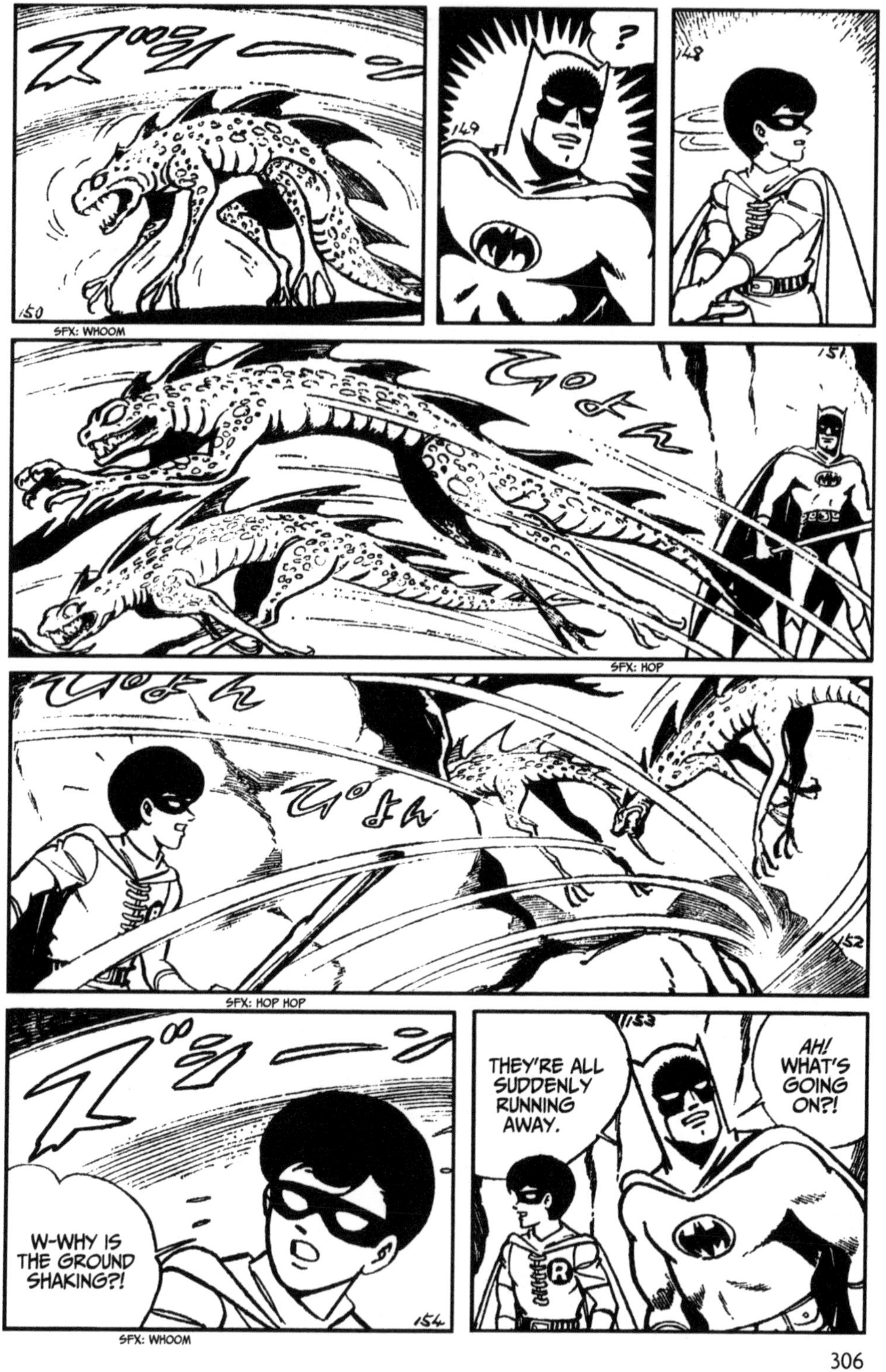
?
SFX: WHOOM
SFX: HOP
SFX: HOP HOP
AH! WHAT'S GOING ON?!
THEY'RE ALL SUDDENLY RUNNING AWAY.
W-WHY IS THE GROUND SHAKING?!
SFX: WHOOM

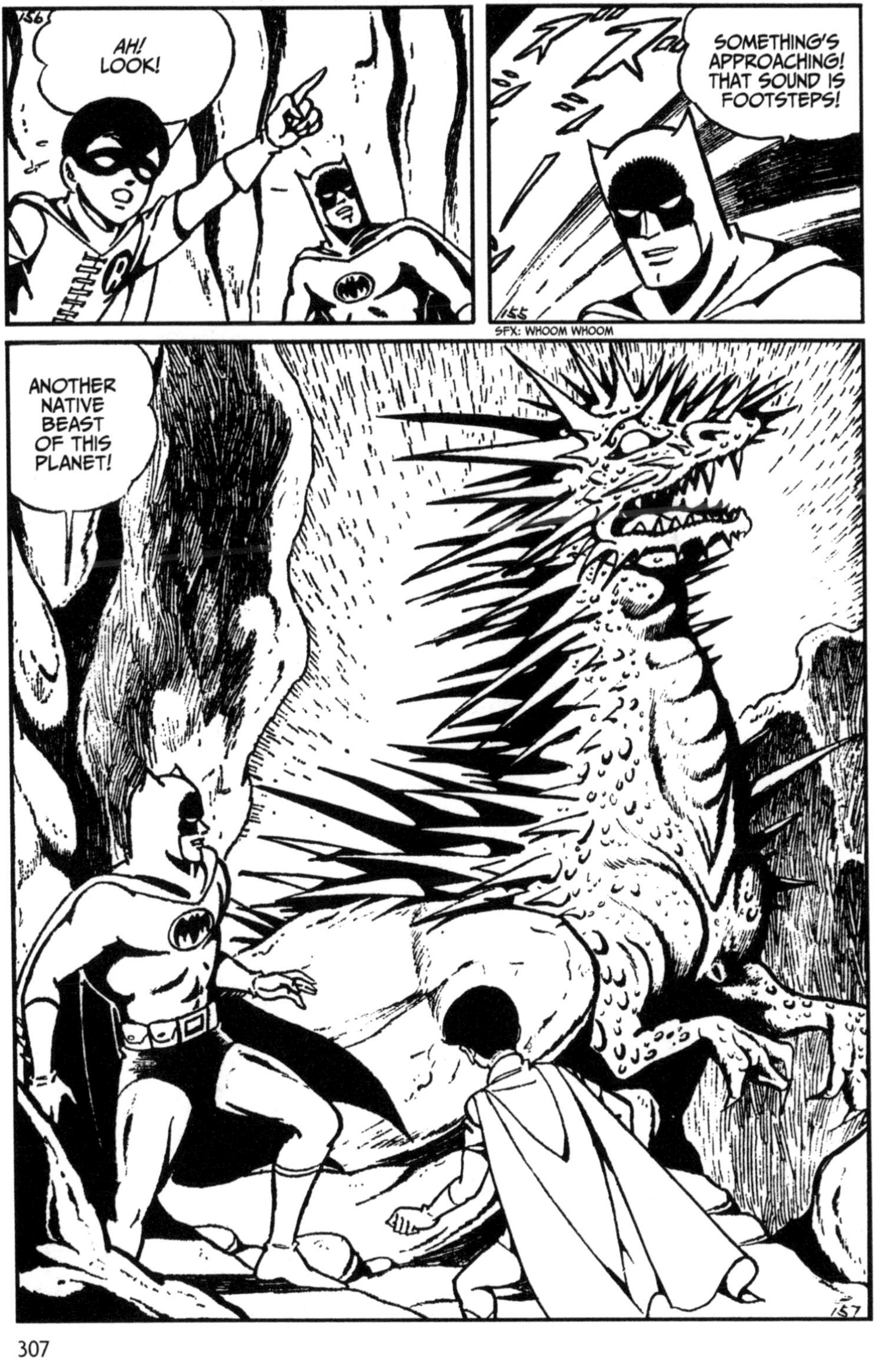
SOMETHING'S APPROACHING! THAT SOUND IS FOOTSTEPS!
SFX: WHOOM WHOOM
AH! LOOK!
ANOTHER NATIVE BEAST OF THIS PLANET!

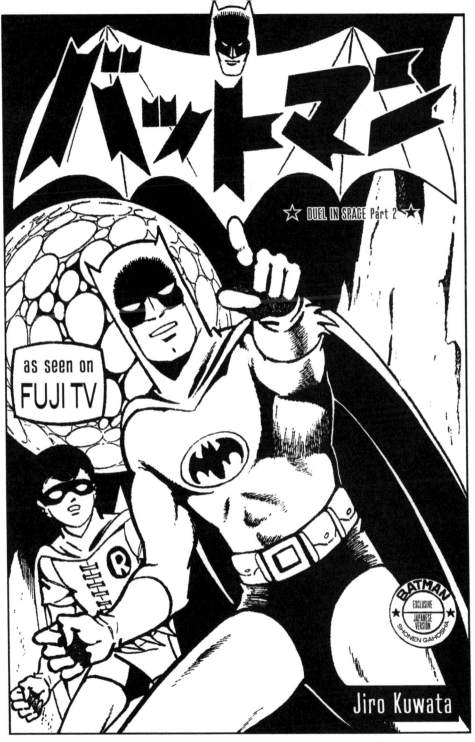

バットマン

☆ DUEL IN SPACE Part 2 ☆

as seen on FUJI TV

BATMAN EXCLUSIVE JAPANESE VERSION SHONEN GAHOSHA

Jiro Kuwata

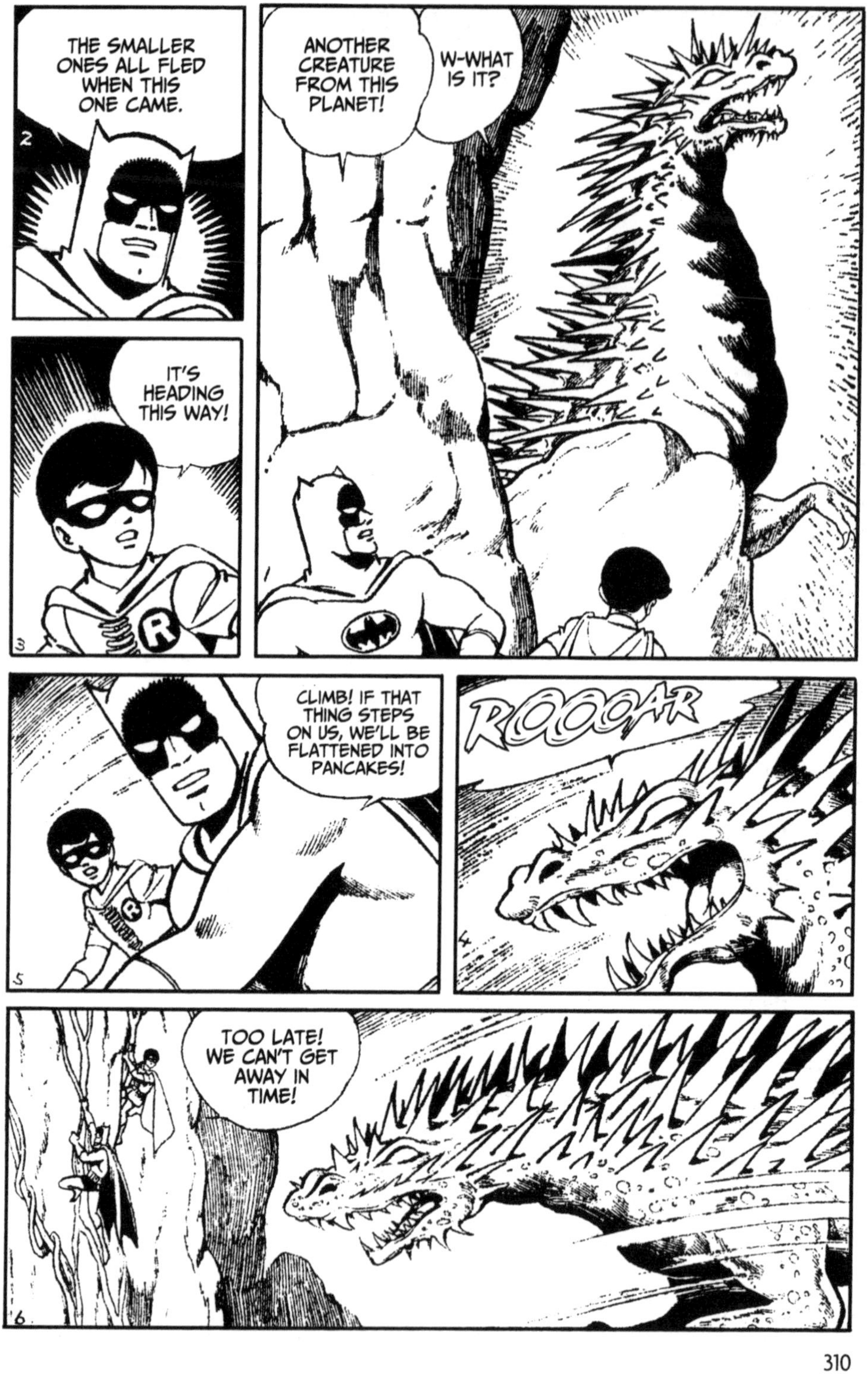
W-WHAT IS IT?
ANOTHER CREATURE FROM THIS PLANET!
THE SMALLER ONES ALL FLED WHEN THIS ONE CAME.
IT'S HEADING THIS WAY!
ROOOAR
CLIMB! IF THAT THING STEPS ON US, WE'LL BE FLATTENED INTO PANCAKES!
TOO LATE! WE CAN'T GET AWAY IN TIME!

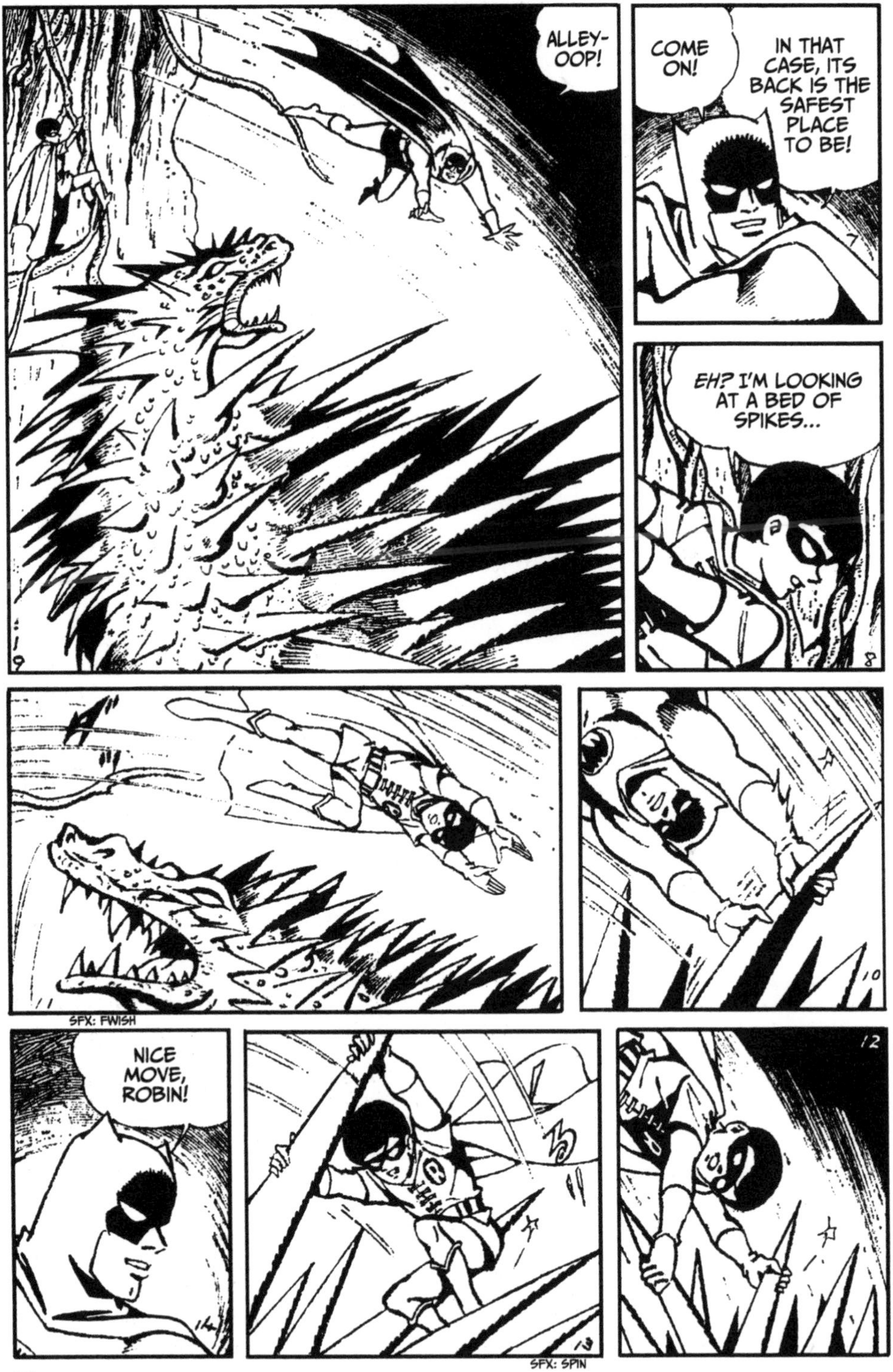
IN THAT CASE, ITS BACK IS THE SAFEST PLACE TO BE!
COME ON!
EH? I'M LOOKING AT A BED OF SPIKES...
ALLEY-OOP!
SFX: FWISH
SFX: SPIN
NICE MOVE, ROBIN!

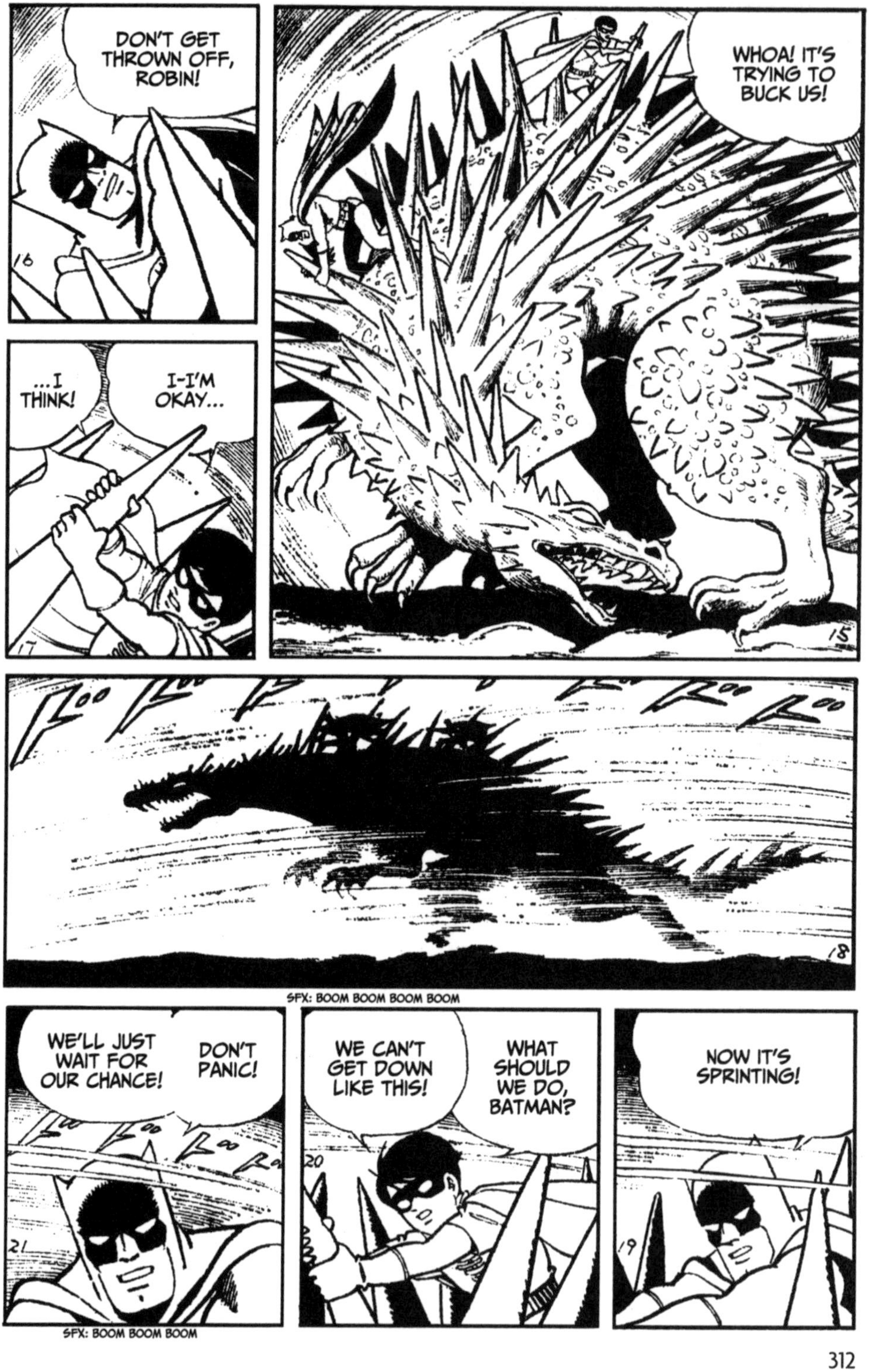
WHOA! IT'S TRYING TO BUCK US!
DON'T GET THROWN OFF, ROBIN!
I-I'M OKAY...
...I THINK!
SFX: BOOM BOOM BOOM BOOM
NOW IT'S SPRINTING!
WHAT SHOULD WE DO, BATMAN?
WE CAN'T GET DOWN LIKE THIS!
DON'T PANIC!
WE'LL JUST WAIT FOR OUR CHANCE!
SFX: BOOM BOOM BOOM

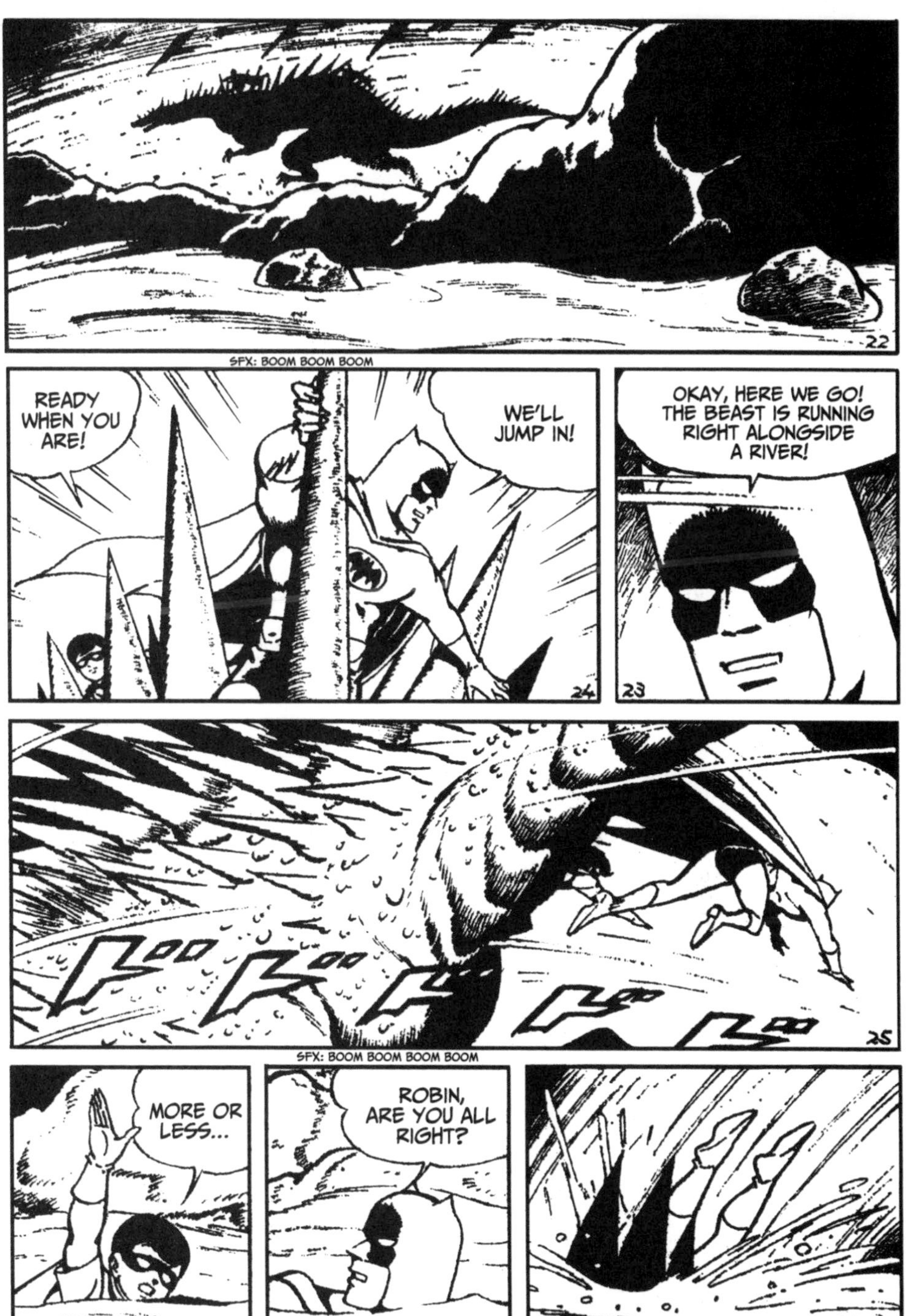
SFX: BOOM BOOM BOOM
OKAY, HERE WE GO! THE BEAST IS RUNNING RIGHT ALONGSIDE A RIVER!
WE'LL JUMP IN!
READY WHEN YOU ARE!
SFX: BOOM BOOM BOOM BOOM
ROBIN, ARE YOU ALL RIGHT?
MORE OR LESS...

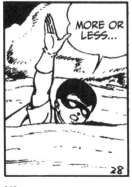

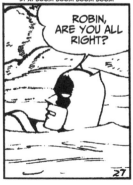

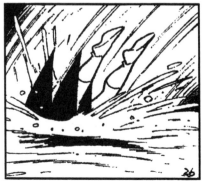

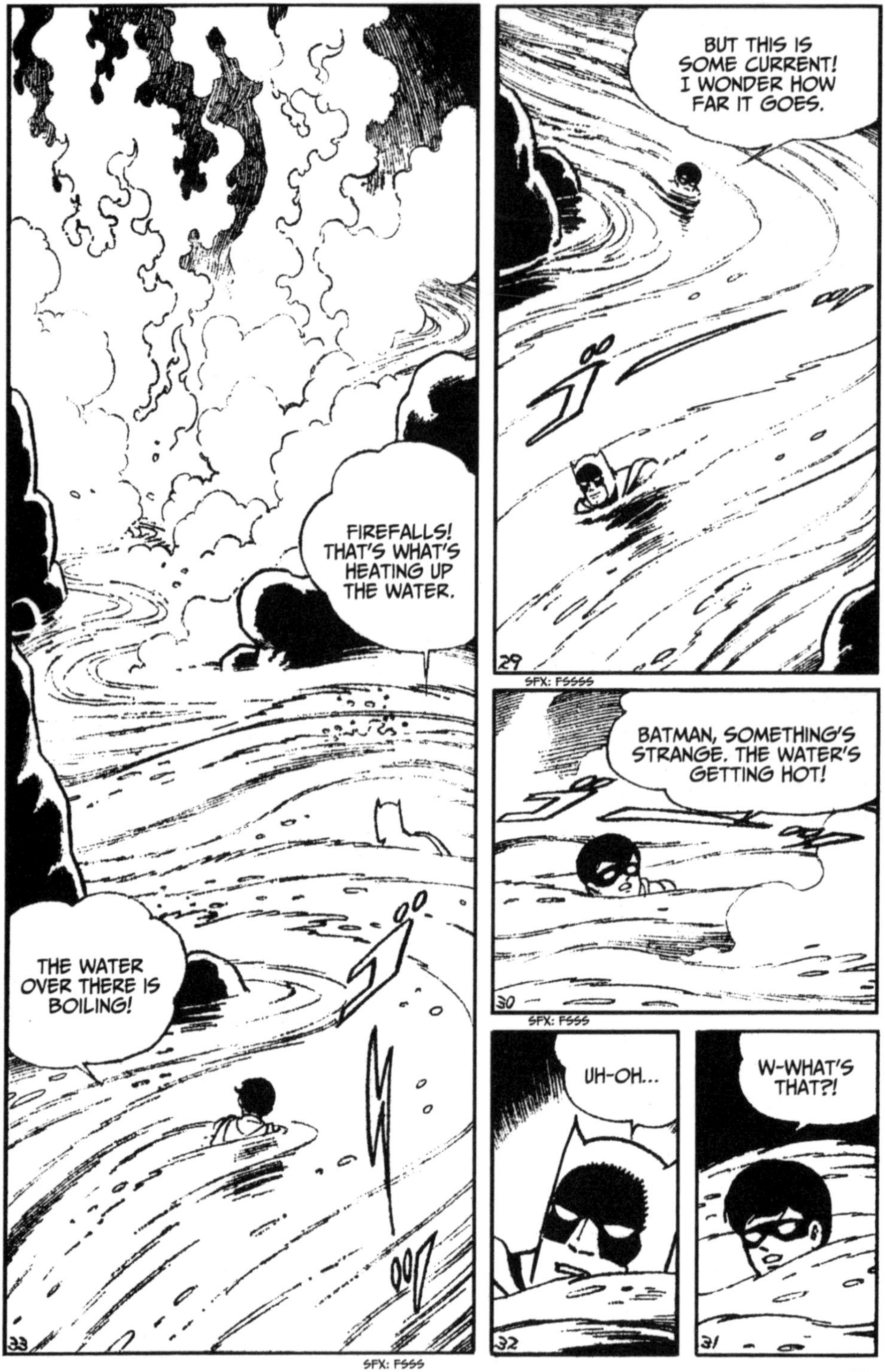
BUT THIS IS SOME CURRENT! I WONDER HOW FAR IT GOES.
SFX: FSSSS
BATMAN, SOMETHING'S STRANGE. THE WATER'S GETTING HOT!
SFX: FSSS
W-WHAT'S THAT?!
UH-OH...
FIREFALLS! THAT'S WHAT'S HEATING UP THE WATER.
THE WATER OVER THERE IS BOILING!
SFX: FSSS

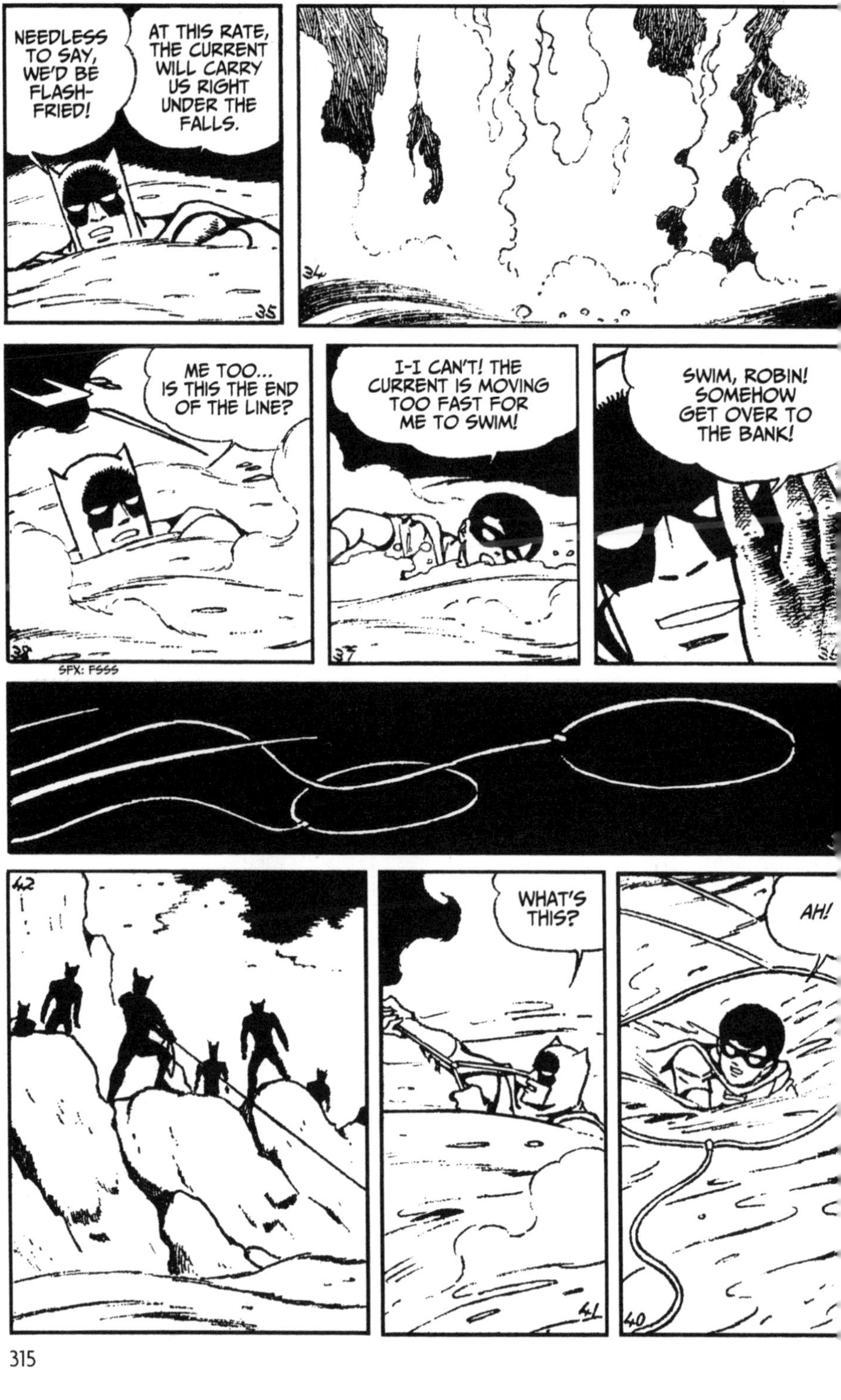
AT THIS RATE, THE CURRENT WILL CARRY US RIGHT UNDER THE FALLS.
NEEDLESS TO SAY, WE'D BE FLASH-FRIED!
SWIM, ROBIN! SOMEHOW GET OVER TO THE BANK!
I-I CAN'T! THE CURRENT IS MOVING TOO FAST FOR ME TO SWIM!
ME TOO... IS THIS THE END OF THE LINE?
SFX: FSSS
AH!
WHAT'S THIS?

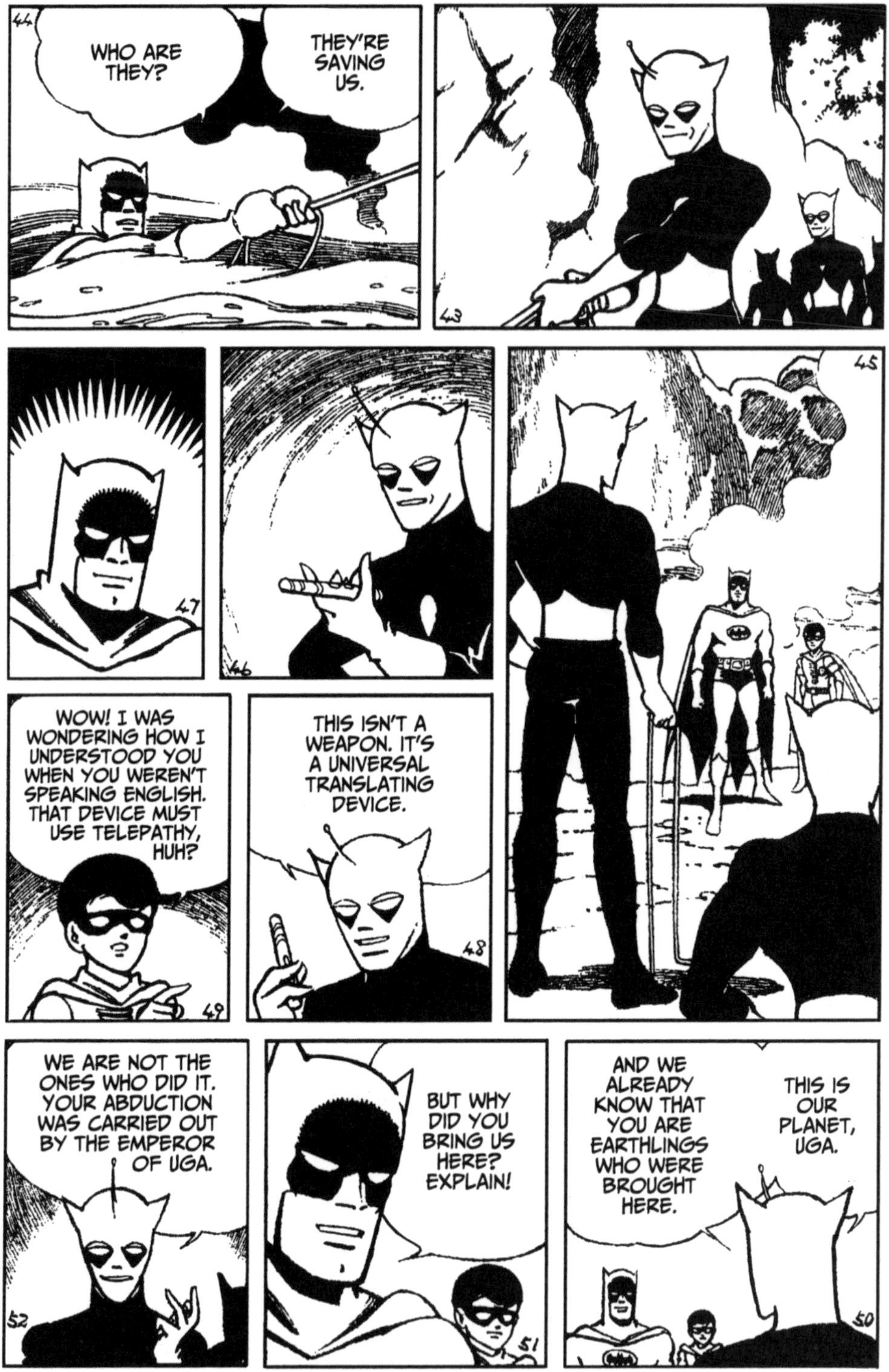
THEY'RE SAVING US.
WHO ARE THEY?
THIS ISN'T A WEAPON. IT'S A UNIVERSAL TRANSLATING DEVICE.
WOW! I WAS WONDERING HOW I UNDERSTOOD YOU WHEN YOU WEREN'T SPEAKING ENGLISH. THAT DEVICE MUST USE TELEPATHY, HUH?
THIS IS OUR PLANET, UGA.
AND WE ALREADY KNOW THAT YOU ARE EARTHLINGS WHO WERE BROUGHT HERE.
BUT WHY DID YOU BRING US HERE? EXPLAIN!
WE ARE NOT THE ONES WHO DID IT. YOUR ABDUCTION WAS CARRIED OUT BY THE EMPEROR OF UGA.

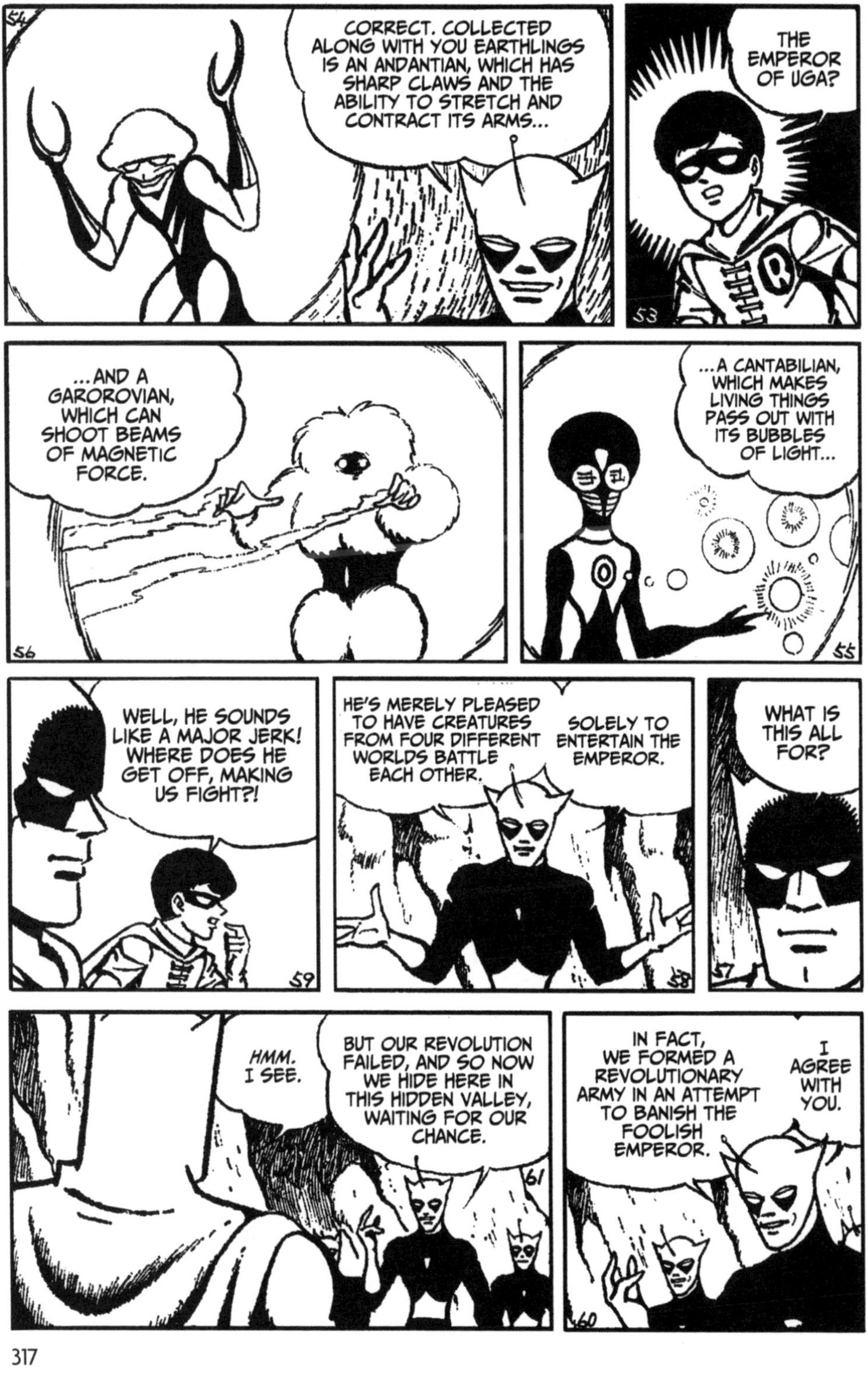
THE EMPEROR OF UGA?
CORRECT. COLLECTED ALONG WITH YOU EARTHLINGS IS AN ANDANTIAN, WHICH HAS SHARP CLAWS AND THE ABILITY TO STRETCH AND CONTRACT ITS ARMS...
...A CANTABILIAN, WHICH MAKES LIVING THINGS PASS OUT WITH ITS BUBBLES OF LIGHT...
...AND A GAROROVIAN, WHICH CAN SHOOT BEAMS OF MAGNETIC FORCE.
WHAT IS THIS ALL FOR?
SOLELY TO ENTERTAIN THE EMPEROR.
HE'S MERELY PLEASED TO HAVE CREATURES FROM FOUR DIFFERENT WORLDS BATTLE EACH OTHER.
WELL, HE SOUNDS LIKE A MAJOR JERK! WHERE DOES HE GET OFF, MAKING US FIGHT?!
I AGREE WITH YOU.
IN FACT, WE FORMED A REVOLUTIONARY ARMY IN AN ATTEMPT TO BANISH THE FOOLISH EMPEROR.
BUT OUR REVOLUTION FAILED, AND SO NOW WE HIDE HERE IN THIS HIDDEN VALLEY, WAITING FOR OUR CHANCE.
HMM. I SEE.

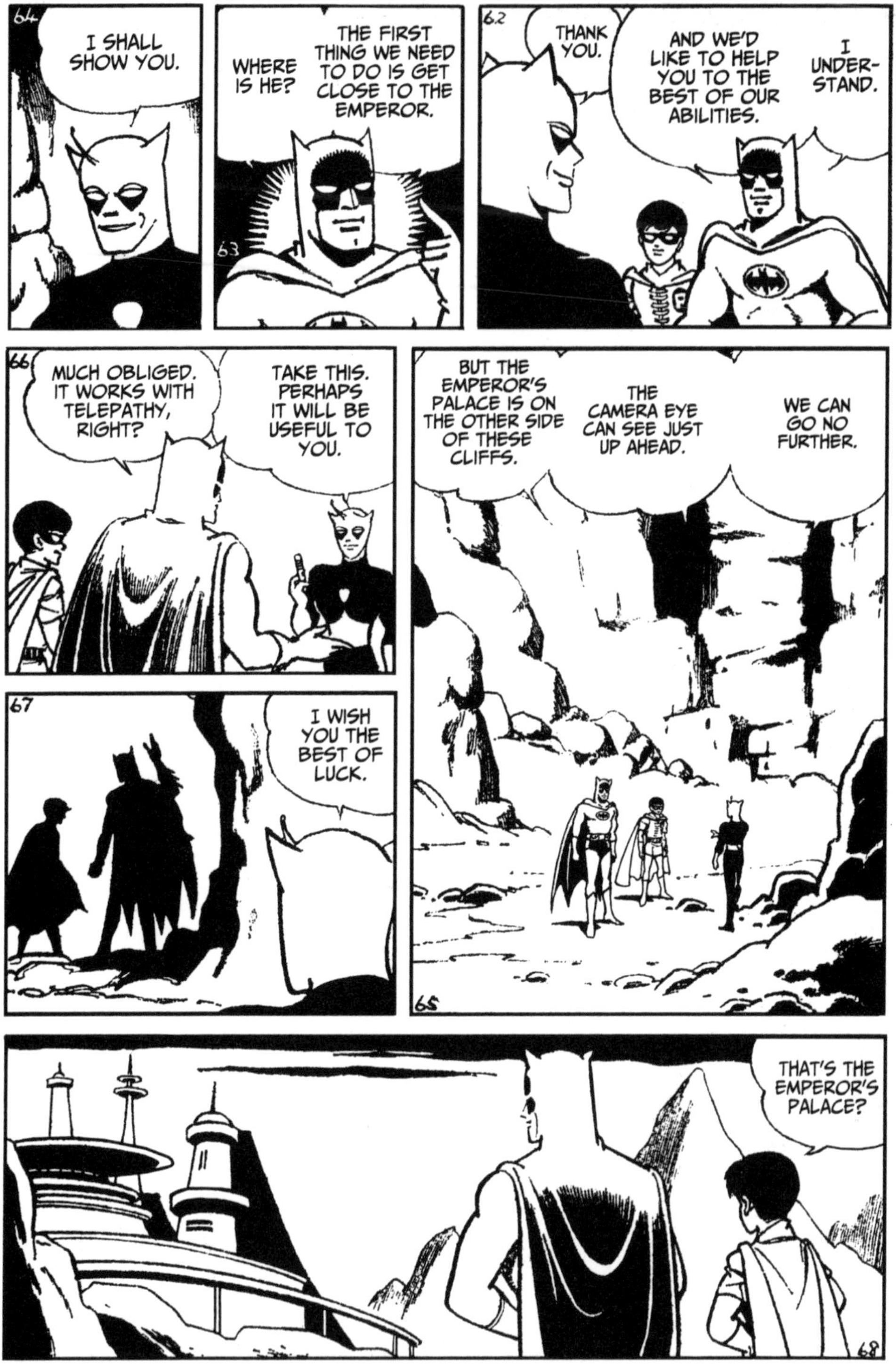
I UNDERSTAND.
AND WE'D LIKE TO HELP YOU TO THE BEST OF OUR ABILITIES.
THANK YOU.
THE FIRST THING WE NEED TO DO IS GET CLOSE TO THE EMPEROR.
WHERE IS HE?
I SHALL SHOW YOU.
WE CAN GO NO FURTHER.
THE CAMERA EYE CAN SEE JUST UP AHEAD.
BUT THE EMPEROR'S PALACE IS ON THE OTHER SIDE OF THESE CLIFFS.
TAKE THIS. PERHAPS IT WILL BE USEFUL TO YOU.
MUCH OBLIGED. IT WORKS WITH TELEPATHY, RIGHT?
I WISH YOU THE BEST OF LUCK.
THAT'S THE EMPEROR'S PALACE?

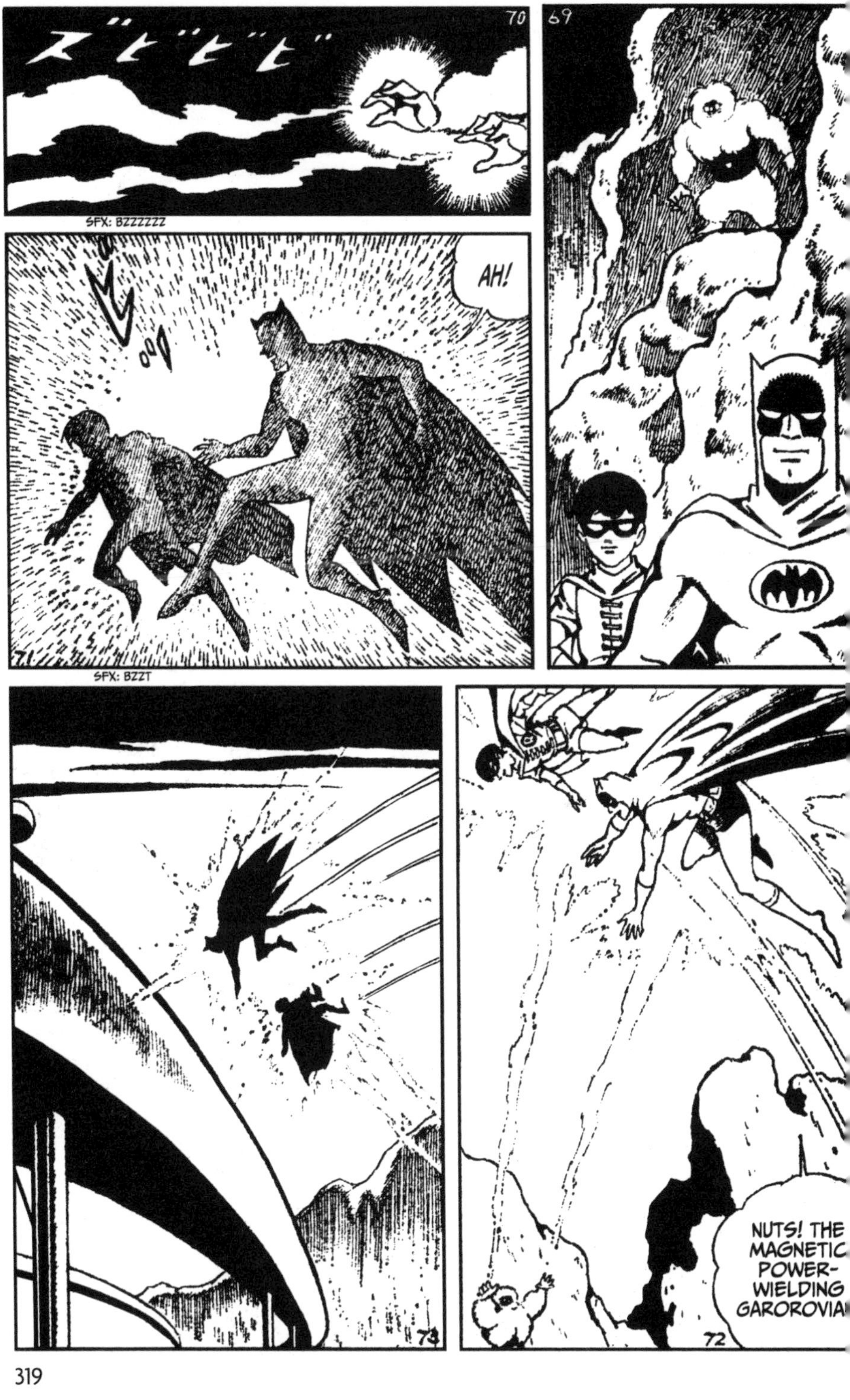
ズドドド
SFX: BZZZZZZ
AH!
SFX: BZZT
NUTS! THE MAGNETIC POWER-WIELDING GAROROVIA

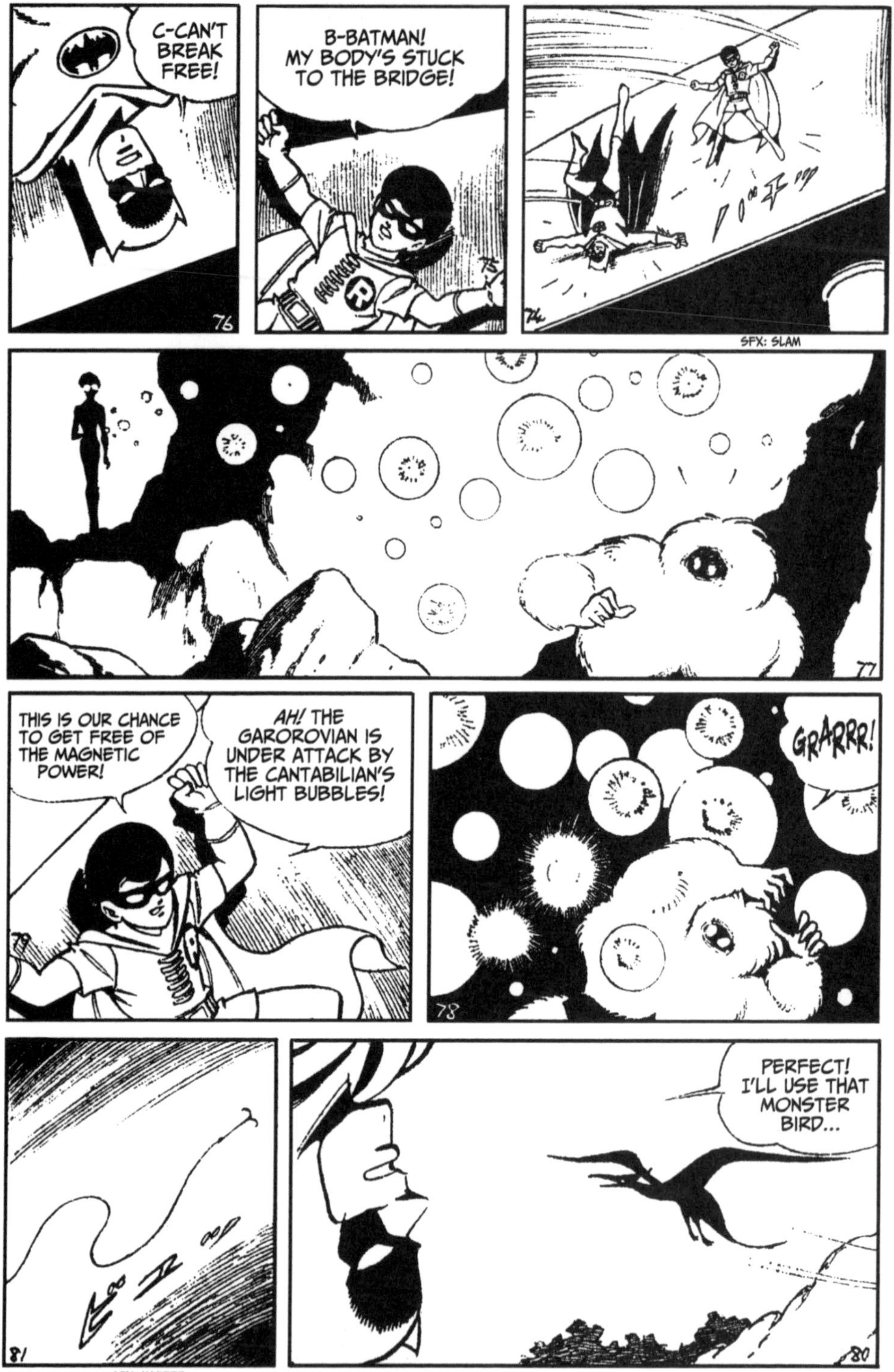
SFX: SLAM
B-BATMAN! MY BODY'S STUCK TO THE BRIDGE!
C-CAN'T BREAK FREE!
GRARRR!
AH! THE GARAROVIAN IS UNDER ATTACK BY THE CANTABILIAN'S LIGHT BUBBLES!
THIS IS OUR CHANCE TO GET FREE OF THE MAGNETIC POWER!
PERFECT! I'LL USE THAT MONSTER BIRD...
SFX: WHIZZZ

MM! IT'S STARTING TO PULL ME OFF!

SHRIEK

NABBED HIM!

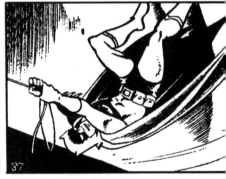

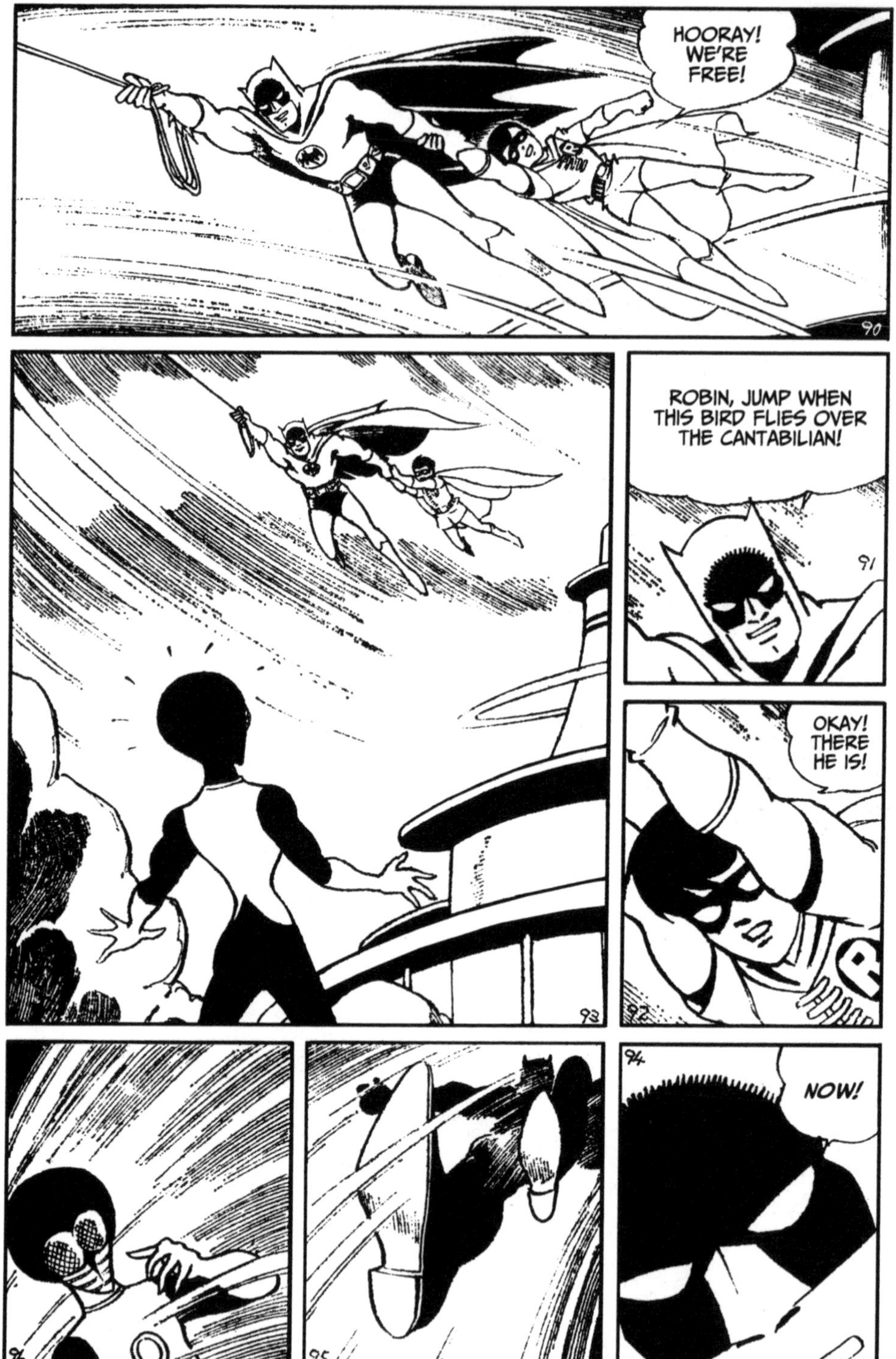
HOORAY! WE'RE FREE!
ROBIN, JUMP WHEN THIS BIRD FLIES OVER THE CANTABILIAN!
OKAY! THERE HE IS!
NOW!

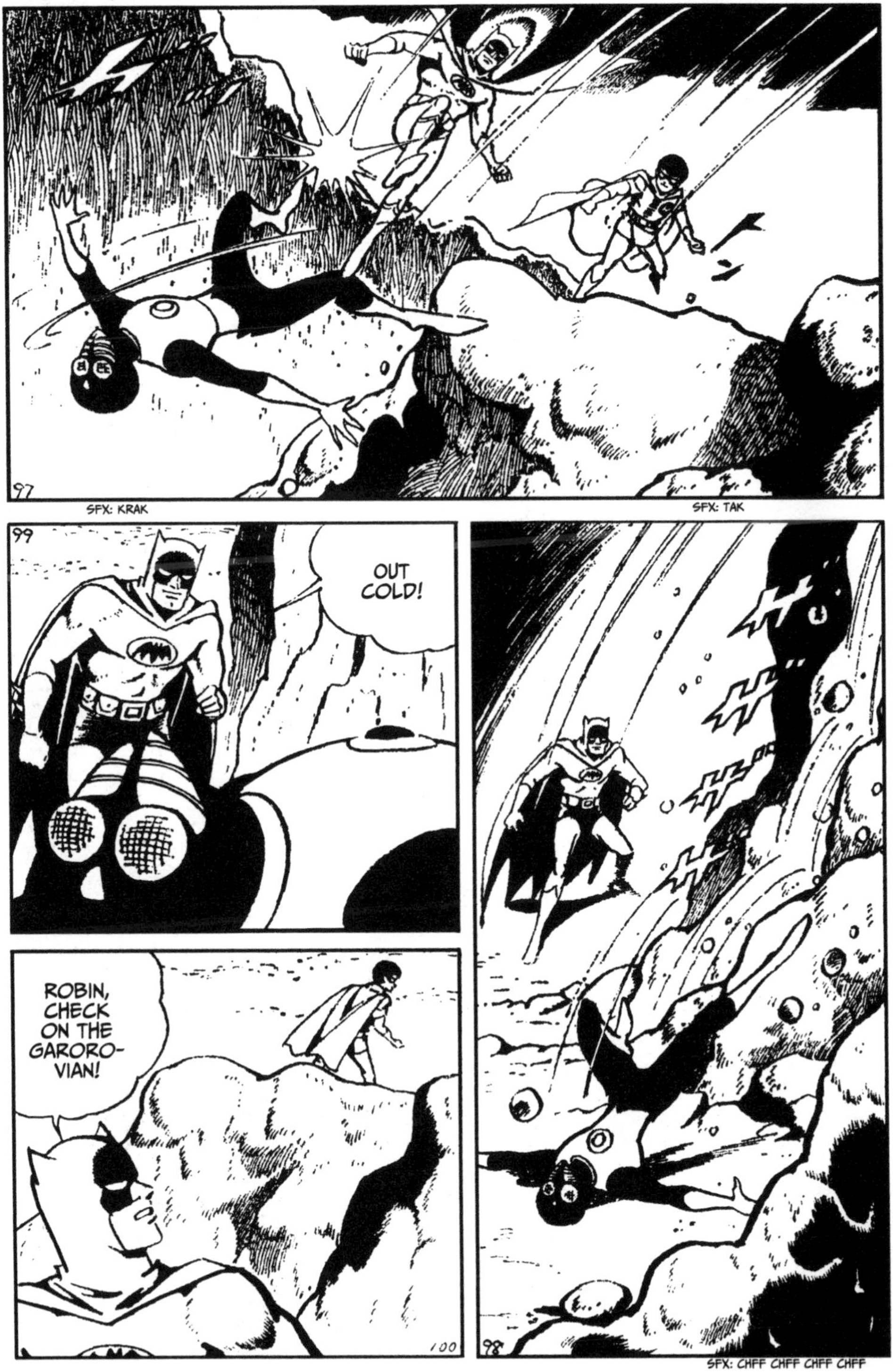
97
SFX: KRAK
SFX: TAK
98
SFX: CHFF CHFF CHFF CHFF
99
OUT COLD!
ROBIN, CHECK ON THE GARORO-VIAN!
100

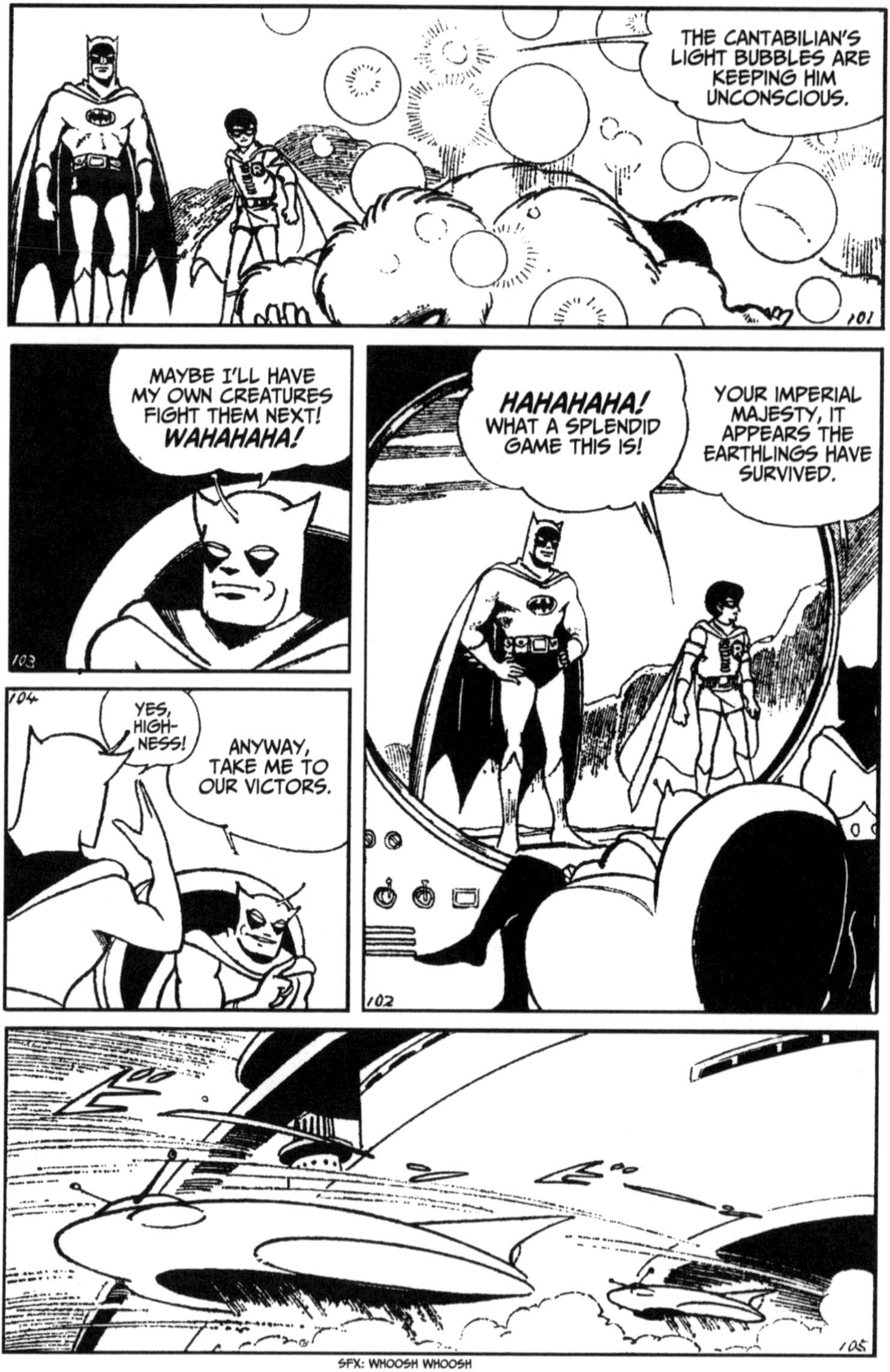
THE CANTABILIAN'S LIGHT BUBBLES ARE KEEPING HIM UNCONSCIOUS.
YOUR IMPERIAL MAJESTY, IT APPEARS THE EARTHLINGS HAVE SURVIVED.
HAHAHAHA! WHAT A SPLENDID GAME THIS IS!
MAYBE I'LL HAVE MY OWN CREATURES FIGHT THEM NEXT! ***WAHAHAHA!***
ANYWAY, TAKE ME TO OUR VICTORS.
YES, HIGH-NESS!

SFX: WHOOSH WHOOSH

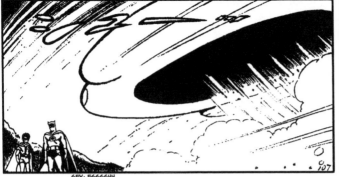

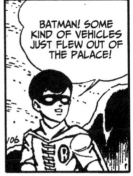

BATMAN! SOME KIND OF VEHICLES JUST FLEW OUT OF THE PALACE!
SFX: FSSSSHH
GET ON BOARD, EARTHLINGS. YOU'RE INVITED TO MY PALACE TO CELEBRATE YOUR VICTORY.
BUT FIRST, PLACE THE THREE UNCONSCIOUS ALIENS ABOARD THE OTHER CRAFT.
WHAT SHOULD WE DO, BATMAN?
MM, LET'S PLAY ALONG FOR NOW.
SFX: FSSSHHH

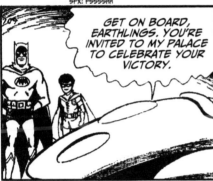

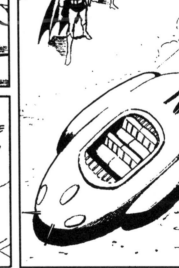

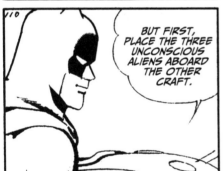

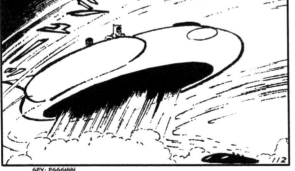

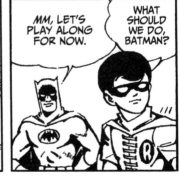

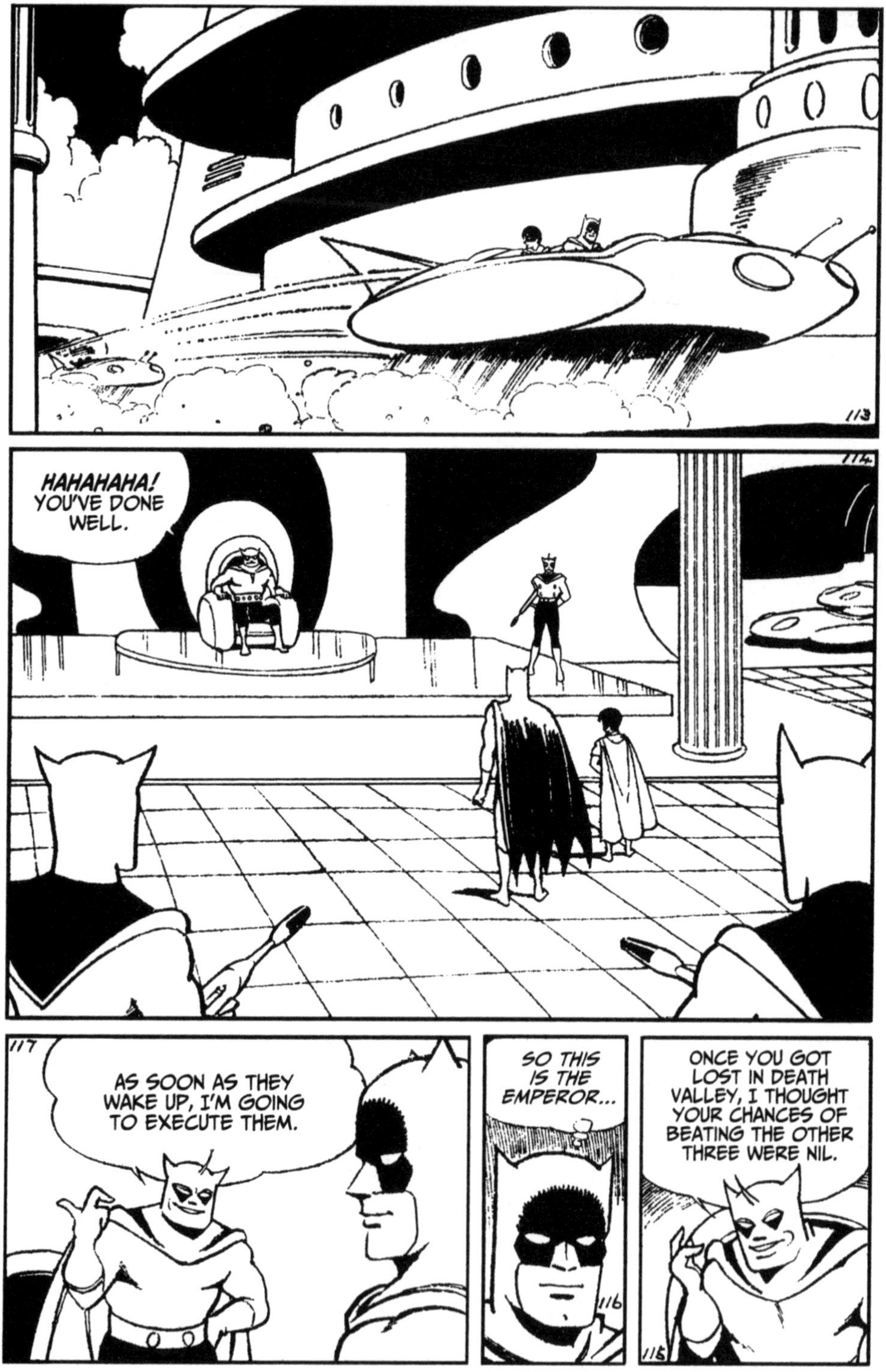
HAHAHAHA! YOU'VE DONE WELL.
ONCE YOU GOT LOST IN DEATH VALLEY, I THOUGHT YOUR CHANCES OF BEATING THE OTHER THREE WERE NIL.
SO THIS IS THE EMPEROR...
AS SOON AS THEY WAKE UP, I'M GOING TO EXECUTE THEM.

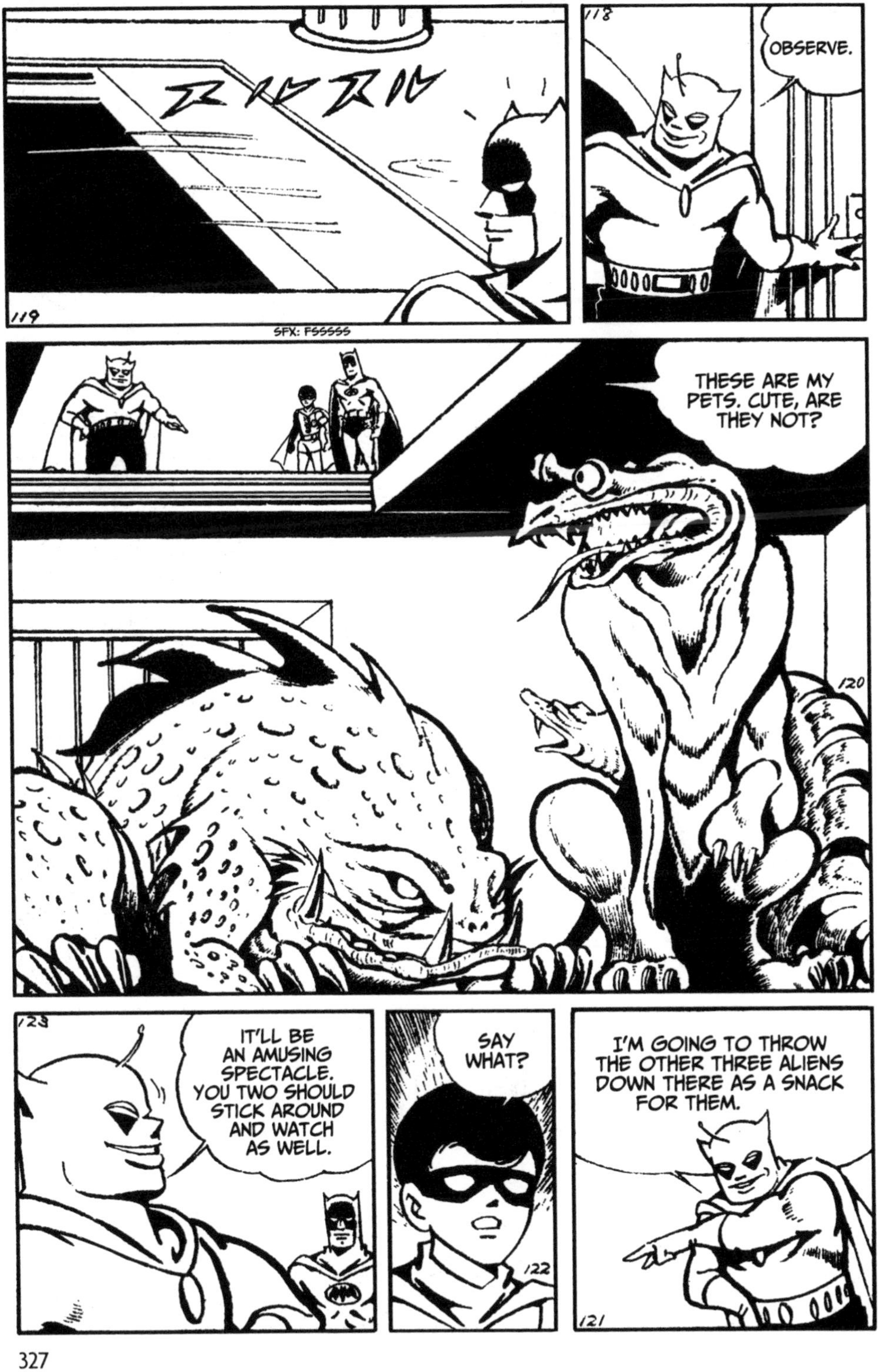
OBSERVE.
SFX: FSSSSS
THESE ARE MY PETS. CUTE, ARE THEY NOT?
I'M GOING TO THROW THE OTHER THREE ALIENS DOWN THERE AS A SNACK FOR THEM.
SAY WHAT?
IT'LL BE AN AMUSING SPECTACLE. YOU TWO SHOULD STICK AROUND AND WATCH AS WELL.

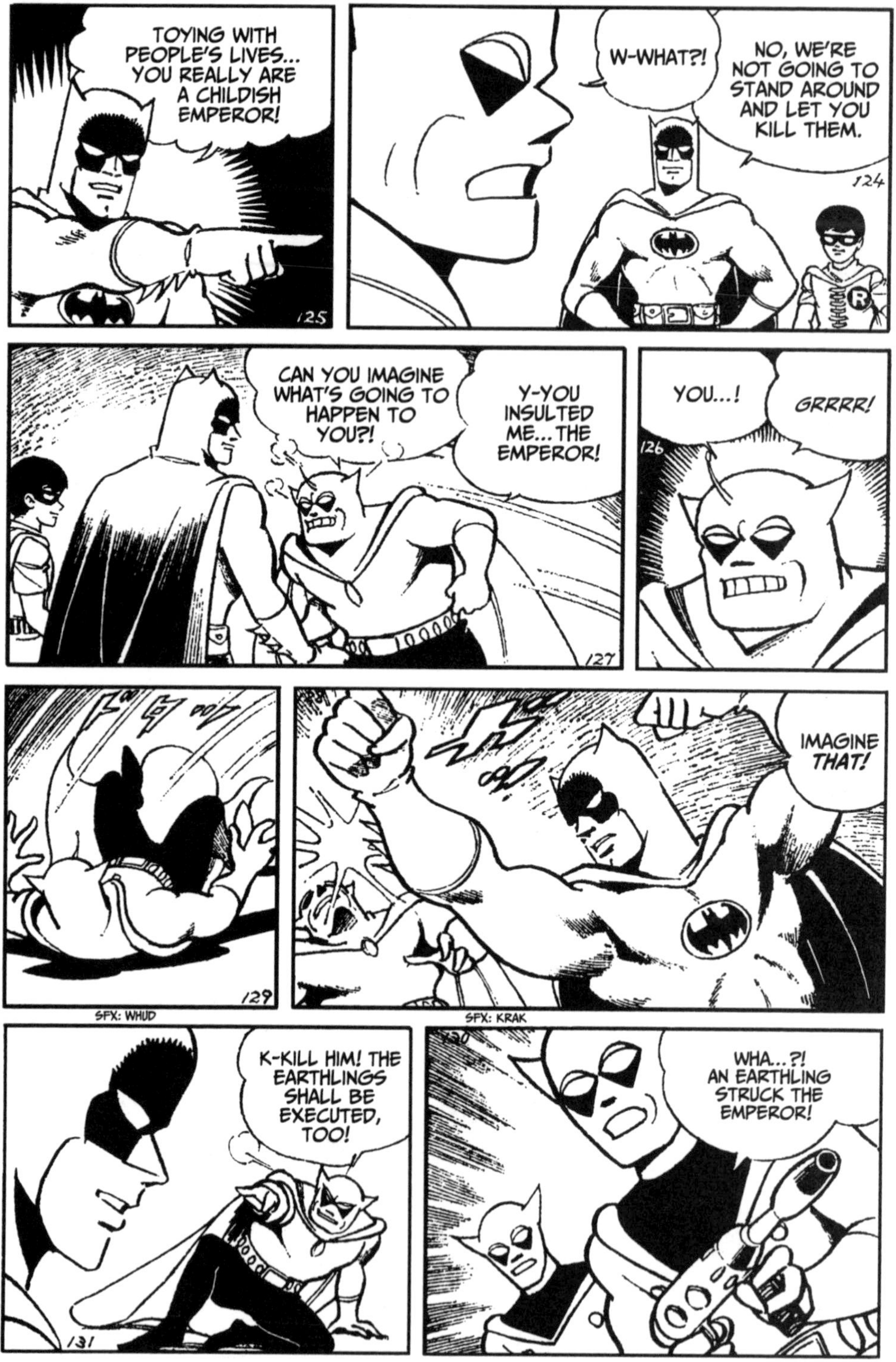
NO, WE'RE NOT GOING TO STAND AROUND AND LET YOU KILL THEM.
W-WHAT?!
TOYING WITH PEOPLE'S LIVES... YOU REALLY ARE A CHILDISH EMPEROR!
GRRRR!
YOU...!
Y-YOU INSULTED ME...THE EMPEROR!
CAN YOU IMAGINE WHAT'S GOING TO HAPPEN TO YOU?!
IMAGINE *THAT!*
SFX: KRAK
SFX: WHUD
WHA...?! AN EARTHLING STRUCK THE EMPEROR!
K-KILL HIM! THE EARTHLINGS SHALL BE EXECUTED, TOO!

SFX: BZZZZ

THE GUNS WERE RIPPED OUT OF OUR HANDS!

134

WAA!

136

OH! THE GAROROVIAN DISARMED THE SOLDIERS!

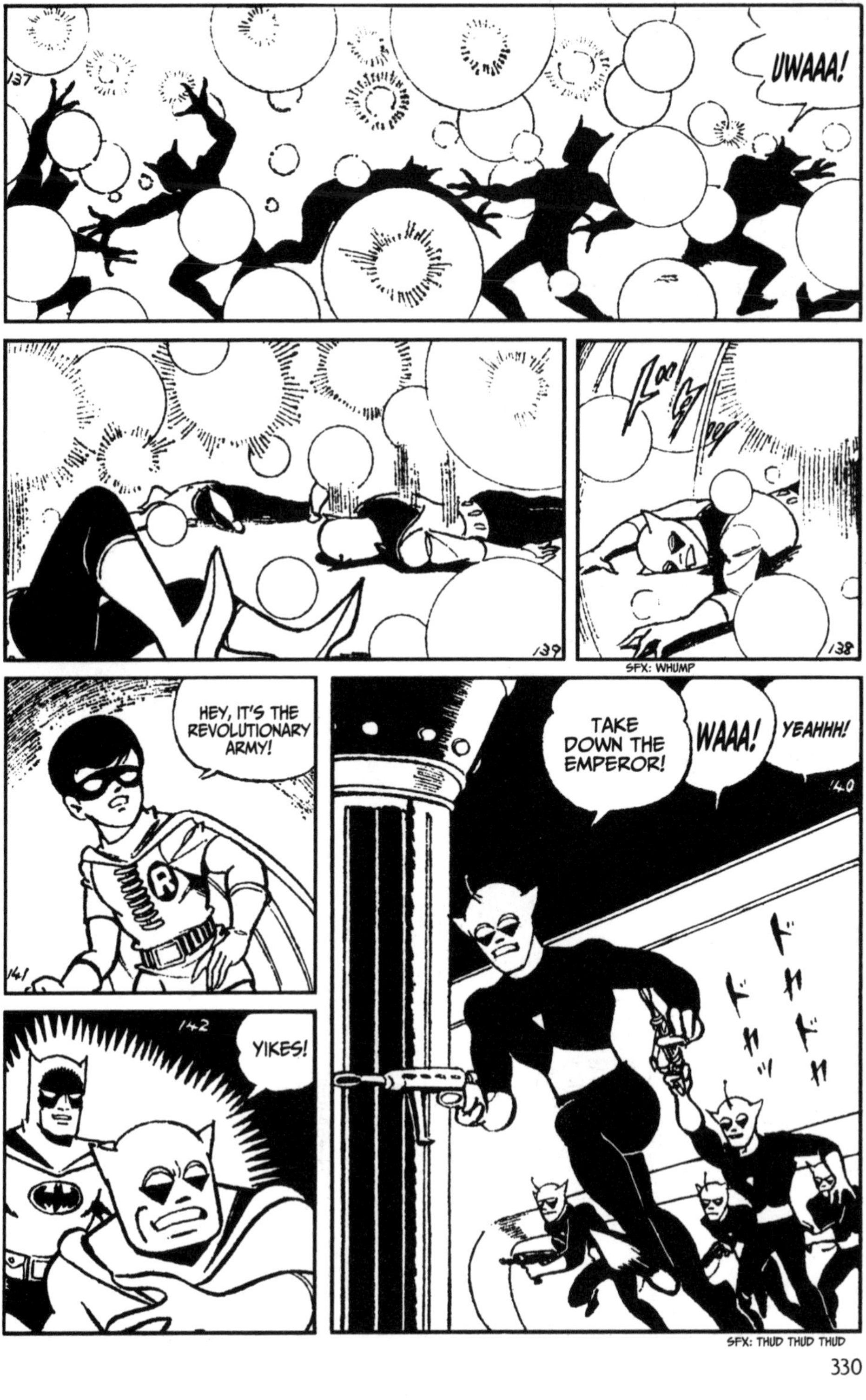
UWAAA!
SFX: WHUMP
YEAHHH!
WAAA!
TAKE DOWN THE EMPEROR!
SFX: THUD THUD THUD
HEY, IT'S THE REVOLUTIONARY ARMY!
YIKES!

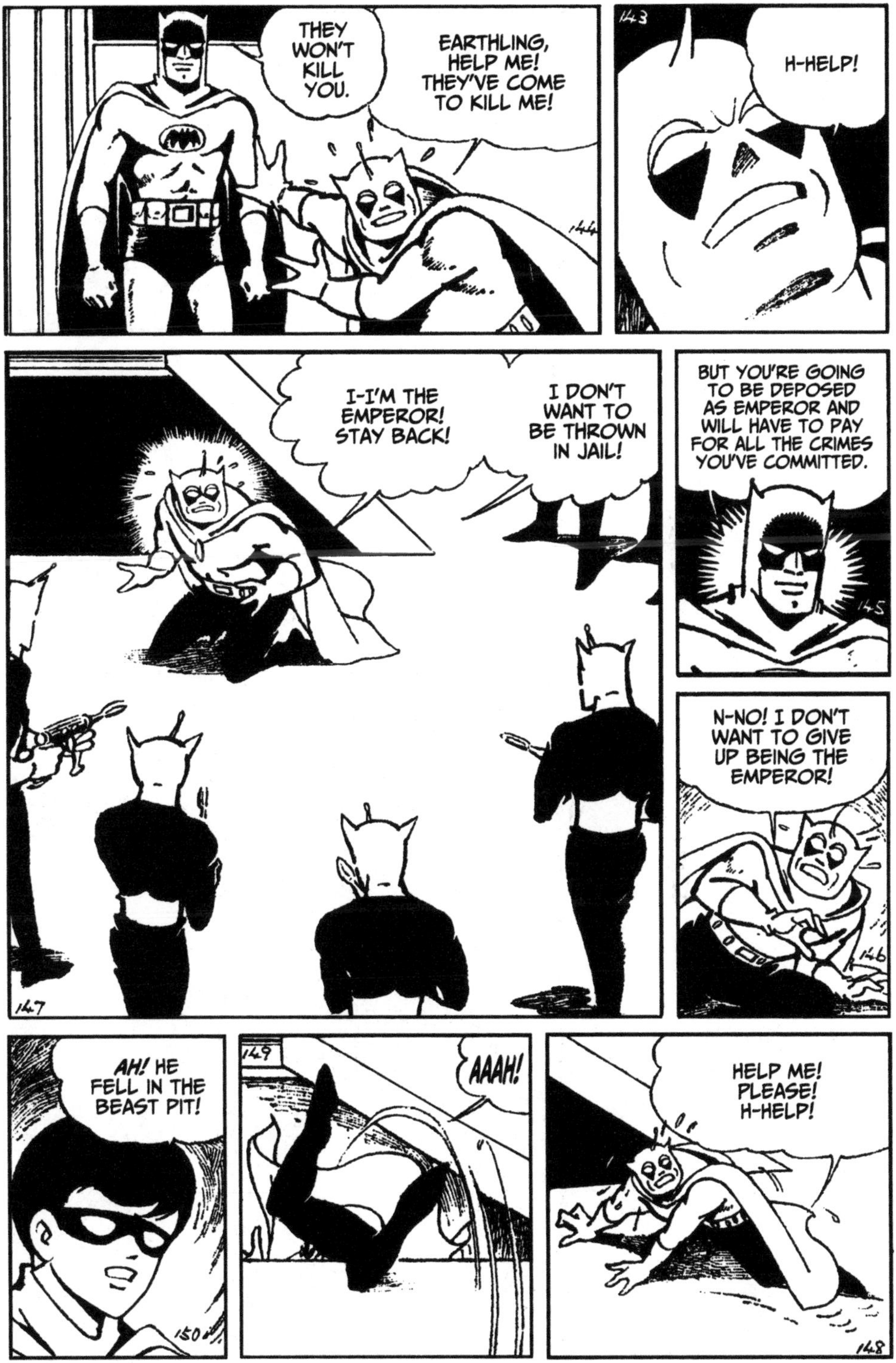
H-HELP!
EARTHLING, HELP ME! THEY'VE COME TO KILL ME!
THEY WON'T KILL YOU.
BUT YOU'RE GOING TO BE DEPOSED AS EMPEROR AND WILL HAVE TO PAY FOR ALL THE CRIMES YOU'VE COMMITTED.
N-NO! I DON'T WANT TO GIVE UP BEING THE EMPEROR!
I DON'T WANT TO BE THROWN IN JAIL!
I-I'M THE EMPEROR! STAY BACK!
HELP ME! PLEASE! H-HELP!
AAAH!
AH! HE FELL IN THE BEAST PIT!

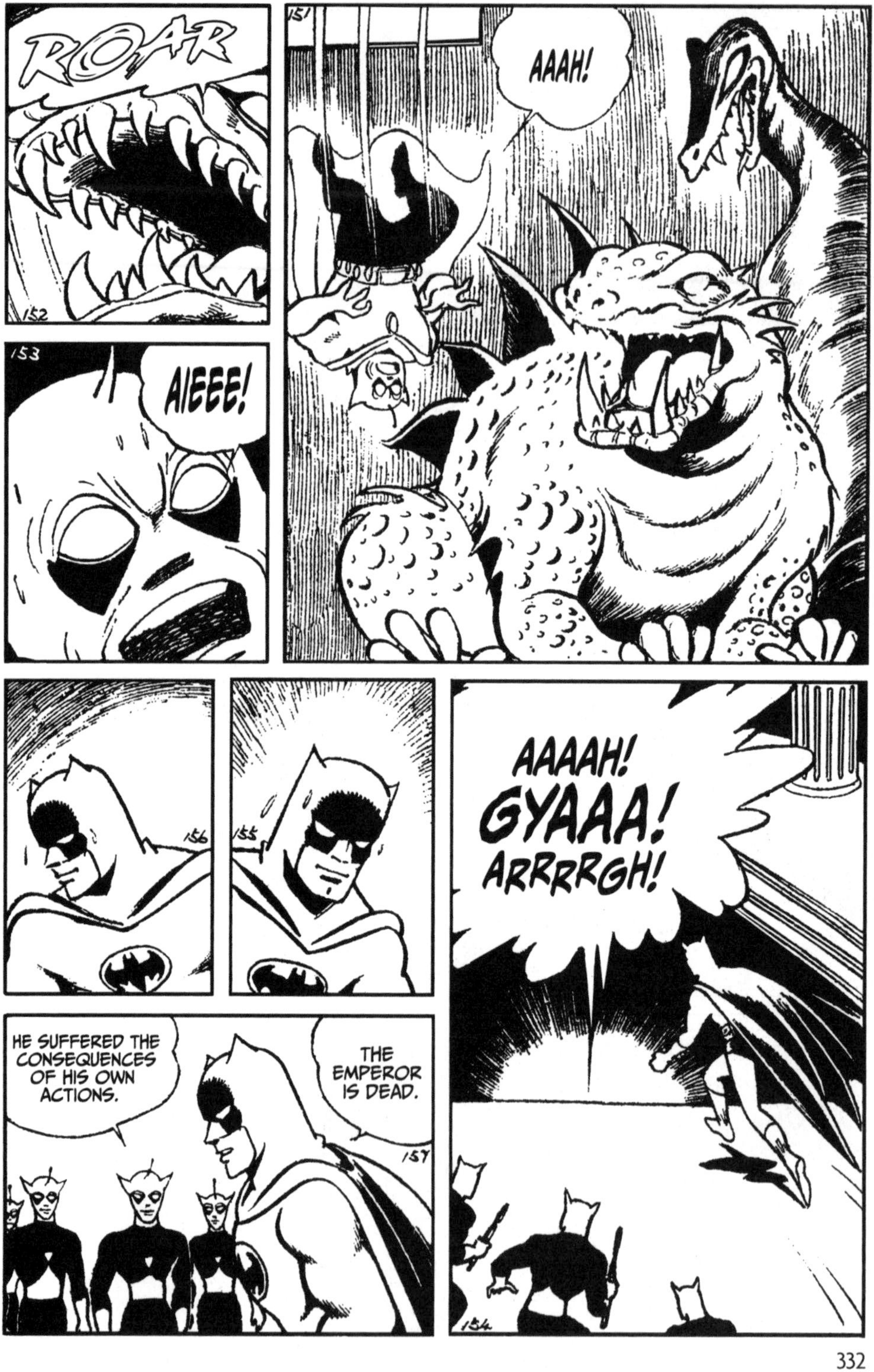
AAAH!
ROAR
AIEEE!
AAAAH!
GYAAA!
ARRRRGH!
THE EMPEROR IS DEAD.
HE SUFFERED THE CONSEQUENCES OF HIS OWN ACTIONS.

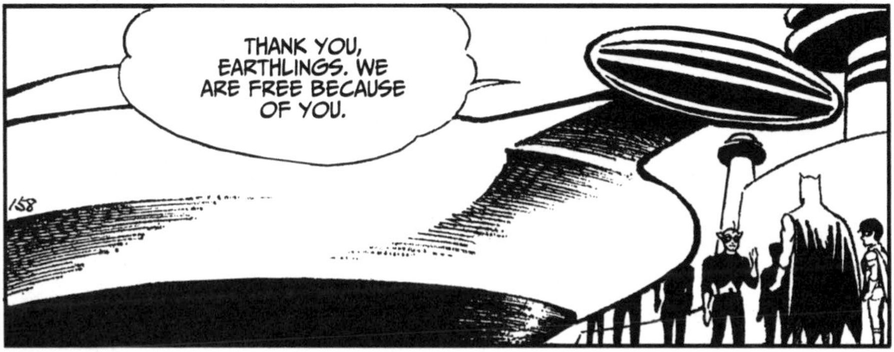
THANK YOU, EARTHLINGS. WE ARE FREE BECAUSE OF YOU.

Soon...

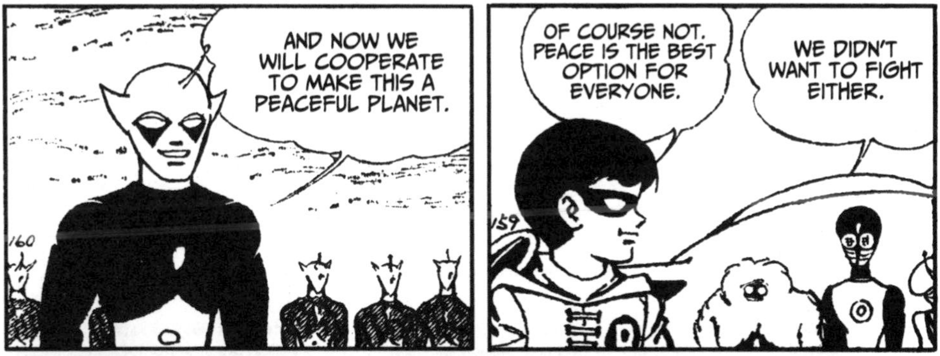
WE DIDN'T WANT TO FIGHT EITHER.
OF COURSE NOT. PEACE IS THE BEST OPTION FOR EVERYONE.
AND NOW WE WILL COOPERATE TO MAKE THIS A PEACEFUL PLANET.

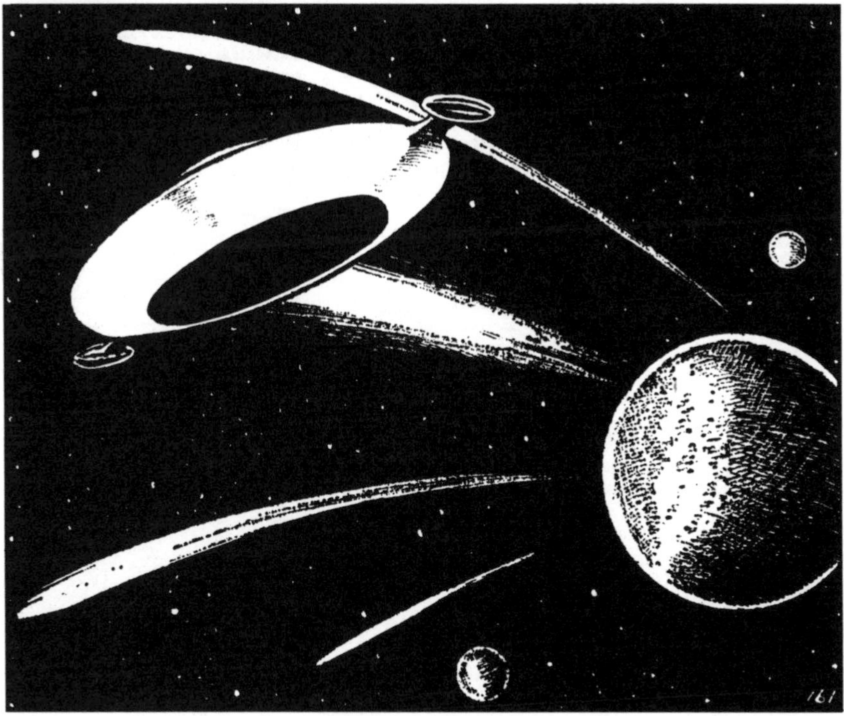

In the end, the flying saucer took home the aliens from all four worlds... including Batman and Robin.

— THE END —

Moonstar magazine ad

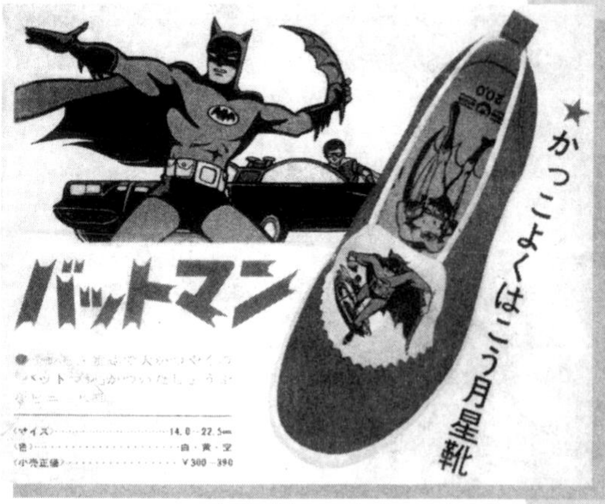
バットマン
かっこよくはこう月星靴

Ad text: These Moonstar Shoes are Cool!

MERCHANDISING

A variety of toys came out to capitalize on the TV show, such as Batman-themed Aoshin tin toys and Imai Kagaku plastic models. While most products were based on the show, the items noted below are confirmed to have been related to the Kuwata version.

Moonstar Shoes: Illustrations on the shoes

Menko: Reproductions from the Kuwata version

Flying Batman: Batarang-style toy

Pasteboard with reproductions from the Kuwata version

Shonen Gaho 20th Anniversary Manga Handkerchief: One illustration

ORIGINAL SOURCE MATERIALS FOR KUWATA'S BATMAN

Lord Death Man	Shonen King #23-25, '66	BATMAN #180
Dr. Faceless	Shonen King #26-28, '66	DETECTIVE COMICS #319
The Human Ball	Shonen King #29-31, '66	DETECTIVE COMICS #347
The Revenge of Professor Gorilla	Shonen King #32-34, '66	DETECTIVE COMICS #339
Go Go the Magician	Shonen King #35-37, '66	DETECTIVE COMICS #353
The Man who Quit Being Human (*3)	Shonen King #38-41, '66	BATMAN #165
The Revenge of Clayface	Shonen King #42-45, '66	DETECTIVE COMICS #304
The Hangman of Terror	Shonen King #46-49, '66	DETECTIVE COMICS #355
Fiend of the Masquerade Festival	Shonen King #50, '66; #1, '67	DETECTIVE COMICS #309
Mystery of the Outsider	Shonen King #2-6, '67	DETECTIVE COMICS #356
The Monster of Gore Bay	Shonen King #7-11, '67	DETECTIVE COMICS #297
The Crimes of Planet King	Shonen King, #12-15, '67	DETECTIVE COMICS #296
Robot Robbers	Shonen Gaho #7-8, '66	BATMAN #42
Clayface	Shonen Gaho #9, '66	DETECTIVE COMICS 298
The Robbery Contest	Shonen Gaho #10-11, '66	BATMAN #152
The Mysterious Catman	Shonen Gaho #12, '66	DETECTIVE COMICS #325
Ghost Batman	Shonen Gaho #1-2, '67	BATMAN #175
Space Duel	Shonen Gaho #3-4, '67	DETECTIVE COMICS #299

SURPRISING ANIME ADAPTATION

On April 1st, 2011, an episode of *Batman: The Brave and the Bold*, airing on America's Cartoon Network, featured the anime adaptation of Kuwata's version of Batman. The episode was markedly different than the rest of the series, with retro touches that closely resembled the 50s and 60s, the ideal episode for an April Fool's joke. The story was inspired by chapters 2 and 3 of the "Lord Death Man" tale published in *Shonen King*. The show's opening was an homage to the *8 Man* anime, while the story had a sepia tone. This is definitely a must-see episode. Currently, it can be seen sporadically in reruns on Japan's Cartoon Network.

(1*) *Bat-Manga! The Secret History of Batman in Japan* (2008). An introduction to Jiro Kuwata's version of Batman and Japan's Batman culture.
(2*) Rocket Tarou (*Interesting Book*, 11/56-11/57). Tarou Temma, who works for the Science Institute of Japan, is actually a descendant of the Atlanteans who went undersea 50,000 years ago. He becomes Rocket Tarou to fight evil.
(3*) The concept for the design of the future human comes from DETECTIVE COMICS #151.

ANALYZING JIRO KUWATA'S "BATMAN"

Mizuki Sugawara (Jiro Kuwata researcher)

PRODUCTION BACKGROUND

At the time, Jiro Kuwata was working on multiple manga series, including *Elite* and *Spade J* for Shonen Gahosha. When *Batman* became a TV series, the same publishing company got an exclusive contract for the rights to adapt the adventures of the Caped Crusader in Japan. Kuwata was tapped to write and draw the series, but to accept the challenge, he had to end his two current series. The editorial department provided Kuwata with the original comics and translated scripts, but he felt they wouldn't go over well as is with Japanese readers, so he used rough approximations of the original stories and scenes, but tailored them for his Japanese audience.

COMPARING TO THE ORIGINAL DC COMICS VERSION

The first memorable episode was published in *Shonen King*, based on the original story from the latest issue of BATMAN at the time, #180. Other current stories were also chosen to be adapted in the pages of *King*. Between the colored title pages, frequent covers of the magazine, introductory articles on the Dark Knight, and many story pages that used two-color printing, it was obvious that Shonen Gahosha was enthusiastic about BATMAN.

The manga version would take the original one-part story and divide it into multiple chapters, devoting about two to three times more pages to the story compared to the original. This allowed dynamic compositions and panel layouts that couldn't be done in the original and made it possible to create a tale with real impact. The merits of this style are especially obvious in "The Man who Quit Being Human." The original story featured a being that resembled the titular *The Amazing Colossal Man*, a movie from 1957, but Kuwata rearranged elements, taking an alien that appeared in a different episode and remaking it into a stylish future human. Kuwata also brought more depth to the tale by adding a daughter that wasn't present in the original.

It took Kuwata about two months to establish his "Batman style" for the series. To present an American superhero comic book atmosphere, he added muscular definition. Back when Kuwata was working on *Elite*, he began drawing scenery in detail, a practice he increased for this series, making the backgrounds even more elaborate. I believe his experience drawing illustrated stories aided him in this regard. Henceforth, the art for all of Kuwata's series had an increasing amount of fine detail, which can probably be traced back to his work on BATMAN.

Hardly any of Batman's regular stable of villains such as the Joker and the Penguin appear in Kuwata's version. It's likely that he deemed characters from nearly 20 years prior to be outdated.

KUWATA'S TAKE ON SUPERMAN

In 1959, before BATMAN, Shonen Gahosha published a Japanese edition of SUPERMAN. Tatsuo Yoshida did the original serialized stories of Superman, but in an interview for *Batmanga!* (*1), Kuwata reveals that he was approached first about doing a Superman series years before BATMAN, but turned the gig down because he was too busy.

Even before that, in 1956, Kuwata did a serialized illustrated story called *Rocket Tarou* (*2). This was Kuwata's first foray into superheroes and was partially an homage to Superman. One can also catch sight of several elements that connect to Kuwata's later hero series.

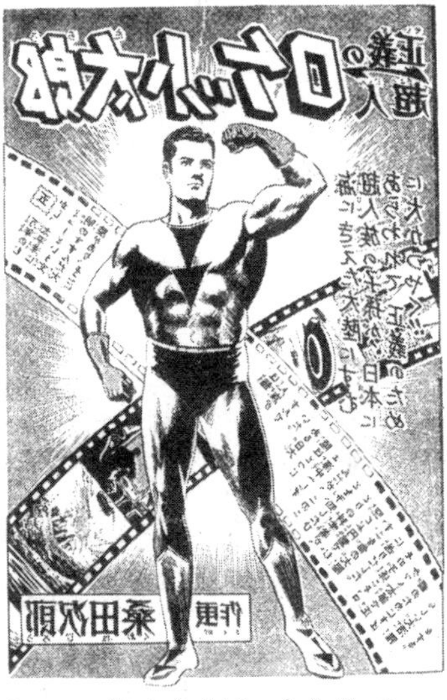

正義の超人
ロケット太郎
作
桑田次郎

***Superman of Justice Rocket Tarou* by Jiro Kuwata**

BA:AC

Jim Chadwick Editor – Translated Series
Jeb Woodard Group Editor – Collected Editions
Liz Erickson Editor – Collected Edition

Bob Harras Senior VP – Editor-in-Chief, DC Comics

Diane Nelson President
Dan DiDio and Jim Lee Co-Publishers
Geoff Johns Chief Creative Officer
Amit Desai Senior VP – Marketing & Global Franchise Management
Nairi Gardiner Senior VP – Finance
Sam Ades VP – Digital Marketing
Bobbie Chase VP – Talent Development
Mark Chiarello Senior VP – Art, Design & Collected Editions
John Cunningham VP – Content Strategy
Anne DePies VP – Strategy Planning & Reporting
Don Falletti VP – Manufacturing Operations
Lawrence Ganem VP – Editorial Administration & Talent Relations
Alison Gill Senior VP – Manufacturing & Operations
Hank Kanalz Senior VP – Editorial Strategy & Administration
Jay Kogan VP – Legal Affairs
Derek Maddalena Senior VP – Sales & Business Development
Jack Mahan VP – Business Affairs
Dan Miron VP – Sales Planning & Trade Development
Nick Napolitano VP – Manufacturing Administration
Carol Roeder VP – Marketing
Eddie Scannell VP – Mass Account & Digital Sales
Courtney Simmons Senior VP – Publicity & Communications
Jim (Ski) Sokolowski VP – Comic Book Specialty & Newsstand Sales
Sandy Yi Senior VP – Global Franchise Management

BATMAN: THE JIRO KUWATA BATMANGA VOLUME 3

Published by DC Comics. Compilation and all new material Copyright © 2016 DC Comics. All
Rights Reserved.

Originally published in single magazine form as BATMAN: THE BATMANGA JIRO KUWATA
EDITION, BATMANGA!, and online as BATMAN: THE JIRO KUWATA BATMANGA Digital
Chapters 40-53 © 1966, 1967, 2013, 2015 DC Comics. All Rights Reserved. All characters, their
distinctive likenesses and related elements featured in this publication are trademarks of DC
Comics. The stories, characters and incidents featured in this publication are entirely fictional.
DC Comics does not read or accept unsolicited ideas, stories or artwork.

Special thanks to Shonengahosha Co. Ltd. (Japan) and Shogakukan Creative Ltd. (Japan)

DC Comics, 2900 West Alameda Avenue Burbank, CA 91505
Printed by RR Donnelley, Crawfordsville, IN, USA. 12/18/15. First Printing.
ISBN: 978-1-4012-5756-9

Library of Congress Cataloging-in-Publication Data

Names: Kuwata, Jiro, 1935-
Title: Batman : the Jiro Kuwata Batmanga. Volume 3 / written & illustrated by
Jiro Kuwata.
Other titles: Batmanga
Description: Burbank, CA : DC Comics, [2016] | "Batman created by Bob Kane."
Identifiers: LCCN 2015037667 | ISBN 9781401257569 (paperback)
Subjects: LCSH: Graphic novels. | BISAC: COMICS & GRAPHIC NOVELS / Manga /
General. | GSAFD: Comic books, strips, etc.
Classification: LCC PN6728.B36 K94 2016 | DDC 741.5/973--dc23 LC record available at http://
lccn.loc.gov/2015037667

MAY — 2017